Hans Conzelmann (1915-1989) dedicated himself to New Testament studies at the universities of Tübingen, Heidelberg, and Göttingen in Germany. His *The Theology of St. Luke* (Fortress Press, 1982) introduced a new epoch in the interpretation of the Synoptic Gospels, followed by landmark studies on Jesus and Paul. Among his many influential works are his three Hermeneia Commentaries on *1 Corinthians* (Fortress Press, 1975), *The Acts of the Apostles* (1987) and, with Martin Dibelius, *The Pastoral Epistles* (1975).

M. Eugene Boring is A. A. Bradford Professor of Religion-Studies at Texas Christian University, Fort Worth, Texas. He is the translator of *Theological Ethics of the New Testament* by Eduard Lohse (Fortress Press, 1991).

GENTILES—JEWS—CHRISTIANS

HANS CONZELMANN

GENTILES
—
JEWS
—
CHRISTIANS

*Polemics and Apologetics in
the Greco-Roman Era*

Translated by
M. Eugene Boring

FORTRESS PRESS MINNEAPOLIS

Translated by M. Eugene Boring from the German *Heiden—Juden—Christen: Ausein-andersetzungen in der Literatur der hellenistisch-römischen Zeit.* Copyright © J. C. B. Mohr (Paul Siebeck). Tübingen 1981.

Scripture quotations, unless otherwise noted, are from the New Revised Standard Version of the Bible, copyright © 1989 by the Division of Christian Education of the National Council of Churches of Christ in the United States of America.

Cover design: *Ned Skubic*
Interior book design: *The HK Scriptorium, Inc.*

Library of Congress Cataloging-in-Publication Data

Conzelmann, Hans.
  [Heiden, Juden, Christen. English]
  Gentiles, Jews, Christians : polemics and apologetics in the
Greco-Roman era / Hans Conzelmann : translated by M. Eugene
Boring.
    p.   cm.
  Translation of: Heiden, Juden, Christen.
  Includes bibliographical references and index.
  ISBN 0-8006-2520-X
  1. Antisemitism—History—Sources. 2. Classical literature—
History and criticism. 3. Jews in literature. 4. Judaism—
Controversial literature—History and criticism. 5. Judaism—
Apologetic works—History and criticism. 6. Greek literature—
Jewish authors—History and criticism. 7. Christianity and
antisemitism—History—Sources. 8. Judaism (Christian theology)—
History of doctrines—Early church, ca. 30–600. I. Title
DS145.C59513 1992
305.892'4—dc20   91-37936
                                      CIP

Manufactured in the U.S.A.   AF 1-3575
96   95   94   93   92   1   2   3   4   5   6   7   8   9   10

CONTENTS

III

THE DEBATE OF HELLENISTIC JUDAISM
WITH THE HELLENISTIC-ROMAN WORLD

IV

CHRISTIANS AND JEWS
FROM THE BEGINNING OF CHRISTIANITY
UNTIL THE TIME OF ORIGEN

PREFACE

This book could not have been completed had I not received much help. First of all, my former assistant who is now my colleague, Andreas Lindemann, has relieved me of much work. The later assistance of Hartmud Plath was extensive and precise. Then Renate Backhaus and Cord Muckelberg helped to carry the project to completion and also read the proofs. I am grateful for the help of Bishop Eduard Lohse and my colleague Axel Freiherr von Campenhausen. To all the above I express my heartfelt thanks.

My colleague Robert Hanhart, whose unselfish friendship and extreme competence were expressed in his careful correction of the proofs, deserves special thanks.

My purpose in writing this book is given in the introduction. Here I need to mention only that I have concentrated on working through the primary sources. The secondary literature was intentionally minimized and surveyed only to the extent that it appeared indispensable for the understanding of the primary sources. References to the second volume of Menahem Stern, *Greek and Latin Authors on Jews and Judaism* (Jerusalem: Israel Academy of Sciences and Humanities, 1980) are missing, since it did not appear until after the manuscript was complete.* On questionable points, everything essential has been derived from other collections of primary sources (e.g., Theodore Reinach, Felix Jacoby).

Last but not least, I thank my wife, who has created for me the setting and working arrangements without which this project could never have been completed.

Hans Conzelmann

---

* [Translator's note: This lack has now been remedied; see the translator's preface.]

TRANSLATOR'S PREFACE

This was Hans Conzelmann's last book, completed in 1981 when he was already struggling with the debilitating effects of his final illness. He considered it one of his most important works—if not his most important—and hoped to live to see the English translation which would introduce the book to much of the academic world, since the German volume had a minimal circulation and few reviews. Some reasons for the limited response to the original publication are clear. The book demanded much of even those readers who could manage German, and it was filled with Greek, Latin, and Hebrew quotations (all of which are translated in the present volume). Other reasons are not so clear. The book was neither well advertised nor consistently distributed to appropriate periodicals; and it was reviewed by only a few of the major journals.[1]

The book was reviewed in the following publications: Kalev Hayam, "Nur die Glaubensfrage," *Reformierte Kirchenzeitung* 122 (1981): 228–30; *Hessens Theol.Literatur-Anzeiger* 81/82, p. 19; H. Weder, *Kirchenblatt für die Reformierte Schweiz* 138/3 (February 1982); *Expository Times* 92 (March 1982): 161–64, as part of a general review article; R. Gradwohl, "Ein Nachschlagewerk von Rang," *Allgemeine jüdische Wochenzeitung* 37 (1982); A. F. J. Klijn, *Novum Testamentum* 24/4 (1982): 375–78; K. M. Woschitz, *Theologisch-praktische Quartalschrift* (Linz) 130 (1982): 1785; Ulrich Hutter, *Homiletische Monatshefte* 2/82–83; Gerhard Ringshausen, *Entwurf* (January 1983); W. Z., *Israelitisches*

---

[1] With no claim to be exhaustive, a thorough check in locations where one would anticipate advertising for the book disclosed announcements only in *Die Zeitschrift für die Neutestamentliche Wissenschaft* (Berlin) and in *Theologische Zeitschrift* (Basel). Of the thirty appropriate major journals checked that list books received, only three indicate that they received *Heiden–Juden–Christen: Journal for the Study of Judaism* (Leiden), *Journal of Biblical Literature* (U.S.A.), and *Recherches de science religieuse* (Strasbourg). Inexplicably, none of the journals that acknowledged receiving it chose to review it—perhaps because reviewers for such a demanding book are not easy to come by.

Wochenblatt Nr. 15 (5 April 1983): 67; Wolfgang Wiefel, *Theologische Literatur-zeitung* 108/6 (1983): 425-28; C. H. Lebram, *Nederlands Archief voor Kerk-geschiedenis* 63/2 (1983); Niels Hyldahl, *Dansk teologisk Tidsskrift* (1983): 144-45; Birger Olsson, *Svensk Exegetisk Årsbok* 48 (1983): 165-68; Giuseppe Segalla, *Studia Patavina* 30 (1983): 136-39; Rudolf Pfisterer, *Deutsches Pfarre-blatt* (June 1984); Z. I. Heiman, *Antonianum* (Rome) (1984): 672-75 (I have not seen this review); R. Oberforcher, *Zeitschrift für katholische Theologie* 106 (1984): 206-8; Clemens Thoma, *Freiburger Rundbrief* 35/36, No. 133-134 (1985): 144-45.
Pier Franco Beatrice, *Christianesimo della Storia* (1985): 606-8; Heikki Solin, *Arctos* 17:152.

Most reviews were generally positive, and some were glowing and enthu-siastic. Only two of the twenty-one were consistently negative (Solin and "Hayam"[2]). Jewish reviews were positive. Most noted the combination of historical and theological perspective, often referring to it as "unique." The aspect of the book most often questioned was the author's forthright declara-tion of the theological perspective from which the book was written, though Jewish authors, who of course did not affirm Conzelmann's perspective as their own, tended to be more positive about the book as a whole than most Chris-tian authors. Conzelmann, of course, had directed the book to Christian theologians, charging some of them with minimizing the substantive issues of faith that separate Jews and Christians and thus hindering real dialogue.

* * *

The translation of the German text of this book was completed in 1983, and it was anticipated that the English edition would appear in 1984. A series of unavoidable circumstances related to translating and editing the many Greek and Latin citations has regrettably delayed publication until now. The world into which this book emerges is a different world from the world in which it was written and to which it was addressed. As examples, one need only think of *peristroika* and *glasnost,* the changed political situation in Europe, the demise of the Berlin wall and the relaxing of tensions between East and West, the different connotations of "communist," the events and changed situation in the Near East, particularly those involving Israel, and the mental distancing of readers from the Six-Day War (still relatively recent when Conzelmann was writing), recent developments and publications in the dialogue between Jews and Christians, and the increased awareness of Islam in such dialogues. Thus

---

[2] This sharply critical review, suggesting that Conzelmann had been angered by something and had written the book to "let off steam," and was "not entirely free of an aversion to Jews," was written pseudonymously. It was only after Andreas Lindemann and Walter Schmithals had written responses, also printed in *RKZ*, to which "Hayam" wrote a response, that it was learned that the author was a Christian theologian.

this book, like all historical documents, needs to be seen in its original context to be appreciated properly, or even understood.

* * *

The original text, though a scholarly monograph, was expressed in the terse, staccato style that characterized the author, who never used two words when one would suffice (see the addresses by Dietz Lange and Eduard Lohse below). This means that even the native German reader must sometimes pause to ponder the several meanings that could inhere in Conzelmann's legendary terseness and straightforwardness. I have thus not always attempted to smooth it out—and lose its force. Particular thanks are due to Professor Robert Hanhart, mentioned by Conzelmann in his preface to the German edition, for his efforts in making it more readable.

I have also left in their original form various historically conditioned expressions that were at home in the original context but are now often said differently. I have, for instance, preserved Conzelmann's term *Spätjudentum* ("late Judaism"), common in his generation to designate the period 165 B.C.E.–135 C.E. but now often replaced by "early Judaism" by Christian scholars since the former term is now often misunderstood to suggest the beginning of Christianity as the orientation point. I have retained it and similar expressions not only for historical accuracy—a translator must resist the temptation to sanitize by being merely "politically correct"—but also because such terms (somewhat ironically) illustrate the point Conzelmann is making about the difficulty of Jewish–Christian dialogue and how each side must engage in it from its own historically and theologically conditioned perspective.

The bibliography has been updated by the addition of some of the more recent publications and editions in the same categories as the original bibliography, and citations in the text and footnotes have been revised to correspond, though retaining the original enumeration. The text itself has been occasionally augmented with references to primary texts not available to Conzelmann but which he intended to include. A few corrections have been made in the German edition's references to ancient sources and to page numbers and notes in secondary literature. I have for the most part used standard translations of Greek and Latin works when they were available (hence some remaining traditional language), but have occasionally made my own translations if Conzelmann's point or nuance seemed to require it.

* * *

Hans Conzelmann was a New Testament scholar. The reader who is familiar with his numerous publications in the field of New Testament, that is, early Christian history, literature, and theology, might wonder why, late in his academic career, he extended himself beyond his previous interests and devoted himself to the subject of this book, which deals with Greek, Latin, and Christian authors from Herodotus to Origen. Without presuming to speak for the author, it may be helpful to point out that one principal reason for writing this book was Hans Conzelmann's conviction that efforts toward dialogue between Christians and Jews were often lacking in historical foundation and theological depth, particularly from the Christian side. In particular, he felt that as a false reaction to the guilt felt by many for the way Jews had been treated during the centuries of Christian history and especially during the Nazi era, some streams of German theology had constructed a view of "salvation history" that incorporated undue political support for the modern state of Israel. Recent events were still fresh in the public memory as Conzelmann wrote these pages, one purpose of which was to set Christian attitudes toward Jews and Judaism in a broader historical context and, from his perspective, in a more legitimate theological setting.

Every book to some extent bears the imprint of its author. That truism is especially the case with this book. To understand and appreciate this book, one must know something of Hans Conzelmann the man. For this reason, and also as a fitting memorial to the author in his final publication, addresses by Dietz Lange and Eduard Lohse, given on the first anniversary of Conzelmann's death, are included in this edition.

TRANSLATOR'S NOTE

I am grateful to Dr. Raymond F. Person, Jr., who did the preliminary bibliographical work, to Dr. Edward J. McMahon for locating English translations of ancient texts, updating the bibliography, and for assistance in the editing process, and to Lana N. Byrd for typing the manuscript and compiling the indexes.

IN MEMORIAM
HANS CONZELMANN*

Dietz Lange

We have come together this morning to honor the memory of a scholar who was one of the most distinguished representatives of New Testament scholarship of the last several decades and a human being who in his own highly individual, straightforward, and angular manner, coupled with his passionate and serious dedication to his work, has left behind an enduring impression on all who had to do with him.

Hans Conzelmann was born on 27 October 1915, in Thailfingen in Württemberg. This geographical datum is already important for understanding the person. As a Schwab, Conzelmann belonged to that lovable branch of the human family that an all-too-cool and poised north German might sometimes find not easy to approach—and I specifically add, Thank God. He was serious, often brooding, and still, at least in his relatively healthy days, filled with the joy of life, a man of enormous will power and iron discipline, a straight thinker secure in his inner independence, direct and explicit almost to the point of rudeness, never merely pleasant, militant but not cantankerous, quick to an anger that was just as quickly gone—like the well-known Schwabian proverb that I here reproduce in proper German and not in its original earthy form: "Was geht mich mein dummes Geschwätz von gestern Abend an?" (Literally, "so what do I care about my dumb prattle of yesterday evening?" Approximately, "so what's the big deal about the dumb things I said last night?").

As the son of parents of modest means, Conzelmann received a scholarship and proceeded along the traditional Württemberg educational course for

---

* Address to the academic memorial celebration on 20 June 1990 in the auditorium of Göttingen University. The academic achievement of Conzelmann was praised by retired Bishop Prof. Dr. Eduard Lohse, in a much more extensive presentation [printed below]. As Dekan (Dean), my task was to commemorate Hans Conzelmann the man.

exceptionally talented members of the rising theological generation, namely, the seminaries (Internate) in Schöntal and Urach, and then after receiving his Abitur (diploma qualifying one for university study) from the famous Stift (Institute) in Tübingen, from which in an earlier time came such illustrious spirits as Schiller, Hegel, and Hölderlin. In Conzelmann's university years—the first years of the Third Reich—there were considerable problems, especially for a nonconformist such as he was. His passion for theology was first kindled when, on the fatherly advice of his friend Ernst Bizer, then pastor of his home church in Thailfingen and later church historian in Bonn, he moved from Tübingen to Marburg to hear Rudolf Bultmann. In this great scholar he found the teacher who became definitive for him, one whose absolute honesty and unsentimental nature with all its north German deliberateness made a deep impression on the young student and evoked a lively resonance in him. It was probably at this time that Conzelmann first formulated the statement that he liked to quote even in his later years to describe his inner relation to the principal object of his research: "The New Testament is always much more fascinating than any detective story."

After his return to Tübingen and passing his first theological examinations with honors, he was denied a position as instructor in the Stift because of the confused circumstances of the time and probably also because of his open disagreement with the Ephorus (Director) of the Stift, who inclined toward National Socialism. He joined the Church Theological Society in Württemberg, a group corresponding to the confessing church elsewhere in Germany, and thus stood clearly in opposition to the current regime. (Later, such renowned theologians as Hermann Diem and Ernst Fuchs belonged to this same group.) Soon after passing the examinations Conzelmann was drafted into the military and had to participate in the greater part of the war first as foot soldier, then as an officer in Russia. He married in 1944. A short time later, when he was again at the front, this time in France, he was severely wounded, and one leg had to be removed. Under the circumstances of the times, it took several years before he was restored to even relative health. He must ever afterward have repeatedly suffered physical pain. He never complained.

For two years after the war, 1946–1948, Conzelmann was a pastoral administrator in Ohnastetten, a small town near Reutlingen. After the requisite examination he became a high school teacher in Ebingen, where he taught religion and—without ever having passed the qualifying examinations for it—history as well. This illustrates already the direction and breadth of his interests, which also extended to literature, especially Horace, Eichendorff, and Mörike, but also to Wilhelm Raabe and to authors such as Fritz Reuter (rather exotic for a Schwab!).

He was a demanding teacher, who required much from his students, but even more from himself, and who thus soon earned the respect of all in his school. As a footnote, I may add in passing that our colleague Professor Baur owes a considerable part of his good knowledge of the New Testament to the instruction he received from his teacher at that time, Hans Conzelmann. It was during this Ebingen period that Conzelmann discovered and worked out the first great theme of his New Testament research: the theology of Luke. The resulting studies led him in quick succession to his doctorate in Tübingen and his *Habilitationsschrift*[1] in Heidelberg under Günther Bornkamm. A little later he was called to Zurich, where in 1954 he became associate professor and in 1956 full professor. His *Habilitationsschrift*, called *Die Mitte der Zeit* ("The Middle of Time"),[2] pioneered a new approach to study of the Synoptic Gospels, namely, the question of the theological conceptions of the individual evangelists, and brought him immediate renown. His lectures were thus crowded already in Heidelberg and later in Zurich. He was very obliging and open in dealing with students, insisting that they challenge his views rather than parroting them back to him. He often enjoyed inviting his seminars to his house, where they profited both from his excellent taste in good wines and from the intense discussions.

I may here perhaps mention that during these Zurich times I myself heard him lecture for two semesters. I was fascinated and impressed by two things: the meticulous conscientiousness with which he had prepared his lectures, which were filled with an overwhelming mass of material but delivered with a clean and clear line of argument, and his absolute honesty that allowed no room for apologetic tricks. The passionate theological concern that drove him often came to unrestrained expression, hidden behind his vehement rejection of every sort of superficial piety. But it was impossible for those who listened closely to fail to notice that here a teacher held forth whose work was not merely a matter of command of the materials, but one who placed his whole person on the line for his theological convictions.

In 1960 Conzelmann accepted a call from Göttingen, to which he remained true despite a later call from Bonn. In the early years his popularity among students continued undiminished. For some years he also preached regularly in Geismar—something that he was firmly persuaded belonged unconditionally to the vocation of a theologian. The upheaval in the academic world of 1968 meant fundamental changes to his life. In Göttingen too, the days were not calm. Once again, Conzelmann was not hesitant to take a stand in his characteristic plain-spoken manner. As in earlier years he had taken the field against every indication of a budding revival of nationalism and obsolete concepts of "honor" among the students, so now he withstood ideologues on the left, in which he saw the same doctrinaire demons as in National Socialism, only with different insignia. His polemic could be directed particularly against that stream of

---

[1] This is the second dissertation required in the German university system to qualify for university teaching.

[2] *Die Mitte der Zeit: Studien zur Theologie des Lukas,* Beiträge zur historischen Theologie 17 (Tübingen: Mohr-Siebeck, 1954; 6th ed. 1977). Eng. trans. *The Theology of St. Luke,* trans. Geoffrey Buswell (New York: Harper & Row, 1961; Fortress Press ed. 1982).

theology then described as Left-wing Protestantism (*Linksprotestantismus*).

His last book, which he had to wrest from the ever more difficult handicaps of his final illness, still manifests the concern and theological passion that governed his life—shows these perhaps more impressively and urgently than many of his other works. I would therefore like to read to you a few sentences that I would simply like to let stand without comment, since they speak for themselves with such force.

> This book has not been written out of that fascination with antiquity as such that is presently enjoying a boom. . . . Precisely as a strictly historical work derived directly from the primary sources, my book is directed to the present. . . . The writing of history . . . must attempt to let the past be what it was. Only then can the study of history serve to provide a better understanding of ourselves in our world. . . .
>
> This book does not direct its attention toward the contemporary world situation in general. It thus stands in fundamental opposition to the machinations of the present-day church, which diligently pursues its own disintegration by means of sonorous pronouncements. By such pronouncements the only word that could really establish the existence of the church, the proclamation of the saving act of God who in Christ has reconciled the world to himself, is pushed aside by the church's own authoritarian announcements. These announcements hold up the false hope that there is some enabling power in them for the transformation of the world into the redeemed community, if only the words of church functionaries are obeyed. All this in the twentieth century! . . .
>
> The result is that faith is replaced by "Christianity," a superficially christianized world view, a world view that can be "promoted" by connecting it with a corporate body, the church. Theologically expressed, this means the replacement of faith by a world view imposed as a law, a law that leads to disaster instead of salvation. . . .
>
> Is this then a call for the church to live its life in the world as a nonparticipating spectator, while people and situations cry out for help?
>
> A stupid question. The answer is already evident when once the mission of the church and the content of its preaching are brought to mind. Then the church will no longer seek a "Christian" politics, but realistic directions in the light of its knowledge that the world exists before God. It will not pronounce a blessing on weapons, nor make a sign of the cross over military programs, which it continues to do here and there even as part of its own program. . . . Against such an approach the only help is the confidence of faith that no "Christian" attempts to exercise force—it is no accident that they turn out so miserably—can break the power of the word of the cross and the hope for the kingdom of God that is not of this world. . . . [There is no other way than] the way of striving for solidarity with sinful humanity, to which Christians belong like everyone else—with only one privilege, that they hear the word of the cross. . . . Precisely as hearers of this word, they [the Christians] continue in human solidarity with non-Christians, learning by experience what they are commanded in the world.[3]

---

[3] H. Conzelmann, *Heiden—Juden—Christen: Auseinandersetzung in der Literatur der hellenistischen-römischen Zeit* (Tübingen: Mohr-Siebeck, 1981) 1–5; see the full English text of the introduction below.

That is the theological legacy of Hans Conzelmann in a nutshell. A clear theological affirmation, delivered with confidence and vigor. He was always a theologian who said what he thought without beating around the bush—an enemy of every lame compromise, and also an enemy of every effort to operate with finesse and intrigue, for which every agitated time offers abundant opportunity. To be sure, his direct manner made him not only friends—a person who has only friends or who alleges that this is the case would be a most suspicious character. He was also respected by those who opposed him on substantive issues, and that is worth more than a cheap and bland approval from everybody.

Hans Conzelmann was relatively early wrenched out of his work. In 1975 he was overtaken with a heart attack, from which he recovered sufficiently to be able to teach for two more years, but then he had to forbear further work in the classroom. Then began a long ordeal: at first an eye problem made it impossible for him to drive a car, then reading became increasingly difficult until he, who had always lived with a wealth of literature, had to give it up completely. Then came a stroke, and then after 1985 a number of severe illnesses, any one of which would have been the end of a man of lesser will. In life he had never made it easy for himself, and he did not die an easy death. He died only after a long struggle against ever more severe physical helplessness during which he maintained a mental alertness that called for a physical expression he could often give only in a limited way. At this point we should not forget the care of Frau Conzelmann, whose constant presence was the decisive factor in his ability to maintain the courage to endure. Until the last few months before his death he still held a seminar for a few trusted colleagues, at the cost of enormous self-exertion and finally only as a silent participant. On 20 June 1989 death delivered him from his suffering.

Hans Conzelmann was a theological teacher who has made a permanent impression on our faculty: by his clear and unsentimental manner as an uncompromising advocate of the Christian faith understood both as Reformation theology and modern critical theology, as a strong personality, and last but not least by his academic teaching and his great scholarly achievements, which precisely in his Göttingen time resulted in an impressive number of theological publications that will occupy the academic world for a long time to come.

THEOLOGY AS EXEGESIS:
IN MEMORY OF
HANS CONZELMANN

Eduard Lohse

It is the task of New Testament scholarship to use all the resources and methods of historical investigation to explain the New Testament as a document of history. But this academic discipline "stands in the service of the New Testament writings under the presupposition that they have something to say to the present."[1] Hans Conzelmann knew himself to be bound by this understanding of what it means to exegete a biblical text, as formulated by Rudolf Bultmann in his classical work on the theology of the New Testament. He had well learned both lessons from his Marburg teacher: the precision with which the meaning of the ancient text is to be pursued, as well as being taken aback by the sense of personal address that sounds forth from the text. This address gives courage and places one under obligation, even as it generates trusting faith, but it also requires one to be a steadfast advocate in testifying to one's perception of what is right and true.

Born on 27 October 1915 in Thailfingen, Württemberg, Hans Conzelmann was already in his early years urged by the pastor of his local church, Ernst Bizer, to render a responsible account of the meaning of the Christian faith. After receiving a superior classical education in the humanities that equipped him with the best tools, he applied himself to the study of theology. It was not, however, in his first semesters in Tübingen, but first in Marburg that he met those academic teachers who both as scholars and as human beings of strong convictions made such a strong impression on the young student and opened the door to his own enduring joy in theological work. In those times, of course,

---

[1] Rudolf Bultmann, *Theology of the New Testament*, trans. Kendrick Grobel (2 vols.; New York: Charles Scribner's Sons, 1951, 1955) 2:251.

this joy was accompanied by suffering and privation. The tense debates that occurred in the university and church during the days of the Third Reich demanded that students of theology take positions and know how to stand by them.

Hans Conzelmann immediately decided to take his stand with the confessing church and discovered the circle of close friends composed of young Württemberger theological students who had formed a society not only for the purpose of struggling toward clarity on the impending issues involving church and politics, but—as adherents of the school of dialectical theology—to engage passionately in doing theology. In this Hans Conzelmann felt himself to be guided especially by his Marburg professors Hans von Soden and Rudolf Bultmann. From them he had learned what must be fundamental for theologians aware of their responsibility: to study the biblical message with conscientious thoroughness, to listen for its affirmations of enduring authority, and to hold fast to the insight attained—precisely because the word of the Bible has something to say to the present.

But before he could dedicate himself to the more intensive academic work toward which he was inclined, the hard years of the war tore the young theologian away from university study and service in the church. Shortly before the end of the war he was severely wounded, but this did not prevent him after the war from turning his great energy and tireless intensity to the tasks called for by his vocation. As a teacher in the gymnasium he sought ways to share with his students the decisive experience he had struggled to attain as the basis for his own theological existence. In 1952 he received the doctor's degree in theology from Tübingen University, and a short time thereafter he completed his *Habilitationsschrift* in the field of New Testament at the University of Heidelberg. In 1954 he became professor in the theological faculty at Zurich, and in 1960 accepted a call from Göttingen, where he worked until his retirement. The Heidelberg theological faculty presented him an honorary doctorate in 1959. A full member of the Göttingen Academy of Science since 1966, he participated in its work, including his service as a member of its Committee on the Septuagint, as long as his health permitted.

* * *

The academic accomplishment of the life work of Hans Conzelmann is documented by a large number of publications appropriate to his vocation, but it is not possible to discuss, or even mention, all of them here. In respect and gratitude, our thoughts will rather be guided by focusing on some central themes that were characteristic of Hans Conzelmann's theology, themes that had been thought through so thoroughly and held with such persistence that the result of his labor has stamped itself on New Testament scholarship and will continue to influence it. This applies in the first place to his pioneering work on the interpretation of the Gospels and the message of Jesus that they contain.

In this field, which has been repeatedly marked off and replowed by an enormous variety of scholarly approaches and questions for more than two hundred years, Hans Conzelmann was able to attain fundamentally new insights and to communicate them with persuasive logic.

With his book *The Theology of St. Luke* (1954) he introduced a new epoch in the interpretation of the Synoptic Gospels. Previous New Testament scholarship had regarded the evangelists primarily as collectors and editors of traditions, but Hans Conzelmann showed that they were to be understood as authors and theologians, each with his characteristic theological point of view. With Luke as his laboratory example, he demonstrated that the way the author arranges and modifies the traditional material allows the student to discern the execution of a characteristic theological program. By studying the redaction of the material in the hand of the evangelist, one cannot, of course, obtain "material for the picture of the Jesus of history," but rather a picture of "the development of the understanding of Christ in the early church."[2] The portrayal of history presented by Luke is determined by the fact that the time of Jesus and the time of the church are represented "as two distinct, but systematically interrelated epochs."[3]

> When Jesus was alive, was the time of salvation; Satan was far away, it was a time without temptation. . . . [But] since the passion, however, Satan is present again, and the disciples of Jesus are again subject to temptation. . . . In view of this distinction, the continuity between the period of Jesus on the one hand and the period of the church on the other, has to be plainly demonstrated. The plan of the whole historical writing serves this purpose. The story of salvation emerges in three stages: I. The period of Israel. II. The period of Jesus' ministry. . . . III. The period since the Ascension, on earth the period of the *ecclesia pressa* during which the virtue of patience is required.[4]

That this outline serves as the framework that not only determines the plan for the entire Lucan two volumes but also determines the redactional formation of individual pericopae is shown through careful detailed work—not only for the theology of the Gospel but later in a learned commentary on Acts.[5] In this commentary he gave detailed documentation for the view that "the continuation of the Gospel by Acts is neither accidental nor is it motivated by purely literary considerations." The presupposition is rather "that the church is a historical entity which has its own particular time; in other words that the

---

[2] Conzelmann, *The Theology of St. Luke*, trans. G. Buswell (New York: Harper & Row, 1961) 12.

[3] Ibid, 14.

[4] Ibid, 16.

[5] H. Conzelmann, *Die Apostelgeschichte* (Tübingen: Mohr-Siebeck, 1963; 2nd ed. 1972). Eng. trans. *The Acts of the Apostles*, trans. J. Limburg, A. T. Kraabel, and D. Juel, Hermeneia (Philadelphia: Fortress Press, 1987).

imminent end of history has been transformed into a portrait of history."[6] The three epochs of salvation history that characterize Luke-Acts are closely connected.

> Each ties up with the preceding and carries it further while also possessing its own additional characteristics. The first is the time of the Law and prophecy, the middle time of the preaching of the kingdom of God (Luke 16:16) and its representation in the acts of Jesus, the third epoch is the time of the church, to which the Spirit has been given and with it the power for the mission to the world.[7]

This thoroughly provocative study of Lucan theology made a great impression on the scholarly world and went into six editions—most unusual for a monograph. The book's theses were widely discussed in academic circles, especially whether the conception of Luke's program of salvation history should be modified here and there. But despite the variety of opinions this discussion called forth,[8] the redaction-critical perspective that had been developed by Hans Conzelmann found almost universal acceptance and development. Since then, this insight has become the common property of New Testament scholarship: that one must speak of the theology of each individual Gospel and that this must be taken into consideration in developing a theology of the New Testament—a matter of which we must speak further.

The sharp eyes Hans Conzelmann developed in analyzing the editorial framework composed by the Evangelist simultaneously allowed him to develop criteria for evaluating the traditional material contained within this framework. The method he used in going behind the Gospels to achieve historically authentic material from the life of Jesus can be seen especially in his article "Jesus Christ" in *RGG*.[9] He formulated extremely strict requirements that traditional material must meet in order to count as historical, explaining: "For the reconstruction of Jesus' teaching the following methodological principle is valid: whatever fits neither into Jewish thought nor the views of the later church can be regarded as authentic. This is the case, above all, for the sayings which express a consciousness of his own situation."[10] By investigating the traditional material with the help of this criterion, he was able to identify a body of sayings of Jesus that could be considered authentic from this point of view

---

[6] Conzelmann, *Acts*, xlv.

[7] Ibid.

[8] See, e.g., the different articles in the anthology edited by G. Braumann, *Das Lukas-Evangelium: Die redaktions- und kompositionsgeschichtliche Forschung* (Darmstadt: Wissenschaftliche Buchgesellschaft, 1974).

[9] *RGG*[3] 3 (1959) 619–53. Eng. trans. *Jesus: The Classic Article from RGG[3] Expanded and Updated,* trans. J. Raymond Lord (Philadelphia: Fortress Press, 1973).

[10] Conzelmann, *Jesus*, 16; see also H. Conzelmann and A. Lindemann, *Arbeitsbuch zum Neuen Testament* (Tübingen: Mohr-Siebeck, 1977; 9th ed. 1988) 346. Eng. trans. *Interpreting the New Testament: An Introduction to the Principles and Methods of N. T. Exegesis,* trans. S. Schatzmann from the 8th rev. German ed. (Peabody, Mass.: Hendrickson Publishers, 1988) 304.

and that could be fitted together into a coherent picture. In Jesus' talk of God, in his ethic, and in his eschatology, "a unified idea of existence can be perceived." "The intention everywhere is for a confrontation of man with God without any intermediary. The shrinking of time in eschatology corresponds to the enlargement of space as the place of faith and obedience in the doctrine of God and eschatology." The unity of these different subjects is given in the person of Jesus.[11]

The much-discussed problem of how Jesus' preaching of the kingdom of God is related to the christological titles used in the Synoptic tradition is attacked with matter-of-fact sharpness by forming historical-critical judgments. Thus he rightly considered decisive the observation "that in the oldest stratum of tradition expectation of the kingdom of God is nowhere connected with the Son of Man. . . ."[12] Since the announcement of the imminent coming of the kingdom of God is certainly to be assigned to the oldest layer of the tradition and attributed to the historical Jesus, it is but a short step to the conclusion that the christological titles are to be attributed not to Jesus himself but to the confession of the early Christian community. They "look back upon the earthly existence of Jesus"; they "acknowledge in the kerygma faith in his resurrection (with which an interpretation of the passion is connected)"; and they "look forward to the parousia."[13]

From this Hans Conzelmann concluded "that Jesus' self-consciousness is not comprehensible in terms of the christological titles."[14] However, in that Jesus confronted human beings directly with God and laid bare the future reality by his announcement of the coming kingdom of God, he claimed a unique position and role for himself, "since after him nothing more 'comes'—but God himself."[15] Thus over against the negative results that resulted from his assigning the christological titles to the early church rather than to the historical Jesus, he places the positive affirmation: Jesus announced the coming of the kingdom of God and proclaimed God's demand directed to human decision and action.

> Thereby a "christology" becomes indirectly visible to the extent that Jesus made a claim to speak authoritatively in behalf of God . . . . [H]is violent death on the cross could be taken as the contradiction of his message by God himself. But in the faith of the Easter message early Christianity confessed its faith that Jesus had not been rejected by God, but on the contrary had been received by him. In that Jesus was confessed as the exalted Lord whom God had raised from the dead, the community made Jesus himself the object of their faith and the content of their confession.[16]

---

[11] Conzelmann, *Jesus,* 59.

[12] Ibid., 45.

[13] Ibid.

[14] Ibid., 49.

[15] Ibid., 50.

[16] Hans Conzelmann, *Grundriss der Theologie des Neues Testament,* 4th ed., ed. Andreas Lindemann (Tübingen: Mohr-Siebeck, 1987) 86–87. [Translator's note: This paragraph was not in the 1969

By critical analysis that is not afraid of rigorous thinking but self-consciously chooses to engage in it, there comes a breakthrough to the essence of the matter itself, as happens in the word of preaching as it is accepted and understood in the confessing response of faith.

* * *

But how is this confession of faith appropriately interpreted? Hans Conzelmann reflected on this question again and again in his engagement with Pauline theology. Here one could speak of a second great emphasis of his theological work. Beginning with his equally careful and expert reworking of Martin Dibelius's commentary on the Pastoral Letters, then through his exegesis of Ephesians and Colossians in the series *Das Neue Testament Deutsch* and the scholarly commentary on 1 Corinthians in the Meyer series and on into his many individual studies of Pauline passages and theology, Hans Conzelmann set forth and defended his understanding of the theology of Paul and the Pauline school with admirable thoroughness.[17] On the one hand, he knew how to show—much more clearly than had been done in previous scholarship—that Paul developed his theology as the exposition of the traditional Christian confession he had inherited. Thus the decisive factor in an appropriate understanding is—as we shall immediately illustrate—"*how* Paul interprets this confession."[18]

On the other hand, Hans Conzelmann was a leader in the scholarly enterprise of critically distinguishing between the authentic Paul and the deutero-Pauline materials, a deliberative task in which his essays repeatedly engaged, expressed in his conviction that there was a Pauline school, founded by Paul in Ephesus that continued after his death, from which the deutero-Pauline literature emerged and/or generated the impulses that created this literature.[19] Because the church's credo must constantly be interpreted afresh, it was inevitable that the apostle himself would give new answers to new questions as they

---

English translation of the 1968 2nd German edition, *An Outline of the Theology of the New Testament,* trans. John Bowden (New York and Evanston: Harper & Row, 1969), but cf. pp. 126–27.]

[17] Martin Dibelius and Hans Conzelmann, *The Pastoral Epistles,* trans. P. Buttolph and A. Yarbro, Hermeneia (Philadelphia: Fortress Press, 1972); Hans Conzelmann, *Der Epheser- und Kolosserbrief,* NTD 8 (Göttingen: Vandenhoeck & Ruprecht, 1962; 9th ed. 1985); idem, *Der erste Brief an die Korinther* (Göttingen: Vandenhoeck & Ruprecht, 1969; 2nd ed. 1981). Eng. trans. *1 Corinthians,* trans. John Leitch, Hermeneia (Philadelphia: Fortress Press, 1987).

[18] Conzelmann and Lindemann, *Interpreting the New Testament,* 370.

[19] See esp. Hans Conzelmann, "Die Schule des Paulus," in *Theologia Crucis–Signum Crucis,* Festschrift für E. Dinkler (Tübingen: Mohr-Siebeck, 1979) 85–96; see also "Paulus und die Weisheit," in *Theologie als Schriftauslegung: Aufsätze zum Neuen Testament* (Munich: Kaiser, 1974) 177–90. [Translator's note: Observe how often "Theology" appears in the titles of Conzelmann's New Testament works. The title of this collection of his essays means "Theology as Biblical Interpretation."]

arose. But also within the Pauline school these answers could not simply be repeated, but the faith had to be newly formulated from time to time.[20]

How did Paul interpret the common confession of early Christianity? In order to present only one example of how Hans Conzelmann grounded his view by an exegetical line of argument, we may briefly consider his interpretation of 1 Thessalonians 4:13-18. These verses deal with the disputed issue of whether members of the Christian community who died before the parousia of the Lord would participate in the future salvation. Paul answers by quoting a traditional word of the Lord that he applies to this question, but first he makes reference to the common Christian confession of faith as the beginning point of his argument: "For since we believe that Jesus died and rose again, even so, through Jesus, God will bring with him those who have died" (1 Thess. 4:14). What may we learn from this brief text? In Conzelmann's view, this: "The statement about Christ is also a statement about the believers. The faith is not understood until it is realized that he is the one who determines our destiny, when it is confessed that 'in Christ' our own future is settled. This is not understood formally as some general future, but exclusively as the future salvation."[21]

The confession to which the apostle refers here and often elsewhere in his letters does not mean for him anything like an unhistorical "dogma,"[22] from which "timeless truths" could be derived. But just as both the content of the confession of faith and the act of confession are historically conditioned, so also when the creed is repeatedly affirmed in history "in the act of confession a historical encounter takes place."[23] That means, however, that the kerygma was interpreted consistently by Paul in the sense of justification by faith. In order to be able to recognize and understand this *cantus firmus* that permeates all the Pauline letters, one must not limit oneself to those passages in which the specific terminology of justification in the narrow sense is to be found, but must also take into one's view how the apostle develops his view of God and humanity throughout. "It becomes apparent, then, that the doctrine of justification in Rom and Gal designates the exact same relationship between God and man, and the same destiny of man in this world, as the theology of the cross in the Corinthian letters."[24]

Hans Conzelmann sought to bring the proof for the correctness of this thesis both in his delineation of Pauline theology as a whole and in the execution of individual exegeses. He thereby focused on 1 Corinthians as the epistle in which it is clearly to be seen that Paul did not understand theology to be merely the

---

[20] See Conzelmann, "Schule des Paulus," 94.

[21] Hans Conzelmann, "Die Rechtfertigungslehre des Paulus," in *Theologie als Schriftauslegung,* 196.

[22] See Conzelmann, "Schule des Paulus," 87.

[23] Ibid.

[24] Conzelmann and Lindemann, *Interpreting the New Testament,* 371.

theoretical development of doctrine. For him theology was "primarily the exposition of the event of salvation that is doctrinally formulated in the creed and actualized in the gospel; that is to say, it expounds the self-understanding of the faith which has its object in the work of salvation."[25] While in Romans Paul interprets and comments on the content of the faith by using traditional creedal material, in 1 Corinthians he engages in practical theology. This means, however, that theology "is here translated into an illumination of the existence of the church and of the individual Christian in it."[26]

So regarded, the ideas developed in Pauline theology are brought into strict consistency. In differing terminology, to be sure, but with consistency with regard to its content, as the apostle faced the questions with which he had to deal, he had time and again to interpret the gospel as the gift of grace that can be received only by faith alone.[27] Every theologian who debates with the Pauline theology that has as its essential and determining content the central doctrine of justification by grace through faith will learn from the encounter that the doctrine of justification cannot be appropriated merely by repeating it, "but only by new formulations for new situations. This is certainly to be set forth as the criterion of what Paul and Luther actually thought."[28]

* * *

As a theologian who was aware of his debt to Paul and Luther more than all other teachers in the church, Hans Conzelmann was at the same time a trained philologist and historian who worked with the strictest academic methods, and knew how to pursue the question of what the texts actually have to say. Our focus on Hans Conzelmann's manner of working thus brings us to a third aspect of our survey dedicated to his life's work. Just as theologians are obligated to exegete the meaning of the scriptural text before them and must not "correct" its intended message according to their own taste, so the writing of history, if it "intends to be taken seriously, that is, if it expects to do something besides merely impose contemporary views on the past, . . . must attempt to let the past be what it was. Only then can the study of history serve to provide a better understanding of ourselves in our world."[29]

The insights attained by a critical method that is equally honest and personally involved in the subject matter make it necessary to correct views of the beginning of the church formed on the basis of later tradition — as Hans Conzelmann has shown in an exemplary fashion in his own history of early Christianity.[30]

---

[25] Conzelmann, 1 Corinthians, 9.

[26] Ibid.

[27] See Conzelmann, Outline of the Theology of the New Testament, 164.

[28] Conzelmann, Theologie als Schriftauslegung, 192 n. 22.

[29] H. Conzelmann, Heiden–Juden–Christen, 1; Eng. trans. below, p. 1.

[30] Hans Conzelmann, History of Primitive Christianity, trans. John E. Steely (Nashville and New York: Abingdon, 1973).

For "the idea of the apostolic age emerged only when people no longer had immediate contact with the early period. . . . That it does not correspond to reality, however, can be shown when one asks where the boundary between the apostolic and the post-apostolic age is supposed to run." If a probing investigation shows that this distinction is a later construction, then the concept of "primitive Christianity" needs to be reformulated in a clarifying way. It will then be seen that "primitive Christianity" was by no means a self-contained unity, but a structure with many layers, which "includes graduations and groupings with tensions that go as far as disputes and open breaks." Yet amid the variety of appearance, "there is one fundamental agreement: the church knows herself to have been founded by the exalted Lord, and that not by way of inner impulses, but by a direct act of communication. And along with the founding the missionary commission is given." In other words, "the church confesses her unity, not only through the various confessions, but also through the epochs of her history, from her founding down to the present; and she believes in this unity on into the future—because her Lord is *one* Lord."[31]

If a critical study of history by no means results only in the demolition of traditional images and opinions, but may instead lead in a positive manner to a sharper grasp of central theological insights, then full credit should be given to the knowledge attained by historical investigation.[32] This is true also for such a difficult theme as the relationship of Christians and Jews, made the more difficult by the burden of the guilty past. Since it is so important to reject an inhuman anti-Semitism and to encourage the formation of a truly human relationship between Christians and Jews, it is indispensable to investigate the history of their mutual relations as precisely as possible.[33] In his historical account, worked out from beginning to end in direct engagement with the primary sources, published in 1981 under the title *Heiden—Juden—Christen* (now translated as the present work), Hans Conzelmann attempted to create the necessary presuppositions for dialogue by urging that the real problematic not be masked by explanations made too quickly. He wanted instead to emphasize the theological significance of the basic issues that bear on the discussion.

Closer observation of the first period in which Jews and Christians attempted dialogue shows that:

the principle difficulty for a mutual understanding between Judaism and Christianity consists precisely in the fact that they have the same fundamental ideas and concepts:

---

[31] Ibid., 18, 19, 41, 13–14.

[32] An example of careful, detailed historical investigation was presented by Hans Conzelmann to the Göttingen Academy of Sciences in their session on 10 November 1967, "Korinth und die Mädchen der Aphrodite: Zur Religionsgeschichte der Stadt Korinth," in *Nachrichten der Akademie der Wissenschaften in Göttingen,* I. Phil.-hist. Klasse, Jahrgang 1987 Nr. 8 (Göttingen: Akademie der Wissenschaften, 1967) 247–61 (in *Theologie als Schriftauslegung,* 152–66).

[33] See below, p. 4.

There is *one* God, who alone may be worshiped, the creator. He has chosen one people for himself and has decreed the statutes by which his elected people must live.

But: although *"one* God" refers to the same God in both religious communities, for the Christians he can be God only to those who "have" him as the Father of Jesus Christ.[34]

From this it follows that "the conflict between church and synagogue is inherent in the founding of the church itself. . . . It did not understand itself as a new religion, but as the true Israel, which believed that the promise to Israel was now being fulfilled."[35] Thus here too attention is focused on the doctrine of justification, since "the only issue between Jews and Christians is the issue of faith," so that within this frame of reference "all human beings, Christian and non-Christian, are directly confronted by God, . . . simply as human beings, i.e., as sinners who must renounce all boasting before God, including boasting that they are Christians, since the renunciation of all such boasting is inherent in faith. All are justified before God in exactly the same way, by faith alone, which Paul in Romans 3:30 bases on the confession that God is *one.*"[36]

By carrying on his theological work with personal commitment that was just as strong as the disciplined precision of the critical academic scholar, he offered his students a model of how exegetical work is to be done on the word of Scripture. One may not prescribe in advance what the Scripture may be allowed to say; one must rather hear what it actually says—and precisely in those cases where it might strike one as unexpected or disquieting.

Hans Conzelmann made use of a terse, precise, and closely argued manner of speech devoid of any unnecessary decoration. By this means he made it clear to his hearers and readers that they were to attend not to the interpreter, but to the word of Scripture. In his commentaries he thus concentrated on providing the readers with all the necessary information, so that they were equipped for critical thinking and could make their own judgments. In this way he resisted the widespread tendency to take over the completed results of other peoples' work. As both teacher and scholar Hans Conzelmann considered it important to discourage such tendencies in students, and to "enable[s] them instead to do their own work on the text."[37] Those who attended his pro-seminar, which he was accustomed to conduct with particular thoroughness, received both a wealth of instruction and, simultaneously, essential help for developing their own competence in the formation of theological judgments.

One literary fruit of his academic instruction is represented by the "workbook for New Testament study" that he wrote in collaboration with his

---

[34] See below, pp. 240–42.
[35] Below, p. 251.
[36] Below, p. 342.
[37] Conzelmann, *Acts,* xiii.

teaching assistant and later colleague, Andreas Lindemann.[38] This textbook, which grew out of rich teaching experience, presents methods and results of critical exegesis to the student in such a way "that the individual steps leading to these results become lucid and can be retraced critically. . . ." He thus proceeds from the conviction "that the historical-critical interpretation of the NT cannot be an end in itself but is to contribute especially to the clarification of what is Christian belief." This means, however, that "an important aspect of exegesis based on scientific criteria is the knowledge and application of methods that aid the explication of what the text says. In principle, the object (text) determines the method and not vice versa; methods are means to an end, never ends in themselves." He matter-of-factly declares that methodologically the biblical texts are not to be treated any differently "than other literary sources. . . . The scientific study of the Bible utilizes the same formal methods as those used in the study of antiquity, namely, classical philology, archaeology, and ancient history." It is not the methods but the texts to which they are applied that are to be distinguished from others, for "the Bible distinguishes itself from other ancient witnesses through its message." It is, after all, "a collection of specific historical documents that attest to and present the [Jewish as well as the] Christian faith."[39]

* * *

But what is it that constitutes the irreplaceable content of this Christian faith? This question comes into view once again in a fourth and final chain of thought, which will allow us to hear Hans Conzelmann's own answer. The "Preface and Foreword" of his *Outline of the Theology of the New Testament* begins with this statement:

> Themes treated in different places and in different ways in discussions over the whole field of New Testament exegesis come together in the study of the "Theology of the New Testament." At any given time, "New Testament Theology" provides as it were a model, presenting a whole theological period in perspective.[40]

If this is a fitting characterization of the discipline that has the task of presenting the interrelated theological ideas of the New Testament, then it is especially appropriate for the life work of the exegete and theologian Hans Conzelmann.

In 1955 the young Zurich professor published a lecture that he gave to the Schweizerischen Freisinnigen Theologentag (Conference of Liberal Theologians) on the theme "What Did Early Christianity Believe?"[41] In this lecture he

---

[38] Conzelmann and Lindemann, *Arbeitsbuch* (see n. 10 above).

[39] Conzelmann and Lindemann, *Interpreting the New Testament*, xvii, 2, 3.

[40] Conzelmann, *Outline of the Theology of the New Testament*, xiii.

[41] Hans Conzelmann, "Was glaubte die früe Christenheit?" *Schweizerische Theologische Umschau* 25 (1955) 61–74 (in *Theologie als Schriftauslegung*, 106–19).

required a high price of his hearers, for he did not answer this question from the perspective of "liberal theology," but developed the insight that the faith of primitive Christianity is expressed in the oldest Christian confessions obtained by form-critical analysis of the earliest Christian literary documents. This confession of faith represents a historical entity that contains an inherent pressure toward constant reinterpretation.

> Even though the confessional statements are brief, still each concept and affirmation contain specific ideas that call for development. When it is said of Jesus that he is the Lord, or that he has been raised from the dead, such statements call for interpretation. In other words: the confession of faith demands theology.[42]

This substance of faith comes to appropriate expression not by the recitation of unchanged vocabulary of traditional formulas, but only as faith constantly renews itself in reaffirmation, which means reinterpretation. But on each occasion of the confession of faith, even in the briefest of formulas, the faith as a whole is contained and expressed.[43] The task of making an appropriate exposition of the creed is, however, only fulfilled "when it is seen that the objective statement about Christ contains a statement about myself (including my future)."[44] If theology is oriented in this way to the confession already given in history and remains aware of this head start as it proceeds in its work, it is protected against every temptation to fall victim to fashionable contemporary currents.[45]

These insights, attained by Hans Conzelmann early in his career and repeatedly advocated, also shaped his understanding of New Testament theology. He conceives of theology in the strict sense as "the interpretation of the faith made at a particular time, . . . as an exegesis of the original *texts* of the faith, the oldest formulations of the creed."[46] Since there could have been no Christian faith prior to Good Friday and Easter, he does not begin, as is usually done, with a delineation of the message of the historical Jesus. The first main part deals instead with the kerygma of the oldest Christian communities and with the theology of the Synoptic Gospels. He treats the message of Jesus within the context of how it was handled within the theology of the evangelists. This outline represents the consistent inferences of his previously attained exegetical insights, including the fundamental importance of the confessions of the first Christians as well as the theological rank to which he assigns the work of the evangelists. Hans Conzelmann thereby intentionally goes

---

[42] Conzelmann, *Theologie als Schriftauslegung,* 108.

[43] Hans Conzelmann, "Zum Überlieferungsproblem des Neuen Testaments," in *Theologie als Schriftauslegung,* 142–51.

[44] Hans Conzelmann, "Zur Analyse der Bekenntnisformel 1 Kor. 15:3-5," in *Theologie als Schrift-auslegung,* 141; Eng. trans. "On the Analysis of the Confessional Formula," *Interpretation* 20 (January 1966): 15–25 (the quotation is from p. 24 of the article).

[45] See also Conzelmann, *Outline of the Theology of the New Testament,* xiv.

[46] Ibid., xv.

beyond the delineation of New Testament theology by Rudolf Bultmann, who does begin with a presentation of the message of Jesus—even though not as a constituent part of New Testament theology but as its presupposition— and who does not treat the content of the Synoptic Gospels under the heading of "theology."[47]

We will have to think further about whether his decision with regard to this problematic, handled in such a variety of ways by other scholars, may be considered completely correct. The issue of how the preaching of Jesus should be incorporated into the structure of a theology of the New Testament has so far found no general agreement, despite vigorous scholarly work.[48] And the discussion of the theology of the Synoptic Gospels might better be located after Paul's theology has been presented.[49] Since the apostle Paul "was the first to interpret the cross of Jesus theologically as the source and ground for the church's proclamation,"[50] the presuppositions were thereby created for the formation of the Gospels, even if there are no historical connections between Paul and any of the Gospels. Both problem areas were not only clearly pointed out by Hans Conzelmann, but by means of the suggestions he developed he pointed the way and described criteria that all who work on the problem must continue to consider if satisfactory solutions are to be found.

Hans Conzelmann perceived that the early Christian confession serves as the binding brackets by which the various documents of the New Testament and their varying theological perspectives are held together within one canon. Thus their very plurality becomes a forceful pointer to the unity of the New Testament. If Paul could already appeal to an early Christian traditional formulation that preceded him, his own accomplishment was "the way in which he thought through the faith theologically."[51] From this grew the fundamental perception of election "by grace alone" and "by faith alone" that leads to the understanding of righteousness by faith "and thus the end of man's own righteousness." Since the credo is the beginning point for the Pauline theology of justification, it thus functioned for the apostle and for his school as "its regulator—not only from outside, but also from within, because theology understands itself to be the interpretation of the creed."[52]

---

[47] Ibid. [Translator's note: The first words of Bultmann's *Theology of the New Testament* were "The message of Jesus is a presupposition for the theology of the New Testament rather than a part of that theology itself" (p. 3)].

[48] See the critical reflections of A. Lindemann, "Jesus in der Theologie des Neuen Testaments," in *Jesus Christus in Historie und Theologie: Festschrift für Hans Conzelmann* (Tübingen: Mohr-Siebeck, 1975) 27–57.

[49] This is the choice of A. Lindemann, "Erwägungen zum Problem einer 'Theologie der synoptischen Evangelien,'" *ZNW* 77 (1986) 1–33.

[50] So C. Demke, "Die Frage nach der Möglichkeit einer Theologie des Neuen Testaments," *ThV* 2 (1970) 129–38, esp. 134–35. Cf. Lindemann, "Erwägungen," 33.

[51] Conzelmann, *Outline of the Theology of the New Testament*, 161.

[52] Ibid., 164, 296.

What can be said of the Pauline theology applies in a similar way for Johannine theology. For "John, too, deliberately takes up the church's tradition"—as can be seen from the first chapter of his book, in which the evangelist "gives a careful survey of the titles that apply to Jesus." It is also the case that the "I am" sayings, in which the Johannine Christology reaches its zenith, have as their starting point "the traditional confession of the community." In that Jesus and no other is confessed and proclaimed as the way, the truth, and the life, an interpretation is given of the confession of faith according to which the light is to be found in him alone, while the world lies in darkness. Thereby a judgment falls on the world; for "the world comes 'to light' for what it is: world."[53]

The theology of the New Testament as outlined by Hans Conzelmann illuminates the special competence of this theological teacher, who began his work by regarding the call of the subject matter as addressed first of all to himself and by responding to it as a binding obligation. He then knew how to do theology as exegesis of the Bible in such a way that his students saw it embodied before them in one radically dedicated to this obligation. This obligation demands, however, that New Testament exegesis, unswerving in the face of fashionable trends of the time, "must stick to its craft like a handworker bent on solid achievement."[54]

Hans Conzelmann knew how to combine unconditional integrity of theological investigation with the force of his own personal commitment. He thereby earned the respect of his colleagues in the world of biblical scholarship and the grateful affection of his students. The foreword of his last major publication concludes with this sentence: "Last but not least, I thank my wife, who has created for me the setting and working arrangements without which this project could never have been completed,"[55] an expression of a deep relationship and sharing of life. His word could always be trusted. He knew how to remain loyal to friends, especially in difficult times. His judgments, sometimes formulated with critical sharpness, always earned an attentive hearing and careful consideration.

As an exegete of the New Testament, Hans Conzelmann knew that suffering is "a fact in the aeon that is passing away, whose end is constituted by the cross and resurrection of Christ."[56] But through suffering God "shatters the props of my self-assertion, leaving me nothing but grace...."[57] What Hans Conzelmann had perceived as an exegete, he had to hold before his own eyes during the last painful years of his long illness. As his days became more and more lonely and the approaching end made itself known, despite many a challenging trial he remained true to the insight he had won—until his death on 20 June

---

[53] Ibid., 336–37, 351, 352.
[54] Conzelmann, *Theologie als Schriftauslegung,* from the foreword.
[55] See above, p. vii.
[56] Conzelmann, *Outline of the Theology of the New Testament,* 281.
[57] Ibid.

1989. For, as he once formulated it himself, "if my justification is the act of God alone and not my own, if my justification is pronounced unconditionally, then I know through the hearing of this message itself that my faith is not my own work, that my faith is not my own accomplishment, that God chose me before I ever believed, that my salvation is 'taken care of.'"[58]

To the circle of friends and students who presented him with an imposing *Festschrift* for his sixtieth birthday,[59] Hans Conzelmann expressed his gratitude by reminding them of a text of Scripture he had adopted as the keynote for his life and work. In the brevity of its affirmation it may even today appropriately state how theology as biblical interpretation is to be worked out and lived out. In the book of Proverbs it is said: "Hold fast to disciplined study and do not let go; guard it well, for it is your life" (Proverbs 4:13).

---

[58] Conzelmann, "Rechtfertigung durch den Glauben," in *Theologie als Schriftauslegung,* 225.

[59] *Jesus Christ in Historie und Theologie* (see n. 48 above).

ABBREVIATIONS

AAB	*Abhandlungen der Deutschen Akademie der Wissenschaften zu Berlin*
AAG	*Abhandlungen der Akademie der Wissenschaften in Göttingen*
ALGJ	Arbeiten zur Literatur und Geschichte des hellenistischen Judentums
ANRW	*Aufstieg und Niedergang der römischen Welt: Geschichte und Kultur Roms im Spiegel der neueren Forschung.* Edited by H. Temporini and W. Haase. Berlin and New York: de Gruyter.
AOT	*The Apocryphal Old Testament.* Edited by H. F. D. Sparks. Oxford: Clarendon Press, 1984.
ARW	*Archiv für Religionswissenschaft*
ASTI	*Annual of the Swedish Theological Institute*
ATANT	Abhandlungen zur Theologie des Alten und Neuen Testaments
BEvT	Beiträge zur evangelische Theologie
Bib	*Biblica*
BJS	Brown Judaic Studies
BKV	Bibliothek der Kirchenväter
CAH	*The Cambridge Ancient History.* 12 vols. Cambridge: Cambridge University Press, 1923ff.
CH	*Corpus Hermeticum*
CIJ	*Corpus Inscriptionum Judaicarum.* Edited by J. B. Frey. 2 vols. Rome: Institute of Christian Archaeology, 1936, 1952.
CIL	*Corpus Inscriptionum Latinarum.*
CPJ	*Corpus Papyrorum Judaicarum.* Edited by V. A. Tcherikover and A. Fuks. 3 vols. Cambridge, Mass.: Harvard University Press, 1957–64.
CQR	*Church Quarterly Review*
CRINT	Compendia rerum iudaicarum ad novum testamentum
DJD	Discoveries in the Judaean Desert
EvT	*Evangelische Theologie*
FGH	F. Jacoby, *Die Fragmente der griechischen Historiker.* Leiden: E. J. Brill, 1923ff.
FHG	*Fragmenta Historicorum Graecorum.* Edited by C. Müller and T. Müller. 1841–72.

FRLANT	Forschungen zur Religion und Literatur des Alten und Neuen Testaments
GCS	Griechische christliche Schriftsteller
GLAJJ	M. Stern, *Greek and Latin Authors on Jews and Judaism*. 3 vols. Jerusalem: Jerusalem Academy Press, 1974–84.
HAT	Handbuch zum Alten Testament
HNT	Handbuch zum Neuen Testament
HTR	*Harvard Theological Review*
HUCA	*Hebrew Union College Annual*
IEJ	*Israel Exploration Journal*
JAOS	*Journal of the American Oriental Society*
JBL	*Journal of Biblical Literature*
JB. Phil. Suppl.	*Theologischer Jahresbericht, Phil. Suppl.*
JEH	*Journal of Ecclesiastical History*
JES	*Journal of Ecumenical Studies*
JJS	*Journal of Jewish Studies*
JQR	*Jewish Quarterly Review*
JR	*Journal of Religion*
JRS	*Journal of Roman Studies*
JSJ	*Journal for the Study of Judaism*
JTS	*Journal of Theological Studies*
KlT	Kleine Texte für theologische und philologische Vorlesungen und Übungen
KlP	Kleine Texte für Philologie
Kl. Pauly	*Der kleine Pauly: Lexikon der Antike von Pauly's Realencyclopädie der classischen Altertumswissenschaft*. Edited by K. Ziegler and W. Sontheimer. Stuttgart: A. Druckenmüller, 1964–75.
LCL	Loeb Classical Library
MGWJ	*Monatsschrift für Geschichte und Wissenschaft des Judentums*
MTZ	*Münchener theologische Zeitschrift*
NovT	*Novum Testamentum*
NovTSup	*Novum Testamentum*, Supplements
NTApoc.	E. Hennecke and W. Schneemelcher, eds. *New Testament Apocrypha*. English translation edited by R. M. Wilson. 2 vols. Philadelphia: Westminster, 1963, 1965.
NTD	Das Neue Testament Deutsch
NTS	*New Testament Studies*
PEQ	*Palestine Exploration Quarterly*
PGM	*Papyri Graecae Magicae*. Edited by K. Preisendanz. 2 vols. 1928.
PW	*Paulys Real-Encyclopädie der classischen Altertumswissenschaft*. Edited by G. Wissowa. Stuttgart: Metzler, 1893–; A. Druckenmüller, 1949–.
PWSup	*PW*, Supplementbände, 1903–.
RAC	*Reallexikon für Antike und Christentum*. Edited by T. Klauser. Stuttgart: Hiersemann, 1950–.
RE	*Realencyklopädie für protestantische Theologie und Kirche*
REJ	*Revue des études juives*

RGG³	*Die Religion in Geschichte und Gegenwart.* Edited by K. Galling. 3rd ed. Tübingen: Mohr-Siebeck, 1957–65.
RHE	*Revue d'histoire ecclésiastique*
RHPR	*Revue d'histoire et de philosophie religieuses*
RHR	*Revue de l'histoire des religions*
RivAC	*Rivista di archeologia cristiana*
RKZ	*Reformierte Kirchenzeitung*
RR	*Review of Religion*
RSR	*Revue des sciences religieuses*
SAH	Sitzungsberichte der Heidelberger Akademie der Wissenschaften Heidelberg
SC	Sources chrétiennes
SPB	Studia postbiblica
ST	*Studia theologica*
St. Patr.	*Studia Patristica*
TAPA	*Transactions of the American Philological Association*
TDNT	*Theological Dictionary of the New Testament.* Edited by G. Kittel and G. Friedrich. Grand Rapids: Eerdmans, 1964–76.
ThV	*Theologia Viatorum*
TLZ	*Theologische Literaturzeitung*
TR	*Theologische Rundschau*
TSK	*Theologische Studien und Kritiken*
TT	*Teologisk Tidsskrift*
TU	Texte und Untersuchungen
TZ	*Theologische Zeitschrift*
VC	*Vigiliae Christianae*
VT	*Vetus Testamentum*
WUNT	Wissenschaftliche Untersuchungen zum Neuen Testament
WZKM	*Wiener Zeitschrift für die Kunde des Morgenlandes*
ZDPV	*Zeitschrift des deutschen Palästina-Vereins*
ZKG	*Zeitschrift für Kirchengeschichte*
ZKT	*Zeitschrift für katholische Theologie*
ZNW	*Zeitschrift für die neutestamentliche Wissenschaft*
ZPE	*Zeitschrift für Papyrologie und Epigraphik*
ZRGG	*Zeitschrift für die Religions- und Geistesgeschichte*
ZTK	*Zeitschrift für Theologie und Kirche*

INTRODUCTION

This book has not been written out of that fascination with antiquity as such that is presently enjoying a boom, as is illustrated, for example, by the "historical" books of the belles-lettres sort. Precisely as a strictly historical work derived directly from the primary sources, my book is directed to the present. If the writing of history intends to be taken seriously, that is, if it expects to do something besides merely impose contemporary views on the past, it must attempt to let the past be what it was. Only then can the study of history serve to provide a better understanding of ourselves in our world.

That is especially the case where relationships, perspectives, and problems manifest a substantial constancy without regard to their particular historical setting, because there is a certain constancy about human being as such through all history. Otherwise historical understanding is impossible.

This book does not direct its attention toward the contemporary world situation in general. It thus stands in fundamental opposition to the machinations of the present-day church, which diligently pursues its own disintegration by means of sonorous pronouncements. By such pronouncements the only word that could really establish the existence of the church, the proclamation of the saving act of God who in Christ has reconciled the world to himself, is pushed aside by the church's own authoritarian announcements. These announcements hold up the false hope that there is some enabling power in them for the transformation of the world into the redeemed community, if only the words of church functionaries are obeyed. All this in the twentieth century!

This is done as though the churches possessed a political insight superior to that, for example, of the Marxist world. But the only superior insight that the church possesses is that knowledge that comes from the kerygma: this world is a fallen world that will come to an end, and precisely this is its hope, because it is the creation of God, who holds it fast despite its fall.

The preaching of this gospel is alleged to be "otherworldly," a hindrance to the kind of real action humanity needs. The gospel is in fact "otherworldly," because the world has alienated itself from God and thereby has become a perverted world. The task of preaching is not, however, to lift up a general lamentation about the misery of the world. Preaching must affirm that the world has indeed abandoned God but God has not abandoned the world, a world that even in its forgetfulness of God owes every day of its existence precisely to this God.

It is symptomatic that a "theology of the Word" is widely disputed and set aside in preaching—and this not by argumentation, nor through the affirmation that the Word is a vehicle of the Spirit, but through clamorous advocacy of slogans that are congenial to the present time. The preacher becomes something of a loudspeaker for a contemporary radio program; the content of the "program" corresponds to this image. This approach justifies itself by the slogan that is heard more and more, that Christian speech is not information drawn from the Bible but from the passing stream of contemporary events, as these are evaluated by theologians from the perspective of their own little treatises. When this happens, listening to the church has lost its value, just as has the church itself.

The result is that faith is replaced by "Christianity," a superficially christianized world view, a world view that can be "promoted" by connecting it with a corporate body, the church. Theologically expressed, this means the replacement of faith by a world view imposed as a law, a law that leads to disaster instead of salvation. Such a perversion can be theologically disguised by replacing the proclamation of Christ by instruction about "salvation history."

This peculiar catchphrase dominates much of fashionable German theology today. Of course, it is the substance of the matter that concerns us, not the terminology. But the widespread use of "salvation-history" terminology signals a complete muddling of the meaning of the proclamation of Christ. Which "salvation" is meant, if it can have a "history"? And which history? The history of the world? How and in what sense can this history, the history of fallen humanity, be the revelation of God? Does the pastor intend to interpret certain historical events as revelation? Does whatever the pastor's finger points to thereby become a saving event, to be accepted in faith?

Or is the history of Israel meant? Which history would this be? That told in the Bible? Or that history reconstructed by the scholars? Then faith would have to be in the theologians. Which events are supposed to be saving? The goings-on of the despot David? The extermination of whole peoples, supposedly at the command of God? Is a certain opinion with regard to the historical Israel a condition of salvation? Not according to the New Testament, in any case, for if the church regarded itself as the true Israel, the historical Israel was no longer for it a "holy people."[1]

---

[1] On the problem of "salvation history," see P. Vielhauer, "Paulus und das Alte Testament," in *Studien zur Geschichte und Theologie der Reformation*, Festschrift E. Bizer, ed. L. Abrahamoski and J. F. Gerhard Goeters (Neukirchen-Vluyn: Neukirchener Verlag, 1969); G. Klein, "Bibel und Heilsgeschichte," *ZNW* 62 (1971): 1ff.; A. H. J. Gunneweg, *Understanding the Old Testament* (Philadelphia: Westminster, 1978).

There are simple, sound tests for any offer of "salvation history" as an object of faith, as is illustrated by the following observations. (1) A discreet silence is maintained concerning the fact that each theologian selects from the Old Testament only that which seems appropriate to him or her. A theological criterion is lacking for distinguishing between law and gospel, between letter and spirit. (2) Proclamation is directly illuminating, saving address. Historical events, on the other hand, can only be *told* and considered in retrospect, with more or less edifying feelings, but cannot be *believed in*. The object of faith does not become visible in events of world history, real or fictitious. "Saving events" are mute, have no word in themselves. If the content of faith were thus to become visible, it would then be subject to human judgment. This content of faith cannot be a multiplicity of "facts," but is the *one* word of God that Christ is and that addresses me directly, bearing its truth within itself, which does not subject itself to our reflective judgment. In the recitation of the history, the person addressed remains his or her old self, becomes a participant involved in a "trial," but loses his or her identity as one who has already received the pronouncement of justification.

If one rejects the theological idea that identifies "salvation history" with the history of Israel (either as told in the Bible or as critically reconstructed), does this not exclude the Old Testament from the Christian Bible? On the contrary! What is rejected is the narrow perception of the Old Testament as a history book. That the Old Testament is a constituent part of the Bible is not denied; that it is this should pose no theological problem at all. But how, and to what extent, is the Old Testament necessary? That it—in part—is a *historical* presupposition of the New Testament is not yet a *theological* datum, but is only a statement within the framework of the history of religions. We reach a genuine theological level only when it is made clear that the Bible, Old Testament and New Testament, is *not* an object of faith. The object of faith is exclusively the witness from God given in Christ. This is the content of faith contained in the Bible (Luther's "what preaches Christ"). That is the principle of selection to be applied to biblical materials. Here is to be found also the reason why the "biblical" theology loudly propagated in recent times only led to drastic confusion with regard to the content of faith and perverted the teaching of the Bible itself.

In what does the unity of the Bible consist? Its unity is found in the identity of the God of the law with the Father of Jesus Christ, who is the end of the law. The law and its end, the gospel, are not to be separated. The gospel does not nullify the validity of the law, but brings out its true nature, namely, the injunction of the creator established in history, not a means of salvation at human disposal.

If we bring the issue of the unity of Scripture into the discussion of the relationship between Jews and Christians, we see that every "salvation-history" theory leads to a dead end. Is it only incidental that the fashionable Jewish–Christian dialogues have sought to bracket out the question of the essential unity of the Old and New Testaments? In such conversations, people are accustomed to harking back to the *man* Jesus, finding parallels between his teaching and Jewish ethics, in order to be able to be nice to each other. This is definitely the wrong road. Whether the man Jesus was a superior example of Judaism, or only a questionable one, the discussion carried on in such terms is already off the track. One indication of this is the hopeless discussion concerning who bears the guilt for Jesus' death.

Two comments on this: (1) If Christians keep quiet about their faith in the saving act of God in Christ, such dialogues carried on between the representatives of two religions are superfluous. It would then be more honest for Christians simply to close up shop. Merely by looking at the man Jesus, no real Jew is going to give up the conviction that we attain salvation by faith (namely, in the *one* God) and by works (namely, the fulfilling of the law). (2) The unbearable, theologically impossible bickerings about the guilt for Jesus' death must cease. If we are talking about the execution of a human being for political reasons, then the question of who is guilty is not a question of one's faith, but is no different from the problem raised by any other judicial murder. But if one speaks of the "murder of God"—then every person, including people today, is equally guilty as a sinner before God.

Should then Jews and Christians continue to stand over against each other, unreconciled, as two hostile fronts? It would be a perverse kind of Christianity that would attempt to burden the Jews with the guilt while letting Christians off rather cheaply. Precisely that is excluded by faith in Jesus' death as God's saving act. Through faith in this saving act, everyone is confronted with the same question of faith. And again, through this faith the necessity to "straighten out" the other is excluded, and the way toward the personal relationship of one human being to another is opened up, whether the person be Christian or not. This is the meaning of the love commandment. Relationships with Jews are thus desacralized and thereby humanized. Israel is, of course, a historically unique people, but not a "holy people" in and of itself. The history of Israel, after all, remains a part of the history of this world. The same is true for the "land" of this people, the present state of Israel. We must be clear about consequences: if one regards political Israel as a holy state or a holy people, then every war in which Israel is involved becomes a religious war on some higher plane than ordinary world history. The dark days of church history are recalled. (One indication of this is the mood that prevailed in Germany during the Six-Day War, as German sympathy for the Israeli cause was subliminally misinterpreted as "overcoming the past.")

The establishing of good human relationships between Christians and Jews presupposes that Israel is understood simply as a secular political reality. Inhuman anti-Semitism, which in the West has included a religious element, cannot be compensated for by a Christian pro-Semitism or even a pro-Zionism. Otherwise, one remains stuck in the realm of "religion," which is the realm of the world, not a matter of revelation. Will not such a misunderstanding actually endanger the political existence of Israel? Will this not lead to the arousal of anti-Jewish feelings in Israel's environment, in which Islam also lives?

Both individual Christians and the churches should keep their fingers out of politics carried on from such a "religious" perspective, which they do not understand anyway. Is this then a call for the church to live its life in the world as a nonparticipating spectator, while people and situations cry out for help?

A stupid question. The answer is already evident once the mission of the church and the content of its preaching are brought to mind. Then the church will no longer seek a "Christian" politics, but realistic directions in the light of its knowledge that the world exists before God. It will not pronounce a blessing on weapons, nor make a sign of the cross over military programs, which it continues to do here and there even as part of its own program. For this would mean that it wants to exercise power itself and avoid the scandalous weakness that is inherent in the gospel. Against such an approach the only help is the confidence of faith that no "Christian" attempts to exercise force—it is no accident that they turn out so miserably—can break the power of the word of the cross and the hope for the kingdom of God that is not of this world. There is only one way in this fallen, tormented world that leads to responsible action appropriate to those who profess faith in God. This is the way of love proclaimed in the gospel, the way of striving for solidarity with sinful humanity, to which Christians belong like everyone else—with only one privilege, that they hear the word of the cross. That they are justified by this word confers no higher worldly status on them. Precisely as hearers of this word, they continue in human solidarity with non-Christians, learning by experience what they are commanded in the world.

I

THE POLITICAL
BACKGROUND

PRELIMINARY REMARKS

Is it only an accident that "anti-Semitism" (please excuse this term that unfortunately has become customary) has not been the subject of even a fairly comprehensive study in recent German scholarship? For a survey of the subject we are still dependent on the (excellent, to be sure) article by I. Heinemann in the Pauly-Wissowa *Realencyclopädie der classischen Altertumswissenschaft* (Stuttgart: Metzler, 1893–; A. Druckenmüller, 1949–). The old collection of primary sources by T. Reinach, *Textes d'auteurs Grecs et Romains relatifs au Judaïsme* (1895), has now been replaced by the collection of critical texts with commentaries edited by M. Stern, *Greek and Latin Authors on Jews and Judaism* (1974–84), which is up to the standards of modern critical editions. These texts are also available in F. Jacoby, *Die Fragmente der griechischen Historiker* (1923–). Recently the Dutch work of J. N. Sevenster, *The Roots of Pagan Anti-Semitism in the Ancient World* (1975), has helped fill some gaps. Although the materials he presents are quite valuable, the perspective is somewhat one-sidedly that of the Gentiles. The theological points of view are thoughtful, but incomplete. And it is precisely these theological points of view that must serve as the foundation for the whole presentation, if it is not to remain merely an inventory of historical data but to have genuine current relevance—particularly if it is to be included in the contemporary discussion of the relation between Jews and Christians.

Formulation of the Question

The goal is historical understanding as such. Using a historical model, we are attempting to study the manner and degree of the acceptance of Judaism by a non-Jewish world and the role that Jews themselves played in the manner in which they were accepted or not accepted. The focus is, of course, on Judaism

7

itself, to the extent that it is constituted by its law.[1] It was precisely through this law that the unity of the people and the religion was established when political freedom had been lost.[2] This brings us to our principal theological theme:[3] monotheism, conceived in terms of the law, as a political problem.

This theme receives its breadth not only through the indissoluble connection between the people and its law and faith, and vice versa, but also through the breadth of the idea of God. God may be primarily the God of Israel. But in any case he is, as such, the God of the world, and his law is the law for the world. This theme has its continuing key position for the relationship of Jews and *Christians* when this God of the whole world is proclaimed as the Father of Jesus, who has made his advent as the crucified Messiah of Israel.

This Messiah likewise has a "people"—of course, of a completely new kind and constituted in a completely new way— which can in no way be synthesized with the old (as Bar Kochba already knew). When the Christians became self-consciously a "people," the Christian claim to universality necessarily led to political complications with a state of the Roman style (though one such as Luke might vainly seek to avoid them). The same self-consciousness and claim would inevitably lead to religious-political problems with Judaism (though Paul wanted—likewise in vain—to regard these problems as only preliminary by means of his inherently incompatible combination of history and eschatology in Romans 9–11).[4]

Delimitation of the Material

The boundaries of the period that we are here considering (ca. 300 B.C.E.–ca. 200 C.E.) derive from the sources and data themselves. The period begins with the hellenizing of the Orient in the time of Alexander the Great (d. 323 B.C.E.). For Judaism this created a fundamentally new situation with regard both to external circumstances (geographical expansion of Judaism, the formation of the Hellenistic diaspora) and internal development.[5] The end of the period we are studying is determined by the disappearance of the literature of Hellenistic

---

[1] See J. N. Sevenster, *The Roots of Pagan Anti-Semitism in the Ancient World* (Leiden: E. J. Brill, 1975), who strongly emphasizes this, especially in the chapter "Strangeness," 89ff., 114.

[2] Political freedom was lost in the Babylonian captivity and never recovered except for the brief Maccabean period.

[3] For the formulation of this theme, see E. Peterson, *Die Kirche aus Juden und Heiden* (1933).

[4] Such protests are in vain if Christians such as Luke and Paul express them without making clear that the Christian consciousness of being a new "people" is completely devoid of any "salvation history" element, and is thus free from any perspective on the future bound up with an understanding of themselves in some national-messianic way, and therefore free from any competition with Israel's history and with Israel's understanding of its history. The only problem was that this attitude necessarily led to the Christians understanding themselves as a "people" in such a way that they would not be incorporated into the Roman political schema.

[5] For differing evaluations of this, compare E. Bickermann and M. Hengel on one side and V. Tcherikover on the other (see below).

Judaism after the second century C.E. and the complete change in legal status brought about by the *Constitutio Antoniana.*

The selection of sources discussed is determined by the way in which the question dealt with in this study is formulated. In Parts III and IV the selection is attuned to the issue of the conscious (!) debate of Judaism with the non-Jewish world, as this was carried on in terms of defense, attack, or "public relations": How did Judaism come to terms with the surrounding world, to the extent that this was possible politically and socially? And how did Judaism project itself intellectually from its stance on the foundations of the necessary presuppositions of its existence, namely, people and law? Which possibilities of dealing with the world did these foundations make possible? Which possibilities were opened, and which were already closed off by these foundations? Could a neutral zone be marked off? What were the effects of experiences with the new Hellenistic states?[6]

We need to point out one limitation on the possibilities open to us: nothing approaching a continuous history of ancient anti-Semitism can be written. This not only is due to the external factor of the limited sources that have been preserved, but is inherent in the subject matter of our study itself. There was no such thing as an ancient anti-Jewish "movement" that exhibited some kind of coherent continuity, but only individual voices, eruptions, culminating points. This was not even changed by the bloody wars that extended far in both space and time. Nor did such wars cause "Judaism" to become a significant theme within Greek and Roman literature. This should occasion no surprise.[7] Before the Maccabean revolt, the Jews had no state of their own, and even afterward not an imposing one. And, after all, they can hardly be said to have had a literature when measured by Greek standards.[8] One result of this is that the description of Judaism by non-Jews was, generally speaking, not made from Jewish sources (at least not written ones). Until near the end of the second century C.E. only one historian known to us demonstrably worked with Jewish sources, Alexander "Polyhistor." Characteristically, excerpts from his writings have been preserved only in the works of Christian authors.[9] Nicholas of Damascus, the court historian of Herod the Great, represents a special case.

---

[6] In Palestine (after the Ptolemies and Seleucids), in the diaspora, in the social life of the Hellenistic cities (Alexandria)?

[7] Josephus gives an extensive explanation of this (*Ag. Ap.* 1.60ff.).

[8] Apart from the vain efforts of Josephus and Philo to produce such literature, there is practically nothing.

[9] Clement of Alexandria and especially Eusebius (*Praeparatio Evangelica*). The use of Alexander Polyhistor by later authors was minimal, to judge by the extant texts, including Josephus. Significant reference is found only in the lexical sources used by the lexicographer Stephanus of Byzantium. The data are given in *FGH* III a, 250f., 257ff. (cf. Teucer of Cyzicus references in *FGH* 274; *GLAJJ,* no. 54).

EXTRINSIC DATA[10]

General Statements
(Concerning the Extent of the Diaspora)[11]

Philo's summary description of the diaspora is well known (*Leg.* 281ff. in the speech of Herod Agrippa I). According to Philo (*Flacc.* 43), no fewer than a million Jews lived in Alexandria and Egypt,[12] while Josephus reports (*J.W.* 7.43) that the Syrian diaspora was the largest. No valuable information for computing the size of the diaspora is to be obtained by investigating its origin by emigration from Palestine and the resettlement policy of the Ptolemies and Seleucids. Of these two, however, the policy of the Ptolemies occurred on a scale and at a time that made it the more important. The Jewish settlement in Egypt had a long tradition that began long before Hellenistic times.[13]

The Ptolemaic Period[14]

The settlement of Jewish prisoners of war in Egypt had already begun with the first Ptolemies.[15] Whether Alexander the Great had already used Jewish mercenaries is disputed.[16]

---

[10] Lists of Jewish diaspora congregations are found in E. Schürer, *A History of the Jewish People in the Time of Jesus* (New York: Charles Scribner's Sons, 1901–1909) 3:2ff.; J. Juster, *Les Juifs dans l'empire Romain, leur condition juridique, économique et sociale,* 2 vols. (New York: Burt Franklin, 1914, 1965) 1:180ff.; T. Hopfner, *Die Judenfrage bei Griechen und Römern* (Prague, 1943) 80ff.; M. Stern,"The Jewish Diaspora," in *The Jewish People in the First Century,* CRINT (Philadelphia: Fortress Press, 1974) 1:117ff. Neither the number of Jews nor their percentage of the whole population can be determined (Stern, "Jewish Diaspora," 119).

[11] Such summaries are a form of apologetic; see further Philo, *Flacc.* 45f. Jewish self-consciousness expressed itself somewhat ambivalently in *Sib. Or.* 3.271ff.: πᾶσα δὲ γαῖα σέθεν πλήρης καὶ πᾶσα θάλασσα· πᾶς δὲ προσοχθίζων ἔσται τοῖς σοῖς ἐθίμοισιν· γαῖα δ' ἔρημος ἅπασα σέθεν ("The whole earth will be filled with you and every sea. Everyone will be offended at your customs. Your whole land will be desolate"). For the date, see n. 144 below. According to Bousset, it does not fit before ca. 140 B.C.E. ("Sibyllen und sibyllinische Bücher," *RE,* 3rd ed. [1906] 18:265ff.)—but on the other hand, cf. Pseudo-Hecataeus.

[12] Philo, *Flacc.* 55: two of the five districts of Alexandria were Jewish. According to Tcherikover, the numbers given in *Ep. Ar.* 12–14 are exaggerated, as is probably the case with Philo's figures in *Flacc.* 43 (*CPJ,* 14).

[13] Jeremiah 42–43; the Elephantine papyri.

[14] The discussion of this period is a special case because our material concerning the social situation of the Jews deals almost exclusively with Egypt, from which it comes. The basic work is Tcherikover's "Prolegomena" in *CPJ* 1; in addition, see *The Jewish People in the First Century,* ed. S. Safrai et al., CRINT (Philadelphia: Fortress Press, 1976) 2:701ff.; Sevenster, *Roots,* 57ff.; P. M. Fraser, *Ptolemaic Alexandria,* 3 vols. (Oxford: Clarendon, 1972).

[15] *Ep. Ar.* 12; cf. Josephus, *Ant.* 12.1ff. This report is confirmed by papyri: *CPJ,* no. 152; documentation and bibliography are given in M. Hengel, *Judaism and Hellenism* (Philadelphia: Fortress Press, 1974).

[16] Elias Bickermann, *Yale Classical Studies* 3 (1932): 68; W. L. Westermann, *Journal of American*

The legal status of the Jews in Alexandria, Egypt, and Cyrene has been much discussed. The discussion must consider the structure of the Ptolemaic state, distinguishing (a) between the Macedonian city of Alexandria, which did not belong to Egypt, and Egypt proper (χώρα, the country), and (b) between the Macedonia-Greek population and the Egyptians, even when the former live in the country outside Alexandria.

In these circumstances, were the Jews regarded as Greeks or Egyptians? Certainly not as Greeks![17] To be sure, according to Josephus (*Ant.* 19.280ff.) Claudius had confirmed the Jews' time-honored status as "Alexandrians" and their ἰσοπολιτεία (political equality), therefore, their civil rights.[18] But that was not actually the case. The decisive evidence is in *PLond.* 1912 (*CPJ* 153).[19] See further Tcherikover (70f.), who shows that Josephus, *Ant.* 19.280ff. is an incorrect reporting of the real edict. See also L. H. Feldman on the Josephus passage.[20] Of course, individual members of the Jewish upper class could—by whatever means—have obtained citizenship.[21] But these would have been

---

Philology 59 (1938): 19ff.; Ralph Marcus in LCL on Josephus, *Ant.* 12.46; Hengel, *Judaism and Hellenism*, 12–13. H. Willrich argues otherwise (*Juden und Griechen vor der Makkabäischen Erhebung* [Göttingen: Vandenhoeck & Ruprecht, 1895] 24): What Pseudo-Aristeas knows about Ptolemy I he obtained from Pseudo-Hecataeus, and can thus be supplemented from the same source. See his discussion of the source issue on p. 25: Josephus, *Ant.* 12.1 is a mixture of Agatharchides, Pseudo-Hecataeus, and Pseudo-Aristeas. The beginning of the Jewish diaspora by Ptolemy I is an invention of Pseudo-Hecataeus. There is a connection to Diodorus 19.86.3, the conquest of Tyre; the character of Ptolemy I: καθ' ὑπερβολὴν ἐπιεικὴς καὶ συγγνωμονικός, ἔτι δ' εὐεργετικός ("For indeed, that prince was exceptionally gentle and forgiving and inclined toward deeds of kindness"). Cf. 18.28.5f., directly or indirectly from Hieronymus of Cardia (*FGH*, 154) (*GLAJJ*, no. 10); Josephus, *Ag. Ap.* 1.213f.: this contemporary of Hecataeus did not mention the Jews, although he was the administrator of Syria. The real Hecataeus, at the time of Ptolemy I, knew nothing of a Jewish colony in Egypt. Rather, he *writes* nothing about this, but he knows Egypt and considers the Jews to have come from there.

Tcherikover (*CPJ* 1:2ff.) rightly warns us to be wary of Josephus's statements (*J.W.* 2.487; *Ag. Ap.* 2:35, 42) that already *Alexander* had settled Jews in Egypt. The earliest authentic evidence is the inscriptions of the necropolis of Ibrahimiya near Alexandria, probably from the time of Ptolemy I or II.

[17] *CPJ*, 60, 70, with n. 45; cf. *PLond.* 1912 and Josephus, *Ant.* 19.280ff. (*GLAJJ*, no. 11).

[18] For the meaning of ἰσοπολιτεία, see, among others, Stern, *GLAJJ*, 279ff.: Josephus means civil rights. For these ideas in general, see S. Applebaum, in *Jewish People in the First Century* 1:420ff.

[19] "Epistula Claudiana"; Eng. trans. in C. K. Barrett, *The New Testament Background: Selected Documents* (1987) no. 48; German trans. in J. Leipoldt and W. Grundmann, *Umwelt des Urchristentums,* 3 vols. (Berlin: Evangelische Verlagsanstalt, 1965–67) no. 269.

[20] *CPJ*, no. 151 (from the time of Augustus): an applicant describes himself as a citizen of Alexandria. This was later corrected to "a Jew of Alexandria." Cf. Tcherikover on this passage, and in *Hellenistic Civilization and the Jews,* 3rd ed. (Philadelphia: Jewish Publication Society of America, 1966) 312; see also Feldman on Josephus, *Ant.* 19.281, in *Josephus* (LCL) vol. 9.

[21] When one compares *CPJ*, no. 142 and no. 143, it turns out to be a matter of a Macedonian Jew in Alexandria. For Jewish names on the lists of *epheboi* from Cyrene from the period 3–28 c.e., see *Revue des études grecques* 75 (1962): 218: a Jew of Nero's time is listed among the city's νομοφύλακες ("guardian of the laws").

exceptions that confirm the rule. One argument for such exceptional cases is the occasional (self-)description of Jews as "Macedonians."[22]

THE SITUATION OF THE JEWS IN EGYPT AND CYRENE[23]

Alexandria

According to Josephus (*Ant.* 14.117) the Jews here had their own ethnarch.[24] Such an official is not mentioned after the time of Augustus.

As already mentioned, the most important document is *PLond.* 1912. Unfortunately it contains many riddles. A few examples of the problems of its interpretation are here given, especially from Josephus (*J. W.*) and the commentary in *CPJ*.[25]

PLond. 1912.52ff. deal with the *epheboi* (as the path toward citizenship). The stance of Claudius on this issue is not completely clear. See *CPJ* on this passage: Jews who had already succeeded in getting registered as *epheboi* are to preserve their civil rights. In any case, the passage confirms that the Jews did not possess full civil rights as such. For line 88, see Josephus, *Ant.* 19.280ff. (see above).

A controversy surrounds the emperor's expression διακούσας ἀμφοτέρων ("having given both a hearing"), which concerns the Greek and Jewish embassies sent from Alexandria to Claudius. The *CPJ* understands it to deal with two Greek embassies, while *PLond.* 1912.88f. reads the Alexandrians and Jews as the two embassies. The sending of their own delegation was prohibited to the Jews.

But the *CPJ* is again on the other side: the *Acta Alexandrinorum* (ed. Musurillo) speaks against this interpretation of two mixed delegations. Rather, there were two Jewish embassies sent (Smallwood, *Jews under Roman Rule*, 248 n. 209: for which they were reprimanded by Claudius), namely, the one known to us from Philo and led by him, and an aggressive counterpart.

Smallwood (*Jews under Roman Rule*, 242ff.) argues that the phrase refers to two embassies, one Greek and one Jewish, sent to Caligula. "Both embassies" that Claudius had given a hearing are not to be identified with the embassies

---

[22] Josephus, *J. W.* 2.487f.; *Ant.* 12.8; *Ag. Ap.* 2.35f. The meaning is disputed. According to Tcherikover (13ff.), what is described is a soldier who belongs to a Macedonian unit; cf. *CPJ*, nos. 30, 142. Thus this theme belongs in the larger context of the social status of the Jews, of which military service was an essential factor until the time of the annexation of the country by the Romans.

[23] Strabo reports that the population of Cyrene consisted of citizens, peasants, resident aliens, and Jews (*FGH*, 91 F 7=Josephus, *Ant.* 14.115 [*GLAJJ*, no. 105]).

[24] With Suetonius, *Life of Augustus*, compare Philo, who speaks of a genarch and a gerousia (*Leg.* 40; *Flacc.* 74ff.).

[25] Again, Tcherikover's "Prolegomena" to *CPJ* is foundational; see also Sevenster, *Roots*, 57ff.; Applebaum, *Jewish People in the First Century* 2:701ff.

that left Alexandria after Caligula's death had become known there. Further, the audience given to both sides is not contradictory to but supplementary to Josephus, *Ant.* 12.279 (Smallwood, *Jews under Roman Rule*, 246 n. 101). We need not be concerned about the other details of the traffic back and forth between Alexandrians, Jews, and Caesars.

The picture needs to be amplified by material from the papyri and inscriptions, for in the literature the upper class is understandably more prominent.

Examples: The Tobiads in the "Tobiad novel" in Josephus, *Ant.* 12.157ff. (Hengel, *Judaism and Hellenism*, 269ff.; Marcus, on Josephus, LCL 7:767f.); the family of Philo, who was brother of the "alabarch" Alexander, the father of the apostate Tiberius Alexander (see J. Schwartz, "Note sur la famille de Philon d'Alexandrie," *Annuaire de l'Institut de philologie et d'histoires orientales et slaves* 13, Mélanges I. Lévy [1953] 591ff.; V. Burr, *Tiberius Iulius Alexander* [Bonn: Rudolph Habelt, 1955]).

From the papyri: *CPJ,* 127a: the career of a certain apostate Dositheos, son of Drimylos (3 Macc. 1:3). Jewish soldiers and military colonists are a special case.[26] After the Roman annexation the Jews were excluded from the military service.

Tcherikover, *CPJ* 1:15ff.: peasants (see 33ff.); 17ff.: positions in the administration (see 48ff.); 16: evidence of Jewish merchants or money changers is lacking in the Hellenistic period.[27] It is remarkable that typical objections to Jews do not reproach them for their wealth or practice of usury. Rather, incidental references to their poverty are more characteristic. See Juvenal; Sevenster (*Roots*, 56), Smallwood (*Jews under Roman Rule*, 223), *CPJ* 1:10ff., 25, 55. Several papyri indicate that Jews possessed only a modest amount of property.[28] The picture of Judaism outside Egypt is supplemented by inscriptions: *CIJ* 556 (near Naples, from the time of Claudius or Nero): a prisoner of war from Jerusalem and a freedman of Claudius; *CIJ* 109 (Rome): a painter; *CIJ* 210 (Rome): a shopkeeper, etc. Similar examples are found in Asia Minor. Inscription 760 presents an example of a municipal civil servant. As a result of the recent excavations, inscriptions from Sardis are currently enjoying special prominence.[29]

---

[26] Tcherikover, 10ff.; see thereto no. 18ff.: *Jewish Soldiers and Military Settlers in the Third and Second Centuries BC.*

[27] This is, of course, related to the fact that no Ptolemaic papyri from Alexandria have been preserved. See the index to *CPJ* 1 under τραπεζῖται. For the practice of Jews loaning money to Jews, contrary to the Old Testament usury laws (Exod. 22:25; Deut. 23:19), see *CPJ,* nos. 20, 24.

[28] *CPJ* 1:464 refers to a Jew (or two Jews) as small tenant farmers; 142 refers to real estate; 143 mentions a legacy of two hundred drachmas; similar sums are mentioned in 148 and 149.

[29] See L. Robert, *Nouvelles inscriptions de Sardes* (Paris, 1964) 41ff., and Hengel's comments in "Die Synagogeninschrift von Stobi," *ZNW* 57 (1966): 171f.; see also A. T. Kraabel, *Judaism in Western Asia Minor in the Roman Empire, with a Preliminary Study of the Jewish Community of Sardis, Lydia* (Leiden: E. J. Brill, 1968; see *HTR* 61 [1968] 42–43): discovery of a large synagogue (2nd cent. C.E.); inscriptions indicating that Jews served in city councils and provincial offices. Kraabel makes connections with the polemic of Melito of Sardis; see below.

If one attempts to summarize these findings, it becomes clear that it is not possible to generalize about "the" social status of the Jews, especially in Egypt. Jews were found in every branch of economic life and in every social stratum. There were some rich Jews both in Alexandria and in the country. "But the general impression resulting from a study of the documents is that of a hard-working people earning its living by tenacious labor" (Tcherikover, *CPJ* 1:19).

The lines were drawn through the Ptolemaic system: on the one side, the political economy and the powerful position of the Greeks; and, on the other, the strength of the indigenous population.

The Jews under the Seleucids[30]

The first phase was the settlement of Jews in the newly established cities. According to Josephus, the Jews received citizenship and equality with the Macedonians and Greeks from Seleucus I in return for their military service (*Ant.* 12.119).[31] Willrich considers the purported settlement of Jews in Asia Minor by Seleucus I to be unhistorical (*Juden und Griechen*, 29ff.). The first Syrian king to play a role in Jewish history was Antiochus III. It appears that it was the Romans who first granted the Jews their privileges.[32] The commentary on the political actions of Antiochus III that were favorable to the Jews is provided by Josephus, *Ant.* 12.[33]

There is no reason to discuss here the attack by Antiochus IV on the essential core of Judaism. This concerns our subject only to the extent that the diaspora attained an increased importance in Judaism as a whole by the formation of a free Jewish state in Palestine. This happened not only through the fundamental change in Jewish self-consciousness with regard to Hellenism but also through the changed geographical aspect of the "diaspora" in view of the new center for Judaism.[34]

---

[30] H. Bengston, *Herrschergestalten des Hellenismus* (1975) 493ff.; Schürer, *History* 3:107ff.

[31] Schürer, *History* 3:122 (without a doubt!). Later Josephus notes that Vespasian and Titus did not infringe upon these rights (at Antioch!)—after the Jewish war.

With regard to Ephesus and the cities of the Ionian coast, see Schürer, *History* 3:124: Citizenship was probably conferred here by Antiochus II Theos (261–245 B.C.E.), as he "reorganized the governments of the Ionian cities, replacing the earlier oligarchies with democratic forms of government." That, of course, is only an inference drawn from Josephus, *Ant.* 12.125, taken together with *Ag. Ap.* 2.39; *Ant.* 12.125 says nothing about citizenship for the Jews; Schürer, *History* 3:124 n. 14.

[32] Hengel, *Judaism and Hellenism*, 15f.

[33] *Ant.* 12.138–53. For the question of authenticity, see Marcus, *Josephus* (LCL) 7.743ff. Even if this be affirmed in general, the complete authenticity of the wording cannot be accepted. In evaluating it, considerable weight must be given to the inscription documented in Robert, *Nouvelles Inscriptions,* no. 1, a decree of Antiochus III. A. T. Kraabel ("Paganism and Judaism: The Sardis Evidence," in *Paganisme, Judaïsme, Christianisme,* Mél. M. Simon [Paris: Boccard, 1978] 13ff.) and Tcherikover (*Hellenistic Civilization and the Jews* [Philadelphia: Jewish Publication Society of America, 1966] 287f.) agree with Robert on the authenticity of the document.

[34] For the lasting influence of Hellenism in Palestine and the fluid boundaries between "Palestinian" and "Hellenistic" Judaism, one may simply refer to Hengel.

The first experience of persecution purely on the basis of Jewish faith gave this faith a new image: the demand for public confession of God the Father and the practice of obedience to the Torah—even to the point of martyrdom.[35] An analysis of the internal situation in Palestine just before and during the outbreak of the crisis can be excluded from our present discussion, which is concerned exclusively with the picture of the situation that resulted from these events.

At the present there are essentially two types of interpretation that confront each other: (1) the traditional view and (2) a novel approach inaugurated by Bickermann that has been taken up also by Hengel, but rejected by Tcherikover. According to Bickermann (*The God of the Maccabees* [Leiden: E. J. Brill, 1979]) it was not at all Antiochus IV who took the initiative, but the Jewish hellenizers, and it was they who carried it through to the bitter end. They had been influenced deeply by the ideas of the Greek enlightenment and wanted to restore the pure form of worship that the human race had originally had (corresponding to the conception of history as "origin" and "degeneration"; Posidonius).

Their program called for the abolition of the Mosaic law and the deuteronomistic centralization of the cult. They had not planned on the introduction of Greek cultic forms. No anthropomorphic cult object was to be set up. Rather, they had proposed the establishment of cultic places (groves) along the lines of the ancient Semitic holy places.[36] In addition, the reformers rejected the (not "original") barbarian separation of Jews from other peoples.

Tcherikover rejects this interpretation.[37] The internal feud between the Seleucid and Ptolemaic parties among the Jews had nothing to do with a cultural and theoretical program. It was at first a purely political struggle for power. It first took on a religious character when the worshipers of a foreign god settled in Jerusalem (1 Macc. 1:34ff.).[38]

For our purposes it is adequate to portray the resulting picture as follows: (1) The presupposition for the existential crisis in the life of the community was the defection of some Jews and the mixing with the Gentile population

---

[35] See 2 and 4 Maccabees; H.-W. Surkau, *Martyrien in jüdischer und frühchristlicher Zeit* (Göttingen: Vandenhoeck & Ruprecht, 1932); E. Lohse, *Märtyrer und Gottesknecht*, 2nd ed. (Göttingen: Vandenhoeck & Ruprecht, 1963) 2.

[36] For the worship of Zeus Olympios, see E. Bickermann, *The God of the Maccabees*, trans. H. R. Moehring (Leiden: E. J. Brill, 1979) 73: "He whose throne stands on Zion" was identified with the Syrian "Baal of the heavens," which of course in Greek would mean "Olympian Zeus." Cf. the cultic worship of Olympian Zeus purportedly supported by Hiram of Tyre, in Dios, *FGH*, 785 F 2 (*GLAJJ*, no. 36) (Josephus, *Ant.* 8.147; *Ag. Ap.* 1.112ff.; cf. Eupolemus, *FGH*, 723 [Eusebius, *Praep. Ev.* 9.34.1b]).

[37] Moses Hadas, *Hellenistic Culture: Fusion and Diffusion* (New York: Columbia University Press, 1959) 43: The Maccabean uprising was originally not a reaction to Hellenism, but a struggle for the high priesthood between equally hellenized aspirants. The decree of Antiochus IV appeared only after the struggle became characterized by religious slogans.

[38] For the political aspects, see Hadas, *Hellenistic Culture*, on 2 Macc. 4:9 and Appendix III, 404ff.

(1 Macc. 1:11; 2 Macc. 4:11). Thereby a theological explanation is provided both for the calamity itself and for the ultimate victory of those who were loyal to the law. (2) The initiative was taken by Antiochus IV, or, at least, in such a situation he could have taken the initiative. (3) The struggle was for the Torah of God and as such was a matter of the existence of the people. The temporary loss of political freedom was understood as a call to repentance. But freedom was in any case expected to be restored, though there was a variety of views on how this was to be achieved: by war, by prayer, by apocalyptic transformation of the world. When Israel's religion is attacked, the primary responsibility of Israel to its God is to resist, in extreme cases even to the death of the last member of the resistance (Masada). From this point of view, the most consistent Jews in the early Christian period were the Zealots. Contrary to his own intention, Josephus confirms this by, on the one hand, his portrayal of his own capitulation (*J.W.* 3.8), and, on the other hand, his portrayal of the battle of Masada (*J.W.* 7.8–9). Compare *J.W.* 7.271ff. with 415ff.

Against this background of the readiness to struggle for God, law, and people, the dimension of Israel's readiness for martyrdom becomes visible precisely in those cases where the possibility of active resistance was excluded.[39] The Jewish idea of martyrdom that thus developed did not permit the Jewish martyr who suffered because of his or her faith to bless the persecutor.[40] What they could do was to regard their destiny as punishment sent by God (2 Macc. 7:18) and believe in the expiatory effect of the sufferings of the righteous.[41]

Does a survey of the diaspora provide any basis for estimating the number of Jews in Hellenistic and Roman times? We must be satisfied with mentioning a few attempts to make such calculations, which only serve to illustrate how little we know.

Speculations with regard to the eastern diaspora are absolute guesswork. For the Roman Empire, A. Harnack estimates four million (*The Mission and Expansion of Christianity* [New York: Harper & Brothers, 1961] 8). Juster reckons on six to seven million out of a total population of ca. eighty million (*Juifs dans l'empire* 1:209ff.). J. Beloch guesses about 7 percent of a total population of fifty-five million (*Die Bevölkerung der griechisch-römischen Welt* [1886]), followed by

---

[39] This was the case for prisoners and women, for example. On martyrdom as passive resistance, see Philo, *Leg.* 223. See also the contrast of the easy death in battle (which, of course, Josephus understood himself to have renounced) and death by torture (*Ag. Ap.* 2.232ff.).

[40] The references cited by Billerbeck say nothing at all (*Kommentar zum Neuen Testament aus Talmud und Midrasch*, 6 vols. [Munich: Beck, 1922–62] 1:370f., on Matt 5:44). 2 Macc. 7:18 expresses the idea exactly. For the stance of the synagogue on martyrdom, see Billerbeck, *Kommentar* 1:221ff., on Matt. 5:10.

[41] Lohse, *Märtyrer und Gottesknecht*; 2 Macc. 7:33, 37f.; G. F. Moore, *Judaism in the First Centuries of the Christian Era: The Age of the Tannaim*, 3 vols. (Cambridge, MA: Harvard University Press, 1927–30) 1:546ff.; M. Hengel, *The Zealots* (Edinburgh: T. & T. Clark, 1989) 267. The idea is stylized in the literary "lives of the prophets"; see T. Schermann, *Propheten- und Apostellegenden*, TU 31.3 (Leipzig: Hinrichs, 1907).

H. Lietzmann (*A History of the Early Church* [Cleveland and New York: World, 1961] 1:76).

The causes of the expansion have been much discussed. In any case, there was a great increase of the Jewish population. The πολυανθρωπία ("population density") of the Jews became a literary topos.[42]

How Judaism Spread

In addition to the politically motivated resettlement programs of the rulers (in the earlier period), voluntary immigration was a factor.[43]

What role did the winning of proselytes play in the spread of Judaism?[44] There are widely different opinions about their number (and status).[45] To what extent can one speak of an active Jewish mission (cf. Matt. 23:15)? Or did groups of proselytes originate simply by the power of attraction of the Jewish religion itself?[46]

Proselytes[47]

This is προσήλυτος ("proselytes") in the LXX, גר in rabbinic usage. With the Gentile reader in mind, Philo prefers ἐπήλυτος ("followers"), among other terms; see, for example, *Spec. Leg.* 1.52f.; he explains the term προσήλυτος in *Spec. Leg.* 1.51. Josephus does not use the substantive, but alludes to it in *Ant.* 18.82: the Roman woman Fulvia, νομίμοις προσεληλυθυῖαν τοῖς Ἰουδαϊκοῖς ("a woman of high rank who had become a Jewish proselyte").

The Jewish attitude toward proselytes was not uniform (M. Simon, *Verus Israel* [Oxford: Oxford University Press, 1986] 274ff.). Positive statements

---

[42] Hecataeus of Abdera, *FGH,* 264 F 6 (*GLAJJ,* no. 11): The Jews have many children, and raise them all to maturity. For the assignment of the passage to Hecataeus (against J. C. H. Lebram), see part II, n. 17. On the subject itself, see Josephus, *Ag. Ap.* 2.199ff. For the prohibition of abortion and the exposure of children, see also *Did.* 2:2 and parallel *Barn.* 19:5.

[43] *CPJ* 1, no. 4: the Jewish immigration into Egypt. Rome: Philo, *Leg.* 155; H. J. Leon, *The Jews of Ancient Rome* (Philadelphia: Jewish Publication Society of America, 1960). The number of Jews in Rome was estimated by Juster at about fifty thousand (*Juifs dans l'empire* 1:209), as also by G. La Piana, "Foreign Groups in Rome," *HTR* 20 (1927): 341ff. According to Josephus, Tiberius recruited four thousand Jews in Rome (*Ant.* 18.84; Tacitus, *Annals* 2.85: Egyptians and Jews).

[44] See n. 47.

[45] The Roman measures against proselytism are a special problem: see below and Smallwood, *Jews under Roman Rule,* index.

[46] H. Kasting, *Die Anfänge der urchristlichen Mission* (Munich: Kaiser, 1969) 11ff., and the comments thereon by M. Hengel, *TLZ* 96 (1971): 913ff. For the significance of the synagogue, see Schrage, "συναγωγή (synagogue)," *TDNT* 7:798ff.; and A. T. Kraabel, "Synagogue," *The New Catholic Encyclopedia* 16:436ff.

[47] Billerbeck, *Kommentar* 2:715ff.; *The Beginnings of Christianity,* ed. F. J. Foakes Jackson and K. Lake, 5 vols. (London: Macmillan, 1920–33) 5:74ff.; K. G. Kuhn and H. Stegemann, "Proselyten" in *PWSup* 9:1248ff.

concerning proselytes are listed in G. F. Moore, *Judaism*, 1:345.[48] The proselyte has become a full convert to Judaism, subject to the whole law; he is regarded by the Jews as a Jew. Proselytes were buried in Jewish cemeteries, but not "God-fearers" (see documentation in *CIJ*). Ἀλλοεθνεῖς (members of other ethnic groups) who kept the law were also called Jews according to Dio 37.17. The "God-fearers" (*metuentes;* יראי שמים) were sympathizers.[49] They were not regarded as Jews, but belonged to the Jewish congregations.

We have little idea of the number of proselytes. Based on the number of tomb inscriptions, the number would seem to be very small: only nine of more than seven hundred in *CIJ!* In the Jewish catacombs: 21, 37 (?), 68, etc. Inscription 68 reads: *Cresce(n)s Sinicerius Iud(a)eus prosel(y)tus.* ("Crescens Sinicerius Jewish proselyte").

But the data are not to be evaluated merely statistically. Frey (*CIJ* I:ix n. 5) points out the accidental character of the material that has been preserved: practically all the inscriptions in volume I have been found in Rome after

---

[48] In addition, see Billerbeck, *Kommentar* 1:929, 102, 107; Moore, *Judaism* 1:323ff. By about the middle of the second century the rabbis no longer understood the meaning of יראי שמים (Billerbeck, *Kommentar* 2:720f.).

An inscription from the theater in Miletus reads (*CIJ* 748; A. Deissmann, *Light from the Ancient East* [London: Hodder & Stoughton, 1911] 451): τόπος Εἰουδαίων τῶν καὶ Θεοσεβῶν ("Place of the Jews, who also are called God-fearing").

[49] Literature: *CIJ* 1:495f.; Juster, *Juifs dans l'empire* 1:460, 2:82; F. Bömer, *Untersuchungen über die Religion der Sklaven in Griechenland und Rom*, Part II, Akademie der Wissenschaften und der Literatur in Mainz in Kommission bei Franz Steiner Verlag GMBH (Wiesbaden: F. Steiner, 1960); Schrage, *TDNT* 7:824. Emancipation in the synagogue: *POxy.* 9.1205.

See also the emancipation inscription from Panticapaeum (1st cent. C.E.), CIRB no. 71; H. Bellen, "Συναγωγή τῶν Ἰουδαιων καὶ θεοσεβῶν: Die Aussage einer bosporanischen Freilassungsinschrift (CIRB 71) zum Problem der 'Gottfürchtigen,'" *Jahrbuch für Antike und Christentum* 8/9 (1965–66) 171ff., 176; Schürer, *History* 3:36):

1. ----κα
2. κου ἀφίημι ἐπὶ τῆς προσευ-
3. χῆς Ἐλπία[ν] ----α. τῆς θρεπτ[ῆς]
4. ὅπως ἐστὶν ἀπαρενόχλητος
5. καὶ ἀνεπίληπτος ἀπὸ παντὸς
6. κληρονόμου χωρὶς τοῦ προσ-
7. καρτερεῖν τῇ προσευχῇ ἐπι-
8. τροπευούσης τῆς συναγω-
9. γῆς τῶν Ἰουδαίων καὶ θεὸν
10. σέβων.

"In the synagogue I hereby free Elpis, a slave brought up in my house. She is (sc. in her freedom) to remain unmolested and unhindered by my heirs; the only condition is that she continue in the synagogue. The congregation of the Jews and God-fearers accepts the responsibility of protecting (her freedom)." An inscription from Gorgippia (Anapa) (Latyschev II, no. 400) begins θεῶι ὑψίστωι παντοκράτορι εὐλογητῷ ("To the most high God, blessed Ruler of all . . .") and is therefore considered by many to be Jewish. It concludes with the oath formula ὑπὸ Δία, Γῆν, Ἥλιον ("by Zeus, earth, heaven") from which Schürer (*History* 3:24) concludes that the inscription is pagan with a Jewish element. Hopfner (*Judenfrage*, 25f.) argues that it is Jewish, the concluding formula only present to make it legally binding.

70 C.E. Simon (*Verus Israel*, 257) says we must reckon with the fact that in Rome conversion from one faith to another was strictly monitored. Six of the eight relevant Roman inscriptions concern women. Names can be an indication of gradual accommodation.[50]

Opposing a widespread view, Simon concluded that after the Jewish war(s) the flow of proselytes by no means ceased. He refers, for example, to the importance of Judaism in Syria, which is confirmed by John Chrysostom (*Verus Israel*, 287ff.). Proselytism is reflected in Christian legislation (p. 334). A conflict between Theodosius II and the patriarch Gamaliel VI was due to the latter's proselyting activities (pp. 130ff.). Concerning Syrian Christianity, see further Georg Strecker (in Walter Bauer, *Orthodoxy and Heresy in Earliest Christianity* [Philadelphia: Fortress Press, 1971] 241–85, esp. 244ff.).

The observation of Simon (*Verus Israel*, 273) is worthy of note, that the spread of Christianity had a positive effect on Judaism: the more Christianity in the second century attracted attention to itself, the more it tended to divert attention from Judaism.[51] The uninterrupted growth of Judaism between the wars is indicated by further evidence.[52]

By such observations Simon correctly opposes the current view of the demise of Hellenistic Judaism as a result of the two wars (or else its destruction by Palestinian Judaism). L. Goppelt argues otherwise: after the second war Hellenistic Judaism is no longer evident as a trend within Judaism (*Christentum und Judentum im ersten und zweiten Jahrhundert* [Gütersloh: Bertelsmann, 1954] 160). Most of the Hellenistic Jewish writings pointed to by Simon originated earlier: 4 Maccabees, *Sib. Or.* 4 (ca. 80 C.E.), *Sib. Or.* 5 (last third of the first century; only nos. 1–51 under the Antonini).

In the (Jewish) collection of prayers in the *Apostolic Constitutions,* the LXX is used. The Hellenistic features of the Jews in Celsus probably derive from the older Hellenistic-Jewish literature. Justin and Origen no longer are acquainted with a Hellenistic Judaism as a contemporary phenomenon worth noting.

Despite Goppelt's argument, for non-Jews, Hellenistic Judaism was always considered to be Judaism. And the idea of a rapid accommodation to Palestinian Judaism, with its patriarch and rabbinic system, is too schematic and takes too little account of the inertia of the masses, the numbers of diaspora Jews, the durability and tenacity of tradition, along with the effect of the Greek language (which continued to be used for the Bible).

---

[50] Elephantine (see Schürer, *History* 3:28): The Jewish woman Neibtalya took the Egyptian As-Hor as her husband in her second marriage. He is later called Nathan, and the children received Jewish names. For other instances of such accommodation, see *CIJ* 749; 499 (mixed marriages). For data on names in general, see the index to *CPJ* and *CPJ* 3:167ff.

[51] With exceptions, of course: Septimius Severus. See Simon, *Verus Israel*, 41f.; P. de Labriolle, *La réaction païenne* (Paris: L'Artisan du Livre, 1934) 458: "a transfer of animosity."

[52] Juvenal; Justin, *Dial.* 23.3.

Jewish Self-Awareness

What historical experiences did the Jews bring into the Hellenistic world with them? As before, they continued to operate under the presupposition that they were the chosen people of God, to whom the future belonged; see Philo, *Praem. Poen.* 79ff. and 162ff.! How did these previous experiences work out in this world that was new to them, not only in terms of anti-Jewish reactions (which for the first time gradually appear) but also in the positive effects of Jewish ideas and customs? How did the old experiences influence the new ones, both the objective situation of the Jews and their subjective response to this changed world in which they found themselves.

Since the Babylonian exile the Jews had known that they could endure periods without political independence in a foreign country without the temple cultus and not lose their identity. And they believed that they could continue to endure such times, if they faithfully continued in obedience to God, or if they would return to him. The one God was the guarantor of this, the one God who is ruler of the world but who had also chosen Israel and given it the law, for it is this God whose law and promise are stamped on every worship service.

This faith and law carried with them a certain mode of separation from all other peoples even if there was considerable room for variation in how this was carried out in practice. This separation could be emphatically proclaimed, even in situations where it disrupted the apologetic goals![53] The law is a wall erected around the people, "in order that we might not mingle at all with any of the other nations."[54] This attitude provoked a Gentile reaction, expressed most sharply in the charge against the Jews that they were "haters of humanity."

Jewish apologetic could offer this defense: the law of Moses was the law of

---

[53] For rabbinic materials, see Billerbeck, *Kommentar* 1:449f.; 2:96; 3:157f., 393f., 802f., 806, 818; 4:860f., 868f., 875, 880ff., 1002, 1004ff., 1203; H. Fuchs cites *Meg.* 13b (*Der geistige Widerstand gegen Rom in der antiken Welt,* 2nd ed. (Berlin: de Gruyter, 1964):
"There is one people." Raba said: There has never been anyone so skilful as Haman at defaming a people. He said to Ahasuerus, Come, let us destroy them. He replied: I am afraid of their God, lest He do to me as He did to my predecessors. He replied: they are "negligent" of thy precepts. He said: There are Rabbis among them. He replied: They are "*one* people." Should you say that I will make a void in your kingdom, I reply they are "scattered abroad among the peoples." Should you say, there is some profit in them, I reply, "they are dispersed" *nifredu,* like an isolated bough *peridah* that does not bear fruit. Should you say that they occupy one province, I reply, "they are in all provinces of thy kingdom." "Their laws are diverse from those of every other people"; they do not eat our food, nor do they marry our women or give us theirs in marriage, "neither keep they the king's laws," since they avoid taxes the whole year by their loitering and sauntering. "Therefore it profiteth not the king to suffer them, " because they eat and drink and despise the throne. For if a fly falls into the cup of one of them, he throws it out and drinks the wine, but if my Lord the king were to touch his cup, he would dash it on the ground and not drink from it" (*Commentary to Esth.* 3:8; *The Babylonian Talmud,* ed. Epstein).
[54] *Ep. Ar.* 139; cf. the reference to the purity laws in 142.

the creator, therefore the law of nature and the cosmos. This argument, how-ever, had little prospect of success, since it is self-contradictory. Hengel (*Judaism and Hellenism*, 12ff.) considers the decisive factor to be that the Jews' first experiences with Hellenism were with its war machinery and administrative organization. But the Hellenistic age was by no means from the very beginning a time of terrors (cf. how Josephus characterizes the time of the struggles between the Ptolemies and the Seleucids [*Ant.* 12.130]). Nor was the accommodation of the Jews to new rulers necessarily always negative, as is seen for example in the legendary account of Alexander (Josephus, *Ant.* 11.325ff.), and the literature from and about Egypt. The Jews had already, of course, had positive experiences with Gentile rulers (and these were already recorded in their Scriptures). The Persians are an example, beginning with Deutero-Isaiah's hope that Cyrus was the "anointed" of Yahweh (Isa. 45:1ff.). See also the books of Ezra-Nehemiah (1 Esdras was used by Josephus in *Ant.* 10–11).[55]

One effect of such experiences was the prayer for the pagan ruler that became traditional.[56] Sacrifice: *Ep. Ar.* 45; 1 Macc. 7:33; 3 Macc. 1:9; Philo, *Leg.* 157, 317; Josephus, *J.W.* 2.196f., 408ff. Prayer: *CPJ* 418a: Κύριε Καῖσα[ρ Οὐεσπ]α[σ]ι-ανὸς εἰς σωτὴρ καὶ ε[ὐεργέτης . . . κύρι]ε σεβαστε′ ("lord Caesar Vespasian, the one savior and benefactor . . . lord Augustus"); *CPJ* 418b; *'Abot* 3.2: Rabbi Hananiah the Prefect of the Priests (Strack, *Introduction to the Talmud and Midrash* [New York: Meridian, 1959] 109: therefore this was still in the time of the second temple): "Pray for the peace of the מלכות ("ruling power"), since but for fear of it people would have swallowed up each other alive." Cf. Philo, *Flacc.* 49.[57]

The official relationship between the ruling power and the Jewish subjects in Egypt is reflected also in the fact that synagogues were sometimes dedicated to the rulers.[58]

According to the account in *Ep. Ar.*, Ptolemy II had the law translated into Greek, and debated with Jewish scholars.[59] This account was taken up by

---

[55] Regarding the alleged religious persecution by the Persians, see Pseudo-Hecataeus; Josephus, *Ant.* 20.160; H. Willrich, *Judaica* (Göttingen: Vandenhoeck & Ruprecht, 1900) 35ff.

[56] Prepared for already by Jer. 29:7; see further the decree of Ezra 6:3ff. For the question of authenticity, see W. Rudolph, *Esra und Nehemiah* (Tübingen: Mohr, 1949) 59: doubt on this subject is not permitted!

[57] Schürer, *History* 1:483f.; 2:360ff.; 3:460, 462; Schürer-Vermes-Millar, *History* 1:379f.; Martin Dibelius and Hans Conzelmann, *The Pastoral Epistles*, trans. P. Buttolph and A. Yarbro, Hermeneia (Philadelphia: Fortress Press, 1972) 37–39 (excursus on 1 Tim. 2:2).

[58] *CIJ*, no. 1440ff. No. 1440 gives the oldest reference to a synagogue in Egypt under Ptolemy III Euergetes (246–221 B.C.E.): ['Υ] πὲρ βασιλέως Πτολεμαίου καὶ βασιλίσσης Βερενίκης ἀδελφῆς καὶ γυναικὸς καὶ τῶν τέκνων τὴν προσευχὴν οἱ Ἰουδαῖοι ("In honor of king Ptolemy and queen Bernice, his sister and wife, and their children, the Jews (have dedicated) this synagogue . . .").

For the ὑπέρ-expressions, see F. C. Taeger, *Studien zur Geschichte des antiken Herrscherkultes* 1:299. *CIJ* no. 1449 refers to the granting of the right of asylum to a synagogue (Ptolemy III).

[59] Willrich, *Judaica*, 99ff.: There are two contradictory tendencies in *Ep. Ar.* regarding the relation of Ptolemy I to the Jews: (1) He was a hard master (see Appian, *Syr.* 50; Agatharchides of

Josephus (*Ant.* 12.2), who adds additional reports.[60]
Are negative experiences in Egypt reflected in 3 Maccabees?

Prophetic Phenomena in the Hellenistic-Roman Age[61]

Contrary to widespread opinion, prophecy was alive and well in this period.[62] In Alexandria prophecy was a "sapiential," nonpolitical phenomenon (Wis. 7:27). For Philo the prophetic gift reached its fulfillment in ecstasy (see *Rer. Div. Her.* 259). The stages toward this full experience are discussed in *Rer. Div. Her.* 249. A completely different type of prophecy is found in Palestine (Josephus!), where prophecy comes to expression in an outspokenly political manner, with prophetic types claiming to be leaders of the nation to salvation (conceived politically). Josephus, of course, represents these as false prophets. Josephus claims to have the genuine prophetic gift himself, and he attributes it to the Essenes as well (*J.W.* 2.159; *Ant.* 13.299f. [Hyrcanus]; 15.373ff. [Menachem]). He knows of prophetic movements that withdraw with their leader into the wilderness, where God was supposed to reveal signs of the coming liberation (*J.W.* 2.258ff., 285; *Ant.* 20.97f., 167ff.). His picture of Jesus ben Ananias is especially impressive, representing him to be very much like the Old Testament prophets (*J.W.* 6.300ff.).

Effects of Judaism on the Gentile World, apart from Anti-Semitism; Syncretistic Phenomena?

Kraabel correctly warns against overestimating the degree of Jewish syncretism[63] that supposedly included the worship of Sabazios and Hypsistos,

---

Knidos [*GLAJJ*, no. 30a]; Josephus, *Ag. Ap.* 1.206ff.; *Ant.* 12.8ff.). (2) He was their patron and benefactor (Josephus, *Ant.* 12.1ff.). The common source is Pseudo-Hecataeus; cf. Josephus, *Ag. Ap.* 2.43ff. From Pseudo-Hecataeus also comes Josephus, *Ant.* 11.207ff.

[60] In the polemic against Apion (Josephus, *Ag. Ap.* 2.4f.); a religious discussion in the presence of Ptolemy VI Philometor (Josephus, *Ant.* 13.74; cf. 12.10).

[61] Rudolf Meyer, "προφήτης κτλ. (prophecy, etc.)," *TDNT* 6:812ff.

[62] Despite a rabbinic theory according to which the place of the prophets had been taken by the wisdom teachers. Meyer correctly argues that the much-discussed texts in 1 Macc. 4:46; 9:27; and 14:41 do not confirm that prophecy was extinct, but are directed toward justifying the priestly leadership of John Hyrcanus.

[63] Morton Smith, *JBL* 86 (1967): 60f.; A. T. Kraabel, *HTR* 61 (1968): 642 (Sardis); Kraabel, "Paganism" (summary of the data presently available). Here Kraabel continues to advocate his negative judgment concerning Jewish syncretism, cautiously avoiding what is merely hypothetical. The main points of his argument are as follows: (1) The inscription mentioned above (Robert, no. 1; see n. 33 above). (2) The archaeological discoveries from the synagogue and its environs. It was part of the same building complex as the gymnasium and the baths, but not connected to them by adjoining halls. The Jews were closely related to the municipal life, but their religion gave no indication of syncretistic amalgamation. (3) This is true also in the furnishings and decorations of the synagogue, which included pagan symbols. So was there syncretism after all? Not according to Kraabel, who interprets: "The Sardis synagogue reflects a *self-confident* Judaism, bold enough to

particularly in Asia Minor, for there are only barely visible traces of this at the most. But a discussion concerning the relationship between Judaism and Gnosticism has been made completely unavoidable by the Nag Hammadi texts, which include documents that interpret essentially Jewish ideas in a Gnostic manner. We already had some examples of this in the magical papyri: *PGM* 4.3019ff.; the "Leiden Cosmogony": *PGM* 13; *PGM* 5.96ff.; the prayer of Adam for salvation from Anagke (fate), *PGM* 1.196ff.; 4.1167ff.

This is not the place for a discussion of the problem of the origins of Gnosticism, but a warning should be given against confusing motif parallels with genetic theories.

External Influences on Hellenistic Judaism

Philo is "Exhibit A." His works often mention specific schools, especially Plato, who virtually lives again in Philo's writings, but also the Stoics. Other passages may define a given idea as "Platonic" or by some other philosophical label. Of course, in that eclectic age precise distinctions were not possible. A case for the strong influence of Pythagoras or Pythagoreanism is made by I. Lévy in *La légende de Pythagore de Grèce en Palestine* (Pythagore, 1927). He reconstructs (from Abaris of Heraclea Pontica) a *Katabasis* of Pythagoras. The life of Moses as portrayed by Artapanos, Philo, and Josephus was modeled on the *Life of Pythagoras*. (See also E. Bréhier, *Les Idées philosophiques et religieuses de Philon d'Aléxandrie*, 3rd ed. [Paris: Vrin, 1950] 18; R. Reitzenstein, *Historia Monachorum und Historia Lausiaca* [1916] 105f., 257f.; for the "two natures," see Jamblich, *Pythagoras*, 31; Philo, *Vit. Mos.* 1.27). The influence of Pythagoras made itself felt on Judaism as a whole, including the rabbis.

Comparisons

Philo: Egyptian science and mathematics, *Vit. Mos.* 1.23; Jamblich. *Pythagoras*, 19; Porphyry, *Vita Pythagorae* 1; Apuleius, Flor. 15. The new Pharoah, *Vit. Mos.* 2.284, with Phalaris against Pythagoras: Jamblich, *Pythagoras*, 215f.; cf.

---

appropriate pagan shapes and symbols for itself" ("Paganism," 21). He supports his interpretation by the references to municipal and provincial functionaries in the synagogue inscriptions (George Hunfmann, "The Ninth Campaign at Sardis"; cf. *BASOR* 187 [1967]: 27ff.). (4) Probably the most important argument for Jewish syncretism in Asia Minor is provided by the names Sabazios and Hypsistos.

The literary data have long been familiar. Concerning the issue of syncretism, see the literature provided in Kraabel, "Paganism," 28f.; see also M. P. Nilsson, *Geschichte der Griechischen Religion*, 2nd ed. (Munich: Beck, 1961) 2:662ff., and Kraabel's comment thereon: "Hypistos" was used in Asia Minor by pagans, Jews, and Christians. The name "Sabatios" in Jewish ears probably connotes "Sabbath" rather than "Sabazios." "There is no evidence in the more than eighty Jewish inscriptions of any interest in Sabazios or knowledge of him" (Kraabel, "Paganism," 29; for two pagan Sabazios inscriptions, see pp. 30f.). Melito of Sardis, who probably would have had good reasons for mentioning Jewish syncretism in this area if it existed, says nothing about it.

Domitian against Apollonius, Philostratus 7.10 and 8.12. The imprisonment of Moses: Artapanos and Philostratus 8.30.

For the rejection of the charge of sorcery and the emphasis on the correspondence of life and teaching, see Philo, *Hypoth.* 6.1; Josephus, *Ag. Ap.* 2.161, 169. For the prohibition of the defamation of foreign gods, see (a) Philo, *Spec. Leg.* 1.53; *Decal.* 63; Josephus, *Ag. Ap.* 2.137, and (b) Philostratus 6.3 (see Eduard Norden, *Agnostos Theos* [Leipzig and Berlin: Teubner, 1913] 42); Plato, *Laws* 4.717a; Porphyry, 39; Pythagoras in Diog. Laert. 8.33.

THE SITUATION OF THE JEWS
IN THE ROMAN EMPIRE[64]

From the very beginning, that is, since the new order inaugurated by Pompey, there had been a fundamental difference between the situation of the Jews and that of the Hellenistic states in general. The basis for the legal position of the Jewish state was its status as a client state (for Herod, see W. Otto, *PWSup* 2:1ff.; Schalit, *König Herodes* [Berlin: de Gruyter, 1969] 146ff.). This included the following: Legal rights were not based on a permanent alliance, but were granted by Rome and could be revoked. Such states were not a part of a Roman province and were not subjected to a Roman governor. But Rome reserved the right to have its governors intervene if, for example, the client king did not (or could not) carry out his responsibilities in the service of the empire. Tribute was imposed. The client state was permitted its own internal government and court system, as well as the right to mint its own (copper) coins. The administration of its own financial affairs included, of course, responsibility for the collection and delivery of tribute.

Obviously the client states were not permitted their own foreign policy, as is illustrated, for example, by the emperor's intervention in the squabbles between Herod and the Nabataeans, who were also Roman clients. Roman legions were not stationed in the client states (see Schalit, *König Herodes,* 164). Of course, in emergencies they could be called upon to intervene (see Josephus, *J.W.* 2.40ff.; *Ant.* 17.250ff.).

The client kingdoms had their own military forces, as the case of Herod makes clear. It was necessary that they have such forces, not because they were relatively independent but in order to serve Rome effectively, since the Roman army was thereby relieved of responsibilities. The client kingdoms were given the responsibility of protecting the borders. In emergencies, they also were expected to supply auxiliary troops (Josephus, *Ant.* 15.317; Strabo 16.780). They also served to maintain the ruler in power. Herod's army included not

---

[64] Sevenster, *Roots,* 145ff.; Smallwood, *Jews under Roman Rule;* M. Brüchlmeier, *Beiträge zur rechtlichen Stellung der Juden im römischen Reich* (diss., Münster, 1939); Applebaum, *Jewish People in the First Century* 1:420ff.

only Jewish troops, of course, but foreign troops as well (*J.W.* 1.672; *Ant.* 17.198; 15.111). (The ominous statements in the dubious documents of Josephus give some grounds for evaluating their accuracy somewhat more positively in this case.)

We now turn to a discussion of the privileges granted the Jews from the time of Caesar and later, which did not basically alter the previously established framework of political rights. However important the later privileges may have been, they should not be evaluated in isolation. But to understand the situation of the Jews under Rome, both those in Palestine and those in the diaspora,[65] one must constantly take into consideration the privileges granted the Jews by Caesar and Augustus, which remained in effect after their time. They constitute the basis for evaluating all the political events of the period we are studying.

For a discussion of a constant problem, the issue of military service required of the Jews, see the pioneering essay of Smallwood (*Jews under Roman Rule*, 41): Caesar did not deal with Palestine as a province, but as a client state, and thus raised no auxiliary troops there.[66]

A major source of information regarding these privileges is provided by Josephus, *Ant.* 14 and 16 (see Smallwood, *Jews under Roman Rule*, 228ff.). The interpretation of this information is difficult because of the nature of the traditions, which are in places only fragmentarily preserved. But there is essential agreement concerning the authenticity of the basic elements, even if we cannot be certain of many of the details. Regarding authenticity, Smallwood notes that stylistic elements of the Roman and municipal documents are present (but these, of course, could simply be a matter of imitation); Greek translations of Roman terms appear in the purportedly Roman sources. For us, it can remain an open question whether Josephus is quoting material that he obtained directly from Roman archives or from Nicholas of Damascus.[67]

During Particular Phases

The introductory phase, according to Smallwood (*Jews under Roman Rule*, 105ff.), was "the transition from client kingdom to province."[68] Despite the

---

[65] For an example of alterations made in the diaspora (Egypt), see Smallwood, *Jews under Roman Rule*, 220ff.: the end of military service for Jews there; Josephus, *Ant.* 14.204, 226ff.

[66] For the political arrangements, see Smallwood, *Jews under Roman Rule*, 41 n. 62, which gives additional literature. No conscription: Josephus, *Ant.* 14.195, 217 (Smallwood, 42 n. 68); see also Sevenster, *Roots*, 153ff.

[67] R. Laqueur argues for archives (*Der jüdische Historiker Flavius Josephus* [Giessen, 1920]), B. Niese for Nicholas (*Flavii Iosephi Opera*. vol. 7 [Berlin, 1895]), opposed by Schürer-Vermes-Millar, *History* 1:272ff.

[68] Smallwood, *Jews under Roman Rule*, 120ff.: "The Diaspora and Jewish Religious Liberty." She affirms the capacity of the Jews to preserve their national identity through the centuries, despite the change of languages, anti-Semitism, and the terribly turbulent events that sometimes occurred.

privileges granted the Jews regarding their legal status in the empire, two points continued to be unsettled: the right to proselytize and the responsibility for military service.[69]

The account of the external history of the times should begin—after the prelude under Pompey and Caesar—with the relationship of Augustus and Herod after they reached an agreement following the battle of Actium, that is, after Herod's success in convincing Octavian that he had switched his allegiance to him.[70]

An especially instructive example is provided by the visit that Herod and Agrippa made together to Asia Minor in 14 B.C.E. (Josephus, *Ant.* 16.16ff.), along with the struggle for the rights of the Jews in the Ionian cities (16.27ff.), the confirmation of these rights by Agrippa (16.58ff.), after the speech on this subject by Nicholas of Damascus (16.51ff.). Regarding Agrippa, see also Josephus, *Ant.* 12.125ff.

From the first century C.E., the time after the death of Herod the Great (4 B.C.E.), we need select only a few events,[71] except for Palestine, where the situation so developed during the course of some decades that the war resulted. Concerning this we will have something to say below, in connection with "the intellectual resistance to Rome."

Sevenster affirms as a general rule that the Jews were only able to live in a pagan society if they were granted certain privileges, among which would be included the acknowledgment of the synagogue as a *collegium* (*Roots*, 145ff.). For Caesar, see Smallwood, *Jews under Roman Rule*, 134f.; the documents in Josephus, *Ant.* 14; for Augustus, see Philo, *Leg.* 156ff.; for protection of the Sabbath, see Josephus, *Ant.* 14.242, 245f. etc.

[69] For proselytes, see Sevenster, *Roots*, 197f.; Smallwood, *Jews under Roman Rule*, passim. For the military, see Applebaum, *Jewish People in the First Century* 1:458f.

[70] The famous prelude, the expulsion of the Jews from Rome in 139 B.C.E. (Valerius Maximus 1.3.3) had no *immediate* sequel. For Herod, see Otto, *PWSup* 2:1ff.; Schalit, *König Herodes;* Schürer-Vermes-Millar, *History* 1.187ff. (bib.). The reports about the origin of the Herodian family do not concern us. The usual comments: Antipater was an Idumaean (Josephus, *J.W.* 1.19, 123, 130f.; *Ant.* 14.8ff., etc.); according to Nicholas he came from one of the leading families of those who returned from the exile—which is not to be taken seriously. On the other hand, the statement that Herod's family came from Ashkelon is worth notice. See Justin, *Dial.* 52; cf. H. Gelzer, *Sextus Julius Africanus und die byzantinische chronographie,* 2 vols. (Leipzig: Hinrichs, 1880–98) 1:258ff., who regards this as historical. Schürer-Vermes-Millar give the opposing view (*History* 1:234 n. 3). A. Schalit considers it a Jewish invention for the purpose of slander ("Die frühchristliche Über-lieferung über die Herkunft der Familie des Herodes," *Annual of the Swedish Theological Institute* 1 [1962]: 109ff.).

[71] Smallwood, *Jews under Roman Rule*, 201ff.: The Jews in Rome under the Julio-Claudians. Josephus, *Ant.* 18.63ff.; Tacitus, *Annals* 2.85 (*GLAJJ*, no. 284); Suetonius, *Tib.* 36 (*GLAJJ*, no. 306); Dio 57.18.5a (*GLAJJ*, no. 419).

Under Individual Emperors

In the First Century C.E.

Tiberius[72]

When Tiberius expelled ("the") Jews from Rome,[73] it was a political measure occasioned by a specific incident (Josephus, *Ant.* 18.81ff.): some Jewish swindlers persuaded a high-ranking woman, Fulvia νομίμοις προσεληλυθυῖαν τοῖς 'Ιουδαϊκοῖς ("a woman of high rank who had become a Jewish proselyte"), to make a considerable gift for the Jerusalem temple and then pocketed the money. Being informed of this by her husband, Tiberius commanded: πᾶν τὸ 'Ιουδαϊκὸν τῆς 'Ρώμης ἀπελθεῖν ("the whole Jewish community to leave"). More than four thousand were conscripted for military service and sent to Sardinia.[74]

According to Philo, during the time of Tiberius a certain Sejanus played an ominous role, for he allegedly proposed a plan for the extermination of the Jews (*Leg.* 159ff.).[75] Further information is lacking. A comparison of Philo's account with the *Acta Alexandrinorum* and Josephus (*Ant.* 19.278) regarding the conduct of the Jews in Alexandria reveals a certain one-sidedness in Philo's account.[76]

Caligula[77]

The most significant event of Caligula's reign was his attempt to make the Caesar cult compulsory for the Jews and the temple in Jerusalem, as it was for others, an act that threatened the very existence of Judaism. It was a prime example of testing the ability of the empire to exercise its authority in an

---

[72] Smallwood, *Jews under Roman Rule*, 201ff.; Schürer, *History* 3:60f.

[73] Josephus, *Ant.* 18.65ff.; 81ff.; according to Tacitus, in 19 C.E. induction of Egyptians and Jews *libertini generis* ("of the class of freedmen"); cf. Suetonius, *Life of Augustus;* this was not ended in the year 30 C.E., as has been inferred from the accounts that Josephus inserted in his account of Pilate's administration; see Feldman on *Ant.* 18.65ff. (*Josephus* [LCL] vol. 9.).

[74] Tacitus, *Annals* 2.85: Actum et de sacris Aegyptiis Iudaicisque pellendis. . . . ("Another debate dealt with the prescription of the Egyptian and Jewish rites.") Dio 57.18.5a (*GLAJJ*, no. 419): τῶν 'Ιουδαίων πολλῶν ἐς τὴν 'Ρώμην συνελθόντων καὶ συχνοὺς τῶν ἐπιχωρίων ἐς τὰ σφέτερα ἔθη μεθιστάντων τοὺς πλείονας ἐξήλασεν ("As the Jews flocked to Rome in great numbers and were converting many of the natives to their ways, he banished most of them"). Concerning proselytizing, see Smallwood, "Some Notes on the Jews under Tiberius," *Latomus* 15 (1956): 314ff.

[75] Eusebius, *Chron. on Abr.* 2050 = Tiberius 21, is dependent on Philo, not an independent source.

[76] Philo, *Leg.* 184ff.; Josephus, *J.W.* 2.184; *Ant.* 18.261ff.; Tacitus, *Hist.* 5.9 (*GLAJJ*, no. 281). Concerning particular persons, see *Acta Alexandrinorum* (*CPJ* 154–56); Smallwood, "Notes on the Jews"; Sevenster, *Roots*, 156; L. H. Feldman, *Josephus* (LCL) 9:60f. See also the chronological chart in Schürer-Vermes-Millar, *History* 1:397 n. 180 (contra Smallwood), cf. pp. 389ff. (Alexandria), 503ff. (Judea).

[77] See Smallwood, *Jews under Roman Rule,* index. For the riots in Alexandria, see Schürer-Vermes-Millar, *History* 1:389.

extreme case, the attempted enforced institutionalization of the Caesar mania, just as it was a test case for the ability of a closed community's ability to withstand the empire. Previously, a head-on collision had been avoided by the simple expedient of the Jewish sacrifices in Jerusalem for the emperor.[78] The event revealed a potential problem for the Jews at the most basic level, which, however, had no immediate consequences for the Jews. The situation was later to become otherwise for the Christians.

Claudius

The close relationship between Claudius and the Jewish prince, later to become King Agrippa I, was influential.[79] The interests of the empire were certainly served by this relationship.[80] For our purposes, the most prominent events were (1) the alleged expulsion of the Jews from Rome and (2) the intervention in Alexandria.

(1) With regard to the expulsion, some sort of drastic action clearly happened, but the details are uncertain. The sources are the following: Suetonius, *Claudius* 25 (date not given): Iudaeos impulsore Chresto assidue tumultuantis Roma expulit ("Since the Jews constantly made disturbances at the instigation of Chrestus, he expelled them from Rome"). Orosius, *Historiae* 7.6.15, dates the event in the ninth year of Claudius (=49 c.e.): Anno eiusdem nono expulsos per Claudium urbe Iudaeos Iosephus refert (Irrtum!). Sed me magis Suetonius movet, qui ait hoc modo . . . ("In the ninth year of the same reign, Josephus reports [a mistake!] that the Jews were expelled from the city by Claudius. But Suetonius convinces me more who speaks in the following manner . . ."). Acts 18:2: It was because of this that Aquila and Priscilla came to Corinth. Tacitus mentions no action against the Roman Jews in the year 49 c.e. (for Claudius's purported attitude toward the Jews at the beginning of his reign, see Josephus, *Ant.* 19.5). The decisive information is from Dio 60.6 (*GLAJJ*, no. 422): τούς τε Ἰουδαίους Πλεονάσαντας αὖθις, ὥστε χαλεπῶς ἂν ἄνευ ταραχῆς ὑπὸ τοῦ ὄχλου σφῶν τῆς πόλεως εἰρχθῆναι, οὐκ ἐξήλασε μέν [clearly a correction of Suetonius], τῷ δὲ δὴ πατρίῳ βίῳ χρωμένους ἐκέλευσε μὴ συναθροίζεσθαι ("As for the Jews, who had again increased so greatly that by reason of their multitude it would have been hard without raising a tumult to bar them from the city, he did not drive them out, but ordered them, while continuing their traditional mode of life, not to hold meetings").

It was thus not a matter of driving out *all* Jews. The existence of the Jewish community continued uninterrupted.

---

[78] Concerning the emperor cult, see Philo, *Leg.* 11ff., 74ff.; Josephus, *Ant.* 18.256, 261ff.; 19.4, 11; Suetonius, *Caligula* 22; Dio 59.26, 28; L. Cerfaux and J. Tondriau, *Le culte des souverains dans la civilisation Gréco-romaine* (1957) 342ff.; Taeger, *Studien zur Geschichte* 2:281ff.

[79] Although Agrippa lived only until 44 c.e.; Josephus, *J.W.* 2.206ff.; *Ant.* 19.236, 242 *et passim*; Dio 60.8.2f. (*GLAJJ*, no. 423); Schürer-Vermes-Millar, *History* 1:397f., 445.

[80] Note the intervention of the emperor and of the Syrian governor Marsus (Josephus, *J.W.* 2.218ff.; 5.147ff.; *Ant.* 19.326f., 338ff.; Schürer-Vermes-Millar, *History* 1:448.

(2) The intervention in Alexandria.[81] In the past it has been customary to refer to Josephus's report of Claudius's edict of tolerance made at the beginning of his reign (*Ant.* 19.279–85; Schürer, *History* 1:502; 3:61f.) The authentic text of Claudius that is now available does not agree with the text of Josephus. Some samples of the confused response of historians to this data are: (a) Tcherikover, *CPJ* 1:70f. n. 45: Josephus has partially falsified the edict. (b) Feldman, *Josephus* (LCL) 9.344ff.: Josephus's version and the authentic letter can be harmonized. (c) *CAH* 10.311f. distinguishes three edicts of toleration: (1) for Alexandria, (2) for the whole empire (Josephus, *Ant.* 19.286ff.), and (3) after he had heard the legation (=*PLond.* 1912). For more light on these events, see *CPJ* 156, the complaint of Isidorus against Agrippa (which, I or II? For Agrippa II in Rome, see Josephus, *J.W.* 2.245; *Ant.* 20.134). Tcherikover reconstructs the events as follows (*CPJ* 1:71ff.):

Act I
1. Influence of Agrippa I.
2. Claudius wants to hear both sides of the matter; two delegations come to Rome.
3. Restoration of the Jewish rights (after the model of Augustus).

Act II
4. Opposition by Isidorus (probably a member of the delegation under Apion).

Act III
5. Alexandrian delegation led by Barbillus and the Jewish counter delegation.

Thus, according to Tcherikover there were two Jewish delegations to Claudius (*CPJ* 1:73). The final result was the end of the cultural "emancipation" of Judaism, along with the attainment of religious freedom (*CPJ* 1:74).

A fantastic reconstruction is proposed by T. Zielinski ("L'empereur Claude et l'idée de la domination mondiale des Juifs," *Revue de l'Université de Bruxelles* 32 [1926–27]: 128ff.): the letter of Claudius was preceded by an oral explanation to both delegations. The expression "a pestilence for the whole world" used of the Jews is nothing other than the Roman view of the Jewish idea of the rulership of the world by the Jewish people, an idea with which Claudius was acquainted. This is supposed to make comprehensible the expulsion of the Jews from Rome, which was supposed to be the center of a planned revolt.

Nero
The discussion centers on Nero's concubine, Poppaea Sabina, who later became his wife (Tacitus, *Annals* 13.45f.; 14.1.60f., etc.; Suetonius, *Nero* 35). She is described by Josephus as Θεοσεβής ("God-fearer" *Ant.* 20.195). On this basis many suppose that she had sympathies for Judaism (Schürer, *History*

---

[81] *PLond.* 1912=*CPJ*, no. 153; Schürer-Vermes-Millar, *History* 1:398.

3:64); Feldman sees the matter otherwise, arguing that the word is not used in the technical sense (on *Ant.* 20.195). This view in turn is opposed by R. Marcus ("The Sebomenoi in Josephus," *Jewish Social Studies* 14 [1952]: 247ff.). Smallwood ("The Alleged Jewish Tendencies of Poppaea Sabina," *JTS* n.s. 10 [1959]: 329ff.) agrees with Feldman: even such a person as Gessius Florus owed his career to his friendship with Poppaea (Josephus, *Ant.* 20.252). There is no real evidence of pro-Jewish sympathies on her part.

There were reports of unrest in Alexandria under Tiberius Alexander (Josephus, *J.W.* 2.492ff.; for the context, cf. 457ff., 490: a plan for an embassy to Nero).

Vespasian and Titus[82]

There is perhaps no clearer indication of the Roman political stance with regard to the Jews than the fact that their legal status throughout the empire was not basically altered by the violent war of 66–70, despite the structural changes that Judaism underwent through the loss of the city and the temple and the reorganization of Palestine as a province. Theodor Mommsen[83] sees the matter quite differently, however: their legal status as a nation was withdrawn from them at this time, and their previous political privileges were reduced to mere religious privileges. Politically, they became *peregrini dediticcii.*[84]

The evidence for this theory is lacking, so that today it can no longer be considered tenable. See the reports of Josephus concerning the preservation of the status of the Jews in Antioch and Alexandria (*J.W.* 7.100ff.; *Ant.* 12.120ff.).[85] The subsequent events also speak against Mommsen's view (Smallwood, *Jews under Roman Rule;* Schürer-Vermes-Millar, *History* 1:514ff.). It is remarkable that the Jews under the Flavians (for Domitian, see below) obviously enjoyed a period of peace and quiet. To be sure, there is the report of a persecution under Vespasian (Hegesippus in Eusebius, *Hist. Eccl.* 3.12), but the value of the report is disputed. Jewish sources are unaware of it. Even if it were not created out of thin air, the incident cannot have been very significant. Was it a matter of some sort of Jewish messianism? There is thus hardly any evidence for a

---

[82] Regarding Palestine, see Schürer-Vermes-Millar, *History* 1:514ff.

[83] *Hist. Zeitschr.* 64 (1890): 424ff.; see Smallwood's comments (*Jews under Roman Rule,* 342 n. 44 [bib.]).

[84] That is, "provincials who had surrendered unconditionally" (Smallwood, *Jews under Roman Rule,* 342), "a class inferior to other provincials and legally incapable of contracting valid marriages or making valid wills."

[85] The thesis is already refuted by the fact that there never was an official status of the Jews as a "nation," and, in terms of civil rights, never could have been. There were privileges. From time to time, these were protected by Rome against attacks. See the documentation in Josephus. Of course, the existence of Palestine had an effect on the rest of the empire, whether as a client state (or states), or as a Roman subprovince.

Jewish uprising after 80 C.E.; in any case, it is unknown to the Jewish tradition.[86]

The decisive matter remains the *fiscus Iudaicus*, the temple tax taken annually from every Jew, which was transferred from the Jewish temple to Jupiter Capitolinus.[87]

Domitian[88]

That under Domitian the *fiscus Iudaicus* was enforced with special rigor (Suetonius, *Domitian* 12) was first of all a *fiscal* concern. See the context in Suetonius: lack of funds and harsh measures to balance the budget (J. Speigl, *Der römische Staat und die Christen: Staat und Kirche von Domitian bis Commodus* [1970] 35ff.). What was at issue was not primarily the status of the Jews as such.[89] Of course, the prohibition of conversion to Judaism was a different matter. The proceedings taken by Domitian against (among others) his relatives Flavius Clemens and his wife Domitilla have been much discussed.[90] Concerning the accusation of "godlessness," an anti-Jewish topos, see the sequel in Dio: ὑφ᾿ ἧς καὶ ἄλλοι ἐς τὰ τῶν Ἰουδαίων ἤθη ἐξοκέλλοντες πολλοὶ κατεδικάσθησαν, καὶ οἱ μὲν ἀπέθανον, οἱ δὲ τῶν γοῦν οὐσιῶν ἐστερήθησαν ἡ δὲ Δομιτίλλα ὑπερωρίσθη μόνον ἐς Πανδατερίαν ("The charge brought against them both was that of atheism, a charge on which many others who drifted into Jewish ways were condemned. Some of those were put to death, and the rest were at least deprived of their property. Domitilla was merely banished to Pandateria").

The existence of the Domitilla Catacombs in Rome gave rise to the supposition that both had been Christians and that this is the reason for their persecution.[91] There is no basis for this in fact.[92]

---

[86] Smallwood, *Jews under Roman Rule,* 352f. (contra Juster, *Juifs dans l'empire* 2:185); Schürer-Vermes-Millar, *History* 1:515f. The ominous-appearing coin portraying *Judea capta* of 85 is best not considered in this regard (contra Juster). See Smallwood, 353 nn. 82, 83.

[87] Josephus, *J.W.* 7.218; Dio 66.7.2 (*GLAJJ,* no. 430); Smallwood, *Jews under Roman Rule,* 371ff.; for illustrative material from the papyri, see *CPJ* 2:113ff., and nos. 160ff., 421. Smallwood gives numerous examples.

[88] Smallwood, *Jews under Roman Rule,* 376ff. Concerning the emperor cult, see Cerfaux and Tondriau, *Le culte,* 355ff.; Taeger, *Studien zur Geschichte* 2:337ff.

[89] The investigation of Jesus' relatives is an entirely different issue (see Hegesippus in Eusebius, *Hist. Eccl.* 3.12 concerning Vespasian).

[90] Dio 67.14 (*GLAJJ,* no. 435) (Xiphilinus-Epitome, 95 C.E.; cf. Suetonius, *Domitian* 15). Smallwood, *Jews under Roman Rule,* 382 n. 94: compare Xiphilinus 71.9.4 with Dio himself 70.15.3 and 72.4.7, "71.9.4 is Xiphilinus' own account of the Christian version of an episode that is explained differently by Dio."

[91] Concerning a different Domitilla, whose existence is very doubtful (Reinach, *Textes d'auteurs Grecs,* 195 n. 5), who was presumably the niece (not wife) of Clemens: see Eusebius, *Hist. Eccl.* 3.18.4 (she had become a Christian). Schürer (*History* 3:168 n. 57) gives credence to this, as does Lietzmann (*History* 2:160; opposed by Sevenster, *Roots,* 98: they were both convicted as proselytes). Cf. Smallwood, *Jews under Roman Rule,* 382.

[92] For archaeological data, see *KIP,* col. 2, 574 (no. 23); P. Styger, *Die römischen Katakomben*

See S. J. Case, "Josephus's Anticipation of a Domitianic Persecution," *JBL* 44 (1925): 10ff.: The increasing gravity of the situation of the Jews under Domitian is reflected in Josephus's *Ant.* when they are compared with *J.W.* Josephus repeatedly points out that the Jews have never lost their religious rights. (See the pro-Jewish documents *Ant.* 16.160ff.; 19.281ff., 303ff.).[93] Smallwood ("Domitian's Attitude toward the Jews and Judaism," *Classical Philology* 51 [1956]: 1ff.) explains: In Dio there is no evidence for an attack on the Jews as such. "Those who lived like Jews" were probably converts. Domitian had extended the tax obligation (a) to nonpracticing Jews, and (b) to proselytes. Domitian tended to regard proselytes as persons who were attempting to avoid paying the emperor the divine honors due him, and as atheists.

The fact remains that the Jews felt themselves to be threatened.

Nerva

Nerva's decrees brought relief (Schürer, *History* 3:118). A familiar example is provided by the coins of 96 C.E. with the inscription: *fisci Iudaici calumnia sublata* ("abolition of the false Jewish tax") (F. W. Madden, *History of the Jewish Coinage* [1864] 199; *CAH* 5, plates, 126f.). This did not mean the abolition of the *fiscus* ("tax") itself. The evidence proves that this remained in force (*CPJ;* see below; Appian, *Syr.* 50; Origen, *Epistula ad Africanum* 14; Tertullian, *Apologeticum* 18). Rather, it was the humiliating procedures and denunciations that his decrees were intended to bring to a halt; see Dio 68.1.2 (*GLAJJ*, no. 436): τοῖς δὲ ἄλλοις οὔτ' ἀσεβείας οὔτ' Ἰουδαϊκοῦ βίου καταιτιᾶσθαί τινας συνεχώρησε ("and no persons were permitted to accuse anybody of *maiestas* or of adopting the Jewish mode of life"). On the basis of this text Speigl (*Der römische Staat*, 26) thinks that Nerva regarded the trials under Domitian as trials of impious persons. Dio correctly reports his source on this matter. I. A. F. Bruce ("Nerva and the Fiscus Judaicus," *PEQ* 96 [1964]: 34ff.) understands Domitian to have extended the tax obligation to include even Italians and Roman citizens, and it was this *calumnia* (=abuse) that Nerva's decrees abolished. This is pure fantasy, with no basis in the legal texts (see Smallwood, *Jews under Roman Rule*, 385 n. 105).

Concerning the emperor cult under Domitian, see Martial 10.72, "You come to me now in vain": dicturus dominum deumque non sum (in contrast to Nerva). ("I think not to address any man as Master and God.")

(1933) 63ff., 100ff.; K. Wessel, "Domitilla," RGG³, 2, col. 238: hardly any evidence for a Domitilla catacomb prior to 200 C.E.; L. Hertling and E. Kirschbaum, *Die ältesten Denkmäler der römischen Kirche*, Festschrift Ak. Göttingen II (1951) 182ff.; Smallwood, *Jews under Roman Rule*, 382 n. 93.

[93] The respective dates of *J.W.* and *Ant.* should be noted! Compare the way Herod is presented in each! Compare *J.W.* 1.404 with *Ant.* 15.339, 288, 291; 16.158. For Domitian–Gaius parallels, see *J.W.* 2.184, 203, 208; *Ant.* 18.257ff. 19.1f., 10f., 209.

In the Second Century C.E. [94]

Preview: There is a considerable gap in our sources between Tacitus and the end of the second century.[95] The extant writings of historians of the period refer to the Jews when they are narrating political struggles (thus mostly rebellions).[96] Herennius Philo wrote about the Jews, according to Origen, *Contra Celsum* 1.15.[97] Apuleius (*Apol.* 90; *GLAJJ*, no. 361) alludes to the supposed connection between Judaism and magic, which is also referred to elsewhere: Acts 13:6ff.; 19:13ff.; Josephus, *Ant.* 8.45ff.; Pliny, *Hist. Nat.* 30.11 (*GLAJJ*, 221). See the data in the magical papyri! Galen contains nothing relevant.[98]

Around the end of the second century changes in the intellectual landscape can be recognized. For the first time, the Bible was studied as a source by a pagan author (Celsus); this marks the beginning of historical reflection on the Bible.[99] It is clear that this development is to be seen in connection with the formation of Christian theology and the completely new historical thinking that belonged to its very substance.

Trajan[100]

Although the struggles during his reign were widespread and vicious (Schürer-Vermes-Millar, *History* 1:529ff.), the fundamental position of the Jews in the empire remained stable. Exceptions are local and occasioned by particular events, for example, the prohibition of Jews from residing on Cyprus after the ferocious revolt (Dio 68.32.2 [*GLAJJ*, no. 437]; Schürer-Vermes-Millar, *History* 1:532).

Under Trajan the revolts of Jews reached both their widest geographical spread and their peak of ferocity. We do not know the occasions for such revolts in the differing localities.[101] Reckless revolts broke out in 115 c.e. in Cyrene[102] and Egypt.[103] How fearfully the rebellion raged in Egypt in

---

[94] Smallwood, *Jews under Roman Rule,* 389ff., 507ff.; Schürer, *History* 1:642ff.; Schürer-Vermes-Millar, *History* 1:514ff.

[95] After Hadrian, western Judaism had only Rome as a substitute center for Jerusalem.

[96] Dio: Reinach, *Texts d'auteurs Grecs,* 179ff.; Appian: Reinach, 151ff.; Florus: Reinach, 333f.

[97] Eusebius, *Praep. Ev.* 1.10 (as part of his Phoenician history?).

[98] Reinach, 160ff.; F. Pfaff, *Hermes* 67 (1932) 356ff.; R. Walzer, *Galen on Jews and Christians* (Oxford, 1949); A. D. Nock, *Gnomon* 23 (1951): 50.

[99] Carl Andresen, *Logos und Nomos: Die Polemik des Kelsos wider das Christentum* (Berlin: de Gruyter, 1955), with the critique of H. Dörrie, *Gnomon* 29 (1957): 185ff.

[100] A. Schalit, *Jews on the Eve of the War against Trajan* (Hebrew), Sinai III, 367ff.

[101] Tcherikover, *CPJ* 1:87f.: The first actions of the Jews were taken against their neighbors; when the army intervened, it became a war against Rome.

[102] Eusebius, *Chron.,* trans. Karst, 219; Dio 68.32.1 (*GLAJJ*, no. 437); Orosius 7.12; the leader was a "king" (a messianic element); for archaeological evidence, see Applebaum, *Jewish People in the First Century;* for bibliography, see Schürer-Vermes-Millar, *History* 1:531f.

[103] Dio 68.32.2 (*GLAJJ*, no. 437). It is doubtful that the Jews in Palestine participated. S. W.

115–117[104] can be seen from the moving documentation preserved in the papyri (*CPJ*).[105] For example: *CPJ*, no. 438: the situation in the country; nos. 436–44, 446: private letters, mostly from the archives of the general Apollonius from Apollinopolis; nos. 445, 447–50, from the time after the revolt. The ostraca from Apollinopolis Magna, Edfu, offer a unique kind of evidence; nos. 160–229 are of particular interest with regard to the question of the Jewish tax.[106]

According to Tcherikover (*CPJ* 1:92f.) the results of the revolt and related events were that the Jewish population was eliminated from many localities. References to Jews almost disappear from the sources. To be sure, the Jewish *politeuma* ("government," "body of citizens") obviously continued to exist as such in Alexandria, but the significance of the city as the center of the Hellenistic-Jewish diaspora was broken.[107]

Smallwood (*Jews under Roman Rule*, 517) notes with regard to a later time (late second century) that there was a certain regeneration of Judaism in Egypt, which then appeared more in religious conflict with Christians than in political conflict with Rome. R. L. Wilken (*Judaism and the Early Christian Mind* [New Haven: Yale, 1971] 39ff.) and Tcherikover (*CPJ* 1:93ff., "The Late Roman and Byzantine Period") note that around 300 c.e. the number of Jewish names increases.

Except for reports of inhuman atrocities, reports of the revolt in other areas offer no further information (see above for Cyrene). Field Marshall Lucius Quietus became a byword because of the barbarisms he committed during the battles in the east (Schürer-Vermes-Millar, *History* 1:533).

Concerning Trajan in general, see *POxy.* 10.1242, lines 42f.: Trajan surrounded by Jews. On this see *CAH* 11.419: this is an exaggeration, but the number of provincials in the senate was in fact considerable. *Acta Hermaisci* 8 (ed. Musurillo): there were two delegations to Trajan; Plotina intervened in behalf of the Jews.

Baron, *A Social and Religious History of the Jews*, 2 vols., 2nd ed. (New York: Columbia University Press, 1952) 2:370 n. 9: *Meg. Ta'an.* (entrance) has little value and is missing in the best manuscripts; H. Lichtenstein, "Die Fast enrolle: Eine Untersuchung zur Jüdisch-Hellenistischen Geschichte," *HUCA* 8/9 (1931/32): 272f., 346.

[104] Concerning the chronology, see Schürer-Vermes-Millar, *History* 1:530 n. 73: in the year 116 the Jews in Thebes were still paying taxes; then the receipts stop.

[105] *CPJ* 2:225ff.; I:85ff.; see also Appian, *BC* 2.90 (who was himself affected by these events).

[106] See *CPJ* 2:108ff. Ostraca are extant for the years up to 116. There are later ones from 151–165, but they report nothing about the Jewish tax. No. 460 contains a tax list that indicates only *one* Jewish tax obligation.

[107] Tcherikover, *CPJ* 1:93: destruction of the great synagogue in Alexandria (*t. Ketub.* 3.1 = *t. Pe'a* 4.6). Apparently a part of the Jewish population was located outside the city proper.

Hadrian (and Antoninus Pius)[108]

Hadrian was an outspoken advocate of Hellenic culture. It is no contradiction of this view of the relation of Greeks and Romans when Spartian (*Hadrian* 21.10) writes: sacra Romana(!) diligentissime curavit, peregrina [in which the Greeks are not counted] comtempsit; see Taeger, *Textes d'auteurs Grecs* 2:370ff. ("He diligently enforced the observances of the Roman religion and forbade the practice of all strange or foreign rites").

The Bar Kochba revolt (132–135) was the most important event of this period for the relationship between Rome and the Jews, as well as for the development of Judaism itself, both internally and externally. The source material is very scanty.[109] For example, we know almost nothing about the fate of Jerusalem during the war. The name is found on coins, and once in a document (DJD 2:135). Appian mentions the conquest of the city (*Syr.* 50). New discoveries have provided a few details (Wadi Murabba'at, Naḥal Ḥever, Naḥal Ṣe'elim) that illuminate the picture somewhat, but it remains without depth.[110]

The occasion of the revolt, according to Spartian (*Hadrian* 13.2): moverunt ea tempestate et Iudaei bellum, quod vetabantur mutilare genitalia ("About this time the Jews revolted against the Romans, because they were not allowed to practice the rite of mutilating the genitals [circumcision]") (see Schürer-Vermes-Millar, *History* 1:536f.). The contrary argument is made by H. Mantel (*JQR* 58 [1968]: 224ff., 274ff.): namely, that Hadrian's prohibition of circumcision was the result of the war, not its cause. On this issue Schürer-Vermes-Millar (*History* 1:539) and Smallwood (*Latomus* 18 [1959]: 334ff.; and 20 [1961]: 93ff.) speak rather cautiously: Spartian's dating of the prohibition before the revolt

---

[108] For bibliography, see Schürer-Vermes-Millar, *History* 1:534; Smallwood, *Jews under Roman Rule*, 428ff.; Y. Yadin, *Bar Kochba* (New York: Random House, 1971); J. A. Fitzmyer, "The Bar Cochba Period," in *The Bible in Current Catholic Thought: Gruenthaler Memorial Volume*, ed. J. L. McKenzie (New York: Herder & Herder, 1962) 133ff.

[109] Dio is to be consulted first; Eusebius, *Chron. on Abr.* 2148 = *Hadrian* 16: "The Jews fell back and disappeared into the Palestinian countryside. . . ." Regarding the next year: "Kochba, the leader of the Jewish revolt, punished many of the Christians with various tortures, since they refused to join his battle against the Romans." Christian sources: Justin, *Apol.* 1.31; Eusebius, *Hist. Eccl.* 4.8.4. Of course they could not acknowledge the Jewish messianic claims (cf. Aqiba concerning Bar Kochba!); see Schürer-Vermes-Millar, *History* 1:543f.; Hengel, *Zealots*, 300–301.

[110] On the discoveries, see DJD 2; Yadin, *Bar Kochba;* Yadin, "Expedition D–The Cave of the Letters," *IEJ* 12 (1962): 235ff.; H. J. Polotsky, "The Greek Papyri from the Cave of the Letters," *IEJ* 12 (1962): 258ff.; Schürer-Vermes-Millar, *History* 1:534f. (bib.); Baron, *Social and Religious History* 2:371 n. 12; Smallwood, *Jews under Roman Rule*, 442. Yadin presents the literary sources and the coins of Bar Kochba, and the Roman coins connected with the founding of Aelia (for the inscriptions on Bar Kochba's coins, see pp. 26f., 86f., 194; on the "caves of terror" in the Naḥal Ḥever, see p. 31; the letters, see pp. 124ff. The pronunciation of the leader's name is revealed from a Greek letter: "Chosiba").

is not supported by any other source—but neither is it contradicted. Even if this prohibition against circumcision were not directed exclusively against the Jews, they were affected by it in a different way than other nations—because of their understanding of the law and also because of the implications for proselytizing. This is seen by the exception that Antoninus Pius made for the Jews and only for them (Modestinus, *Digesta* 48.8.11; *GLAJJ*, 3:64).[111]

The passage in Dio 69.12.1f. (*GLAJJ*, no. 440) is especially important (see F. Millar, *A Study of Cassius Dio* [Oxford: Clarendon Press, 1964] 60ff.): When it became known that Hadrian intended to build a new city, Aelia Capitolina, on the site of Jerusalem, and to erect a new temple to Zeus where the Jewish temple had stood, a great war broke out. The Jews remained quiet so long as Hadrian remained in Egypt and Syria (Schürer-Vermes-Millar, *History* 1:541 n. 120), but after his departure open resistance began.[112]

The severity of the struggle is described by Fronto (*De bello Parthico* 2 [*GLAJJ*, no. 342])[113] (for the comfort of Marcus Aurelius): avo vestro Hadriano imperium obtinente quantum militum a Iudaeis, quantum ab Britannis caesum ("Again under the rule of your grandfather Hadrian what a number of soldiers were killed by the Jews, what a number by the Britons!"). Dio 69.14.3 notes that Hadrian, in his report to the senate after the end of the war, omitted the usual introductory formula: ἐγὼ καὶ τὰ στρατεύματα ὑγιαίνομεν ("I and the legions enjoy good health") (Schürer-Vermes-Millar, *History* 1:553 n. 176).

Concerning Jewish martyrs from the time of Hadrian, see Billerbeck, *Kommentar* 1:223ff.; Schürer-Vermes-Millar, *History* 1:552. Concerning Bar Kochba and Aqiba, see the index in Hengel, *Zealots;* concerning the results of the war, see Dio 69.4.1f.: ὀλίγοι γοῦν κομιδῇ περιεγένοντο ("Very few of them in fact survived"). There was an enormous devastation.[114]

Aelia Capitolina was completely paganized.[115] A temple to Jupiter

---

[111] Ulpian, *Digesta* 48.8.4.2: "Divus Hadrianus rescripsit: constitutum quidem est, ne spadones fierent, eos autem, qui hoc crimine arguerentur. Corneliae legis poena teneri" ("The same deified Hadrian wrote in a rescript: 'It is laid down, in order to end the practice of making eunuchs, that those who are found guilty of this crime are to be liable to the penalty of the lex Cornelia'"). Circumcision is not mentioned. Cf. Iulius Paulus Sententiarius 5.22.3. Juvenal mentions circumcision, but not its prohibition.

[112] The legendary notices concerning Hadrian's plans for temple construction may remain outside our consideration (see Schürer-Vermes-Millar, *History* 1:536), as can the hopeless debate about *Barn.* 16:4. The debates concerning the beginning of the conflict are to be supplemented by the hypothesis of J. T. Milik in DJD 2:125 (the beginning was already in 131); on this, see Schürer-Vermes-Millar, *History* 1:542 n. 126; rejected also by Yadin, *Bar Kochba*, 183.

[113] Reinach, *Textes d'auteurs Grecs,* 335; Fronto, *De Bello Parthico,* ed. M. P. J. Van den Hout (1954) 206.

[114] Schürer-Vermes-Millar, *History* 1:554ff.; Smallwood, *Jews under Roman Rule,* 457ff.

[115] Concerning this paganization, see in addition Justin, *Dial.* 16.2; 92.2; *Apol.* 1.47.6; Tertullian, *Apol.* 21.5; *Adv. Iud.* 13.4. Further information is in Smallwood, *Jews under Roman Rule,* 460 n. 128. Note also the Jupiter temple on Gerizim. For coins under Antoninus Pius, see Smallwood, 462 n. 137; for the Antonine period, pp. 467ff. The decree forbidding Jews to enter the city appears to have been relaxed somewhat later (Smallwood, 499f.). Its continued existence seems still to be

Capitolinus occupied the site of the Jewish temple. Jews were forbidden to enter the city. (This prohibition included Jewish Christians, although Christians had not participated in the revolt; see Schürer-Vermes-Millar, *History* 1:553 n. 181.) The church fathers sometimes used this prohibition as an argument against the Jews (see part IV below).

Digesta 50 15.1.6: In Palaestina duae fuerunt coloniae, Caesariensis et Aelia Capitolina, sed neutra ius Italicum habet ("In Palestine there were two colonies, Caesarea and Aelia Capitolina, but neither has the jus Italicum"). After Hadrian: The *Historia Augusta* on Antoninus Pius speaks of a Jewish revolt under Antoninus, but we have no other reports of this.

The Situation of the Jews after the War[116]

We must now turn our view more toward the east, for this is where Judaism now has its centers: in the vigorous Babylonian Jewish community (J. Neusner) and in Galilee (although the city of Rome continued to be a significant factor). This, of course, had an effect on the western diaspora. The changes that took place there, however, are mostly represented in the sources one-sidedly from the perspective of the east.

In Palestine, Judaism was reorganized after the first war of 66–70 and brought into closer conformity with the dominant surviving Pharisaism. An even more thorough reorganization took place after the second war of 132–135. The results included the regulation of the teaching office, the fixing of the canon, and the sharpening of the lines by which fringe groups were separated. Rejection of heretics was made a part of the liturgy. Public discussions were to be avoided. Baron labels this "closing the ranks," which included a return to the Hebrew language (*Social and Religious History* 2:129ff., 145ff.). On the one hand, suspicion of proselytes prevailed (2:147ff.); but then a semiproselytism flourished, which can even be called "Hellenistic Jewry's New Religion" (2:162).

But when and how did these renewing influences become effective in the Greco-Roman diaspora as well? If one looks at the matter from the point of view of the final results, a somber picture can emerge.[117] General considerations, however, make it unlikely that any sort of abrupt severing of relations with Jewish Hellenism occurred. This general impression is supported by particular data: outside the arena of conflict, the status of the Jews was undamaged – despite the temporary prohibition of circumcision. The growth

---

presupposed by Tertullian – of course, with a strong apologetic emphasis against the Jews.

[116] Schürer-Vermes-Millar, *History* 1:556f.; for the Babylonian Jews, see J. Neusner, *A History of the Jews in Babylonia* I, SPB 9 (Leiden: E. J. Brill, 1965).

[117] Lietzmann, *History* 1:75ff.: Jewish Hellenism was systematically stamped out by talmudic Judaism. Its literature was destroyed. Only that has been preserved which the Christians adopted (and reworked): the LXX, Philo, Josephus, the Apocrypha, all of which could be adapted to Christian usage. This is correct: but in which period did this process take place?

of Judaism did not cease, despite this prohibition.[118] The process of helleniza-tion continued in Palestine itself (see Schürer-Vermes-Millar, *History* 1:556).[119] The production of literature in the Hellenistic style progressed.[120] The narrow standpoint prevailed only after an extended period (Simon, *Verus Israel,* 30). In fact, the attractive power of Judaism increased with time, a phenomenon that should be seen in conjunction with the general orientalizing of late antiquity (the age of the Severi!).[121]

The annexation of the diaspora onto the Jewish "headquarters" in Palestine first became effective after the final establishment of the patriarchate.[122] Even then, the development should not be thought of too schematically.[123] The pos-sibilities for travel and communication available in those days should be kept in mind, as well as the fact that such cultural exchange was limited to the cities!

On the other hand, homogenization was facilitated by the concentration of Jews in a few dominant centers: Galilee, Rome, and Babylon. The previous temple tax was replaced by a tax for the patriarchate. A new kind of orthodoxy was able to develop.

What were the consequences of these developments to be for the competition with Christianity? Simon suggests the result with his formula "The Conflict of Orthodoxies" (*Verus Israel,* 133ff.).[124]

The Reflection of Roman Rule in the Jewish Consciousness (Types and Phases)

By "phases" I do not mean that there was a consistent development of the Jewish political consciousness against Rome, nor that there was a uniformity

---

[118] So Simon, *Verus Israel.* For the increase (!) in the diaspora congregations and the connection with the ancient development in general, see J. Vogt, "Kaiser Julian und das Judentum," *Morgenland* 30 (1939): 46ff.

[119] And in any case outside Palestine. With regard to the penetration of pictorial art in the synagogue, for Dura Europos see E. R. Goodenough, *Jewish Symbols in the Greco-Roman Period* vols. 9–11 (New York: Pantheon Books, 1953ff.); for Rome, see H. J. Leon, *The Jews of Ancient Rome* (Philadelphia: Jewish Publication Society of America, 1960) 195ff.; Simon, *Verus Israel,* 51ff.; see also the works of Kraabel.

[120] See the *Sibylline Oracles* (!) as well as the prayers in the *Apostolic Constitutions* 7 (although the LXX is no longer used; Bousset, "Sibyllen und sibyllinische Bücher," *RE,* 3rd ed. [1906] 18:265ff.).

[121] Hadas, *Hellenistic Culture;* Vogt, "Kaiser Julian," 9ff.

[122] From about the second half of the second century; Juster, *Juifs dans l'empire* 1:391ff. See M. Avi-Yonah, *Geschichte der Juden im Zeitalter des Talmud* (Berlin: Walter de Gruyter, 1962).

[123] A solitary bit of illumination is provided in M. Hengel, "Die Synagogeninschrift von Stobi," *ZNW* 57 (1966): 145ff.

[124] Simon, *Verus Israel,* 62ff.: Judaism constituted itself henceforth as a church. Simon, *Verus Israel,* 378, with Harnack, *Mission* 1:17: A national religion can become a universal religion in two ways: either through reduction to a few fundamental elements or through enrichment by the ideas of those it wishes to win. Judaism practiced both methods, but the second disappeared with the advent of Christianity, with its incorporation of a salvation mysticism (mediated by the mystery religions). Judaism could not compete: its tie to one people became a hindrance. See also Vogt, "Kaiser Julian," 18ff.

in the Jewish attitude. That was not the case, but there were certainly iden-
tifiable types, culminating points, and lasting changes of attitude in response
to the ebb and flow of events. Space permits only a few characteristic examples.

The abhorrence that was felt in response to the report that after the conquest
of Jerusalem Pompey entered the temple is expressed in *Ps. Sol.* (2; cf. 17:11ff.;
Josephus, *Ant.* 14.71; *J.W.* 1.152), although he did not bother the temple
treasury.[125]

Juster gives a one-sidedly positive evaluation (*Juifs dans l'empire* 1:213ff.); the
Jews wanted above all to be Roman subjects; they formed one element of the
unity of the Roman Empire. Juster relies heavily on the speech of Nicholas of
Damascus (Josephus, *Ant.* 16.31ff.). This speech is a remarkable item of
evidence, whether it be taken as relating to the official program of Herod (!)[126]
or to the view of Josephus sometime after the Jewish war.

The speech places the relationship between Rome and the Jews in a comprehensive framework of (a) Roman tolerance for the particular practices of *every*
nation; and (b) Roman rule over the Greek cities, a rule that could not annul
rights that had been conferred by Rome itself.[127] The speech is well seasoned
with the theme that it was from Rome that they had first received their
freedom—after the tyranny of their earlier rulers.

The Jews demand no more than the right to practice their own traditions
handed down from their ancestors. These are a matter of public knowledge:
the Jews practice no secret rites.[128]

The relationship between the Jews and Rome had a firm basis in that Rome
acknowledged the Jews to be a nation. This position is also documented by the
sacrifice that had been regularly offered in Jerusalem for the emperor since the
days of Augustus.[129] The suspension of this signaled the beginning of the revolt
(*J.W.* 2.409).

---

[125] Cicero, *Pro Flacco* 28.68; Josephus, *Ant.* 14.72. T. Hopfner, *Die Judenfrage* 13: The Jews, who
had been transported to Rome as prisoners and slaves, must for the most part have been granted
their freedom scarcely four years later. See Cicero, *Pro Flacco;* this must mean redemption by their
fellow countrymen.

[126] Schalit (*König Herodes*, 426ff.), concerning the speech: The basic ideas are for the most part
taken from the memoirs of Herod. S. L. Guterman, *Religious Toleration and Persecution in Ancient
Rome* (London: Aiglon Press, 1951).

[127] Here is the origin of a typical tension: on the one hand, the Jewish practices must be seen
to be old, handed down from the fathers, like those of other peoples. On the other hand, because
of attacks by the Greek cities on the rights of the Jews it must be explained that these have been
granted by the Romans. See especially the conclusion, *Ant.* 16.57.

[128] This is a defense against the typical charge against the Jews of hostility to the human race,
and sounds more like Josephus than Nicholas (or even Herod). On the other hand, we find in §42
(from Nicholas, who was a Gentile): "If the deity enjoys being worshipped . . . ," then a basic principle of the generally accepted religiosity is being claimed for the Jews.

[129] According to Philo, *Leg.* 157, the emperor himself bore the expense of this; according to
Josephus, *J.W.* 2.197; *Ag. Ap.* 2.77, they were provided by the Jews themselves. In both cases the
apologetic note is clear.

A Counterbalance

The opposite point of view is to be seen in the formation of the Zealot movement (Hengel, *Zealots*), which also appeared in parts of the diaspora.[130]

We have seen in the discussion above that the basic legal position of Jews in the empire was not changed by the war. But two new factors had a continuing effect: (1) the destruction of the temple,[131] and (2) that one of the possibilities offered by Pharisaism as a way of making theological sense of the catastrophe was to interpret it as punishment for the disobedience of Israel. Within this point of view one could come to the conclusion that Jews needed only to endure their destiny in patient waiting on God and the ultimate restoration of Israel. Both possibilities, the Zealot and the "peaceful" Pharisaic, were reflected in politics as well as in literature.[132] Any evaluation must take account of the broad context: the "intellectual resistance against Rome" (Fuchs) was not only a Jewish phenomenon (even if in Judaism from time to time it did result in extraordinary measures), but a broadly based protest against the continued expansion of the Roman world power, its forms and its methods. The Greeks had been involved in this struggle long before the Jews and had experienced humiliation at the hands of the Romans in completely different ways than had the Jews (Antiochus III and IV; Perseus of Macedon). Those who had lost their political power could at least defend themselves intellectually.[133] In 156 B.C.E. a scholar in Rome representing the Athenians gave two antithetical speeches, first affirming and then denying that justice prevailed in the empire.[134] The Romans owed their rule to their rapacity and injustice.[135]

---

[130] In the painful aftermath of the Jewish war; Josephus, *J.W.* 7.407ff., 437ff.

[131] Josephus, *J.W.* 6.267ff. In 4 Ezra and *Syr. Bar.* Rome becomes "Babylon" (C.-H. Hunziger, "Babylon als Deckname für Rom und die Datierung des 1. Petrusbriefes," in *Gottes Wort und Gottes Land*, Festschrift H.-W. Hertzberg [Göttingen: Vandenhoeck & Ruprecht, 1965] 67ff.). Cf. *Sib. Or.* 4:125ff.; 5:145ff.; and Fuchs, *Der geistige Widerstand*, 66f. On the analysis: *Sib. Or.* 4 was composed after the destruction of Jerusalem (115–127) and after the eruption of Vesuvius in 79 C.E. (130ff.), which was interpreted as punishment for the destruction of Jerusalem. The book is Jewish, containing no specifically Christian elements (Schürer, *History* 3.579f.). Bousset, "Sibyllen und sibyllinische Bücher," *RE*, 18:265ff.: The polemic against sacrifice (vv. 27–29) indicates how quickly Judaism was able to dispense with the idea of sacrifice after the destruction of the temple. But the author has only sacrificial worship of idols in view! G. Alon (*Jews, Judaism and the Classical World* [Jerusalem, 1977] 252ff.) thinks that it refers to the burning of the temple. This is against Josephus, who states that the temple was burned at the command of Titus to eliminate the center of Judaism.

[132] The *Sibylline Oracles* may be taken as representative of the extent to which active propaganda against Rome had developed.

[133] For rich material with excellent interpretations, see Fuchs, *Der geistige Widerstand*.

[134] Cicero, *Resp.* 3 characteristically reverses the order.

[135] Cicero, *Resp.* 3.14–17, 20–22, 24; cf. thereto Augustine, *Civ. Dei* 4.4. Concerning the rapacity of the Romans, see the letter of Mithradates to Arsakes, in Sallust, *Hist. Fr.* 4.69.5, 17, 20; cf. Josephus, *J.W.;* Minucius Felix delivers himself of a vehement invective, *Oct.* 25 (Fuchs, *Der geistige Widerstand*, 85f.).

There was an interesting interplay between moral judgment and prophecy. A remarkable prophecy was ascribed to the "peripatetic" Antisthenes:[136] an army from Asia will devastate Rome. This is only one variation of a broad tradition of such prophesyings. Apocalyptic streams also existed outside Judaism. The best-known documents are the oracle of Hystaspes[137] and the Egyptian "potter oracle."[138] In different variations there appears the man who is to march against Rome from the east as Nero *redivivus,* Antichrist, etc. The historicizing variant that secondarily was referred to Vespasian was especially familiar.[139]

There emerged a style of writing history that was hostile to Rome. It was still innocuous when Greek historians explained the success of Rome in terms of accident and gifts of Tyche.[140] Those variations went further that spoke of the struggle against "tyrants" and the Caesar cult.[141]

Jewish Contributions

The first contacts between the Jews and Rome were represented positively in Jewish sources. In 1 Maccabees the Romans are extolled for their subjection of

---

[136] Phlegon Mirabilia, *FGH* 257 F 36 III (Fuchs, *Der geistige Widerstand,* 5ff., 29f.).

[137] H. Windisch, "Die Orakel des Hystaspes," *Koninklijke Akademia von Wetenschappen,* AFD. Letterkunde 28, no. 3 (1929); J. Bidez and F. Cumont, *Les Mages Hellénisés,* 2 vols. (Paris: Belles Lettres, 1938); cf. Fuchs, *Der geistige Widerstand,* 31ff.

[138] Fuchs, *Der geistige Widerstand;* Text: POxy. 22.2332; R. Reitzenstein and H. H. Schaeder, *Studien zum antiken Synkretismus* (Leipzig: Teubner, 1926) 38ff. For further discussion, see Hengel, *Judaism and Hellenism,* 181 n. 497.

[139] Josephus, *J.W.* 6.312f.; Tacitus, *Hist.* 5.13 (*GLAJJ,* no. 281); Suetonius, *Vespasian* 4 (*GLAJJ,* no. 312). E. Norden, "Josephus und Tacitus über Jesus Christus und eine messianische Prophetie," *Neue Jahrbücher für das klass. Altertum* 31 (1913): 656ff.; W. Weber, *Josephus und Vespasian* (Stuttgart: Kohlhammer, 1921) 15ff.; Windisch, "Orakel," 65ff. Fuchs asks (*Der geistige Widerstand,* 9, with 37 n. 24) whether Sallust, *Ep. ad Caes.* 1.5 alludes to a corresponding oracle. Horatius Flaccus appears in the Epode 16 about the flight from Rome and the salvation of the pious on the island of the blessed to have had an oracle before him in the style of Hystaspes. In any case, Horatius is also acquainted with the *moral* polemic against Rome (see Epode 7, about the murder of Romulus and the depth of Roman guilt). The church fathers fall in this category (for Minucius Felix, see above; Augustine). Greeks against Rome: J. Geffcken, *Der Ausgang des griechisch-römischen Heidentums* (Heidelberg: C. Winter, 1920) 162ff.; the *Acta Alexandrinorum.*

[140] See the polemical response to this by Polybius 1.63.9; 18.28.5. Dionysius of Halicarnassus, 1.4.2ff. (quoted in Fuchs, *Der geistige Widerstand,* 41) combats anti-Roman portrayals of the story of Rome's origin: The original Romans had been homeless nomads, who fell in with each other only by accident; they lived by robbery and hunting. Their true name had not been "Aborigines," but "Aberrigines." Some of them had been runaway slaves. Sallust, *Cat.* 6.1; Livy 1.8.3ff.; 5.53.9; Ovid, *Fast.* 3.433, etc.; Pompeius Trogus 28.2.8ff.; 29.2.2ff.; 38.6.7ff. Roman self-criticism: Tacitus; Juvenal.

The Romans were aware of the hatred for them: Cicero, *De prov. cons.* 6; *De imp. Cn. Pomp.* 65.

[141] Dio Chrysostom; Apollonius Molon; Lucian, *Demonax, Nigrinus;* Taeger, *Studien zur Geschichte, passim.*

other nations—not surprisingly, since the enemies of the Jews were included.[142]

An opposing, but still Jewish, view is found in *Sib. Or.* 3.167ff.:[143] the high-spirited, rather bawdy Greeks and Macedonians are followed by an empire from the west that is oppressive, insolent, and godless. This section obviously originated in the time of Ptolemy VII Physkon. Then judgments against Rome are taken up such as the one ascribed to Mithradates.[144]

Nero, who was supposed to have fled beyond the Euphrates (*Sib. Or.* 4.119ff.),[145] is coming back (4.137ff.; 5.363ff.). Rome will have to repay its debt to Asia (4.145ff.; cf. 3.350ff.); Fuchs, *Der geistige Widerstand,* 66ff.

Concerning the Analysis of Sib. Or. 5 (esp. 155ff.)

It is no surprise that the interpretation of this section is very disputed, for that is the case with the *Sibylline Oracles* generally. For example:[146] (1) Bleek: Lines 286–332 are Jewish, having originated in Asia Minor soon after 20 C.E. Lines 260–85 and 484–531 were written by an Alexandrian Jew around the middle of the second century before Christ. (2) A. Hilgenfeld, *Die jüdische Apokalyptik in ihrer geschichtlichen Entwicklung* (Jena, 1857); Geffcken: Lines 52–531 are Jewish, a few years before 80 C.E. (3) Schürer: A loose conglomeration; the time and place of origin of the individual sections cannot be determined. The major part is Jewish; lines 256–59 are Christian. Mostly from the first century, because of lamentation over the temple. (4) Bousset: In three related sections, lines 137–78, 214–85, 361–446 one finds respectively the returning of Nero; the messianic age (Jerusalem); threats against Babylon/Rome. Cf. Revelation 17; 18; 21. The author has himself experienced the destruction of the temple. See 4.115ff., 125ff. (5) Fuchs: The major sections of book 5 were composed about twenty years after book 4, by an Alexandrian Jew.

---

[142] 1 Macc. 8:1ff.; 2 Macc. 11:34ff. Pompeius Trogus contains a biting commentary. Fuchs, *Der geistige Widerstand,* 46.

[143] Cf. further *Sib. Or.* 3.350ff., 520ff., 638ff., 652ff.; Fuchs, *Der geistige Widerstand,* 30ff.

[144] Again the analyses differ: for *Sib. Or.* 3, see Schürer, *History* 3.571ff. (bibliographical information for the authors mentioned is found in Schürer 3.591f.). (1) F. Bleek ("Über die Entstehung und Zusammensetzung der uns in acht Büchern erhaltenen Sammlung sibyllinischer Orakel," *TZ* 1 [1819]: 120ff.; 2 [1820]: 172ff.): *Sib. Or.* 3 is Jewish (up to the Christian interpolation in 350–80), by an Alexandrian Jew, but with Gentile elements worked in (97–161, 433–88). (2) C. Alexandre (*Oracula Sibyllina* [Paris, 1856]): by an Alexandrian Jew, around 168 B.C.E., 295–488 is Christian. (3) Bousset ("Sibyllen und sibyllinische Bücher," *RE* 18): 167–195 is an older Jewish element, worked in by the composer of the *Sibyllines.* (4) J. Geffcken (*Komposition und Entstehungszeit der Oracula Sibyllina,* TU 23/1 [Leipzig: Hinrichs, 1902]): strike out the reference to Ptolemy VII in 192f. as a later scribal interpolation (because it does not fit the situation and because of 608). Bousset opposes this. (5) Fuchs with Geffcken: Then 181 must be struck; cf. 520ff., 638ff. . . . In *Sib. Or.* 4 the destruction of the temple is God's punishment on the Jews, which then becomes punishment on the Romans.

[145] Cf. 5.28ff., 138ff., 216ff., 363ff.; 7.70ff., 140ff.

[146] For the following, see Schürer, *History* 3:581ff.; Fuchs, *Der geistige Widerstand,* 66ff. and A. Rzach, *PW* 2 A 2:2137ff.

487ff.). Little information about our subject is known from their time. Particular measures taken by Septimius Severus are a part of his struggle against Pescennius Niger. On the one hand, he forbade (once again) conversion to Judaism; on the other hand, he is reported to have had a positive attitude toward the Jews.[147]

With the grand intervention of the *Constitutio Antoniana* we reach a good chronological division. With it comes complete Jewish equality (Dio 37.17.1-3).

For a survey of the diaspora of the second and third centuries, see Smallwood, *Jews under Roman Rule*, 507ff. Sardis enjoys considerable attention because of the excavations there (for bibliography, see Smallwood, 509 n. 16; see especially the works of Kraabel).

---

[147] Smallwood, *Jews under Roman Rule*, 500: That is no real contradiction. As before, Judaism continues to be permitted but is not to expand beyond its own membership.

II

THE EVALUATION OF JUDAISM IN GRECO-ROMAN LITERATURE

PRELIMINARY REMARKS

The Principal Objections Raised against the Jews

These have been summarized by Juster (*Juifs dans l'empire* 1:45 n. 1). When he remarks, however, that almost all of these were used by the Christians, he does not do justice to the specifically Christian element in the Christian objections, which must be distinguished from that which is specifically Jewish.

A more recent survey is given by Sevenster (*Roots*, 88ff.) under the descriptive rubric "Strangeness." In his view the principal factor is the Jewish loyalty to the Torah, for this is what separates Jews from other peoples.[1]

These objections are to be sorted out into various categories in a number of different ways, including the temporal. There is no prevalent hostility against the Jews in the earlier writers, e.g., Theophrastus, Clearchus, and Megasthenes (see below). Josephus gives an extensive, but still colorless, enumeration of authors who had written about the Jews (*Ag. Ap.* 1.215f.). It is more informative concerning Josephus's acquaintance with the literature than informative about the views of the authors he lists.

Another way to categorize the material is in terms of the degree of

---

[1] For example: ἀμιξία ("unsociableness") (Manetho) cf. Apollonius Molon, who also reproaches the Jews for being the first atheists (Josephus, *Ag. Ap.* 2.148; *GLAJJ*, no. 49; Lysimachus) (hatred for the human race); Pompeius Trogus.

To this correspond the references to the internal solidarity of the Jews (Tacitus); cf. Josephus, *Ag. Ap.* 2.68. The Sabbath was always noticed. Circumcision and the lack of images in worship could be judged ambivalently. For circumcision, note the reference below that it was also practiced by other peoples. With regard to images in worship, see Terentius Varro below.

acquaintance of the various pagan authors with Judaism. What do they know about Jewish history in general? The figure of Abraham, for example, is little known, though he is referred to by Nicholas of Damascus (not surprisingly), Apollonius Molon, and Pompeius Trogus. Moses is generally known (see J. G. Gager, *Moses in Greco-Roman Paganism* [Nashville: Abingdon, 1972]), but what is related concerning him is generally unbiblical. Authors were aware of events of contemporary history involving the Jews, especially the Seleucid era, and then of course the Herodian times. The Jewish War formed a special case (Tacitus).

The objections are of different quality. That the Jews keep themselves separate from others is an objective fact, emphasized by the Jews themselves. But how this fact is evaluated is mostly subjective: one can simply note it, condemn it, ridicule it, even admire it (though the admiration may be hostile, as in Tacitus). The customs of circumcision and the Sabbath were noticed. It was natural that ritual customs first attracted attention, for example, that the Jews closed their shops on the Sabbath (see Sevenster, *Roots,* 152). Circumcision, of course, does not attract public attention, but people were aware of it as a Jewish custom; the roman satirists present drastic examples. People were aware of the Jewish dietary rules. Paying the temple tax could become a problematic practice (Cicero; see Smallwood, *Jews under Roman Rule,* index under *didrachmon* ["two drachmae tax"], Jewish tax, temple tax). Later, a specifically *Christian* critique would be developed concerning the ritual laws (see below).

The charge of *atheism* is in a completely different category.[2] This charge was in fact made on two grounds: the lack of images of a god and the refusal of the Jews to participate in other cults.

Many of the charges against the Jews are of one piece with the charges against other peoples; but against the Jews they received an especially sharp focus. To be sure, every people had its peculiarities, among them such comical ones as the Egyptians have. But no other people had anything corresponding to the Jewish law, this fundamental principle of separation, corresponding to their internal solidarity. The Jews themselves seemed to hinder efforts to understand them from outside. A person such as Philo might interpret the Torah as the law of nature and of humanity in general. Nonetheless, it constituted a certain distancing from the Gentile world.

On the other side, certain limitations must also be seen. So long as the monotheistic confession as such was not challenged and the Jews were not kept from observing their own prescribed rituals or compelled to observe the rituals

---

[2] A. Harnack, *Der Vorwurf des Atheismus in den ersten drei Jahrhunderten,* TU n.F. 18.4 (Leipzig: Hinrichs, 1905); E. Sandvoss, "Asebie und Atheismus im klassischen Zeitalter," *Saeculum* 19 (1968): 312ff. For the expression ἀνόσιοι ᾿Ιουδαῖοι ("unholiness of the Jews") and related matters, see, e.g., *Acta Alexandrinorum,* index.

With regard to Domitian, see below. For a Jewish defense, see Philo against the Egyptians: *Leg.* 163; *Vit. Mos.* 2.193, 196; *Poster. Caini* 2; *LA* 3.112; *Rer. Div. Her.* 2.103; *Fug.* 114, 180; *Vit. Cont.* 8f. See Sevenster, *Roots,* 97.

of others, there remained a large neutral area in which the Jews could come to terms with their environment—a larger area than for Christianity, whose God, to be sure, did not separate himself from the world by ritual laws (*Epistle to Diognetus*), but who involved the Christians in conflict through the confession of Christ. This was a distinctively Christian conflict in which pure Jewish monotheism did not have to get involved.

A special case was represented by the atrocity propaganda which charged the Jews with worshiping the head of an ass and with ritual murder. Both charges were later to be transferred to the Christians. Tacitus illustrates how tenacious this story was and also notes the imageless worship of the Jews. Tertullian (*Apol.* 16) documents this contradiction sarcastically.

Our sources[3] begin with "Mnaseas" (the name has been corrupted in the manuscripts, restored by Niese according to Josephus, *Ant.* 1.94; *Ag. Ap.* 1.216) from Patara in Lycia (*FGH* 3:149ff.; concerning his place of origin, see *POxy.* 13.1611 col. 1:128f.; *GLAJJ,* 97ff.; for additional information, see Josephus, *Ag. Ap.* 1.215f.; 2.112ff.; *GLAJJ,* no. 28. The lexicon *Suda* (a Byzantine lexicon of the tenth cent. C.E.) indicates that he was a pupil of Eratosthenes (ca. 200 B.C.E.). He wrote a *Perihegesis* (travelogue) which emphasized θαυμάσια ("the miraculous") and euhemeristic interpretation of myths, and which was used by Apion (cf. §112). Bib.: *GLAJJ,* 98, esp. E. Bickermann, "Ritualmord und Eselskult," *MGWJ* 71 (1927): 255ff.: in the year 5/4 B.C.E. an account of a military stratagem was transferred from the Idumeans to the Jews and introduced by Mnaseas into Greek literature. D. Flusser, "The Ritual Murder Slander against the Jews in the Light of Outlooks in the Hellenistic Period," in *The Essays in Mem. Joh. Lewy* [Hebrew] 104ff.; I. Heinemann, "Antisemitismus," *PWSup* 5:29; Schürer, *History* 3:152 n. 9; J. Yoyotte, "L'Égypte ancienne et les origines de l'anti-judaïsme," *RHR* 147 (1963): 133ff.: the story existed already before the time of Alexander, against Jewish soldiers and their loyalty to the Persian empire. The ancient ass-cult is related to the identification of Seth with this animal. Within the broad perspective of a history-of-religions approach, W. Fauth deals with Seth-Typhon, Onoel, and the ass-headed Sabaoth (*Oriens Christianus* 57 [1973]: 79ff.).

Further sources and discussions of the history of the affair: Mnaseas tells a fable of the war of the Jews against the Idumeans ("Jews" in the tradition). Through a military stratagem the golden ass's head was stolen from the Jewish temple.

The combination of the ass-head story and ritual murder was brought into the *Suda* by Damocritus in the first century C.E. (*FGH* 730 F 1; *GLAJJ,* no. 247). Δαμόκριτος: Ἱστορικός. Τακτικὰ ἐν βιβλίοις Β'. Περὶ Ἰουδαίων. ἐν ᾧ φησιν, ὅτι χρυσῆν ὄνου κεφαλὴν προσεκύνουν καὶ κατὰ ἑπταετίαν ξένον ἀγρεύοντες

---

[3] For collection of sources, see T. Reinach, *Textes d'auteurs Grecs; GLAJJ.* For a brief survey, see M. Stern, "The Jews in Greek and Latin Literature," in *The Jewish People in the First Century,* vol. 2, ed. S. Safrai and M. Stern, CRINT (Philadelphia: Fortress Press, 1976) 1101ff.

προσέφερον καὶ κατὰ λεπτὰ τὰς σάρκας διέξαινον καὶ οὕτως ἀνῇρουν ("Damocritus, a historian. He wrote a work about tactics in two volumes and a work *On Jews*. In the latter he states that they used to worship an asinine golden head and that every seventh year they caught a foreigner and sacrificed him. They used to kill him by carding his flesh into small pieces"). Do the verbs in the imperfect tense indicate that Damocritus did not write until after the destruction of Jerusalem? E. Schwartz ("Damokritos," *PW* 4:2070) dates the writing in the first century B.C.E., with 70 C.E. as the latest possible date.

As a supplementary observation we should note that in Tacitus (*Hist.* 4.2; *GLAJJ*, no. 281) certain ambiguities exist: effigiem animalis, quo monstrante errorem sitimque depulerant, penetrali sacravere, caeso ariete velut in contemeliam Hammonis; bos quoque immolatur, quia Aegyptii Apin colunt. Sue abstinent . . . ("They dedicated, in a shrine, a statue of that creature whose guidance enabled them to put an end to their wandering and thirst, sacrificing a ram, apparently in derision of Ammon. They likewise offer the ox, because the Egyptians worship Apis. They abstain . . ."). Does Tacitus have in mind a single, unique act of dedication of the image (without reflecting on the circumstances at the time of the Jewish War), or is he thinking about a continuing worship of the object—which, however, would not fit his statement about the lack of images in Jewish worship. This contradiction does not count for much, however, since Tacitus reports the opinions of different authors. In any case, there is a certain conflict between the present tenses of *immolatur* and *abstinent* and the perfect tense *sacravere*.

W. Friedrich has suggested (orally) that a comma not be placed after *sacravere*, but a period after *Hammonis* and a semicolon after *colunt*.

We can now offer something of a summary: A principal objection against the Jews was the charge of "hatred of the human race," provoked by their law and their exclusiveness in external relations (in connection with which their internal solidarity was often noted). See Hecataeus of Abdera; Posidonius 87 F 109 (Diodorus 34.1.3; *GLAJJ*, no. 63) τὸ μῖσος τὸ πρὸς ἀνθρώπους ("hatred of the human race"); Pompeius Trogus 36.2 (*GLAJJ*, no. 137); Philostratus, *Vit. Apoll.* 5.33 (*GLAJJ*, no. 403); Origen, *Contr. Cels.* 5.43; Lysimachus 621 F 1; Josephus, *Ag. Ap.* 1.309 (*GLAJJ*, no. 158). A neat summary is given by Josephus, *Ag. Ap.* 2.145ff. (Apollonius Molon, Lysimachus, Apion). Tacitus's comment is classic: . . . apud ipsos fides obstinata, misericordia in promptu, sed adversus omnes alios hostile odium ("the Jews are extremely loyal toward one another, and always ready to show compassion, but toward every other people they feel only hate and enmity") (*Hist.* 5.1; *GLAJJ*, no. 281). They are constantly inclined to rebel (Apion 616 F 4g.; Josephus, *Ag. Ap.* 2.68; Origen, *Contr. Cels.* 3.5). They are a rather useless people, who have contributed nothing to the cultural accomplishments of the present (Apollonius Molon 728 F 3a; Josephus, *Ag. Ap.* 2.248 [*GLAJJ*, no. 49]; Apion 616 F 4n; Josephus, *Ag. Ap.* 2.135; 2.182; Celsus in Origen, *Contr. Cels.* 4.31).

Along with the Syrians, they seem to have been created to be slaves (Cicero,

De prov. cons. 5.10; *GLAJJ*, no. 70). This was the standard assessment of Roman politicians concerning Orientals: . . . Iudaeis et Syris nationibus natis servituti (". . . Jews and Syrians, peoples born to be slaves").

Cicero further comments (*Pro Flacco* 28.69; *GLAJJ*, no. 68): The fate of the Jews illustrates their value to the gods. Other authors also regard the enslavement of the Jews as their destiny based on their religion (Tacitus, *Hist.* 5.8, *GLAJJ*, no. 281: Titus, in Josephus, *J.W.* 6.42; Apion 616 F 4m, Josephus, *Ag. Ap.* 2.125).

This religious argument against the Jews, explaining their political destiny on religious grounds, will be found later, with characteristic changes, among the Christians: they bear the burden of punishment for their treatment of Jesus (see part IV passim).

EXCURSUS: RITUAL MURDER AND CANNIBALISM

See Stern, 97f.

Perhaps the oldest reference to ritual murder is that of Damocritus. According to Apion (616 F 4i=Josephus, *Ag. Ap.* 2.88ff.; *GLAJJ*, no. 171), it took place annually (Damocritus: every seven years; *GLAJJ*, no. 247). Reinach attempts to trace both versions back to Molon (*Textes*, 121 n. 3).

Concerning Typhon, see Josephus, *Ag. Ap.* 1.237; *GLAJJ*, no. 21 (Manetho). Typhon and the ass: G. Michaelis, *Aegyptus* 32 (1952): 45ff.; L. Vischer, *RHR* 139 (1951): 14ff. Fauth, *Oriens Christianus* 57 (1973): 79ff. The ass is the sacred animal of Typhon; Typhon was often represented with an ass's head (cf. Plutarch, *Is. Os.* 30, 50).

The whole business is further developed by Plutarch, who knows yet another explanation (*Quaest. Conv.;* see *GLAJJ*, no. 258): The Jews worship the ass, which once led them to a spring of water, and refrain from eating rabbits because of their similarity to the ass. Still another variant is found in *Is. Os.* 31 (*GLAJJ*, no. 259): Typhon once made his escape on an ass, which he rode for seven days. After his escape, he begot two sons, "Jerusalem" and "Judea" (cf. Tacitus, *Hist.* 5.2, 3).

A further variation is found in Posidonius, *FGH* 87 F 109 (*GLAJJ*, no. 63): During the siege of Jerusalem by Antiochus VII, his friends reminded the king of the visit which Antiochus IV made to the temple, to the secret inner chamber itself: εὑρὼν δὲ ἐν αὐτῶι λίθινον ἄγαλμα ἀνδρὸς βαθυπώγωνος καθήμενον ἐπ᾽ ὄνου, μετὰ χεῖρας ἔχον βιβλίον, τοῦτο μὲν ὑπέλαβε Μωυσέως εἶναι τοῦ κτίσαντος τὰ Ἱεροσόλυμα καὶ συστησαμένου τὸ ἔθνος, πρὸς δὲ τούτοις νομοθετήσαντος τὰ μισάνθρωπα καὶ παράνομα ἔθη τοῖς Ἰουδαίοις ("finding there a marble statue of a heavily bearded man seated on an ass, with a book in his hands, he supposed it to be an image of Moses, the founder of Jerusalem and organizer of the nation, the man, moreover, who had ordained for the Jews their misanthropic and lawless customs"). Concerning cannibalism as the primitive practice of the human race, see the Isis aretalogy of Andros, 44ff. On the ending of cannibalism, see Kyme Hymn, line 21 (p. 302 in *Ich Bin Isis* [ed. J. Bergman; Uppsala, 1968]). D. Müller (*Isisaretalogien* in *Ägypten und die griechischen Isis–Aretalogien* [Berlin, 1961] ad. loc.) argues that the idea was not Egyptian but Greek, in agreement with A.-J. Festugière ("A propos des aretalogies d'Isis," *HTR* 42 [1949]: 209ff.) against R. Harder ("Karpokrates von Chalkis und die memphitische Isispropaganda," *Abhandlungen der Deutschen Akademie der Wissenschaften zu Berlin* [1943], phil.-hist. Kl. 14, 1944). Concerning cannibalism in myth, legend, folklore, ethnography, see Polyphemus, Homer, *Od.* 10. Individual atrocity stories in mythology: Thyest etc. See Theophilus, *Autol.* 3.3 and Athenagoras 35. For a Stoic perspective, see Diog. Laert. 7.121.

The current picture of the matter needs supplementation. As a characteristic and official document we may take the letter of Claudius to the Alexandrians in the year 41: that is, a letter written into the very center of anti-Jewish agitation (*PLond.* 1912; *CPJ* 153). It was directed against the assumption by Jews of certain rights to which they were not entitled, and against the streaming in of Jewish reinforcements (lines 99f.). καθάπερ κοινήν τεινα τῆς οἰκουμένης νόσον ἐξεγείροντας ("I shall proceed against them in every way as fomenting a common plague for the whole world"). See John Chrysostom, *Contr. Iud. et gent.* 1 (*PG* 48: 852): ὡς κοινὴν λύμην καὶ νόσον τῆς οἰκουμένης ἁπάσης ("they are the common disgrace and infection of the whole world"). The comparison is instructive. The decree of Claudius is no general judgment concerning Judaism as such. The inhabitants of Alexandria must conduct themselves in relation to the Jews (lines 82f.) πραέως καὶ φιλανθρώπως ("gently and kindly"). This decree in its stern style refers solely to a possible Jewish action from outside. Chrysostom, on the other hand, ignites an argument that concerns an entire world view.

A study of such models reveals characteristics that are not merely incidental but correspond to the ancient style in both politics and thought as a whole: there was a deep hatred on both sides, which broke out in atrocious ways, e.g., in the eruption of the Jewish War and the uprisings that followed it under Trajan and Hadrian (Schürer, *History* 1:661ff.); cf. the papyri from the time of the struggles in Egypt under Trajan. But there was no formalized anti-Jewish ideology and thus no general program for extermination of the Jews as such. The primitive anecdote (about Antiochus VII, in Posidonius 87 F 109; Diodorus Siculus 34; *GLAJJ*, no. 63) is no proof to the contrary, but it confirms the point.

Outside the war zone and areas immediately affected by it, the privileges of the Jews were unaffected. (See the program in Damascus at the beginning of the Jewish War [Josephus, *J.W.* 2.559ff.] and similar things in other cities [*J.W.* 2.477], but 2.479 reports that the Jews were treated with consideration in Antioch.) Despite the *fiscus Iudaicus,* the privileges of the Jews remained intact even after the great war of 132–135.

The failure of a developed ideological program to emerge must be seen in a broader context: there was an ancient philosophical "enlightenment." But this ancient enlightenment did not reach the level of modern reflection in the autonomous Enlightenment itself. This is why it did not develop any thoroughgoing critique of religion as such, and no philosophy of history at all. There were particular political theories, political utopias that were developed in a theoretical way, and the concept of human equality. There were revolutions and class conflicts, but none based on an ideology that had fundamentally rethought everything and then come to expression as a radicalized political or social revolutionary movement. The slave uprisings were not this, including the famous one of Spartacus (though now and then individual theologians celebrate it as such, in sovereign ignorance of the texts). The same was the case with anti-Semitism.

Developments in Hellenistic History Writing

(We will first discuss these writings quite apart from their statements about the Jews, which have already been mentioned, in order to understand such statements better by placing them in their proper historiographical frame of reference.)

A special place must be given to those two sources which introduce a completely new style of writing history, and which deal with the Jews only incidentally by means of secondary interpretation or reworking of traditional sources: Berosus (or Berossus) of Babylon (*FGH* 680) and the Egyptian Manetho of Sebennytos (*FGH* 609).

Berosus[4] dedicated his history of Babylonia to Antiochus I Soter (coregent

---

[4] *GLAJJ,* 55ff.: Berosus was a priest of Bel in the time of Alexander; see T 1=Eusebius, *Chron.* 6, 14; T 2=Tatian 36; Eusebius, *Praep. Ev.* 10.11.8 (Tatian according to Juba *FGH* 275 F 4); T 3=Josephus, *Ag. Ap.* 1.128-31; T 8=Josephus, *Ant.* 1.107 (*FGH* 680 F 14); Tertullian, *Apol.* 19 (*FGH* 609 T 6b). *GLAJJ,* 79: Josephus uses Berosus indirectly through Alexander Polyhistor, changing the extracts from him into direct speech.

Further: J. Freudenthal, *Hellenistische Studien,* 2 vols. (Breslau: H. Skutsch, 1874, 1875) 1:27f.; P. Schnabel, *Berossos und die babylonisch-hellenistische Literatur* (Berlin: Teubner, 1923) 166f.: it is clear that the largest block of material in Josephus from Berosus (concerning Nebuchadnezzar) is dependent on Alexander. Cf. Abydenus (*FGH* 685), who introduces a fragment of Megasthenes about Nebuchadnezzar in the same place (common source, sc., Polybius); see A. v. Gutschmid, *Kleine Schriften,* 5 vols. (Leipzig, 1889-94) 4:527; E. Schwartz, "Abydenos," *PW* 1:129, "Alexandros," 1:1451, "Berossos," 3.315.

Schnabel, *Berossos,* 28: Until Polyhistor and Juba, Berosus had no influence on the Greek historians, with the exception of a note in Cleitarchus and the use of the astronomical part of book 1 by Posidonius. Jacoby, *FGH* IIIa:289: the excerpts from Berosus in Juba are not exclusively from Polyhistor.

We are interested in only one point: the point of contact between Berosus and the Jews, namely, the flood story; *FGH* 680 F 4c=Josephus, *Ant.* 1.93 (95) (Eusebius, *Praep. Ev.* 9.11). F 6=Josephus, *Ant.* 1.158 (Eusebius, *Praep. Ev.* 9.16.2=*FGH* 737 F 2): Berosus mentions Abraham. This is inferred

with Seleucus I beginning in 293 B.C.E.), see T 2=Tatian 36 (*GLAJJ*, no. 18) (see also the note of Juba of Mauretania, *FGH* 275 F 4). His book includes cosmogony, anthropogony, the ten primeval kings before the flood, and thereafter a history of the dynasties until the time of Alexander the Great. The bulk of what has been preserved can be found in Josephus (especially in *Ag. Ap.*) and Eusebius, *Chron.*, as well as in excerpts in Alexander Polyhistor, from whom Eusebius also draws. His chronology of primeval history results in enormous spans of time. He claims to use books which had been preserved in Babylon for 215 (?) myriads (Eusebius, *Chron.* 6ff.=*FGH* 680 F 1; Syncellus indicates only fifteen myriads—still quite enough!). The time span of the ten primeval kings requires 120 *sares*, with each *sare* reckoned at 3,600 years (cf. *AOT*, 247ff.). No one will be surprised that Josephus was able to harmonize this chronology with his biblical data about Nebuchadnezzar in Egypt and the Jewish captivity.

At the request of Ptolemy II (285 or 283–246), Manetho composed a history of Egypt. It contains the list of Egyptian kings, the dynasties; see W. Helck, *Untersuchungen zu Manetho und den ägyptischen Königslisten* (Berlin, 1956). Excerpts have been preserved, especially in Josephus and Eusebius. Josephus, however, used a text that had been reedited, perhaps more than once. Jews changed the numbers, in order to bring them into agreement with the Bible. A summary (of the changed text) is provided by the list of kings, upon which both Africanus and Eusebius are dependent.

At the beginning of things there was an epoch of gods and heroes, lasting 24,900 (?) years (F3a). For other numbers, see appendix II in *FGH* III C, 64f. Eusebius adjusts it to the biblical chronology (*Chron.* 63f.). Then follow the dynasties, which comprise more than 5,500 years (Eusebius, *Chron.* 65ff.). This goes far beyond what the Greek historians have room for (cf. Herodotus, Plat.; *FGH* 665). We must return later to the problem of Manetho and the Jewish interpretations and harmonizations provided by Josephus (see below).

The question of how much influence these oriental historians had on the Greeks has, in the case of Berosus, already been answered by Schnabel. Cf. Jacoby (*FGH* II D, 719): works such as Berosus's, Manetho's, and those of the Jewish aspirants to history writing remained for a long time without any great influence. The influence of the Oriental dynasty lists which were reworked in the Persika of Ktesia, among other places, in the form in which we find them in the Jewish-Christian chronography, does not occur until the work of Castor, Alexander Polyhistor, and the falsification issued in the name of Apollodorus (F 83–87), dated by E. Schwartz in 100 B.C.E.

With regard to Jacoby one should note that the appreciation of Egyptian wisdom by the Greeks does not indicate any direct use of Egyptian literature. The Greeks did not learn foreign languages, which would have allowed them to circulate a literature of translated works. An exception, not quantitatively

---

from the enumeration of the *tenth* generation. We may limit ourselves to the reflection of Berosus in Josephus. See further F 7a=*Ant.* 10.20; F 7b=*Ant.* 10.34; and F 8a, b, c, 9a.

significant, was provided by the casual attention given to the Orient in incidental publications devoted to such subjects as Greek astrologers, the oracle of Hystaspes, Zoroaster, the *Hermetica,* and the magical papyri.

In view of the later Christian development of chronography, its beginnings in the writings of the Hellenistic historians are especially worthy of our notice. The comparison reveals, however, the deep changes that had taken place in the overall picture of the world and history. We need only think of the significance of the "proof of antiquity" for the development of the Christian consciousness of history, with the attendant increased self awareness in general, which we find in the church fathers, apologists, and chronographers—a matter that must be pursued later.

In the light of the preceding preview provided by the Oriental historians, we must now turn to the specific Greek developments, to which Jacoby has given special attention. He documents an illuminating twin development in Ephorus of Cyme, which he dates in the fourth century (*FGH* 70). According to Niese, the first books of this thirty-volume work were written after 334. In Jacoby's view (*FGH* II C, 24f.), the writing of history broadens out to become universal history; at the same time the individual disciplines become independent. In his fourth (*Europe,* 70 F 30–42) and fifth (*Asia* F 43–53) books Ephorus gives an independent geographical survey.

Jacoby: "In the two books which he [Ephorus] appears to have dedicated to political geography (T 18) he thus executes a separation between geography as merely an auxiliary discipline for the historian and history as such, and then unites the indispensable element in the former discipline with his history writing in a way which influenced Polybius, among others (T 12)" (*FGH* II C, 25). This was the prelude to the development of historical, ethnological, and other kinds of monographs, including monographs concerning the Jews: Apollonius Molon stands in this line, as does Alexander Polyhistor at a later date, as well as the still later development of biography. See A. Dihle, "Zur hellenistischen Ethnographie" in *Grecs et barbares, Entretiens Hardt* 8 (1962): 207ff.

We come now to the development of those individual disciplines which are of special importance to our subject (in all four parts): chronography in its types and phases.

In addition to the real chronographical works, we should especially note *lists* (of rulers, inventors, etc.). An early example of chronological tables is provided by the Marble Parium (*FGH* 239), according to Jacoby probably erected in 264/263. Apart from the fragments of historians (*FGH* 239–61), the most important work is Eusebius's *Chronicon.* For its structure, see the sketch in Jacoby (*FGH* II D, 661ff.): first comes the *official* chronology with its major headings. In the official, political usage, the eras of the individual states or cities (beginning with the real or supposed date of their founding) provide the chronological divisions, e.g., the Seleucid era, the era *ab urbe condita,* the Augustan era of documented events.

The dominant factor in the scholarly chronography was the Olympian periods (from 776 B.C.E.). See *FGH* II D 663: they prevail in the chronological schemes of Timaeus and Eratosthenes; "the Olympiad was *the* chronological reference point of antiquity." (Cf. Timaeus F 125/6 and the commentary thereto.) In general, the work of Timaeus of Tauromenium (*FGH* 566) is to be considered epoch-making (4th–3rd cents. B.C.E.). He calculated the time from Troy (1194/1193) to the First Olympiad to be 417 years (F 80, 125). This approach was continued by Eratosthenes of Cyrene (*FGH* 241) (ca. 285–205 B.C.E.). He composed a chronography which became foundational.

By counting back from the First Olympiad one comes to the second "canonical" date, the fall of Troy, which was established as 1184/1183. The Greeks generally presupposed that this was the oldest historical date that could be established. It separated historical times from the mythical or heroic.[5] This situation was changed by a writer who became very influential,[6] Castor of Rhodes (*FGH* 250, 1st cent. B.C.E.).[7] His chronology begins with Ninus (2123/2122) and extends to the fourth year of the 179th Olympiad (61/60 B.C.E.). Contemporary with Ninus was Aigialeus, the first king of Sikyon.[8] Castor thus also surveyed Oriental history—of course from a "Greek" perspective.

According to Jacoby (*FGH* II B, 816), Castor appears for Varro (F 9; quoted *FGH* II B, 709) "to have been the actual handbook to which he perhaps owed the analysis of the tradition into the three epoches of ἄδηλον, μυθικόν, ἱστο-ρικόν ("uncertain, mythological, historic" time) (Censorinus, *De d. n.* 21.1-2, cf. F 4 par 1139.26; 1142.31ff.).

The text:

Hic enim [sc. Varro] tria discrimina temporum esse tradit: primum ab hominum principio ad cataclysmum priorem,[9] quod propter ignorantiam vocatur adelon; secundum a cataclysmo priore ad olympiadem primam, quod quia multa in eo fabulosa referuntur, mythicon nominatur; tertium a prima olympiade ad nos, quod dicitur historicon, quia res in eo gestae veris historiis continentur. Primum tempus, sive habuit initium seu semper fuit, certe quot annorum est, non potest comprehendi. Secundum non plane quidem scitur, sed tamen ad mille circiter et sescentos annos esse creditur. A priore scilicet cataclysmo, quem dicunt et Ogygii, ad Inachi regnum[10] annos circiter CCCC computarunt, hinc ad excidium Troiae

---

[5] Apollodorus of Athens (2nd cent. B.C.E.) was also influential (*FGH* 244; *GLAJJ*, no. 34; with Pseudo-Apollodorus, 83–87).

[6] Castor was influential on, among others, Varro (see below), Thallus, Abydos, Julius Africanus, and Eusebius.

[7] For bibliography, see, besides Jacoby, E. Schwartz, *Die Königslisten des Eratosthenes und Kastor* (1894); H. Gelzer, *Sextus Julius Africanus* 1:209ff.; 2:63ff.

[8] F 2 = Eusebius, *Chron.* 81ff.

[9] Here in good Greek (and Roman) style a number of floods are presupposed—a favorite controversial point of Jewish apologetic. Wacholder, *Essays on Jewish Chronology,* 118: the flood meant here is that of Ogygus, in 2376; after that there were 400 years until Inachus, 800 years until Troy, and then 400 years until the First Olympiad.

[10] For the synchronism of Inachus with Moses, see below pp. 148 n. 51, 309.

annos DCCC, hinc ad olympiadem primam paulo plus CCCC; quos solos, quam-
vis mythici temporius postremos, tamen quia a memoria scriptorum proximos,
quidam certius definire voluerunt.

This author divides time into three periods; the first extends from the origin of
man to the first cataclysm, and he calls it uncertain, on account of the obscurity
in which it is concealed. The second extends from the first cataclysm to the First
Olympiad and as it has given rise to numerous fables he calls it mythological. The
third extends from the First Olympiad to our time. He calls this historic, because
the events which transpired during this interval are related in reliable histories. As
to the first period, whether or not it had a commencement, or of how many years
it consisted, we can never know. As to the second, we cannot say exactly, but we
may believe that it covered about six hundred years. From the first cataclysm,
which is called that of Ogygus, until the reign of Inachus [Bacchus] about four
hundred years are counted; from that time until the First Olympiad, a little more
than four hundred are counted. And as these events, although belonging to the end
of the mythical period, approach the historical, several writers have attempted to
give the number more exactly.

Among Gentiles of this period, there is no evidence for any reading of the
Bible worthy of the name. This is indicated by the paucity and confusion of
the data. From the Jewish past, at the most the figure of Moses (with much confusion) was generally known, along with the awareness that the Jews had spent
some time in Egypt, though this was sometimes accompanied with horribly
distorted fantasies concerning their expulsion and settlement in Judea. The first
Gentiles to which any degree of knowledge of the Hebrew and Christian Scriptures can be attributed appear at the end of the second century C.E.: Celsus (in
his conflict with the Christians), and perhaps to a certain extent the philosopher Numenius of Apamea.

Excursus: Acquaintance with the Bible among Gentiles?

(Except for the possibility of allusions, which more or less must be laboriously
tracked down one at a time.)

J. Geffcken (*Zwei griechische Apologeten* [Leipzig and Berlin: Teubner, 1907]
xxviiff.) believes that traces of Gentile polemic against the Scriptures, and thus
their having been read among the Gentiles, can already be recognized in Philo.
Geffcken's documentation is hardly compelling:

(a) *Op. Mund.* 157: Ἔστι δὲ ταῦτα οὐ μύθου πλάσματα . . . ἀλλὰ δείγματα
τύπων ἐπ' ἀλληγορίαν παρακαλοῦντα κατὰ τὰς δὲ ὑπονοιῶν ἀποδόσεις ("Now
these are no mythical fictions . . . but modes of making ideas visible, bidding
us resort to allegorical interpretation guided in our renderings by what lies
beneath the surface"). This could be simply a matter of discussions carried on
within Judaism, or by apologetes for it.

(b) *Conf. Ling.* 2f. (similar to *LA* 3.205f.): οἱ μὲν δυσχεραίνοντες τῇ πατρίῳ πολιτείᾳ . . . ("Persons who cherish a dislike of the institutions of our fathers . . ."). Thus: *Jews* appropriated the ideas of the Greek enlightenment and applied its critical approach to religious ideas to Judaism. In the Old Testament God swears (*LA* 3.203ff.: Gen. 22:16f.). One can make a "rational" argument against this: εἰ δὴ ὄμνυσιν ὁ θεός, ἑαυτῷ μαρτυρεῖ, ὅπερ ἐστὶν ἄτοπον . . . ("so if it is God that swears, He bears witness to Himself, which is absurd . . ."). The objection is countered by Philo's exegesis. This objection is in fact of the same kind which Celsus, for example, could have raised later. But it is here raised and answered by Philo himself—for the benefit of hoped-for Gentile readers of the Bible? (See E. R. Goodenough, *By Light, Light* [New Haven: Yale University Press, 1935]: "The 'allegory' is intended for Jews, the 'exposition' to which the *Op. Mund.* belongs for Gentiles.")

(c) A corresponding result is derived from *Deus Imm.* 31, 60ff.: anthropomorphisms are explained by the fundamental principle: οὐχ ὡς ἄνθρωπος ὁ θεός ("God is not like man") (Num. 23:19); cf. *Deus Imm.* 53. Exactly the same is found in *Poster. Caini* 1ff., with a reference to the Epicurean ἀσέβεια ("impiety") and Egyptian ἀθεότης ("godlessness"); cf. *Rer. Div. Her.* 90ff.

(d) *Agric.* 157: a limitation on dissolving the commandments into mere allegories, with no apparent Gentile polemic visible.

The argument of F. Dornseiff (*Echtheitsfragen antik-griechischer Literatur* [Berlin, 1939] 50) is not persuasive: The supposed Pseudo-Phocylides is in fact genuine; there was already in that time a Greek translation of the Old Testament (cf. Aristobulus, Clement of Alexandria, *Strom.* 1.22); it was based on a parallel tradition of the Pentateuch.

Some scholars perceive a knowledge of the Bible to be present in Hecataeus of Abdera, especially W. Jaeger (*Diokles Von Karystos* [Berlin, 1938] 146f.): his references to the law and the death of Moses (cf. Deut. 29:1ff.) would then be the first quotation from the Bible in Greek literature. Of course, one cannot speak strictly of a "quotation." Note *FGH* 264 F 6 (Diodorus 40.6) (*GLAJJ*, no. 11): προσγέγραπται δὲ καὶ τοῖς νόμοις ἐπὶ τελευτῆς ὅτι Μωυσῆς ἀκούσας τοῦ θεοῦ τάδε λέγει τοῖς Ἰουδαίοις ("And at the end of their laws there is even appended the statement: 'These are the words that Moses heard from God and declares unto the Jews'"). Compare this with the last clause of Lev. 27:34: αὗταί εἰσιν αἱ ἐντολαί, ἃς ἐνετείλατο κύριος τῷ Μωϋσῇ πρὸς τοὺς υἱοὺς Ἰσραὴλ ἐν τῷ ὄρει Σινᾷ ("These are the commandments which the Lord commanded Moses for the sons of Israel in Mount Sina") (cf. Lev. 26:46). The similarity is not all that close. (For further echoes of the Old Testament text, see *GLAJJ*, 32).

By and large, Greek writers on Judaism betray no knowledge of the Bible. This judgment is not changed by incidental (real or supposed) traces of the biblical creation story.

A question of much more importance is whether the Bible was used by Alexander Polyhistor. Jacoby (*FGH* IIIa, 253): Do the numerous references belong to Alexander himself? ("I cannot really believe so.") The material is scanty. (Concerning the tower-building sibyllinum, see below.)

FGH 273 F 102 = Josephus, *Ant.* 1.240 (Eusebius, *Praep. Ev.* 9.20) μαρτυρεῖ δέ μου τῶι λόγωι ᾿Αλέξανδρος ὁ Πολυίστωρ λέγων οὕτως· Κλεόδημός φησιν ὁ προφήτης, ὁ καὶ Μάλχος, ἱστορῶν τὰ Περὶ ᾿Ιουδαίων ("And my statement is confirmed by Alexander Polyhistor, who speaks thus: 'But Cleodemus the prophet, who is also called Malchas, in narrating the history of the Jews . . . says'") (*FGH 727* F 1), καθὼς καὶ Μωϋσῆς ἱστόρησεν ὁ νομοθέτης αὐτῶν, ὅτι ἐκ τῆς Κατούρας ᾿Αβράμωι ἐγένοντο παῖδες ἱκανοί ("even as Moses their lawgiver has narrated it, that by Chettura Abraham had many sons") (see Gen. 25:1-4).

F 19a (*GLAJJ*, no. 51a) (Eusebius, *Praep. Ev.* 9.39): Alexander mentions Jeremiah and the Babylonian captivity, a reference probably derived from Eupolemus.

F 101b (Pseudo-Justin, *Cohortatio* 9); cf. F 101a (Eusebius, *Praep. Ev.* 10.10.7): Alexander is, among other things, a witness for the old age of Moses — but that proves no personal knowledge of the Bible on his part.

There remains the famous citation of Pseudo-Longinus, *De subl.* 9.9 (ed. with commentary by D. A. Russell; Oxford: Clarendon Press, 1964); *GLAJJ*, no. 148, p. 361ff.: Ταύτῃ καὶ ὁ τῶν ᾿Ιουδαίων θεσμοθέτης, οὐχ ὁ τυχὼν ἀνήρ, ἐπειδὴ τὴν τοῦ θεοῦ δύναμιν κατὰ τὴν ἀξίαν ἐχώρησε κἀξέφηνεν, εὐθὺς ἐν τῇ εἰσβολῇ γράψας τῶν νόμων· "εἶπεν ὁ Θεός," φησί,—τί; "γενέσθω φῶς, καὶ ἐγένετο· γενέσθω γῆ, καὶ ἐγένετο" ("A similar effect was achieved by the lawgiver of the Jews — no mean genius, for he both understood and gave expression to the power of the divinity as it deserved — when he wrote at the very beginning of his laws, I quote his words: 'God said' — what? 'Let there be light. And there was. Let there be earth. And there was'").

A summary of the results: If the use of the Bible by Alexander Polyhistor is thus so questionable, we find ourselves confronted with the fact that prior to the end of the second century C.E. no Gentile author known to us was familiar with the Bible, i.e., no one before the philosophers (not historians) Celsus and Numenius of Apamea (see below).

GREEK AUTHORS

Herodotus[11]

The first Greek historian does not mention the Jews, although his horizon includes the Orient;[12] in fact, the struggle between the Orient (Persia) and the Greeks is his principal theme.

---

[11] M. Pohlenz, *Herodot* (Leipzig: Teubner, 1937); for bibliography, see *Kl. Pauly*, s.v.; A. Lesky, *History of Greek Literature* (New York: Crowell, 1966) 306–7.

[12] 2.4.109 (which also includes the Babylonians). Real barbarians in the cultural sense are also discussed, for example, Scythians (4.1ff.; 4.18: cannibalism); 4.62: human sacrifice; cf. 4.103 (the Taurians). The invention of the alphabet by the Phoenicians (5, no. 58) belongs to cultural history. The Greeks remained continually aware of this inheritance, reminded of it from time to time by Jewish apologetic.

In view of the later Hellenistic tendency to divide history into periods, it is notable that in Herodotus's purpose the distinction between the historical and the mythical ages plays practically no role, for he commits himself to that which is subject to investigation, to "history" (*Historie*).[13]

His view of the extent of world history becomes visible in 2.2–4, which indicates that Egypt played a dominant role in the early period.[14]

Two passages which deal with the Jews: 2.104 (cited by Josephus, *Ag. Ap.* 1.168ff. and *Ant.* 8.262) and 2.159. The first deals with the Egyptian origin of people of Colchis: both peoples practice circumcision. And: Φοίνικες δὲ καὶ Σύριοι οἱ ἐν τῇ Παλαιστίνῃ [cf. 7.89] καὶ αὐτοὶ ὁμολογέουσι παρ' Αἰγυπτίων μεμαθηκέναι ("The Phoenicians and the Syrians of Palestine acknowledge of themselves that they learned the custom from the Egyptians") (*GLAJJ*, no. 1). Of course Josephus understands these Syrians to be Jews, since the Syrians themselves do not practice circumcision. We may ignore the question of who these "Syrians" really were, since it suffices for us that Herodotus does not name the Jews. The same applies to the second passage (not mentioned by Josephus) (*GLAJJ*, no. 2): Pharoah Neco besieged the Syrians at Magdolos and conquered Kadytis. Even if one identifies Magdolos with Megiddo, there is still no mention of Jews (Josiah).

---

[13] 1.95; cf. 130, 214.

[14] Rich documentation of the relation of Greeks to Egyptians, through which the Greeks became acquainted with an era of history that made the Greek period sink into relative insignificance: *FGH* 665 ("Appendix": note the authors who deal with Egypt, especially Herodotus; Plato, *Timaeus* 23; and Diodorus).

More concerning Egypt (and other material dealing with the Orient) from Greek literature can be found especially in the lengthy work on Egypt by Diodorus I, which for its part draws extensively on the *History of Egypt* of Hecataeus of Abdera. Hecataeus wrote in the time of Ptolemy I in behalf of, as is to be expected, the Ptolemaic cultural propaganda. Egypt also plays the dominant role from the point of view of our study, since the relation of Jews to Egypt belongs to the principal themes of the body of literature concerned with the Jews.

A selection: Diodorus 1.12.4: The Egyptians call the earth "mother," identified with Demeter, i.e., Isis; cf. 1.13.5; 1.25.1. Isis is identified with the earth: Plutarch, *Is. Os.* 366A; 374C. Diodorus 1.27.4: Ἐγὼ Ἰσίς εἰμι ἡ βασίλισσα πάσης χώρας, ἡ παιδευθεῖσα ὑπὸ Ἑρμοῦ ("I am Isis, the queen of every land, she who was instructed by Hermes"). Cf. 1.17.3 (euhemeristic). Diodorus 1.16: inventions of Hermes; 43: of Isis. With regard to both, see also 20.6; Plutarch, *Is. Os.* 352.

The worship of certain animals in certain regions is pointed out in Diodorus 1.21.6, 9, which gives occasion for remarks on the usefulness of animals; 21.10f.: Gods once changed themselves into animal forms; 1.86.3: in the battle against human beings (giants); cf. Plutarch, *Is. Os.* 379EF (against Typhon). Egyptian animal worship gave an inexhaustible theme for ridicule by Greek and Roman authors, as well as for Jewish and Christian apologetic.

Oriental thinkers were included in the history of Greek philosophy. Cf. W. Jaeger, *Aristotle* (Oxford, 1934) 130ff., and the "Introduction" by Diogenes Laertes.

An interesting, emphatically anti-Greek version is presented by the Christian "barbarian philosopher" Tatian.

Theophrastus

The oldest significant observation concerning the Jews comes from Theophrastus (ca. 370–285 B.C.E.), a disciple of Aristotle (*GLAJJ*, 8–17). To be sure, Jaeger (*Diokles,* 114ff.) advocates the thesis that Theophrastus was dependent on Hecataeus of Abdera, to whom he also attributes his information about the Jews. Even if the former be accepted, the latter is still to be proved (see *GLAJJ*, 8ff.; W. Pötscher, *Theophrastus,* Περὶ Εὐσεβείας ("On Piety") [Leiden, 1964] 123).[15] As evidence for his hypothesis Jaeger refers to the fact that (in Theophrastus) the discussion of the Jews is followed immediately by a comment on the animal worship of the Egyptians (Porphyry, *De Abst.* 2.26; cf. Diodorus 1.83–90); in both places animal sacrifice is regarded as exceptional in particular circumstances. If one compares the reports further, the agreement is not very extensive.

Megasthenes

FGH 715 F 3 = *GLAJJ*, no. 24; Bib.: Jaeger, "Greeks," 132 n. 14; idem, *Diokles;* Hengel, *Judaism and Hellenism,* 141f., 257.

Around 300/290 Megasthenes was the envoy of Seleucus I in India, and wrote Ἰνδικά (*India*). See also F 1a=Josephus, *Ant.* 10.227; *Ag. Ap.* 1.144; F 1b=Eusebius, *Chron.* 19.32, trans. Karst (Eusebius, *Praep. Ev.* 9.41.1); *FGH* 721 F 20= Clement of Alexandria, *Strom.* 1.71.3ff. According to Megasthenes, philosophy began among the barbarians: the Egyptian prophets, the astrologers ("Chaldeans") of the Assyrians, the druids among the Celts . . . but by far the oldest are the Jews; see Philon the Pythagorean and Aristobulus the Peripatetic. In the third book of his Ἰνδικά (*India*) is found the declaration that everything that was said by the ancient Greeks concerning nature can also be found in the non-Greek philosophers, either in the Brahmans among the Indians, or in the Jews among the Syrians. Hengel (*Judaism and Hellenism*) argues that Megasthenes gives a stoicizing representation of the Brahman philosophy (?). But he also probably knew certain basic teachings of Judaism. Clearchus, who also is to be numbered among the admirers of Oriental wisdom, is also dependent on Megasthenes.

Clearchus of Soli

Only F 1 and 7: Josephus, *Ag. Ap.* 1.176ff. For the rest, see F. Wehrli, *Die Schule des Aristoteles* III: *Klearchus* (Basel, 1948). F 6 Wehrli = *GLAJJ*, no. 15. Bib.: H. Lewy, "Aristotle and the Jewish Sage according to Clearchus of Soli," *HTR* 31 (1938): 205–35; Hengel, *Judaism and Hellenism,* 257-58.

---

[15] W. Jaeger ("Greeks and Jews," *JR* 18 [1938]: 127ff.; idem, *Diokles,* 134ff.) discusses Theophrastus and the oldest Greek reports about the Jews. Concerning the connection with general theories about the origins of culture (with which here we are not particularly concerned), see W. Graf Uxkull-Gyllenband, *Griechische Kulturentstehungslehren* (1924); J. Haussleiter, *Der Vegetarismus in der Antike* (Religionsgeschichtliche Versuche und Vorarbeiten 24 [1935]).

Clearchus was a pupil of Aristotle. He repeats an alleged story of Aristotle about an encounter with a Jew from Coele-Syria: The Jews were descended from the Indian philosophers, called "Calanoi"; in Syria philosophers were called "Jews."

Hecataeus of Abdera (Teos)[16]

The oldest connected account of the Jews derives from Hecataeus, which, according to Jacoby, was still in the style of the old ethnography. Hecataeus lived in the time of Ptolemy I (until 283/282 B.C.E.; T 1=Josephus, *Ag. Ap.* 1.183). He wrote a history of Egypt and had a personal knowledge of the country (cf. T 4=Diodorus 1.28.2).

Pseudo-Hecataeus belongs in the category of Jewish documents, not to the Gentile category (F 21–23 or 24). See below.

According to Jaeger and others, Theophrastus was dependent on Hecataeus (see above). This was also the case with Megasthenes, and especially so in the case of the excursus on the Jews found in Strabo. This latter is usually ascribed to Posidonius, whose reworked version replaced Hecataeus's own report in all ancient authors except Diodorus (even though Posidonius was among the major sources of Diodorus). According to Willrich (*Judaica*, 86ff. ["Hekataios von Abdera und die Jüdische Literatur," 99]), Hecataeus is also the source of the explanation of why the Greeks had taken no notice of Jewish literature (*Ep. Ar.* 31). Josephus, who knows *Ep. Ar.*, discusses this subject himself in *Ag. Ap.* 1.1ff.

Stern (*GLAJJ*, 21) supposes that Hecataeus also used an oral Jewish tradition. He bases this conclusion on the way Moses is evaluated and on echoes of biblical language. We will here renounce purely speculative guesses and limit ourselves to presenting the major content of his "Excursus on the Jews."

THE EXCURSUS CONCERNING THE JEWS
(F 6=DIODORUS 40.3)[17]

Foreigners were driven out of Egypt because of a plague,[18] for a demonic spirit was believed to be the reason for the plague. *All* foreigners were expelled, whose religious practices tended to replace those of Egypt. The ἐπιφανέστατοι

---

[16] *FGH* 264; *GLAJJ*, 20–44.

[17] For the allocation to the Abderites, see Jacoby, *FGH* IIIa, 46ff.; Jaeger, "Greeks"; idem, *Diokles,* 144ff.; K. Reinhardt, *Poseidonios über Ursprung und Entartung* (Heidelberg: C. Winter, 1928). Jacoby: The Milesian is excluded by §8b (reference to the Macedonian rulers). And if that should turn out to be an addition by Diodorus: The Jews first appeared in the Greek horizon of thought in the time of Alexander documented by references to their knowledge of the law of Moses. Derivation of the Jews from Egypt is also reflected in F 25=Diodorus 1.28.2. The attitude of the "Excursus" in the book of Hecataeus cannot be determined with certainty.

[18] For the plague, see Chaeremon, Josephus, *Ag. Ap.* 1.288ff. (*GLAJJ*, no. 178); for the development of the anti-Semitic version, see also his successors.

("most outstanding") and δραστικώτατοι ("most active") emigrated to Greece, under leaders such as Danaus and Cadmus (*GLAJJ*, no. 11). The vast majority moved to Judea under the leadership of Moses.

A tension is apparent in this story: Cadmus comes from Egypt (cf. Diodorus 1.23.4: from the Egyptian city of Thebes), but he is a foreigner there. This should be compared with the "colonization version" (F 25 with Diodorus 1.38), which, however, mentions only Danaus.

Jacoby declares there is simply a contradiction in Hecataeus: (a) F 6 ξενηλα-τουμένων τῶν ἀλλοεθνῶν ("the aliens were driven from the country")–which still was not present in Hecataeus's idealized Egypt; (b) real colonization extending from Egypt. We have here two variations of an original story. The central core of the story, which is similar to the version promoted by the Egyptian priests, portrays the Egyptians as the original teachers of the Greeks: all life derives from the Nile Valley. Egypt is idealized, without being really hostile to foreigners. The second variation manifests no particular interest in setting Egypt in relationship to other peoples; "it idealizes, in a theoretical manner, but unlike Hecataeus does not deal systematically with the Greeks at all, when it speaks of the Egyptians; rather, it concretizes the Egyptian tradition of the expulsion of the 'contaminated.'" That is, it is the expression of the hatred of the Egyptian priesthood for everything foreign and shows that this hatred gained a new impetus through the Greek conquest (Jacoby, *FGH* IIIa, 50).

The question of the sources which Hecataeus used for his information concerning Moses is raised by Wacholder (*Eupolemus*, 91), by I. Heinemann ("Moses," *PW* 16.361, and "Antisemitismus," *PWSup* 5:32ff.): No Gentile author from Hecataeus to Posidonius, Cicero, Strabo, and Tacitus had direct access to the Bible. The opposite side is argued by E. Bickermann (*MGWJ* 71 [1927]: 177) (see the preceding excursus, pp. 55-57 above); cf. the quotation [*sic!*] of a Mosaic text in Diodorus 40.3.6; Jaeger, *Diokles*, 144; Gager, *Moses*, 26ff.; Wacholder, *Eupolemus*, 95f.

He possesses φρόνησις ("wisdom") and ἀνδρεία ("courage") (on which see Bidez and Cumont, *Les Mages Hellénisés* 1:241 n. 2): but not εὐσέβεια ("piety"); cf. §5: selection of priests according to φρόνησις ("wisdom") and ἀρετή ("virtue"). He founds Jerusalem and the temple (Moses pictured as the "founder"!). Thus Hecataeus does not know the Bible. Concerning his cult and his political organization: he gives no picture of God, διὰ τὸ μὴ νομίζειν ἀνθρωπόμορφον εἶναι τὸν θεόν, ἀλλὰ τὸν περιέχοντα τὴν γῆν οὐρανὸν μόνον εἶναι θεὸν καὶ τῶν ὅλων κύριον ("being of the opinion that God is not in human form; rather the Heaven that surrounds the earth is alone divine, and rules the universe"). Reinhardt (*Poseidonios*, 9f.): This is not yet the picture of the all-encompassing that encompasses *us* which we have in Posidonius (cf. Strabo). The comparison is rather to be made with the Egyptian heavenly gods (Diodorus 1.11). The cultus and customs are different than among other peoples, for in remembrance of the expulsion (Moses) ἀπάνθρωπόν τινα καὶ μισόξενον βίον εἰσηγήσατο ("he introduced an unsocial and intolerant mode of life"). The Jews are thus given something of an excuse for their behavior. But one can recognize seeds that can later germinate: the observation concerning the imageless worship can later lead to the charge of atheism; "hatred of humanity" becomes a firm motif. The cultic peculiarities were considered as indignities which later made the rumors of ritual murder and the worship of an ass's head easy to evoke.

According to Hecataeus, the Jews never had kings—a further indication that he was not acquainted with the Bible. Lebram finds here a pro-Hasmonean note, from the time before the Hasmoneans adopted the royal title. But what about the biblical historical writings?

At the head of the government stood the ἀρχιερεύς ("priest"). He is selected on the basis of intrinsic merit. The Jews consider him to be ἄγγελος τῶν τοῦ θεοῦ προσταγμάτων ("messenger to them of God's commandments"). When he gives his exposition of these laws, people fall down before him. At the conclusion of his discussion of the law, he remarks ὅτι Μωσῆς ἀκούσας τοῦ θεοῦ τάδε λέγει τοῖς Ἰουδαίοις ("These are the words that Moses heard from God and declares unto the Jews") (cf. Lev. 27:34, often described as a "quotation"; see above p. 56).

There are further reports about military training, conquests under Moses' leadership, and the division of the land into equal shares (only the priests receiving larger portions), which could not be sold. Children may not be exposed, but must be nurtured to maturity. This point we find—on both sides—as a topos (polyandry of the Jews; see Josephus, Ag. Ap. 2.202). This is the reason their race is always numerous.

Then follow the laws for marriage and burial. But: κατὰ δὲ τὰς ὕστερον γενομένας ἐπικρατείας ἐκ τῆς τῶν ἀλλοφύλων ἐπιμιξίας ἐπί τε τῆς τῶν Περσῶν ἡγεμονίας καὶ τῶν ταύτην καταλυσάντων Μακεδόνων, πολλὰ τῶν πατρίων τοῖς Ἰουδαίοις νομίμων ἐκινήθη ("But later, when they became subject to foreign rule, as a result of their mingling with men of other nations (both under Persian rule and under that of the Macedonians who overthrew the Persians), many of their traditional practices were disturbed") (GLAJJ, no. 11).

Individual "Minor" Authors

(1) Agatharchides of Cnidos (FGH 86 F 20; GLAJJ, no. 30ab = Josephus, Ag. Ap. 1.205–211, abbreviated in Ant. 12.5f.) (2nd cent. B.C.E.) was a Peripatetic (Strabo 14.656). Josephus portrays him as writing derisively about Judaism: the Jews are a good example of δεισιδαιμονία ("superstition") (cf. Plutarch, De Superst. 8) (GLAJJ, no. 30a). One of his examples: the Jews have the strongest fortress, Jerusalem (often praised as such: Eusebius, Praep. Ev. 9.35; Tacitus). But since they observe the Sabbath,[19] and refused to bear arms on that day (cf. 1 Maccabees), Ptolemy I Soter was able to capture the city. The Jews lost their freedom, and the absurdity of their religion was revealed (similarly Plutarch, Nicholas of Damascus, Josephus, Ant. 13.252; Dio Cassius 37.16, 49; 66.7).

---

[19] He is the first Gentile to mention Sabbath rest. Fraser (Ptolemaic Alexandria 1:517, 2:783 n. 204) assumes that his writing on the Red Sea presupposes a knowledge of the LXX.

(2) Polybius (end of 3rd cent. B.C.E.)[20] narrates events of contemporary Palestinian history, especially from the struggles between the Ptolemies and the Seleucids (*GLAJJ*, nos. 31–33).[21] Josephus (*Ant.* 12.135) takes over the report of the conquest of Palestine by Antiochus III from Polybius 16, and the report of the plundering of the temple by Antiochus IV (*Ag. Ap.* 2.83f.) from Polybius and others (Strabo, Nicholas of Damascus, etc.). See Schürer, *History*, vol. 1, for a general discussion of these events. (So also, the geographical data, especially concerning Jerusalem and the Dead Sea, are only occasionally relevant for our discussion here.) The events named above are also dealt with by Apollodorus of Athens (*FGH* 244; 2nd cent. B.C.E.; Josephus, *Ag. Ap.* 2.83f.; *GLAJJ*, no. 34).

(3) There follows a noteworthy group of reports concerning Solomon and Hiram, which are of interest to us only because of the perspective on Jewish history which they offer. Josephus (*Ag. Ap.* 1.116ff.) contains a fragment from Menander of Ephesus (*FGH* 783; *GLAJJ*, no. 35), who was a second-century B.C.E. author of a history of Greeks and barbarians. Menander used sources, the importance of which lies in their derivation from the archives of Tyre (Josephus, *Ant.* 8.144ff., 324; 9.283ff.). It deals with the dedication of a golden column in the temple of Jupiter in Tyre. Herodotus also knows of such a column (2.44), as well as an emerald one in the temple of Hercules. Cf. Theophrastus in Pliny, *Hist. Nat.* 37.19. It is found in anecdotal form: riddles were interchanged, and Solomon regularly lost (the same also in Dios, see below). Concerning the golden column and further points of contact between Solomon and Hiram, see in addition the Jewish historian Eupolemus (*FGH* 723). The dating of the construction of the temple is also of interest: 143 years before the founding of Carthage. Among the authors of anecdotes worthy of note we may also mention the composer of a Phoenician history, Dios (*FGH* 785; Josephus, *Ag. Ap.* 1.112ff.; *Ant.* 8.147ff.; *GLAJJ*, no. 36), who relates a story about a statue of the king's daughter who was finally married by Hiram. As a final member of this group we may mention Laitos (?), the obscure author of a Phoenician history (*FGH* 784; *GLAJJ*, no. 39) (2nd cent. B.C.E.; cf. also Tatian 37; Eusebius, *Praep. Ev.* 10.11.10ff.; Clement of Alexandria, *Strom.* 1.114.2).

Diodorus Siculus

In the first century before Christ Diodorus composed a "historical library," a universal history, which is extremely valuable because of the sources contained in it (*GLAJJ*, nos. 55–66). He begins with Egypt. Book 1.28.1–3 indicates that he is acquainted with the departure of Danus from Egypt (the Argivite Version); he is also aware, from Herodotus 2.104, of the derivation of the people of Colchis from the Egyptians (circumcision!), from which he infers

---

[20] "Minor," of course, only for his reports concerning the Jews.

[21] He passes over the Jews in his report concerning the fourth Syrian war.

that this was also the case with the Jews. (Herodotus in fact locates the Phoenicians and Syrians in Palestine, while Diodorus locates the Jews between Arabia and Syria). See also 1.55.5.

Book 1.94 contains a list of those who gave laws to the Greeks and other peoples, beginning with the Egyptian Mneves, with the divine patron from whom they received their laws: Zathraustes, Zalmoxis, παρὰ δὲ τοῖς Ἰουδαίοις Μωυσῆν τὸν Ἰαὼ ἐπικαλούμενον θεόν ("among the Jews Moyses referred his laws to the god who is invoked as Iao") (GLAJJ, no. 58). (The name "Yahweh" appears here for the first time in Greek literature; some would want to derive it from Hecataeus. The name also emerges in Varro; see GLAJJ, no. 75). In Diodorus 19 we begin to get reports of events. The Jewish κτίσις ("creation") stands in its characteristic place (40.3 = GLAJJ, no. 65), comparable to the ethnographic excursus in the other historians: Ἡμεῖς δὲ μέλλοντες ἀναγράφειν τὸν πρὸς Ἰουδαίους πόλεμον, οἰκεῖον εἶναι διαλαμβάνομεν προδιελθεῖν ἐν κεφαλαίοις τήν τε τοῦ ἔθνους τούτου ἐξ ἀρχῆς κτίσιν, καὶ τὰ παρ' αὐτοῖς νόμιμα. κατὰ τὴν Αἴγυπτον τὸ παλαιὸν λοιμικῆς περιστάσεως γενομένης ἀνέπεμπον οἱ πολλοὶ τὴν αἰτίαν τῶν κακῶν ἐπὶ τὸ δαιμόνιον . . . περὶ μὲν τῶν Ἰουδαίων Ἑκαταῖος ὁ Ἀβδηρίτης ταῦτα ἱστόρηκεν ("Now that we are about to record the war against the Jews, we consider it appropriate to give first a summary account of the establishment of the nation, from its origins, and of the practices observed among them. When in ancient times a pestilence arose in Egypt, the common people ascribed their troubles to the working of a divine agency. . . . Such is the account of Hecataeus of Abdera in regard to the Jews").

The problem passage is Diodorus 34.1, which is usually ascribed to Posidonius (FGH 87 F 109); W. Aly (Strabon von Amaseia, Strabonis Geographica [Bonn, 1957] 199f.) offers a dissenting opinion. This is the familiar anecdote of the siege of Jerusalem by Antiochus VII and the demand of his friends to exterminate the loathsome Jewish people; the story of the worship of the ass's head is also included in this. The passage is anti-Semitic, but that is not the tendency of the author himself. Antiochus rejected the irrational request, μεγαλόψυχος ὤν ("being magnanimous") according to Diodorus (see also Josephus, Ant. 13.242ff.; GLAJJ, no. 63).

The reasons for ascribing the passage to Posidonius, who is not named in the section, are discussed by Stern (GLAJJ, 1.143, 184): In book 30ff., Diodorus is chiefly dependent on Posidonius. According to Josephus, Ag. Ap. 2.79, Apion derived the story of the ass's head from Posidonius and Apollonius Molon. The parallel in Josephus, Ant. 13.236 has no changes (common source?). In any case, Josephus had not read Posidonius himself. (Concerning Posidonius see Josephus, Ag. Ap. 2.79ff. = FGH 87 F 69 = Edelstein and Kidd F 278; GLAJJ, no. 44). FGH II C, 197. Suspicor Josephum—(who has himself never looked into Posidonius)—in universum tantummodo Posidonium inimicum tamquam Iudaeorum cognovisse ("I imagine that Josephus, generally speaking, got to know Posidonius merely as an enemy, so to speak, of the Jews").

Stern, *GLAJJ*, 1.141ff.: Josephus supposes that Apion obtained his slanderous reports about the Jews from Posidonius and Apollonius Molon. It could be that Apollonius Molon was dependent on Posidonius. It is also possible that Apion appealed to both authors in order to give his pronouncements more authority.

In the following, questions of authenticity of authorship will for the most part be kept in the background, since it is less a matter of declarations by individual authors than of the picture as a whole which was widespread in the public domain—though of course individual authors played a role in shaping this picture. In any case, it is characteristic that from so influential an author as Posidonius we receive no clear picture of the Jews. That is especially true of the great excursus about the Jews in Strabo, which has often been ascribed to Posidonius due to the influence of the views of E. Norden and K. Reinhardt.

With regard to tracing back the material to Posidonius, I am grateful for the instruction I have received from my respected colleague H. Dörrie of Münster (letter of 2 March 1976). To be sure, Posidonius was used by Strabo, who incidentally would have had occasion to note Posidonius's comments about the Jews. But in Strabo's great excursus on the Jews there is nothing particularly characteristic of Posidonius. The central point for Posidonius was the Jews' rejection of foreign cults, and this is lacking in Strabo.

Even though one must proceed carefully, we include the excursus in Strabo, especially since Jacoby is too uncertain, printing it in his Posidonius-fragments in fine print (F 70) (see below, pp. 69ff.).

Nicholas of Damascus

FGH 90; *GLAJJ*, nos. 83–97; B. Z. Wacholder, *Nicolaus of Damascus*, University of California Publ. in History 75 (Berkeley and Los Angeles: University of California Press, 1962). Bib. also in Schürer-Vermes-Millar, *History* 1:28ff.

Nicholas is primarily a source for the history of the times. The great apologetic speeches attributed to him by Josephus, in which he advocated the political rights of the Jews and which were fundamental to Josephus's own defense of the Jews' place within the empire, were of course composed by Josephus himself (*Ant.* 12.235ff.; 16.27ff.; *GLAJJ*, no. 86). Josephus is particularly dependent on Nicholas for his portrayal of Herod. A sample of Josephus's dependence on Nicholas: most of the details of the account of the plundering of the temple by Antiochus IV in *Ag. Ap.* 2.83f. (=*FGH* 90 F 91; *GLAJJ*, no. 87) are derived entirely from Nicholas.

Nicholas was a philosopher (Peripatetic) and diplomat, serving Anthony and Cleopatra during his thirties, who was later the respected friend and court historian of Herod, where he also participated in important diplomatic missions until Herod's death (cf. T 12=Josephus, *Ant.* 16.183f.) (*GLAJJ*, no. 93). For the relation of these two, see further T 4=Josephus, *Ant.* 16.29; F 133 (*GLAJJ*, no. 94); F 134 (*GLAJJ*, no. 95); F 235 (*GLAJJ*, no. 96): Nicholas was instrumental in getting Herod interested in the study of history, while Herod in turn encouraged Nicholas in the writing of history. He composed a biography of Augustus (with whom he already enjoyed something of a reputation), an autobiography, and a history of the world in 144 volumes. It is disputed whether this history extended until shortly before or shortly after the death of Herod, but for our purposes the issue is unimportant.

He is unique because he is a highly educated Gentile who has a firsthand knowledge of Judaism (examples from his biblical history F 20 = Josephus, *Ant.* 7.101ff.) (*GLAJJ*, no. 84). F 72 = Josephus, *Ant.* 1.93ff. (*GLAJJ*, no. 85): he refers the story of the flood to Moses, the lawgiver of the Jews. Wacholder (*Nicolaus,* 57) supposes that he gave extensive descriptions of the biblical heroes. But he also departs from the biblical story: Abraham came out of Chaldea with an army, became king of Damascus, Nicholas's hometown (F 19 = Josephus, *Ant.* 1.159f.; *GLAJJ*, no. 83, cf. Pompeius Trogus 36.2).

It is very important to remember that Nicholas was the major source used by Josephus for the Hasmonean time and, most important of all, for the time of Herod. (Wacholder, contrary to the general opinion, argues that Josephus used Nicholas more in *Ant.* than in *J.W.,* for in the former Jewish history is more interwoven in general Hellenistic history.) It is debated whether Josephus used Nicholas *directly* (so Hölscher ["Josephus" in *PW* 9:1934–2000], Schürer) or through an intermediary source (Otto, "Herodes," *PW* 9:2513; "Herodes," *PWSup.* 2:6ff.; Jacoby), an anonymous Jewish author (*FGH* II C, 230 on T 12 = Josephus, *Ant.* 16.183ff.; *GLAJJ*, no. 93 – which is supposed to account for the unfavorable judgment on Nicholas!).

The evaluation of Herod in *J.W.* is positive; in *Ant.* hostile elements are woven in. Thus the idea arose (Hölscher) that here an anti-Herodian compilation by Nicholas and a second source (Ptolemy) were utilized. It could be, of course, that Josephus's opinion about Herod simply changed. Compare the fact that Nicholas himself, in his autobiography written after Herod's death, seems to have evaluated Herod less favorably than before (F 136, 2–4; cf. *FGH* II C, 255). R. J. H. Shutt asks whether the unfavorable judgments concerning Herod were inserted after the death of Agrippa II (*Studies in Josephus* [London: SPCK, 1961] 90).

Since Schlatter (*Geschichte Israels,* 169) does not trouble himself with source analysis, he is very confident in making judgments concerning the political theories of Nicholas. But we cannot dare to simply transfer the picture which Josephus gives of the standing which Jews had in the Roman Empire (see above) to Nicholas. We need not doubt that Nicholas, working in Herod's court, also sought to clarify the position of Jews in the empire: that was Herod's interests. Schalit (*König Herodes,* 426ff.) judges the contribution of Nicholas very positively. That corresponds to his total evaluation of the political ideas of Herod, and may underestimate the tendentious view of Josephus (who lived in a changed political situation!). The argument of the

Ionians is certainly historical, to the effect that political equality must presuppose the worship of the city gods—a political issue of the first magnitude (*Ant.* 12.126) (*GLAJJ*, no. 86).

Strabo of Amaseia

FGH 91; Stern, *GLAJJ*, 261ff. (nos. 98–124)

Strabo was both historian and geographer; he lived from 64/63 B.C.E. until at least 23 C.E. His historical work was done before that of Nicholas of Damascus. It is important to consider him at this point, especially because of the great "Excursus concerning the Jews" in his *Geography*, but also because of the fragments of the historical work, which provide rich material concerning the history of the times (used by Josephus; Jacoby, *FGH* II C, 291, characterizes the work as "banal," but useful because of the sources which Strabo lists and includes). Josephus, who takes advantage of it for his portrayal of Hasmonean times, incidentally confirms its agreement with Nicholas, who of course wrote at about the same time (e.g., F 13=Josephus, *Ant.* 14.104; *GLAJJ*, no. 104). The agreements probably are the result of using the same sources (cf. Schürer-Vermes-Millar, *History* 1:26). But Jacoby claims that Strabo used Nicholas of Damascus (*FGH* II C, 231; cf. also 90 F 100, Strabo, *Geog.* 15.1.73—but really from the *Historical Sketches?*).

Strabo constructs a geographical framework: Syria is divided into the areas of Coele-Syria, Syria proper, and Phoenicia, among which four peoples are distributed: Jews, Idumeans, and the peoples of Gaza and Azotus. The (confused) description of the land is related by him to the mixed character of the population—a mixture of Egyptians, Arabs, and Phoenicians, which again is to be seen in the context of the idea of the Egyptian origin of the Jews (F 7; *GLAJJ*, no. 105).

The problem is that the "Excursus on the Jews" is often ascribed to Posidonius (see above). In connection with Strabo we will here review all the material, referring to the various interpretations of the Posidonius hypothesis. We will deal first with the individual references, then the great excursus.

F 4=Josephus, *Ant.* 13.287 (*GLAJJ*, no. 99): Josephus deals with the time when Ptolemy VIII (Lathyrus) and his mother Cleopatra were engaged in war 108/107 B.C.E.). Most of Cleopatra's troops deserted to her son's side; but the Egyptian Jews remained loyal to her (cf. Josephus, *Ag. Ap.* 2.49).

F 6=*Ant.* 14.111ff. (*GLAJJ*, no. 102): an episode from the same time, not important for our considerations here.

F 7=*Ant.* 14.114–18 (*GLAJJ*, no. 105): Concerning the political standing of the Jews (with comments on their worldwide dispersion) in Cyrenaica, where they formed one of the four classes of the population, in Egypt and Alexandria (their ethnarch).[22] Originally they were Egyptians, who then settled the

---

[22] See part III; Tcherikover, *Civilization*, 362; Schürer, *History* 3:76ff.

borders of the country. This much is correct, that the Cyrenian Jews came from Egypt, which has been confirmed by inscriptions (see S. Applebaum, "Cyrenesia Judaica," *JJS* 13 [1962]: 34; concerning Cyrene, see Josephus, *Ag. Ap.* 2.44, as well as *Supplementum Epigraphicum Graecum* XVII, no. 823 etc.). On §115: . . . μηδ' ἐπικρατεῖται ὑπ' αὐτοῦ. (a) "and in which it has not made its power felt" (Stern, *GLAJJ*, 278), (b) "where Jews were not accepted and could not hold their own" (Heinemann, "Antisemitismus," *PWSup* 5:16).

F 10 = Josephus, *Ag. Ap.* 2.83f. (*GLAJJ*, no. 98): Strabo listed among a series of witnesses for the time of Antiochus IV.

F 11 = *Ant.* 13.319 (*GLAJJ*, no. 100): Josephus cites Timagenes (88 F 5) concerning Aristobulus.

F 12 = *Ant.* 13.345 (*GLAJJ*, no. 101) also from Timagenes, a blood-curdling story of the boiled flesh of women and children and atrocities against prisoners (*GLAJJ*, 272).

F 13 = *Ant.* 14.104 (*GLAJJ*, no. 106) only mentions briefly the expedition of Gabinius and Pompey against the Jews (64/63), with references to Nicholas of Damascus (*FGH* 90 F 97) and Strabo.

F 14 = *Ant.* 14.35f. (*GLAJJ*, no. 103): refers to gifts to Pompey which were displayed in Rome in the temple of Jupiter Capitolinus, including one with the inscription of "Aristobulus" the son of Alexander the king of the Jews. The text is uncertain. (See Niese ad loc.)

F 15 = *Ant.* 14.66 (cf. 487) (*GLAJJ*, no. 104): the taking of Jerusalem on a Fast Day—a frequent topos (Stern, *GLAJJ*, 276f.).

F 16 = *Ant.* 14.138 (*GLAJJ*, no. 107) names the high priest Hyrcanus and F 17 = *Ant.* 14.139 Antipater as ἐπιμελητής ("procurator") of Judea (cf. Hypsicrates) as participants in a military campaign against the Egyptians (Nicholas [Josephus, *Ant.* 14.68] does not mention Hyrcanus).

F 18 = *Ant.* 15.8–10 (*GLAJJ*, no. 108): Antigonus, the last Hasmonean ruler, was taken captive by Sosius and Herod during the capture of Jerusalem in 37 B.C.E. Antonius had him taken in chains to Antioch and beheaded (cf. Plutarch, *Ant.* 36). He was the first Roman who had a subject king beheaded. Strabo's reasons for this are interesting:

Antonius acted on the basis of political reasoning. He saw no other means of separating the Jews from their dependence on Antigonus and transferring it to Herod. The perspective of this report is pro-Hasmonean. An anti-Herodian source is obvious in Josephus, *Ant.* 14.490: the execution occurred at the instigation of Herod. On the other hand, a pro-Herodian version appears in *J.W.* 1.357, where there is no mention of Herod's initiative, but rather a disparaging comment about Antigonus.

In conclusion we may mention the note in *Geography* 16.4.23, which lists Jews among the soldiers in the Roman army. In 25/24 B.C.E. the prefect of Egypt, at the command of Augustus, undertook an expedition against Arabia. Ten thousand troops marched under his command τῶν ἐκ τῆς Αἰγύπτου Ῥωμαίων καὶ τῶν συμμάχων, ὧν ἦσαν Ἰουδαῖοι μὲν πεντακόσιοι, Ναβαταῖοι δὲ χίλιοι μετὰ τοῦ Συλλαίου ("consisting of Romans in Egypt, as also of Roman allies, among whom were five hundred Jews and one thousand Nabataeans under Syllaeus") (*GLAJJ*, no. 120). Josephus, *Ant.* 15.317 contains a pro-Herodian comment on this: these five hundred were a selected company sent by Herod (Schürer-Vermes-Millar, *History* 1:290 n. 8).

We now come to the great ethnographic excursus of Strabo concerning the Jews, which Jacoby attributes to Posidonius—with an obviously bad conscience (*FGH* 87 F 70; *GLAJJ*, no. 115).[23] The time of Posidonius was about 150–135 B.C.E. Rhodes was the primary setting for his work. Josephus counted him among the anti-Semitic writers (see *Ag. Ap.* 2.79; see especially F 109, the episode with Antiochus VIII mentioned above). To Rhodes also belongs Apollonius Molon. Thus it happens that this island appears in the literature as second only to Alexandria as a nest of anti-Semitism in the ancient world. If one gives up on Posidonius as a source and works only with the relatively moderate statements of Josephus concerning Apollonius, many historians would judge that the picture has become rather dim.

Only fragments remain of the enormous work of Posidonius. Nonetheless, he has left behind many traces of his work in other authors (see Schürer-Vermes-Millar, *History* 1:20ff.).

Some of the arguments, in my opinion unpersuasive, that have been introduced for attributing the excursus to Posidonius, are as follows: (a) The excursus is purported to be composed according to the Posidonian scheme of "generation and degeneration" (cf. Seneca, *Ep.* 90!). (b) The concept of God attributed to Moses is supposedly that of Posidonius. Gager argues to the contrary (*Moses*, 44): it was the general Stoic view; the similarity with Cicero, *De div.* (Reinhardt, *Poseidonios*) is in fact minimal. We mention it only for the sake of curiosity: A. D. Nock (*JRS* 49 [1959] 8): the source was a Jew who was acquainted with Posidonius.

One of the major literary problems is that of the relation of the historical outline to the following description of the land of Judea (see on the one side Jacoby [all belongs to Posidonius], and Stern on the other side). The decisive thing, in my opinion, is that we receive a comprehensive picture of Judaism from the Gentile perspective. This would still be true even if one accepted a Jewish source that would have been used by Posidonius for the historical part; see Nock (*JRS* 49 [1959] 8); Gager, *Moses*, 38ff., J. C. Lebram, "Der Idealstaat der Juden," in *Josephus-Studien*, Festschrift O. Michel (ed. O. Betz, K. Haacker, M. Hengel; Göttingen: Vandenhoeck & Ruprecht, 1974) 233–55; cf. the review by Stern, *GLAJJ*, 265f., who accepts a Gentile source, but which Strabo adopted only with modifications. If the source were Jewish, then Alexander Polyhistor would not have been the only historian who read Jewish authors. But no such source can be proved for Strabo. This view requires in addition

---

[23] L. Edelstein and I. G. Kidd, *Posidonius I. The Fragments* (Cambridge: Cambridge University Press, 1972).

that one posit a considerable ignorance of the Bible by the purported Jewish authority supposed to stand in the background. See especially the argument against derivation from Posidonius by Aly (*Strabon*, 201), who excises §§38f. from the historical excursus. But if this is regarded as an insertion, the question arises: By whose hand? And is it an interruption in the author's thought at all? Jacoby's additional hypothesis that Posidonius was used by an intermediate source, i.e., Timagenes (cf. Josephus, *Ag. Ap.* 2.83f.), which was also the source for Pompeius Trogus 36 (contra Reinhardt, *Poseidonios*, 26, 29 n. 1) does not clarify things but produces further complications. The further question as to where Posidonius would have included this excursus in his own historical work seems to me to dispose of this hypothesis. In this connection the literary form of "foundation accounts" is important (e.g., because of the proposal to excise §§38f.). On this form, cf. Pompeius Trogus and Tacitus. According to Jacoby (*FGH* II C, 196):

> the description of the land is however closely related to that of the essential features of the people themselves, their composition and their history, as is seen not only in Strabo, but also in Justin and Tacitus, as well as Dio Cass. XXXVII 16:5. There is, of course, a well known form of ethnographically-interested history, and even in view of the way in which Strabo uses sources, it is not advisable to see a change of sources at §39. Positing such an alternation of sources is in fact prohibited by the connections between 40 on the one hand and §36, par 264, 33, and 37 on the other, for such connections were obviously not first made by Strabo himself.

Contents: Strabo (§34) introduces his historical report with a survey of the population of Judea: it is a mixture. Cf. in this connection Hecataeus (F 6) on the one hand: the expulsion of non-Egyptians; and, on the other hand, the anti-Semitic version of the expulsion of the unclean (*leprous*): Chaeremon, Lysimachus, Apion, who also is acquainted with Posidonius (87 F 109).

Then follows the historical report (§35) (*GLAJJ*, no. 115). Again a thorough comparison is to be made with Hecataeus. Moses was an Egyptian priest (cf. "Manetho" in Josephus, *Ag. Ap.* 1.250, *GLAJJ*, no. 21; Chaeremon, Josephus, *Ag. Ap.* 1.290, *GLAJJ*, no. 178). He possessed a part of lower Egypt, but left that country because of his rejection of the prevailing religion, that is, both the Egyptian animal worship and the Greek anthropomorphism. Thus the way is prepared for the later description of the Jewish cult.

Many worshipers of the Divine Being (πολλοὶ τιμῶντες τὸ θεῖον) left with Moses. Some scholars hear the overtones of a Jewish author in this; but the expression is not typically Jewish, and the context likewise gives no indication of Jewish authorship. Moses' positive doctrine of God is given as εἴη γὰρ ἕν τοῦτο μόνον θεὸς τὸ περιέχον ἡμᾶς ἅπαντας καὶ γῆν καὶ θάλατταν, ὃ καλοῦμεν οὐρανὸν καὶ κόσμον καὶ τὴν τῶν ὄντων φύσιν ("for, according to him, God is the one thing alone that encompasses us all and encompasses land and sea—the thing which we call heaven, or universe, or the nature of all that exists")

(*GLAJJ*, no. 115). (This concept of God is—despite or because of Philo—completely un-Jewish.)

This does remind one of Hecataeus (see above). But two points should be noted: (a) The inference drawn by Strabo: there can be no images of God, though there can be shrines: τούτου δὴ τίς ἂν εἰκόνα πλάττειν θαρρήσειε νοῦν ἔχων ὅμοιαν τινὶ τῶν παρ᾿ ἡμῖν; ᾿αλλ᾿ ἐᾶν δεῖν πᾶσαν ξοανοποιίαν, τέμενος ‹δ᾿› ἀφορίσαντας καὶ σηκὸν ἀξιόλογον τιμᾶν ἔδους χωρίς ("What man, then, if he has sense, could be bold enough to fabricate an image of God resembling any creature amongst us? Nay, people should leave off all image-carving, and, setting apart a sacred precinct and a worthy sanctuary, should worship God without an image") (cf. Tacitus, *Hist.* 5.5; Dio 17.2). (b) Concerning περιέχον ("encompass") Jacoby considers it possible that Posidonius [*sic!*] knows Hecataeus; but then the differences become important. This can be seen precisely in the concept of περιέχον (cf. Reinhardt, *Poseidonios*, 10ff. and esp. 13 no. 1): Aristotle, *Met.* 1074b3: . . . καὶ περιέχει τὸ θεῖον τὴν ὅλην φύσιν ("the divine encloses the whole of nature"). Similarly in Cornutus 1; Philo, *LA* 3.6: ὁ φαῦλος δοκεῖ εἶναι τὸν θεὸν ἐν τόπῳ, μὴ περιέχοντα, ἀλλὰ περιεχόμενον ("The bad man thinks that God is in a place, not containing but contained") (*LA* 1.44, 51).

Reinhardt (*Poseidonios*, 10), who interprets τὸ περιέχον ("encompass") in Strabo "posidonically" and in contrast to Hecataeus, understands the contrast to be not "superrational/rational," but "the all-encompassing"/"the limitations of temporal objects." Concerning this pantheism, Reinhardt remarks (*Poseidonios*, 15): "The God of Moses is the God of Posidonius," for whom pantheism was the primeval religion. This "primeval" perspective then sets up the following excursus on Greeks and Barbarians, §§38f. regarded by Aly as an addendum. But the text cannot be understood in terms of a "primeval religion." Regarding Posidonius's concept of God, see also the annotation to Lucan, *Pharsalia* 9.578 (Posidonius); cf. Aly, *Strabon*, 196: θεός ἐστι πνεῦμα νοερὸν διῆκον δι᾿ ἁπάσης οὐσίας ("God is a rational spirit that pervades all that is").

After the plan for the erection of a shrine is given, there follows a remarkable note concerning Jerusalem (placed in brackets by Jacoby, since neither grammar nor content seems to fit the context; αὐτούς ["them"] has no antecedent. . . . And the content is appropriate to Posidonius; cf. Cicero, *De div.* 1.64); ἐγκοιμᾶσθαι δὲ καὶ αὐτοὺς ὑπὲρ ἑαυτῶν καὶ ὑπὲρ τῶν ἄλλων ἄλλους τοὺς εὐονείρους ("people who have good dreams should sleep in the sanctuary, not only themselves on their own behalf, but also others for the rest of the people"). And the σωφρόνως ("self-restrained") who live righteously may expect to be rewarded by God.

Reinhardt (*Poseidonois*, 14) considers the questionable passage to be stylistically appropriate: after the doctrine of the universal God follows the teaching concerning divination. Again he turns to the excursus in §§38f. for support:

how could Posidonius (!) have placed Moses beside Trophonius and Amphiaraus, unless he had described him as the founder of an oracle that functioned by the interpretation of dreams (is this logic?)? For the connection gods—providence—revelation (manticism), see Chrysippus.

By his teaching Moses persuaded εὐγνώμονας ἄνδρας οὐκ ὀλίγους ("not a few thoughtful men") (§36) (*GLAJJ*, no. 115). He captured the site on which Jerusalem now stands. (A brief conventional geographical characterization is given: the place has rocky cliffs, is located in an arid district, but is itself well provided with water.)

He won over people not with weapons, but by instruction concerning the cultus and the deity, promising a cult without pomp or ecstatic excitement.

The story reaches a certain climax in §37: After Moses, his followers remained faithful for a while to the arrangements he had instituted, but then the priestly office (!) fell into the hands of leaders who developed it in a superstitious way, and then into the hands of tyrants.[24]

It was from this superstition that the food laws developed, as well as περιτομαί ("circumcisions"), ἐκτομαί ("excisions," i.e., cuttings of the female body), etc.,[25] and from this tyranny that the banditry, revolts, and conquests derived.[26] But the veneration for their acropolis continues, which they revere as a holy place.

The first part of the excursus comes to an end with this report about Moses and the degeneration that followed him. It is in itself, as many interpreters recognize, a neutral report, which can be evaluated only in the framework of its wider context.[27]

The following excursus in §§38f. has already been mentioned repeatedly

---

[24] Reinhardt, of course, interprets the data in terms of Posidonius's scheme of generation and degeneration. Lebram ("Idealstaat," 237) objects that the Greek theory of culture is lacking. "The contrast between Moses and his successors is not determined by cultural factors, or factors in developmental history, but personal factors." The whole is an encomium to Moses.—An inadequate argument.

[25] Strabo, *Geog.* 17.2.5 (*GLAJJ*, no. 124) concerning the Egyptians: τὸ πάντα τρέφειν τὰ γεννώμενα παιδία καὶ τὸ περιτέμνειν καὶ τὰ θήλεα ἐκτέμνειν ("they rear every child that is born, and circumcise the males and excise the females"); so also the Jews (see 16.4.9).

[26] It is obvious that this refers to the Hasmoneans. Lysimachus ascribes such conduct to the Jews from the very beginning; this is why their city was called Hierosyla, *FGH* 621 F 1=Josephus, *Ag. Ap.* 1.304ff. (*GLAJJ*, no. 158). Concerning banditry: "Manetho," *FGH* 609 F 10=Josephus, *Ag. Ap.* 1.248ff. (*GLAJJ*, no. 21); Strabo, *Geog.* 16.2.28 (*GLAJJ*, no. 114); Pompeius Trogus 39 Prol. (*GLAJJ*, no. 138); 40.2.4 (*GLAJJ*, no. 139).

[27] Lebram goes his own way here, finding the tendency to protect Moses from anti-Semitic criticisms, although with anti-Hasmonean elements included. He finds biblical elements: the Israelites in lower Egypt; revelation of God to Moses. Concerning weaponless [*sic!*] combat, cf. the battle at Rephidim (Exod. 17:8ff., etc.; Exod. 17:13 "with the edge of the sword"). And: this report is supposed to be the source for the pro-Hasmonean version, which was wrongly attributed to Hecataeus.—This fantasy is disposed of by the texts mentioned above.

from different points of view.[28] It concludes: τοιοῦτος δέ τις [i.e., like the listed mantics] ἦν καὶ ὁ Μωσῆς καὶ οἱ διαδεξάμενοι ἐκεῖνον, τὰς μὲν ἀρχὰς λαβόντες οὐ φαύλας, ἐκτραπόμενοι δ' ἐπὶ τὸ χεῖρον ("Moses was such a person as these, as also his successors, who, with no bad beginning, turned out for the worse").[29] Then the report returns to the subject of tyranny, which is illustrated by the Hasmoneans until Pompey established order.[30] Another comment about Jerusalem is included here: it was conquered on the fast day (i.e., the Sabbath).[31] Pompey destroyed the ληστήρια ("haunts of robbers") and the γαζοφυλακεῖα ("treasure-holds") of the tyrants.[32] In the appended description of the land, Posidonius is named as the source (§43).

In addition, an episode that does not derive from Strabo, but from Diodorus, though scholars like to ascribe it to Posidonius (*FGH* 87 F 109), has already been mentioned above.[33] The comment made there is to be here augmented from a particular point of view. Quite apart from the question of authorship, what we have here is a small compendium of anti-Semitic material, which as such belongs to the following section. If it should turn out to derive from Posidonius, it would be significant that he knew the anti-Semitic version, but did not adopt it himself: the compendium shows how indiscriminately one author copied from another, and how thus here and there a picture was rather haphazardly accumulated, which then had an effect on the public at large. We have here in one passage, in an unusually concentrated density, all the sloganistic phrases that were effectively used against the Jews: The friends of Antiochus VII advised him during his siege of Jerusalem to storm the city and exterminate the γένος ("race") of the Jews (*GLAJJ*, no. 63): μόνους γὰρ ἀπάντων ἐθνῶν ἀκοινωνήτους εἶναι τῆς πρὸς ἄλλο ἔθνος ἐπιμιξίας καὶ πολεμίους ὑπολαμβάνειν πάντας ("since they alone of all nations avoided dealings with any other people and looked upon all men as their enemies").[34] Their ancestors were

---

[28] Reinhardt bases his argument precisely on this section. He refers to the "parallels" in Cicero, *De div.* 1.88, which are derived from Posidonius; but Moses is not mentioned. Reinhardt: they derive from the *older* work of Posidonius on manticism. — But in this way one can prove whatever one wishes.

[29] No argument can be based on this comment.

[30] Jacoby does not attribute §40 to Posidonius, but to Timagenes, in order to be able to affirm that no alteration of sources is present in Strabo.

[31] The Sabbath is also elsewhere mistaken for a fast day, which in reality it certainly was not. Suetonius, *Aug.* 76, etc.; Dio 37.16: on the "Kronos day." Josephus, *Ant.* 14.66 naturally understands Strabo to be speaking of Yom Kippur; cf. *J.W.* 1.146. Concerning conquest on the Sabbath, see Agatharchides (from the point of view of the Jewish δεισιδαιμονία ["superstition"]; Josephus, *Ag. Ap.* 1.209f.; *GLAJJ*, no. 30a). See further Dio 49.27 (Herod); Sosius 66.7 (Titus).

[32] Lysimachus; Pompeius Trogus 39 Praef.

[33] The attribution of *FGH* 87 F 109 to Posidonius remains uncertain. For purposes of evaluation, the context of Diodorus 34 should be observed. Jacoby, *FGH* II C, 208 characterizes the section as "a tendentious, but complete (!) ethnography to the point of describing the land."

[34] Cf. Hecataeus as the "kernel." Separation, from the Jewish point of view, *Ep. Ar.* 139ff.

driven out of Egypt ὡς ἀσεβεῖς καὶ μισουμένους ὑπὸ τῶν θεῶν ("men who were impious and detested by the gods").[35] The ἀλφοὺς ἢ λέπρας ἔχοντας ("persons who had white or leprous marks") were driven out for the sake of the purity of the land.

Thus two reasons for the expulsion were combined: godlessness and leprosy. Ἄλφα ("white marks") white blotches on the skin; other versions of ἄλφα are found in Nicarchus, son of Ammonius (*FGH* 731 F 1, *GLAJJ*, no. 248); Ptolemy Chennos (Reinach, *Textes*, 361); Helladius (*FGH* 635) the text also in Philo of Byblos (*FGH* 790 F 11; Reinach, *Textes*, 362f.).

Alexander Polyhistor

FGH 273; commentary in *FGH* IIIa, 248ff.; *GLAJJ*, no. 51-53.[36]

According to Jacoby, Alexander must have played a certain role in the intellectual life of the Ciceronian period (first cent. B.C.E.). He was brought to Rome as a slave, and there became a freedman. On the other hand, the perceptible use of his works by the Romans is quite small. Jacoby explains this easily enough on the supposition that his material had already been taken over by Varro and Hyginus. Juba (*FGH* 275) was obviously of more interest to the Romans. An exception: Extensive use was made of Alexander's literary bequest in the lexical sources of the lexicographer Stephanus of Byzantium (sixth cent. C.E.)—but he excludes the Chaldaica and the works concerning the Jews. From the book dealing with the Jews, Jacoby (F 19) presents only the bare skeleton (as does Stern, *GLAJJ*, no. 51a), because the Jewish historians excerpted by Alexander must later be presented under their own names anyway (part III; *FGH* 722ff.). The excerpts are preserved, because Alexander was excerpted in turn by Clement of Alexandria and especially by Eusebius (*Praep. Ev.* 9.17-39). Eusebius probably quoted the main items verbatim, but that concerns only quotations that he actually looked up. The outline is recklessly compressed. According to Jacoby (*FGH* IIIa, 15):

> [Alexander] made the Romans aware of peoples and literature, the very existence of which they had previously hardly been aware, and which nonetheless in a certain sense had to form the very center of their concern. For it is difficult to conceive how the impulse which led to these books could be separated from Varro's Sibyls and Vergil's Fourth Eclogue—to mention only these two; although the foreign policy from Sulla to Caesar's latest plans for the most part call for the same kind of consideration. . . . Rome's view [despite Caesar's Gallic intermezzo] was at that time directed to the East. . . . In the acceptance of Chaldeans and Jews, as also in Alexander's Pythagoreanism (F 93/4), we can trace the fundamental historical turning point in which philosophical and scientific thought begins to

---

[35] Cf. Apollonius Molon and again the kernel in Hecataeus.

[36] Bib.: J. Freudenthal, *Hellenistische Studien*; B. Z. Wacholder, *Eupolemus: A Study of Judaeo-Greek Literature* (Cleveland: Hebrew Union College-Jewish Institute of Religion, 1974) 44ff.

turn back in the direction of the longing after primeval, revealed wisdom. But this was certainly not for Alexander a self-conscious change of direction. . . .

Of his voluminous writings, his monograph on the Jews has unique significance for us, because Alexander is the first (so far as we can discern) and for a long time the only author who studied and excerpted Jewish sources.[37] He used in addition non-Jewish authors, among others Apollonius Molon F 19a §19 (Eusebius, *Praep. Ev.* 9.19.1) (*GLAJJ*, no. 51a) and Timochares §35 (Eusebius, *Praep. Ev.* 9.35). The scope of his work is not clear: Eusebius does not follow Polyhistor after the Babylonian exile, but Berosus (*FGH* 680 F 8=Josephus, *Ag. Ap.* 1.130ff. [on 1.135ff. (*GLAJJ*, no. 17), see *Ant.* 10.220ff.] Eusebius, *Praep. Ev.,* 9.40). But it is unlikely that Alexander ended with the Babylonian captivity; more probably he extended his work to the time of Pompey. Of course that cannot be proved.[38] Josephus mentions him only in *Ant.* 1.240f.[39]

In Eusebius the chronology follows the course of events of Jewish history from Abraham on.[40]

There are only scanty additional materials concerning the Jews in Polyhistor (F 79 = Eusebius, *Chron.* 4ff.): Polyhistor writes about the flood, in dependence on Berosus (*FGH* 680 F 4; *GLAJJ*, no. 17; Josephus, *Ant.* 1.104ff.) and about the Tower of Babel in dependence on Jewish sources.[41]

The remarkable statement in F 70 (Suda; *GLAJJ*, no. 52) cannot be unexplained: Καὶ περὶ Ῥώμης βιβλία έ. ἐν τούτοις λέγει, ὡς γυνὴ γέγονεν Ἑβραία Μωσώ, ἧς ἐστι σύγγραμμα ὁ παρ' Ἑβραίοις νόμος ("And about Rome five books, in which he states that there lived a Hebrew woman Moso, who composed the law of the Hebrews").[42]

F 121 from Stephanus of Byzantium s.v. Ἰουδαία ("Juda") (*GLAJJ*, no. 53): Ἀλέξανδρος ὁ Πολυΐστωρ ἀπὸ τῶν παίδων Σεμιράμιδος Ἰούδα καὶ Ἰδουμαία ‹ς?› ("Judea.—Alexander Polyhistor says that the name derives from the children of Semiramis Judas and Idumea [?]"). The continuation proceeds through Claudius Iolaus (1st cent. c.e.?; *FGH* 788 F 4; *GLAJJ*, no. 249): ὡς δὲ

---

[37] On whether he himself knew the Bible, see pp. 56–57 above.

[38] Berosus was also named by Tatian (36) as a source of information on Nebuchadnezzar and the Babylonian captivity (Eusebius, *Praep. Ev.* 9.39; Berosus *FGH* 680 F 8b; so also Juba of Mauretania *FGH* 275 F 2).

[39] Jacoby (*FGH* I 1, 269) against deriving Josephus's discussion of the major parties from Polyhistor, contra Hölscher (*Die Quellen des Josephus* [Leipzig, 1904]). See now Hölscher himself, "Josephus," *PW* 9:1966. Josephus cites Cleodemus Malchus.

[40] 17ff., 19 from Molon; 19:4 again from Polyhistor: Isaac's sacrifice; 20ff.: Babel, Joseph; 26ff.: Moses etc. to Jeremiah 39 and the exile.

[41] Concerning the "Sibyl and the Building of the Tower," which Polyhistor allegedly derived from non-Jewish sources, but in fact does not have at all, see *Sib. Or.;* Josephus, *Ant.* 1.118f.

[42] One can speculate on whether behind Μωσώ ("Moso") a Sibyl is to be found; but, even so, no progress has been made. Heinemann ("Moses," *PW* 16:360) sees only spite in the remark. Then Polyhistor must have used an anti-Jewish source.

Κλαύδιος Ἰόλαος, ἀπὸ Οὐδαίου Σπάρτων ἑνὸς ἐκ Θήβης μετὰ Διονύσου ἐστρα-
τευχότος ("According, however, to Claudius Iolaus, it comes from that of
Udaeus, one of the 'Sown-men' at Thebes, who was among the military
companions of Dionysius"). (Concerning the Spartan Udaeus, see Stern,
GLAJJ, 535).[43]

Polyhistor appears also as the authority for the chronology of Africanus
(Eusebius, *Praep. Ev.* 10.10, F 101a; cf. Pseudo-Justin, *Coh.* 9; E. Bickermann,
Chronologie [Ithaca: Cornell University Press, 1968]).[44] We have here a certain
transitional period in the literature (of course, not in the sense of a consistent
development).

To this point, we have found a pronounced anti-Judaism in the sources only
in Josephus's report of Posidonius's anecdote about Antiochus VII (which
Josephus lists in *Ag. Ap.* 2.79 among those hostile to Jews), an evaluation which
Posidonius does not adopt himself. In addition, there was only stupid gossip
like that of Mnaseas of Patara (Stern, *GLAJJ*, 97f.), along with expressions of
surprise which resulted from the self-chosen separation of the Jews. A factor
in later verdicts about the Jews was the picture of Judaism offered by the
Hasmonean state (and this not only for Hellenistic historians, but this was also
finally the case for Roman historians who were at first associated with them).

These expressions[45] became sharper with time, without becoming consistent.
From the later perspective[46] Josephus divides authors into two groups depend-
ing on their attitude to the Jews: ἀνοήτους ("mindless") and τετυφωμένους
("fools"), naming Apollonius Molon[47] as their model, and the κατ᾿ ἀλήθειαν
φιλοσοφήσαντας ("genuine exponents of Greek philosophy") who confirm
Josephus's own portrayal (*Ag. Ap.* 2.255). The archenemy is of course Apion
(2.88), who belongs to the Alexandrian group and thus is not to be discussed
until later.

Whatever was the case with Posidonius himself, he and Apollonius, from
their base on Rhodes, exercised an influence on Romans who came to study
under them. And Apollonius wrote the first monograph concerning the Jews

---

[43] For Semiramis as queen of the Orient, see Diodorus 2.14.1.

[44] About the same time as Polyhistor, a certain Teucer of Cyzicus (*FGH* 274) wrote, in addition
to other works, a history of the Jews in six books (T 1, Suda). Stern, *GLAJJ*, 165f.

The Stoic Cleomedes (according to Posidonius) wrote the following concerning the way (among
other things) the disciples of the Epicureans expressed themselves (a perspective on the social
standard of the Jews); see Sevenster, *Roots*, 82: τὰ δὲ ἀπὸ μέσης τῆς προσευχῆς καὶ τῶν ἐπ᾿ αὐταῖς
προσαιτούντων, Ἰουδαϊκά τινα καὶ παρακεχαραγμένα καὶ κατὰ πολὺ τῶν ἑρπερῶν ταπεινότερα
("Epicurus learned his particular way of putting things in the synagogue, or among the individuals
who begged in its vicinity: 'a Jewish jargon of poor quality, lower than all that creeps on the
ground'") (Reinach, *Textes*, no. 121).

[45] And no wonder, in view of the growth of the diaspora and the development of the Jewish
state.

[46] Some time after the Jewish War.

[47] In stark contrast to the respect in which he was held not only on Rhodes, but also among
the Romans.

known to us. He was known to Polyhistor, and thus could have been discussed previously. But since the lines from Alexander Polyhistor to the later authors can be traced more clearly, we have discussed him first.

Apollonius Molon[48]

He was a famous rhetorician and grammarian, taught on Rhodes and was highly respected by many peoples, including the Romans;[49] Cicero and Caesar, among others, were numbered among his hearers.[50] In Josephus he seems to have been shifted into the same context as the Alexandrians: there follows (again) a report about Apion, with the stories of the ass's head (Ag. Ap. 2.80) and ritual murder (Ag. Ap. 2.91ff.). Concerning Apollonius, Josephus grants (Ag. Ap. 2.148) that he does not, like Apion, summarize his charges into one passage, but scatters them throughout his work. Thus they would be read somewhat differently than in Josephus's own summary of them. That the work offered an unfavorable picture of the Jews is not, of course, to be doubted.[51]

Eusebius (Praep. Ev. 9.19) describes Apollonius's work (like that of Porphyry) as συσκευή (lit., "equipment," especially for the theater, thus "slight-of-hand," "illusion").

Apollonius anticipates Polyhistor in that he refers back to the period prior to Moses, to Abraham.[52] After the flood, the survivor (no name!) wandered from Armenia to the mountainous part of Syria οὖσαν ἔρημον. μετὰ δὲ τρεῖς (!) γενεὰς ᾿Αβραὰμ γενέσθαι ("which was desolate. After three generations Abraam was born") (GLAJJ, no. 46).[53] He had twelve sons by his Egyptian slave, who moved to Arabia and became rulers;[54] by his real wife he had one son named Γέλως ("Gelos"="laughter, joke"). This one, i.e., Isaac, had eleven sons καὶ δωδέκατον ᾿Ιωσήφ, καὶ ἀπὸ τοῦδε τρίτον Μωσῆν ("and a twelfth one Joseph. His grandson was Moses").[55] Apollonius thus knows etymologies of names, which must ultimately have come from Jewish sources;[56] cf. also Abraham, ὅν δὴ

---

[48] Actually: Apollonius, son of Molon; Stern, GLAJJ, 148ff.; Kl. Pauly s.v. Molon.

[49] See Cicero concerning him (in Brutus) and cf. Josephus, Ag. Ap. 2.255.

[50] Plutarch, Cic. 4; Caes. 3.

[51] Josephus, Ag. Ap. 2.79, 145ff., 236, 255, 295.

[52] In F 1, which Eusebius took from Polyhistor κατὰ ᾿Ιουδαίων ("On the Jews"); Willrich, Judaica, 86ff.: as the first known non-Jew.

[53] Three; otherwise, ten.

[54] Cf. Gen 25:13ff. (the twelve sons of Ishmael).

[55] Jacob is thus passed over. The reports are thus fragmentary (cf. also the comment about Joseph). Still, traces of biblical influence become unmistakably stronger. There are yet other indications of this.

[56] Schlatter, Geschichte Israels, 196 and 422 n. 183: The (Jewish) book of names which is apparent in Apollonius (?) has been preserved in later revisions, especially in Origen and Jerome; the source used by Molon had translated the names of Abraham and Isaac into Greek.

μεθερμηνεύεσθαι πατρὸς φίλον ("whose name signifies the friend of the father").[57]
It is to be emphasized that in this portrayal the Jews do not come from Egypt.
Abraham is also the patriarch of the Arabian princess. And he is characterized:
ὅν δὴ σοφὸν γενόμενον τὴν ἐρημίαν μεταδιώκειν ("This man was wise and eagerly
went to the desert").[58]

The evaluation of Moses (Josephus, *Ag. Ap.* 2.145; *GLAJJ*, no. 49) sounds
somewhat different than that of the "international" Abraham. He is described
as a sorcerer. The continuation in Josephus (*Ag. Ap.* 2.248) fits this wholesale
description. It is not a direct quotation, nor does it contain them, but is
Josephus's own summary, which of course contains reliable material from
statements currently in circulation about the Jews. The additional charge, in
which the perspective of the cultivated Greek is revealed, is especially characteristic: λέγει δὲ καὶ ἀφυεστάτους εἶναι τῶν βαρβάρων καὶ διὰ τοῦτο μηδὲν εἰς
τὸν βίον εὕρημα συμβεβλῆσθαι μόνους ("He adds that we are the most witless
of all barbarians, and are consequently the only people who have contributed
no useful invention to civilization") (*GLAJJ*, no. 49). This picture must be
compared with: (a) the Greeks' self-confidence in their culture taken as a whole,
which includes the topos that Greeks are aware that they have learned something from the Orient (especially from the Egyptians)—but still not from the
Jews! (b) On the other hand, the picture drawn by the Jewish apologetes of
Abraham and Moses as inventors (in view of the significance which the Greek
doctrine of the origins of culture attributed to the category "inventor"!).
(c) Finally, Josephus's own refutation and "explanation" of this charge (*Ag. Ap.*
2.152ff.): the Jews have remained from the very beginning true to their origins;
this is the reason for the lack of innovations among them. He also works in
his defense against ἀθεότης ("atheism") and μισανθρωπία ("hatred of humanity"):
ὅτι μὴ παραδεχόμεθα τοὺς ἄλλαις προκατειλημμένους δόξαις περὶ θεοῦ μηδὲ
κοινωνεῖν ἐθέλομεν τοῖς καθ᾽ ἑτέραν συνήθειαν βίου ζῆν προαιρουμένοις ("he condemned us for refusing admission to persons with other preconceived ideas
about God, and for declining to associate with those who have chosen to adopt
a different mode of life") (*Ag. Ap.* 2.258; *GLAJJ*, no. 50).

Summary: it seems that what one can say about Molon as a whole is to be
placed more in the category of astonishment at and disdain for "barbarians"
than a matter of hatred. This is still reflected in the writings of Josephus. The
charges remain moderate, provoked by Jewish practices themselves, the kind
of typical charges which a Greek rhetorician brings against the uneducated for
the benefit of the reader's own education. One also sees here how limited is the

---

[57] Many suppose a connection with Aramaic רחם, others with Isa. 41:8 זרע אברהם אהבי and
2 Chron. 20:7 (see Stern ad loc.).

[58] Apollonius thus takes over without criticism the traditional picture of Abraham as sage. And
he had heard something to the effect that Abraham was a traveler. There are some hints of the
wilderness motive. Josephus's comment in *Ag. Ap.* 2.16 does not really provide any information
(the Gentile historians contradict each other on the date of the Exodus; Molon is mentioned
among others.

understanding of the Jews expressed in this series of stereotypes. The new element in the authors that we are now to discuss is the activation of hatred, and this is connected with Alexandria.[59] In placing these authors together, we need also to backtrack somewhat chronologically;[60] in this we are following Josephus (but not only him). The first Alexandrian author who was apparently an anti-Semite was Manetho (in the 3rd cent. B.C.E.). We say "apparently": he had such a reputation. But the question is whether in fact he was concerned with the Jews at all. It is thus necessary to treat him at some length. The problems that will emerge in the course of our presentation can hardly be solved here, but hypotheses will be suggested.

Manetho[61]

As an Egyptian priest (3rd cent. B.C.E.), he was commissioned by Ptolemy II to write a history of Egypt in the Greek language, for which he used Egyptian sources.[62] We are not particularly interested in his significance for the writing of Egyptian history, although Josephus's utilization of Manetho's work makes a few comments necessary. The problem of the history of the materials is opaque to the nonspecialist and controversial among the specialists. There is consensus, however, that Josephus did not read the original Manetho, but only reworked excerpts.[63] In these he found elements hostile to Judaism. In this manner he made his judgment about Manetho—rather, about the version of Manetho he possessed (*Ag. Ap.* 1.223, 227ff.). Paradoxically, a Jewish, pre-Josephus revision thus becomes visible.[64] This conflict in Josephus's writings is revealed not only in the way he apportions his excerpts, but also in his use of Manetho himself: on the one hand, as an apologetic witness; on the other hand, carrying on a polemic against him.

---

[59] Concerning the political organization of Egypt, see Fraser, *Ptolemaic Alexandria* 1:38ff. 1:169: The earliest anti-Semitic document (see index under "Anti-Semitism"), *CPJ* 141, is not directly connected with Alexandria; it is a matter of a letter that cannot be interpreted with confidence.

[60] See the outline of Josephus: He discusses Molon after Manetho and his contemporaries, on the basis of his perspective; see *Ag. Ap.* 1.73: Ἄρξομαι δὴ πρῶτον ἀπὸ τῶν παρ᾽ Αἰγυπτίοις γραμμάτων ("I will begin first with the Egyptian documents"). And here, of course, Manetho is the first author. Then in 1.106: the Phoenicians follow, then in 1.128 the Chaldeans. Josephus thus holds to the traditional order of the three acknowledged Oriental peoples who had exercised a major influence on the world and its culture. Then follow the Greeks (from 1.161 on). With regard to placing the Egyptians first, see further *Ag. Ap.* 1.232.

[61] *Stern, GLAJJ*, 62ff. On the forms of the names in the tradition, see *FGH* III C, 5f. Bib.: R. Laqueur, "Manethon," *PW* 14:1069ff.; Heinemann, "Antisemitismus," *PWSup.* 5:3ff. (cf. W. Helck, "Chronography").

[62] Cf. the characterization in Josephus, *Ag. Ap.* 1.73: He was familiar with Greek culture, wrote on his own authority on the basis of local sacred Scriptures, and blamed Herodotus for false information. See further *Ag. Ap.* 1.228.

[63] See, e.g., *Ag. Ap.* 1.91f., 250; Jacoby, *FGH* III C, 84.

[64] See, e.g., Helck, *Untersuchungen zu Manetho*: Jews changed dates, rearranging the chronology in order to be able to make Menes a contemporary of Adam.

Sample Evaluations

(1) E. Meyer (*Aegyptische Chronologie* [Berlin, 1904]; cf. Jacoby, *FGH* III C, 84): The following in Josephus is authentic, though sometimes a bit distorted (but it is precisely these distortions that concern us): *Ag. Ap.* 1.75–82, 98–101, 232–51, perhaps the core of the pseudo-Manetho section 84–90, "but with the insertion of the name Amosis." The list of kings (as an excerpt; Jacoby, 88) is also authentic, but it does not concern us.

(2) Laqueur ("Manethon," *PW* 14:1064ff.): The authentic material is 75–82, 84–90,[65] 94–102a, 232–49, 251. Alongside this we find a rationalistic polemical writing of an Egyptian polytheist against Manetho: 254–61,[66] 267–69, 271–74, 276f. Additions by Josephus are 262–66, 270, 275.[67]

(3) Heinemann ("Antisemitismus," *PWSup.* 5:3ff.): A report of the temporary victory and ultimate suppression of sun worship (Manetho and Chaeremon) was connected with the Jews in the third or second century. That could have actually been the case.

(4) Jacoby (*FGH* 84; see Meyer above): Josephus does not know Manetho himself (cf. *Ag. Ap.* 1.91f., 250), who spoke neither of the exodus from Egypt, their leader Moses (cf. Heinemann), nor of the "Hyksos," but only of "shepherds" (concerning "Hyksos," see *Ag. Ap.* 1.82, and below).

(5) Tcherikover (*Civilization*, 361ff.): Even if one bases nothing on *Ag. Ap.* 1.250,[68] anti-Semitism remains: who are these "Hyksos" who come from Jerusalem to Egypt, if not the Jews?[69]

(6) Wacholder (*Eupolemus*, 94f.): Manetho's version intends to correct Hecataeus[70] and justify the expulsion. He identifies the Jews with the Hyksos. He is *not* anti-Semitic, but, in dependence on Hecataeus, wants to affirm the superiority of Egyptian culture. What in Hecataeus and Manetho is merely intellectual speculation does take on an anti-Semitic character in Lysimachus (95 n. 116).

(7) Stern (*GLAJJ*, 62ff.): He ascribes the "Hyksos" to Manetho (see above, Jacoby). There is no reason to deny the Osarsiph episode (*Ag. Ap.* 1.237ff.) to

---

[65] 84-90 indirect speech, thus no direct quotation!

[66] Cf. 255 (νὴ Δία) ("yes, by Zeus"); μάντις ("the seer"); 256ff.; 256: The gods are angry over ἀσεβήματα ("impiety"), not over ἐλαττώματα τῶν σωμάτων ("physical deformities").

[67] Jacoby, *FGH* III C, 84: This hypothesis only contributes to the confusion.

[68] Which Stern, for example, does not do, but who is still not able to avoid affirming that it was an addition to the main story.

[69] Nonetheless, see Jacoby: *Ag. Ap.* 1.82, which has "Hyksos," is not Manetho, neither is 230–32; cf. the fact that the king's brothers bear different names than in 98ff. (F 8), "which proves that there were different authors, which Manetho used" (91). In 241 (*GLAJJ*, no. 21) ὑπὸ Τεθμώσεως ("by Tethmosis") and εἰς πόλιν τὴν καλουμένην Ἱεροσόλυμα ("in the city called Jerusalem") is placed in brackets by Jacoby; he also brackets Σολυμῖται ("Solymites") in 248. Thus Judea and Jerusalem remain in 90. The more authentic form is in 77 (where both are lacking); on the introduction of Judea, cf. *Ag. Ap.* 2.21 (*FGH* 616 F 4b).

[70] For the connection of Manetho and Hecataeus, see *FGH* 609 F 19=Hecataeus *FGH* 264 F 4 (cf. F 25); Plutarch, *Is. Os.* 354 CD.

Manetho;[71] cf. the prophesying of the lamb and the potter oracle[72] (cf. *AOT,* 48ff.). The combination "contaminated people" and "Jews" was easily made and may have already been current in the time of Manetho (there was an anti-Jewish atmosphere in Egypt already in the Persian period!). The reference to the Assyrians is anachronistic and corresponds to the *Greek* idea of the Assyrian empire (indeed!). To be sure, Manetho does not speak directly of "the Jews"; but they may be implied in the reference to the founding of Jerusalem. Cf. Hecataeus, who considers Moses to have been the founder of the city and knows nothing of its pre-Jewish existence.[73]

From the perspective of our study it is immaterial whether the historical Manetho was an anti-Semite or whether he spoke of the Jews at all; it is important to see that to the literary public he was considered to be the initiator of the anti-Semitic movement which had its center in Alexandria.

The Manetho of Josephus

In *Ag. Ap.* 1.74-92 (F 8) and 93-105 (F 9) Josephus claims his version of Manetho as a positive witness for the antiquity of the Jews and for their sojourn in Egypt.[74] In its extant form we have a report concerning the invasion of an unknown people (the "shepherds" from the east).[75] They ravaged Egypt with extreme ferocity, destroyed the cities and temples, killed or enslaved the population, and attained mastery of the country until the Egyptians were gradually able to mount a counterattack. They finally withdrew to Syria. These "shepherds" were thus identified with the ancestors of the Jews. Josephus accepts this

---

[71] Indeed! See Jacoby, *FGH* III C, 93ff.

[72] Of doubtful interpretation is *CPJ* 519. The "potter oracle": *CPJ* 520; L. Koenen, *ZPE* 2 (1968): 178ff.; Stern, "Jews," 1113f: An anti-Semitic coloring cannot be given to this.

[73] Stern, "Jews," 1112ff.: Even if Manetho does not directly name the Jews together with the Hyksos, we must still conclude that he identifies them: migration of the Hyksos to "Judea"; the founding of Jerusalem; the conduct of the "Solymites!" Manetho is anti-Semitic. Already before Manetho, Egyptian traditions about the exodus had been combined with Jewish ones by Hecataeus.—When one reads Manetho, it is good to keep in mind how an Egyptian contemporary would probably have understood him.

[74] Toward a critical analysis: It is clear that 83 and 92 are not from Manetho, but are Jewish comments that have been inserted. Laqueur still ascribes 82 (and thereby the term "Hyksos") to Manetho. Jacoby argues against this, that 82 is not from Manetho (see 75!) but belongs to the interpolated source of Josephus. Concerning the last sentence of 82 τινὲς δὲ λέγουσιν αὐτοὺς Ἄραβας εἶναι ("Some say that they were Arabs") and 83 (*GLAJJ,* no. 19), cf. Meyer: This derives from Josephus's source, which includes authentic material from Manetho; regarding the analogous case in 91: this is from a copy that has been edited by a Jew.—But: Is βίβλος ("Book") (91) the same as ἀντίγραφον ("copy") (83)? See Stern, *GLAJJ,* 72.

[75] See the discussion above as to whether or not these were already described by Manetho as "Hyksos." On the Hyksos, see W. Helck, *Die Beziehungen Aegyptens zu Vorderasien im 3. und 2. v. C.* (Wiesbaden, 1962).

version of the history (92).[76] Further (90) (*GLAJJ*, no. 19): from fear of the Assyrian empire (see Stern above) ἐν τῇ νῦν Ἰουδαίᾳ καλουμένῃ πόλιν οἰκοδο-μησαμένους . . . Ἱεροσόλυμα ταύτην ὀνομάσαι ("They built in the land now called Judea a city . . . and gave it the name of Jerusalem"). In another book of his Αἰγυπτιακά (*History of Egypt*) Manetho says that the Jews were described as "captives" (Josephus, *Ag. Ap.* 1.91). That is an addition to Manetho, but presents Josephus a point of contact: for him it is a reference to the captive Joseph (92).

Josephus can account for the reports of the atrocities of the Hyksos: in such cases Egyptian hatred for the Jews is expressed (*Ag. Ap.* 1.223ff.). Josephus includes the sequel, an excerpt from the Egyptian list of kings (*Ag. Ap.* 1.93–105; F 9), because it supports his view of the chronology, providing a proof for the antiquity of the Jews. We need only to note par. 102, which iden-tifies an Egyptian prince Harmais with a certain Danaus who fled from Egypt. This is supposed to provide evidence for the antiquity of the Jews, for the exodus took place 393 years before the flight of Danaus (103; cf. 2.16), the first king of Argos.[77]

The results are summarized (104): Manetho confirms our arrival in Egypt and our exodus from there almost a thousand years before the Trojan War. At this point (the exodus), however, Manetho abandons his sources and tells fables (105). Here Josephus too abandons the story line temporarily. The second great excerpt follows, 1.227ff.;[78] Josephus returns to the Egyptians (*Ag. Ap.* 1.223, 228–53; F 10a), beginning with their slanders about the Jews. The basis for their hatred was of course the fact that the Jews had once been rulers of their country, then the manner in which the Jews flourished after their return to Israel, and then the religious difference which is so vast, ὅσον θεοῦ φύσις ζῴων ἀλόγων διέστηκε (224) ("as is the nature of God from that of irrational beasts"). This allusion to the apologetic topos of Egyptian animal worship is elaborated in 225.

The Egyptian hatred for the Jews is so deep that it causes Egyptian authors to contradict their own chronicles and to compose contradictory accounts themselves (226), for example, in statements of chronology. Then follows the section in which Manetho promulgates lies: ἔπειτα δὲ δοὺς ἐξουσίαν αὐτῷ διὰ τοῦ φάναι γράφειν τὰ μυθευόμενα καὶ λεγόμενα περὶ τῶν Ἰουδαίων ("thereafter, by offering to record the legends and current talk about the Jews") (cf. the concluding remark in 287). ἀναμῖξαι βουλόμενος ἡμῖν πλῆθος Αἰγυπτίων λεπρῶν καὶ ἐπὶ ἄλλοις ἀρρωστήμασιν, ὥς φησιν, φυγεῖν ἐκ τῆς Αἰγύπτου κατα-γνωσθέντων ("he took the liberty of interpolating improbable tales in his desire to confuse us with a crowd of Egyptians, who for leprosy and other maladies

---

[76] 84-90 indirect speech, thus a summary, not a quotation (see above, note 72).

[77] The most ancient king of Argos in the Greek tradition, Inachos, is ignored; cf. 231.

[78] Previously: the Phoenicians, etc.

had been condemned, he says, to banishment from Egypt") (229; *GLAJJ*, no. 21).[79]

Then comes a narration of Egyptian character,[80] which has nothing to do with the Jews (at first summarized, then from 237 on as a direct quotation): The king Amenophis[81] wanted (like his predecessors) to see the gods. He learned from a man of God (μάντις ["seer"], 256ff., 267) that he would have to purify the land ἀπό τε λεπρῶν καὶ τῶν ἄλλων μιαρῶν ἀνθρώπων ("from lepers and other polluted persons") (233).[82] These, including leprous priests, were deported and compelled to work in the stone quarries east of the Nile. Then complications enter the story: the deportees were granted the city of Auaris, once a stronghold of the "shepherds." But they rebelled and chose for their leader a priest from Hierapolis, Osarsiph.[83]

This Osarsiph gave them their law (239) μήτε προσκυνεῖν θεούς ("they should neither worship the gods") (hence the apologetic topos of the ἀθεότης ["atheism"] of the Jews), and that they should abstain from eating the sacred animals of Egypt, συνάπτεσθαι δὲ μηδενὶ πλὴν τῶν συν(ομ)ωμοσμένων ("and that they should have intercourse with none save those of their own confederacy") (text according to the conjecture of Niese; here we have the topos of ἀμιξία, ἀπανθρωπία, "unsociableness, inhumanity"). This Osarsiph called for help from the "shepherds," who had previously been driven out of Auaris.[84] They respond to this invitation by invading Egypt, with terrible devastation.[85] The Egyptian king fled to Ethiopia. And thus it is said that Osarsephus (so in 238; 250 has Osarsiph) adopted the name "Moses."[86]

Taken as a whole, Josephus's "refutation" of Manetho (251 or 254–86) is picky and banal; the stress is on the absurdity of Manetho's report. A short summary is introduced en route in 278, concerning the derivation of the Jews: Manetho

---

[79] For a characterization of the fragment, see Jacoby, *FGH* III C, 91: "F 10 presupposes the identification of pro-Semitic (Jews = Ποιμένες ["shepherds"] and Hyksos) and anti-Semitic (Osarseph = Josephus [*sic!*]), of which F 8 (*GLAJJ*, no. 19) (contra §228 τοὺς ἡμετέρους προγόνους ["our ancestors"]) knows nothing; §231 gives different names to the royal brothers than F 9 §§98ff. (which indicates different authors used by Manetho as sources); also the "verbatim" quotation of §§237ff. is commandeered as evidence (in §241 Τέθμωσις ["Tethmosis"] and Ἱεροσόλυμα ["Jerusalem"] [Σολυμῖται ("Solymites") §245] are not Manetho's style)."

[80] See Meyer, quoted in Jacoby, *FGH* III C, 91.

[81] Cf. Chaeremon. Josephus declares that this king was an invention of Manetho—a proof that he had not read Manetho himself (*Ag. Ap.* 1.230).

[82] Posidonius F 109; Chaeremon *Ag. Ap.* 1.288ff. = F 1; Lysimachus *Ag. Ap.* 1.304ff., 2.20 = F 1, 3; Apion *Ag. Ap.* 2.15 = F 4 (*GLAJJ*, no. 21); cf. Tacitus.

[83] Concerning the name, see 238, 250, 265, 286. This name for the Jewish lawgiver (which at first calls Josephus to mind; in Chaeremon, *Ag. Ap.* 1.290 alongside Moses) is not found elsewhere. But in Strabo Moses is an Egyptian priest. According to Apion, Moses was from Hierapolis.

[84] In 241 Jacoby brackets ὑπὸ Τεθμώσεως ("by Tethmosis") and εἰς πόλιν τὴν καλουμένην Ἱεροσόλυμα ("in the city called Jerusalem"), then in 248 Σολυμῖται ("Solymites") (*GLAJJ*, no. 21).

[85] A doublet of the earlier version.

[86] Again, this is not Manetho.

himself affirms (unintentionally, cf. 229!) οὔτε ἐκ τῆς Αἰγύπτου τὸ γένος ἡμῶν ἐστιν οὔτε τῶν ἐκεῖθέν τινες ἀνεμίχθησαν ("our race was not of Egyptian origin, and that there was no mixture of the races"). For the Egyptians associated with them died in the quarries, battles, and especially in the flight that followed. He meets the allegation of leprosy by citing the Jewish legal prescriptions on this subject (281ff.). Manetho's statements concerning (Osarseph) Moses are refuted (279ff.) by a critical analysis of the chronology (280).

Summary

The authentic Manetho may not have been concerned with the Jews. But that he intended the Jews by his reports about the "shepherds" is still the most likely hypothesis, and this is the way he would have been understood by his readers. To this extent he belongs to the history of Alexandrian anti-Semitism (see further Sevenster, *Roots,* 186).[87] And one can get some idea of the embittered literary give and take in Alexandria by observing the use made of older (Gentile) authors on both sides. This picture will be filled in as we now come to those authors who expressed hostility to Judaism not merely by revising previous literature, but who emphasize it in their own writings.

Lysimachus

FGH 621; *GLAJJ*, nos. 158–62; Reinach, *Textes,* no. 59.

The identity and thus the date of this author cannot be determined with confidence. He is sometimes identified with a grammarian and mythographer of the same name[88] (ὁ Ἀλεξανδρεύς, "the Alexandrian"; place of origin unknown; ca. 200 B.C.E.), and sometimes distinguished from him.[89] If the latter view is correct, we know about him only what is contained in Josephus, namely, a few incidental comments:

Ag. Ap. 2.16=F 2 (*GLAJJ*, no. 159), not a fragment of Lysimachus's work, but only a reference to him in a list of authors.

Ag. Ap. 2.20=F 3 (*GLAJJ*, no. 160), an isolated note on the number of those driven out of Egypt (120,000; so also Apion, F 4=Josephus, *Ag. Ap.* 2.20).

Ag. Ap. 2.245=F 4 (*GLAJJ*, no. 161), a general comment (together with Apollonius Molon, with whom he is also mentioned in 2.236=T 1b).

---

[87] An oracular fragment (Hellenistic period) announces the expulsion of the "lawless" Jews from Egypt by the wrath of Isis (cf. Chaeremon in Josephus, *Ag. Ap.* 1.289f.), *CPJ* 520; cf. n. 123; see Hengel, *Judaism and Hellenism,* 185.

[88] A. Gudemann, "Lysimachos," *PW* 14.32ff.; F. Kudlien, "Lysimachos," *Kl. Pauly* 3.841: "very probably."

[89] Jacoby (the other Lysimachus *FGH* 382). According to Cosmas Indicopleustes he wrote Αἰγυπτιακά (*Aegyptiaca*) (T 2); but that is obviously inferred from Josephus; in any case, no monograph on the Jews is visible. Fraser, *Ptolemaic Alexandria* 2:1092 n. 475.

Ag. Ap. 1.304–11=F 1 (*GLAJJ*, no. 158), a review of his version of the exodus story, unfortunately not a verbatim quotation, but a description that is permeated with confusion.[90]

Josephus places Lysimachus after Chaeremon and expressly associates him with both Manetho and Chaeremon (*Ag. Ap.* 1.304); but he surpasses them in fabricating anti-Jewish material, and in hatred. Josephus arranges them in increasing order of intensity—with Apion as the climax.

Lysimachus represents a third Egyptian version alongside those already named. He goes astray chronologically, placing the exodus under king Bocchoris (*Ag. Ap.* 1.305; 2.16; so also Tacitus).[91]

The identity of this Bocchoris is a disputed point: there was a Bocchoris who was the only king of the 24th dynasty (8th cent. B.C.E.; see *FGH* 609 F 2/3). In addition, Diodorus refers to a primeval king of the same name, immediately after the construction of the pyramids, who was a lawgiver (Diodorus, 1.45.2; 65; 79.1; 94.5).[92] According to Josephus, the exodus had taken place 1,200 years earlier.

Lysimachus also is acquainted with the version of the story about leprous and diseased people but in a special variant, which in Josephus's retelling has become unclear and self-contradictory: the Jewish people in Egypt, afflicted with leprosy and scurvy, fled into the temple and lived by begging. Due to the great number of people who were diseased, ἀκαρπία ("impurity") entered (*Ag. Ap.* 1.306; *GLAJJ*, no. 158). The king inquired of the oracle of Ammon and received the command to purify the temple from the impure and godless people and to drive them out into the wilderness (308: where they were to perish; Josephus's additional note?) while the diseased were to be drowned, because they were repugnant to the sun. Both events occurred.

Those who had been driven out deliberated on their situation and celebrated a kind of nocturnal ceremony: at nightfall they ignited a bonfire and torches (λύχνους). Then they fasted and implored the gods for deliverance. The next day, a certain Moses appeared (he does not appear here as an Egyptian priest, as is also the case in Tacitus) and encouraged them to march forth until they reached some inhabited country. He commanded (Josephus, *Ag. Ap.* 1.309):

---

[90] Contacts with Apion make it likely that he wrote before Apion. Stern, cautiously: Is Apion dependent on Lysimachus himself, or on the same Egyptian tradition? The question can hardly be answered on the basis of the material in Josephus.

[91] Stern, *GLAJJ*, 385: because the prophesying of the lamb is connected with this (by the Egyptian subjection to foreign rule)? That can concern only the tradition that lay before Lysimachus, who of course says nothing of foreign rule in connection with Bocchoris; that is apparent even from this brief excerpt.

[92] C. Müller (*FGH*) and Reinach (*Textes*, 118 n. 1) conclude that Lysimachus intends this legendary Bocchoris. Against this Wacholder ("Biblical Chronology in the Hellenistic World Chronicles," *HTR* 61 [1968]: 451ff.) holds that there is an anti-Semitic chronology present: Lysimachus means the historical Bocchoris, thereby forcing the exodus down into the eighth century B.C.E., as does Apion, in order to refute the Jewish claim of the antiquity of Moses.

μήτε ἀνθρώπων τινὶ εὐνοήσειν μήτε ἄριστα συμβουλεύσειν ἀλλὰ τὰ χείρονα θεῶν τε ναοὺς καὶ βωμούς, οἷς ἂν περιτύχωσιν, ἀνατρέπειν ("to show goodwill to no man, to offer not the best but the worst advice, and to overthrow any temples and altars of the gods which they found").[93] They were to proceed . . . τούς τε ἀνθρώπους ὑβρίζοντας καὶ τὰ ἱερὰ συλῶντας ("there they maltreated the population, and plundered and set fire to the temples")[94] . . . and to establish a city, which people called, in accordance with their conduct, Ἱερόσυλα ("temple robbers"). After they had risen to power, they changed the name to Ἱεροσόλυμα ("Jerusalem") and called themselves Jerusalemites.[95]

If we have rightly understood §309, the polemic of Lysimachus is more acute and pointed than that of his predecessors. But this scanty excerpt does not provide the basis for any more detailed observation.

If we attempt to pursue further this Egyptian, or rather Alexandrian, line of development, we must note that, politically speaking, Alexandria does not belong to Egypt. Politically, Alexandria is a "Macedonian," i.e., Greek city, to be distinguished from Egypt as the χώρα ("country") (cf. the sharp distinction made in Josephus, Ag. Ap. 2.41, 72). And the cultural life was naturally concentrated in the city (especially so since there was a formidable language barrier). Still, the boundary was somewhat perforated, especially since the governing power for the country was itself located in the city. Manetho already offers an example of the influence of Hellenistic elements in the "country"; Apion also immediately comes to mind. Cf. also the multitude of Egyptian histories (FGH 608ff.). The immigration of Greeks and other foreigners is also a factor that should not be ignored.

When this line is extended, it reaches toward Rome (earlier, we have noted a similar line from Rhodes pointing in the same direction). The realities of everyday politics now emerge into full view. We thus come to the center of Josephus's polemic, namely, Apion, by which name Josephus's apology is today known.

Apion of Oasis and Alexandria

FGH 616; GLAJJ, nos. 163–77. He was nicknamed Πλειστονίκης ("victor in many contests") (Suda: the son of Πλειστονίκης [Pleistonikes] is not to be preferred against the other witnesses) and Μόχθος ("hardship") (GLAJJ, no. 163b).

Apion was a versatile and successful teacher and author in the first century

---

[93] The topos μισανθρωπία! ("hatred of humanity") Apion FGH 616 F 4 1=Ag. Ap. 2.121; GLAJJ, no. 173: the Jews swear μηδενὶ εὐνοήσειν ἀλλοφύλῳ ("to show no goodwill to a single alien") especially not to the Greeks. Cf. Deut. 12:2f.; Josephus, Ant. 4.192. Cf. also the doings of the "Shepherds" in Manetho FGH 609 F 10=Ag. Ap. 1.249; GLAJJ, no. 21.

[94] Stern, GLAJJ, 386: an echo of the revolt against the religious policy of the Hasmoneans; Alexander Janneus! Schürer-Vermes-Millar, History 1:228.

[95] Apion also attempted to make a joke of the name (Ag. Ap. 2.49).

C.E. His activity is well documented.[96] Josephus (*Ag. Ap.* 2.28ff.) considers it a meritorious point that he was an Egyptian and not an Alexandrian: his native city was Oasis in Egypt. That information is disputed in some quarters, since it is documented only in Josephus, and particularly on the basis of *Ag. Ap.* 2.48 (*GLAJJ*, no. 167), where Josephus himself obviously acknowledges Apion's Macedonian origin: οἱ τῶν προγόνων αὐτοῦ Μακεδόνων βασιλεῖς ("the kings of his Macedonian ancestors") (so Willrich, *Juden und Griechen*, 172ff.; contra Schürer, *History* 3.539: Μακεδόνων ("Macedonian") is not to be connected with προγόνων ("ancestors").

In any case he attained citizenship in Alexandria (Josephus, *Ag. Ap.* 2.32, reluctantly [*GLAJJ*, no. 166]; cf. 28–31 and esp. 41, 72), and came to be highly respected: he was chosen to be a member of the Alexandrian delegation against the Jews which appeared before Caligula in 40 C.E. The opposing delegation was led by Philo, who reported his account of it in the *Legatio* (cf. Josephus, *Ant.* 18.257ff.; T 6).

Though probable, it is disputed whether Apion's writing κατὰ Ἰουδαίων (*Against the Jews*) was a part of his Αἰγυπτιακά (*Egyptian History*) or an independent work. The tradition is ambiguous.[97]

In Apion we find the material that had previously been scattered in various writings summarized in one document and directed to an immediate political goal (the position of the Jews in Alexandria). He is thus for Josephus the archenemy. Apion needs only to repeat what others have reported. Thus his literary method becomes apparent (which can be read off the surface in F 4): In his summaries he emphasizes only what is peculiar to himself; otherwise he

---

[96] See the fragments in Jacoby! Concerning his propaganda itself, cf. T 10. The emperor Tiberius names him *cymbalum mundi* ("the world's cymbal"). Regarding his influence on literature, see I. Lévy, "Tacite et l'origine du peuple juif," *Latomus* 5 (1946): 339f.; 10 (1951): 161.

[97] (a) *Ag. Ap.* 2.8ff. (F1; *GLAJJ*, no. 164): Apion's writings concerning Moses appear in the third book of his Αἰγυπτιακά.

(b) Clement of Alexandria, *Strom.* 1.101.3f. (T 11b and F 2b; *GLAJJ*, no. 163b): ἐν τῇ τετάρτῃ (!) τῶν Αἰγυπτιακῶν ἱστοριῶν . . . ὡς καὶ κατὰ Ἰουδαίων συντάξεσθαι βιβλίον ("in the fourth [!] book of his Egyptian History . . . so as to compose a book 'Against the Jews'"). On this, Jacoby comments: ὡς . . . means precisely this fourth book; that however had already been misunderstood by Africanus; see Schürer, *History* 3:540ff.; correspondingly Jacoby arranges the Apion fragments of Josephus (except for F 1) under book 4 of the Αἰγυπτιακά.

(c) Africanus in Eusebius, *Praep. Ev.* 10.10.16; *GLAJJ*, no. 163c: Ἀπίων . . . ἐν τῇ κατὰ Ἰουδαίων βίβλῳ καὶ (!) ἐν τῇ τετάρτῃ τῶν ἱστοριῶν ("Apion, in his book 'Against the Jews,' and [!] in the fourth book of his History"). Is the "καί" ("and") to be bracketed, or is it a misunderstanding of Africanus?

[Translator's note: An additional possibility is to take the καί as epexegetical, as in the LCL translation: "Apion, in his book 'Against the Jews,' which constitutes the fourth book of his History."]

(d) *Ag. Ap.* 2.4 (*GLAJJ*, no. 164): Despite his aversion, Josephus must deal with Apion, κατηγορίαν ἡμῶν ἄντικρυς ὡς ἐν δίκῃ γεγραφότα ("who has written an indictment of us formal enough for a court of law"). An indication here of a particular book after all?

makes only brief comments, sometimes with extensive polemics.[98] He outlines his report as follows (*Ag. Ap.* 2.6ff.; *GLAJJ*, no. 164):

(1) What others have already said about the exodus; cf. Apion himself on his sources (*Ag. Ap.* 2.10, F 1; *GLAJJ*, no. 164): ὡς ἤκουσα παρὰ τῶν πρεσβυτέρων τῶν Αἰγυπτιακῶν ("as I have heard from old people in Egypt").

(2) Attack on the Jews in Alexandria; that is new material (cf. *Ag. Ap.* 2.28; *GLAJJ*, no. 165).

(3) On the Jewish cult and their other νόμιμα ("customs").

The Content of Apion's Charges and Josephus's Polemical Response

(1) The *chronology* already serves Apion's polemical purpose: the exodus took place in the first year of the Seventh Olympiad (752–749 B.C.E.) (*Ag. Ap.* 2.17), i.e., the (alleged) year of the founding of Carthage. Thereby the age of the Jewish people is radically abbreviated.[99]

(2) *Moses and the exodus* (*Ag. Ap.* 2.8ff.=F 1).[100] Moses came from Hierapolis.[101] But according to Apion he was not an Egyptian, but set up cultic worship centers representing his own ancestral traditions (Jewish? Or does it appear so only because of Josephus's abbreviation?) In *Ag. Ap.* 2.15ff. (F 4; *GLAJJ*, no. 165) Josephus's abbreviations are apparent; supplementary information must be derived from other authors.

Moses led a group of leprous people out of Egypt. In Apion's eyes the Jews are simply originally Egyptians (*Ag. Ap.* 2.28). But Moses? Josephus pounces on this point: Apion of all people, who himself was an Egyptian *par excellence!* The number of those expelled Apion incidentally registers—like Lysimachus (F 3)—at 110,000 (*Ag. Ap.* 2.20).

Then follows a variation peculiar to Apion (*Ag. Ap.* 2.21): ὁδεύσαντες γάρ φησιν ἓξ ἡμερῶν ὁδὸν βουβῶνας ἔσχον, καὶ διὰ ταύτην τὴν αἰτίαν ἐν τῇ ἑβδόμῃ

---

[98] *Ag. Ap.* 2.3 (*GLAJJ*, no. 164): τὰ μὲν γάρ ἐστι τῶν ὑπ' αὐτοῦ γεγραμμένων τοῖς ὑπ' ἄλλων εἰρημένοις ὅμοια, τὰ δὲ λίαν ψυχρῶς προσέθηκεν, τὰ πλεῖστα δὲ βωμολοχίαν ("Some of these resemble the allegations made by others, some are very indifferent additions of his own; most of them are pure buffoonery [burlesque; toadyism]) ἔχει καὶ πολλήν, εἰ δεῖ τἀληθὲς εἰπεῖν, ἀπαιδευσίαν ("and, to tell the truth, display the gross ignorance of their author"). Apion is a demagogue. *Ag. Ap.* 2.32: He wrote a letter of appreciation to the Alexandrians for the conferral of citizenship.

[99] Cf. above, Wacholder on Lysimachus. Timaeus (*FGH* 566 F 60) dates the founding of Carthage in 814 B.C.E. Josephus (*Ag. Ap.* 2.28f.; cf. 1.126) introduces the Phoenicians as an argument: Hirma lived over 150 years before the founding of Carthage and was a contemporary of Solomon. But Solomon's founding of the temple was 612 years after the exodus (see *Ant.* 20.230; differently in 1 Kings 6:1; *Ant.* 8.61). (In any case, Wacholder misunderstands the relation of Apion to Dionysius of Halicarnassus, who refers to Timaeus but does not refer to him in regard to the date of the founding of Carthage and Rome.)

[100] *GLAJJ*, no. 164 is to be noted. Gager, *Moses*, 122ff.

[101] Manetho, Josephus, *Ag. Ap.* 1.238, 250, etc.

ἡμέρᾳ ἀνεπαύσαντο, σωθέντες εἰς τὴν χώραν τὴν νῦν Ἰουδαίαν λεγομένην, καὶ ἐκάλεσαν τὴν ἡμέραν σάββατον, σῴζοντες τὴν Αἰγυπτίων γλῶσσαν· τὸ γὰρ βουβῶνος ἄλγος καλοῦσιν Αἰγύπτιοι σαββάτωσις ("'After a six days' march,' he says, 'they developed tumors in the groin, and that was why, after safely reaching the country now called Judea, they rested on the seventh day, and called that day Sabbaton, preserving the Egyptian terminology; for disease of the groin in Egypt is called sabbatosis'").[102]

Apion further relates (*Ag. Ap.* 2.25) that Moses remained forty days on Mount Sinai. Josephus notes the contradiction with Apion's view of the six-day march to Judea.

Now comes the most relevant part of Josephus's account: Apion's charges against the Alexandrian Jews (*Ag. Ap.* 2.33ff.) and his polemic against the Jewish religion. We will deal with this latter polemic first.

(3) *Judaism according to Apion* (*Ag. Ap.* 2.79ff.) (the text is permeated with Josephus's own counterpolemic). At the beginning stands the familiar tale of the ass's head in the Jewish temple (*Ag. Ap.* 2.79f.; *GLAJJ*, no. 170, cf. Mnaseas, *Ag. Ap.* 2.112ff.; *GLAJJ*, no. 28; Tacitus). Josephus refutes the story by calling on the testimony of the Romans, who entered the temple, and by many historians. He refers generally to Posidonius and Apollonius Molon. He does not miss the opportunity to land a blow against *Egyptian* animal worship.

Then follows the rumor of ritual murder (*Ag. Ap.* 2.89ff.; *GLAJJ*, no. 171).[103] The topos of hatred of humanity appears in *Ag. Ap.* 2.121 (*GLAJJ*, no. 173): The Jews swear by the god who made heaven, earth, and sea (echo of biblical language!), μηδενὶ εὐνοήσειν ἀλλοφύλῳ, μάλιστα δὲ ῞Ελλησιν ("to show no goodwill to a single alien, above all to Greeks") (cf. Lysimachus; "especially the Greeks": the Alexandrians are in view). There is also a variation on the theme of ἀθεότης ("godlessness") (*Ag. Ap.* 2.125). Josephus opposes this by introducing historical facts (the Egyptians, the Greeks).[104]

Nor is the argument from cultural history lacking: the Jews have produced no significant people (*Ag. Ap.* 2.135; *GLAJJ*, no. 175; cf. Molon, *Ag. Ap.* 2.148; *GLAJJ*, no. 49).

Josephus summarizes Apion's version of the Jewish religion (*Ag. Ap.* 2.137; *GLAJJ*, no. 176): ἐγκαλεῖ γὰρ ὅτι ζῷα θύομεν ("For he denounces us for sacrificing domestic animals") (supply ἡμέρᾳ, "daily"; Latin: *animalia consueta*, "the

---

[102] Cf. *Ag. Ap.* 2.26f., where Josephus writes σαββώ ("a disease of the groin"); see E. Lohse, "σάββατον," *TDNT* 7:18 n. 138; M. Scheller, *Glotta* 34 (1955): 298ff. On the explanation of "Sabbath," see also Plutarch, *Quaest. Conv.* 4.6.2 (*GLAJJ*, no. 258): the name is derived from the Bacchai, who were also called Σάβοι ("persons dedicated to the service of Sabazius") (see Stern, *GLAJJ*, 562).

[103] Bickermann, "Ritualmord und Eselskult," 171ff.; cf. Damocritus, *FGH* 730 F 1 = Stern, *GLAJJ*, 530f.; F. Schwenn, *Das Menschenopfer bei den Griechen und Romern* (Giessen, 1915).

[104] On Apion's argument, see Cicero, *Pro Flacco* 28.69 (*GLAJJ*, no. 68); Cicero, *De prov. cons.* 5.10 (*GLAJJ*, no. 70): Iudaeis et Syris nationibus natis servituti ("Jews and Syrians, themselves peoples born to be slaves"). On the Syrians and Asiatic Greeks, see Livy 36.17.5.

usual animals") καὶ χοῖρον οὐκ ἐσθίομεν καὶ τὴν τῶν αἰδοίων χλευάζει περιτομήν ("and for not eating pork, and he derides the practice of circumcision"). Josephus's response: Critique of animal sacrifice is typically Egyptian (*Ag. Ap.* 2.138; an insulting blow aimed at Apion's Egyptian extraction); their priests are circumcised and eat no pork. Apion was therefore criticizing his own ancestral laws—and therefore justifiably suffered a gruesome death (*Ag. Ap.* 2.143; the motif of the death of the blasphemer!).

(4) *The currently relevant political polemic* (*Ag. Ap.* 2.33ff.): The Alexandrian Jews came from Syria (are therefore not Alexandrians). This statement is then illustrated by the familiar letter from Claudius to the Alexandrian Jews (*PLond.* 1912 = *CPJ* 153 lines 96f.): μηδὲ ἐπάγεσθαι ἢ προσείεσθαι ἀπὸ Συρίας ἢ Αἰγύπ ‹τ› ου καταπλέοντας ᾿Ιουδαίους ("Nor are they to bring in or invite Jews coming from Syria or Egypt"). Josephus responds (2.38; *GLAJJ*, no. 166) that Apion is an ignoramus if he is surprised that Jews in Alexandria are called Alexandrians. But Apion had the best of this argument.

In Apion, too, the religious exclusivism of the Jews is made into a political argument (*Ag. Ap.* 2.65; *GLAJJ*, no. 169), as it is in other writers (cf. the Ionians, Josephus, *Ant.* 12.125, 16.37ff.). Josephus strikes back: How about you Egyptians and your religion? Further, the unrest in Alexandria derives from the incursion of Egyptian elements.

A dangerous element enters the argument when the appeal is made to the Romans to observe that the Jews refuse to venerate the image of Caesar (*Ag. Ap.* 2.73; *GLAJJ*, no. 169). Cf. the events under Caligula! (Philo, *Leg.*; Josephus, *J.W.* 2.284ff.; *Ant.* 18.261ff.). In this context Josephus appeals to the *universality* of the Jewish prohibition of images (*Ag. Ap.* 2.75) and to the Jewish sacrifices made for the emperor—and for him only, for no other human being (*Ag. Ap.* 2.77).

Chaeremon of Alexandria

FGH 618; *GLAJJ*, no. 178; the collection of fragments: H. R. Schwyzer, *Chairemon* (Leipzig, 1932) (on Josephus = F 1, see 57ff.).

He was a first-century C.E. ἱερογραμματεύς ("priestly scribe") (T 4, Porphyry in Eusebius, *Praep. Ev.* 5.10.5; cf. T 6) and Stoic philosopher (T 8, Eusebius, *Hist. Eccl.* 6.19.8; T 9, Porphyry, *De abst.* 4.8), probably director of the museum in Alexandria,[105] as well as tutor of Nero.[106] His *Egyptian History* was obviously heavily mythological (cf. the fragments in Porphyry: H. Dörrie, *Kl. Pauly* 1:1121). Josephus offers only a summary review of it (*Ag. Ap.* 1.288–92 = F 1), following his account of Manetho. This arrangement is based on the

---

[105] After Apion and before Dionysius Glaucon; see T 3.

[106] Suda see above ᾿Αλέξανδρος Αἰγαῖος ("a leading Alexandrian"). Since the name was common in Egypt, it is useless to ask whether he is identical with the Chaeremon in the letter of Claudius (*PLond.* 1912 = *CPJ* 153, line 17).

subject matter: for Josephus, Chaeremon stands in the Manetho tradition (cf. Schürer, *History* 3:536ff.); this is seen in the agreement in the royal names Amenophis and Ramesses (*Ag. Ap.* 1.288; cf. Manetho, F 10; *GLAJJ*, no. 21 = Josephus, *Ag. Ap.* 1.230), since Josephus regards the name Amenophis to be an invention of Manetho. Thus in his refutation (*Ag. Ap.* 1.293ff.), Josephus presents the substantive contradictions between the two with all the more relish. He has, however, a unique variation of the exodus story:[107] Isis appeared to Amenophis in a dream and scolded him because her temple had been destroyed in the war. What to do? The ἱερογραμματεύς ("priestly scribe") Phritibautes (in Manetho Amenophis the son of Paapis) explained to the king (*Ag. Ap.* 1.289) ἐὰν τῶν τοὺς μολυσμοὺς ἐχόντων ἀνδρῶν καθάρῃ τὴν Αἴγυπτον, παύσεσθαι τῆς πτόας αὐτόν ("if he purged Egypt of its contaminated population, he might cease to be alarmed") (*GLAJJ*, no. 178).[108] The parasites were driven out, numbering 250,000. Their leaders were the γραμματεύς ("scribe") Moses and Joseph, the ἱερογραμματεύς ("priestly scribe") (as contemporaries!). Their Egyptian names were Tisithes and Peteseph. Cf. the strange Osarseph of Manetho![109]

In Pelusium they met 380,000 people who had been left there by Amenophis, ἃς οὐ θέλειν εἰς τὴν Αἴγυπτον διακομίζειν ("who [i.e., the 380,000] refused them permission to cross the Egyptian frontier"). (According to Josephus, *Ag. Ap.* 1.298 the subject is Amenophis.)

These two groups united and attacked Egypt. The king fled to Ethiopia (cf. Manetho, F 10; *Ag. Ap.* 1.237ff.). He left his pregnant wife behind, who bore Ramesses, the savior-child, who as an adult drove the Jews (200,000) into Syria and brought his father home from Ethiopia.

Alexandria proved to be an independent center; there were connections with Rome.

Plutarch

Before we discuss the situation in Rome, we need to round off the picture by considering the information gleaned from a representative advocate of Greek culture, who, moreover, had close contacts with Rome:[110] Plutarch (Stern, *GLAJJ*, 545ff., nos. 255–72).

---

[107] Gager (*Moses*, 120ff.) accepts the unrest in Alexandria in 38–40 c.e. as the background. He concludes that originally two Egyptian stories of expulsion from the country existed, on the basis of similarities, differences, and that two versions appear already in Manetho—which relies too simply on a literary approach.

[108] Stern (*GLAJJ*, 417f.) appropriately remarks that a connection is missing here between the wrath of Isis and this prescription, probably due to the abbreviated version of the story (Josephus had only this abbreviated version before him).

[109] Joseph is incidentally mentioned also by Molon (*GLAJJ*, no. 46) and Justin, *Historiae Phillippicae* 36.2.6 (*GLAJJ*, no. 137).

[110] And who already looks back on the Jewish War, but of course knows older sources. Retrospective view of the war: *Vit. Galb.* 13 (*GLAJJ*, no. 270); *Vit. Oth.* 4 (*GLAJJ*, no. 271), 25 (*GLAJJ*,

We may leave aside purely historical comments on the history of the times (Pompey, *GLAJJ*, no. 261f.; Antonius, *GLAJJ*, no. 264ff.). They are not concerned with Judaism but with political figures, especially Herod the Great, and should at least be mentioned as the significant figures under which the political life of the Jews under Rome stood. There are a few customary comments (*De superst.* 3, ed. Paton 166a; *GLAJJ*, no. 255): Plutarch cites Euripides *Tro.* 764, according to which the Greeks took over κακά ("evil ways") from the barbarians; they did that on the basis of δεισιδαιμονία ("superstition"); among such, σαββατισμοί ("keeping of the Sabbath") is mentioned—an example of the attractive power of the Sabbath for Gentiles. *Superst.* 8, ed. Paton 169c (*GLAJJ*, no. 256) presents the familiar example of Jewish superstition: they will not fight on the Sabbath, alluded to in reference to the conquest of Jerusalem on the Sabbath by Ptolemy I Pompeius (Dio 37.16), Herod (Dio 49.22), Titus (Dio 66.7).[111] The comment in *De Stoic. rep.* 38 Pohlenz [revised, E. Westman] p. 1051 e (*GLAJJ*, no. 257) is very general: "Ορα γὰρ οἷα ᾿Ιουδαῖοι καὶ Σύροι περὶ θεῶν φρονοῦσιν ("See the opinions held on gods by Jews and Syrians"). *Is. Os.* 31 (ed. W. Sieveking, p. 363 C-D; *FGH* 737 F 11; *GLAJJ*, no. 259; Source? K. Ziegler, "Plutarchos," *PW* 21.843ff.) obviously contains a variation of the tale of the ass's head: there are writers who confuse τὰ ᾿Ιουδαϊκά and the myth of Typhon, who fled on an ass for seven days (cf. Apion, Tacitus). After his escape he begat two sons, Hierosolymos and Ioudaios.[112]

Vit. Cic. 7 (*GLAJJ*, no. 263) presents an anecdote: a freedman named Caecilius, ἔνοχος ἰουδαΐζειν ("suspected of Jewish practices"), wants to take legal action against Verres (Verres is the Latin equivalent of χοῖρος, "boar," "young pig").[113] Cicero, the prosecutor, jokes about it: τί ᾿Ιουδαίῳ πρὸς χοῖρον; quid Iudaeo cum verre/Verre?) ("What has a Jew to do with Verres / with a pig?'")[114]

The passage in *Quaest. Conv.* 4.4.4–6.2 p. 669C–672B (*GLAJJ*, no. 258) is instructive:

(1) One of the participants in the discussion mentions his grandfather's scorn for the Jews because they would eat no pork, τὸ δικαιότατον κρέας ("the most proper type of meat").[115] There is a debate as to whether this is due to veneration

---

no. 272): Otho believed, among other things, that Asia, Syria, Egypt, and the troops with which the Jews fought, were all on his side.

[111] Cf. Agatharchides, Josephus, *Ag. Ap.* 1.205ff.; *GLAJJ*, no. 30a; Frontinus 2.1.27; *GLAJJ*, no. 229.

[112] Cf. (Tacitus, *Hist.* 5.2) Alexander Polyhistor 273 F 121 (*GLAJJ*, no. 53): The sons of Semiramis were Juda and Idumaea (?); from these the name ᾿Ιουδαία ("Judea") is derived.

[113] Cf. Cicero's speech against Verres; according to him it was, to be sure, a matter concerning Caecilius, who had been Verres' Quaestor.

[114] Schürer, *History* 3:632; Stern, *GLAJJ*, 566.

[115] Porphyry, *De abst.* 1.14: And swine are hardly good for anything else. The Phoenicians and Jews refrain from eating them, because they do not thrive in their country.—Another explanation is given in Aelian, *Hist.* 10.16 (Stern, *GLAJJ*, 559).

or abhorrence.[116] The custom is finally explained as due to their fear of leprosy.[117] The Jews, like all barbarians, try to avoid τὰς ἐπιλευκίας, which means "white scale" or "white rash"; or should we conjecture τὰς ἐπὶ ‹χρωτὸς› λεύκας καὶ λέπρας ("the white and leprous spot on ‹the skin›)?

(2) They worship the ass, because it once revealed the location of a spring to them.[118]

(3) Who is the god of the Jews? Their most important festival[119] occurs at the same time as that of the Bacchus cult.[120] This fits the pattern of their other ritual practices. "Levites"[121] are derived from Lysius or Euius. "Sabbath" is related to the Σάβα=Bacchai; it is celebrated with banquets and carousing.[122] Finally even the robes of the high priest are introduced as an argument.[123]

Epictetus

He presents hardly anything worthy of note.[124] Diss. 1.11.12f. (GLAJJ, no. 252) mentions the differing views concerning what may be eaten among the Jews, Syrians, Egyptians, and Romans, under the rubric: Is everything which is considered right actually right in reality? The opinions contradict each other. Similarly Diss. 1.22.4 concerning pork (GLAJJ, no. 253). Diss. 2.9.19–21 (GLAJJ, no. 254) is somewhat interesting, in that the passage obviously presupposes "God-fearers" and proselytes, and is possibly evidence for proselyte baptism.[125] "Why do you play the role of a Jew, although you are a Greek?" When someone is half this, half that we usually say οὐκ ἔστιν ᾿Ιουδαῖος, ἀλλ᾿ ὑποκρίνεται. ὅταν δ᾿ ἀναλάβῃ τὸ πάθος τὸ τοῦ βεβαμμένου καὶ ἡρημένου,[126] τότε καὶ ἔστι τῷ ὄντι καὶ καλεῖται ᾿Ιουδαῖος. οὕτως καὶ ἡμεῖς παραβαπτισταί, λόγῳ μὲν ᾿Ιουδαῖοι, ἔργῳ δ᾿ ἄλλο τι[127] ("'he is not a Jew, he is only acting the part.' But when he adopts the attitude of mind of the man who has been [wrongly] baptized and has made his choice, then he both is a Jew in fact and is also called one").

---

[116] Cf. Stern, GLAJJ, 558f. "veneration": the Cretans abstain, because a pig once rendered some service to Zeus; Athen. 9.18, par 376A (Agathokles, FGH 472 F 1a; Neanthes, FGH 84 F 15). A satirical comment on veneration of swine: Petronius, F 37 (GLAJJ, no. 195).

[117] A reminiscence of the saga of the lepers in Tacitus, Hist. 5.4?

[118] Tacitus, Hist. 5.3.

[119] νηστεία! ("fast")! The first day of which was called σκήνη ("Tabernacles"); thus Booths, called by the Jews simply "the feast." Plutarch confuses the Day of Atonement and the feast of Booths (which he also gets in the wrong order).

[120] Extremely to the contrary Tacitus, Hist. 5.5.

[121] Only here in Gentile literature.

[122] More on this theme and the spread of Sabbath observance in Nilsson, Geschichte 2:665ff.

[123] Schürer, History 3:219.

[124] We may here disregard a comment on the "Galileans" (Diss. 4.7.6); he certainly means the Christians.

[125] So Schürer, History 3:184 n. 87.

[126] Meaning? W. A. Oldfather (trans.): "But when he adopts the attitude of mind of the man who has been baptized and made his choice" (GLAJJ, no. 254).

[127] Should ᾿Ιουδαῖοι ("Jews") be read instead of Στωϊκοί ("Stoics")?

Dio Cassius[128]

He offers a variety of instructive material:

(1) 37.15–18 (*GLAJJ*, no. 406): Pompey took advantage of the Saturdays in his siege of Jerusalem, taking the temple[129] (which he plundered[130]) on a Saturday.

(2) 37.17 (*GLAJJ*, no. 406): People of all nations are called "Jews," if they observe the Jewish laws.

(3) Though often decimated, they have recovered their numbers again and again.

(4) They have achieved recognition of their customs and have been permitted to practice them freely.[131]

(5) Concerning separation from other peoples through their manner of life and their religion: they acknowledge only *one* God and no images at all. Their dedication to their god is very intense.

(6) 66.1 (*GLAJJ*, no. 429): The prophetic experiences of Josephus.

In sum: Dio Cassius has no empathy with the Jews, but does not repeat the slanders against them. One can also perceive a certain respect for their worship practices.

Celsus (concerning the Jews)[132]

Celsus (ca. 178 c.e.)[133] was described by Origen as an Epicurean (*Praef.* 4 and often). His own statements, however, indicate that he was a Platonist.[134] To the extent that he was a Platonic-theistic philosopher,[135] he must have fundamentally rejected the biblical concepts of God common to Jews and Christians

---

[128] The period of the Severii. [Translator's note: See now *GLAJJ*, nos. 406–42, 2:347–407.]

[129] Agatharchides; Plutarch; so also Dio 49.22 (*GLAJJ*, no. 414) concerning Herod, 66.7 concerning Titus (not so in Josephus). Pompey: Josephus, *Ant.* 14.64ff. (according to Strabo, *FGH* 91 F 15 [*GLAJJ*, no. 104] and Nicholas of Damascus, *FGH* 90 F 98 [*GLAJJ*, no. 91]). Schürer, *History* 1:298 n. 23 (cf. Schürer-Vermes-Millar, *History* 1:239 n. 23): Josephus misunderstood his Gentile source. The source intended the Sabbath, and misunderstood it, as often happened, as a fast day; cf. Strabo 16.2.40 (*GLAJJ*, no. 115); Suetonius, *Aug.* 76 (*GLAJJ*, no. 303); Pompeius Trogus 36.2.14 (*GLAJJ*, no. 137).

[130] Otherwise Josephus and Cicero.

[131] 60.6: Claudius's edict forbidding assembly.

[132] Origen, *Contra Cels.*, ed. P. Koetschau; German trans. by Koetschau (Bibl. der Kirchenväter, 1926/27); Eng. trans. H. Chadwick (Cambridge: Cambridge University Press, 1953). Reconstruction of Celsus: R. Bader, *Der ΑΛΗΘΗΣ ΛΟΓΟΣ* [True Doctrine] *des Kelsos* (Stuttgart and Berlin: Kohlhammer, 1940). [Translator's note: See now Stern, *GLAJJ*, 375.]

[133] See 8.69, 71: Persecution would indicate the time of Marcus Aurelius; οἱ βασιλεύοντες ("the rulers") would point to shared government (Marcus Aurelius and Commodus 177–80) (*GLAJJ*, no. 375).

[134] C. Andresen, *Logos;* H. Dörrie, *Gnomon* 29 (1957): 185–96 (review of Andresen, *Logos und Nomos*).

[135] Cf., e.g., 6.3ff. on the essence of the supreme deity according to Plato, *Ep.* 341 cd (concepts of God and epistemology; concerning epistemology, see 7.45 and Origen's response).

(5.59; 6.29).[136] He recognized the similarities and differences. His opposition was directed not only against what was distinctively new in Christianity but also against what was common to both religions: their points of contact with Platonism (see especially *Tim.* 4.52ff.):[137] God created nothing mortal; the immortal *soul* is his work.[138] From the point of view of his philosophical idea of God, the idea of a descent of a god or son of a god is impossible (5.3) and absurd (4.3). Such a descent would contradict his nature; it would mean a change toward the worse. But God is changeless (4.14).[139] This argument (for God as well as for the son of God) applies to both Jews and Christians. The argument between them does not concern the idea of a descent (of the Messiah) as such, but only the time of it: whether it has already happened or is still to be expected.

From the perspective of a philosophical idea of God it is also immaterial by which *name* one addresses God (5.45; 6.65). Thus, Celsus stands within a widely accepted philosophic-monotheistic viewpoint in the Greco-Roman style.[140] And thereby a fundamental conflict is revealed, just as fundamental for the Jews (despite isolated lapses such as *Ep. Ar.*) as for the Christians. The issue is whether monotheism can be incorporated into a syncretism.

The segregating law provided the Jewish means of defense (*Ep. Ar.*), while this role was played among the Christians by binding faith to the fact that the Son of God had come. Thereby the Christian faith became historical in a qualitatively different way than that of the Jews.

It was both the fundamental denial of the descent of a god and locating the decisive point in the argument between Jews and Christians which led Celsus into a *historical* argumentation. For an ancient philosopher who thinks unhistorically, how is that possible? More precisely: that he can *also* argue historically is nothing new (Posidonius). But that history and metaphysics have anything to do with each other is an idea that was absolutely foreign to ancient philosophy. So Celsus deals with history only for the sake of the argument (Dörrie, *Gnomon* 29 [1957]: 185–96).

In this respect he at least comes to the edge of the problem. Andresen in particular has explored this theme in Celsus's work (see *Logos*, 303ff., Andresen's

---

[136] E.g., 6.64: God has no σχῆμα ("form") no χρῶμα ("skin"), does not participate in any οὐσία ("substance"); cf. Plato, *Resp.* 509b.

[137] 4.52 in the first instance with reference to the Christian dialogue between Papiskos and Jason (Ariston of Pella; see Chadwick, 227 n. 1).

[138] Thereby, of course, the resurrection is also disputed; cf. 5.14; 7.28; *GLAJJ*, no. 375: it is a distortion of the Greek idea of reincarnation.

[139] The possibilities at a deity's disposal are determined by the concept of deity as such. 5.14 (in the argument against the resurrection of the flesh): τὰ αἰσχρά ("the shameful") the deity *can* not do τὰ παρὰ φύσιν ("what is contrary to nature") (*GLAJJ*, no. 375). What sort of god must rest after the work of creation! 5.59; 6.61.

[140] Examples: Seneca, *Benef.* 4.7.1; *De mundo* 7; Dio Chrysostom 31.11; Maximus of Tyre 39.5.2.5. Namelessness: 6.65; 7.42; Chadwick, *Contra Celsum*, 380 n. 7; Philo: Wolfson, *Philo* 2:110ff.; God has all names and none: Festugière, *Révélation* 4:65ff.

discussion of the relation of Celsus and Justin): In Celsus there is a "fundamental reflection on history, in which the phenomenon of history has become
a constitutive element of his thinking." He is unique in this (*Logos,* 303f.). The
occasion for this turn toward historical thinking must have been some external
pressure.

In Middle Platonism there were, in fact, no tendencies in this direction.[141]
But how then did it happen that philosophy came to be influenced by impulses
from historical thinking? We obviously find ourselves at this point in a changed
intellectual situation.[142]

Excursus: Celsus and Justin[143]

Andresen responds to the question of the source of Celsus's stimulation in this
direction by referring to Justin, with whom Celsus was acquainted and whom
he opposed.[144] He bases this on the similar construction of their polemical
argument with regard to history: in each case the picture of history is developed in conjunction with the concepts of *Logos* (Reason) and *Nomos* (Law,
Principle).

Justin: The Logos was active in philosophers and lawgivers. By becoming
incarnate, the Logos demonstrated the primacy of Christianity.

Celsus: Christianity has no independent standing; it really means the degeneration of the ideas of Logos and Nomos.[145]

---

[141] Cf. Plutarch, *Moralia* 377D, 378A; Maximus of Tyre: Eternal reason is the supreme authority.
Celsus: the authority of the divine poets, sages, and philosophers (7.41), to which Origen
comments that of course he would name no one besides Plato; still, cf. 1.16b (see below).

[142] H. Jonas (*Gnosis und spätantiker Geist I* [Göttingen: Vandenhoeck & Ruprecht, 1934]) would
have liked to understand this new situation from the point of view that Gnosticism was *the*
specifically new element of the "spirit of antiquity." He has in fact thrown new light on the matter.
But it is precisely the historical elements in the new situation for which Gnosticism cannot be
regarded as the key element. The documentation of the new mode of thinking is provided by the
patristic literature after the middle of the second century C.E.

[143] Andresen, *Logos;* see below; critically evaluated by Dörrie, *Gnomon* 29 (1957): 185–96.

[144] Andresen, *Logos,* 303ff. In agreement, A. D. Nock, review of *Logos und Nomos, JTS* n.s. 7
(1956): 314ff.; H. Chadwick, *Early Christian Thought and the Classical Tradition* (Oxford: Oxford
University Press, 1966) 22ff.

[145] Cf. Justin, *Apol.* 2.10 with *Contra Cels.* 7.41–45. Plato, *Tim.* 28C! Chadwick (*Contra Celsum,*
429 n. 1) comments thereon: "perhaps the most hackneyed quotation from Plato in Hellenistic
writers"; cf. Geffcken, *Apologeten,* 174f. For interpretation in the schools, see Chadwick, *Contra
Celsum,* 429 n. 4; Festugière, *Révélation,* 4.94. Andresen: the most exclusive circle of initiates, to
whom knowledge of god was accessible, meant for Celsus, differently than for his school, not only
Plato and his disciples but also the ancient poets and sages (7.41). Justin: Through Christ this
knowledge has been made available to all, ἐπεὶ δύναμίς ἐστι τοῦ ἀρρήτου πατρὸς καὶ οὐχὶ ἀνθρωπείου
λόγου κατασκευή ("since it is the power of the Unspeakable Father and not the contrivance of
human reason") (so Otto; some MSS read τὰ σκεύη, "the vessels" [of human reason]. This reading
is adopted by Preuschen in his translation).

Justin: The spread of Christianity is the direct, organic result of its understanding of revelation.[146]

Celsus: The contradiction between knowledge of God mediated by historical events (7.41f.) and the mental vision of God (7.45) remains unresolved.

Several of Celsus's arguments are understandable only as answers to Justin (350).[147] If the authority of the ancient sages is acknowledged (1.14) (*GLAJJ,* no. 375), the twin basic principles must be granted: (1) The *true* Logos is the *ancient* Logos.[148] (2) The ancient Logos was at once both Logos and Nomos.[149] But corruption[150] takes place in history, and that in two different forms: (a) The Logos is *misunderstood,* i.e., deprivation.[151] (b) The Nomos is (not "falsified" but) demolished.[152]

In accord with these principles, it is possible to assign a high rank to Judaism, and then play it off against Christianity. But Celsus loses the unity of his argument by doing the latter while disputing the former.

He thus uses the trick of introducing a Jew into the discussion and allowing him to argue against Christianity;[153] but this has been preceded by a polemic against Judaism, which is also, of course, aimed against Christianity. Both Christianity and Judaism for him are religions of defection, upstart religions against which the ancient truth must be defended. Against the Jews, he takes up the old topos of their rebellious character (see 3.5). In any case, Celsus characteristically uses arguments that deal with the origins of the Jewish people, not evidence from Roman history: the Jewish revolts.

Celsus begins with their claim to antiquity, which corresponds to his own self-understanding, just as it formed one of the principal points in the Jewish and Christian representation of themselves and their claims (1.14). He documents that many ancient peoples had συγγένεια τοῦ αὐτοῦ λόγου ("an affinity in

---

[146] See n. 145.

[147] *Contra Cels.* 1.16: The literary works of the sages, which were regarded as sources of revelation; cf. Justin, *Apol.* 1.30ff. (Old Testament prophecies).

[148] Dörrie: thereby the historicity of the Logos is excluded. Cf. *Contra Cels.* 3.16b; cf. Plato, *Leg.* 4.716 CD. Judaism: e.g., Philo, *Spec. Leg.* 1.6, 8.

[149] On the continuity of the Logos/Nomos thinking in the peoples of antiquity, cf. 1.24 with 6.80 (*GLAJJ,* no. 375).

[150] On "corruption," "degeneration," see Posidonius. For understanding Celsus's own point of view and contribution, see Andresen, *Logos,* 239ff. ("Das Problem der Geschichte im mittleren Platonismus"). Plutarch (*Is. Os.*) has, alongside each other, both the idea of cultural progress (379A) and the theory of the fall (379C). Cf. Posidonius: (a) technical progress through the inventions of philosophy (Seneca, *Ep.* 90); (b) religious-moral decadence. In Plutarch the consistency of the decadence theory is demolished.

[151] 4.11; extensively in 6.1–7.58; Andresen, *Logos,* 146ff. Or it is falsified (7.28, Moses, Jesus).

[152] 5.25, cf. 8.68 (by the Caesar cult: λύειν τὸ δόγμα) ("overthrow the doctrine"); Andresen, *Logos,* 209.

[153] 1.28. There is a break here: the proem ends at 1.27 (Bader; Wifstrand, "Die wahre Lehre des Kelsos," *Bulletin de la Société Royale des Lettres de Lund* [1941–42]: 391ff.; Andresen, *Logos,* 34). The method changes after this point. Chadwick on 1.28: Origen probably wrote the first sentence of this chapter before the foreword to the whole work.

that they hold the same doctrine") (*GLAJJ*, no. 375). These ancient, wise peoples are enumerated, beginning with the Egyptians, Assyrians, Indians, Persians . . . the Jews are, of course, missing from the list.[154] It is just as clear that Moses is missing from the lists of ancient sages (1.16). Moses' false cosmology (cf. 4.36) makes the age of the world laughably short (1.19).[155] He borrowed his teaching from the wise peoples and sages of antiquity, falsified it (4.21, 41), and won a δαιμόνιον ὄνομα ("name for divine power") for himself (1.21).[156] He got circumcision from the Egyptians.[157] One can detect a constant modification of the old topoi: he duped the shepherds who followed him ἀγροικαῖς ἀπάταις ("by clumsy deceits") and enticed them into believing in *one* god and thus to depart from the worship of the gods (1.23).[158] The Jews worship angels, practice superstitious magic,[159] and have lapsed into error (4.33).

With 1.28, the introduction of the Jews, a new style of argument begins[160]

---

[154] Cf. 4.31: The Greek authors are silent about the Jews (on this, cf. Josephus's apology, *Ag. Ap.* 1). 4.33, 35: these add genealogies. 4.36: they do not fulfill the requirements of wisdom (*GLAJJ*, no. 375). They are unacquainted with the cosmology of Hesiod and with countless inspired authors. But in any case the foolishness of the Jews is an old anti-Semitic topos: cf. Apollonius Molon (Josephus, *Ag. Ap.* 2.148; *GLAJJ*, no. 49). Origen responds by citing Numenius, Hermippus, etc. (*GLAJJ*, no. 25; Josephus, *Ag. Ap.* 1.263ff., 183ff.) (1.25), as well as Hecataeus, who praises the Jews so highly that Herennius Philo at first doubted the text's authenticity (thus obviously our Pseudo-Hecataeus).

[155] 6.49ff. (*GLAJJ*, no. 375): It is "very naïve." The philosopher's theory is supported by the ἐκπυρώσεις ("conflagrations") (finally: Phaethon, 1.19; 4.21) and ἐπικλύσεις ("floods") (finally Deucalion, 1.29; 4.11, 41).

[156] Andresen, *Logos*, 11f.: Are magical abilities or theological doctrine intended? In the literature, both are predicated of him: wisdom (Strabo); magic (Pliny, *Hist. Nat.*; Apuleius). In the context in Celsus, it can only be interpreted to mean magic; cf. 1.26 and Origen's comments on the magical use of the names of the patriarchs (1.22). Of course, there is in this passage an obvious lack of agreement with the preceding section (caused by Origen's abbreviation?): in the preceding the doctrine of Moses was false; here it appears to be tolerable, but not original (and thus to lack the dignity of age); cf. the way the passage continues. A certain adjustment is made in 4.21 (cf. 41): Moses spoils the Greek traditions. There is thus an alternation between the topoi of (a) stupidity (imitation) and (b) falsification.

[157] 5.41; see above: Egyptian origin has been posited since Herodotus 2.204; Josephus, *Ag. Ap.* 1.168, etc.

[158] This appears abruptly. 3.5 shows that Celsus uses an extracanonical version of the exodus; 1.23 functions rather as an anticipation than as a result of Origen's abbreviation. Defection: 5.41 (current!); Lysimachus, Josephus, *Ag. Ap.* 1.309 (*GLAJJ*, no. 158); Tacitus, *Hist.* 5.4 (*GLAJJ*, no. 281). Deception: Apollonius Molon; Lysimachus, Josephus, *Ag. Ap.* 2.145 (*GLAJJ*, no. 161). The accusation of rebellion is to be added to this passage; it is explicitly emphasized in a later context, 3.6.

[159] Angel worship: Acts 7:42; *Ker. Petr.* 2; Aristides, *Apol.* 24; *Contra Cels.* 5.6: And they worship heaven, but not the constellations. On the worship of heaven, see Hecataeus, Strabo. *Contra Cels.* 5.41: they did not invent the worship of heaven themselves; the Persians already did this.

[160] M. Freimann, "Wortführer III," *MGWJ* 56 (1912): 49ff., 164ff.: The Jew in Celsus's writing is historical; he never slips out of his role. To be precise, he is a Hellenistic Jew, while Origen is unacquainted with any surviving Hellenistic Judaism (but Celsus?). Thus he is surprised at the Greek education of the Jew in Celsus's writings (1.67). This Jew is an advocate of the Logos

(see above). The Jews are of Egyptian origin,[161] and were compelled to leave Egypt as political and religious rebels (3.5).[162] Here we have the motif which Celsus elevates to a fundamental principle: the root of Judaism, as later of Christianity, was στάσις ("revolt").[163] Moses took over Greek traditions, which he then perverted (4.11, 21, 41).[164] This reproach is leveled at both Jews and Christians; he ridicules both at the same time (4.23). All the same, Celsus knows how to indicate the decisive difference between them and does so in this same passage: for the Christians the Son of God has already come.[165]

Celsus probes deeper into the ancestral history (4.43ff.). He finds objectionable features in Old Testament morality—the incest of Lot and his daughters (4.45), the hatred of enemies, which the Old Testament encourages (4.46)—and uses these as countercharges against the ethical criticisms which Jews and Christians had raised against the immorality of the Greek myths. This is of one piece with his attack on allegorical interpretation (4.48ff.; cf. already in 38): φησὶν ὅτι καὶ Ἰουδαίων καὶ Χριστιανῶν οἱ ἐπιεικέστεροι τοῦτ' ἀλληγοροῦσι ("he says that the more reasonable Jews and Christians try somehow to allegorize them"): they take refuge in allegory αἰσχυνομένους ἐπὶ τούτοις ("ashamed of these things").[166]

Celsus also argues on the basis of the idea of god as such (4.52ff., first part of book 5). So far, both Jews and Christians have been the object of his critique. But if his attack is to hit the latter, he must call their understanding of history into the fray. And it was not difficult for him to find a decisive point which

---

doctrine (2.31), which the Pharisaic Jews could not acknowledge. Freimann, "Wortführer," 173: the only unhistorical thing about the Jew is his statement about the resurrection; thus someone has duped Celsus. Really!

[161] An anti-Semitic version without regard to the (close of Genesis and the) book of Exodus. But in 4.47 the author takes advantage of the Joseph story for polemical purposes.

[162] Cf. 4.31, where the supplementary note is added that they, released slaves, have never accomplished anything worthy of note (Apollonius Molon, Josephus, Ag. Ap. 1.148 (GLAJJ, no. 49; Apion, Josephus, Ag. Ap. 2.135; GLAJJ, no. 175). Also, their numerical size is insignificant. Is that an Egyptian impression in the time after Trajan?

[163] Cf. the comment concerning Christians in 3.7. In Strabo, the rebellious character of the Jews was still considered an indication of degeneration. Tacitus; Philostratus, Vit. Apoll. 5.33 (Reinach, Textes, no. 96).

[164] The Tower of Babel: Aloadae; Sodom and Gomorrah: Phaethon; Flood: Deucalion (cf. Philo, Praem. Poen. 23; Justin, Apol. 2.7.2; Theophilus, 3.19).

[165] In anticipation of part IV we may note Origen's response (4.31) (a) He praises the Jewish legal ordering of life. The life of the Jews was (!) a reflection of the heavenly life itself; they worshiped only the highest God, no images. (b) And (32), concerning "degeneration": providence finally modified the Jewish system to make it appropriate to all humanity. Here Origen inserts an apologetic summary which repudiates the main points of the current anti-Semitism. With regard to the relative acknowledgment of the Jews and the distancing of the Christians from them, see 7.26, where the aspect of salvation history appears: the difference in the requirement of the Old Testament in the pre- and post-Christian era, a difference the Jews did not acknowledge, which caused their state and cult to be destroyed. Cf. Justin; see n. 164.

[166] In his defense of allegorizing, Origen appeals to Numenius, 4.51 (see below).

the Christians would have to concede. For the Christians claimed, of course, to be a people (*Volk*), whether as the "true Israel" or the "third race" (see part IV below). Nevertheless, Celsus fell into difficulties, as the comparison with Justin shows (Andresen, *Logos,* 303ff.):

Justin (*Apol.* 1.64) explains pagan cultic practices as having originated from misunderstandings of Scripture; theology of history is thus transformed into historical polemic. Celsus to the contrary (6.15): the Christian practice of penance originated as a misunderstanding of a text in Plato (*Leg.* 4.715E/716A). In Celsus this remains an isolated argument. Justin and Celsus use (Ps-) Plato, *Ep.* 2.312 DE (Justin, *Apol.* 1.60.6f.; *Contra Cels.* 6.18). The use of this passage by Justin is understandable, but not by Celsus.[167] Celsus presupposes Christian apologetic, an apologetic that is directed both to the emperor and to the Roman people. That is correct only for Justin (*Apol.* 1.1.1). And Justin is the source of Celsus's reference to the fate of the Jews, for Justin is the only one of the apologists to deal with that subject (cf. later, e.g., Tertullian, *Apol.* 21; Minucius Felix 10.33).

Summary: "Celsus responded to the first Christian attempt to connect the history of Rome and its fortunes with the history of Christianity" (Andresen, *Logos,* 362). It corresponds to the unreconciled duality of Celsus's mode of thought (arguments based on both timeless philosophical-rational principles and on historical data) that he demanded a literal interpretation of the Old Testament, to which Origen must object.

He also had difficulty in his historical argument with the Jews, which he tried to get around by means of a literary device: the Jews became a separate people and gave themselves the kind of laws customary in their country, laws that they preserved until the present, and they had their worship customs which they inherited from their ancestors ("however they may have actually originated"). In these things they were like other nations (5.25f.). The idea of the origin and preservation of these things is explicitly emphasized (5.34). At the same time, of course, the priority of the Jews is disputed (5.50; cf. 41, 44). And the conversion of non-Jews, who are henceforth obligated to keep these traditions, can be branded as an abominable innovation. This last, of course, is especially directed at the Christians (5.35, first part). The Christians represent a defection from tradition and are not a true nation or people (*Volk*). They have οὐδεμίαν ἀρχὴν (3.14: no ὑπόθεσις) τοῦ δόγματος ("no authority [foundation] for their doctrine") (5.65). Against this, Origen affirms (a) the critique of the ethical relativism which must prevail if all the original views of the nations (peoples = *Völker*) are acknowledged (2.27f.); (b) the critique of the written law from the perspective of the natural law, which is the law of God (5.37). He thereby makes use of a Stoic commonplace, which he, however, reformulates in the sense of biblical monotheism: the law of nature is in fact the (written!) biblical

---

[167] It is simply taken from the school tradition; see Chadwick, *Contra Celsum,* 331 n. 3; Numenius in Eusebius, *Praep. Ev.* 11.18.

law. (Philo) (c) If Celsus agrees with Pindar that the law is king, Origen asks: Which law?

5.41 presents a kind of summary, in which the aspect of the argument based on a philosophy of history remains hidden behind commonplaces: (a) The Jewish customs are not original with them (see above). (b) It is immaterial which name one uses in worshiping God (Origen's response, 5.45). This is no contradiction to the philosophical thesis that God is nameless. On the contrary, it is the fundamental namelessness of God which allows for any number of historical names for the gods.

Numenius of Apamea[168]

Fragments: 1 Eusebius, *Praep. Ev.* 14.4ff.
  9a 9.7
  9b Origen, *Contra Cels.* 1.25 (*GLAJJ*, no. 364b)
  10 Clement of Alexandria, *Strom.* 1.22 = Eusebius, *Praep. Ev.* 9.6 (*GLAJJ*, no. 363a)
  11 Eusebius, *Praep. Ev.* 11.21
  12 15.17
  13 15.17
  14 11.9; ibid. 15, 16, 17
  18 9.8
  19 Origen, *Contra Cels.* 4.51 (*GLAJJ*, no. 366)
  20 Eusebius, *Praep. Ev.* 11.17 – etc.

The fragments of Numenius suffice to disprove the idea that Hellenistic Judaism had been exterminated in the second century, an idea that does not correspond to the reality of history, but to the perspective of *eastern* Judaism.

(Pseudo-) Ecphantus[169]

Was he influenced by Genesis 1? Cf. Stobaeus, *Ecl.* 4.6.22 (*GLAJJ*, no. 564a) on this question. Burkert asks whether this text contains Jewish ideas. The idea

---

[168] E. A. Leemans, "Studie over den wijsgeer Numenius van Apamea," *Kon. Belgische Akademie, Afdeeling Letteren, enz.*, Verh. 37 (1937); Reinach, *Textes*, no. 95; R. Beutler, "Numenios," *PWSup.* 7.664ff.; H. Dörrie, "Numenios," *Kl. Pauly* 4:192ff.: Pythagoras and Moses are the real models for him. Clement of Alexandria, *Strom.* 1.150.4; Origen, *Contra Cels.* 4.51; cf. 1.15.

[169] W. Burkert in *Pseudepigrapha I*, Fondation Hardt (Vandoevres-Genève, 1972) 23ff., on which see Hengel, *Judaism and Hellenism*, 308 n. 2 and the discussion on 315. H. Thesleff, *An Introduction to the Pythagorean Writings of the Hellenistic Period*, Act. Acad. Aboensis. Ser. A 24, 3 (Abo, 1961) 68; idem, *The Pythagorean Texts of the Hellenistic Period*, Act. Acad. Aboensis. Ser. A 30, 1 (Abo, 1965) 79ff.

Time of the Severii? Otherwise Thesleff: the *Doric* Pythagorean texts derive from the Hellenistic period; Ecphantus at the earliest from the Seleucid-Ptolemaic. Dörrie, "Ekphantos," *Kl. Pauly* 2: 400 B.C.E..

that a human being is a combination of body and soul is banal Platonism, with the idea of the divine "breath" as a Stoic touch. The equation of "eternal life form" and the divine world reflects the *Timaeus.* The mother (internal equilibrium and the vision of the Father): the earth (cf. Gen. 2:7; Philo, *Op. Mund.* 135; *LA* 1.38; *Det. Pot. Ins.* 86); the speculations concerning the repose and internal equilibrium of Adam.[170]

Porphyry[171]

He rarely mentions Moses, but respects him and the Jews, praising their religious customs.[172]

ROMAN AUTHORS[173]

Preliminary Remarks

Reinach organizes the texts according to Greek-Latin authors. Stern chooses an arrangement based on the chronological order of the texts — so far as this can be determined — without regard to language or political affiliation. There are good reasons based on content for treating the Roman authors together. In dealing with them, we are in a completely different situation with regard to the state of the extant sources than with the sources treated previously, for here we are able for the most part to obtain our data directly from extant authors, statesmen (Cicero), historians (Tacitus), and poets. From such sources we can obtain a clear picture of the role of Jews played in Roman literature (namely, how small a role this in fact was).

---

[170] Cf. "The Hypostasis of the Archons" in Robinson, *Nag Hammadi Library,* 161ff.

[171] Gager, *Moses,* 69ff.; E. R. Dodds, *Pagan and Christian in an Age of Anxiety* (Cambridge: Cambridge University Press, 1968) 125ff.; J. Vogt, *Kaiser Julian,* 16f.; Eusebius, *Hist. Eccl.* 6.19.4; Augustine, *Civ. Dei* 19.23; Lactantius, *Ira.* 23.12. [Translator's note: See now *GLAJJ,* nos. 423–66, esp. nos. 454, 455, 458.]

[172] Porphyry saw the fall of Jerusalem differently from his predecessors in that he did not regard it as proof of the inferiority of the Jews or of their rejection by the gods. "All in all, Porphyry's evaluation of the Jews is a consistent development from his fundamental view of the prerogatives of national religious practices. A guiding principle of his thought and that of his whole school is expressed in the statement: 'The best fruits of piety are to be found in worshipping the Deity in accordance with the customs of the fathers' (*Ad Marc.* 18). This view, and the demand implicit in it, was the unifying factor among all the opponents of Christianity. 'This polytheistic cult of deities equivalent to the religious heritage of all nations' was called by them, as aptly defined by Eus. (*Dem. Ev.* 12), 'Hellenism.' This late form of Hellenism believed that it was able to incorporate Judaism into itself and to obtain special help from it as a privileged mediator of divine wisdom" (Vogt, 17).

[173] R. L. Wilken, "Judaism in Roman and Christian Society," *JR* 47 (1967): 314ff.; A. N. Sherwin-White, *Racial Prejudice in Imperial Rome* (Cambridge: Cambridge University Press, 1967); here a wider horizon is outlined: the northern barbarians in Strabo, *Caesar;* Tacitus on the barbarians, etc. 86ff.: Anti-Semitism in the Roman world. Sevenster, *Roots,* 145ff.; Smallwood, *Jews under Roman Rule.*

Despite all the similarities with the Greek writings there are unmistakable Roman stylistic elements. The most important of these is that in the Roman authors the evaluation of the Jews is determined from a political perspective which is quite absent from the Greek writings.[174] It is in fact the political factor that is the most important aspect in the Roman relation to the Jews, especially for the Caesar, Augustus, but also his successors (Claudius).

Of course new aspects arose due to the Jewish revolts.[175] *Iudaea capta;* the ashes of Jerusalem, which was a very famous city also in the West,[176] the *fiscus Iudaicus* (to *Jupiter Capitolinus*).[177] But these developments, including even the Jewish wars, never determined the Roman policy to the Jews as a whole.

One part of the *agreements* between Greek and Roman authors requires no explanation. In both cases Jews came to their attention because of their distinctiveness:[178] a combination of external separation and the strongest internal coherence, their food laws and especially their Sabbath observance.[179] People were aware that they practiced circumcision, and that this could provoke imperial measures against it (Hadrian), and knew that their cult contained no images of the deity.[180] In addition to their own observations, of course, the

---

[174] Of course there is also an element of pure gossip here. On the other hand where among the Greeks (such as Apion), we also find political attacks, the difference in style is also noticeable. Roman politics is of a different order from Alexandrian city squabbles.

Tib., *Sen. Ep.* 108.22 (Stern, *GLAJJ*, 189). Compare Smallwood, *Jews under Roman Rule,* 202, to Tacitus, *Annals* 2.85. On the Roman, political aspect: Sevenster, *Roots,* 145ff.; Smallwood, passim, esp. 344ff.

[175] Tacitus; the poets; the Flavian dynasty's understanding of itself.

[176] Pliny, *Hist. Nat.* 5.70: the most famous city of the Orient; Tacitus.

[177] Varro: Jupiter Capitolinus is identical with the god of the Jews.

[178] Sevenster gives an extensive discussion: "Essentially the conflict with the ancient world was always centered on the law" (*Roots,* 89ff., 108).

[179] Examples concerning the Sabbath: Tibullus mentions *Saturni sacram diem* ("the accursed day of Saturn") (1.3.18) (U5 [*GLAJJ*, no. 126]); Horace, *Serm.* 1.9 (*GLAJJ*, no. 129), see below, 105; Ovid, *Ars Am.* 1.76, 415f. (*GLAJJ*, no. 141). Such passages document the impression the Sabbath made on non-Jews, precisely by their incidental nature. See Josephus, *Ag. Ap.* 2.282; Tertullian, *Ad nat.* 1.13. [Translator's addition: For Greek authors, see Meleager, in *GLAJJ*, no. 43.]

[180] In addition, there was the Greek gossip about the image of an ass in the temple; Tacitus can mention each alongside the other. Imageless worship: Livy in Lydus, *De Mensibus* 4.53 (*GLAJJ*, no. 134): Livy says, ἄγνωστον τὸ ἐκεῖ τιμώμενον . . . ("the God worshiped there [Jerusalem] is unknown"). Norden, *Agnostos Theos,* 59. Livy in *Scholia in Lucanum,* ed. Usener, 2:593 (*GLAJJ*, no. 133): Incerti Iudaea dei. Livius de Iudaeis: "Hierosolymis fanum cuius deorum sit non nominant, neque ullum ibi simulacrum est, neque enim esse dei figuram putant" ("And Judaea given over to the worship of an unknown God. Livy on Jews: 'They do not state to which deity pertains the temple at Jerusalem, nor is any image found there, since they do not think the God partakes of any figure'"). Livy, *Perlochae* 102 (*GLAJJ*, no. 131): Cn. Pompeius Iudaeos subegit, fanum eorum Hierosolyma, inviolatum ante id tempus (!), cepit ("Cn. Pompeius conquered the Jews and captured their temple (!) Jerusalem, never invaded before").

Josephus, *Ant.* 14.71: The temple was ἄβατος or ἀόρατος ("never before been entered or seen"). (Stern, *GLAJJ*, 329: Livy and Josephus used the same source [?]). Concerning the Jerusalem sanctuary, see also Polybius (Josephus, *Ant.* 12.135f.).

Concerning Titus: *CIL* 6, no. 944 (80 C.E.): gentem Iudaeorum domuit et urbem Hierosolymam,

Romans also had the "knowledge" of the Greek writers at their disposal.[181] Examples of simply adopting such "knowledge": the Sabbath was regarded erroneously as a day of fasting.[182] The Jews are considered (since Hecataeus) a rebellious people and a superstitious one.[183]

A typical Roman nuance was added by the satirical genre (Horace, Martial, Juvenal).

The Jews in Roman Satire

We can treat the satirists together, because they are all dominated by the motifs just named: Sabbath, circumcision, abstention from pork. The political aspect recedes—despite the political commitments of Horace.

Horace[184]

The Jews appear three (or four?) times in the *Satires*, except for the reference to the palm groves of Herod (*Ep.* 2.2.183f.) (*GLAJJ*, no. 130).

(1) *Serm.* 1.4 (*GLAJJ*, no. 127): Once when he had dished out ridicule a little too strongly, he asks the friendly reader's indulgence, for one of my minor weaknesses is to jot down my random thoughts on paper . . . "cui si concedere nolis, multa poetarum veniat manus, auxilio quae sit mihi: nam multo plures sumus, ac veluti te Iudaei cogemus in hanc concedere turbam" ("and if you should make no allowance for it, then would a big band of poets come to my aid—for we are the big majority—and we, like the Jews, will compel you to

---

omnibus ante se ducibus regibus gentibus aut frustra petitam aut omnino intemptatem, deleuit ("[Titus] destroyed the city of Jerusalem, which by all previous commanders, kings, and peoples had either been vainly sought or futilely attempted").

[181] We have seen that Rhodes was one center for such exchange (Posidonius? Molon); Rome itself was another (Apion; Chaeremon). With reference to the latter, cf. L. H. Feldman, "Asinius Pollio and his Jewish Interests," *TAPA* 84 (1953): 73ff.: Timagenes (*FGH* 88; *GLAJJ*, 222ff.; cf. Josephus, *Ant.* 13.319, 344; *Ag. Ap.* 2.84) has contacts with Asinius Pollio (Seneca, *De ira.* 3.23). Otherwise, there is no indication that anyone was interested in the Jewish sources of Polyhistor.

[182] Strabo; Pompeius Trogus; see Schürer, *History* 1:298 n. 23; Schürer-Vermes-Millar, *History* 1:239 n. 23.

[183] *Superstitio* is *the* standard Roman characterization of the Jews (and later for the Christians, as it was for foreign, suspicious cults in general). On this concept, see R. Freudenberger, *Das Verhalten der römischen Behörden gegen die Christen im 2. Jh.* (Munich: Beck, 1967) 189ff. On the accusation of rebelliousness, compare Apion, *FGH* 616 F 4m (Josephus, *Ag. Ap.* 2.125) "the Jews were always a subject people" with the Roman style expressed in Cicero, *De prov. cons.* 5.10: ". . . Iudaeis et Syris, nationibus natis servituti" ("he handed them over as slaves to Jews and Syrians, themselves peoples born to be slaves") (*GLAJJ*, no. 70). One is reminded of Vergil's "Tu regere imperio populos, Romane, memento" ("Remember, Roman, to rule the people under law").

[184] 65-8 B.C.E.; Stern, *GLAJJ*, 321ff. (incorrectly 321, "an emancipated slave"; he was rather the son of an emancipated slave. In any case, he was temporarily a commander in the Legion during the civil war).

become one of our throng") (140ff.)—a reference to the proselytizing zeal of Jewish missionaries.

(2) *Serm.* 1.5 (*GLAJJ*, no. 128): The famous travelogue of the trip to Brundisium. In Gnatia the inhabitants try to convince tourists that frank-incense melts without fire at the temple. "Credat Iudaeus Apella, non ego" ("Apella the Jew may believe it; not I"). Then follows an Epicurean motto.

(3) *Serm.* 1.9 (*GLAJJ*, no. 129): Today is not a day for discussions . . . "hodie tricensima sabbata: vin tu curtis Iudaeis oppedere?" ("Today is the thirtieth day, a Sabbath. Would you affront the circumcised Jews?") (69f.).[185]

(4) *Serm.* 2.3, 288ff. is disputed: a woman solemnly promises Jupiter that if her sick child is healed, the next day, on the morning of the day in which people fast in Jupiter's honor, the child would stand naked in the Tiber. But since there is no fast day in Jupiter's honor, it has sometimes been asked whether the Jewish God was the one intended.

Persius[186]

Sat. 5 deals with the true, inner freedom of the philosophers. Such things as superstition enslave people. As his first example he names the Sabbath (179ff.; *GLAJJ*, no. 190): "at cum Herodis venere dies unctaque fenestra[187] dispositae pinguem nebulam vomuere lucernae[188] portantes violas rubrumque amplexa catinum cauda natet thynni, tumet alba fidelia vino,[189] labra moves tacitus recutitaque sabbata palles.[190] ("But when the day of Herod comes round, when the lamps wreathed with violets and ranged round the greasy window-sills have spat forth their thick clouds of smoke, when the floppy tunnies' tails are curled round the dishes of red ware, and the white jars are swollen out with wine, you silently twitch your lips, turning pale at the Sabbath of the circumcised").

Here we have another example of the extent of Sabbath customs.

---

[185] The form *sabbata* is correct Jewish-Greek. But what is *tricensima sabbata*? Stern places a comma between the two words ("the thirtieth day, a sabbath"). According to the annotators who wrote the scholia, Utricensima was usually understood to mean "new moon." Thus, new moon as Sabbath = "day of rest"; see Stern ad loc.

[186] 34–62 C.E., a Stoic author of satires.

[187] "Herod's Day" is, as the context makes clear, the Sabbath.

[188] Concerning Sabbath lights, cf. *m. Shab.* 2:6f.; contra Seneca, *Ep.* 95.47 (*GLAJJ*, no. 188): "Quomodo sint dii colendi solet praecipi. Accendere aliquem lucernas sabbatis prohibeamus, quoniam nec lumine dii egent et ne homines quidem delectantur fuligine" ("Precepts are commonly given as to how the gods should be worshiped. But let us forbid lamps to be lighted on the Sabbath, since the gods do not need light, neither do men take pleasure in soot").

[189] Fish on Friday evening: see Stern, ad loc.

[190] "Recutita sabbata" = sabbata recutiturom; palles ("turning pale at the Sabbath of the circum-cised"). (a) Reinach: from fasting (thus the familiar error concerning the Sabbath). (b) Stern: from fear, see Juvenal 14.96 (*GLAJJ*, no. 301): metuentem sabbata ("who reveres the Sabbath").

Petronius[191]

This author (Stern, *GLAJJ*, 441ff.) is hardly worth mentioning; his writings include ridicule of circumcision.[192] "Iudaeus licet et porcinum numen adoret[193] et caeli summas advocet auriculas,[194] ni tamen et ferro succiderit inguinis oram et nisi nodatum solverit arte caput, exemptus populo Graias migrabit ad urbes et non ieiuna sabbata lege tremet"[195] (*GLAJJ*, no. 195). ("The Jew may worship his pig-god and clamor in the ears of high heaven, but unless he also cuts back his foreskin with the knife, he shall go forth from the people and emigrate to Greek cities, and shall not tremble at the fasts of Sabbath imposed by the law").

Martial[196]

Here too the satire is limited to circumcision and Sabbath (*GLAJJ*, nos. 238–46). In addition, he has a quick glance at the Jewish War; he does after all have connections with the Flavians—but this is to anticipate later material.[197] Of greater interest are a few passages in his younger contemporary Juvenal.

Juvenal

On the Porta Capena: "Hic ubi nocturnae Numa constituebat amicae [sc. the Nymph Egeria] nunc sacri fontis nemus et delubra locantur Iudaeis, quorum cophinus faenumque supellex. Omnis enim populo mercedem pendere iussa est

---

[191] Probably first century C.E. It is disputed whether he is identical with Nero's "arbiter elegantiarum" ("fastidious observer, elegant judge"). His *Satyricon* is a novel-parody (which includes the well-known dinner party of Trimalchio).

[192] 68:4-8 (*GLAJJ*, no. 193) in the dinner party scene: a slave has only two faults: circumcision and snoring; 102:13f. (*GLAJJ*, no. 194); F 37 (*GLAJJ*, no. 195).

[193] Cf. Epiphanius, *Pan.* 26.10.6 concerning the Barbeliotites: φασὶ δὲ τὸν Σαβαὼθ οἱ μὲν ὄνου μορφὴν ἔχειν, οἱ δὲ χοίρου ("Some say Sabaoth looks like an ass, others, like a pig"). W. Fauth, *Oriens Christianus* 57 (1973): 89.

[194] On the veneration of heaven, see Hecataeus.

[195] Again, Sabbath fasting.

[196] Ca. 40-103/104 C.E.; author of epigrams; lived in the Flavian court (Domitian).

[197] *Epigr.* 2.2 (*GLAJJ*, no. 238), to Domitian (on his success over the Germans) including. Frater Idumaeos meruit cum patre triumphos ("Along with his sire thy brother won his Idumaean triumph" [Idumea is used for Judea, as often by Roman authors]). Additional references: 4.4 (*GLAJJ*, no. 239): disparaging comment about a foul-smelling woman, which compares her, among other things, to the women who fast on the Sabbath; 7.30 (*GLAJJ*, no. 240): concerning a harlot, who gives herself to one and all: nec recutitorum fugis inguina Iudaeorum ("of the breath of fasting Sabbatarian women"); 7.35 (*GLAJJ*, no. 241): ridicule of a slave who had kept his genitals covered; 7.55 (*GLAJJ*, no. 242): an obscenity, which refers to the destroyed Jerusalem and Jewish tribute; 7.82 (*GLAJJ*, no. 243) concerning an actor who had concealed the fact that he had been circumcised; 11.94 (*GLAJJ*, no. 245): against a Jewish poet, who purportedly was sexually involved with Martial's *puer* (boy, son, slave?), but who denied it; 12.57 (*GLAJJ*, no. 246): in Rome one is always bothered by Jewish beggars, who learned begging from their mothers.

arbor et eiectis mendicat silva Camenis" ("Here Numa held his nightly assig-
nations with his mistress; but now the holy fount and grove and shrine are let
out to Jews, who possess a basket and a truss of hay[198] for all their furnishings.
For as every tree nowadays has to play toll to the people, the Muses have been
ejected, and the wood has to go a-begging") (*Satire* 3.10ff.; *GLAJJ*, no. 296).

See further 6.508ff., which provides an extremely interesting insight into the
syncretism in Rome. 6.542ff. (*GLAJJ*, no. 299): The superstitious woman chases
around after all sorts of oriental Jews. Jewish women also appear as objects of
smug satire in this connection: "cophino foenoque relicto arcanam Iudaea
tremens mendicat in aurem, interpres *legum Solymarum* et magna sacerdos
arboris ac *summi fida internuntia caeli*"[199] ("a palsied Jewess, leaving her basket
and her truss of hay, comes begging to her secret ear; she is an interpreter of
the laws of Jerusalem, a high priestess of the tree, a trusty go-between of highest
heaven"). "Implet et illa manum, sed parcius: aere minuto qualicacumque voles
Iudaei somnia vendunt"[200] ("She, too [the superstitious woman], fills her palm,
but more sparingly, for a Jew will tell you dreams of any kind you please for
the minutest of coins").

Of special significance is the picture of the spread of the Jewish religion (even
after the Jewish War!) and/or the progressive conversion to it (*GLAJJ*, no. 301):
"Quidam sortiti metuentem sabbata patrem nil praeter nubes et caeli numen
adorant, nec distare putant humana carne suillam qua pater *abstinuit;* mox et
praeputia ponunt. *Romanas autem soliti contemnere leges,* Iudaicum ediscunt et
servant ac metuunt ius tradidit arcano quodcumque volumine Moses: non
monstrare vias eadem nisi sacra colenti" ("Some who have had a father who
reveres the Sabbath, worship nothing but the clouds, and the divinity of the
heavens, and see no difference between eating swine's flesh, from which their
father abstained and that of man; and in time they take to circumcision. Having
been wont to flout the laws of Rome, they learn and practice and revere the
Jewish law, and all that Moses handed down in his secret tome, forbidding to
point out the way to any not worshiping the same rites"). An echo of Lysimachus: Never give good advice! "Quaesitum ad fontem solos deducere verpos.
Sed pater in causa, cui septima quaeque fuit lux ignava et partem vitae non
attigit ullam" ("and conducting none but the circumcised to the desired foun-
tain. For all which the father was to blame, who gave up every seventh day
to idleness, keeping it apart from all the concerns of life") (14.96ff.; *GLAJJ*,
no. 301).

A real compendium!

Concerning using the Sabbath as an occasion for the neglect of duties, cf. the

---

[198] Basket and hay as beggar's equipment: cf. 6.542f.

[199] "Sacerdos arboris" ("a high priestess of the tree")? An allusion to the beggar in the grove of
Numa (see above), where the tree is mentioned?

[200] The Jews and manticism: rich illustrative material is offered by the magical papyri. And: The
Jews have cheaper rates.

moralizing version of Seneca F 593 (Augustine, *Civ. Dei* 6.11): "Hic [sc. Seneca] inter alias civilis theologiae superstitiones reprehendit etiam sacramenta Iudaeorum et maxime sabbata, inutiliter eos facere adfirmans, quod per illos singulos septenis interpositos dies septimam fere partem aetatis suae perdant vacando et multa in tempore urgentia non agendo laedantur" ("Along with other superstitions of the civil theology Seneca also censures the sacred institutions of the Jews, especially the Sabbath. He declares that their practice is inexpedient, because by introducing one day of rest in every seven they lose in idleness almost a seventh of their life, and by failing to act in times of urgency they often suffer loss") (*GLAJJ*, no. 186).

Sherwin-White (*Racial Prejudice*, 98f.): Juvenal is not afraid that the Jews will ascend to prominent places in Roman society (like the Greeks). Although they could become Roman citizens, the normal way of social ascendancy—military service—was blocked for them. The Jewish colony in Rome was rather proletarian. [Translator's note: See now *GLAJJ*, nos. 297-98.]

Other Poets

References to Jews do not amount to much. Prior to the Flavian period *one* allusion to the Jewish religion is found. After that—but still only in a few places—the Flavian aspect becomes more clearly visible. The emphasis is not on Judaism or the Jewish people as such, but on the destruction of Jerusalem and the subjugation of Palestine as the event through which the Flavian dynasty was constituted.

Lucan (*GLAJJ*, 438ff.)[201]

In his historical epic *Pharsalia* (*Bellum Civile*), he portrays Pompey as making a speech in which he says: "Me domitus cognovit Arabs . . . Cappadoces mea signa timent et dedita sacris incerti Iudaea dei"[202] ("The Arab acknowledges me as conqueror. . . . My standards overawe Cappadocia, and Judea given over to the worship of an unknown god") (2.590ff.; *GLAJJ*, no. 191).

The following three prevailed in the Flavian period:

C. Valerius Flaccus (*GLAJJ*, 502ff.)

This writer of mythological epics composed the *Argonautica*. He introduces it with a panegyrical proem on the Flavian dynasty.[203] The point of departure

---

[201] M. Annaeus Lucanus (39-65 C.E.) was a nephew of Seneca, and like his uncle was forced to commit suicide by Nero. On his political tendency, see *Kl. Pauly*, s.v.

[202] On the "di incerti" ("unknown god"), see Varro, who, however, does not reckon the Jewish god among them.

[203] The date of the writing of the proem is disputed: in the time of Vespasian, Titus, or Domitian; relevant literature is given in Stern.

for their rise to power is also included (1.1–20; *GLAJJ*, no. 226): The offspring of Phoebus (Apollo), Domitian, is supposed to announce it: "Versam proles tua pandet Idumen (namque potest): Solymo nigrantem pulvere fratrem (Titus) spargentemque faces et in omni turre furentem"[204] ("Thy son shall tell of the overthrow of Idume [Judea]—for well he can—of his brother foul with dust of Solyma, as he hurls the brands and spreads havoc in every tower") (1.12–14).

Silius Italicus (*GLAJJ*, 506ff.)

This author (ca. 25–100 C.E.) composed the historical epic *Punica.* In book 3 Jupiter prophesies concerning the Flavian dynasty: "palmiferamque senex bello domitabit Idymen. . . . Tum iuvenis, magno praecellens robore mentis, excipiet patriam molem celsusque feretur, aequatum imperio tollens caput. Hic fera gentis bella Palaestinae primo delebit in aevo" ("he shall subdue in war the palm-groves of Idume [Judea]. . . . Then his son, unrivalled in mighty strength of mind, shall take up his father's task and move on in majesty, raising his head as high as his power. While yet a youth, he shall put an end to war with the fierce people of Palestine") (3.597ff.; *GLAJJ*, no. 227).

P. Papinius Statius (*GLAJJ*, 515ff.)

P. Papinius Statius (ca. 40–96 C.E.) was a lyric poet (*Silvae*) and a writer of mythological epics. In his *Silvae* he mentions the prestige of the Idumaean triumph (3.3.240; *GLAJJ*, no. 235). To a young officer: "Where would you like to fulfill your military service?" ". . . an Solymum cinerem palmetaque capta subibis non sibi felices silvas ponentis Idymes?" ("Wilt thou tread the dust of Solyma, and the captive palm-groves of Idume [Judea], who not for herself did plant her fruitful orchards?") (5.2.138ff.; *GLAJJ*, no. 237).

The stage was set for Roman–Jewish relationships[205] by Pompey's intervention in the East. Then followed the civil wars until their final culmination in the battle of Actium (31 B.C.E.),[206] wars that also included the East. Both of Cicero's comments on the Jews (only two!) come from the time of Pompey.

This was not the first time, of course, that the Jews had come to the attention of people in Rome. The earliest known reference to the Jews in Roman literature occurred in 139 B.C.E.[207] The passage (*Valerius Maximus* 1.3.3) is preserved

---

[204] Cf. Josephus, likewise in the service of the Flavians, but as a Jew: he would like to save Titus from the charge that he wanted to burn the temple.

[205] After a historically insignificant diplomatic prelude in the time of the Maccabees (cf. the biting comments on this by Pompeius Trogus).

[206] After Herod had obtained reconciliation with Augustus.

[207] The year of the embassy from Simon the Maccabean to Rome? Schürer, *History* 3:59; Schürer-Vermes-Millar, *History* 1:197; Stern, *GLAJJ*, 360: the embassy was probably in 142 B.C.E.

only in two epitomizers. The more extensive version: "Cn. Cornelius Hispalus [correctly: Cn. Cornelius Scipio Hispanus] praetor peregrinus M. Popilio Laenate L. [correctly: Cn.] Calpurnio coss. [i.e., 139 B.C.E.] edicto Chaldaeos citra decimum diem abire ex urbe atque Italia iussit. . . . Idem Iudaeos, qui Sabazi Iovis cultu Romanos inficere mores conati erant, repetere domos suas coegit" ("Cn. Cornelius Hispalus, *praetor peregrinus* in the year of the consulate of P. Popilius Laenas and L. Calpurnius, ordered the astrologers by an edict to leave Rome and Italy within ten days. . . . The same praetor compelled the Jews, who attempted to infect the Roman customs with the cult of Jupiter Sabazius, to return to their homes") (*GLAJJ*, no. 147b).

Schürer understands the expression to mean that they were not yet settled residents (*History* 3:58f.; differently K. Latte, *Röminische Religionsgeschichte* [Munich, 1960] 275). It could have reference to those who accompanied the embassy from Simon. But the other version should be noted: "Iudaeos quoque, qui Romanis tradere sacra sua conati erant, idem Hispalus urbe exterminavit arasque privatas e publicis locis abiecit" ("The same Hispalus banished the Jews from Rome, because they attempted to transmit their sacred rites to the Romans, and he cast down their private altars from public places") (*GLAJJ*, no. 147a).

The "sabazios" of the Jews (identified with Dionysus; cf. Plutarch) is obviously related to "Sabbath" (Schürer, *History* 3:58f.); differently Nilsson, *Geschichte* 2:662: Sabazios was the god of the Sabbath, which was celebrated by the Jews "Dionysus-like" (cf. Plutarch).

The passage is supposed to support the thesis that there were syncretistic, Jewish-pagan cults (Cumont, *The Oriental Religions in Roman Paganism* [Chicago: Open Court, 1911]; Nilsson, *Geschichte*; I. Léwy, *Studies in Jewish Hellenism* [Jerusalem, 1960] 166).

Cicero

The data are very meager: the Jews appear in a total of two passages.[208]

(1) *Pro Flacco* 28.66–69 (*GLAJJ*, no. 68): The speech was given in 59 B.C.E..

The situation is that the former proconsul of Asia, L. Valerius Flaccus, was accused *de repetundis*. One charge against him was that he confiscated "the Jewish gold," obviously the depository for the Jerusalem temple tax. Cicero defended him: the senate had forbidden the export of gold from Italy, a measure undertaken, after all, under its own consulate. That was, of course, a matter of economic policy, not a special measure against the Jews. The same also applies in the case of Flaccus. But obviously the measure evoked agitation among the Jews in Rome.

Cicero accused the prosecutor, Laelius, of intentionally arranging to have the

---

[208] Stern, *GLAJJ*, 194: "It is noteworthy that in spite of his sojourn at Rhodos and his connections with Apollonius Molon, Cicero did not take recourse to any of the specific arguments of Hellenistic anti-Semitism . . ." (misanthropy, etc.).

trial in a location where the Jews would be able to vent their hostility, in order to exert pressure on the court: "scis quanta sit manus, quanta *concordia*, quantum valeat in contionibus"[209] ("You know what a big crowd it is, *how they stick together,* how influential they are in informal assemblies").

And in particular concerning the Jews: "huic autem barbarae superstitioni resistere severitatis, multitudinem Iudaeorum flagrantem non numquam in contionibus pro re publica contemnere gravitatis summae fuit" ("But to resist this barbaric superstition was an act of firmness, to defy the crowd of Jews, when sometimes in our assemblies they were hot with passion, for the welfare of the state was an act of the greatest seriousness").

An objection: When Pompey conquered Jerusalem, he touched nothing in the temple (see Josephus, *J. W.* 1.253; *Ant.* 14.72). Cicero: That was a wise move on his part; he did not allow any suspicion to arise "in tam suspiciosa ac maledica civitate" ("in a state so given to suspicion and calumny"). Then comes the typically Roman aspect: "Sua cuique civitati religio, Laeli, est, nostra nobis. Stantibus Hierosolymis pacatisque Iudaeis tamen istorum religio sacrorum a splendore huius imperi, gravitate nominis nostri, maiorum institutis abhorrebat; nunc vero hoc magis, quod illa gens quid de nostro imperio sentiret ostendit armis; quam cara dis immortalibus esset docuit, quod est victa, quod elocata, quod serva facta" ("Each state, Laelius, has its own religious scruples, we have ours. Even while Jerusalem was standing, and the Jews were at peace with us, the practice of their sacred rites was at variance with the glory of our empire, the dignity of our name, the customs of our ancestors. But now it is even more so, when that nation by its armed resistance has shown what it thinks of our rule; how dear it was to the immortal gods is shown by the fact that it has been conquered, let out for taxes, made a slave") (*GLAJJ*, no. 68).

In the background stands the Roman conviction that the Romans owed their domination to *pietas.*[210]

In evaluating this data, it is to be kept in mind that this is a speech made before the court. In the same speech, the citizens of Asia do not come off very well either — just as is the case with other national groups in other speeches.[211]

(2) *De prov. cons.* 5.10 (*GLAJJ*, no. 70): This is the location of the witticism already mentioned: "Iudaeis et Syris, nationibus natis servituti" ("Jews and Syrians, themselves peoples born to be slaves").[212]

---

[209] A fleeting glimpse of Judaism in Rome exaggerated, of course, in the rhetoric of the courtroom; Cicero dramatizes, claiming that he must speak only loud enough for the judge to hear him, but not the people.

[210] On the argument with the god, cf. Apion (Josephus, *Ag. Ap.* 2.125; *GLAJJ*, no. 175); Minucius Felix 10.4; Tertullian, *Apol.* 25.2; and cf. the Jewish interpretation of the fate of the nation.

[211] Stern, *GLAJJ*, 294: "Thus little is left of Cicero's supposed anti-Semitism." That makes the matter appear for him a little more harmless than he in fact believed it to be, for he regarded the Jews throughout the empire and in Rome in a different light than he did the Sardians.

[212] Cf. Livy 36.17.5, and see above, 104 n. 183.

That is all Cicero offers on our subject. The next author (in his *Antiquitatum*) provides information about the early imperial period and the time just preceding it.

Varro

Varro[213] (116–27 B.C.E.) was a comprehensive scholar with amazing productivity in many different areas,[214] from agriculture to linguistics, including influential philosophical and antiquarian studies. Nevertheless, his most important work, *Antiquitates rerum humanarum et divinarum,*[215] has been only fragmentarily preserved.[216]

Though he had learned much from the Greeks, his national consciousness was thoroughly Roman,[217] and had a powerful effect in the Augustinian reformation.[218] His Roman perspective is expressed, for example, in his critical stance to oriental cults.[219] His extant statements concerning the Jews are all the more worthy of note.[220] They are to be understood in the framework of his theology, a theological framework that is discussed by Augustine in *Civ. Dei* 6.2ff.

A quotation in Johannes Lydus is neutral (*De Mensibus* 4.53, p. 109; Wünsch-*FGH* 790 F 7); Norden, *Agnostos Theos,* 58ff. (see above): This is certainly taken from an attached scholion. Lydus reports different opinions concerning the god of the Hebrews: ὁ δὲ Ῥωμαῖος Βάρρων περὶ αὐτοῦ διαλαβών φησι παρὰ Χαλδαίος ἐν τοῖς μυστικοῖς αὐτὸν λέγεσθαι Ἰάω ἀντὶ τοῦ φῶς νοητὸν τῇ Φοινίκων γλώσσῃ, ὥς φησιν Ἐρέννιος ("The Roman Varro defining him says

---

[213] *GLAJJ,* 207ff.

[214] Seneca, *Helv.* 8.1: doctissimus Romanorum ("the most learned of the Romans"). See Augustine below.

[215] Dedicated to Caesar as *Pontifex Maximus.*

[216] Concerning the fragments, see R. Agahd, *Jahrbuch für classische Philologie* Suppl. 24 (1898); A. G. Condemi, *M. Terrentii Varronis Antiquitates Rerum Divinarum librorum I–II Fragmenta* (Bologna, 1964). On the arrangement, Augustine (*Civ. Dei* 6.3) notes: twenty-five books on human themes, the rest on divine themes.

This is characteristic of Varro's thinking, since the national groups were there first, and only later the religious institutions they established. He explicitly renounces the claim to write on the nature of the gods as such (otherwise he would have found it necessary to decide to treat the subjects in the opposite order).

[217] K. Sellmann, "Varro," *Kl. Pauly* 5:1139: "Greek science offered the method and form of presentation; but Varro remained nonetheless almost more Roman than Cicero."

[218] Latte (*Röminische Religionsgeschichte,* 291ff.) emphasizes romanticism and rationalism. For editions of the text and bibliography, see *Kl. Pauly* 5:1139; H. Dahlmann, "M. Terentivs Varro," *PWSup.* 6.1172ff.

[219] Servius in *Aen.* 8.698: Varro indignatur Alexandrinos deos Romae coli ("Varro is offended that the Alexandrians cultivate the worship of the Roman gods") (see Latte, *Röminische Religionsgeschichte,* 282 n. 3).

[220] Where does he get his information? Alexander Polyhistor wrote somewhat later than the *Ant. div.* Norden (*Agnostos Theos,* 672) thinks of Posidonius.

that he is called Iao in the Chaldaean mysteries. That means in the Phoenician language the 'intelligible light' according to Herennius"). (See Herennius Philo of Byblos, *FGH* 790 F 7; *GLAJJ*, no. 324, from the period ca. 56–142 C.E.; see *GLAJJ*, no. 75). On the name Ἰάω ("Iao"), see Diodorus 1.94, and *GLAJJ*, no. 58, and, of course, the magical papyri.

According to *Civ. Dei* 6.3 (Agahd, 3; Condemi, 1): In the last three books of the *Ant. div.* Varro distinguished among the gods as follows: "in primo dei certi, in secundo incerti [cf. 7.17; Norden, *Agnostos Theos*, 61, 58ff.], in tertio cunctorum novissimo dii praecipui atque selecti" [cf. 7.2] ("in the first book are the 'certain gods'; in the second the 'uncertain gods'; and in the third and last of all the 'principal and select gods'").

Civ. Dei 6.5 (Condemi, 23): There are three *genera theologiae* ("kinds of theology") (according to Pohlenz [*Stoa* (Göttingen: Vandenhoeck & Ruprecht, 1919) 1:276ff.], this is taken from Panaetius) "id est rationis quae de diis explicatur, eorumque unum mythicon appellari, alterum physicon, tertium civile" ("Of these one is called mythical, another physical, and the third, civil"). The first contains much that has been fabricated. On the second: the disputes among the philosophers are to be kept away from the common people. "Prima, inquit theologia maxime accommodata est ad theatrum, secunda ad mundum, tertia ad urbem" ("'The first theology,' he says, 'is chiefly suited to the theater, the second to the universe, the third to the city'") (Agahd, 53; Condemi, 28).

Varro was a monotheist in the style of classical antiquity. He stood in the academic and Stoic tradition, with Neopythagorean influences. "Jupiter" was for him a collective name, a generic term: "Hi omnes dii deaeque sit unus Iuppiter" ("Let the one god Jupiter be all this") (*Civ. Dei* 4.11; Agahd, 15b; Condemi, 53).

Civ. Dei 4.9 (Agahd, 58f.; Condemi, 47): "Hunc [sc. Jupiter] Varro credit etiam ab his coli, qui *unum deum solum sine simulacro* colunt, sed ab alio nomine nuncupari" ("Varro believes that he [Jupiter] is worshiped even by those who worship one God only, without an image, though he is called by another name").

That can be referred to the Jews: Augustine, *Cons. Ev.* 1.22.30 (Agahd, 58b; Condemi, 48): "Varro autem ipsorum, quo doctiorem apud se neminem inveniunt, *deum Iudaeorum* Iovem putavit nihil interesse censens, quo nomine nuncupetur, dum eadem res intellegatur. . . . Nam quia nihil superius solent colere Romani quam Iovem, quod Capitolium eorum satis aperteque testatur, eumque regem omnium deorum arbitrantur, cum animadverteret Iudaeos summum deum colere, nihil aliud potuit suspicari quam Iovem" ("Yet Varro, one of themselves—to a more learned man they cannot point—thought the God of the Jews to be the same as Jupiter, thinking that it makes no difference by which name he is called, so long as the same thing is understood. . . . Since the Romans habitually worship nothing superior to Jupiter, a fact attested well and openly by their Capitol, and they consider him the king of all the gods, and as he perceived that the Jews worship the highest God, he could not but identify him with Jupiter") (*GLAJJ*, no. 72b). Augustine refers, of course, to the Roman worship of images: "Si deum Israhel Iovem putant, sicut Varro scripsit, interim ut secundum eorum opinionem loquar, cur ergo Iovi non credunt idola esse delenda?" ("If they think Jupiter to be the god of Israel, as Varro wrote, let me speak meanwhile according to their opinion, why therefore don't they believe Jupiter that idols ought to be destroyed") (*Cons. Ev.* 1.27, 42; *GLAJJ*, no. 72d).

But, of course, Varro rejects these images, which expresses both his critical stance toward religion[221] and his commitment to Roman history (*Civ. Dei* 4.31; Agahd, 59; Condemi, 76): "eum [sc. deum] esse animam motu ac ratione mundum gubernantem. . . . dicit etiam antiquos Romanos plus annos centum et septuaginta deos sine simulacro coluisse" ("he, God, is the soul which governs the world by a movement that accords with reason. . . . He also says that for more than 170 years the ancient Romans worshiped the gods without an image") (cf. Plutarch, *Numa* 8; Pythagorean)."Quod si adhuc, inquit, mansisset, castius dii observarentur" [thus "origin and degeneration"]. "Cuius sententiae suae testem adhibet inter cetera etiam gentem Iudaeam" ("'If this usage had continued to our own day,' he says, 'our worship of the gods would be more devout.' And in support of his opinion he adduces, among other things, the testimony of the Jewish race") (cf. *GLAJJ*, no. 72a).

Pompeius Trogus

As a historian of the Augustinian period, Pompeius Trogus[222] composed *Historiae Philippicae*, as part of a universal history. He is of particular importance to us, because his work includes one of the four great excursuses on the Jews and because in his work it is possible to evaluate the proportionate amount of space within his total work which he devoted to the Jews. To be sure, the value of his work is impaired for us because only summaries of the individual books have been preserved by a certain Justin (but we have them for each of the forty-four volumes) in addition to the prologues of the individual books.

By virtue of the fact that he used Greek sources, it may be clearly seen that he stands in the tradition of Greek history writing. This may be seen all the more clearly in the excursus on the Jews. But he consciously develops his own program (see Seel), in which the Roman perspective is clearly recognizable.[223]

---

[221] This critique is, among other things, based on good Stoic doctrine; cf., e.g., the treatment of Seneca's *De superst.* in Augustine, *Civ. Dei* 6.11; 7.5; the question (Maximus of Tyre 2): εἰ θεοῖς ἀγάλματα ἱδρυτέον ("Being then God's offspring"); cf. Acts 17:29; B. v. Borries, *Quid veteres philosophi de idolatria senserint* (Göttingen: Dieterich, 1918); Pohlenz, *Stoa* 1:267f.

[222] O. Seel, ed. *Die Praefatio des Pompeius Trogus* (Erlangen, 1955); Stern, *GLAJJ*, 332ff.

[223] Alongside his use of anti-Roman sources. Against the hypothesis that Pompeius Trogus himself was anti-Roman, see Fuchs, *Der geistige Widerstand*, 42f., 45 (on the anti-Roman speeches).

He takes over the schema of the four pre-Roman world empires as the framework for his own presentation.[224]

When a new people comes within the field of view of the story as it progresses, he customarily (like his Hellenistic predecessors; cf. Tacitus) deals with their origin, land, and history in an excursus.[225]

The Jews (and Palestine) in Book 36[226]

(1) *Location in the work as a whole:* In relation to the subjection of the Jews through Antioch VII Sidetes.[227]

The situation of the Jews prior to this point in history: "Iudaeos quoque, qui in Macedonico imperio sub Demetrio [sc. I] patre armis se in libertatem vindicaverant, subegit. Quorum vires tantae fuere, ut post haec nullum Macedonum regem tulerint domesticisque imperiis usi Syriam magnis bellis infestaverint" ("He also reduced the Jews, who during the Macedonian rule under his father Demetrius had recovered their liberty by force of arms and whose strength was such that they would submit to no Macedonian king afterwards, but commanded by rulers of their own nation harassed Syria with fierce wars") (1.10).

(2) *Structure:* (a) origin 36.2.1; (b) the land 36.3.1ff.; (c) history 36.3.8f.: the Jews were first subjugated by Xerxes (thus no knowledge of the Bible is reflected! Cf. Josephus, *J.W.* 4.176: they were never subjugated either by the Egyptians or by the Medes, i.e., Persians). Then follows the rule of the Macedonians until the time of Demetrius. Then they break away from him and successfully seek friendship with the Romans: "primi omnium ex Orientalibus libertatem acceperunt, facile tunc Romanis de alieno largientibus" ("They were the first of all the eastern peoples that regained their liberty, the Romans then readily bestowing what was not their own") (3.9).[228]

With reference to the origin of the Jews, Pompeius Trogus first gives an "eastern" version: "origo Damascena,[229] . . . unde et Assyriis regibus genus ex

---

Concerning the anti-Roman version of the origins of Rome, cf. Christian authors, especially Minucius Felix, Tertullian, Augustine; cf. Fuchs, 85ff.

[224] Stern, *GLAJJ*, 541ff. He makes no distinction between the mythical and the historical age. The pattern origin/degeneration appears in several places. On the structure as a whole, see P. L. Schmidt, "Pompeius," *Kl. Pauly* 4:1032: "a clearly arranged structure, oriented by the principle of the *Translatio imperii* (cf. Inst. I 3:6)."

[225] Examples: general (books, 1–2); the oldest peoples (2); Athens (18.3ff.); Carthage (43.1): initia (a) *Romanae urbis,* (b) *Romani imperii,* beginning with the aborigines and King Saturn (euhemerism!); the golden age (primitive communism).

[226] *GLAJJ,* no. 137. Cf. the prologue (*GLAJJ,* no. 136). Stern ("Jews," 1146ff.) posits three sources for the "Excursus on the Jews": (1) one that is similar to the biblical account, (2) a Damascus tradition, and (3) a Greek-Egyptian anti-Semitic tradition.

[227] Cf. Hecataeus, and Josephus, *Ant.* 13.236ff.; Diodorus (Posidonius; *GLAJJ,* no. 63); Plutarch 184 E (*GLAJJ,* no. 260).

[228] In the background, an anti-Roman source.

[229] Nicholas of Damascus, *FGH* 90 F 19; *GLAJJ,* no. 83)=Josephus, *Ant.* 1.159ff.

regina Samirami fuit" ("The origin of the Jews was from Damascus . . . whence also the stock of the Assyrian kings through queen Samiramis had sprung")[230] (2.1). The name of the city was given by King Damascus. His successor was "Azelus (Hasael), mox Adores (Hadad),[231] et Abrahames[232] et Israhel reges fuere" ("Azelus, and then Adores, Abraham, and Israhel were their kings") (2.3). Abraham had ten (!) sons, divided his people into ten kingdoms,[233] and named them all "Jews," after his son Judah who had died prematurely ("cuius portio omnibus accesserat"; 2.5).[234] ("whose portion was added to theirs").

The youngest (!) son, Joseph,[235] was sold by his brothers because they were jealous of his great talent,[236] and was taken to Egypt, where he learned magic and expertise in occult arts ". . . et somniorum primus intelligentiam condidit,[237] nihilque divini iuris humanique ei incognitum videbatur"[238] ("he was the first to establish the science of interpreting dreams; and nothing indeed of divine or human law seemed to have been unknown to him") (2.8). He predicted a famine, "tantaque experimenta eius fuerunt, ut non ab homine, sed a deo responsa dari viderentur" ("such being the proofs of his knowledge that his admonitions seemed to proceed, not from a mortal, but a god")[239] (2.10). His son (!) was Moses, who became the heir of his father's special knowledge. His beauty is praised as well.[240]

At this point (between 2.11 and 2.12) there comes a break:[241] here, without being harmonized with what precedes, begins the Egyptian version of the expulsion of the lepers[242]—the continuation is remarkable: "Dux igitur (!)[243]

---

[230] On Semiramis in the Jewish genealogy, see Alexander Polyhistor.

[231] On both, see Josephus, *Ant.* 9.93.

[232] A variation in Nicholas of Damascus, *FGH* 90 F 19: Abraham comes to Damascus from the East.

[233] Hecataeus, *FGH* 264 F 6 (*GLAJJ*, no. 11): Moses divided the people into twelve tribes.

[234] On the relationship between origin and name, cf. Tacitus.

[235] Molon likewise mentions Joseph—as the twelfth son of Gelos (Isaac).

[236] This is obviously a tradition which has no relation to the story of dividing the people into twelve tribes.

[237] Demetrius the Chronographer; Philo the writer of epic poetry. Does the motif of Joseph as an inventor indicate a Jewish source? Cf. the portrayal of Abraham, and especially Moses, by Jewish writers.

[238] Joseph as lawgiver!

[239] Tertullian, *Ad nat.* 2.8; Firmicus Maternus, *Err.* 23; *Suda*, s.v. Sarapis: In Egypt Joseph was worshiped as divine, under the name Sarapis.

[240] Likewise a Jewish topos; LXX; Philo, *Vit. Mos.* 1.18; Josephus, *Ant.* 2.231; Acts 7:20.

[241] Whatever Justin may have omitted by way of abbreviation, the immigration of the Jews into Egypt is lacking here.

[242] Elsewhere it is the Egyptians who are sick; here it is those who are exiled. In addition, only the Jews are expelled (see Gager, *Moses*, 48ff.). The cause of the plague is not foreign religious practices, but the presence of an unclean people.

[243] A clear indication of the abbreviation of the source.

exulum factus [sc. Mose] sacra Aegyptiorum furto abstulit,[244] quae repetentes armis Aegyptii domum redire tempestatibus conpulsi sunt"[245] ("Accordingly, becoming leader of the exiles, he carried off by stealth the sacred utensils of the Egyptians, who, trying to recover them by force of arms, were compelled by tempests to return home") (2.13). Worthy of notice is the continuation,[246] "Itaque (!) Moyses Damascena, antiqua patria, repetita montem Sinam occupat,[247] in quo septem dierum ieiunio per deserta Arabiae cum populo suo fatigatus cum tandem venisset, septimum diem more gentis Sabbata appellatum in omne aevum ieiunio[248] sacravit, quoniam illa dies famem illis erroremque finierat" ("Thus Moyses, having reached Damascus, his ancestral home, took possession of mount Sinai, on his arrival at which, after having suffered together with his followers, from a seven days' fast in the deserts of Arabia, he, for all time consecrated the seventh day, which used to be called Sabbath by the custom of the nation, for a fast-day, because that day had ended at once their hunger and their wanderings") (2:14).

Then follows a rationalistic (not unfriendly) version of the ἀπανθρωπία ("unsociability"): "Et quoniam metu contagionis pulsos se ab Aegypto meminerant, ne eadem causa invisi apud incolas forent, caverunt, ne cum peregrinis conviverent; quod ex causa factum paulatim in disciplinam religionemque convertit. Post Moysen etiam filius (!) eius Arruas sacerdos sacris Aegyptiis, mox rex creatur; semperque exinde hic mos apud Iudaeos fuit, ut eosdem reges et sacerdotes haberent, quorum iustitia religione permixta incredibile quantum coaluere" ("And as they remembered that they had been driven from Egypt for fear of spreading infection, they took care, in order that they might not become odious, from the same cause, to their neighbors, to have no communication with strangers; a rule which, from having been adopted on that particular occasion, gradually became a religious institution. After Moyses, his son Arruas, was made priest to supervise the Egyptian rites, and soon after created king; and ever afterwards it was a custom among the Jews to have the same persons both for kings and priests; and by their justice combined with religion, it is almost incredible how powerful they became") (2.15f.).

Next (3.1ff.) comes the description of the land, and after that a brief note on the later history of Demetrius I (see above).[249] In sum: The report is clearly a

---

[244] Cf. Lysimachus ("Hierosyla"!). Does the tradition of Moses as an Egyptian priest here shimmer in the background (but cf. 2.16; Aaron)? The inference must then be that the Jewish religion is the (of course perverted) continuation of the Egyptian (so Tacitus).

[245] For a rationalistic explanation of the Reed Sea miracle, see Artapanos, *FGH* 726 F 3.

[246] This now switches back to the Damascus version.

[247] Most simply explained as a mistake of the epitomizer; the fact that the continuation of the passage is most easily read when this explanation is adopted also argues for the correctness of this solution. Or was there already a mixture of source material by Pompeius himself, or had one of his sources already made this combination? A decision is not possible.

[248] Once again! For example, Apion, *FGH* 616 F 4b; *GLAJJ*, no. 165 (Josephus, *Ag. Ap.* 2.21); Tacitus, *Hist.* 5.4 (*GLAJJ*, no. 281).

[249] Cf. further the prologue to book 39 (*GLAJJ*, no. 238) and the note in 40.2.4 (*GLAJJ*, no. 139).

mixture of different sources, which includes one friendly to Jews as well as a hostile tradition.[250]

Seneca[251]

He spent a part of his youth in Egypt,[252] and thus wrote *De situ et de sacris Aegyptiorum*.[253] He shared the general aversion to oriental religions.[254] His statements concerning the Jews were written during the sixth decade of the first century (thus during a high point of the proselyte movement and the proliferation of Jewish customs). Augustine (*De superstitione, Civ. Dei* 6.11; *GLAJJ*, no. 186) notes that Seneca included in his list of theological superstitions the "sacramenta Iudaeorum et maxime sabbata" ("sacred institutions of the Jews, especially the Sabbath") by which one seventh of one's life was lost. "Cum interim usque eo sceleratissimae gentis consuetudo convaluit, ut per omnes iam terras recepta sit; victi victoribus leges dederunt"[255] ("Meanwhile the customs of the accursed race have gained such influence that they are now received throughout all the world. The vanquished have given laws to their victors"). "Illi [the Jews] tamen causas ritus sui noverunt; maior pars populi[256] facit, quod cur faciat ignorat" ("The Jews, however, are unaware of the origin and meaning of their rites. The greater part of the people go through a ritual not knowing why they do so").

Ep. 95.47 (*GLAJJ*, no. 188; see above pp. 105 n. 188): The Sabbath lamps should be forbidden: the gods need no lamps.

Tacitus

Tacitus (ca. 55 until the time of Trajan) was a good example of the typical Roman political leader, who wrote a history of the empire that extended through the Flavian period. His two principal historical works are the *Historiae* (except for a few fragments, only the first five books have been preserved; they begin after the death of Nero) and the *Annals,* which cover the period from Augustus to Nero (the middle section has been lost).

The section in which we are primarily interested, the "Excursus on the Jews," is found in the fifth book of the *Historiae*. This is the most important text on ancient anti-Semitism, because of the material it contains and because of the

---

[250] Stern (*GLAJJ*, 332) wants to combine a biblical source, a Damascus source, and a hostile Greek-Egyptian version. But one should not speak of a "biblical" source—at the most, of elements from the biblical story.

[251] *GLAJJ*, 429ff.

[252] L. Cantarelli, *Aegyptus* 8 (1927): 89ff.

[253] Servius in *Aen.* 6.154.

[254] Isis, Cybel; *Vit. beat.* 26.8; Augustine, *Civ. Dei* 6.10.

[255] Elsewhere Seneca can appreciate the value of a day of rest, *Tranq.* 17.7.

[256] Non-Jews who adopt Jewish customs.

personal and political evaluations made by the author, who looks back on the Jewish War. It is this concern with the Jewish War that caused him to deal so extensively with the Jews. This excursus summarizes practically everything that previous authors had said and contains new material as well.[257]

Sources[258]

Although the question of sources must of course be raised, it turns out to be of limited value in this case; see Pöschl in Sontheimer, 10: Tacitus presses everything into service for his own viewpoint. The question of sources is only more important in the "Excursus on the Jews" than elsewhere because, and to the extent that, Tacitus himself comments on it several times.

Tacitus and Josephus

The relation of Tacitus to Josephus, who wrote earlier, poses a difficult problem.[259] Tacitus collects oral traditions, for example, from his friend Pliny the Younger (*Ep.* 6.16, 20; *Hist.* 3.38.75; 5.13: *accepimus*). He can also use official documents (*Ann.* 15.74; "reperio in commentariis senatus," "records of the senate"). Groag considers the primary source for parts of the *Historiae,* including the "Excursus on the Jews," to have been Pliny the Elder. His arguments are questionable, however.[260] Groag himself admits that in much of the material Tacitus stands closer to Josephus than to Pliny, but he still argues that

---

[257] Editions of the *Historiae:* E. Koestermann (Heidelberg: C. Winter, 1957); I²/II¹⁻² (1964/ 1969). Latin-German: F. Borst (2nd ed. 1969) (Tusculum); German: W. Sontheimer (1959); F. Eckstein (1960). For further editions and bibliography, see *Kl. Pauly* 5, under Tacitus. Bibliography: L. Schwabe, *PW* 4.1566ff.; R. Syme, *Tacitus,* 2 vols. (Oxford: Clarendon, 1958); *Tacitus,* ed. V. Pöschl, Wege der Forschung 97 (Darmstadt, 1969); commentary on the *Historiae,* by H. Heubner, 5 vols. (Heidelberg, 1963–82). On the "Excursus on the Jews," see A. M. A. Hospers-Jansen, *Tacitus over de Joden* (Gröningen, 1949).

[258] P. Fabia, *Les sources de Tacite dans les Histoires et les Annales* (Paris, 1893); E. Groag, "Zur Kritik von Tacitus' Quellen in den Historien," *Jahrbuch für classische Philologie* Suppl. 23 (1897): 709ff. [Translator's note: See now *GLAJJ,* nos. 273–94.]

[259] E. Norden, "Josephus und Tacitus"; F. Dornseiff, "Lukas der Schriftsteller: Mit einem Anhang: Josephus und Tacitus" *ZNW* 35 (1936): 129–55, 143-55; A. Briessmann, *Tacitus und das flavische Geschichtsbild,* Hermes Einzelschriften 10 (Wiesbaden, 1955).

[260] The alleged peculiar arrangement does not imply anything significant, e.g., that Pliny is the source, for the arrangement itself is not all that remarkable; cf. the structure of the other ethnographic excursuses. If the appeal is made to observations which presumably could only come from eyewitnesses, it should still be noted that it is doubtful whether Pliny himself is such an eyewitness. In addition, shortly after 70 c.e. a literature appeared concerning the war, see *J.W.* 1.1ff., 7f., and Stern, *GLAJJ,* 455 (no. 200). We know of the "Commentaries" of Vespasian (Josephus, *Vita* 358; *Ag. Ap.* 1.56), of a work by a certain Antonius Julianus (from Minucius Felix 33; cf. Josephus, *J.W.* 6.238?) and of the work of Justus of Tiberius, with whom Josephus debated in his *Vita.* Tacitus had correct information concerning the Jews which perhaps came to him via Pliny concerning his superior Tiberius Alexander—for example, concerning monotheism. But he is well known in the literature—and then what would be the source of the stupid anti-Semitic gossip in Tacitus?

Tacitus used a source that had some contacts with Josephus, but that Tacitus himself had certainly not read Josephus ("Zur Kritik," 784).

This latter hypothesis has practically become the general consensus, especially through Eduard Norden. By means of a comparative study made on a broader base, Breissmann came to the conclusion that Tacitus knew the same traditions as Josephus, but more precisely. Compare, for example, Josephus, *J.W.* 4.499 ("Achaia") with Tacitus, *Hist.* 2.1.3 ("Corinth"); and further, *J.W.* 4.98ff. with Tacitus, *Hist.* 2.1.1ff. It is especially instructive to note *J.W.* 4.602 vs. *Hist.* 2.74.2; *J.W.* 4.586 vs. *Hist.* 2.93.1; *J.W.* 4.654 vs. *Hist.* 4.1.1; *J.W.* 7.78f. vs. *Hist.* 4.54.

Tacitus is regarded by Schürer (*History* 2:604) as dependent on Josephus. Dornseiff calls attention to the similarity between *Hist.* 5.7 (Sodom and the Dead Sea) and *J.W.* 4.483f., on which Norden had already commented earlier: "And yet there is no literary dependence, for Tacitus gives different and more precise data regarding the vegetation" ("Josephus and Tacitus," 663). That is, of course, a questionable argument; Dornseiff responds (of course, just as problematically in terms of method): "Really? More precise?" What Tacitus undertook to do has become a rhetorical debate. Cf. Josephus: ἔτι δὲ κἀν τοῖς καρποῖς σποδιὰν ἀναγεννωμένην, οἳ χροιὰν μὲν ἔχουσι τῶν ἐδωδίμων ὁμοίαν, δρεφαμένων δὲ χερσὶν εἰς καπνὸν διαλύονται καὶ τέφραν ("Still, too, may one see ashes reproduced in the fruits, which from their outward appearance would be thought edible, but on being plucked with the hand dissolve into smoke and ashes") Tacitus: "nam cuncta sponte edita aut manu sata, sive herba tenus aut flore seu solidam in speciem adolevere, atra et inania velut in cinerem vanescunt" ("In fact, all the plants there, whether wild or cultivated, turn black, become sterile and seem to wither into dust, either in leaf or in flower or after they have reached their usual mature form") (*GLAJJ*, no. 281).

The supernatural phenomena which both Tacitus and Josephus include in their respective works have played a considerable role in the discussion concerning sources. A survey:

J.W. 6

289:    A constellation resembling a star and a comet visible for a year.

290:    At the Passover in 66 a light shone around the altar and the temple—which was understood as an evil omen.

292:    At the same Passover a cow gave birth to a lamb within the temple area.

293:    The eastern gate of the city opened by itself.

297ff.:   The armies of heaven.

299f.:   (Pentecost) "We are departing."

300ff.:   The prophet Jesus.

312–13:   A χρησμὸς ἀμφίβολος ("ambiguous oracle") also to be found in the sacred Scriptures, ὡς κατὰ τὸν καιρὸν ἐκεῖνον ἀπὸ τῆς χώρας αὐτῶν τις ἄρξει τῆς οἰκουμένης. τοῦθ' οἱ μὲν ὡς οἰκεῖον ἐξέλαβον; ἐδήλου δ' ἄρα τὴν Οὐεσπασιανοῦ τὸ λόγιον ἡγεμονίαν ἀποδειχθέντος ἐπὶ

'Ιουδαίας αὐτοκράτορος ("to the effect that at that time one from their country would become ruler of the world. This they understood to mean someone of their own race. . . . The oracle, however, in reality signified the sovereignty of Vespasian, who was proclaimed Emperor on Jewish soil").

Tacitus, *Hist.* 2.78 (*GLAJJ*, no. 278):

Recursabant (to Vespasian) animo vetera omina. . . . Est Iudaeam inter Syriamque Carmelus: ita vocant montem deumque. Nec simulacrum deo aut templum—sic tradidere maiores—ara tantum et reverentia. Illic sacrificanti Vespasiano . . . Basilides sacerdos inspectis identidem extis: (Quidquid est) inquit, Vespasiane, quod paras . . . datur tibi magna sedes, ingentes termini, multum hominum.

Old omens came back to his mind. . . . Between Judaea and Syria lies Carmel: this is the name given to both the mountain and the divinity. The god has no image or temple—such is the rule handed down by the fathers; there is only an altar and the worship of the god. When Vespasian was sacrificing . . . Basilides, after repeated inspection of the victim's vitals, said to him: "Whatever you are planning, Vespasian, the god grants you a large home, limitless bounds, and a multitude of men."

Hist. 5.13 (*GLAJJ*, no. 281):

Evenerant prodigia, quae neque hostiis neque votis piare fas habet gens superstitioni obnoxia, religionibus adversa. Visa per caelum concurrere acies, rutilantia arma, et subito nubium igne collucere templum. Apertae repente delubri fores et audita maior humana vox, excedere deos; simul ingens motus excedentium. Quae pauci in metum trahebant: pluribus persuasio inerat *antiquis sacerdotum litteris contineri*, eo ipso tempore fore ut valesceret Oriens, profectique Iudaea rerum potirentur. Quae *ambages* Vespasianum ac Titum praedixerat; sed volgus, more humanae cupidinis, sibi tantam fatorum altitudinem interpretati, ne adversis quidem ad vera mutabantur.

Prodigies had indeed occurred, but to avert them either by victims or by vows is held unlawful by a people which, though prone to superstition, is opposed to all propitiatory rites. Contending hosts were seen meeting in the skies, arms flashed and suddenly the temple was illuminated with fire from the clouds. Of a sudden the doors of the shrine opened and a superhuman voice cried: "The gods are departing": at the same moment the mighty stir of their gong was heard. Few interpreted these omens as fearful; the majority firmly believed that their ancient priestly writings contained the prophecy that this was the very time when the East should grow strong and that men starting from Judaea should possess the world. This mysterious prophecy had in reality pointed to Vespasian and Titus, but the common people, as is the way of human ambition, interpreted these great destinies in their own favour, and could not be turned to the truth even by adversity.

Suetonius, *Vesp.* 4f. (*GLAJJ*, no. 312–13):

Percrebruerat Oriente toto vetus et constans opinio esse in fatis ut eo tempore Iudaea profecti rerum potirentur. Id de imperatore Romano, quantum postea eventu paruit, praedictum Iudaei ad se trahentes rebellarunt. . . . Apud Iudaeam Carmeli dei oraculum consulentem ita confirmavere sortes, ut quidquid cogitaret volveretque animo quamlibet magnum, id esse proventurum pollicerentur. Et unus ex nobilibus captivis, Iosephus, cum coiceretur in vincula, constantissime asseveravit fore ut ab eodem brevi solveretur, verum iam imperatore.

There had spread over all the Orient an old and established belief, that it was fated at that time for men coming from Judaea to rule the world. This prediction, referring to the emperor of Rome, as afterwards appeared from the event, the people of Judaea took to themselves; accordingly they revolted. . . . When he [Vespasian] consulted the oracle of the god of Carmel in Judaea, the lots were highly encouraging, promising that whatever he planned or wished, howsoever great it might be, would come to pass; and one of his high-born prisoners, Josephus by name, as he was being put in chains, declared most confidently that he would soon be released by the same man, who would then, however, be emperor.

The supernatural phenomena that are found scattered throughout Josephus are brought together by Tacitus.[261] Structure: (1) The history of the origins of the Jews, of which he gives six versions, with emphasis on the last, most detailed version (plurimi . . . , 5.3; here no longer *oratio obliqua*); (2) description of the land;[262] (3) religion and customs.[263] Tacitus himself gives his reason

---

[261] P. Corssen ("Die Zeugnisse des Tacitus und Pseudo-Josephus über christus," *ZNW* 15 [1914]: 114–40) also argues for the priority of the account in Josephus, affirming that Tacitus can be derived from Josephus, but not the opposite. O. Michel and O. Bauernfeind comment on *J. W.* 6.312: Josephus has the singular; Tacitus 5.13 and Suetonius, *Vesp.* 4 the plural. But in the interpretation, Tacitus switches over to the singular; Josephus thus "no doubt provides the literary source" (*De bello Judaico* [Munich: Kösel, 1959–69] 2:2, 190ff.). Dornseiff: The plural in Tacitus (profecti Iudaea) ("men starting from Judaea") does not refer to Vespasian and Titus, but aloofly to the Messiah and his satellites. On "fore ut valesceret Oriens" ("the East should grown strong") cf. the oracle of Hystaspes and the *Sibyllines*. It is understandable that the court historian Josephus does not record that, but the echo is still there in οἱ μέν ὡς οἰκεῖον ἐξέλαβον ("someone of their own race").

[262] Reinhardt, *Poseidonios,* 60ff.: It is not possible to regard Posidonius as the common source for Josephus, Strabo, Trogus, and Tacitus. The agreements in their arrangement are not sufficient proof, for they derive from Hellenistic history writing in general. This does not necessarily mean that the *content* could not derive from the same source.

Tacitus's critique: "Sic veteres auctores, sed gnari locorum (Plinius?) tradunt" ("Such is the story told by ancient writers, but those who are acquainted with the country aver") (5.6) *J. W.?* Cf. further Strabo 16.2.42; Diodorus 2.48; 19.98f.

Hospers-Jansen, *Tacitus,* 150ff.: Tacitus 5.7 is most probably from Posidonius; *Tacitus,* 147: Pliny and Josephus report without critique matters on which Strabo and Tacitus express doubts; thus Pliny is not intended to be included in the *gnari locorum*.

[263] Cf. the earlier ethnographers and Tacitus on Germany and Britain. E. Wolff in *Tacitus* (Berlin, 1914) 261f. concerning the descriptions of national groups by the Roman historians: in the "Excursus on the Jews" Tacitus deliberately places the description of the origins before the description of the land. Cf. Strabo, Trogus. Reinhardt (*Poseidonios*) considers the scheme to be from Hellenistic history writing.

H. Schreckenberg, *Die Flavius-Josephus-Tradition in Antike und Mittelalter,* Arb. Lit. Gesch. des Hell. Judentums 5 (Leiden: E. J. Brill, 1972): the agreements between Tacitus and Josephus usually

for placing this excursus at this particular point in his work (5.2): it is an introduction to the report of the destruction of Jerusalem (which has been lost).[264]

The Excursus[265]

5.1: Introduction.[266]

Titus takes the initiative and surrounds Jerusalem with his troops.

5.2: "Sed quoniam famosae urbis supremum diem tradituri sumus, congruens videtur, primordia eius aperire" ("However, as I am about to describe the last days of a famous city, it seems proper for me to give some account of its origin").[267]

Then follows, in an extremely objective style, Tacitus's survey of the various hypotheses.

(1) *Memorant* (there is no known parallel to this version): the Jews moved into the remote parts of Libya as refugees from Crete,[268] at the same time as the expulsion of Saturn by Jupiter (5.4: Saturn was expelled *with* Jupiter), i.e., in the mythical times understood euhemeristically. This derivation of the Jews from Crete is based on the name *Iudaei*, which was supposed to be a barbarian development of *Idaei*[269] (a word derived from the mountain "Ida" on Crete).[270]

---

may be explained in terms of the use of a common source (69), cf. *J.W.* 4.483f. with *Hist.* 5.6; *J.W.* 6.312 with *Hist.* 5.13; *Ant.* 18.63f. with *Ann.* 15.44.

[264] Cf. Polybius on Carthage. Reinhardt (*Poseidonios,* 30ff.) contra Jacoby: this is the normal position. Trogus departs arbitrarily from the pattern by sometimes introducing his excursuses at the first reference to a particular national group. He seems to have no problems concerning the consistency of this "pattern." The more recent studies come to mind, e.g., W. Steidle, *Sueton und die antike Biographie* (Munich, 1951), with their doubts concerning whether there was a fixed form for the ancient biography.

[265] Stern, "Jews," 1156; Bib.: E. Paratore, *Tacito,* 2nd ed. (Rome, 1962) 653ff.

[266] Cf. 4.51; Josephus, *J.W.* (4.656ff.; cf. 5.39ff.): Vespasian departs for Rome in order to assume the imperial power.

[267] Suetonius, *Nero* 40 (*GLAJJ,* no. 309): Predictions were made for Nero that in case he should lose his imperial throne, he would receive the rulership of the Orient. Some of these prophecies mentioned Jerusalem in particular, while others predicted that he would be restored to his former power. Cf. Livy, *Per.* 102; *GLAJJ,* no. 131.

[268] What is meant? This is mostly interpreted as referring to that part of Libya on the west, farthest removed from the Mediterranean. Conversely, Borst (see n. 257) understands it to refer to the coastal area of Libya. Regarding Libya, cf. Josephus, *Ant.* 1.240f., and Cleodemus Malchus, *FGH* 727. On the African wife of Moses, see Ezekiel the tragedian (Eusebius, *Praep. Ev.* 9.28.4).

[269] So Koestermann and others; mss read Iudaei.

[270] R. Reitzenstein, *Poimandres* (Leipzig and Berlin: Teubner, 1904) 112: connecting the Jews with the Idaians already presupposes the identification of the Jewish God with Kronos.

Other explanations of the name: according to Alexander Polyhistor (*GLAJJ,* no. 53): derived from the name of a son of Semiramis; according to Trogus 36.2 (*GLAJJ,* no. 137) and Claudius Iolaus, *FGH* 788 F 4 (*GLAJJ,* no. 249), derived from the name of one of the Spartans, Udaios. Plutarch, *Is. Os.* 31; see below, Josephus, *Ant.* 11.173.

The source of this singular version can no longer be determined. What is clear is that the second explanation of the Sabbath (or Sabbath year?) in 5.4 derives from the same source.[271]

(2) *Quidam:* During the time when Isis ruled,[272] the Egyptians unburdened themselves of the unwanted elements in the overflowing population by discharging them into the surrounding countries, under the leadership of Hierosolymus and Iudas.[273]

(3) *Plerique:*[274] "*Aethiopum* prolem, quos rege Cepheo metus atque odium mutare sedes perpulerit" ("Many others think that they were an Ethiopian stock, which in the reign of Cepheus was forced to migrate by fear and hatred").[275] This version too is singular.[276]

(4) "Sunt qui tradant *Assyrios* convenas" ("Still others report that they were Assyrian refugees");[277] since they lacked adequate farmland, the Jews seized a part of Egypt.[278] "Mox proprias urbes Hebraeasque terras et propiora Syriae coluisse" ("Then later they had their own cities and lived in the Hebrew territory and the nearer parts of Syria").[279]

---

[271] Hospers-Jansen, *Tacitus*, 111ff.: The explanation of the Cretan origination of the Jews cannot be derived from 2 Sam. 8:18 (contra C. Meiser, *Tacitus Histoires* [1884]; and H. Goelzer, *Tacitus Histoires* [Paris: Coll. des Univ. de France, 1920]). The objection is to be accepted. In addition, the source was Latin, for it is easier to derive Iudaei from Idaei than from the corresponding Greek form; cf. Iulus/Ilus (Vergil, *Aen.* 1.267f.). This derivation is in fact clearly Roman, for it is intended to point to the Julians. Dio 37.17 indicates that he does not know how the name "Jew" originated.

[272] An analogous euhemerism.

[273] Cf. Diodorus 1.28 (*GLAJJ*, no. 55); Plutarch, *Is. Os.* 31.363 D (*GLAJJ*, no. 259; authors who are criticized by Plutarch): several authors believe that Hierosolymos and Iudaios were the sons of Typhon: αὐτόθεν εἰσὶ κατάδηλοι τὰ Ἰουδαϊκὰ παρέλχοντες εἰς τὸν μῦθον ([These authors] "are manifestly, as the very names show, attempting to draw Jewish traditions into legend"). Is this an indication of an anti-Jewish source (Typhon!) or merely pure speculation? No firm decision can be made. Hospers-Jansen, *Tacitus*, 133ff.: Plutarch polemicizes against a variation of Tacitus's version (cf. Stern, *GLAJJ*, 563: from circles hostile to Judaism). In any case, the source can no longer be determined (Apion as such could not have been the source; K. Ziegler, "Plutarchos," *PW* 21.845).

[274] This represents an intensification, then (4) and (5) a sort of catching of the breath in preparation for the climax of the whole list in no. 6.

[275] Haraeus: metus ("fear") ipsorum ("of ourselves"); odium ("hatred") popularium Aethiopum ("of the people of Ethiopia"); Cepheus: Father of Andromache; mostly an Ethiopian setting; on Joppa, see Pliny, *Hist. Nat.* 5.69; Josephus, *J.W.* 3.420; Pausanias 4.35.9; the mythographer Konon, *FGH* 26 F 1 (*GLAJJ*, no. 145).

[276] Hospers-Jansen, *Tacitus*, 115f.: It is supposed that the environs of Joppa were governed by Ethiopia. Cf. the birthplace of Cepheus (Pliny, *Hist. Nat.* 6.182). Has "Ethiopia" been derived rather fancifully from such passages as Herodotus 2.104 (*GLAJJ*, no. 1; circumcision of the Colchians, Egyptians, Ethiopians, Phoenicians, and Syrians)? Cf. Josephus, *Ant.* 8.161; and in addition the legend of the Ethiopian military campaign of Moses; cf. Artapanus; Josephus, *Ant.* 2.239ff.

[277] A variation of the "eastern" tradition. Alexander Polyhistor: descended from Semiramis; in addition, Nicholas of Damascus, *FGH* 90 F 19 (Josephus, *Ant.* 1.159; *GLAJJ*, no. 83); see also Pompeius Trogus 36.2 (*GLAJJ*, no. 137).

[278] Cf. on the one side Jewish writers on Joseph and Moses, and on the other side "Manetho" on the "shepherds."

[279] Pompeius Trogus 36.2: Moses returns to Damascus, the ancient homeland of the people.

(5) *alii:* The Jews enjoyed an illustrious origin, for they were in fact identical with Homer's Solymians,[280] who founded a city which they named Hierosolyma.[281]

(6) 5.3: *"Plurimi* auctores consentiunt" ("Many authors agree").[282] Here appears the Alexandrian version of the expulsion of the leprous under Bokchoris after the oracle of Hammon had been consulted.[283] Moyses, one of those who had been expelled, declared to the others that they should expect no help from either God or humanity, since they have been abandoned by both.[284] "Et sibimet duce [cj. duci; et duci; ut duci] caelesti crederent, primo cuius auxilio praesentes miserias pepulissent.[285] Adsensere atque omnium

---

Pliny, *Hist. Nat.* 5.67 (*GLAJJ*, no. 204): some authors regard Idumaea and Judea as a part of Syria; 5.70: "pars eius [sc. Judäas] Syriae iuncta Galilaea vocatur" ("The part of Judaea adjoining Syria is called Galilee").

[280] Homer, *Il.* 6.184, 204; *Od.* 5.282; cf. Choerilus of Samos, *FGH* 696 F 34e (Josephus, *Ag. Ap.* 1.172f.; Eusebius, *Praep. Ev.* 9.9: Choerilus refers to soldiers in Xerxes' army, including those who speak Phoenician, inhabitants of the Solymer mountains. Josephus considers them to be Jews. For the location of the Solymer mountains, see Strabo 14.3.9.

[281] Hierosolyma=Solyma: Josephus, *J. W.* 4.438f.; *Ant.* 7.67 (cf. 180). Solyma: Pausanius 8.16.4; Philostratus, *Vit. Apoll.* 6.29, etc.; Latin poets (metrically!).

[282] The most extensive account of a version with which Tacitus himself is in agreement can be found most easily in Lysimachus (*GLAJJ*, no. 158); Hospers-Jansen, *Tacitus,* 119ff.; I. Lévy, "Tacite," *Latomus* 5 (1946): 339.

[283] See Lysimachus on the chronological question. Tacitus does not trouble himself with the date of Bokchoris. For additional data concerning the period and the names of the kings, see the survey in Josephus, *Ag. Ap.* 2.15–17 (*GLAJJ*, no. 165) (esp. "Manetho" and Apion); Ptolemy of Mendes, *FGH* 611 F 1a, from Tatian 38 (*GLAJJ*, no. 157a) and Clement of Alexandria, *Strom.* 1.101.5 synchronizes Amosis (cf. "Manetho") and Inachos (rejected by Apion). Alexander Polyhistor, *FGH* 273 F 101a–b: Moses was a contemporary of Ogygus, i.e., 1770 or 1775 b.c.e.; cf. Josephus and Lysimachus.

[284] Manetho (*FGH* 609 F 10; Josephus, *Ag. Ap.* 1.239; *GLAJJ*, no. 21): Osarsiph gives the νόμος, μήτε προσκυεῖν Θεούς ("law that they should neither worship the gods"). See Lysimachus, *FGH* 621 F 1 (Josephus, *Ag. Ap.* 1.309; *GLAJJ*, no. 158); Apion, *FGH* 616 F 41 (Josephus, *Ag. Ap.* 2.121; *GLAJJ*, no. 173). Thus one can also perceive Alexandrian tradition in Tacitus; cf. also what follows.

[285] The meaning? (1) Heraeus: *pepulissent* "is to be understood as a future subjunctive with a view to the present"; see 1.74 *legisset;* 3.63, Livy 23.19 *abscessisset.* (2) Reinach: "sibi, [ut] duci caelesti; . . . mais de se fier à lui comme à un guide envoyé par le ciel et le premier (!) qui eût soulagé leurs misères présentes" ("but to put their trust in him as a guide sent by heaven and the first who had eased their present distress"). (3) Bornecque: "sed sibi ut duci caelesti . . . mais de se fier à lui comme à un guide céleste, le premier qui, leur procurant de secours, les délivrerait des maux présents" ("but to put their trust in him as a heavenly guide, the first who, procuring for them and, delivered them from a bad present"). (4) Sontheimer: "They should rather have been confident in themselves, under the guidance of God, for above all it is with his help that they could have averted the present troubles." This is a correct translation of *pepulissent,* even though there is nothing in the text about such a preceding averting of troubles.

On *sibimet,* etc.: This would then have to mean that the idea shimmers through Tacitus's text that Moses teaches about a new God. But is that really the meaning? Does not *sibimet* refer to the speaker, in *oratio obliqua* (oblique speech), i.e., Moses, who presents *himself* as the heavenly leader. Then, of course, *(ut) duci* must be read. (5) Eckstein: ". . . but rather to trust in him as a leader sent by heaven, who was the first one to help them out of their present troubles." But where is *sibimet*

ignari fortuitum iter incipiunt" ("But to trust to themselves, regarding as a guide sent from heaven the one whose assistance should first give them escape from their present distress. They agreed, and then set out on their journey in utter ignorance, but trusting to chance").

They suffered much from thirst. But a herd of wild asses appeared, which the Jews followed and "coniectura herbidi soli largas aquarum venas aperit" ("conjecturing the truth from the grassy ground discovered abundant streams of water").[286] (Bible, Josephus, Lysimachus).[287]

(4) *Customs:* Moses introduced: (with the goal) "quo sibi in posterum gentem firmaret) *novos ritus contrariosque ceteris mortalibus*" ("to establish his influence over this people for all time, *new religious practices, quite opposed to those of all other religions*"). Here the rule applies: "Profana illic omnia quae apud nos sacra, rursum concessa apud illos quae nobis incesta" ("The Jews regard as profane all that we hold sacred; on the other hand, they permit all that we abhor").[288]

---

and *pepulissent* in this translation? (6) Borst: "They should rather, in view of the heavenly leadership under which they stood, trust in themselves; it is above all through this heavenly helper that they will be able to overcome the present misery." But here too: does *pepulissent* get an adequate translation? (7) C. J. Classen (in a letter dated 22 March 1976): "In my opinion there is no problem in seeing Moses as having referred to earlier event—*praesentes miseriae* can well be those 'immediately pressing worries and cares' (not only those that are objectively present at the moment), even if Tacitus had not previously spoken of these events. One of my colleagues considers this a possible shifting of tenses (cf. the grammar of Kühner-Stegmann, *Syntax* I, 141); but this is not documented in Tacitus. I would thus exclude this interpretation."

Tacitus's manner of expression appears to be best understood as an abbreviation of a text such as that of Lysimachus (Josephus, *Ag. Ap.* 1.308f.; *GLAJJ*, no. 158); cf. also Pompeius Trogus 36.2.13 (*GLAJJ*, no. 137): [Moses] "dux igitur exulum factus" ("Becoming leader, accordingly, of the exiles").... Deliverance from the pursuing Egyptians. Tacitus could have omitted some such phrase as this. In any case, *pepulissent* refers to something previous.

[286] A distortion of Exod. 15:22ff.; Num. 33:8f. *Venas aperit:* Does this mean "find" or "open"? The first makes the better sense, for asses of course drink. Reinach: "He uncovered." Bornecque: "il devine et ouvre" ("he predicted and opened"). Sontheimer: "found." Eckstein: "discovered." Reinach: Although the episode is not found in the extant MSS of Lysimachus and Apion, it is certainly derived from an Alexandrian author; cf. the allusion in Plutarch, *Quaest. Conv.* 4.5.2 (*GLAJJ*, no. 258).

[287] Concerning the ass, and Typhons seven-day flight on an ass, see Plutarch, *Is. Os.* 31 (*GLAJJ*, no. 259); Apion; Pompeius Trogus 36.2.14 (*GLAJJ*, no. 137).

[288] That is a (typically Roman!) variation of the topos of ἀπανθρωπία "apud nos" ("misanthropy among *us*")! "res novae [contra] mos maiorum" ("a new thing contrary to the custom of our revered ancestors!"). Cf. 5.5, where there is somewhat of a self-correction! That then there was a conscious attitude of the Jews against the Egyptians here illustrated is another indication of the source of the materials which are here used. (But cf. also what is said regarding the Egyptians in 5.5).

See Hecataeus, *FGH* 264 F 6.4 (Diodorus 40.3) (*GLAJJ*, no. 11): The peculiarity of the laws is based, on the one hand, on the experience of being expelled and, on the other hand, on providing for the future. See further Apollonius Molon and Lysimachus (Josephus, *Ag. Ap.* 2.145; *GLAJJ*, no. 161); Posidonius, *FGH* 87 F 109.2 (Diodorus 34); "Manetho" (Josephus, *Ag. Ap.* 1.240, 248ff.; *GLAJJ*, no. 21); Lysimachus (Josephus, *Ag. Ap.* 1.309; *GLAJJ*, no. 158); Apion (Josephus, *Ag. Ap.* 2.121). Trogus gives as explanations for the peculiarity of their laws (a) isolation because of anxiety

Characteristically, the story of the image of the ass comes as the high point of the narrative: "effigiem animalis, quo monstrante errorem sitimque depulerant, penetrali scravere,[289] caeso ariete velut in contumeliam Hammonis.[290] Bos quoque immolatur quia [or, better, *quoniam*] Aegyptii Apin colunt; sue abstinent"[291] ("They dedicated, in a shrine, a statue of that creature whose guidance enabled them to put an end to their wandering and thirst, sacrificing a ram, apparently in derision of Ammon. They likewise offer the ox, because the Egyptians worship Apis. They abstain from pork"). This abstention is historically grounded, with a reference to leprosy.[292]

The Jews have frequent fasts—in memory of the long period of hunger they had suffered.[293] "Jewish bread" contains no leaven—a memorial of the fruits of which they were once robbed.[294] The seventh day is celebrated by resting, "quia is finem laborum tulerit" ("because that day ended their toils").[295]

Since the Jews had developed a taste for idleness, they also observed every seventh *year* as a year of rest.[296] Another explanation comes from the same source as 5.2 (Cretan-Idan origin).[297] The Sabbath is observed in honor of

---

about being infected and (b) from what was once a relevant reason for such laws there gradually developed *mos* and *religio* ("custom and religion").

[289] We thus have, as in the case of Hecataeus, a historical grounding, and thus a contradiction to §9. According to the principle of contrast with the Egyptians, we would expect Typhon to be mentioned here, but he is absent. A peculiarity (and an indication of the origin) is the argument based on a consistent contrast with the Egyptians.

[290] Does this refer merely to a dedication ceremony for an image of an ass which occurred only once? Cf. the *penetrali sacravere* ("sacrificing a ram").

[291] The Egyptian origin of this explanation is clear. Cf. 5.3 above: the reproach against the Egyptian gods. Cf. also the variations of Manetho, *FGH* 609 F 10 (Josephus, *Ag. Ap.* 1.239; *GLAJJ*, no. 21): the Jews do not practice any abstention from eating the meat of the sacred animals of Egypt.

[292] Eating pork is regarded as the same as leprosy; Manetho, *FGH* 609 F 23 (Aelian, *De Natura Animalium* 10.16); Plutarch, *Quest. Conv.* 4.5.3 (*GLAJJ*, 559). That the Egyptian priests also abstain from pork is affirmed by Sextus Empiricus, *Pyr.* 3.223 (Reinach, *Textes*, 170).

[293] "*Longam olim famem.*" Above it was seven days; a contamination of the source? But see Pompeius Trogus: they fast on the Sabbath because the famine was over after seven days (36.2.14; *GLAJJ*, no. 137).

[294] But nothing had been said about this; thus once again a source has been abbreviated. Obviously Tacitus thinks that the Jews eat only such bread.

[295] Cf. Pompeius Trogus 36.2.14; differently Apion.

[296] Reinach, *Textes*, 306 n. 1: This is the only reference to the Sabbath year in pagan literature. Schürer, *History* 1:35f.: it was already referred to by the pagan author used by Josephus (*J.W.* 1.60=*Ant.* 13.234). But this "use" is improbable. Democritus, *FGH* 730 F 1 (*GLAJJ*, no. 247): every seven years there was a ritual sacrifice.

[297] What follows is not a second explanation of the Sabbath *year*, as might be supposed from the way the text is worded, but an explanation of the Sabbath, which was of course the day of Saturn; Tibullus (*GLAJJ*, no. 126); Dio 64.7 (the conquest of Jerusalem on the day of Kronos); Frontinus (*GLAJJ*, no. 229): "Divus Augustus Vespasianus Iudaeos Saturni die, quo eis nefas est quicquam seriae rei agere, adortus superavit" ("The deified Augustus Vespasian attacked the Jews on the day of Saturn, a day on which it is sinful for them to do any business, and defeated them").

Saturn,[298] either because the origins of their religion came to them by means
of the Idains or because of the seven stars that rule over mortals (text: *mortales;*
Nipperday: *mortalia*). Saturn rotates in the highest sphere and with special
power[299] "and directs the orbits and rotation of most of the heavenly bodies
according to a pattern based on the number seven."

5.5: "Hi ritus, quoquo modo inducti, *antiquitate defenduntur*" ("Whatever
their origin, these rites are *maintained by their antiquity*"). The contrast is
strongly emphasized: *"cetera instituta,* sinistra foeda, pravitate valuere. Nam
pessimus quisque, *spretis religionibus patriis,* tributa et stipes illuc congerebant,
unde auctae Iudaeorum res" ("the other customs of the Jews are base and
abominable, and owe their persistence to their depravity: for the worst rascals
among other peoples, renouncing their ancestral religions, always kept sending
tribute and contributing to Jerusalem, thereby increasing the wealth of the Jews").

That refers, of course, to proselytes (cf. Philo, *Spec. Leg.* 1.309) and the temple
tax (although Tacitus wrote in the period when the *fiscus Iudaicus* was already
in effect); but it was normally the case that ancient historians continued to
repeat inadequate information which was contained in their sources.

We can hardly ask whether Tacitus also thought of the image of the ass in
connection with the time-honored rites; cf. the ambiguity of the expression in
5.4 and the contradiction between 4 and 9.

Hospers-Jansen (*Tacitus,* 130ff.) assumes that there was influence from Posidonius (contra Reinhardt, *Poseidonios,* 61). There is no indication that evolu-
tion, in the sense of a theory or history, played any role in Tacitus's thinking.
His respect for ancient tradition is not based on the stoic philosophical understanding but is simply that of the average Roman.

One may compare Tacitus with Quintilian, who is satisfied to determine the
beginning of the *superstitio:* "Et est conditoribus urbium infame contraxisse
aliquam perniciosam ceteris gentem, qualis est primus Iudaicae superstitionis
auctor" ("Founders of cities are detested for concentrating a race which is a
curse to others, as for example the founder of the Jewish superstition") (*Inst.*
3.7.21; *GLAJJ,* no. 230). For Celsus's relatively defensive stance with reference
to ancient Judaism vis-à-vis the new Christian religion, see above.

Next follows Tacitus's picture of contemporary Judaism: among themselves
they practice *misericordia* ("compassion")[300] but against all others hostile *odium*
("enmity"):[301] "separati epulis, discreti cubilibus,[302] proiectissima ad libidinem

---

[298] Thus a Greek or Roman interpretation: the Jewish god Saturn.

[299] Here there is a seam in the text, and the Cretan source ends.

[300] The familiar topos of the inner cohesion of the Jews (Rome: Cicero!), in which the Jews
themselves took pride; Josephus, *Ag. Ap.* 2.175ff., 279ff.; Aristides, *Apol.* 14.3.

[301] This topos too has been present from the beginning in descriptions of the Jews and debates
concerning them: Manetho, Hecataeus, Posidonius, *FGH* 87 F 109 (μίσος, no table fellowship);
Apollonius Molon (ὡς ἀθέους καὶ μισανθρώπους) ("as atheists and misanthropes") (*GLAJJ,* no. 49);
Lysimachus (Josephus, *Ag. Ap.* 1.309; *GLAJJ,* no. 158); Apion (Josephus, *Ag. Ap.* 2.121; *GLAJJ,* no.
173); Origen, *Contra Cels.* 5.41. Contra, e.g., Josephus, *Ag. Ap.* 2.146, 209; Philo, *Virt.* 51ff.

[302] That is the Jewish law: Josephus, *Ant.* 8.191; Gal. 2:12; John 4:9f.; Acts 10:28. On Jewish

gens alienarum concubitu abstinent,[303] inter se nihil inlicitum"[304] ("They sit apart at meals and they sleep apart, and although as a race, they are prone to lust, they abstain from intercourse with foreign women; yet among themselves nothing is unlawful").

They practice circumcision as a distinctive badge by which they recognize each other.[305] Proselytes are taught "contemnere deos,[306] exuere patriam,[307] parentes liberos fratres vilia habere"[308] ("to despise the gods, to disown their country, and to regard their parents, children, and brothers as of little account").

And they are interested in the numerical growth of their own national group: "nam et necare quemquam ex agnatis nefas,[309] animosque proelio aut suppliciis peremptorum aeternos putant: hinc generandi amor et moriendi contemptus"[310] ("for they regard it as a crime to kill any late-born child, and they believe that the souls of those who are killed in battle or by the executioner are immortal; hence comes their passion for begetting children, and their scorn of death").

Tacitus describes the religious metaphysic of the Jews in comparison to the religion of Egypt: the Jews derived their views concerning the netherworld and their burial practices from the Egyptians.[311] This is contrasted with their views of the *caelestia* ("heavenly things"): The Egyptians worship animals and images.

---

social regulations concerning association with non-Jews, see Billerbeck, *Kommentar* 4:353ff., 374ff.; *connubium* 378f.; Philo, *Spec. Leg.* 3.29. G. Kittel, *Das Konnubium mit den Nicht-Juden im antiken Judentum*, Forschungen zur Judenfrage II (Hamburg, 1938) 30ff.; *Jub.* 30:7; *Testament of Levi* 24:5-8; Josephus, *Ag. Ap.* 2.199ff. meanders apologetically through this issue (209f.). That would have been for Tacitus a confirmation of his evaluation of proselytes.

[303] Sexual relations with non-Jewish women: Billerbeck, *Kommentar* 1:298.

[304] The reproach of libertinism is singular, but obviously not first introduced by Tacitus himself; cf. the representation of Jewish sexual morality, which is obviously tinged with apologetic motifs in Philo, *Spec. Leg.* 3.7ff.; Josephus, *Ant.* 3.274ff.; *Ag. Ap.* 2.199ff.

[305] In Strabo (Posidonius, *FGH* 87 F 70.37) this is an indication of degeneration. Tacitus says nothing of the Egyptian origin of the same (cf. Dio 1.28; *GLAJJ*, no. 55, etc.); this would, of course, not fit his idea that Jewish customs stood in tension with those of the Egyptians (of course, the present text refers only to the ancient customs, among which circumcision was not included). Circumcision did in fact play a role as an identification mark when it had to be established whether or not one was subject to the obligation of paying the *fiscus Iudaicus* (Suetonius, *Domitian* 12; *GLAJJ*, no. 320).

[306] Another instance of the topos of "godlessness," which derived from Jewish monotheism and rejection of images. Philo and Josephus emphasize that Jews are not permitted to slander foreign gods (Philo, *Vit. Mos.* 2.205; *Spec. Leg.* 1.53; Josephus, *Ag. Ap.* 2.237; cf. *Ant.* 4.207).

[307] That means something different for a Roman than for a Greek urbanite in the East.

[308] Mark 10:29; Philo, *Vit. Cont.* 18.

[309] *agnatis:* Koestermann; Heraeus: cf. Gloss Philox: *agnati=epigonoi*. On the commandment to raise all their children (i.e., not to expose them) and the topos on the polyanthropy of the people, cf. Hecataeus, *FGH* 264 F 6.8; Josephus, *Ag. Ap.* 2.202f.

[310] Martyrdom: 2 and 4 Maccabees; Pseudo-Hecataeus; Josephus, *Ag. Ap.* 1.190ff. (*GLAJJ*, no. 12; Josephus, *J.W.* 2.152f. (Essenes); *Ag. Ap.* 2.232; cf. 1.42; 2.279ff.; cf. 2.283; Schlatter, *Theologie des Judentums*, 134. The battle for Jerusalem offered Tacitus illustrative material.

[311] The latter can be understood only as an emphasis on the rejection of cremation.

"Iudaei *mente sola*,[312] *unumque numen* intellegunt"[313] ("the Jews conceive of one god only, and that with the mind only") "profanos, qui deum imagines mortalibus materiis in species hominum effingant; summum illud et aeternum neque imitabile neque interiturum"[314] ("they regard as impious those who make from perishable materials representations of gods in man's image; that supreme and eternal being is to them incapable of representation and without end").

Tacitus perceives the political implications of this: "igitur nulla simulacra urbibus suis nedum templis sistunt; non regibus haec adulatio, non Caesaribus honor"[315] ("Therefore they set up no statues in their cities, still less in their temples; this flattery is not paid their kings, nor this honor given to the Caesars").

The polemic that follows returns to a nonpolitical perspective: on the basis of some of their cultic practices,[316] it is supposed by some that they worship

---

[312] Cicero, *Tusc.* 1.66: "mens soluta quaedam et libera, segregata ab omni concretione mortali" ("a mind unfettered and free, severed from all perishable matter").

[313] That corresponds to the first commandment in its Hellenistic-Jewish exposition; Philo, *Monarch.* (*Spec. Leg.* 1, etc.); Josephus, *Ag. Ap.* 2.193, etc.; Philo, *Decal.*

"*Mente sola*": usually the contradiction with §4 (image of the ass) is pointed out here. There can be no doubt that there are inconsistencies, for example, through combination of sources; cf. §9. But we may ask whether Tacitus does not intend to refer to the distant past, differently than his source (despite §5.1).

[314] We may here once again call to mind the most important references:

(1) Hecataeus: No image of the deity is possible. God is not anthropomorphic, but only the sky itself.

(2) Strabo (Posidonius, *FGH* 87 F 70.35): God is in the form of neither animals (Egypt) nor of humans (Greeks), but rather τὸ περιέχον ἡμᾶς ἅπαντας ("the one thing alone that encompasses us all"). Reinhardt (*Poseidonios,* 12 n. 1) on Tacitus and Dio 37.17.2; *GLAJJ,* no. 406: "The 'inexpressible,' 'invisible' God, 'pure Spirit,' in contrast to 'perishable matter': this God is foreign to Posidonius, so foreign that he also does not recognize him in the God of Jews, in whom he would have had to have recognized him, if he had recognized him at all." This argument is incomprehensible to me.

(3) On imageless representation among the Romans, see above under Varro.

(4) Dio Cassius 37.17.1f.; *GLAJJ,* no. 406: Writing after the constitution of Caracallas, he acknowledges his own ignorance of the origin of the name "Jews," confirms the spread of Judaism also among the Romans, despite frequent repressive measures, ὥστε καὶ ἐς παρρησίαν τῆς νομίσεως ἐκνικῆσαι· κεχωρίδαται δὲ ἀπὸ τῶν λοιπῶν ἀνθρώπων ἔς τε τἆλλα τὰ περὶ τὴν δίαιταν πάνθ' ὡς εἰπεῖν, καὶ μάλισθ' ὅτι τῶν μὲν ἄλλων θεῶν οὐδένα τιμῶσιν, ἕνα δέ τινα ἰσχυρῶς σέβουσιν. οὐδ' ἄγαλμα οὐδὲν [οὐδ'] ἐν αὐτοῖς ποτε τοῖς Ἱεροσολύμοις ἔσχον, ἄρρητον δὲ δὴ καὶ ἀειδῆ αὐτὸν νομίζοντες εἶναι περισσότατα ἀνθρώπων θρησκεύουσι ("and has won its way to the right of freedom in its observances. They are distinguished from the rest of humanity in practically every detail of life, and especially by the fact that they do not honor any of the usual gods, but show extreme reverence for one particular divinity. They never had any statue of him even in Jerusalem itself, but believing him to be unnamable and invisible, they worship him in the most extravagant fashion on earth"). On ἄρρητος ("unutterable") and the like, see Norden, *Agnostos Theos,* 56ff.

[315] Cf. Apion and the defense of Josephus in *Ag. Ap.* 2.73 (*GLAJJ,* no. 169); Tacitus, 5.9 (*GLAJJ,* no. 281): Caligula.

[316] The priests made music and made ivy crowns for themselves; a golden vine was found in the temple (see Josephus, *J.W.* 5.210; *Ant.* 15.395; *b. Middot* 3.8c).

the Liber pater-Bacchus (Plutarch, *Quaest. Conv.* 4.6.2; *GLAJJ*, 560), the conqueror of the Orient. By no means! "Quippe Liber festos laetosque ritus posuit, Iudaeorum mos absurdus sordidusque" ("For Liber established festive rites for a joyous nature, while the ways of the Jews are preposterous and mean").

5.6–8: The description of the land now follows, corresponding to the common pattern. This flows into a short description of Jerusalem and the temple, which reads at first as though they had not been destroyed. But then Tacitus shifts to the imperfect: "ad fores tantum Iudaeis aditus, limine, praeter sacerdotes, arcebantur"[317] ("Only a Jew might approach its doors, and all save the priests were forbidden to cross the threshold").

This is followed by an outline of the history of the Jews, again in accordance with the usual pattern (on the pattern, see Pompeius Trogus 36). Tacitus too includes the series of the four pre-Roman empires—Assyrians, Medes, Persians, Macedonians—with his own characteristic nuance: under the rulership of the first three, the Jews were "despectissima pars servientium" ("regarded as the meanest of their subject").

Then came the Macedonians. "Rex Antiochus demere superstitionem et mores Graecorum dare adnisus, quominus taeterrimam gentem in melius mutaret, Parthorum bello prohibitus est" ("King Antiochus endeavored to abolish Jewish superstition and to introduce Greek civilization; the war with the Parthians, however, prevented his improving this basest of peoples").

The Jews took advantage of the weakness of the Macedonians, just as they did that of the Parthians, who were just beginning to emerge,[318] and crowned kings for themselves. This in turn led to a situation of anarchy and criminality: the kings were dethroned and driven out, then returned and committed the most heinous atrocities against the people (this is in good Tacitus style, his typical view of kings). But they cultivated "superstitio, quia honor sacerdotii firmamentum potentiae adsumebatur"[319] ("the national superstition, for they had assumed the priesthood to support their civil authority").

Then Pompey conquered the Jews; he entered the temple, "iure victoriae,[320] inde vulgatum nulla intus dei effigie vacuam sedem et inania arcana"[321] ("by

---

[317] Thus Tacitus has in fact no accurate idea of the factual relationships: see Philo, *Leg.* 212; Josephus, *J.W.* 5.186f., 193f., 219; 6.124ff.; *Ant.* 15.391ff., 417; *Ag. Ap.* 2.103ff.; the familiar table of prohibitions.

[318] "Et Romani procul erant" ("and keeping their distance from the Romans"). Contra Pompeius Trogus 36.3.9: The Jews were the first Orientals to win the friendship of the Romans, and freedom (*GLAJJ*, no. 137).

[319] The unity of the kingship and the priestly office: Pompeius Trogus 36.2.16 (but: from the beginning).

[320] Cf. Josephus, *J.W.* 1.152 (*Ant.* 14.72); Livy, *Per.* 102 (*GLAJJ*, no. 131): "inviolatum ante id tempus" ("Jerusalem, never invaded before"); not in Strabo, Appian.

[321] Sontheimer: The place was empty and had nothing to do with the secret cult of the Jews. Josephus, *J.W.* 5.219.

right of conquest, thereafter it was a matter of common knowledge that there were no representations of the gods within, but that the place was empty and the secret shrine contained nothing").

The historical sketch then quickly proceeds to the siege of Jerusalem.[322] With this, the section on supernatural wonders (5.13; see above) rounds off the chapter and brings the subject temporarily to a close.

The scene shifts to the simultaneous military events in the northwest (the revolt of the Batavi under Civilis). The remaining account of the Jewish War has been lost.[323]

With this, we have the most complete summary to be found in the ancient "anti-Semitic" literature.[324]

SUMMARY: ANCIENT "ANTI-SEMITISM"

The thesis of Sevenster affirms that it was the Jewish law that provoked the most opposition in ancient "anti-Semitism." It is, of course, incontestable that the law was an essential factor.

But to what extent? The first commandment was that of monotheism, and the other nine were related to it, e.g., the prohibition of images. But other legal prescriptions were not so related, e.g., the prohibition against eating pork. So distinctions must be made. The ancient world was able here and there to come to terms with the Jewish insistence on monotheism—even, to take an extreme example, their refusal to participate in the Caesar cult. An anti-Jewish "movement" existed in antiquity only from time to time, and in certain localities. Thus there was no such thing in antiquity as a continuing anti-Semitic stream,

---

[322] The following are excerpted from the events mentioned by Tacitus:

The prelude was formed by Simon's attempt at usurpation after the death of Herod (he was defeated by Varus); Josephus, *J.W.* 2.57ff.; *Ant.* 17.273ff. The deposing of Archelaus and the installing of the first prefect are not mentioned, although Tacitus knows of Pilate (*Ann.* 15.44: the execution of Christ).

The decree of Caligula to place his image in the temple; cf. Philo, *Leg.* 207ff.

The transfer of Judea to the authority of a Roman governor by Claudius. Felix is accentuated (with the famous characterization).—As though this was the first time for such governors.

[323] Without a trace? Some suppose that Tacitus stands behind two notes of the Christian author Sulpicius Severus, one describing the siege of the Jerusalem and the other a note concerning the military council of Titus immediately prior to the destruction of the city: Titus and others wanted to destroy the temple in order to abolish the religion of the Jews (and the Christians). Differently Josephus, *J.W.* 1.28; cf. 6.220ff., 228, 238ff. Michel and Bauernfeind, *De bello Judaico* 2:2, 173f. n. 108.

[324] Sherwin-White, *Racial Prejudice,* 99: "You may call the attitude of Juvenal and Tacitus anti-Semitic, because it is a dislike of the Jews based on their way of life. But it is a negative anti-Semitism. No violent action followed from it, if only because the Jews were knocking on no Roman doors." E. H. Flannery, *The Anguish of the Jews* (New York: Macmillan, 1965) 19: The real anti-Semites in the Roman Empire were neither the emperor nor the people, but the intelligentsia.

but rather the continuity of the Jewish people with their consciousness of being an elected people, which included the readiness to accept the consequences of such a self-understanding. There was continuity in their awareness of their duty to be loyal to the Torah. Even today this Jewish consciousness cannot be encroached upon by any attempt at Christian–Jewish rapprochement.

For Christians, there can be no acknowledgment of the people of Israel as an especially holy people, nor of Israel's law. But instead of attempting to find a basis for religious agreement, it is thoroughly possible to attempt a rapprochement on human grounds, since Christians stand under the commandment of love, which is the end of the law.

III

THE DEBATE OF HELLENISTIC JUDAISM WITH THE HELLENISTIC-ROMAN WORLD

PRELIMINARY REMARKS

Basic Features of Hellenistic-Jewish Thought

How was the content of faith[1] related to the methods of intellectual and political self-expression available to one in a foreign (and often hostile) world, if faith in the *one* God was simply inseparable from obedience to his law (a law partly already written and partly still in the process of oral transmission and expansion)? How was this possible if God and the existence of the Jewish people as a cohesive religious community were considered to be simply inseparable? Was there any other possibility than that of keeping one's distance from such a world (amixia)?

On the other hand, there were other, more *positive* possibilities, since this God was the creator and ruler of the world and of all humanity, and since his law was also the law of the world and of nature.[2]

Within this framework of thought, how far did the neutral field extend, that area within which one could cultivate not only social but also intellectual associations with Gentiles? There was considerable room for discretionary decisions within the Jewish way of life, and that due to the nature of the Jewish faith itself. One only has to think of the different Jewish groups! There was

---

[1] D. Lührmann, "Pistis im Judentum," *ZNW* 64 (1973): 19–38: to the extent that the word does not mean "loyalty" in general (Pseudo-Hecataeus, Josephus, *Ag. Ap.* 2.43; thus essentially in Josephus), it is in any case not a specifically missionary term (contra Bultmann, *TDNT* 6:197, 202). On Philo, esp. *Abr.* 262ff. (on Gen. 15:6) and *Rer. Div. Her.* See H. Thyen, *TR* n.F. 23 (1955): 237ff.; H. Braun, *Wie man über Gott nicht Denken soll* (Tübingen: Mohr-Siebeck, 1971) 79ff.

[2] See below, esp. Philo, *Decal.* and, for the specifically Jewish regulations, *Spec. Leg.*

no structured systematic theology. But where was the boundary that must not be crossed if that which was distinctively Jewish was not to be surrendered? Which themes had to be pressed forward in the debate, and which could be kept in the background? That in this process opportunistic tactics played a certain role is obvious, and from the point of view of Jewish presuppositions themselves to a certain extent even legitimate. For the extent to which the Jewish political expectation of an ultimate world rulership could be suppressed (without giving it up entirely!) can be seen in Philo (cf. his intimations of this in *Praem. Poen.* 79ff., 162f.) and in Josephus.

Whatever differentiation there may have been on this point, there was one core affirmation that was not open to discussion: faith in the *one* God and his law (along with his people).[3] This is true quite apart from the fact that ancient Israel as yet had no idea of any theoretical monotheism (which was in fact impossible within the structure of their thinking). It was rather a matter of how this was concretely expressed in practice: it was enough to forbid the *worship* of other gods and to prohibit making images of the one God. In a polytheistic milieu this monolatry was then developed into a theoretical monotheism (W. Bousset and H. Gressmann, *Die Religion des Judentums im späthellenistischen Zeitalter,* 3rd ed. [Tübingen: Mohr-Siebeck, 1926] 302ff.), in the context of the polemic against polytheism. In this polemic, fixed forms of debate were developed, preliminary forms of the apologetic that was later to be developed more formally and methodologically. The most important of these were showing the foolishness of idolatry and the (literary) preaching of repentance. The critique focused relatively early on the making of images (in accord with the Decalogue; cf. Deutero-Isaiah) and on the worship of the gods through sacrifice (which included even human sacrifice). The critique of images could be combined with the similar critique found in Gentile authors.[4] Ridicule was one of the chief weapons.[5]

---

[3] *Ep. Ar.* 132; *Sib. Or.* proem (Theophilus, *Autol.* 2.36); Aristobulus; Philo, *Op. Mund.* 171; *Decal.* 51; *Spec. Leg.* 1.30 ("Monarchy"). In a specifically apologetic context, Josephus, *Ag. Ap.* 2.167, 251ff. Christian: 1 Cor. 8:6; Rom. 3:30; Eph. 4:6; Hermas, *Mandates* 1; *2 Clem.* 1:4ff.; Ignatius, *Magn.* 8:2, *Ker. Petr.* 2; Aristides, *Apol.* 15.3; Greek: Xenophanes B 23.

[4] Seneca in Augustine, *Civ. Dei* 6.10: "sacros . . . immortales inviolabiles in materia vilissima atque immobili dedicant, habitus illis hominum *ferarumque* et piscium . . . induunt; numina vocant, quae si spiritu accepto subito occurrerent, monstra haberentur" ("They dedicate images of the inviolable immortals in most worthless and motionless matter. They give them the appearance of man, beasts, and fish. . . . They call them deities, when they are such that if they should get breath, they would be held to be monsters"). Plutarch, *De superst.* 167D; Lucian, *Jup. Conf.* 8 (images can be stolen). Concerning the material of which the images were made, see Lucian, *Jup. Trag.* 7; see Herodotus 2.172, who had already made such statements (they became a widely circulated topos). The tradition of this motif: Philo, *Vit. Cont.* 7; Athenagoras 26; Minucius Felix; see J. Geffcken, "Der Bilderstreit des heidnischen Altertums," *ARW* 19 (1919): 286ff.; B. v. Borries; "Kultbild," *PWSup.* 5:472ff.

[5] Elijah! For the later period the main points were already established by Isaiah 44: (a) the manufacturers of the images are human beings; (b) the process of manufacture! (c) the material,

This faith in the one God became the uncrossable boundary between Judaism and every form of non-Judaism and the basic theme of all its polemic. In the process—if even in a marginal way—contact could be made with the monotheistic tendencies present in some streams of Gentile religion and culture,[6] and these points of contact could be utilized for apologetic purposes. This was the case, for example, with the view that the one God had many names or that the many names in fact all refer to one supreme being.[7]

For a Jew, such utilization of pagan ideas was, of course, questionable from several points of view.[8] It could lead to a blurring of the contours of what one means by "God." The same argument could also, of course, be used by the Gentiles, as when Celsus used it against the Christians (Origen, *Contra Cels.* 1.24). Josephus, *Ant.* 2.275f: The name of God may not be discussed.[9]

The point of reference for monotheism was provided by the first commandment.[10] The picture of the *essential nature* of God is determined by the Bible. Philo never grew tired of emphasizing that the human intellect is incapable of attaining to this. God is the One, the creator, the ruler of the world, the giver of the law, the one who has elected Israel. His lordship fills the whole earth (*Ep. Ar.* 132ff.). It is nevertheless true that he has a special relationship to Israel.

The possibility existed that the Jewish idea of God as the one whose sovereign authority permeated the whole universe could be constructively related to the Stoic idea of God. This concept of God presents certain inherent conceptual problems: What is the relationship between (a) the absolute

---

and the helplessness of the images. H. D. Preuss, *Verspottung fremder Religionen im Alten Testament* (Stuttgart: Kohlhammer, 1971) (193f.: Isa. 40:19f., from Deutero-Isaiah); 192ff.: Deutero-Isaiah and the late exilic texts that are directly dependent on him.

[6] *Ep. Ar.* 16 (cf. Josephus, *Ant.* 12.21f.) can commend, as a point of contact, the fundamental agreement concerning the *one* God, worshiped among the Greeks as Dis and Zeus. Cf. Aristobulus F 4.

[7] Philo, *De mundo 7* (on this, see N. Walter, *Der Thoraausleger Aristobulos*, TU 86 [Berlin: Akademie-Verlag, 1964] 101, 112f.); Dio Chrysostom, *Or.* 12.75ff.; Seneca, *Nat. quaest.* 2.43; *CH* 5.1, 10.

[8] Philo, *Abr.* 51: God needs no name; "God" is not a proper name (*Mut. Nom.* 11ff.; *Somn.* 1.230). On *Ep. Ar.* 16, see M. Hadas, *Letter of Aristeas* (New York: Harper & Brothers, 1951) ad loc.: "The Jewish Hellenistic writers have no objection to describing God by general Greek terms for the gods, but never apply to God the proper name of any Greek deity; only because Aristeas is represented as a non-Jew and a philosopher can he be made to speak of Zeus as meaning the same as the God worshipped by Jews." Wolfson, *Philo,* 2 vols. (Cambridge, Mass.: Harvard University Press, 1948) 1:15. Cf. Aristobulus F 4 in Eusebius, *Praep. Ev.* 13.12.7.

[9] On the namelessness of God, see Norden, *Agnostos Theos,* 52ff., 83ff., 115ff.; Bickermann, *God,* 62–65; idem, *RHR* 115 (1937): 211ff.; idem, "Anonymous Gods," *Journal of the Wartburg Inst.* 1 (1937/38): 187ff.

Christians: Aristides, *Apol.* 1.5: God has no name; the existence of a name is already an indication of idolatry. Justin, *Apol.* 2.6.3; Tatian 4; Pseudo-Melito 2; Pseudo-Justin, *Coh.* 21, 24; Minucius Felix 18.20. The polemic of Origen against Celsus forms a high point.

[10] Philo, *Decal.; Spec. Leg.* He misses a good opportunity to cite the *Shema*—which is not found at all in his writings. Cf. Josephus, *Ag. Ap.* 2.190.

sovereignty of God and providence[11] and (b) God's absolute sovereignty and human free will?[12] These questions would be brought over into Christian theology as puzzles that are in principle unsolvable, and would continue to plague it to the extent that thinking about God remains isolated from Christology.

Since in principle Jewish monotheism can be combined with a natural theology (Wisdom 13; Philo *passim*),[13] ideas from Greek religious philosophy (e.g., euhemerism) were taken over and used for apologetic purposes. It may be objected that this leads to a dehistoricizing of the Old Testament ideas of God and the people of God. It is not to be doubted that such a development did make its appearance. But did this necessarily spring the basic framework of Judaism? In a historical description such as is here attempted, it would be out of place to make a normative theological judgment that the structure of the Jewish concept of God must be limited to the conceptuality of the Old Testament and that of the rabbis (who, or course, did not always think historically themselves).

The general religious philosophy provided the following pattern that could be adopted: (a) *that* God exists is discernible from the world, but (b) his *essential nature* remains unknown or can be only dimly perceived.[14] The concept of God can be enriched with Greek ideas—from cosmology, for example: the idea of one God leads to the idea that there is *one* world (Philo, *Op. Mund.* 170ff.).

If God is the creator, then his existence (Philo: but not his essential nature) can be inferred from his works. On the basis of the possibility of such a natural theology, the question was then raised whether the Jewish God was identical with the "*one* god" of Greek faith (see above, *Ep. Ar.*). Implicit tendencies toward answering this question in the affirmative are in fact found in the appeal to (genuine or fabricated ad hoc) pagan documents.[15] Josephus has Vespasian sacrifice to "the providence of God" (*J.W.* 3.144f.) and to God; cf. Claudius, *J.W.* 2.414. Epicurean and euhemeristic criticisms of myths were assimilated for apologetic purposes.[16]

But the line of demarcation for such adoption was always drawn at the point of *worship* of God. Here there was an uncompromising exclusiveness. This is

---

[11] Josephus, *J.W.* 4.297, 622; Philo, *De providentia.*

[12] Philo: Moore, *Judaism* 1:458f.; H. A. Wolfson, "Philo on Free Will"; Josephus: see his review of the Jewish "philosophical schools." Schlatter, *Theologie*, 33ff.; Billerbeck, *Kommentar* 1:583; G. Mayer, "Aspekte des Abrahambildes in der hellenistisch-jüdischen Literatur," *EvT* 32 (1972): 118ff.

[13] This does not become impossible until the understanding of God is constructed by means of Christology. Wherever Christian theology still holds on to the idea of natural theology, this is an indication that the connection between Christology and the concept of God has been relaxed, and that an ideological component has forced its way into the concept of God.

[14] Cicero, *Nat. Deor.* 2.1; Philo, *Op. Mund.* 170f.; *Spec. Leg.* 1.13ff., 32, 41.

[15] Pseudo-Orpheus in Aristobulus and Pseudo-Justin, *Coh.* 15 (on the different recensions, see Walter, *Aristobulos*); Pseudo-Sophocles from Pseudo-Hecataeus and Pseudo-Justin, *De monarchia* 2f.; Clement of Alexandria, *Strom.* 5.113; Eusebius, *Praep. Ev.* 13.13.40. See Schürer, *History* 3:595f.

[16] Widespread; Artapanos; Wisdom 13–15; Geffcken, *Apologeten*, XVIIIff.

no more discussable than the unity of God himself. This constituted a fundamental difference over against all the traces of monotheism found among the Gentiles. Neither does *Ep. Ar.* discuss monotheism as such. Since the whole course of everyday life was interwoven with cultic relationships, the radical separation of the Jews from all Gentile cultic associations led in fact to their strict isolation from the rest of society. This isolation belonged to the very substance of their existence, however harmonious their coexistence with their Gentile neighbors may have been in many other respects.

This is seen in an impressive way in *Ep. Ar.*: Alongside the adaptation in §16 (see above), extravagant praise is also given to the Jews for their separation from the Gentiles through the law (§139). This is a tension that no apologetic was ever able to resolve, nor can it do so. It constantly, necessarily and hopelessly, stood in the way of any real apologetic. A further example: the attempt to identify the Torah with the law of nature (Schlatter, *Theologie*, 15; Josephus, *Ant.* 1.24; 16.176f.) by means of allegorical explanations can never be persuasive, because at the same time literal compliance with its precepts is required. Philo's efforts show how difficult this can be. The attempt to base the validity of the law on arguments from examples of Jewish loyalty to it even to the point of martyrdom (2 and 4 Maccabees; Josephus, *J.W.* 1.653; 2.152; 7.417; *Ant.* 15.248) must in fact strengthen the contrary view, both in theory—that is, in the literary apologetic—and in practice, as in the Jewish War.

Hellenistic-Jewish Apologetic

There has been considerable talk of Jewish "missionary literature." Tcherikover objects[17] that this literature was intended primarily for use within the Jewish community for purposes of edification. But is this really a proper alternative? See, for instance, Philo's *Decal.!* Tcherikover wants to establish his thesis precisely from the document that others would like to regard as written for a "missionary" goal, namely, the *Letter of Aristeas*.

The sources that are indispensable for the investigation of this subject are the following: (1) the writings of the LXX not found in the Hebrew canon, to the extent that they were composed (primarily or secondarily) for apologetic purposes; (2) Pseudepigrapha from the Jewish diaspora—selected on the same

---

[17] V. Tcherikover, "Jewish Apologetic Literature Reconsidered," *Eos* 48 (1956): 169ff.: idem, "The Ideology of the Letter of Aristeas," *HTR* 51 (1958): 59ff., followed to a considerable extent by Hengel, "Anonymität, Pseudepigraphie und 'Literarische Fälschung' in der jüdisch-hellenistischen Literatur," in *Pseudepigrapha* (Geneva: Fondation Hardt, 1972) 1:306f., as is the case with N. Walter, "Historische und legendarische Erzählungen," in *Jüdischen Schriften* (Gütersloh: Mohn, 1980) 1:97 n. 14. The apologetic motive is regarded as stronger by W. Speyer, *Die literarische Fälschung im heidischen und christlichen Altertum*, Handbücher der klass. Altertumswissenschaft (Munich: Beck, 1971) 155ff.

basis;[18] (3) the fragments excerpted by Alexander Polyhistor, those preserved in Clement of Alexandria, and especially those in Eusebius, *Praep. Ev.* 9.17–39[19] (Alexander is the only pagan author before Celsus [ca. 180 C.E.] who demonstrably read Jewish sources, though obviously the Bible was not among these [see above]); (4) the apologetic writings of Philo and Josephus (to which practically all of Josephus belongs); (5) the literature listed in Schürer, *History,* 3:553ff.[20]

Definition of Terms

(1) We will use the term "apology" and "apologetic" independently of the dubious alternative mentioned above, which questions whether a Jewish writing that deals thematically with paganism was intended for the internal use of the Jewish community for edification and the strengthening of its own self-confidence, or whether it was intended for Gentile readers with a view to winning them over to Judaism.[21]

(2) That Gentile readers did not in fact become very aware of this literature is no argument against the idea that Jewish authors hoped that what they wrote would be read by Gentile readers and that they wrote specifically with this in mind. It is clear enough that a Philo or a Josephus sought such a readership— but in vain. The fact that these writings were ignored by the Greeks need not rest on some particular aversion to the Jews, but only on the general mentality of the Greeks, which was inclined away from everything "barbarian": it is also the case that authors such as Manetho and Berosus made no impression on the Greeks. For the educated Greek, what they wrote was not "literature."

Even Alexander Polyhistor cannot be adduced as an exception. His excerpts from Jewish authors seem to have had no effect on his Gentile readers. A passage such as Hermippus's note (probably about 200 B.C.E. in Alexandria; Josephus, *Ag. Ap.* 1.164f.; Origen, *Contra Cels.* 1.15) that Pythagoras adopted teachings from the Jews and the Thracians, is hardly anything to get excited about (Schürer, *History,* 3:625f.; Stern, *GLAJJ,* 93ff.). M. Friedländer would like

---

[18] Editions of the individual writings: A.-M. Denis, *Fragmenta Pseudepigraphorum* (Leiden: E. J. Brill, 1970). German: E. Kautzsch, *Die Apokryphen und Pseudepigraphen des Alten Testaments,* 2 vols. (Tübingen: Mohr-Siebeck, 1900); P. Riessler, *Altjüdisches Schrifttum ausserhalb der Bibel* (Heidelberg: Augsburg, 1928) [unreliable]; *Jüdische Schriften aus hellenistisch-römischer Zeit,* ed. W. G. Kümmel et al. (Gütersloh: Mohn, 1973-). English: R. H. Charles, *The Apocrypha and Pseudepigrapha of the Old Testament,* 2 vols. (Oxford: Clarendon Press, 1913); J. H. Charlesworth, ed., *The Old Testament Pseudepigrapha,* 2 vols. (Garden City, NY: Doubleday, 1983, 1985).

[19] Freudenthal (*Hellenistische Studien*) is still indispensable.

[20] Schürer (*History* 3:420ff., 528ff.) is still indispensable; O. Eissfeldt, *The Old Testament: An Introduction* (New York: Harper & Row, 1965); R. H. Pfeiffer, *History of New Testament Times* (New York: Harper & Brothers, 1949); L. Rost, *Einleitung in die alttestamentlichen Apokryphen und Pseudepigraphen einschliesslich der grossen Qumran-Handschriften* (Heidelberg: Quelle & Meyer, 1971) [too brief].

[21] Simon, *Verus Israel,* 391–92; Sevenster, *Roots,* 209 n. 140.

to believe that at the time of Philo, the writings of Moses were a subject of lively interest among educated Greeks[22] (B. Z. Wacholder has recently argued a similar view with regard to the writings of the Greek chronographers).

(3) An important consideration is the issue of how one defines literary types and forms. There was no consistent development, and yet certain high points are visible: Philo, Josephus.

(4) *Preview:* What sort of modifications had to be made in Jewish apologetic when it was adopted and adapted by the Christians? Points of continuity in both form and content were easily at hand.[23] That was, of course, because of the identification of the Christian God with the Jewish God.

But we are interested in precisely the characteristic differences: Which modifications had to be made if the Jewish idea of God was not only taken over but also christologically reinterpreted? Would it lose its mooring in a specific people? Would the Christian community give up the objective identifying mark of Judaism that was visible to the Gentiles—namely, the law[24]—but nonetheless claim to be a specific people—namely, the true Israel?

It appears, of course, to be absurd: the Christians did not observe the Jewish laws that set them apart from other people and thus appeared—quite in contrast to the Jews—to be able to coexist with other people—a theme of the *Epistle to Diognetus.* But that was in fact not the case. Despite their laws, the Jews were one national group among others, even if they were exceptional. They carried on a propaganda campaign and attempted to win converts from the Gentiles. But mission was not a *conditio sine qua non* of their existence. The church, on the other hand, could only exist as a missionary institution. Jews were related to the world by the very fact that they were Jews and the world was the creation of their God, and Israel had an eschatological hope in and for this world. Christians also lived in a world created by this God, but they believed their true citizenship to be in heaven (this was true also for Jews, but in another sense: Philo, *Conf. Lang.* 78; and this quite apart from the fact that Philo's understanding of the individual Jew's relationship to the world was not typical of Judaism). The Christians proclaimed Jesus, the Jew crucified by a Roman governor, as the only possibility of coming to terms with this God and this world—and this meant for the Romans primarily their own, political world.

---

[22] The "proof": Philo, *Leg.* 209ff. (concerning Petronius!); Josephus, *J. W.* proem 2, 6; *Ant.* 3.317; Acts 8:27f.(!). The Christian apologists credit the Caesars with knowledge of the Bible, as Justin and Tatian (note the time!) attribute knowledge of the Christian movement itself to them. In sum: the process of giving "proofs" is a case of *lucus a non lucendo,* that is, establishing false and fantastic "points of contact." The Jewish influence on Gnosticism and the magical writings is a completely different matter, outside the literary sphere.

[23] The standard work is still Geffcken, *Apologeten.*

[24] Not only such matters as the Sabbath, but especially amixia, the rejection of table fellowship, and *konnubium.*

Survey of the Essential Forms and Materials of Apologetic

There is still a lot of work to be done in the area of the analysis of the forms and motifs of this apologetic literature. Preliminary studies with regard to the form can be found, for example, in P. Wendland (*Die Therapeuten und die philonische Schrift vom beschaulichen Leben* [Leipzig, 1896]); the task of collecting these motifs has essentially already been done by Geffcken, but not really pursued historically and worked through theologically. But that the evaluation expressed above is nevertheless valid is seen by examining such helpful monographs as those of N. Walter on Aristobulus (*Der Thoraausleger Aristobulos*) and B. Mack (*Logos und Sophia* [Göttingen: Vandenhoeck & Ruprecht, 1973]) on the types of wisdom in the Wisdom of Solomon and Philo. An important step forward was made by Hengel's classification in his article "Anonymität und Pseudonymität": the predominance of these two types of writing in the literature of the Jewish diaspora indicates a cultural lag, an undeveloped consciousness of their own intellectual resources. Hengel suggests a rule of thumb: Literature that appears under the author's own name engages its Hellenistic environment *directly*, historically or philosophically, in order to set forth the superiority of Judaism. That hardly happens in the anonymous and pseudonymous literature. But there are notable exceptions, such as the *Letter of Aristeas* and the Wisdom of Solomon.

Themes and Methods [25]

The themes of the apologetic literature derive mostly from the points on which the Jews were attacked and the points at which the peculiarity of their faith and law became publicly visible because of their way of life.

Examples: The numerical growth of the Jews evoked hostility (*Sib. Or.* 3.271f.). A Jewish counterargument was that their growth as a people was due to the fact that Jews raise all their children (=do not practice infanticide), and that their increasing numbers was an indication of the significance of their nation. This was not simply a defensive reaction, but also served to increase the people's own self-awareness and self-confidence. And that means throughout the whole literature: the self-awareness of being *the* elect people is the basis of *all* apologetic. It is in connection with this idea that the ideal description of the people, among other things, is found (*Sib. Or.* 3.218ff., 234ff., 573ff.). The whole literary corpus of both Philo and Josephus makes use of it. The perspective on the future (*Sib. Or.* 2.217ff., 319ff.) also belongs to this world of ideas, whence is derived the hope for the final (political) restoration.

---

[25] M. Friedländer, *Geschichte der jüdischen Apologetik* (Amsterdam: Philo Press, 1903); Wendland, *Die hellenistisch-römische Kultur*; Geffcken, *Apologeten*; Willrich, *Judaica*; Schürer, *History* 3:545ff.; P. Krüger, *Philo und Josephus als Apologeten des Judentums* (Leipzig, 1906).

The biblical creation story is lauded as being superior to all the theological and cosmological myths (Philo, *Op. Mund.*). This story lays the foundation for a perspective on humanity as a single whole (Philo, *Virt.* 116ff.; *Spec. Leg.* 1.51ff.), for which monotheism (the "monarchy") is the necessary condition (Philo, *Virt.* 175ff; Josephus, *Ag. Ap.* 2.279ff.). At the same time, the supremacy of the Jews is already grounded in cosmology. Since the creator and the lawgiver are one and the same, the Torah can be identified with the law of nature and humanity.[26]

The concept of the law of nature could of course not emerge until Greek ideas began to be adopted by the Jews.

Now the difficulty is, of course, that the Torah was not proclaimed by Moses until long after the creation, but, of course, ways out of this dilemma were found. According to *Jubilees,* the law was already created at the beginning. Philo (*Decal.*) distinguishes the laws that were promulgated directly by God from those that he gave indirectly through his mediator Moses.

This doctrine of God provided a basis to respond to an especially grievous objection, that of "godlessness."[27] This was a particularly dangerous issue, because atheism was not simply a private matter (isolated philosophical exceptions such as the "atheist" Diagoras can be disregarded), but an extremely political matter, having to do with the cult of ruler and state. In the Roman period, this meant the worship of Roma and the Caesar.

The Jews responded with an attack on the pagan gods,[28] especially on their multiplicity and the insoluble problems associated therewith (Which is the highest? How can the power of a god be limited by others?) and the disgusting qualities of the myths associated with them.

But the attack cut even deeper: the Gentile polytheistic worship was a worship of the creation rather than the creator (Rom. 1:18ff), the material of the universe, temporary perishable things. *The* indication of this is that the gods must be manufactured by the worshipers themselves, the images, the nothings.[29] It was precisely in regard to their monotheism that the Jews sought to demonstrate their political loyalty (*Ep. Ar.* 15): they prayed to the Almighty

---

[26] Philo, *Vit. Mos.* 2.137ff.; Josephus, *Ag. Ap.* 2.39; *Sib. Or.* 3.234ff., 283ff., 274ff., 580.

[27] According to the opinion of Josephus, Posidonius (whom he had not read) was one who made this charge; cf. Apollonius Molon; Apion; Pliny, *Hist. Nat.* 13.9.46: "gens contumelia numinum insignis" ("a race remarkable for their contempt for the divine powers"). Preview: This accusation will fall even more heavily on the Christians, and it will be more difficult for them to defend themselves against it, since they had no temple or visible cult. See Harnack, *Der Vorwurf des Atheismus.*

[28] Also with the help of euhemeristic critique. [Translator's note: "The rationalistic system of Euhemerus, who explained mythology as the deification of earthborn kings and heroes, and denied the existence of divine beings" (Funk & Wagnalls, s.v. "euhemerism").]

[29] A particularly opportune case is that of the Egyptian animal worship, which was also rejected and ridiculed by Gentile authors, a topos that is found repeatedly.

in behalf of the emperor, offering sacrifices to the one God for the Caesar.[30]

The Jews responded to slander concerning their origins[31] by reciting the story of creation and the account of their own history as a people, and answer the charge of amixia[32] by referring to their law. But this resulted—once again—in their falling into a contradiction: on the one hand, they defended themselves against the charge; on the other hand, their very defense emphasized it all the more. And they could not have done otherwise.[33]

The charge was made that the Jews had not accomplished anything in the sphere of culture.[34] It was especially Moses who was set forth as the answer to this charge (Gager, *Moses*), since among other things he was the model lawgiver[35] and demonstrated that in comparison with other peoples it was the Jews who were the people of true wisdom.[36] The same argument was made for Abraham (see below) and Joseph (see below).[37]

Chronography[38]

Chronography had become an independent discipline in the Hellenistic period and formed an essential part of apologetic. A formal presupposition for this was provided by the enormous increase in the knowledge of other lands and peoples. This brought with it a fundamental change in the way history was perceived. Among the Hellenistic historians, history became universal history. A prominent means of organizing such a universal history was devised, in which there were four world empires[39]—a scheme that also penetrated Judaism

---

[30] See Harnack, *Der Vorwurf des Atheismus*, 39, 84, 136 n. 56. This was taken over by the Christians (without sacrifice, of course): 1 Tim. 2:2; *1 Clem.* 61; Athenagoras in his conclusion; Theophilus 1.11; 3.14, Tertullian, *Apol.* 10, 28, 30, 34.

[31] E.g., that they had been driven out of Egypt because they were lepers; cf. Lysimachus, Chaeremon.

[32] From Hecataeus of Abdera on. Philo, *Spec. Leg.* 2.167: prayers, festivals for all humanity; *Virt.* 51ff.: φιλανθρωπία ("friendship for humanity"). They are forbidden to revile other peoples and their gods.

[33] *Ep. Ar.* 139, 151: isolation for the sake of ritual purity; Philo, *Spec. Leg.* 3.7ff. (sexual morality); 3.110ff. (prohibition against exposing children); 4.234 (peacefulness).

[34] Apollonius Molon; Apion. The force of this argument can be perceived only when one remembers the role played by *inventors* in the Greek understanding of culture. Josephus, *Ant.* 1.60ff.: Cain was a perverse inventor; but the opposite picture is given of Seth (1.68ff.).

[35] In any case a principal figure in the Greek cultural history.

[36] Philo, *Spec. Leg.* 4.179f.; Eupolemus: he was the first sage, the inventor of alphabetical writing; Artapanos: he brought astrology to the Egyptians (see below, Abraham); Aristobulus: Moses and philosophy.

[37] Moses as miracle worker: D. L. Tiede, *The Charismatic Figure as Miracle Worker*, SBLDS (Missoula, Mont.: Scholars Press, 1972).

[38] On the characteristics of the general Hellenistic chronography, see part I; *FGH* II D, 661ff. Here we need to note only a few things concerning the way in which Jewish apologetic played a role in this; see B. Z. Wacholder, "Biblical Chronology."

[39] Diodorus; Appian, *Punica* 132.

(Daniel; modified in *Testament of Naphthali* 5:9). We cannot discuss here the origin of this scheme, nor how it came to be that the *myth* of the four ages of the world was related to the four metals.[40]

Jacoby, *FGH* II D, 662: "The fundamental problem of this scientific chronography ... was the establishing of a universally valid era, a universally acceptable dating of events" – which would transcend the local systems. The final result was that the pivotal date became the First Olympiad (calculated at 776 B.C.E.), and then beyond that the fall of Troy (set at 1184/1183). That was as far back as historical time could be calculated.

The manner in which chronology was established was very different among the Orientals, Egyptians (cf. Manetho), the Babylonians (cf. Berosus), the Phoenicians (cf. Herennius Philo of Byblos [*FGH* 790; 1st or 2nd cent. C.E.]).[41] Their influence on the Greeks is minimal (*FGH* II D, 719). But they were used by the Jews for apologetic purposes: cf. Josephus. But that Josephus already had predecessors in this regard is clear from the fact that prior to him there was already a (pro-)Jewish reworking of Manetho.

The Jews Respond with Their Own Calculations

On the basis of their Bible, the Jews were able to bring forward their own chronography as an alternative counterproposal, which was plausible in itself and more reasonable than the others. (It is another question whether it became generally known and acknowledged.) They had compiled this chronography in *one* clearly arranged document that had been carefully and officially transmitted. The rather harmless differences between the Hebrew and the Greek versions could safely be ignored, especially since non-Jews were ignorant of both.

At the beginning of his polemical composition against Apion, Josephus took advantage of the multiplicity and arbitrariness of the chronographical schemes of the Hellenistic historians. In the Bible we have a firm chronology, with no gaps from the creation of the world until contemporary times. There is no need to get lost in some vague prehistorical mythical period in the Greek style (before Troy), nor for the fantastic number of years attributed to the primeval kings by Berosus, in comparison to which the number of years attributed to the early generations in the Bible seem rather human. At the same time, Josephus points out that some data in the Greek historians provides points of contact for the support of his own position: the flood story of Berosus and the

---

[40] E. Meyer, *Ursprung und Anfänge des Christentums* (Stuttgart: J. G. Cotta, 1925) 2:189ff.; H. Fuchs, *Basler Zeitschrift für Geschichte und Altertumskunde* 42 (1943): 49ff.; J. W. Swain, "The Theory of the Four Monarchies," *Classical Philology* 32 (1940): 1ff.; Schalit, *König Herodes*, 524f.

[41] His source, Sanchuniathon, is supposed to have lived even before the Trojan War; Eusebius, *Praep. Ev.* 1.9.20ff.

Greek legends about the primeval flood.[42] So Judaism was able to feel rather good about its situation in this regard, rather than being harassed by some ἄδηλον ("unknown and unknowable quantity"). Besides, the Trojan War could not serve as a pivotal date, since its own date could not be determined: Eusebius, *Chron.* 42 (according to the LXX): the time from Adam to the flood was 2,242 years, from Adam to Abraham 3,184 years; *Chron.* 171: Troy fell 835 years after Abraham=411 years after the birth of Moses.

With the help of the Bible, the "proof for the antiquity of the Jews" can be given: where there are parallels between Jewish and Greek teachings, the creative, older teacher is in fact the Jew: Moses preceded Orpheus and Greek philosophy. And where there are obvious contradictions — Homer, for example, can simply be called a liar — appeal can even be made to Plato for confirmation (and Plato, in turn, had received his wisdom by reading Moses). Moses was the central figure (Gager, *Moses*), but, of course, others could be included in the argument — for example, Abraham, who in these apologetic writings becomes an inventor.[43]

Motifs in the Picture of Abraham

(1) Universal fatherhood. Through Ishmael, Abraham became the progenitor of the Nabateans, and through the sons of Keturah the ancestor of the Trogodytae.[44]

(2) The bringer of culture. Abraham invented astrology (Josephus, *Ant.* 1.156, 167; *Jub.* 12, 16, but, on the other hand, cf. chap. 17), which from the point of view of Jewish presuppositions was hardly to his credit anyway.[45] He was a teacher (on the education of Isaac, see Josephus, *Ant.* 1.215; Artapanus; Pseudo-Eupolemus) and an inventor (Pseudo-Eupolemus; *Jubilees*).

---

[42] When Varro regards the flood as a decisive hiatus between the three ages of history (the historical, the heroic, and the mythical — ἄδηλον "unknown and unknowable"), Wacholder supposes that he has been influenced by the biblical tradition — not however directly from Genesis but only via an earlier (purely hypothetical) chronography. Pure speculation. In the Jewish tradition there is not a hint that the time before the flood was all ἄδηλον ("unknown and unknowable").

[43] Gager, *Moses*, 145, 148; Josephus, *Ant.* 1.248ff.; Pseudo-Eupolemus; Aristobulus. See G. Mayer, "Aspekte des Abrahambildes," 118ff.; N. Walter, "Zur Überlieferung einiger Reste früher jüdisch-hellenistischer Literatur bei Josephus, Clemens und Euseb," *St. Patr.* 7 (1966): 314–43.

According to Josephus, *Ant.* 1.158ff., Abraham is mentioned by Berosus, Hecataeus, and Nicholas of Damascus. See further Alexander Polyhistor; Apollonius Molon; Pompeius Trogus.

[44] Josephus, *Ant.* 1.220f., 239ff. Abraham was the ancestral father-in-law of Hercules and thus an ancestor of the Mauretanians, and of the Spartans (1 Macc. 12:21).

[45] Philo, *Abr.* 82; on the ethical use of astronomy, see the negative observations in *Mut. Nom.* 72f. There is a frank rejection of astrology in *Sib. Or.* 3.218ff., 227f.

(3) In addition, he became a philosopher,[46] and the ideal ruler.[47] The ideal of the νόμος ἔμψυχος ("living law") was attributed to him.[48]

EXCURSUS: B. Z. WACHOLDER ON
THE DEVELOPMENT OF JEWISH CHRONOLOGY

Wacholder distinguishes three stages. This suggests a development that did not in fact take place, at least not in a straight line. It is better to speak of types, which could be of heuristic interest, but in fact hardly are even that, for they must be constructed in too artificial a manner. According to Wacholder, the first stage was formed by the working out of an adjusted biblical chronology; this is demonstrated in the case of Demetrius (*Eupolemus: A Study of Judaeo-Greek Literature* [Cleveland, Oh.: Hebrew Union College–Jewish Institute of Religion, 1974] 98ff.).[49] The second phase includes the mixing of biblical data with extrabiblical mythology.[50] In the third stage the biblical events have become a part of a universal chronology of world history (evidence?).

Examples of Jewish chronology in non-Jewish documents (for the dates, see Josephus, *Ag. Ap.* 2.16):

(1) Ptolemy of Mendes, *FGH* 611 (Stern, *GLAJJ*, 379ff.); time: prior to Apion, who used him (see Tatian 38; Apion, *FGH* 616 F 2; see further below). He dates the exodus at the time of Pharaoh Amosis, who was a contemporary of Inachus. Wacholder regards him as the author of the chronological note (*Eupolemus;* cf. Eupolemus, *FGH* 723 F 4; Walter, F 5). Pure speculation.

(2) Thrasyllos of Mendes (*FGH* III, 501ff.; Reinach, *Textes,* 113) can be mentioned only with reservations. Reinach asks whether the reference to Moses and the Jews does not come from Clement of Alexandria (*Strom.* 1.145) within which it is transmitted. (Inachos is found here too; see further Kastor, *FGH* 250 F 3; *FGH* II D, 821.)

---

[46] L. H. Feldman, "Abraham the Greek Philosopher in Josephus," *TAPA* 59 (1968): 145ff.

[47] Aristocracy: Pseudo-Eupolemus; cf. Josephus, *Ant.* 1.278. Military leadership: Philo, *Abr.* 232ff. Righteousness, love of peace: Philo, *Abr.* 208ff., 225. Philanthropy: Philo, *Abr.* 107. He released prisoners: Josephus, *Ant.* 1.182.

[48] I. Heinemann, *Philons griechische und jüdische Bildung* (Hildesheim: G. Olms, 1932) 182ff.; E. R. Goodenough, *The Politics of Philo Judaeus* (New Haven: Yale University Press, 1938); W. Völker, "Das Abrahambild bei Philo, Origenes, und Ambrosius," *TSK* 103 (1931): 199ff. He refers to the fashioning of the picture according to the Stoic idea of προκοπή ("progress, progression"): from astrologer via self-understanding (*Migr. Abr.* 134, 184ff.), to the insight that there is *one* who rules the world (*Abr.* 70; *Mut. Nom.* 16, 76) to final perfection in virtue (*Migr. Abr.* 53ff.).

[49] Schürer, *History* 3:473: use of the LXX Pentateuch; M. Gaster, "Demetrius and the Seder Olam," in *Festkrift i anledning af Prof. David Simonsens 70-aarige Fodelsdag,* ed. J. Fischer (Copenhagen: Hertz's Bogtrykkeri, 1923) 243ff.

[50] Pseudo-Eupolemus (the older Belos corresponds to Noah, etc.); Artapanus; Eupolemus (none of the mythical Greek kings is older than Moses).

(3) Although Apion is dependent on Ptolemy of Mendes, he does not adopt the latter's dating, but places Moses in the time of Bokchoris (see Tacitus) and postpones the exodus until the year of the founding of Carthage (Josephus, *Ag. Ap.* 2.17). Is that a consciously anti-Jewish chronology?[51]

THE SCRIPTURES: PREPARATION IN THE LXX (EXCEPT WISDOM)[52]

The Book of Baruch

This writing does not belong to the apologetic literature but is mentioned here because of a particular disputed point. Baruch is not a single integrated document, nor is the historical situation artificially constructed for it a unity (partly after the first deportation under Jehoiachin, partly after the destruction of the temple).

The events are interpreted as punishment of the exiles for their revolt against the (Gentile!) rulers, which God himself had set over them (2:21ff.). The exiles urge those who are left behind to pray and offer sacrifice for Nebuchadnezzar and his son [*sic!*] Balthasar (1:10f.).

Schürer (*History* 3:462) assumes that the purported situation for this writing would not be appropriate until after the destruction of Jerusalem in 70 C.E., when the Jews rebelled against their Gentile rulers. The author or authors would then belong not to the Babylonian diaspora, but perhaps in the circle of disciples of Johanan ben Zakkai (see Rost, *Einleitung*, 53). It will be remembered that at that time the revolt began with the cessation of sacrifices for the emperor (Josephus, *J.W.* 2.408ff.). Nebuchadnezzar and Balthasar would then be code names for Vespasian and Titus.[53]

Should this late dating be correct,[54] then we would have an extremely interesting document relating to the political adjustment made to Rome from the time of the Jewish War, which should then be seen in connection with

---

[51] Stern, *GLAJJ*, 397: in Apion the different sources are not harmonized; cf. *GLAJJ*, 340 on Pompeius Trogus 36.2.12.

On Josephus, *Ag. Ap.* 1.103ff., see A. v. Gutschmid, *Kleine Schriften* 4:460: not Danaos, but Inachos was considered to be the oldest king of Argos (Tatian 39). Correspondingly, the church fathers made Inachos the contemporary of Amosis and of the departure of the Hyksos. This would lead to the equation: Hyksos=Israelites, Moses was a contemporary of Inachos. "Thus Josephus suffered a lapse of memory."

[52] The book of Wisdom is in a special category and is to be discussed among the individual apologists.

[53] Eissfeldt objects that the exhortation to prayer and sacrifice can be explained from the letter of Jer. 29:5-7 (*Introduction*, 594). To be sure, the reference to sacrifice is missing there. (Of course! This is after the destruction of the temple.)

[54] Rost also supposes that the whole was "compiled and provided with a historical introduction only after 70 C.E." (*Einleitung*, 53).

Josephus and his group, who did not want to participate in the revolt. The fact that the book is not a literary unity tends to support this assessment, for the *political* point would come to expression precisely in this final redaction.

The Third Book of Maccabees[55]

This legend is of interest here only because of its apologetic elements. Does any historical event at all stand behind it (the Ptolemaic period?) (Rost considers it possible [*Einleitung*, 79]; Eissfeldt is doubtful [*Introduction*, 789]). We can go into this question only to the extent that it deals with the apologetic situation that obtained at the time it was composed (under the Ptolemies or the Romans?) (see Hadas, "Third Maccabees"; Tcherikover, "Third Book of Maccabees").

Ptolemy IV Philopator (221–204 B.C.E.) offers sacrifice in Jerusalem to the most high God,[56] but he cannot, of course, enter the temple.[57] Thus he persecutes the Jews. He demotes them to the legal status of the native population (3 Macc. 2:28) and commands that they be branded with the sign of the ivy leaf, the symbol of Dionysus (the household god of the Ptolemies) (2:29). But the Jews remain loyal to their religion and receive some help through the bribery of officials (2:32). It is presupposed that the action of the king corresponds to the sentiment of the population in general.

To what situation does this book belong? To any real historical context at all? Behind the introduction (1:1–7) lie reports concerning the battle of Raphia (217 B.C.E.), which are also dealt with in Polybius 5.79ff.[58] If dependence on Polybius could be confirmed, we would at least have a *terminus post quem*,[59] but certainly no more than that. Nor do we get more conclusive results from other indications.[60] To be sure, Hadas believes that he is able to date it exactly

---

[55] Greek-English: M. Hadas, ed., *The Third and Fourth Books of Maccabees* (New York: Harper & Brothers, 1953). See also H. Willrich, "Der historische Kern des III Makkabäerbuches," *Hermes* 39 (1904): 244ff.; M. Hadas, "III Maccabees and Greek Romance," *Review of Religion* 13 (1949): 155ff.; V. Tcherikover, "The Third Book of Maccabees as a Historical Source of Augustus' Time," *Scripta Hierosolymitana* 7 (1961): 1ff.

[56] In Jerusalem until the beginning of the war in 66 C.E., not only was sacrifice made for the emperor, but offerings from non-Jews were accepted (Josephus, *J.W.* 2.408ff.; *Ant.* 11.87). Regulations concerning sacrifices from Gentiles are found in *J.W.* 2.549ff. Stories are told of sacrifices made precisely by Gentile rulers: Alexander the Great (*Ant.* 11.336), Ptolemy III (*Ag. Ap.* 2.48), Agrippa (*Ant.* 16.14); see Schürer, *History* 2:357ff. On sacrifice by foreigners, see Schürer-Vermes-Millar, *History* 2:309ff.

[57] Entered by Antiochus IV (1 Macc. 1:21; cf. Josephus, *Ant.* 12.250), Pompey (Josephus, *J.W.* 1.152; *Ant.* 14.71f.; *Pss. Sol.* 2), Titus (*J.W.* 5.260).

[58] Polybius 5.81: attack by Theodotus (but without the help of a Jew); 5.83: Arsinoe incites to battle; 5.86: reception of Philopator by the Syrians (3 Macc.: the Jews).

[59] Thus Willrich (*Juden und Griechen*, 38), but according to Tcherikover, some details extend beyond Polybius; thus he is not the source, but some other Greek historian.

[60] Kautzsch refers to the acquaintance with the additions to Daniel (*Apokryphen*); Josephus does not know the book; the temple is still standing: thus it originated at the beginning of the Christian period at the earliest.

to 25/24 B.C.E., when the civil rights of the Jews in Egypt were threatened.[61] Tcherikover's analysis follows the style of the older source criticism: 1:1–7 is supposed to derive from a good source (insignificant for us); 2:28f. is from an official Ptolemaic source;[62] 2:30 is from the author of the book, and betrays a certain ignorance (as if everyone had access to the mysteries—an argument?). 1:8–2:24 is pure legend—this information is not exactly new.

There are contradictions in the report of the persecution in Alexandria (2:25f.). On the one hand, the persecution is in the city; on the other hand, the surrounding countryside is the scene of the persecution. The report of the elimination of the Jews from the countryside is only elaboration, not an independent report from a more extensive source. The persecution is said to be carried on at the initiative of the king, but then also at the initiative of the courtiers (2:28 vs. 3:1). An account of the enslaving of all Jews is juxtaposed with another in which only a certain group is exterminated in the Hippodrome (see Josephus, *Ag. Ap.* 2.53ff. concerning Ptolemy VII Physkon).

Josephus knew at least two versions (cf. the different names for the mistresses, Attica and Eirene). 3 Maccabees is yet a third version, in which the author himself was the first to combine the legend with the events in Palestine. The author's own trimmings are found in 2:12ff. and 7:1–9 (see above: from a good source). *When* do the Jews first see themselves standing before the alternative of either being enslaved or receiving the rights of citizens? This happened for the first time when the *laographia* made a distinction between Greek citizens and subject peoples. The author understood the *laographia* in terms of *Roman* relationships—namely, not as a census but as a head tax. Thus the time of the author is later than 24/23 (cf. Hadas above). If one strikes the assumptions out of this source "analysis," hardly any literary results remain.

Chapter 3 contains an apologetic schema: (a) although loyalty is to the king (3:3; cf. Pseudo-Hecataeus, Josephus, *Ag. Ap.* 2.43f.), this loyalty is of course expressed in such a way that loyalty to God and the law is preserved (3:4); (b) from this attitude the inference was drawn that the Jews were hostile to the state, which resulted in their being hated (3:7, 24); (c) there was the additional factor of the segregation of the Jews because of their dietary laws (topos); (d) but the Jews behaved themselves well nonetheless, which caused them to be well thought of by all (*Ep. Ar.* 140; Josephus, *Ag. Ap.* 2.273ff.). However peculiar it may sound, it was precisely the contradiction between (b) and (d) that formed a constituent part of the schema that was supposed to avert the hatred of outsiders and generate good will. The attempt was made to mitigate it: the ἀλλόφυλοι ("aliens") would not have anything to do with the good will of the Jews—as if the problem could be disposed of in this way! The main

---

[61] Through the census; see *PTebt.* 163 (U. Wilcken, *Grundzüge und Chrestomathie der Papyruskunde* 1/1 [1912; reprint, 1963] 288; see Tcherikover below).

[62] Nor do I understand how C. C. Edgar and A. S. Hunt support this thesis (*Select Papyri* I [Cambridge, Mass.: Harvard University Press, 1952]; II [1956] nos. 109, 110).

points of the controversy were reaffirmed in the conclusion: the worship practices and the dietary laws.

Esther LXX[63]

The Hebrew book of Esther also belongs in the period being considered, and in any case shows the influence of the Hellenistic-Roman style.[64] According to the signature on the Greek version, it was translated by a resident of Jerusalem named Lysimachus and was brought to Egypt in the fourth year of Ptolemy and Cleopatra.[65] But the following questions remain: Which Ptolemy and which Cleopatra? What historical value may be attributed to the signature? How much historical knowledge did the author of the note possess? How much time came between the composition of the Hebrew book, the Greek additions, and the bringing of the book to Egypt? Were the additions made in Jerusalem or not until the book arrived in Egypt?[66] Today the opinion of E. Bickermann ("The Colophon of the Greek Book of Esther," *JBL* 63 [1944]: 339ff; cf., Hanhart, *Esther*, 96 n. 1) is generally accepted: The colophon was probably added by the librarian in Alexandria when the book was catalogued in the library there, in 78/77 B.C.E. (see below).

Concerning the relationship of the LXX passages to the original composition: their original language was certainly Greek (Hanhart, *Esther*, 96). One should not be deceived by the oriental coloring in the prayer style. According to Bardtke, the Greek recension originated between the first successes of Judas Maccabeus (167 B.C.E.) and the transformation of the feast of Purim into Mordecai Day.

The Greek additions to Esther offer a small but instructive example (a) for the interrelationships of Palestine and Hellenism, (b) for the variations in

---

[63] Text according to R. Hanhart, *Esther*, Septuaginta, Acad. Litt. Gott. 8,3 (Göttingen: Vandenhoeck & Ruprecht, 1966). Translation of the Additions: Victor Ryssel in Kautzsch, *Apokryphen*; H. Bardtke, "Zusätze zu Esther," in *Jüdische Schriften* 1/1; Eissfeldt, *Introduction*, 511; "Additional Literature and Notes," in Rost, *Einleitung*, 61ff.; Pfeiffer, *History*, 304ff.; R. Stiehl, "Das Buch Esther," *Wiener Zeitschrift für die Kunde des Morgenlandes* 53 (1957): 4–22; C. A. Moore, "On the Origins of the LXX Additions to the Book of Esther," *JBL* 92 (1973) 382ff.; H. Bardtke, "Der Mardochäustag" in *Tradition und Glaube*, Festschrift K. G. Kuhn (Göttingen: Vandenhoeck & Ruprecht, 1971) 97ff.

[64] So R. Stiehl. This conclusion still stands despite the objections of Hengel (*Judaism and Hellenism*, 110–12), who refers to the oriental novelistic material. Cf. already the title from Kerényi (*Die griechisch-orientalische Romanliteratur in religionsgeschichtlicher Beleuchtung* [Darmstadt: Wissenschaftliche Buchgesellschaft, 1962])!

[65] On the flow of Palestinian literature into Egypt, see V. Tcherikover, "Third Book of Maccabees."

[66] Ryssel: The translation reflects Egyptian circumstances. Contra Hengel (*Judaism and Hellenism*, 101): in Rest of Esther 16:10, 14 Haman is described as a Macedonian, a designation that can hardly have originated in Alexandria, where many Jews proudly called themselves this. But this is not a persuasive argument. On Jerusalem, see also Bardtke, "Zusätze zu Esther." 57ff.

Jewish polemic and apologetic, and (c) for the inseparable connection between the Jews' own self-edification and defense against the objections of outsiders (see on *Ep. Ar.*). "Domestic policy" (whereby the elect, and thereby segregated people of God had their own self-understanding strengthened and confirmed) and the "foreign policy" (defense and attack over against the hostile surrounding world) were a unity (a unity in which, of course, from case to case one or the other factor could be emphasized).

The following motifs and topoi may be perceived in the additions to Esther:

(a) Rest of Esther 13:4ff. RSV is precisely a compendium of anti-Jewish polemic in the Alexandrian style, assembled for the purpose of apologetic, in which the familiar objections appear: segregation by their own laws, which stand in contradiction to the laws of all other peoples; hatred of humanity; political opposition, and this not just in particular situations, but as a fundamental principle. This people thus cannot be integrated politically into the rest of society. This results in the demand that they be exterminated (cf. the discussion of Posidonius above); this demand was already anticipated in 12:6; see also 14:9.

(b) The dominant theme in the prayer of Mordecai (Rest of Esther 13:8–17) is that of reassuring themselves of their own sense of election during the time of danger: God's omnipotence, election, salvation; similarly in Esther's prayer in 14:3–19 with the confession of the sin of the people, especially the sin *par excellence,* that of idolatry. The punishment, grounded in God's righteousness, corresponds to this spiritual self-annihilation of Judaism (14:9)

In turn, prayer as such is the proof that there is a basis for hope: it is directed to the *one* God (14:3), the Almighty (13:9ff.), and in its light the gods are seen to be nonexistent.

The date of the colophon need not concern us. Some estimates: Ptolemy VIII (170–163 [Bardtke, "Zusätze zu Esther," 57]); Ptolemy IX and Soter II (116–107 and 88–80) and Cleopatra III; Ptolemy XII (80–51) XIII (51–47) and Cleopatra VII (51–30). On Ptolemy XII, see Bickermann ("Colophon") and Eissfeldt (*Introduction*). The guessing game will continue.

1 Esdras

The book itself does not belong within our field of interest, but we mention it here because of its use by Josephus, who makes a few apologetic emphases in connection with it.[67]

---

[67] On the relationship between 1 Esdras and Josephus, see K.-F. Pohlmann, *Studien zum dritten Esra: Ein Beitrag zur Frage nach dem ursprünglichen Schluss des chronistischen Geschichtswerkes* (Göttingen: Vandenhoeck & Ruprecht, 1970) 113: all the additions can be explained as the editorializing of Josephus.

HELLENISTIC-JEWISH LITERATURE OUTSIDE THE BIBLE[68]

Preliminary Comment on the Sources

Since a chronological history of this literature is not possible, the writings from the LXX will be dealt with first, then the extrabiblical writings (fragmentarily).

The Hellenistic-Jewish literature disappears from our field of view in the first or second century C.E. (on the special situation of *Sib. Or.*, see below), that is, at that point in time when it had not yet become aware of Christianity. Josephus, who stood at the end of this period, was indeed aware of Christianity, but avoided any debate with it (that holds true, even if the *testimonium Flavianum* [*Ant.* 18.63] should turn out to be authentic, in whole or in some undeterminable part—which is hardly possible). In any case, we possess no Hellenistic-Jewish literature that is concerned with Christianity. Whether such may have existed anyway is an idle question. In any case there cannot have been very much. This can be inferred from the few scattered traces in the Christian literature.

The Christian dialogue literature[69] presupposes at least *oral* conversations between Christians and Jews. But to what extent is that a Christian fiction that arose from the necessity that Christians had to be involved with the Jews and with the *Bible?* Can valid inferences be made on the relationship of these two groups in the diaspora? May Jewish material be inferred from the Christian writings?[70]

G. C. O'Ceallaigh ("Marcinnus' Aristide on the Worship of God," *HTR* 51 [1958]: 227–54; Speigl agrees [*Der römische Staat*, 94]) supposes that the *Apology* of Aristides was a Christian reworking of a Jewish document. Simon (*Verus Israel*, XV, 49–50) wants to accept the view (proposed by others) that behind Pseudo-Clement, *Hom.* 4–6 a Jewish source is to be found. (Apion, the opponent of the Jews made notorious by Josephus, here emerges [*Hom.* 4.7, 23;

[68] Still indispensable: J. Freudenthal. *Hellenistische Studien* I, II (1874, 1875); Schürer, *History* 3:468ff.; G. Vermes, *Scripture and Tradition in Judaism* (Leiden: E. J. Brill, 1961). German: N. Walter, "Fragmente jüdisch-hellenistischer Exegeten," in *Jüdische Schriften* 3/2:280ff.

[69] M. Hoffmann, *Der Dialog bei den christlichen Schriftstellern der ersten vier Jahrhunderte*, TU 96 (Berlin: Akademie-Verlag, 1966). Dialogues: Justin; Ariston of Pella; cf. Tertullian, *Adversus Iudaeos* (on the question of authenticity, see below, Part IV).

[70] Speigl's evaluation (*Der römische Staat*, 5ff.): In Rome at the time of Nero and the Flavians, the dominant trend was in the direction of friendliness toward Rome (see Romans 13), and a peaceful coexistence obtained. That is documented on the one hand by Josephus and on the other by Acts, which holds on to the favorable climate that prevailed under the Flavians—e.g., in the way the trial of Paul is presented, which emphasizes the role of Agrippa II and Bernice, friends of the Flavians. Both Josephus and Luke distance themselves from the rebellious Jews (where?). *1 Clement* is also squeezed into this situation, in which the influence of the Jewish tradition favorable to Rome is supposed to be effective (chap. 17). —Response: (1) Josephus and the Christians! (2) The conclusion of Acts and the localities mentioned in the book. (3) Would the time of Domitian be an opportune time to mention Bernice?

5.23ff., 38]). He considers it approximately contemporary with 4 Maccabees.[71] If this were the case, we would possess an extremely valuable document. But G. Strecker (*Das Judenchristentum in den Pseudoklementinen,* TU 70 [Göttingen: Vandenhoeck & Ruprecht, 1958] 78ff.) comes to the conclusion that the Apion sections neither stood in the document that formed the basis of the Pseudo-Clementines nor were they taken from any source at all.

There remains the question of the Jewish sources used by the Gentile Celsus. But the Jew he introduces for the purpose of arguing with Christians is no historical figure, but a literary fiction.

Once again, the perspective from which the survey is seen is: "Monotheism as a political problem."[72] It is not only a question of the problems that monotheism poses for a world that not only *believes* polytheistically, but is structured in such a way that religion and the political order were most closely woven together. Nor is it only a matter of the other question of the problems posed for monotheism in such a world; it is also a question of the grounding of monotheism in the program of monarchy.[73] One must, of course, be aware of the ambivalence of this argument: *De mundo* illustrates the relation of God to the world by the analogy of the emperor; but the same argument can be made for polytheism: the gods are satraps of the highest god.[74]

Demetrius the Chronographer[75]

Nothing is known about the author. Josephus (*Ant.* 12.12ff.; cf. *Ag. Ap.* 2.46) identifies him with Demetrius of Phaleron, whom he knows from *Ep. Ar.* as the initiator of the LXX; so he considers him (along with Philo the Elder and Eupolemus) to be a Gentile (*Ag. Ap.* 1.218).[76]

---

[71] He follows Dupont-Sommer (*Le Quatrième Livre des Machabées* [Paris, 1939]), placing 4 Maccabees after the revolt under Trajan. Bickermann dates it around 35 C.E.; Eissfeldt is undecided; Rost places it in 82, since the temple appears still to be standing.

[72] E. Peterson, *Der Monotheismus als politisches Problem* (1935) (= *Theologische Traktate* [1951] 45ff.).

[73] Ibid., 64. In this connection reference is constantly made to Homer, *Iliad* 2.204: οὐκ ἀγαθὸν πολυκοιρανίη· εἷς κοίρανος ἔστω, εἷς βασιλεύς ("No good thing is a multitude of lords; let there be one lord, one king") Philo, *Conf. Ling.* 170; Origen, *Contra Cels.* 8.68.

[74] Peterson, *Der Monotheismus,* 112 n. 35: *De mundo* was not written by a Jew (as is sometimes supposed): a Jew would have used the picture of the God-king and his officials to combat the polytheistic cult. Philo, *Decal.* 61; *Spec. Leg.* 1.31; Tertullian, *Apol.* 24; Celsus 8.2.35, contra Origen, *Contra Cels.* 8.35f.

[75] Freudenthal, *Hellenistische Studien,* 35ff., 205ff.; Schürer, *History* 3:472ff.; A.-M. Denis, *Introduction aux Pseudepigraphes Grecs d'Ancien Testament* (Leiden: E. J. Brill, 1970) 248ff.; German: N. Walter, "Fragmente Exegeten," in *Jüdische Schriften* 3/2 (1975) 280ff.; and in *Untersuchungen zu den Fragmenten der jüdisch-hellenistischen Historiker* (Habilitionsschrift [masch.], Halle, 1968) 15ff. E. J. Bickermann, "The Jewish Historian Demetrius," in *Christianity, Judaism and Other Greco-Roman Cults,* Festschrift M. Smith (Leiden: E. J. Brill, 1975) 3:72ff. (chronological material).

[76] Demetrius and Josephus: Walter, "Fragmente Exegeten," 280 n. 3: F 6 (Clement of Alexandria, *Strom.* 1.141) from an intermediate source also used by Josephus, *Ag. Ap.* 1.218. – That can be

Time

Clement of Alexandria names Ptolemy IV Philopator (221–204) (*Strom.* 1.141.1–2); the title is also found here: περὶ τῶν ἐν τῇ Ἰουδαίᾳ βασιλέων ("On the Kings in Judea").[77] The book makes it completely clear that it was written by a Jew: it is directed entirely toward the internal concerns of the Jews, with no external orientation at all, either missionary or apologetic. The use of the Bible as a historical source by a Gentile in this period would be unique. And individual comments are entirely Jewish.[78]

Content

The content is an outline of biblical history, with an effort to fit everything into one continuous story by means of chronological adjustments. The source is the LXX. Demetrius is in fact the first author known to us who clearly used this version of the Bible.

The language is primitive, both in sentence construction and vocabulary (Freudenthal: the latter almost entirely within the linguistic environment of the LXX). Some authors see Hellenistic influence present in the stylistic form "questions and answers": F 1.13f.; F 5; cf. *Ep. Ar.;* H. Dörrie, "Methodik" and "Erotapokriseis" in *RAC* 6:342ff. One need not seek literary models.

Chronology

The chronology corresponds to the LXX. The author reckons time from the date of the deportation of the ten tribes and from the deportation of the tribes of Judah and Benjamin up to the time of Ptolemy IV (F 6), and thereby betrays his own date. Unfortunately this fragment has been poorly transmitted. The most probable reconstruction (according to Schürer, *History* 3:473; cf. Walter, "Fragmente," 292) is: from the first deportation until Ptolemy IV, 573 years, and from the second deportation 438 years (the text has 338); this is a good 70 years too long.[79]

---

derived from the garbled fragment and the scanty note by Josephus only by an imagination untroubled by methodology.

[77] Walter, "Fragmente Exegeten," 280: the title does not indicate the comprehensive nature of the work (in fact), or if another work is intended (pure supposition). We will not trouble ourselves with conjectures concerning where Demetrius wrote.

[78] F 1.16: "Since Abraham was chosen from among the Gentiles." F 1.7: The "angel" with whom Joseph wrestled. On the haggadic expansions of the Bible, see below.

[79] Cf. Dan. 9:24-27; Josephus, *J.W.* 6.437ff.; cf. *Ag. Ap.* 2.226; –Schürer, *History* 3:266f. For the relationship to the LXX, cf. Gen. 30:1ff. with F 1.3; Gen. 32:25ff. with F 1.7 (Philo, *Ebr.* 82; *Mut. Nom.* 187; *Somn.* 1.130; Josephus, *Ant.* 1.331ff.); Exod. 22ff. with F 4 (Philo, *Fug.* 183; *Congr.* 162; *Poster. Caini* 155f.; *Vit. Mos.* 1.181; Josephus, *Ant.* 3.1ff.).

Haggadic Material

F 5 (cf. Josephus, *Ant.* 2.349) is an example of "questions and answers" of the type that arise among Bible readers: after the exodus from Egypt, how did the Israelites get weapons?[80] A few typical motifs, chosen at random: Jacob's wrestling with the angel (Hos. 12:4-7; Josephus [see above]; Justin, *Dial.* 58, etc.); Joseph the interpreter of dreams (Philo the epic poet F 2; Artapanus; Justin, *Dial.* 22, etc.); his activities in Egypt.

Moses. Of course, in this book the period of Moses was also calculated. His Ethiopian wife (Num. 11:35) is mentioned (F 3), whereby Midian and Ethiopia are identified, as in Ezekiel the Tragedian. The Jews were shepherds, who were detested by the Egyptians (Gen. 46:34); this is introduced as the reason for Joseph's apparent lack of concern for his father for so long—one of the "questions and answers" (cf. Philo, *Sacr.* 51; *Agric.* 57; Josephus, *Ant.* 2.146).

Although chronology is quite important for Demetrius, concern for chronology is still present for him only in a preliminary form. He does not yet synchronize the biblical data with other systems, but is simply interested in calculating the biblical dates themselves: from Adam until the entrance into Egypt, 3,624 (Hebr. 2,238) years, of which 215 were in Canaan; from Adam to the settlement in Canaan, 1,360 (Hebr. 580). The stay in Egypt was 215 (Hebr. 430) years; thus Canaan and Egypt together, 430 years (see Exod. 12:40 LXX; Josephus, *Ant.* 2.318f).[81]

Cleodemus Malchas (Malchus)

FGH 727 (only one fragment).[82]

He is described by Alexander Polyhistor as the "prophet" Cleodemus, with the epithet Malchas (better documented as Malchus). Whether this fragment derives from his book on the Jews, as is usually supposed, is immaterial for our present concern. (N. Walter argues that this fragment is not from the book on the Jews, because Eusebius quotes from this book, but interrupts the citation with a quotation from this fragment.) The short excerpt reports the marriage of a granddaughter of Keturah to Heracles in Libya, thus creating a genealogical connection between the Jews and the people in or around Carthage (where the author perhaps lives).[83]

---

[80] There is no *literary* connection between Demetrius and Josephus; see the continuation of the passage; cf. Wis. 10:19f.

[81] On the numbers, see the footnote by N. Walter. Wacholder (*Eupolemus,* 98 n. 7): Josephus follows the LXX up to the flood (*Ant.* 1.148–50), except in the manuscripts R and O, which are mistakenly preferred by Niese and Thackeray.

[82] From Alexander Polyhistor in Josephus, *Ant.* 1.239ff., from which Eusebius then draws, *Praep. Ev.* 9.20.2–4. German trans. by N. Walter in "Fragmente jüdisch-hellenistischer Historiker," in *Jüdische Schriften* 1/2 (1976) 115ff.; N. Walter, *Untersuchungen;* Freudenthal, *Hellenistische Studien,* 13ff., 130ff.; Schürer, *History* 3:481; Denis, *Introduction,* 259ff.

[83] On Heracles and Africa, see Juba, *FGH* 275 T, where the name Sophax appears, which Cleodemus also has.

Concerning these primitive attempts to establish family connections between the Jews and other peoples, and thereby improve their station in the world, see 1 Macc. 12:5; Artapanus, Pseudo-Eupolemus. The Jews naturally have the priority: Abraham is a universal ancestor (of the Assyrians as well, according to Cleodemus).

Philo the Epic Poet (the Elder)

Only one item is important for us here: Jews begin to attempt to appropriate Greek literary forms. (See *FGH* 729).

Eupolemus[84]

The author. Josephus considers him too to be a Gentile, and thus does not identify him with the Eupolemus of 1 Macc. 8:17; 2 Macc. 4:11 (*Ant.* 12.419).

The tradition. This poses a problem: Eusebius, *Praep. Ev.* 9.17 is to be excluded: Pseudo-Eupolemus, *FGH* 724 F 1 (cf. Eusebius 9.18.2=724 F 2).

The title. According to Clement of Alexandria (*Strom.* 1.153 [=F 1a]), the title is Περὶ τῶν ἐν τῇ ᾽Ιουδαίᾳ βασιλέων ("On the Kings in Judea").

Time. In a fragment in Clement of Alexandria (*Strom.* 1.141.4 [F 4]), the time is calculated from Adam and from Moses until the fifth year of Demetrius=the twelfth year of Ptolemy: from the exodus on (i.e., to the time of Eupolemus himself) there were 2,580 years (which should be corrected to 1,580).[85]

A. v. Gutschmid (*Kleine Schriften* 2:191ff.): "As Ptolemy ruled the twelfth year in Egypt" was added by Clement from Julius Cassianus (on Cassianus, see Harnack, *Geschichte der altchristlichen Literatur bis Eusebius* [Leipzig, 1893] 1:202f.; Schürer, *History,* 3:476). Without this secondary note, the synchronism and thus the composition of the work are to be dated in the time of Demetrius I

---

[84] *FGH* 723. Text also in Denis, *Fragmenta,* 179ff. German trans. by Walter in "Fragmente Historiker," in *Jüdische Schriften* 1/2 (1976) 93ff. Freudenthal, *Hellenistische Studien,* 105ff.; Schürer, *History* 3:474ff.; J. Giblet, "Eupolème et l'historiographie du Judaisme hellénistique," in *Mélanges G. Ryckmans* (Louvain, 1963) 39ff.; Walter, *Untersuchungen,* 37ff., 156ff.; Hengel, *Judaism and Hellenism,* 92–94; Denis, *Introduction,* 252ff.; Wacholder, *Eupolemus.*
   In Eusebius, *Praep. Ev.* 9.30–34, Demetrius stands in front (F 5). Then follows Theophilus, *FGH* 733 F 1 (34:19), then Eupolemus F 4 (Clement of Alexandria, *Strom.* 1.141=N. Walter, F 5). F 5 (Eusebius, *Praep. Ev.* 9.39) is disputed, since no author's name has been transmitted with it; on the other hand Walter, "Fragmente Historiker," 93 n. 2: The fragment is not anonymous. Eusebius, in fact, has neglected to include the introduction ("Eupolemus says"), but has indicated the author's name in the title to the chapter.

[85] Schürer, *History* 3:476; Walter, "Fragmente Historiker," 95 n. 7; differently Wacholder ("Biblical Chronology," 462), who holds firm to 2,530. Thereby one can remain nearer the Hebrew text for the period from Adam to the exodus; but see Walter: then the second epoch is unexplainably lengthened.

Soter (162–150 B.C.E.) and Ptolemy VIII Euergetes Physkon, who ruled after 170 B.C.E., thus in the year 158 B.C.E.[86]

Use of the Bible. Eupolemus's text was the LXX. Freudenthal, *Hellenistische Studien;* Wacholder, *Eupolemus,* 252: in addition he made use of the Hebrew text (2 Chronicles 2–3). Wacholder, *Eupolemus,* 253: Eupolemus is the only Greek-Jewish author whose knowledge of Hebrew is firmly established. "Eupolemus' approach to history bears a greater resemblance to the style of the priestly authors of the Old Testament than to that of Hellenistic historiography" (p. 217)—but see below (Wacholder, *Eupolemus,* 255f.).

For example. Eupolemus should be compared with 1 Kings 5:21; 2 Chron. 2:11f.; 1 Kings 7:1f., 13f.

The theological position. This is somewhat similar to that of the Maccabees. The book is for the purpose of internal Jewish edification, hardly for missionary or apologetic goals. (Wacholder, *Eupolemus,* 71: F 1, unlike the other fragments, is in fact directed to outsiders, in a polemical tone; the others are priestly).

But the fact is that one cannot here speak of "missionary literature." Nevertheless, tendencies in that direction do appear, with the proof of the antiquity of the Jews: Moses was the first sage (F 1); he introduced the alphabet among the Jews, from whom the Phoenicians obtained it, and the Greeks in turn from them. Thus, the claim is made for the priority of the Jews on a decisive point in the history of culture, not only over against the Phoenicians but also over against the Greeks. Then comes the additional topos: Moses was the first to give laws to the Jews; he was a prophet (F 2). Other prophets followed him; then came the kings.

The power of David is portrayed very vividly (he is regarded as the son of Saul; an error of Alexander Polyhistor?). He is in fact portrayed precisely as the founder of a world empire.

The political picture reflected in the book is that of the Maccabean period: expansion in Palestine-Samaria, which was supported by a good relationship to Egypt; cf. the letters. Further: David's empire expanded to the north and east, but friendship prevailed in the relationship with Egypt (Vaphres from Jer. 51:30 LXX; the time is ignored).

Pseudo-Eupolemus ("An Anonymous Samaritan")[87]

Alexander Polyhistor transmits a fragment under the name of Eupolemus that creates difficulties if it is in fact assigned to him: *FGH* 724 F 1 = Eusebius, *Praep.*

---

[86] Walter, "Fragmente Historiker," 95f. That would fit the Eupolemus of the 1–2 Maccabees.

[87] *FGH* 724. German trans. by Walter in "Fragmente Historiker," 137ff.; Freudenthal, *Hellenistische Studien,* 82ff.; Schürer, *History* 3:482; B. Z. Wacholder, "Pseudo-Eupolemus' Two Greek Fragments on the Life of Abraham," *HUCA* 34 (1963): 83ff.; N. Walter, "Zu Pseudo-Eupolemus," *Klio* 43–45 (1965): 328ff.; idem, *Untersuchungen,* 112ff., 236ff.; Hengel, *Judaism and Hellenism,* 88–92; Denis, *Introduction,* 261f.

Ev. 9.17. There are tensions between the fragment and Eupolemus's own work that can hardly be explained simply as the use of different sources by the same author.[88]

Difficulties. One of the arguments usually brought forward against the authenticity of this fragment is in fact uncertain: the fragment has contacts with another (Eusebius, *Praep. Ev.* 18.2), which Polyhistor introduces as ἀδέσποτον ("anonymous"). How are these two fragments related to each other? Do they in fact belong to the same (i.e., unknown) author, so that neither is from Eupolemus?[89]

On the one hand, there are certain agreements between them: the name Belus, the punishment of the giants, Abraham's descent from them; Abraham as the instructor in astrology, as the first one to communicate this to the Phoenicians; his emigration to Egypt. At this point the fragment F 2 breaks off. But alongside these agreements stand not only differences but also contradictions. This evaluation is made the more difficult by the fact that fragment F 1 is itself confused. At first Abraham is presented as the inventor of astrology etc., who also instructs the Egyptians in this art.[90] But then Abraham explains to them that the Babylonians and he himself had invented astrology, based on Enoch's original knowledge – and not the Egyptians.[91] That fits better in fragment F 2 than in the framework of F 1.[92] Enoch, in turn, fits into F 1: the reference to him fits together with the synchronization with the Eastern-Greek mythology: Enoch is identified with Atlas, who was known among the Greeks as, among other things, both astronomer and mathematician (*PW* 2, see entry "Henoch").[93]

The substance of F 2 (i.e., the first half, which is denied to Pseudo-Eupolemus by N. Walter; see above) is polytheistic: the giants were destroyed by "the gods." It contains an amalgamation of the Greek myth of the Titans and the

---

[88] Freudenthal, whose view has generally prevailed. For ascription to Eupolemus, see, e.g., Bousset-Gressmann, *Die Religion des Judentums,* 21 n. 2: Eupolemus copies a source that also is used by Eusebius (*Praep. Ev.* 9.18.2); it is of Samaritan derivation (see below).

[89] Walter ("Zu Pseudo-Eupolemos," 284) nevertheless raises the question whether the second fragment might come from Pseudo-Eupolemus. He sees the difficulty: the style is different from that of the first fragment. He nevertheless holds fast to the view that the fragment belongs to Pseudo-Eupolemus, arguing that the first half of F 2 is a summary made by Polyhistor from Babylonian legendary material, the second a brief excerpt from parts of F 1. – But Polyhistor subsumes both parts under *one* (the unknown) source.

[90] On Abraham as teacher of the Egyptians: Artapanus F 1; Pseudo-Hecataeus; Josephus, *Ant.* 1.167 (arithmetic and astronomy).

[91] Thus an anti-Egyptian point? That is not certain. It can also simply be based on the "historical" series Babylon – Phoenicia – Egypt.

[92] Abraham was educated in astrology, brought it to the Phoenicians, and then went to Egypt.

[93] Enoch: *Jub.* 4:17ff.; *Eth. En.* 41ff., 72ff.; 1QapGen 2:19ff.; see the commentary by J. A. Fitzmyer, *The Genesis Apocryphon of Qumran Cave I,* BibOr 18A, 2nd ed. (Rome: Biblical Institute Press, 1971). As intermediate agent, Methuselah: *1 Enoch* 106; 1QapGen 2:19ff.

Babylonian version of the saga of building the tower.[94] Of course, one may not appeal to Berosus for the Babylonian story of the tower building.[95] There is no mention of the flood, nor of a collapse of the tower (the giant Belus continues to live in it).

Attempts to explain the absence of both motifs can be made, for example, by claiming that an earlier source was abbreviated by Polyhistor or a predecessor, especially since F 2 is a tiny fragment. But, of course, speculation remains speculation.

Portrayal of history. The portrayal of history is different in the two fragments: F 2 portrays the war of the giants (in which Belus escapes from death). Then the story of Abraham follows abruptly, obviously added through a Jewish or Samaritan reworking of the Gentile text.

The relationship of Abraham to the giants is different than in F 1, in which Jewish and Babylonian traditions are united: flood and tower. Monotheism prevails. The order of events is: flood, then the giants who are saved. Here confusion begins: contrary to the biblical story, the giants appear after the flood: Genesis 6 and 11 are amalgamated or confused.[96]

In the following, F 2 is thus not used to interpret F 1, on methodological grounds.

Some additional comments on the problem of authenticity: The stronger argument against the attribution of the fragment to Eupolemus (however one evaluates their mutual relation) is the fact that Gerizim is "the mountain of the Most High"[97] and that Melchizedek is transferred there as "priest of God" and king.[98] Thus the author is a Samaritan. It is worthy of note that he uses the LXX, as can be seen from the form of the names. Whether he used the Hebrew

---

[94] The name is Babylonian. Belus in F 1 is identical with Chronos—one of the euhemeristic elements. The identification of Belus and Chronos is singular. In F 2 Belus is one of the giants who escapes the destruction and builds a tower in Babylon. On Belus and Babylon, see Abydenus, *FGH* 685 F 1.

[95] Contra Freudenthal, *Hellenistische Studien;* see *Sib. Or.* 3:97ff. (Nikiprowetzky, *Le Troisième Sibylle*).

[96] See further Gen. 10:9f. LXX: the giant Nebroth, ruler of Babylon. Hengel, *Judaism and Hellenism,* 88–92: (a) Compare the combination of flood/founding of Babylon with Berosus and the revolt of the Titans in Hesiod. (b) The founding of Babylon according to Gen. 10:10 (Nimrod). In Pseudo-Eupolemus are Noah (the one who escaped from the flood), Nimrod, Belus, and Chronos all intentionally identified? (Hengel, 89 n. 244) —But there is no connection between the giant Belus and the flood. And how is the giant to be related to the god of the same name? (c) *Sib. Or.* 3 is dependent on Pseudo-Eupolemus; so also Wacholder (see Geffcken, *Komposition,* above).

[97] Freudenthal: the author understands הר עריץ instead of גרזים. Cf. the interpretation of Οὐρίη as "City of the Chaldeans" on the basis of a misunderstood transcription: אור was transcribed as עיר. But, according to Walter, Ur of the Chaldees is represented in the LXX with χώρα τῶν Χαλδαίων ("country of the Chaldeans"); Pseudo-Eupolemus considers Ur to be a city, and he knows that Gerizim is a mountain.

[98] Compare this with the role of the Solomonic temple in Eupolemus. We obviously find ourselves in a time of sharp rivalry between Samaritans and Jews.

text in addition (so Wacholder, *Eupolemus,* 187ff.) is not a significant issue for us.

Time. Egypt is disparaged over against Phoenicia.[99] Since as yet the synthesis with non-Jewish culture remained unbroken, the author is often placed in the pre-Maccabean period. But this is not a valid argument, not only because the author is a Samaritan but because the "cultural synthesis" (how much of this is found in these tiny texts!) did not cease when the Maccabean period began.[100]

Provenance. The provenance is mostly taken to be Syria/Phoenicia/Palestine. Note the emphasis on the Phoenicians and their identification with the Canaanites.[101]

Literary relationships. These cannot be established.[102]

General characteristics. There is a tendency toward making things more rational: historicizing myths and associating them with events in Jewish history. Euhemeristic identifications are made for this purpose: for example, the genealogy of Belus/Chronos is traced via Ham to Canaan, etc. A universalistic tendency is symbolized by Abraham.[103] But one should not describe the attitude as syncretistic (with Hengel against Freudenthal). A polytheistic remnant, resulting from the use of Polyhistor, is found only at the beginning of F 2. The euhemerism is merely an apologetic aid. According to Wacholder, the identifications are no concession to syncretism, but serve to glorify Abraham.—The alternative?

Motifs. (1) Flood, tower building, Babylon.[104] On the flood tradition, see *Sib. Or.* 3.97ff.: the tower was built in the tenth generation after the flood; it was destroyed by a storm. Chronos, Titan, Japetos were rulers; there was a struggle between Chronos and Titan.[105] The relationship of these motifs, within all the

---

[99] According to Walter, that can also indicate struggles in the time of the author. —But there is no indication of this in the text.

[100] Hengel, *Judaism and Hellenism;* according to Walter, there is not yet anything here of the destruction of the temple on Gerizim by John Hyrcanus in 129 B.C.E.

[101] Hengel, *Judaism and Hellenism:* On the role of the Phoenicians in Palestine during the Persian and early Hellenistic period, see Exod. 6:15; Josh. 5:1 LXX; Josephus, *Ant.* 1.258, 260.

[102] Walter: Pseudo-Eupolemus could have used Berosus; so P. Schnabel in 1912, but he retracts this in his 1923 work, *Berossos* (cf. 67–79 in the former with 246 in the latter). Compare F 1 with Berosus, *FGH* 680 F 6=Josephus, *Ant.* 1.158. The reminiscences of the Titans do not come directly from Hesiod (Wacholder [*Eupolemus,* 104f.] obviously has a different view).

[103] Walter: an effort at bridging the gap between the cultures on a biblical basis. For the picture of Abraham, see 1QapGen cols. 19–21, with the commentary by Fitzmyer.

[104] P. Schnabel, *Berossos,* 67ff.: Berosus and Pseudo-Eupolemus count Abraham as the tenth generation; Χοὺμ ῎Ασβολος=the second king after the flood in Berosus Χωμάσβηλος (68); the giants are also from Berosus (Schnabel, *Berossos,* 69ff.): Berosus and the Sibyl. On "tower-building/sibyllinism," see *Sib. Or.*

[105] Cf. Abydenus, *FGH* 685 F 4b (Eusebius, *Praep. Ev.* 9.14). Josephus, *Ant.* 1.93–95; *Ag. Ap.* 1.128ff. (Berosus); Thallus, *FGH* 256; Castor, *FGH* 250 F 1a (Eusebius, *Chron.* 26f.): the giants rose up against the gods and were crushed. —After his death Belus was regarded as a god; Ninus was his successor.

peculiar features that characterize every ancient mythological text, is just as clear as the euhemerism that is so widespread in the flood literature (cf., e.g., Castor, *FGH* 250 F 1; Thallus, *FGH* 256 F 2, 6:—N. Walter). Synchronization: Theophilus, *Autol.* 3.29, according to Thallus, *FGH* 256 F 2, 3: Belus was 322 years before the Trojan War. That must be a mistake; see *Autol.* 3.28: from the flood to the conception of Isaac was 1,036 years. Did the previous passage then read 932?

(2) Abraham. He belonged to the tenth generation (obviously, "after the fall of the giants" is to be understood; on the tenth generation, see above *Sib. Or.* 3). Only F 2 makes anything of his *relationship* to the giants. He is the instructor in astrology; but it is clear that originally he was its inventor. That is now artfully painted over—from the perspective of a Jewish evaluation.

Jewish evaluations of astrology:[106] negative (*Jub.* 12:15, 17; Philo, *Abr.* 69ff.); intensively negative (*Sib. Or.* 3:221ff.; according to Geffcken, *Komposition,* a direct polemic against (Pseudo-)Eupolemus is here present); ambivalent (negatively Pseudo-Philo 4:16 against Gentile astrology, but with a characteristic Jewish adaptation: God revealed to Abraham the arrangement of all the stars [18:5]). The witness for the adoption of astronomical knowledge as a constituent part of the knowledge of the world of the creator is provided by the sections in *1 Enoch* dealing with astronomy.

The rabbinical data are indicated in Billerbeck, *Kommentar* 2:403f.; 3:212f.

Artapanus [107]

Time. Before Polyhistor. The existence of the Jewish temple in Leontopolis is presupposed[108] (from ca. 160 B.C.E. under Ptolemy VI Philometor).

Literary character. It is a historical novel of sorts, spun out of biblical stories, but it reworks these on a rather low level.[109] If one were to take the work seriously, it could be described as a document of pioneering syncretism, but that would pay it too much respect. We may regard it as the work of a Jew with literary ambitions, whose work could still be tolerated by Jews.

The author uses the LXX, as is clear, for example, from Exod. 4:2: ῥάβδον ἐκβαλόντα ὄφιν ποιῆσαι ("He [Moses] threw down the rod that he had and made a serpent").

---

[106] Walter, *Aristobulos,* 226f. n. 5; 233 n. 3; Hengel, *Judaism and Hellenism,* 236–39.

[107] *FGH* 726. The text is also found in Denis, *Introduction aux Pseudepigraphes Grecs* IIIb, 186ff.; German trans.: Walter in "Fragmente Historiker," 121ff.; Freudenthal, *Hellenistische Studien,* 143ff.; Schürer, *History* 3:477ff.; Willrich, *Judaica,* 111ff.; Walter, *Untersuchungen,* 57ff., 176ff.; Denis, *Introduction,* 255ff.

[108] Freudenthal: The author was Jewish, but disguises himself as an Egyptian priest. Artapanus is a pseudonym. Pseudo-Artapanus is identical with Pseudo-Aristeas. But the perspective on the Egyptian religion in which animals were worshiped already argues against this, for according to Artapanus this was instituted by Moses. Cf. *Ep. Ar.* 138.

[109] Wendland, *Die Therapeuten,* 71f.: the organization is from the perspective of the Greek primeval history.

Contents. (1) An explanation of the name "Jews" is given: they are called "Hermiut," which in Greek becomes 'Ιουδαῖοι. They designate themselves as "Hebrews," 'Εβραῖοι, after Abraamos. On "Hermiut," see Freudenthal, *Hellenistische Studien*, 153a: the name characterizes the Jews as "Mosesites," through the identification of Moses and Hermes (see below). The word has an Egyptian tone. Or does it represent ארם יהודה (*'ărām-yĕhûdâ*); cf. ארם דמשׂק (*'ărām-dammeseq*), etc., and thus mean Syrian-Jews?

"Hebrew" of Abraham: see also Charax of Pergamum (*FGH* 103 F 52; *GLAJJ*, no. 335; Reinach, *Textes*, 158; differently Josephus, *Ant.* 1.146). Greek authors later use "Hebrews" for the Jews more often (W. Gutbrod ['Ισραήλ, *TDNT* 3:372]: "rare," but he surveys only a small amount of literature): Alexander Polyhistor, Plutarch, Antonius Diogenes (Reinach, *Textes*, 159) Pausanias *passim*, Porphyry, etc.

"Jews" is used by *Alexander Polyhistor* (*FGH* 273 F 121 = Stephanus of Byzantium; see under the entry 'Ιουδαία, "Jews"). The name derives from the sons of Semiramis, 'Ιούδα καὶ 'Ιδουμαία ("Judas and Idumaea"). The text is damaged. Jacoby (*Fragmente* III a 303): obviously from a book that presupposes the unification of Judea and Idumea (126 B.C.E.). (On Idumea, see the Roman writers below.) The book can hardly be regarded as Jewish, since Jews understand the genealogy in the opposite manner. (Cf. Josephus, *Ant.* 1.240ff.; *FGH* 273 F 102). But the passage probably comes from Alexander Polyhistor Περὶ 'Ιουδαίων ("On the Jews"), who would not have limited himself completely to Jewish sources.

Claudius Iolaus (*FGH* 788 F 4; continued by Alexander Polyhistor F 121 in Steph. of Byz.): ὡς δὲ Κλαύδιος 'Ιόλαος, ἀπὸ Οὐδαίου Σπάρτων ⟨ἐν⟩ ὃς ἐκ Θήβης μετὰ Διονύσου ἐστρατευκότος ("According, however, to Claudius Iolaus, it comes from that of Udaeus, one of the 'Sown-men' of Thebes, who was among the military companions of Dionysus") (see *GLAJJ*, no. 249, 535, and Alexander Polyhistor).

Pompeius Trogus. The king Israhel [*sic*] divided his people into ten kingdoms, corresponding to his ten sons, and called them all Jews . . . "ex nomine Iuda, qui post divisionem decesserat, Iudaeos" ("From Judas, who died soon after this division") (36.2.5).

Plutarch Is. Os. 363 C/D: Typhon fled on an ass for seven days; he became the father of two sons, 'Ιεροσόλυμος (Hierosolymus) and 'Ιουδαῖος (Judaeus). *GLAJJ*, nos. 259 and 563: the story originated in anti-Jewish circles, who charged the Jews with worshiping an ass (Tacitus, etc.).

(2) Abraham came from Babylonia[110] to Egypt and was a teacher of astrology (cf. Pseudo-Eupolemos). He later returned to Syria (Syria included Judea).

(3) Joseph was followed by his father and brothers. The Syrians multiplied

---

[110] Josephus, *Ant.* 1.158 = *FGH* 264 F 3a: Abraham is mentioned also by Berosus; Hecataeus wrote a book about him.

in Egypt. They, the so-called Hermiut, established a temple in Heliopolis[111] and "Athos" (=Pithom?).[112]

(4) Joseph, son of Jacob, grandson (!) of Abraham, outclassed his brothers in σύνεσις ("knowledge") and φρόνησις ("practical wisdom") and fled to Egypt with the help of Arabs.[113] He is portrayed as the bringer of culture. He was the first to devise the system of measurements and divided up the land. In Eusebius, *Praep. Ev.* 9.23.2, social motive appears: he eliminated the discrimination against the weak by the powerful. He was the διοικητής ("governor")[114] of Egypt.

(5) *The period after Joseph* (F 3). Then the oppression of the Jews begins.

(6) *Moses.* There is only one point in the muddled reports concerning Egypt in this part that concerns us: the daughter of Pharaoh, Merris,[115] married but childless, claimed one of the Jewish children as her own and named him Moysos.[116] But after he became an adult, he was called *Musaios* by the Greeks. This Moysos became the teacher of Orpheus (Orpheus: Diodorus 7.1.1, contemporary with Heracles, one hundred years before the Trojan War). His activity in Egypt was carried on in the interests of securing the position of King Chenephres, the husband of Merris. He eliminated the prevailing anarchy. He was an *inventor* in the realm of technology and the originator of philosophy. He established (the Egyptian!) religion.

This is the most uninhibited piece of writing that any Jewish author known to us has allowed himself. (Schlatter [*Geschichte Israels*, 195] asks if Artapanus wants to humiliate the Egyptians. A strange question!) Moses assigns to every district of Egypt the god that is to be worshiped there: cats and dogs and ibisses.[117] Remarkably, the king takes countermeasures (Apis; cf. Diodorus

---

[111] Pseudo-Eupolemus F 1: Abraham lived in Heliopolis with the Egyptian priests and instructed them; Josephus, *Ant.* 2.188: assigned to Jacob and his family as their place of residence.

[112] At the time of Joseph (F 2). Freudenthal, *Hellenistische Studien*, 158: Artapanus egyptianizes the geographical names of the Bible: Pi-thom (Herodotus 2.258: Pathumas) by detaching the article: Ἀθώς (Athos). Exod. 1:11 LXX: the construction of fortresses: Pithom, Ramesses, Om, ἥ ἐστιν Ἡλίου πόλις ("which is the city of the Sun").

[113] The Arabian kings are the descendants of Israel (or Ishmael?), sons of Abraham, brothers of Isaac; Molon, *FGH* 728 F 1; *GLAJJ*, no. 46: Abraham had twelve sons by his Egyptian wife, and they went to Arabia and became rulers. He had another son, Gelos, by his principal wife. This Gelos had twelve sons, the twelfth of which was Joseph, whose third son was Moses.

[114] And Ruler (23:4); N. Walter ("Fragmente Historiker," 128 n. 4 c and "Fragmente Exegeten," 287 n. 12 c) wants to ascribe the passage to Demetrius.

[115] Freudenthal (*Hellenistische Studien*, 154) has an extensive discussion about this, in the interests of his hypothesis that the author disguises himself as an Egyptian priest. Merris (Josephus, *Ant.* 2.224) is Isis. Cf. the tomb of Merris in Meroë, and Diodorus's comments (1.22): a tomb of Isis in Memphis, and still another on the Ethiopian border. —But why would the author encode this equation (Merris=Isis) so carefully?

[116] Later follows a description of the person; cf. Diodorus 1.44.4: letters, in which every Egyptian king is described.

[117] The usefulness of the animals is given as the reason for their worship: Diodorus 1.87, 89. In our case, the usefulness of the ibis is demonstrated during Moses' military campaign against

1.84, 85; Eusebius, *Praep. Ev.* 9.27.12). Thereby Moses secures the monarchy and establishes order. Of course, this causes him to be loved by the people, and the priests, to whom he had distributed choice land, bestow divine honors upon him.[118] He was called *Hermes* because he interpreted the hieroglyphics and allocated the sacred writings to the priests (*Praep. Ev.* 27.6). On top of all this, he was a *general* in the war with Ethiopia, which ended in friendship with the Ethiopians.[119] Finally, there comes the war with Egypt (27:22, according to Sträuben, contra Raguelos, 27:19), and then the exodus. The miracles that happen during the exodus are, of course, related to the miracle stories in the Bible, but with modifications—an increase in the miraculous element—and with additions: 27:20: Chenephres became the first man to die of elephantiasis (on elephantiasis, see Deut. 28:27 Symm.), because he compelled the Jews to wear linen clothing as an identifying mark. In 27:21 a variation of the story of the burning bush is reported, and in 27:23 the miraculous freeing of Moses from prison. In 27:32 Moses' staff, with which he had done several miracles—including the creation of vermin—is related in a remarkable way to the staff used as the cultic symbol of Isis: Isis is the earth, who causes miracles to happen when brought in contact with the staff. In 27:35 there is the suggestion of a rationalistic explanation of the crossing of the Red Sea (ascribed to the Memphites).[120] Only a few places deal more closely with the—hardly developed—idea of God, who is thought of as intervening from time to time. That is practically the only specific motif that is at all developed. The document is completely silent about cult and law.

The characteristic feature is formed by the instances where the power of the *name of God* is illustrated. In 27:25 it has a numinous-psychical effect on the king; in 27:26 the (written) name has a fatal effect on a priest.

We can thus hardly speak of "theology." The *goal* is the glorification of Judaism (though, to be sure, in a peculiar manner), especially through what is said concerning Moses.[121]

Ethiopia (hardly understandable in Artapanus, but cf. Josephus, *Ant.* 2.238ff.).

[118] The same is reported of Joseph in F 2. The context for understanding the political division of the land according to *nomoi* and religious (to each *nomos* its god) becomes understandable first in Diodorus (1.89): thereby a united course of action among the population becomes impossible. —Cf. Diodorus 1.54 (Sesostris); 1.94. Artapanus has been so abbreviated in Polyhistor that he is no longer understandable.

[119] Moses = Tut (Hermes) indicates an awareness of the name Tut-Moses. Tut-Hermes the inventor of writing: Plato, *Phaedr.* 247f.; see R. Hanhart, "Fragen um die Entstehung der LXX," *VT* 12 (1962) 143 n. 1; Diodorus 1.16, 43; Philon of Byblos, *FGH* 790 F 1; Cicero, *Nat. Deor.* 3.22; inventor of art and science, Diodorus 1.16, 43; Plutarch, *Is. Os.* 3; the promoter of the worship of the Egyptian gods, Diodorus 1.20. His sacred animal is the ibis.

[120] Details of Artapanus (who has obviously been abbreviated by Polyhistor) should be supplemented from Josephus, *Ant.* 2.238ff.; Walter, "Fragmente Historiker," 130f.

[121] Walter, "Fragmente Historiker," 124: Artapanus reveals "a picture of an Egyptian Jew who deviates noticeably from strict Judaism and is quite open to syncretism." —Nonetheless, there is never a question of *Jews* worshiping foreign gods, including participation in the Egyptian animal

Sources. The quest for sources would be hopeless, because of the nature of the work. One can only establish relationships between the content and that of Hecataeus of Abdera, Pseudo-Hecataeus, and especially the reports in Diodorus and Plutarch.

Evaluations of the book. Freudenthal remains general: the sections on Orpheus and Musaios in Egypt are from Greek sources (cf. Diodorus 1.23, 92, 96; Hecataeus of Abdera, *FGH* 264 F 25). The division of the land: Diodorus 1.54. Willrich (*Judaica*, 111ff.): Does Artapanus share reports from a common source (i.e., Hecataeus?) with Diodorus and Plutarch? Compare the list of the disciples of the Egyptians in Hecataeus and Plutarch, *Is. Os.* 10.

On the whole work, see Josephus, *Ant.* 2.238ff.—which in any case is not to be derived directly from our version of Artapanus, but more probably variations of the Moses legend.

Ezekiel the Tragedian [122]

Title. 'Εξαγωγή ("Exagoge") Eusebius, *Praep. Ev.* 9.29.14; Clement of Alexandria, *Strom.* 1.155).

Form. The author attempts the form of a drama, but is only minimally successful. There are dramatic scenes (Snell, *Szenen aus griechischen Dramen*), but the work as a whole is predominantly monological with rudimentary dialogical elements. According to Snell, the verse structure indicates that the author has some familiarity with Euripides, and Snell asks whether Ezekiel knows the Persians of Aeschylus. Schürer denies that the play was ever actually intended to be presented on stage, but Snell keeps the possibility open.

Audience. For whom was the work intended? Several scholars suppose that this work was not written for Jews, since those Passover regulations that were offensive to Gentiles were omitted. Among the passages omitted are Exod. 12:23; 4:5; 7:10 and the like (and thus the idea that God proves his divinity by means of miracles). According to Snell, the author obviously supports the idea of a certain kind of coexistence between Judaism and paganism. But that is not in the text; at most what we have is a certain consideration for Gentile readers.

A Philosophical Essay: Aristobulus [123]

We are interested in this essay only from the one point of view, "forms of apologetic." But in this regard Aristobulus is of particular interest, because here

---

cult, even if this was instituted by Moses himself. Precisely this is what is clear. That can be seen from the way in which the relationships between Moses and the Egyptians are developed.

[122] Schürer, *History* 3:500ff.; Dalbert, *Die Theologie der hellenistisch-jüdischen Missionsliteratur*, 52ff.; B. Snell, *Szenen aus griechischen Dramen* (1971), 170ff.

[123] Text (for extant quantity, see below): Denis, *Fragmenta*, 217ff. German: N. Walter in *Jüdische Schriften* 3/2:261ff.; —A. Elter, *De Gnomologiorum Graecorum historia atque origine commentatio I–IX* (Bonn: Universitätsprogramme, 1893–95); Schürer, *History* 3:512ff.; Denis, *Introduction*, 277ff.; Hengel, *Judaism and Hellenism*, 163–69. See especially N. Walter, *Der Thoraausleger Aristobulos.*

nascent forms of both apologetic and Hellenistic-Jewish exegesis can be perceived: the first signs of the "proof of the antiquity" and the use of allegory to dispose of anthropomorphisms, though still in the beginning phase of its development. Nor is this the only method employed, for midrashic expositions are found alongside the more hellenizing approach.[124]

The Quantity of Transmitted Material

Clement of Alexandria, *Strom.* 5.97.7: Aristobulus composed βιβλία ἱκανά ("many books").[125]

The Enumeration of the Fragments

K. Mras's edition of Eusebius, *Praep. Ev.* numbers 7.14 as F 1. But that is a part of F 5. Hence Walter, *Aristobulos*, 7: Eusebius, *Hist. Eccl.* 7.32.16–18 (according to Anatolius) is to be numbered F 1. Then the further enumeration of Mras can be preserved.

The Problem of Authenticity (see Walter, *Aristobulos*, 35ff.)

If the work is authentic, when was it composed? Which of the Ptolemies is meant? F 3b (Eusebius, *Praep. Ev.* 12.12.2) speaks of the king as a descendant of Philadelphus (Ptolemy II, the supposed sponsor of the translation of the LXX). Thus the report of Eusebius (*Hist. Eccl.* 7.32.16) that a beginning was made under Philadelphus by Anatolius (in which Aristobulus was one of the seventy translators) is false. According to Clement of Alexandria and Eusebius, the book was prepared for Ptolemy VI Philometor;[126] he was the sole ruler in the years 176–170; prior to that he shared the reign with his mother, and after that with his (brother and) sister. (See Clement of Alexandria, *Strom.*

---

[124] Walter, "Fragmente Exegeten," 265: Aristobulus is not yet familiar with Philo's understanding of the double sense of Scripture and does not yet have any ethical-psychological exposition. Wendland in Elter, *De Gnomologiorum Graecorum historia* 9:229ff.: The book is Christian and dependent on Philo (a view also opposed by Bousset-Gressmann, *Die Religion des Judentums*, 28f.).

[125] Schürer, *History* 3:513: That probably does not mean several works, but *one* comprehensive book. Clement identifies the author with the Aristobulus in the fictional letter of 2 Macc. 1:10 (cf. Eusebius, *Praep. Ev.* 8.9.38, where he appears as teacher of Ptolemy in the fictional framework: Ptolemy VI Philometor). Walter, "Fragmente Exegeten," 261: a free invention by the composer of the fictional letter; confidently opposed by Hengel, *Judaism and Hellenism*, 163 n. 373.

[126] Schürer, *History* 3:512f.; Hengel, 164 n. 378. Walter, *Fragmente Exegeten*, 262: We can still recognize from Clement of Alexandria (*Strom.* 5.97.7) that the identification with Philometor is simply derived from 2 Macc. 1:10. — It still may be correct. Hengel, 164 n. 378: Assignment to the time of Ptolemy VIII (IX) Lathyrus (116–108 and 88–80) is unlikely, because of his hostility to the Jews. Lathyrus: Josephus, *J. W.* 1.86; *Ant.* 13.284-87, 328ff., 356, 358f., 370; Schürer-Vermes-Millar, *History* 1:219ff.; *CPJ* 1 no. 24f.; *Kl. Pauly,* under Ptolemaios, no. 12.

1.150=Eusebius, *Praep. Ev.* 9.6.6; Eusebius, *Chron. ad Olymp.* 151; 176–172 B.C.E.) The situation of the Jews under Philometor was good.[127] But things began to get worse under Ptolemy VII Physkon.[128]

Purpose

The dedication already indicates that the author writes primarily for Gentile readers. According to Walter (*Aristobulos,* 29), the primary purpose is not the proving of the high age of the Jewish philosophy but the justification of Judaism before the bar of Greek thought.[129] In fact, the "proof of antiquity" has not yet been consistently constructed. To be sure, Greek philosophy is dependent on Moses. But (see Walter, *Aristobulos,* 44) Aristobulus does not yet affirm that *all* Greek wisdom derives from the Jews (see Artapanus on this point). It is nonetheless remarkable how many names are found in the few extant fragments: Socrates, Plato, Pythagoras, Orpheus, (Musaios), Arat, Hesiod, Linus, Homer. On the other hand, one must concede Walter's point that Clement and Eusebius both regarded this text from the perspective of the "proof of antiquity" and sought it out and preserved it for this reason.[130]

Content

The content is the exposition of the Mosaic laws (Eusebius, *Praep. Ev.* 7.13.7). The work is, in point of fact, a philosophical exposition, intended for readers with a Greek education. Eusebius, *Praep. Ev.* 8.9.38: Aristobulus combined the philosophy of Aristotle with that of the fathers. There are incidental explanations of the legal prescriptions as such (see F 1; Eusebius, *Hist. Eccl.* 7.32.17f.).[131] The description "Peripatetic" does not prove that he was an Aristotelian in the strict sense. This is seen even in his method of exposition: he follows the

---

[127] Josephus, *Ant.* 12.387f.; 13.62ff.: *Ag. Ap.* 2.48f.; —Schürer, *History* 3:131, 144f.; Walter, *Aristobulos,* 35ff.; Bengtson, *Herrschergestalten,* 465ff.; *CPJ* 1 no. 20f. Hostility to Antiochus IV: Josephus, *Ant.* 12.235, 242ff.; *J.W.* 1.31ff.

[128] Josephus, *Ag. Ap.* 2.51ff. In 3 Maccabees the hostility is transferred to Ptolemy IV. Schürer, *History* 3:108 n. 32: despite the legendary character of 3 Maccabees, it correctly reflects the hostile attitude of Physkon, since the Jews supported his rival Cleopatra. Willrich (*Juden und Griechen,* 142ff.) understands the matter in exactly the opposite fashion: Physkon was the friend of the Jews. This is rejected by Schürer.

[129] An alternative view? Walter, *Aristobulos,* 28f.: Eusebius took pains to find passages in Aristobulus that he could use for the major theme he developed in *Praep. Ev.* 11–13 (namely, the "proof of antiquity").

[130] But did both possess the unabbreviated form of the work? Affirmed by Walter, *Aristobulos,* 27 n. 1, 34 n. 6, and 97ff. Doubted by Hengel, *Judaism and Hellenism,* 164 n. 374.

[131] On the method of exposition, see Schürer, *History* 3:513f.: "Analogous material . . . is not found in the allegorical commentaries of Philo on individual texts, but rather in Philo's systematic presentation of the Mosaic giving of the law. . . ." In the doctrine of creation, *wisdom* is a characteristic Jewish factor (Proverbs 8; Wisdom of Solomon; Sirach 24; Philo).

(Pergamenic-Stoic) allegorical method, not the (Alexandrian) Peripatetic philological method.[132] Incorrectly quoted bits of poetry were pressed into service for his purposes.[133]

When one considers the work of Aristobulus as a whole, Walter's point (*Aristobulos*, 129) must be granted: The relationship of Aristobulus to the Bible must be fundamentally distinguished from that of every Greek to Homer: one cannot play around with mythology (cf. Eusebius, *Praep. Ev.* 8.10.2). Monotheism is presupposed. One only has to take the trouble to find it in the text.

Summary

Is it possible to construct a summary? The structure (see Eusebius, *Praep. Ev.* 8.10.1) appears to indicate a certain schema: (1) Confirming the correct view of God, with a rejection of everything mythological and anthropomorphic; *one* God, Creator, and Lord—from which the stability of the world is derived. Revelation. (2) Method: Pressing poets and philosophers into the service of his own purpose. (3) The law, with a tendency toward ethicizing. (4) The creation; the Sabbath; the motif of stability occurs also here. Thus the beginnings of an apologetic are present: the Gentile is referred to the Bible, and the "proof of antiquity" is hinted at. Even though the argument is not chronologically structured, that is appropriate to the character of the book, which in any case does not claim to be a history.

A Literary Essay: The Letter of Aristeas[134]

According to Tcherikover ("Ideology") the addressees are Jews. We must later ask whether the literary character of the document justifies this conclusion. Despite the literary ambition of the author (imitation of the symposia literature, discussion with sages, imitation of the genre Περὶ βασιλείας ("On Kingship"), the manner of argument is thoroughly naïve.

The document is pseudonymous. The author pretends to be a high official of Ptolemy II Philadelphus (coruler 285–283, then sole ruler until 246), who writes to his brother Philocrates, the explicit subject of the letter being the

---

[132] On philology, see Wendland, *Kultur*, 112ff.; K. Müller, "Allegorische Dichter erklärung," *PWSup*. 4:16ff.; Walter, *Aristobulos*, 124ff.

[133] A matter of debate: which Pseudo-Orpheus text was originally present in Aristobulus? Cf. Walter, "Fragmente Exegeten," 265; idem, *Aristobulos*, 103ff.: Aristobulus originally cited a different Pseudo-Orphic poem; accepted by Hengel, "Anonymität," 292ff.

[134] Editions of the text: P. Wendland (*Aristeae ad Philocratem* [Leipzig, 1900]); M. Hadas (1951) (with commentary); M. Pelletier, SC 89 (Paris: Cerf, 1962) (with French translation); Wendland, in Kautzsch, *Die Apokryphen und Pseudepigraphen des Alten Testaments* 2:1ff. (German translation); N. Meisner, "Aristeasbrief," in *Jüdische Schriften* 2/1:35ff. —N. Meisner, *Untersuchungen zum Aristeasbrief* (Diss., Berlin, 1973, duplicated) 2:93ff.

translation of the Jewish law into Greek for the library in Alexandria at the suggestion of Demetrius of Phaleron (§9).

Date

There is great variety among the various suggestions for dating:

(1) Wendland: The Palestinian conditions alluded to presuppose a date between 96 B.C.E. (the rule of Alexander Janneus over the coastal area; see §115) and 63 (Pompey). The provenance is determined to be the island Pharos (Alexandria); the island had been deserted since the time of Caesar (Strabo 17.6).

(2) Willrich, *Judaica:* The picture of Palestine (with harbors) fits only the time of the Roman province; at that time the harbors were all controlled by one central authority. Measures against informers (§167) had existed since Tiberius (33 C.E.; contra Meisner, "Aristeasbrief," 66 n. 167). The question and answer (§§282f.) are appropriate to the time of Herod and Augustus (?).

(3) E. Bickermann ("Die Datierung des Pseudo-Aristeas," *ZNW* 29 [1930]: 280ff.) investigated the use of Ptolemaic titles and formal expressions and arrived at a date of 145-127 B.C.E.—an uncertain criterion, when a book is written by a layperson who understands little of the language of politics and protocol and who was probably dependent on various sources of undeterminable dates anyway. On Egypt and Palestine, see further the Zenon Papyri; *PCairoZenon* 59003 and 56075 (letters of Tobias to Apollonius and Ptolemy) are especially interesting. See Hadas, *Aristeas,* 46f.

(4) Pelletier: the beginning of the second century B.C.E.

(5) Eissfeldt, *Introduction,* 705: not prior to the end of the second century B.C.E.

(6) Meisner affirms a special situation between 127 and 118/117 B.C.E. (with keen perception, but without any basis in the text): the threatening times under Ptolemy VII Physkon. Contra S. Jellicoe ("Aristeas, Philo and the Septuagint Vorlage," *JTS* n.s. 12 [1961]: 261ff.): prior to the ultimatum of Popilius Laenas (168 B.C.E.).

A special problem derives from the appeal to Hecataeus (§31), who wrote an excursus on the Jews in his *Egyptica* (*FGH* 264 F 6 = Diodorus 40.3) (*GLAJJ,* no. 11). Wendland and Geffcken (*Apologeten*) in fact consider Hecataeus to be the source. But what is contained therein cannot have been written by the real Hecataeus, so the Jewish apologist Pseudo-Hecataeus must be intended (see further §312ff.).

On the irksome Hecataeus problem, see further §§12ff. and 22ff.

Ptolemy I overran Syria and Phoenicia and deported one hundred thousand Jews to Egypt; a part of them were settled there as military colonists. For a contrary view, see Josephus, *Ag. Ap.* 1.186 according to Pseudo-Hecataeus: after the battle of Gaza Ptolemy I also occupied Syria. Many of the inhabitants there wanted to relocate voluntarily in Egypt; Josephus, *Ag. Ap.* 1.194 (Pseudo-Hecataeus).[135]

---

[135] Conquest of Jerusalem by Ptolemy I: Josephus, *Ag. Ap.* 1.209ff. = *Ant.* 12.3f. = Agatharchides,

Contents

The apologetic style is especially clear at the very beginning, in the address of the fictitious Gentile (!) author to the king concerning Judaism. The Jewish faith is summarized: *one* God and *one* law (§§15f. 132). With this phrase the uniqueness of Judaism is expressed in the shortest possible summary, with which two items of information are given: The God of Israel is the God whom all other people worship, only it is under the name Zeus (Zena, Dia; Zeus, zen; Diodorus 3.61.1, etc.). Thus the author (who is operating as a "Gentile") falls back on the favorite Greek (especially Stoic) etymological explanations of the names of the gods, which we will meet even more often later (Cornutus is only one example); cf. Abydenus (Eusebius, *Praep. Ev.* 9.12.2). And Aristeas can bestow the same attributes on his God as the Greeks do on theirs: goodness (Stoics; Geffcken on Aristides 1.3); he presides over the whole world (§254, cf. 201); he is the governor of human thinking (§§17, 227, 246).

We have here both an attempt to hold fast to monotheism and a tactic to commend it to others (see Josephus, *Ant.* 12.22): it can be said to the king that this God also rules *his* kingdom and that the king owes him a debt of thanksgiving (§§35ff.). None of the Jewish claims is in reality given up. Fundamentally, this "Zeus" is really Yahweh, the God of the Torah. But is he, really? In any case, a problem that is to be present for some time here emerges, the problem of the *name* of God: can God in fact be worshiped under different names? Does he then remain the same?

Is it possible with the help of these ideas from the philosophy of religion for Jews (and Christians) and Gentiles to come to a mutual understanding? Origen will thoroughly discuss this issue in his debate with Celsus—and will deny the possibility. At first we need only to press the question of whether such a concession does not necessarily dissolve the Jewish understanding of God. And does the way in which the doctrine of monotheism is formulated in Judaism offer any means of defense? If so, which?

In §31 we come to the edge of the theme of the Jewish apologists: Judaism does not "go over well" with the Gentiles.[136] Then the apology proper begins in §131, with the motifs and structures that have already become familiar to us, here arranged in a catechetical form.

(1) An introduction of sorts (§§128ff.) deals with the regulations concerning abstinence (on §129, see Philo, *Op. Mund.*): Jews are commanded to abstain from certain things, even though the world is still regarded as God's creation.

(2) The lawgiver: a man of piety and justice.

FGH 86 F 20 (*GLAJJ*, no. 30a); Appian, *Syr.* 50. Further on §13: there were already Jewish mercenaries under the Persians and previously (Psammetich).

[136] Jews explained this as the result of the fact that Gentiles did not really know Judaism; Philo, *Vit. Mos.* 1.2f.: They are acquainted with the person Moses, but nothing beyond that. See also Josephus, *Ag. Ap.* 1. "Jerusalem" provided a certain point of contact, for the city was just as well known as the nature and essence of Judaism were ignored or misunderstood (Pliny, *Hist. Nat.* 5.7; Tacitus, *Hist.* 5.2).

(3) The main thing: There is *one* God, *one* ruler (cf. the other apologetes). Along with this affirmation comes the polemic against (a) polytheism and (b) the worship of images, and the irrationality of this error is illustrated: the worship of images not only of human beings, but even of animals (the Egyptians)! One is immediately reminded of Wisdom 13ff.[137]

(4) The positive counterpart is the praise of the Jews as a "godly people" alongside other people.

Section §139 appears as something of an erratic block in this context (cf. the opposing view in §§15f.): the purpose of the law is the separation of the Jews from all other peoples; it is the protective wall around the Jewish nation. This is also the reason for the regulations concerning ritual purity (§142).

It appears that this exposition can be understood only on the hypothesis (see above) that the book was not written for missionary purposes, but was intended for Jews. On the other hand, the point of view can suddenly change: it is precisely this segregation that allows the Jews to be considered godly people in the eyes of the Egyptian priests (immediately after the Egyptians had been classified as the most evil of the worshipers of false gods). In any case, here is a seam in the text. Even if it is impossible to reconstruct different sources, we cannot fail to observe the somewhat inconsistent juxtaposition of different sources.

Another case: the metaphorical exposition of biblical cult traditions in §144, which likewise was already traditional, fits poorly with §142.[138] The author looks for arguments wherever he thinks he can find any. In this Hellenistic Judaism it is possible to make use of a jumble of elements of Jewish and Greek wisdom willy-nilly (cf. the rulers' code as a Greek example; see Meisner on §§188f., 258; cf. Diodorus 1.56).

Audience

Can we *summarize* the argument over the question of the intended readership of the book? The contributions to the discussion may be listed:

(1) G. Stählin, "Josephus und der Aristeasbrief," *TSK* 102 (1930): 323ff.: The apologetic is also directed to *insiders*, serving the purpose of justifying the LXX in the eyes of the Jewish community. Josephus is not interested in this. —What now? What is the logic here?

(2) G. Zuntz, "Aristeas-Studies," *JJS* 4 (1959): 21ff., 109ff.: Primarily intended for *Greek* readers, used as a model by Pseudo-Hecataeus. Zuntz convincingly establishes that the letter was concerned only with the translation of the Torah. —But what does this prove?

---

[137] Cf. *Sib. Or.* frag. 1; 3:11ff.; frag. 3; Pseudo-Justin, *Coh.* 16.
[138] Philo, *Det. Pot. Ins.* 4–7; Hadas, *Aristeas:* a response to the charge of isolation, like Esth. 3:8 and 3 Macc. 3:4.

(3) V. Tcherikover, "The Ideology of the Letter of Aristeas," *HTR* 51 (1958): 59ff.: For Jewish readers; see §§139ff. It is true enough that the Jewish apologetic literature was a reaction to anti-Semitism. But there is no evidence of Greek anti-Semitic writings before the time of the Maccabees. Manetho was an Egyptian. Was there any interest among the Gentiles in the refutation? (§§130–69). –But that is no argument: the question is whether it was such in the opinion of the author.

Tcherikover elaborates on the internal polemic of §122. The author wants to instruct Jews that there is no yawning chasm that separates Jews and non-Jews, that Jews can in fact associate with Gentiles; he sketches the picture of ideal Judaism. The ideal portrayal of Palestine is intended to teach that one should be bound not to the Hasmonean Palestine but to the pure, holy land. It is only the law that opens the door to culture for the Jews (by means of a fundamental isolation?), because it makes clear to the Greeks (indeed!) the superiority of the Jews to the barbarians. Thus the Jews should hold fast to it, even when it leads to isolation from the other nations (and from the Greeks?) (§139).

Despite the enormous failure of logic inherent in Tcherikover's argument, one can still well affirm the conclusion that the alternative "or" was not present. The literary form itself already speaks for the view that the author wrote for Jews *and* Greeks–whether the form achieved its intended purpose or not.

The Wisdom of Solomon[139]

This is the most significant document in the development of the apology as a literary type prior to Philo. That is not to say that literary dependence existed between Philo and Wisdom, but that they used related traditions and that there was a continuity of the *literary* type, for which, to be sure, Wisdom provided a widely used model (and Wisdom itself already stood in such a tradition).

The question of *authorship* has no prospect of an answer. The further question as to whether a part of the book was originally composed in Hebrew (so, e.g., Focke, *Entstehung,* 74ff., today denied by practically all) is not important for our concern. Likewise the question of the *literary unity*[140] of the book

---

[139] Text and commentary: J. Reider, *The Book of Wisdom* (New York: Harper, 1957); German: K. Siegfried in Kautzsch, *Apokryphen,* 476ff. Commentaries: C. L. W. Grimm, *Das Buch der Weisheit erklärt* (Leipzig, 1860); J. Fichtner, *Die Weisheit Salomos,* HAT (Tübingen: Mohr-Siebeck, 1938). Lit.: Schürer, *History* 3:505ff.; F. Focke, *Die Entstehung der Weisheit Salomos* (Göttingen: Vandenhoeck & Ruprecht, 1913); Pfeiffer, *History,* 313ff.; Eissfeldt, *Introduction,* 600, 772; Rost, *Einleitung,* 41ff.; J. M. Reese, "Plan and Structure of the Book of Wisdom," *CBQ* 27 (1965): 391ff.; F. Ricken, "Gab es eine hellenistische Vorlage für Weish 13–15?" *Bib* 49 (1968): 54ff.

[140] Fichtner, *Weisheit,* 7. Perspective: In Part I (chaps. 1–5) the hope of immortality; this is lacking in Part III (chaps. 10–19), except for 15:3. It is possible that this is to be accounted for, of course, by the subject matter of this section. Philosophical material is practically limited to Part II (chaps. 6–9); here too the theme dealt with offers an explanation for the data.

is a secondary concern for us, since we are dealing with the final form of the book, and in fact with an independent unit within it. The objections against the unity are in any case not convincing in my opinion. Such objections in part confuse change in motifs with a change of authorship.

Regarding the date, it is clear that the *terminus post quem* is the LXX. Compared to Philo, the book functions in a rather archaic manner in the reception of philosophical elements and in its exegetical procedures, which are not allegorical but a strangely encoded history of Israel. The Logos doctrine is barely hinted at (once, 18:15) rather than being developed didactically, though it is true enough that the idea of hypostatized wisdom is utilized.

For our purposes, the usual division of the book into three parts is satisfactory.

1. Chapters 1-5: Polemic

This is directed against the infiltration of Greek thought patterns and life-style into Hellenistic Judaism, especially (of course) in the upper class, and departures from the Jewish rule of faith and practice. The addressees are (despite 1:1ff.: the rulers) the endangered Jewish community as such—endangered by the seductive enticements being offered by Epicureanism (more as an attitude toward life than as a philosophical system) and sophistry (with its view of the world and the resulting ethical consequences). The world came into being accidentally (thus not through the work of a Creator—which also invalidates his law; the connection of creation and the giving of the law will also be a primary theme of Philo). Thereby the idea that pleasure is the goal of life is given free reign (2:6), along with the sophist morality that "might makes right" (2:11).[141]

There are some specifically Jewish elements: the polemic (3:8) formed through the view of the future, the judgment, and the future Jewish rulership over all nations. Eschatology makes its appearance.[142]

Here (alongside 1 Macc. 1:11ff.; 2 Maccabees 4; Philo, *passim*) we get an insight into the fundamental problematic inherent in the existence of the Jews within the culturally superior Hellenistic world, with its ceaselessly fascinating attitude toward life.[143] This is of fundamental value in the recognition of the historical presuppositions of the Jewish apologetic and its literary form. This apologetic does not necessarily presuppose "anti-Semitic" attacks from outside. It is too often seen from the perspective that it was a defense against such assumed attacks.

Of course, the Jewish apologists did write defenses against such attacks, a defense that reached its high point in the last such writing of which we are aware—Josephus. But it reveals its *primarily theological* character in the fact (which can be seen already in the structure of Wisdom) that its *first* goal was

---

[141] Callicles in Plato, *Georg.* 483.

[142] See the eschatological elements in chaps. 10–19.

[143] Along with the suffering of the righteous and God's ultimate intervention for them.

to present the Jewish concept of monotheism with its consequences (Wisdom 1–5: righteousness/justice) and the destruction of polytheism with its worship of images and the perversion of morality that necessarily follows.

Thus it is—contrary to the alternative of Tcherikover and others mentioned above—precisely because of its basic, positive-theological impulse to be called "missionary literature." The *one* God is the God of the whole world, and his order is the order of the world and humanity as a whole. The inner struggle of Judaism concerning its existence demands both together: Jewish parenesis that was both a defense against paganism and at the same time an effort to win the pagans over, a struggle against both its internal influence and its attack from without, a parenesis that demonstrated that the connection between religion and morality in the world existed at all.[144]

2. Chapters 6–9: The Praise of Wisdom and Her Works

It is customary to point out the influence of Greek philosophical thought in this section, but elements of the "rulers' code" (cf. *Ep. Ar.*) should also be noted. In chaps. 7 and 8 the author attempts to become chummy with his (real or hoped-for) public, that is, the Greek public that includes the Jews. This latter is intended expressly to make the point that the general public can be addressed without surrendering the substance of Judaism. In material purportedly addressed to Gentiles, the Jewish people is held up as *the* example of a place where Wisdom truly rules. The tendencies toward a hypostatization of the picture of Wisdom as the wisdom of *God* (7:22ff.) belong to a broad stream of Jewish tradition (Proverbs 8; Sirach 24, continued in the New Testament). To this stream of tradition belongs also the stylistic form of the hymn of praise (for the New Testament, see commentaries on 1 Corinthians 13).

From the very beginning, the dominant thread of the argument was provided by the motif of monotheism in the discussion of wisdom itself, and then in the next chapters.

3. Chapters 10–19: The Unseen Rule of Wisdom in the History of Israel

The passage that primarily interests us, chaps. 13–15, is found in this section. It is inserted into the context somewhat forcibly: the connection between chaps. 12 and 16 is interrupted by it.[145]

---

[144] This was done while holding fast to the idea of the prerogatives of Israel, which, incidentally, can be soft-pedaled for tactical reasons (Philo).

[145] Though this is quietly prepared for by the reference to the philanthropy of the Jews in 12:19 and the preliminary polemic against animal worship in 12:24; and see later the transition from 15:15f. to chap. 16. Despite such seams, the unity of the book is to be maintained.

In themselves these three chapters represent a self-contained unit, a complete, formally correct apology. Thus both features are to be observed: the formal rigidity of the apology as a literary type, which is an interpolation into the larger framework of internal Jewish polemic and edification, and the bipartite proof of the hidden rule of Wisdom.

The Apology, chapters 13–15. This is the most significant and most stylistically pure document of this literary genre prior to Philo, a document that already has taken up traditional ideas of the struggle against idolatry. (This struggle had been going on since Deutero-Isaiah, Ep. Jer., the LXX additions to Daniel). Development in the genre is seen in the way the tradition is incorporated within the connection between the *knowledge* of God and the *worship* of God. This connection had developed the relation between religious perversion and ethical perversity much more strongly and more systematically than previously.[146] The "theoretical" foundation for the whole apology is laid in 13:1-9: establishing the "vanity" (a key word in the polemic against idolatry) of paganism resulting from the ignorance of a humanity that does not know how to distinguish the creator from the material objects of creation. Here, too, basic ideas of Greek religious philosophy are adopted, although their theoretical character is attenuated. 13:1: Μάταιοι μὲν γὰρ πάντες ἄνθρωποι φύσει, οἷς παρῆν θεοῦ ἀγνωσία καὶ ἐκ τῶν ὁρωμένων ἀγαθῶν οὐκ ἴσχυσαν εἰδέναι τὸν ὄντα οὔτε τοῖς ἔργοις προσέχοντες ἐπέγνωσαν τὸν τεχνίτην ("What born fools all men were who lived in ignorance of God, who from good things before their eyes could not learn to know him who really is, and failed to recognize the artificer though they observed his works!" [NEB]).

That does not mean, for example, that human beings in principle, or because of their essential nature, are incapable of coming to a knowledge of God; the capacity for this is in fact given (v. 5). But they have not realized this potential. Thus on the one hand they are guilty (13:8), but on the other hand they are to a certain extent excused (13:6), since they nevertheless are seeking God, however erroneously.

The passage is a *locus classicus* for the unavoidable association of all monotheistic thinking with a natural theology, unless this monotheism is anchored in a historical act of revelation. Wisdom of Solomon does then in fact draw the conclusion that is given in its presuppositions: the existing error can be overcome by instruction, since a true knowledge of God is a realizable possibility for humanity as such. Whether the individual person does in fact realize this potential is quite another matter.

Although it may be an unfashionable idea, we might nonetheless say that "paganism" in all its varieties is not to be overcome by such a monotheism, however consistent it may be, for in both cases a true relationship to God is considered to be a possibility inherent in humanity as such. Objection: But

---

[146] Rom. 1:18ff.; see Lietzmann, *An die Römer,* 5th ed., HNT (Tübingen: Mohr-Siebeck, 1971) *ad loc.*

what about the Jewish concept of revelation? Here too the central problem of the concept of God remains unresolved, because the revelation occurs in empirical events (or events believed to be such)—therefore, in events that are available for general examination. Thus the affirmation that or how revelation from God is present in some special sense is dependent on an interpreter of the events—even if one also ascribes supernatural "prophetic" capacities to such interpreters. Between God and humanity a third intermediary human agent emerges, who becomes a supplement to faith, a supplement that eliminates the *sola fide* so essential to the gospel as understood within the Protestant perspective. This supplementary understanding of faith demands a legalistic accomplishment, even if this "work" is only an intellectual one. Thereby the possibility is opened for God to become the object of critical examination within the context of human religion, for example, in the style that is excluded by Paul in Rom. 1:18ff.

A firm schema emerges: the worship of images, stars, and the elements, or, more systematically: the world/elements, matter/images. Thereby the path that leads to the emperor cult is already hinted at (along with the taking up of some euhemeristic elements for polemical purposes, which thus uses them in a sense contrary to their original euhemeristic intention). There is a concluding polemic against the worship of animals (here we find ourselves in an Egyptian milieu). The following sections of this book will show how constant this type is, as we discuss Philo, *Hypoth., Decal., Vit. Cont.*[147]

It is no surprise that repeatedly a special point of the polemic is always against the Egyptian animal cult (also hinted at in Rom. 1:18ff.). For this theme also, Wisdom of Solomon forms the prelude (15:18f.); here too are found the recurring indications that especially repulsive animals were preferred as the objects of such worship (one thinks of R. Otto; Wisdom of Solomon 12:24). On this point, the apologetes were able to refer especially well to pagan examples: Egyptian religion was a popular subject in the ethnographic literature.[148]

---

[147] See further examples below: *Ep. Ar.* 135ff.; *Sib. Or. passim; Ep. Jer.*: Images are ephemeral; they get dusty and are incapable of taking care of themselves. This becomes a *topos:* images are subject to bats and other varmints. Ridicule is a solid weapon; see Preuss, *Verspottung.*

These *topoi* then become a part of the arsenal of Christian apologetes: on bats, etc., see Minucius Felix, Tertullian; see Geffcken, *Apologeten*, XVIf., 276. But can one who is supposedly in the service of a christologically conceived monotheism use ridicule as a weapon? Here is a question concerning the concept of God held by Christian apologists!

[148] Egypt: Hecataeus of Miletus, *FGH* 1; Herodotus *passim* (2.46, 143); Hecataeus of Abdera, *FGH* 264; Diodorus, book 1; Plutarch, *Is. Os.;* Celsus 3.19. Geffcken, *Apologeten* 11, 27: the examination of Egyptian animal worship was a firm part of Hellenistic religious tractates. Cicero, *Nat. Deor.* 1.16.43; Sextus Empiricus, *Hyp.* 3.219; Maximus of Tyre 8.5; Lucian, *Jup. Trag.* 42; *Deorum conc.* 10. Jews: *Ep. Ar.* 238; *Sib. Or.* 3:30; 5:77ff., frag. 3:22; Philo: *Ebr.* 95; *Decal.* 76; *Vit. Cont.* 8; *Leg.* 139; Josephus, *Ag. Ap.* 1.224f.; 2.66, 86, 139. Christians: *Ker. Petr.;* Athenagoras 1; Theophilus, *Autol.* 1.10; *Acta Apollonii* 17; Tertullian, *Ad nat.* 2.8.8; Minucius Felix 28.

In any case, it is no softening of the sharpness of the point of monotheism, but a confirmation of its exclusiveness, when it is incidentally mentioned in an apologetic context that the Jews may not revile foreign gods.[149]

Wisdom of Solomon is also representative of the *preaching of repentance* and its connection with missionary preaching. The basis for the positive side of the argument is the tradition of Israel deposited in the Scripture,[150] for which Moses is the guarantor.[151] Within the description of the law there belongs also a description of the lawgiver or law mediator. (On the relationship of lawgiver and law mediator, see Philo, *Decal.*)[152]

As one would expect, Greek motifs influence the picture of Moses (Philo, *Vit. Mos.*): Moses is *the* divine man, wise man, miracle worker, political leader, general, inventor,[153] initiator,[154] philosopher, and founder of Greek wisdom.

An Ethnographic Apology: Pseudo-Hecataeus[155]

In *Ag. Ap.* 1.183-204; 2.43 Josephus quotes extensively the historian Hecataeus of Abdera. The question is disputed whether the quotation really derives from Hecataeus (the time of Ptolemy I) or from a Jewish imitator who composed an apology for the Jews, using as a point of contact the fact that Hecataeus had in fact written about the Jews (Stern, *GLAJJ,* 20ff.). The following scholars argue for the authenticity of the section: Wendland (*Hellenistisch-römische Kultur;* though he reckons with a falsification by Josephus, as does Schürer, *History* 3:604ff.); Stern, *GLAJJ,* 23 (Stern, *Jewish People in the First Century* 2:109: Josephus could have read a copy of Hecataeus's work on the Jews that

---

[149] Philo, *Vit. Mos.* 2.205 stands in relationship with his exposition of Lev. 24:15f.: Reviling the images is forbidden, so that the name of God will not be misused; cf. *Spec. Leg.* 1.53; *Hypoth.* 7.4. On Josephus, *Ag. Ap.* 2.237 and *Ant.* 4.207 cf. Exod. 22:27 and 23:13 LXX; *Ant.* 4.207: βλασφημείτω δὲ μηδεὶς θεοὺς οὓς πόλεις ἄλλαι νομίζουσι. μηδὲ συλᾶν ἱερὰ ξενικά, μηδ᾽ ἂν ἐπωνομασμένον ᾖ τινι θεῷ κειμήλιον λαμβάνειν ("Let none blaspheme the gods that other cities revere, nor rob foreign temples, nor take treasure that has been dedicated in the name of any god"). Josephus knows how to suck apologetic honey out of this theologoumenon. Origen, *Contra Cels.* 8.38; the counterpart is found in Minucius Felix 8.4.

[150] Form-critical analysis: Norden, *Agnostos Theos;* see further *Sib. Or.* 1:125ff. (Noah); Philo, *Decal.* 52ff.

[151] The idea of inspiration had understandably received a much sharper profile in the diaspora than in the rabbinic literature; see Billerbeck, *Kommentar* 4:435ff. Philo: see Bousset-Gressman, *Die Religion des Judentums,* 149f. There was no need for a binding theory of inspiration to be generally accepted. The conviction of the truth of the tradition concerning Israel's election, law, and history was all that was needed.

[152] Philo, *Vit. Mos.* —I. Heinemann, "Moses," PW 16:365ff.; W. Gutbrod, "νόμος," TDNT 4:1052–54; Gager, *Moses.*

[153] K. Thraede, "Erfinder," *RAC* 5.1242ff.

[154] He was regarded by the Gentile authors as the founder of the Jewish nation; see part II above.

[155] Text: Josephus, *Ag. Ap.* 1.183-204; 2.43 (–47); *FGH* 264, F 21–24; Stern, *GLAJJ,* 35ff. German: N. Walter, "Fragmente Historiker," in *Jüdische Schriften* 1/2:144ff.

had already been reworked by Jewish predecessors); especially H. Lewy (see below); Gager, *Moses*. Against authenticity: Willrich, *Judaica*, 86ff.; *Juden und Griechen*, 20ff.; B. Schaller, "Hekataios von Abdera über die Juden: Zur Frage der Echtheit und Datierung," *ZNW* 54 (1963): 15–31; Hengel, "Anonymität," 301ff.).[156]

The Evidence

(1) *FGH* 264 F 23 = *Ep. Ar.* 31: Hecataeus explains why the Greek authors do not mention the law of the Jews, namely, because of its holiness; cf. in this connection the tales in *Ep. Ar.* 313–16; Josephus, *Ag. Ap.* 1.60ff.; Willrich, *Juden und Griechen*, 24: Pseudo-Aristeas derives this theme from Pseudo-Hecataeus.

(2) Josephus, *Ag. Ap.* 1.183: A book concerning the Jews.

(3) Josephus, *Ant.* 1.159: Hecataeus wrote a book concerning Abraham.

(4) Clement of Alexandria, *Strom.* 5.113 (Eusebius, *Praep. Ev.* 13.13.40): From Hecataeus's book κατ᾿ Ἄβραμον καὶ τοὺς Αἰγυπτίους ("On Abraham and the Egyptians") Pseudo-Sophocles is quoted: εἷς ταῖς ἀληθείαισιν, εἷς ἐστιν θεός, ὃς οὐρανόν τε ἔτευξεν καὶ γαῖαν μακρὴν ("One, truly one is god who made both heaven and the wide earth").[157] Thus how many book titles are here present?

Reinach (*Textes*) doubts the existence of the second book. Stern (*GLAJJ*, 22) considers it a work of Jewish propaganda. Schürer (*History* 3:606): the two books (concerning the Jews and concerning Abraham) are probably identical. On the other hand, Jacoby distinguishes between Περὶ Ἰουδαίων ("On the Jews") = *FGH* 264 F 21–23 (see Josephus, *Ag. Ap.* 1.183, 213f.), Herennius Philo in Origen, *Contra Cels.* 1.15 and the book about Abraham and the Egyptians (F 24). The book about the Jews is free from such clumsy imitations as the Sophoclean verses and from such horror stories as *Ep. Ar.* 312ff.

Schaller holds that both books are probably by the same author; thus the argument concerning the Sophoclean verses is valid also for the book concerning the Jews. Further, Jacoby (*FGH* III a, 75): Josephus betrays an awareness of the Abraham book in his *Antiquities;* thus he could have taken much from it in the following text. Cf. Willrich, *Judaica*, 86ff., 108ff.: from Pseudo-Hecataeus also comes Josephus, *Ant.* 1.161, 165f., perhaps 207ff., and all the quotations in *Ag. Ap.* 1.166–83.

W. Spoerri ("Hekataios," *Kl. Pauly* 2:981f.): Pseudo-Aristides and Artapanus could have used the authentic book of Hecataeus about Egypt. The two inauthentic works on the Jews and on Abraham/the Egyptians are, however, in reality two different books, not necessarily by the same author. According to Wacholder (*Eupolemus*, 262ff.), Josephus, *Ag. Ap.* 1.183–205 and 2.44–47 are

---

[156] Additional literature: A. T. Olmstead, "Intertestamental Studies," *JAOS* 56 (1936): 243f.; Walter, *Aristobulos* (bibliography); Stern, *GLAJJ*, 25; Jaeger, "Greeks and Jews."

[157] The affirmation of *one* God is also ascribed by Aristobulus to a Greek, i.e., to (Pseudo-) Orpheus.

not from the same author. *Ag. Ap.* 1.183ff. is from an eyewitness; the former refers to Judea, the latter to Jerusalem; the former refers to Ptolemy I, the latter to Ptolemy II. We should thus distinguish three different authors: (a) Pseudo-Hecataeus I (ca. 300 B.C.E.): Josephus, *Ag. Ap.* 1.183ff., 213f.; *Ep. Ar.* 83–120; (b) Pseudo-Hecataeus II (after *Ep. Ar.*, but before Josephus): *Ag. Ap.* 2.43–47; *Ant.* 12.3–8; *Ep. Ar.* 12–27, 31; (c) Pseudo-Hecataeus III (prior to Aristobulus): *Ant.* 1.159; Clement of Alexandria, *Strom.* 5.113.1–2; Herennius Philo.

Pseudo-Hecataeus I contains the oldest remnants of a Jewish author who writes Greek, more precisely a Palestinian priest (because of the description of the temple). Josephus, *Ag. Ap.* 1.183 is probably the beginning of the book (the primary theme: the faithfulness of the Jewish people to the law; cf. 1.190.). On the description of Ptolemy I, see Diodorus 19.86.3 (Willrich, *Juden und Griechen,* 26). The principal model for this was the genuine Hecataeus (Diodorus 40.40.3; see Jacoby, *FGH* IIIa, 46ff.; contrast Agatharchides, *FGH* 86 F 20; Josephus, *Ag. Ap.* 1.209ff.; *GLAJJ,* no. 30a), with the intent of "correcting" some negative statements of the authentic Hecataeus. The description of the temple indicates no dependence on the LXX version of the Pentateuch (cf. Willrich, *Judaica,* 99: Pseudo-Hecataeus does not yet know the LXX legends). The author gave up his priestly office in order to serve with Mosollanus in the army. According to N. Walter, Pseudo-Hecataeus I (on the Jews) and II (on Abraham) are to be distinguished. Both works were provoked by Hecataeus's excursus on the Jews.

Ep. Ar. 31 (Hengel, "Anonymität," 313ff.) has no recognizable connection with either of the pseudonymous writings. There is a relationship, but literary dependence is not confirmed. In *Ep. Ar.,* "Hecataeus" is a freely composed fiction. Schürer (*History* 3:604), Schaller, and Meisner relate the quotation to Pseudo-Hecataeus. N. Walter: In Pseudo-Aristides Ptolemy I is represented as being anti-Jewish, so there is probably no influence from Pseudo-Hecataeus. In summary, it remains the case that the temporal relations have not been clarified.

On the Sophoclean verses, see N. Walter, in *Jüdische Schriften,* 1/2:151. See also the continuing series of pseudepigraphical writings under Hecataeus's name, all of which are related to each other, probably originally a gnomological document written by a dramatic poet (with commentary), more or less unchanged in Pseudo-Justin, *De monarchia* 2–4, where nothing from Hecataeus is found. Pseudo-Hecataeus quoted one of these poems.

Arguments for and against Authenticity

The favorable evaluation of the Jews is a principal argument against authenticity.[158] Willrich: Pseudo-Hecataeus, in comparison with Eupolemus,

---

[158] Origen (*Contra Cels.* 1.15) already notes that the Phoenician historian Herennius Philo (of Byblos, 2nd cent. C.E., *FGH* 790 F 9) expressed doubt as to its authenticity.

represents a later form of propaganda.[159] In *Juden und Griechen* (p. 21), Willrich argues that the emphasis on faithfulness to the law points to the Maccabean period (?). The description of persecution by the Persians (cf. *Ep. Ar.* 13) presupposes that of the Syrians. The author must transfer this Syrian persecution to the Persians, since he claims to be a contemporary of Alexander. None of the authors preserved in Alexander Polyhistor represents Greek princes as guardian patrons of the Jews; Pseudo-Hecataeus is the first to do that; thus he is later than Alexander Polyhistor.

The most vigorous recent advocate of authenticity is H. Lewy ("Hekataios von Abdera Περὶ Ἰουδαίων," *ZNW* 31 [1932]).[160] That the author is an uninformed Gentile is already indicated by the report of the deportation of the Jews by the Persians (see Wacholder, *Eupolemus*, 270: 2 Macc. 1:19 is a similar lapse made by a Hellenistic Jew). Lewy adds that the contrast between the objective evaluation in Diodorus=Hecataeus and the praise in Josephus does not prove inauthenticity. The dominant factor is a utopian-protreptic tendency (logic?). The texts in Josephus and Clement of Alexandria respectively hardly derive from the same document.

No conclusions can be drawn concerning the one from the false Sophoclean verses of the other. In *Ep. Ar.*, only the saying about the sacredness of Scripture belongs to Hecataeus, not the whole apologetic section (but, on the other hand, the horror stories in 313ff.). The author does know the Alexandrian period well. Of course, the statement in Josephus, *Ag. Ap.* 2.43, that Alexander assigned Samaria to the Jews is difficult. Further, the author does not know the Jews well, which points to a Gentile author. His way of looking at things is Greek, as can be seen, for example, in the way he represents Ezechias and Mosollamus. (It is not clear how this is an argument.) He describes Jerusalem as though it were laid out like a Greek city (artificially so, if he himself lives in a Greek city). A Jewish pseudepigraphist would have pretended to be an eyewitness (but he does do this!).

Schaller: The assigning of Samaria to the Jews by Alexander is noticeably similar to the taking over of the three districts in 1 Macc. 10:29ff. Nevertheless, the identification of both events remains uncertain. In Josephus, *Ag. Ap.* 1.188, "Hecataeus" speaks of the tithes for the priests. But these were not transferred

---

But Lewy, *Studies in Jewish Hellenism* (Jerusalem, 1960): Philo no longer understands the early Hellenistic period. He lives in the time of hatred for the Jews. —Not a sound argument.

[159] He presupposes a consistent, unilinear development. Schaller, "Hekataios," 28: the two cannot be compared; the one portrays Jewish *history*, the other the relationships and customs of the Jews. Events are only touched upon "to the extent that they illustrate the characteristic features of the Jews, especially their loyalty to the law."

[160] Walter, "Fragmente Historiker," 144f.: Lewy has not overcome the force of Willrich's argument based on references that indicate connections of Pseudo-Hecataeus with the Maccabean period, and has not sufficiently taken into account the fact that the fragments do not merely have a positive attitude toward the Jews but are explicitly propagandistic.

from the Levites to the priests until the Maccabean period. The document thus could not have been written prior to the second century B.C.E.[161]

Gager: The only effective argument against authenticity is Josephus, *Ag. Ap.* 2.43. But it remains to be noted that the Samaritans revolted against Alexander in 331.[162] On 1 Macc. 11:34, see Thackeray on *Ag. Ap.* 2.43 (LCL): Demetrius may have confirmed an earlier donation. Schaller overlooks an early Hellenistic coin from Beth Zur.[163]

Preliminary Comments on the History-of-Religions Problem

In the summary of the most important apologetic motifs in Pseudo-Hecataeus (for the moment making no distinctions among the different authors included in this designation), we have a basic stock of materials that is met again and again in the other apologists. In the details, Pseudo-Hecataeus represents a somewhat primitive stage in the development of the defense. That applies, for example, to the topos "ridicule" (the Mosollamus episode, Josephus, *Ag. Ap.* 1.201ff.). It is still incidental, not yet a central motif in establishing the validity of monotheism. Also, the resources made available by the Greek critique of religion are at the most only embryonically present. We then have the next step in Aristobulus.

Nevertheless, the schema that is already becoming traditional can be recognized: against the worship of nature/the elements (etymologies of the names of the gods—e.g., Hera="air"—were later developed, a process that had already begun earlier); the worship of images (on which see the ridicule literature referred to above); the worship of animals.

A few examples from the material collected by Geffcken, *Apologeten* XIXff.:

(a) Worship of the stars and the elements of nature: Carneades; Sextus Empiricus, *Math.* 9.39, 121; Cicero, *Nat. Deor.* 3.9.23 (the academician Cotta against the Stoics: "non est igitur mundus deus" ["therefore the world is not god"]).

---

[161] Contra Stern, *GLAJJ*, 41: This change could have already occurred in the Persian period. His primary evidence, Tob. 1:7 S, is of course fragile. J. G. Gager, "Pseudo-Hecataeus Again," *ZNW* 60 (1969): 137f.: The author makes no distinction at all between priests and Levites; as a Gentile he appears to be quite ignorant on this point.

[162] Curtius Rufus 4.8f.; Eusebius, *Chron.* 123d. See now the caves in the Wadi ed Daliyeh (about fourteen km. north of Jericho) that contain the remnants of about two hundred skeletons and evidence from the Samaria of the fourth century B.C.E.; F. M. Cross, *The Ancient Library of Qumran and Modern Biblical Studies,* rev. ed. (Garden City, N.Y.: Doubleday, 1961) 172–73.

[163] A. Reifenberg, *Ancient Jewish Coins,* 4th ed. (Jerusalem: Rubin Mass, 1965) 9, 93; M. Avi-Yonah (*The Holy Land from the Persian to the Arab Conquests (536 B.C. to A.D. 640)* [Grand Rapids: Baker, 1966] 35) reads יהוד (Yehud) and יחזקיה (Yehezqiah). One is tempted to identify him with the otherwise unknown high priest Ezechias of Josephus, *Ag. Ap.* 1.187. O. R. Sellers (*The Citadel of Beth-zur* [Philadelphia, 1933] 73f.), to be sure, reads חזקיה (Hezeqiah), but acknowledges that the reading is doubtful, and rejects the identification of the Ezechias of Josephus. Thus the matter remains uncertain.

(b) Stars, heroes: Cicero, *Nat. Deor.* 3.12.30f.; 24.62; 16.41: Cf. Philo, *Congr.* 133: elements, stars, world; *Conf. Ling.* 173; *Spec. Leg.* 2.255; *Op. Mund.* 7ff. Heroes: *Omn. Prob. Lib.* 105ff.

(c) Images: Seneca in Lactantius, *Div. Inst.* 2.2.14; in Augustine, *Civ. Dei* 6.10: "in materia villissima atque immobili" ("[They consecrate] images of the cheapest inert material"). Cicero, *Nat. Deor.* 1.27.77; 36.101; Plutarch, *De superst.* 167D; Lucian, *Jup. Trag.* 7; cf. H. D. Betz, *Lukian von Samosata und das Neue Testament*, TU 76 (Berlin: Akademie-Verlag, 1961) 40. The *material* of the images: Herodotus 2.172 became a classical topos; Athenagoras, 26. Geffcken: probably from a handbook.

Geffcken also established that a firm stylistic element of the Hellenistic handbook was present in the topos of the ridicule of animal worship: Cicero, *Nat. Deor.* 1.16.43; cf. 3.19.47; Sextus Empiricus, *Hyp.* 3.219; Maximus of Tyre 8.5; Lucian, *Jup. Trag.* 42; *Deorum conc.* 10; Philo, *passim;* Geffcken, *Apologeten,* 73ff., on Aristides 12. Wendland (*Die Therapeuten und die philonische Schrift vom beschaulichen Leben* [Leipzig, 1896] 713) gives references and indicates firm apologetic forms existed. The dependence of Josephus and Philo on the Jewish-Hellenistic authors must in fact be much greater than we can recognize.

Structure and Content

Jacoby first marks off a framework narrative, F 21: §§186/189, 200/204, characterized by the I-style and personal experiences. Jacoby, *FGH* III a, 66: it was probably told that Hecataeus accompanied Ptolemy on the Syrian military campaign. Cf. F 25 (Diodorus 1.82.3; 84.3), which knows of a trip to the Red Sea.

The objectivity of the authentic Hecataeus should now be compared with this subjective report! Josephus abbreviates, severely and unevenly. The founding of the Jewish community in Alexandria is omitted, a report that the author experienced as an eyewitness. §186 confirms the ἠπιότης ("kindness") and φιλανθρωπία ("humanity") of Ptolemy I; see Diodorus 19.86.3. Many wanted to move to Egypt; Josephus, *Ag. Ap.* 2.12f.: forced resettlement. §187 follows the praise of the "high priest" Ezechias.[164] This section must represent an abbreviation; cf. §189: πάλιν ("reverting"). Then followed the preserved remnants of the real apology: κατοίκησις ("settlement") and πολιτεία ("constitution").

§§188f.: Ezechias assembles his own people around him. The author hints at a personal acquaintance with him: συνήθης ἡμῖν ("in touch with us"); cf. §200. The number of priests who receive these is reported to be 1,500. Cf. the other numbers reported in Ezra 2:36ff.; Neh. 7:39ff. Jacoby, *FGH* III a, 72f.: Pseudo-Hecataeus has better information than Hecataeus F 6 §7 (Diodorus 40.3.6). On

---

[164] Regarding the coins of Beth-zur, see also R. Marcus on *Ant.* 12.9 (Josephus, *Antiquities,* LCL). Of course not too much can come from that. But if one insists, then the most that can be affirmed is that "Hecataeus" was a Jew.

the composition: καὶ τὰ κοινὰ διοικοῦντες ("and administer public affairs"): this corresponds to the author's present. The gap between §§188 and 189 is bothersome (see above: πάλιν, "reverting").

The account of the real establishment does not come until this point in the narrative. According to Jacoby, κατοίκησις ("settlement") does not mean that which is described by the phrase τῆς χώρας ἣν κατοικοῦμεν ("of the country that we inhabit") (195), but the establishment of their residence in the land, thus to the antiquity of the people and Moses' giving of the law (cf. F 6 §3), which belongs here.

§189 is also difficult: παραλαβών τινας τῶν μεθ' ἑαυτοῦ τήν τε διαφορὰν ἀνέγνω πᾶσαν αὐτοῖς ("[This man] assembled some of his friends and read to them his whole scroll").

Wendland: "The special furnishings"; that would fit F 6 (Diodorus 40:3).

Willrich, *Judaica*, 91: "He settled all the differences among them": no longer comprehensible due to abbreviation of the text?

Blum: ". . . and explained (*exposa*) to them all the peculiarities of his nation" (with the note that the text is corrupt).

Jacoby: Should αὐτοῖς ("to them") be retained (because of the reference to τῶν μεθ' ἑαυτοῦ ("some of his friends"), or should ἡμῖν ("to us") be adopted as a conjectural emendation of the text? Or is it a case of Josephus's hurried style at this point or a misunderstanding of his secretary? The *meaning* can be derived from the context: Ezechias has writings concerning the διοίκησις ("administering") and the πολιτεία ("constitution"); that is, he reads the Torah (F 6 §6 also knows of this). The details have become vague because of Josephus's abbreviation.

Thackeray: ". . . and read to them a statement showing all the advantages of emigration." Abbreviation of the text?

Stern: adopts the conjecture of H. Lewy ("Hekataios," 123), which substitutes διφθέραν (". . . and read to them his whole scroll") for διαφοράν ("spread abroad . . .").

§§190–193:[165] Their conduct with regard to the law. This, and their willingness to suffer for it, is demonstrated by their persecution by the Persians ([*sic!*])[166] §194); to this are added several examples of τῆς ἰσχυρογνωμοσύνης τῆς

---

[165] εἶτα . . . πάλιν ("In another passage . . . Again") once more points to a lacuna. Jacoby, *FGH* IIIa 68: Pseudo-Hecataeus picks out something that is not "law" in the narrow sense: the cult of the *one* God. Thereby the law becomes a central concern in a completely different sense than in Hecataeus, where the Jewish understanding of God is only the first in a series of *nomoi* (as in the usual ethnographies). Has something fallen out here? Cf. §192f.

[166] Cf. *Ep. Ar.* 13. Persians: (a) in the repetition of Esther in Josephus, *Ant.* 12.45; (b) *Sib. Or.* 3:599; 5:93ff. Jacoby: The Persian rule is brought into relationship to the attempt of Antiochus IV in the Jewish literature generally. "Persian" refers also to the rule of the Assyrians and Babylonians. The distinction is no longer significant for Pseudo-Hecataeus. Perhaps he intentionally blurs it(?). Then the attitude of (Alexander and) the Ptolemies can be brought out by contrast.

περὶ τῶν νόμων ("obstinacy in defense of their laws"); the Jews deserve admiration.[167]

§194: the πολυανθρωπία ("vast population") of the nation is documented as a topos since Hecataeus of Abdera.[168]

Next comes the description of the land: Palestine (§§194f.), Jerusalem (§§195f.), temple and cult (§§198f.). In an apologetic document, these are also factors in the intellectual self-affirmation of diaspora Jews.[169]

An appendix (§200) mentions battles in which Jews fought alongside Alexander and his successors and ridicules pagan superstitions.

Now we may summarize the *principal motifs* (keeping in mind the standard topoi of other apologetes): (1) the surpassing wisdom of the Jews; (2) their great number; (3) hostility; (4) loyalty to the law; readiness to suffer; (5) ridicule of pagan superstition; (6) the political loyalty of the Jews (which was rewarded by Alexander); (7) defense against the charge of ἀπανθρωπία ("misanthropy").[170]

MODELS FOR THE TYPOLOGY OF APOLOGIES

Philo

Hypothetica (Apology for the Jews)

Only two fragments have been preserved from this apology: (1) Eusebius, *Praep. Ev.* 8.6.1-9; 7.1-20; (2) *Praep. Ev.* 11.1-18. Only the first is directly related to our subject. (On the second, see below.)

The authenticity is disputed.[171] In any case, the first excerpt, whether

---

[167] Jacoby, *FGH* IIIa, 72: That does not fit Hecataeus: ἀπάνθρωπός τις καὶ μισόξενος βίος. The emphasis on the cult of the *one* God and the rejection of foreign cults fits a time when this cult was threatened. Cf. Willrich above: the time of the Seleucids.

[168] Hecataeus F 6 §8; Philo; Josephus, *Ag. Ap.* 2.202f.; *Sib. Or.* 3:271. Their large numbers were seen in connection with the fact that the Jews raise all their children; Tacitus, *Hist.* 5.5. Hecataeus sees it as a result of a prescription of Moses; Pseudo-Hecataeus confirms it as a fact within the framework of his ethnographical discussion.

[169] Jacoby: In §§169-99 there is nothing that a Gentile could not have written. On the Jewish concept of God, see Hecataeus; the most that Pseudo-Hecataeus could have done is to have argued against it. But Josephus preserves no polemic.

[170] See Jacoby: Hecataeus gives a historical-ethnographical report on the *beginnings* of the nation, while Pseudo-Hecataeus deals with the *present*. He describes a kind of return to Egypt. His intention is not to emphasize the isolation of the Jews, but their associations with other nations. Of course, the emphasizing of *both* in the Jewish apologetic literature, in a contradictory way, is precisely the possibility that is practically unavoidable.

[171] Cautiously Colson, *Philo* (LCL) 9:407. The text is missing in the large edition by Cohn; it is given in the small edition as an appendix to vol. 6. The German translation also omits it. Cohn expresses doubt concerning its authenticity because of differences between it and *Spec. Leg.* Heinemann finds the doubts not to be convincing, since *Spec. Leg.* is not consistent with itself. On the similarities to Josephus, *Ag. Ap.*, see Colson, 409 and *passim*. Eusebius adds it on to the first excerpt from Josephus, *Ag. Ap.* 2.163-228.

authentic or not, contains a type of apology in its pure form. With this as a basis, we can recognize whole sections or elements of the same type in other passages as well.[172]

Title: Eusebius (*Hist. Eccl.* 2.18.6) mentions among Philo's works one called Περὶ Ἰουδαίων ("On the Jews"). In the introduction, he cites the first excerpt, the apology, as ἀπὸ τοῦ πρώτου συγγράμματος ὧν ἐπέγραψεν Ὑποθετικῶν ("quoting from the first book of what he entitled *Hypothetica*") (*Praep. Ev.* 8.5.11). The meaning of this title is not clear. The standard *text* is now the edition of Eusebius, *Praep. Ev.*, by K. Mras (GCS 43, 1.2 [Berlin: Akademie-Verlag, 1954, 1956]).[173]

Summary of Contents

Two parts may be distinguished in the first fragment: (1) from the national history (6.1-9), an excerpt that concentrates on Moses (the exodus and the taking of the land); (2) the law (6.10; 7.1-20). Each of the two parts could be seen as a complete apology in itself. But their combination, in this order, is typical for Philo, as can be seen in other passages, for example, *Vit. Mos.*

The historical part. Colson (LCL) establishes the rationalistic character of this portrayal of history and asks why Philo (and Eusebius) would be interested in this. The answer is not difficult to determine, when one sees his portrayal in conjunction with (a) the anti-Jewish polemic (which essentially limited their argument to the exodus, in the historical parts of their argument), and (b) with the Jewish tradition (see the fragments of the Alexandrians above). The repulsion of attacks and the portrayal of the (idealized) Jewish history and the Jewish way of life belong together.

The ethnographic topos "origin" is indicated by naming the ancestors (Jacob, not Abraham, as the continuation shows): the ancestral patriarch was a Chaldean. Thus the claim that the Jews were originally Egyptians is quickly disposed of; on the eastern origin of the Jews, see Pompeius Trogus 36.2 (*GLAJJ*, no. 137); Nicholas of Damascus (Josephus, *Ant.* 1.159f.; *GLAJJ*, no. 83). Likewise, the migration from Syria to Egypt is mentioned only briefly and incidentally (Jacob is not mentioned at all).

After mention of a gap in the excerpt,[174] the exodus becomes the principle theme. It is explained rationally (it must be read in the light of the hostile portrayals of the same events). One reason for it was that the nation's population had become so numerous. No mention is made of the oppression of the people, nor of Pharaoh. But, of course, we do not know what might have been contained in the omitted section (between Jacob and Moses). The second

---

[172] Here the allusions to the opposing literature are especially clear.

[173] Older editions: Cohn, Wendland, smaller edition, vol. 6; Colson (LCL) 9:405ff. (with 539f.).

[174] 6:2 καὶ μετὰ βραχέα φησίν ("and a little later he says"). The end of Genesis and the beginning of Exodus are omitted.

explanation is provided by the character of the people (which must also have impressed the Gentiles), and the longing to return to their old homeland.

Finally, divine revelations are mentioned as a factor. These are referred to as though they belonged in the category of ancient manticism, which would be congenial to Gentile ears. The *miracles* are passed over in silence!

The exodus account is narrated altogether in connection with Moses. His first characterization is to be explained from apologetic motives: he is no different from ordinary human beings; this fits in with the ignoring of the miracles (note the contrast on this point found in *Vit. Mos.*). Thus Philo counters the opposing description of Moses as a *goēs* ("wizard").[175] Philo opposes this hostile view of Moses by emphasizing the human abilities of Moses: leading the people out of Egypt called for unusual (but still human) qualities, qualities that allowed him to guide the people through the wilderness and (contrary to the Bible) to maintain their unity and obedience.

The judgment concerning the proportionate role played by Moses, the Jewish characters, and, lastly, God is left to the discretion of the Gentile reader—a thinly disguised apologetic.[176]

Gentile writers who are unacquainted with the Bible consider the taking of the land to be an important part of the exodus events, and they attribute it to Moses. That is impossible for a Jew. Philo simplifies the matter merely by failing to mention Moses. Instead, he offers two explanations for the taking of the land and allows the Gentile readers to make up their own minds: The Jews either took the land by force, even after the losses they had sustained during the desert journey, which would argue for the superiority of the Jews. Or the land was occupied by the Jews by virtue of an agreement they had worked out with the inhabitants, which reveals something of the nature of the Jewish people, if they were accepted as neighbors by people who would be their enemies in the natural course of things.

Then Philo himself incidentally points out that the second alternative is the correct one (6.8), as he lauds the virtues of the Jews and suggests the relationship between virtue and getting along well in the world. This was a view that, generally speaking, gave the apologists some trouble, in view of the actual experience of the Jews (one has only to think of Josephus).

The major concern of the Jews as they began their residence in the land had to do with their cultic institutions (6.6). This is what determined the relationship of the Jews to the native inhabitants. And these cultic institutions included especially the particular Jewish way of life—expressed in terms of the Greek doctrine of virtue (cf. the catalogue of virtues in 6:8)—which was traced back to Moses.

---

[175] Josephus, *Ag. Ap.* 2.145 (*GLAJJ*, no. 49) (Molon and Lysimachus: γόητα καὶ ἀπατεῶνα ("charlatan and impostor"). Philo has the anti-Jewish, Alexandrian literature in view.

[176] 6:4 is unclear; see Colson, ad loc. The best solution is to punctuate as does Mras (cf. Colson): a question mark after φῶμεν ("Shall we say"); a decision is called for.

The presentation often consciously shimmers in changing colors: apparently the Gentile readers were left to make up their own minds. But along with this the "correct" answer was given, for example, in the question whether Moses devised this unparalleled law from his own thinking or whether it came from divine inspiration. (For the Jews themselves, of course, there could be no alternative to this last answer as the correct explanation for Moses, the divine man and prophet.) In any case, the Jews attributed this law to God and had been faithful to it for two thousand years,[177] so faithful, in fact, that not a word had been changed.[178]

The part concerning the law. Eusebius (6.10) notes the transition to the law in this second part of the apology. The beginning at 7.1 shows that Eusebius omits something, mainly a reference to the conduct of the Gentiles, which was there in order to make the behavior of the Jews all the clearer by contrast.

Here too one sees something of the character of apologetic: that it is not merely defensive, that it is not limited to warding off objections, but also is interested in spreading the knowledge of what Judaism, and thus God and his will, is really like. The accents are placed to correspond to this purpose: the Jewish law knows no halfheartedness. This is related to the fact that the law is clear, simple, and known to every Jew; on this see Josephus, *Ag. Ap.* and 7.1 in the text under discussion.

How serious and severe the law is can be seen, for example, in the imposition of the death penalty for a wide variety of offenses.[179] The emphasis on the criminal code and the moral law and neglect of the esoteric cultic regulations provided a good point of contact with Gentile readers.

In 7.3 there is a transition to other "rules," within which appear the elements (but no more) of a table of household rules (*Haustafel*).[180]

In addition to the written law, the Jews have the unwritten traditional usages (among which the "golden rule" is not missing [A. Dihle, *Die goldene Regel* (Göttingen: Vandenhoeck & Ruprecht, 1962)]). It is remarkable how frequent the prohibition of ἱεροσυλία ("robbing temples") is found (7.4).[181]

---

[177] A chronological wrinkle that is apparently relativized by the author: as though he does not know the exact number of years. Of course he knows it. But he is satisfied, for the benefit of the nonhistorian and nonchronographer, simply to affirm the great age of the law of Moses and thereby the high quality of Jewish piety.

[178] Cf. the manner in which Josephus plays on the variety and changeableness of the Greek laws (*Ant.* 1.18ff.).

[179] Particular exaggerations over against the Bible (and *Spec. Leg.*), such as the death penalty for stealing and such (7.2; see Colson on 7.1), are not to be used as evidence against authenticity.

[180] Ad. loc. and Josephus, *Ag. Ap.* 2.190ff.: J. E. Crouch, *The Origin and Intention of the Colossian Haustafel*, FRLANT 109 (Göttingen: Vandenhoeck & Ruprecht, 1972) 84ff. That Philo (even if polemically) works with Greek material is seen, for example, by a glance at the commandments of the Buzyges (Crouch, *Origin*, 87): Josephus does not mention the name, but his list in *Ag. Ap.* 2.211 is more complete than that of Philo (Colson, 539f.).

[181] Philo, *Vit. Mos.* 2.205; *Spec. Leg.* 1.53; Josephus, *Ant.* 4.207; *Ag. Ap.* 2.237; Acts 19:37; Rom. 2:22.

In 7.7 we find the Jewish topos, also known to the Gentiles, which prohibits sterilization, abortion, and the killing of newborn infants. This provided the explanation for the large population of the Jewish people (the explanation was common from the time of Hecataeus of Abdera; Josephus, *Ag. Ap.* 2.203; Tacitus, *Hist.* 5.5). At 7.10 there is again a gap, which must have spoken of the Sabbath. The Sabbath *per se* is a purely internal Jewish matter, but it is not surprising that it required an apology. The custom of Sabbath observance was probably the best-known Jewish custom among the Gentiles (and often adopted by them, and constituted *the* mark of Judaism (alongside the practice of circumcision, which was not generally publicly noticeable). Religious instruction and the general familiarity of the Jews with the laws are advertised by Philo (as later by Josephus, intensively). A noteworthy item is the rational explanation of the Sabbatical year as an indication of the reasonableness and philanthropy of the law (the fruit that grows by itself in this year is given to the needy).

The second excerpt (*Praep. Ev.* 8.11.1–18; 10.19) divides the Jewish people into two groups: the masses, who live by the literal sense of the law of Moses, and the philosophers, who strive for a higher understanding. It is not an apology (despite Eusebius), nor a fragment of any such writing, but describes the life of the *Essenes*. (At the conclusion of this section, Eusebius cites the corresponding description from *Omn. Prob. Lib.* 75ff.). In order to understand why it stands in an "apology," one must notice the general style (another example of the fact that the alternative "edification literature or missionary literature" misunderstands the situation): Philo holds before the eyes of the Greeks a Jewish group that can remind them of related religious-social groups or ideas: the Pythagoreans. (We find ourselves in the time of Neopythagoreanism. On Pythagoras, see Philo's references in *Op. Mund.* 100; *LA* 1.15; *Omn. Prob. Lib.* 2; *Aet. Mund.* 12).

The apologetic works of Philo to be discussed below will allow his apologetic conception as whole to be seen more clearly.

De Vita Contemplativa [182]

It is here presupposed that the writing is authentic[183] (with Colson, 108, Bormann, 46). If the document should turn out not to be authentic, the firmness of the literary type would be confirmed even more strongly, especially through a comparison with *Decal.*

Material for comparison is found in the description of the Essenes in *Hypoth.* (see above) and *Omn. Prob. Lib.* 75ff. (cf. the cross-reference §1). The descriptions

---

[182] Editions besides Cohn and Colson: F. Daumas and P.-J.-L. Miquel (Greek-French; *De vita contemplativa,* Les oeuvres de Philon d'Alexandrie [Paris: Cerf, 1963]); German: K. Bormann, in *Philonis Alexandrini Opera,* ed. L. Cohn and P. Wendland (Berlin: Reimer, 1927) 7:44ff., who also discusses the tradition of the title.

[183] Contested by Schürer, *History* 3:687f.; defended by Wendland, *Therapeuten;* Bormann, 45f.

supplement each other as representations of two exemplary forms of the ideal life, the practical life of the Essenes and the contemplative life of the Therapeutae (in whom Eusebius, *Hist. Eccl.* 2.17 sees the first Christians in Egypt).[184]

We confine our comments to those parts of the document that represent the literary type of the apology. Here again he makes use of the idea of an exemplary Jewish group: Philo presents a Jewish community that he considers to be of general interest to people everywhere.[185] But the special feature of this writing is that Philo precedes the description of the Therapeutae with the complete scheme of an apology. He introduces this with a general observation concerning these Therapeutae, who are so called *either* because they understand the healing arts better than others (because they are not concerned with the body only but with the soul as well), *or* because of their worship of God.

With this point of contact, the topoi of the apology follow: (1) The worship of the elements of the world (§§3f.; cf. *Decal.* 53) with a reference to the familiar Stoic etymologies (Hera=air, etc.; *Decal.* 54). This worship is a "sophistic" invention. The elements are soulless matter, subject to the Creator. (2) The stars (§5), products of a demiurge (cf. *Congr.* 131ff.; *Conf. Ling.* 173; *Spec. Leg.* 1.13). The designation of the stars as ἀποτελέσματα ("created objects") is explained (on στοιχεῖα ["elementary"] and ἀποτελέσματα ["completed"] as contrasting terms, see *Rer. Div. Her.* 209). (3) Demigods (§6). The idea of worshiping them is laughable. One need only think of the legends of their birth.[186] (4) The images (§7).[187] Of course, there must be a reference to the materials themselves from which the images are made, just as there must be a reference to: (5) The Egyptians (cf. the repeated references since Wisdom).

This concludes the apology. The way it is worked into the outline of the whole already signals the next section: the Therapeutae, of course, live in Egypt. Thus the Egyptians, advocates of the most debased form of religion, become the foil for his presentation of the model form of the worship of God.

Appendix: P. Wendland, one of the forerunners of form criticism, also studied the apology as a literary type and confirmed the regularity of its contents (*Therapeuten,* 707ff.). Selected from his references: see especially *Decal.* (see below). 709: A selection from the legal prescriptions is made, from the point of view of agreement with Gentile laws: Pseudo-Phocylides; Philo, *Hypoth.;* Josephus, *Ag. Ap.* 2.188–219 (712f.: Josephus used Philo); cf. Eusebius, *Praep. Ev.* 8.7.2/Pseudo-Phocylides 183 (lacking in the Torah); 7.6/Josephus *Ag. Ap.* 2.221; Pseudo-Phocylides 22, 24; 7.9/213; Pseudo-Phocylides 84f.; 7.1/207, 215;

---

[184] Cohn (see Bormann, 44): *Vit. Cont.* is the second part of a work on the Essenes. Bormann: §1 cannot be related either to *Omn. Prob. Lib.* or to *Hypoth.* (Daumas-Miquel [12, and on §1] relate it to *Hypoth.*).

[185] He can relate his material to Greek ideals; Aristotle, *Eth. Nic.* 1095b 19; Epicurus.

[186] *Omn. Prob. Lib.* 105ff.

[187] Josephus, *Ag. Ap.* 2.74f., 252; *Sib. Or.* 3 *passim; Decal.* 7, etc.; and throughout the whole apologetic.

7.3/201, 206; Pseudo-Phocylides 8; *Sib. Or.* 3.593f.; Josephus, *Ag. Ap.* 2.209/
Pseudo-Phocylides 39; Josephus, *Ag. Ap.* 2.218/Pseudo-Phocylides 104.

De Decalogo[188]

Some will object to including this writing in the category "apology."[189] It
belongs to Philo's systematic work on the law that begins with the *Op.
Mund.*, which continues with the biographies of the patriarchs (which have been only
partially preserved; cf. *Abr.* 3) and connects with the Joseph story (§1).[190] The
exposition of the laws begins with the Decalogue, which prepares for the
"special" laws. Of course, both expositions serve the purpose of offering instruction to the Jews, but also instruct Gentiles. The law is presented as the law of
humanity and the natural law in general, which is already indicated by placing
Op. Mund. programmatically at the beginning. (Thus 96ff. makes the Sabbath
obligatory for all humanity since it is grounded in the structure of the cosmos
itself.) This is another example of how false it would be to pose the alternative
"edification literature or missionary literature." Thus I. Heinemann (*Philons
griechische und jüdische Bildung* [Hildesheim: G. Olms, 1932]) is on target in his
observation that even in *Spec. Leg.*, which is primarily concerned with specific
Jewish regulations, the Greek reader is also kept in view; one need only note
the defense of circumcision over against Greek ideas on the subject (*Spec. Leg.*
1.1f.). And Cohn (LCL) refers to the apologetic character of *Virt.* (cf. the
apologetic topos *Virt.* 141), which, formally speaking, has nothing to do with
the literary type of apologetic; but Cohn correctly sees that instruction in the
law is presented as instruction in the Greek concept of virtue.

Content. The preliminaries (to §49) deal with the question of why the Decalogue was promulgated in the wilderness. The reasons presented are characterized as human "hypotheses" (§18). But Nikiprowetzky's interpretation is
correct: this does not mean a mere probability (as, for example, in the sense
of the Sophists) with regard to the correctness of the information, which is in
fact considered to be near to the truth. They are called "conjectures" only in
regard to human weakness, not with reference to the facts themselves.

Then follows the fundamental distinction (which is maintained consistently
throughout *Decal.* and *Spec. Leg.*) between the commandments that God

---

[188] Greek-French: V. Nikiprowetzky, *De Decalogo* (Paris: Cerf, 1965); German: L. Treitel, *Die
Werke Philo von Alexandria in deutscher Übersetzung* 1:369ff.

[189] Nikiprowetzky (29ff.): As an exegetical work, the book is intended for Jewish readers. Still,
Nikiprowetzky must acknowledge that compromises with Hellenism are made. —Precisely this
double character is significant.

[190] Schürer, *History* 3:666 picks out *Vit. Mos.* as a special work; similarly Treitel. In any case,
Decal. is not directly connected with the *Vit. Mos.*, the cross-reference to Moses in §18 notwith-
standing. It is noticeable that in *Decal.* the Sinai theophany is dealt with extensively, while it is
only softly hinted at in the *Vit. Mos.* (2.70f.). Cohn asks if the account in *Vit. Mos.* might have been
lost—but no evidence to support such an assumption exists.

himself gave (the Decalogue) and those he gave through Moses as a mediator. A commentary on the distinctions between different modes of revelation is found in *Vit. Mos.* 2.188ff., 246, 258.

In this context is found the famous discussion—not about the voice of God, for God cannot have a voice—but about the miraculous articulation of the heavenly voice (§§32–35, 46), which is frequently found in expositions of the Pentecost story in Acts 2.

This preparatory section already includes (in connection with a small diatribe on Typhos [§§4ff.], which becomes exposition at §7) typical motifs and topoi of apologetic, beginning with a polemic in the usual style against images (§§7f.) and polytheism (§8). The apologetic motifs and topoi are collected in the brief anticipatory summary of the Decalogue that follows (which then receives a commentary, resulting in doublets) (§§50f.).

The concept of "monarchy" is used as the point of contact with which to begin the discussion. Monotheism is grounded in the first commandment. The *Shema* is, however, not found at all in Philo (but it would not be appropriate for pagan ears).

Then follows topos on topos, in the order of the Decalogue, each with such a rich commentary that we can in fact speak of a model apology conceived from the first word with the whole world (§52) and the cardinal error of humanity in view. Using both the Decalogue and the apologetic typology as the structure of his discussion (a combination already present in the Decalogue itself to some extent) leads to the repetition of familiar themes: polemic against the deification of the elements, the stars, the sky, the world (and parts thereof); cf. *Congr.* 131ff.; *Conf. Ling.* 173; *Spec. Leg.* 2.255. Nor can the etymologies of the names of the gods be omitted (§54 is a particularly good example); then comes the expected critique of the myths (§55). Reference to the abominations in the Greek myths is made in §156. This later becomes an extensive theme of Christian apologetes.

Appeal is made to reason: whoever has really learned how to think will not be able to confuse God and the world, Creator and creation (§§58ff.). This "natural theology" is constructed throughout within the realm of Jewish monotheism[191] and can be applied as an apologetic argument. Within the arena in which this argument functions, appeal is made also to an awareness of the internal contradiction found in polytheism (§59).[192]

When the replacement of the Creator by the creation is called ἀσέβεια ("ungodliness") (§§62f.), an anti-Jewish topos is returned unopened to its Gentile sender.

---

[191] To be sure, the Sinai revelation was promulgated in the desert, far removed from cities (the places of idolatry [8]), and thus from the world. But it belongs to all nations (37); there is equality before the law of God, for nature is the common property of all humanity (40f.).

[192] This is excluded only when the pattern of thought is constructed on a christological-historical base (Paul).

In §§65ff. topoi are repeated in a more intense manner: the worship of images is compared with the worship of the elements of the world, and the former is found to be worse, because in this case it is not something that exists that is worshiped, but "gods" that are manufactured (cf. *Spec. Leg.* 1.21ff.).[193]

Philo, like the Jews in general, does not distinguish the god and the image, thus does not really address the religion of the educated Greeks, though (as the *pagan* ridicule of the images of the gods shows) his understanding of idolatry is approximately that of the masses.

He tries his hand at ridicule (without much luck): (a) The Gentiles should at least be consistent and worship the craftsman or his tools rather than his product. (b) The highest good is, of course, to be like God. He thus suggests that pagans pray to become like their gods: to have eyes that do not see, etc. (§§73ff.; *Spec. Leg.* 2.256).

A topos made familiar by the Wisdom of Solomon and especially through the analysis of Rom. 1:18ff. is the connection between religious error and moral perversity (§91): ἀθεότης ("godlessness") is the root of all unrighteousness (again, an anti-Jewish topos is thrown back in the face of those who originally used this term of the Jews). Once again the Egyptians provide the climactic example (§§76f.).

A concluding summary once more emphasizes the rejection of all this sort of idolatry and the necessity of the worship of the true God (§81). The concluding remarks (§§176ff.) contain yet another noteworthy feature: a justification of the fact that no punishments are threatened in the Decalogue. This is in contrast to those passages that advertise the severity of the Jewish criminal code.

In sum: In the exposition of the first two commandments we have a typical, complete apology. It is followed in *Spec. Leg.* 1 by a related example.

De Specialibus Legibus

The apology in the *Decal.* is complete in itself, but the book is planned with a continuation in mind. And the further development begins immediately, *Spec. Leg.* 1 (cf. *Decal.* 18f.). This not only appears to be considerably more esoterically Jewish than the *Decal.*, but is in fact so. But also here we find not only ideas that are common in apologetic (and why not?), but also the formal and structural elements of apologetic, though, of course, they are widely scattered, so that our presentation must gather them up and deal with them in a more compressed manner than they actually appear in the text. But the discussion of them is worth the effort, for thereby several additional aspects come to light.

---

[193] As an example he introduces the argument that must arise on the basis of polytheism of who the greatest god would be—an argument that could have made no impression on even a pre-Socratic philosopher.

The juxtaposition of the two books is probably the strongest proof that in Philo "domestic policy" and "foreign policy" are inseparable and that not only does apologetics have a theological character as an external tactic but it is inherently an essentially theological enterprise.

The outline itself makes this clear, no less so in the case of the *Spec. Leg.* than in the *Decal.:* After the introduction (1.1–11), Philo immediately discusses the appropriateness of the structure (1.12): It is fitting to begin with the concept of "monarchy" (cf. 1.30). That is the typical beginning point of an apology, a theme that is immediately traced through further topoi, in the traditional order: against the worship of the stars (1.13ff.), the worship of images with a reference to the material of which they are made, gold and silver (1.21), along with a critique of the cultic institutions, particularly of the temples,[194] supplemented by a moral component (1.23ff.): against worshiping πλοῦτος ("wealth") and δόξα ("glory") as divine.[195] The moralistic critique fades into the critique of the myths (1.28). The critique of images is then supplemented by a warning against perversions deriving from a taste for music and art (seduction not only through what one sees, but by what one hears).

The issue posed by the concept of God is also "standard": God is not easy to perceive, but one should not conclude from this that the quest should be given up as hopeless—on the contrary (1.36; cf. Acts 17:27). The issue is then subdivided according to the usual schema:

(a) Whether God exists; the critique of atheism is later (1.330) attached to this question. Again the familiar charge against the Jews is returned to the sender (cf. *Praem. Poen.* 162).

(b) What his *essential nature* is (discussed further in 1.36ff.). 1.60 polemicizes against manticism, showing that faith in the true God reveals it to be superstition (cf. 1.315: against false prophecy and other phenomena that have the external appearance of being religious, i.e., enthusiasm).

1.197ff.: *Universalism* is emphatically underscored, because just as there is *one* God, so there is only one *cult* (!), the Jewish, which is valid not only for all people but also for nature as the creation of God (cf. 2.162ff., 168).

Monotheism, when it is thought through, is itself a universalistic concept; for God is not only the God of human beings but of the gods (1.307).[196] Thus the

---

[194] In regard to this, note also the comment in 1.66: God's temple is the world—which was already a commonplace of Gentile thought. On using the pagan critique of the construction of temples as a point of contact, see the commentaries of Acts 7:48.

Once again the Jewish apologetic reaches a certain boundary situation: it must find a way to exclude its own temple from such critique. The answer: one God, one temple (1.68f.).

[195] Against the lack of relationship between the Greek mysteries and ethics, which was also criticized by the Greeks.

[196] We cannot, of course, interpret this comment so as to find a residual amount of polytheism still unconsciously present in Philo himself. In the first place, the manner of expression is borrowed from the Old Testament, and, second, he intends to say that god is the God of those who are falsely called gods by others but who have no power of their *own* (1.13).

role of the Jewish people as the advocates of this God is a role in the service of humanity as a whole, and the absurdity of the charge of hatred of humanity is clear (2.166f.; 165).

But in reality, with these arguments the conflict between Jewish universalism and Jewish segregation is not overcome, but only glossed over. It is precisely the *one*, the universal God, who commands the segregation. But Philo makes progress in at least one point: faith must be available to all. Monotheism and secret (mystery cult) rituals are mutually exclusive (1.320ff.). The Jews have succeeded where other peoples had the opportunity and failed, in that which is most important of all (2.165).

A Current Political Defense: In Flaccum *and* Legatio ad Gaium [197]

In Flaccum

In the literature, this invective has been used primarily as a source for the situation and destiny of the Jews in Alexandria during a limited period. Since the events narrated are of a very special sort, this account is only marginally important for our theme (see part I). On the other hand, *Legatio* goes right to the heart of our concern,[198] although for historical information the book is to be used only with care.[199]

Gerschmann characterizes *Flaccum* and *Legatio* as documents written for the encouragement of fellow believers. They are certainly that. But when they are perceived as a whole, it is clear that they are concerned with the religious-political conflict with which Jewish existence was confronted, seen in its broadest perspective. An apologetic intention can be seen in the fact that Philo's presentation in *Flacc.* does not suggest any *necessary* conflict between the

---

The universalism implicit in monotheism is introduced by Paul in Rom. 3:29f. as a fundamental principle of soteriology.

[197] German: *Flacc.:* K.-H. Gerschmann, in *Philo,* ed. Cohn and Wendland 7:122ff., *Leg.:* F. W. Kohnke, in *Philo,* ed. Cohn and Wendland, 7:166ff. See Schürer, *History* 3:677ff.; Goodenough, *Politics.* On the literary and historical problems of both books, see E. M. Smallwood, ed., *Philonis Alexandrini Legatio ad Gaium* (Leiden: E. J. Brill, 1961) (there is an attempt on pp. 40ff. to reconstruct the five books on virtue [so Eusebius] from the present form of *Leg.;* which is unsuccessful; cf. Kohnke, 169). On the historical aspects, see further Smallwood, *Jews under Roman Rule,* 235ff.

[198] On *Flacc.,* see Goodenough, *Politics: Somn.* 2.81–92 is a key: the Roman officials are encouraged to proceed with caution: it is written for a Gentile who is not acquainted with Alexandria.

[199] Sevenster, *Roots,* 21f.; V. Tcherikover, "The Decline and Fall of the Jewish Diaspora in Egypt in the Roman Period," *JJS* 14 (1963): 17: Philo is not obligated to report everything; nor was it always in his interest to write only the truth. One must read between the lines.

Gerschmann refers to the formal elements of ancient biography, which can only to a limited extent be considered a historical genre (in addition, the formal consistency of this genre has long been overrated), and to elements of the novel; see especially the concluding part. Moreover, to speak in terms of a strict generic form is here not appropriate.

Jewish and Roman ways of life, but leaves the way open for a harmonious relationship. Flaccus's hostility to the Jews did not derive from any political necessity. For years the government had functioned smoothly without any problems with the Jews (cf. also *Leg.* 161). The problems originated with Flaccus's personal ambition and thus rested on a violation of his official duty. The persecutors of the Jews—Sejanus (*Flacc.* 1; we must assume that a preceding reference to Sejanus has unfortunately been lost; note nevertheless *Leg.* 159ff.), Flaccus, and then especially Gaius—are *degenerate* advocates of what Rome really stands for—a degeneration that has infected even the palace of Caesar.

A few details remain to be noticed. In the first writing Philo remained essentially within the framework of the local Alexandrian situation, though he drew wider implications from it.[200] The broader political aspects are hinted at in §48; the Jews are described as peaceful by nature (which includes their religion). But there is a line beyond which they cannot allow themselves to be pushed—the line that constitutes their very being as Jews. They are willing to die rather than be forced beyond this line.[201] Precisely this attitude had a positive political consequence, which should have been clear to the Romans too: depriving the Jews of their houses of prayer means at the same time depriving them of the possibility of reverence for the state.

Although the Jews are a peaceful folk, they are also human (§121). After the fall of Flaccus, they certainly thanked God for their rescue. But they take no pleasure in his punishment; for their laws teach them to have compassion for their fellow human beings.

But there must be adequate and appropriate punishment nonetheless (§189; cf. 146). This is an indication of God's concern for his people (§190). For just as monotheism has something that properly corresponds to it in the one law, so also there is something that corresponds to monotheism in the justice that is present in the way things happen in the world. This correspondence to the Jewish doctrine of the one God who rules the whole world is something that is subject to empirical observation, something that can in principle be documented by observing the way things within the world are ruled—though one may have to wait a while to see it.

There is no room in the Jewish concept of God for the Christian understanding according to which the manifestation of the justice and righteousness of God are realized in the cross of Christ, a righteousness that is from God *sub specie contrarii* but that becomes visible only through faith in Christ.[202] On the

---

[200] Is there a particularly malicious element in §29, in that Philo (who knows the difference well enough) includes the Alexandrians in the same category with the Egyptians? Cf. *Leg.* 162ff. with 166.

[201] *Leg.* 233: on martyrdom without resistance, cf. Josephus, *Ant.* 18.271.

[202] There is thus no comprehension of Paul's doctrine of the righteousness of God, which the Jew will ultimately declare to be an affirmation of his own faith against Christianity (=Christianity in the Pauline style); in fact, to be consistent he *must* do so.

basis of the Jewish concept of God it is possible to have the appropriate humanitarian attitude described in §121.

Legatio ad Gaium[203]

Kohnke (p. 170) emphasizes that the fundamental thing in *Legatio* is the collision between the political organization and Judaism with its faith (and throne in Jerusalem). The observation is correct but one-sided. *Flacc.* also contains an apologetic slant directed to outsiders. Despite the absolute opposition that exists between Jewish faith and the Caesar cult, *Legatio* wants nonetheless to hold fast to the possibility of the peaceful coexistence of the two, which had in fact obtained until it was disturbed by the madness of Gaius. In §§2f., the reader's view is directed to the future of the Jews (though in an allusion that is hardly understandable to the non-Jewish reader), on the basis of faith in the providential care of God for his people (a care that is hardly visible to the casual observer) and for its political situation as the race that is always begging for protection (cf. §§8ff.). The situation of the empire after the death of Tiberius (of whom Philo had a favorable opinion) is painted in ideal colors (§8), in order to provide a foil. No political critique is directly expressed, but rather the Roman idea of a welfare state that embraces the whole civilized world (through Q. Naevius Cordus Sutorius Macro, the praetorian prefect, *Legatio* 49; cf. Kohnke, 187 n. 1), in tones that are reminiscent of the inscriptions about Augustus (§§143ff.) and of the speech of Nicholas of Damascus in Josephus, *Ant.* 16. The law of equality prevails. Masters and slaves enjoy the same general state of well-being.

If we now pursue our study of the document with the question of apologetic in mind, we discover that the familiar topoi of apologetic are in fact there. To be sure, their intended purpose is to address the political issue, which is developed in a two-fold manner: (a) as a defense of the Jews relevant to the current political situation, and especially (b) as the *theological* basis for the whole Jewish political problem. In view of the emphasis on monotheism, there is, however, one noticeable peculiarity that shows what means can be pressed into the service of apologetic: Philo argues here as a *Gentile* against the emperor cult[204] (§§ 76–113 are an exceptionally strong example).

The first step in the self-deification of Gaius was his equating himself with the demigods, Heracles (§81), Dionysus (§82), etc. But their great deeds of

---

[203] See bib. on *Flacc.;* German: F. W. Kohnke, in *Philo,* ed. Cohn and Wendland, 7:166ff.

[204] Kohnke, 195: The debate here does not follow as a consequence of the standpoint of Jewish monotheism. "Thus we apparently have here a united front of Jews and Gentiles." W. L. Knox, *Some Hellenistic Elements in Primitive Christianity* (London: H. Milford, 1944) 48f.: The section is a satire, from a Gentile source (the same as §§141–51). But the situation is different in the second passage. Smallwood (on §76, differently from those named above) points to the Jewish character of this section, when Gaius is charged with ἀθεότης ("godlessness"). But Philo could have sharpened his source on this point.

charity stand in stark contrast to the nondeeds of Gaius. This line of argument contains nothing specifically Jewish. But does it not at least lie within the circle of what is possible for Jewish polemic—according to Jewish criteria (like the adoption of euhemerism for political purposes)?

The second stage (§§93ff.) is the elevation of Gaius to the stature of a full-fledged god. Here too the dominant mode of argument is a caricature without "Jewish" arguments.[205]

Next in turn (§§115ff.) come the consequences for the Jews, the only nation that does not participate in emperor worship and that also cannot make the smallest compromise on this point. The readiness of the Jews to die for their faith extends even to such "minor details"; for giving in on the smallest point finally leads to destruction of the whole (§117). It is precisely with the secular-caricaturing section (§§76–113) as background that the crucial religious point stands out all the more sharply.

Here too it remains clear that Philo is not attempting to withdraw from the Roman state and the emperor as such, but marks himself off from the perversions (even according to Roman standards) that developed when the barbarian praying to the emperor as a god was introduced into Rome (§116). The threat to the Jews posed by the Roman state, supposedly in its own interest, derives exclusively from this non-Roman self-deification. This is corroborated by a reference to the rabble of Alexandria (§§120–27, 162).[206] An additional light is thrown on the issue by mentioning again the Egyptian animal cult.[207]

Knox argues that the section §§141–51 is derived from the same (Gentile) source as §§76–113. There is no point in arguing whether in fact the same source is used or not, for in any case its secular character is undeniable. Tiberius and especially Augustus are contrasted to Gaius. The discussion has a Roman-monarchical slant (§149). He acknowledges without criticism that "Olympian" honors are paid to Augustus, as evidenced by temples and other buildings, "especially in our Alexandria" (§150).

That what we have here is a self-contained unit of pro-Roman propaganda is indicated by the transition in §§145ff.[208] There follows, with a formally firm connection, the Jewish point: despite the honors paid to Caesar, the Jews were not bothered. For it was understood that Augustus was concerned for the preservation of the traditions of the Jewish people and was honored by them precisely for this reason. He refused to be addressed as a god (§154) and thus

---

[205] Incidentally: Philo's witty comment that it would be easier to think of God becoming a man than a man becoming God (§118) is, of course, not to be exploited theologically—as though Philo made some distant reference to the idea of an incarnation.

[206] Cf. *Flacc.* 41–96. There the real blame is laid at the door of the excesses of Flaccus, while here the emperor is blamed.

[207] Smallwood: Philo consciously charges the Alexandrians with this, who are thereby morally degraded.

[208] Of course the style of the ruler encomium ("this"+definite article+participle) is not Greek but oriental; Norden, *Agnostos Theos*, 223 (cf. 187); see on Acts 7:37f.

was able to get along with the Jews. He instituted the offering for the emperor in Jerusalem, at his own expense (§317).[209] Thereby the Jews were acknowledged politically.[210]

In addition, the famous affair of the planned erection of a Gaius/Jupiter statue in the Jerusalem temple is told at length.[211] The readiness of the Jews to die for their faith is reaffirmed once more (in §233 with the nuance: defenselessly), and again the Jewish national consciousness is bound to the existence of Jerusalem (§281). Here is the seat of their political loyalty (§§231, 288).

Now the tone becomes sharper: the attitude of the Jews, their relationship to the law and the temple (§§290ff.), their great numbers, and their dispersion throughout the Roman Empire and the rest of the world (danger could threaten from the East [§§216f.], which is something for the Syrian governor Petronius to think about), along with the Jews' corporate and intellectual qualities, constitute for Rome a political factor. Here notes are sounded that (when one reads Josephus) will be linked together to become a song pointing in the direction of the future war. Rome is advised of the political loyalty of the Jews (§§281f.; Flacc. 45f.).[212] But they are a peace-loving, unarmed people who, when they go to Petronius, are loyal (§§230f.).[213] They must not be made into enemies by attacking their faith, but that is precisely what Rome does—if the first and second commandments are violated by the erection of an image to Caesar in the sacred national center of Judaism. One passage in Gaius's discussion with the Jewish legation summarizes the problem well (§357); Gaius: "You have indeed offered sacrifice, but to another, even if for me." That is certainly the most that Jews were capable of doing, and the most they did do. The riddle posed by the conclusion, the announcement that a "palinode" (what is meant?) must follow, is a matter that we cannot discuss here. Only for the sake of a survey do we now introduce a political monograph.

De Josepho [214]

According to Goodenough, the purpose of this writing is "to insinuate to its Gentile readers the political philosophy that Jews wished Gentiles to believe

---

[209] Josephus, J.W. 2.10, cf. Ag. Ap. 2.6 fin: the sacrifice was at Jewish expense. Even so, their political recognition remains.

[210] The time will come when the beginning of the Jewish War will be signaled by the cessation of this sacrifice.

[211] Parallel Josephus, J.W. 2.181ff.; Ant. 18.257ff. (259f. is the only passage where Josephus names Philo—as part of the legation to Gaius).

[212] Goodenough (Politics, 19f.) hears threats against Rome already in §§136–61.

[213] Allusions to the Jewish theocratic movements, which fundamentally rejected the Roman rule, are avoided, but shimmer in the background anyway. In Josephus, Ant. 14.278, the Alexandrian Jews are not so harmless.

[214] German: L. Cohn, in Philo, ed. Cohn and Wendland, 1:155ff.; Greek-French: J. Laporte (De Josepho. 21. Les oeuvres de Philon d'Alexandrie [Paris: Cerf, 1964]).

was theirs" (*Politics*, 62). B. Badt (in *Philo*, ed. Cohn and Wendland, 1:217ff.) comments on the form of the presentation: In *De Josepho* as in *De Abrahamo*, first the events are reported and then the symbolic meaning is given (cf. Cohn, *Philo* 1:155). This is different from *Vit. Mos.*, which is a kind of historical novel (like Xenophon's *Cyropaedia*), though of course symbolic elements are also found there (e.g., the burning bush, 1.67ff.).

The only item here that is of present interest to us is the picture of Judaism that the document wants to suggest. Among the features that have an apologetic goal is, of course, the presentation of Jewish morality (which is related to their political capacity [§§37ff., 54]). As for the rest, the rulers' code can at the most show that in this point the Jews have no other ideal than the Greek political philosophers. If there is anything specifically Jewish here, it must be sought out with a magnifying glass.

An apologetic trait is first revealed with the help of the anti-Jewish literature: Here we have a Jew, a man of a noble family (§248), as the chief administrative officer of Egypt (§242).

A Historical, Apologetic Monograph: De Vita Mosis [215]

The book has, to be sure, a thoroughly apologetic goal, but is of a literary type completely different from all the apologetic writings of Philo previously discussed.[216] Although there are points of contact with the works on the exposition of the law and the biographies of the patriarchs, this work can be interpreted as a unit in itself.

Although Alexandrian Jews had long attempted to write Jewish history according to Greek models, this work stands in a different kind of literary tradition: the Greek biography[217] and historical monograph.[218] Still, Philo attains such a high level that his product can also be presented to Greek readers.[219]

Here it is not the individual motifs and episodes that are very apologetic, taken by themselves, but the book as such, which presents the basic elements of Judaism in an exemplary perspective.

The rough outline is as follows (1.334; cf. the modification in 2.1ff.; for purposes of comparison, cf. *Praem. Poen.* 1ff. for a thematic, not literary, outline):

---

[215] German: B. Badt, in *Philo*, ed. Cohn and Wendland, 1:217ff.

[216] Ibid., 218: A novel of sorts, like Xenophon's *Cyropaedia*.

[217] There was a special tradition of Greek biography precisely in Alexandria, though this was of course primarily literary, not historical. Embryonic elements of biographical form can be seen, e.g., in 1.5, 7 and 2.1.

[218] It is no longer possible today to treat ancient biography as though it were such a rigid genre and to separate it so sharply from the composition of historical monographs, as was the usual practice for a long time (following F. Leo).

[219] Whether they read them and found them to their taste is another question; see Philo's complaint, 1.2.

Book 1: Kingship
Book 2: (a) Priesthood
        (b) Giving of the law (see 2.3, 8)
The account of the priesthood generally follows the Bible. Although Aaron is not ignored, he has only a minor role (1.84ff.; high priesthood, 2.142, 176ff.; his sons do not succeed him in this office). He is not mentioned at all in the story of the golden calf (2.162).

A dilemma appears already in the first sentence; in Greek categories Moses is thought of as a law *giver* (and then the laws are really *his* laws). But in the Jewish categories that represent Moses as he really was—to which the Greeks must be introduced—Moses is the transmitter and translator of the *sacred* laws. We have seen in an earlier passage (*Decal.*) how Philo attempts a balance between these two.

The *form* allows Philo to leave the question of *meaning* open. This is pure strategy. Once he makes use of the concept of the νόμος ἔμψυχος ("living imper-sonation of law") (1.162). This is a Greek expression, but the meaning for Philo is determined not by the Greek understanding of nature and law but rather by the concept of a transcendent God, in which nature is conceived of as his crea-tion and the law as the statutes of the Creator.

This greatest and most perfect specimen of humanity must be made known, in view of the absurd fact that his law is famous throughout the whole civilized world (see also 2.17), but the man himself is practically unknown—an impossi-ble situation, since the law is constituted for what it really is only by its connec-tion with Moses. This is due to the relationship between Moses, the prophet and friend of God (1.156), and God himself.

The primitive explanation for Moses' remaining unknown: partly from jeal-ousy (similarly Josephus, *Ag. Ap.* 1.213); the second explanation—from the con-trast to the laws of other states—again exposes the weak point of the apologetic.

Now concerning this person who has inexcusably remained unknown: Moses was educated in all the arts of the Egyptians,[220] Greeks, Assyrians, and Chaldeans (astronomy), but remained nonetheless true to the traditions of the ancestors (1.32).[221] In case the Gentile slander that the Jews were originally deported (leprous) Egyptians (is there an allusion to this in 1.39?) has been heard, it is countered by the emphasis with which the Jews are presented as *foreigners* in Egypt (1.34), in concert with the Bible.

So once again we have the old dilemma that the diaspora Jews must repeat-edly explain: living together with other peoples and at the same time remaining

---

[220] On Egyptian education among the Greeks, see Herodotus; Plato, *Laws* 656D, etc.; the description of Egypt by Strabo and Diodorus; and the firmly established motif of educational trips to Egypt by famous Greek scholars.

[221] In the cutting remarks against backsliding that precede (1.31), Badt finds an allusion to events in Philo's immediate vicinity (Tiberius Alexander).

separate from them.[222] Philo's version of the Balaam story (1.278) is nothing short of a classical discussion of this problem. A number of things must be seen together: The Jews are the scattered and isolated nation; this life necessarily involves a kind of isolation, but the worldwide context of the dispersion must be kept in mind. The Jewish laws thus stand out by contrast wherever they are, but they also thereby enjoy a worldwide respect (2.17ff.; cf. Josephus, *Ag. Ap.* 2.282). This facilitates the desired goal (2.44) of emphasizing the universalism that is implicit in monotheism (1.147ff.) that is made as opportunity permits.

Further: Moses voluntarily gave up the rulership of Egypt in order to become the leader of a stronger people, a nation chosen to be priests for the whole world. Thereby the political claim of the Jews is at once established and camouflaged.

The section is rounded off with a brief rulers' code. Once Moses' position has been established, the leading of the people to their later homeland can follow. The way leads through the desert—for purposes of discipline and education (1.164). Here we find both overlappings and discrepancies with the *Decal.*[223] The beginning of book 2 is related to book 1 in that again the figure of the ideal king is sketched. The consequences that follow from the office of kingship are given (with a reference to Plato, *Resp.* 5.473D on kings and philosophers). In addition to the Greek ideal of kingship we find discussions of (a) the giving of the law,[224] (b) the high priesthood, and (c) prophecy.

On the giving of the law: After the enumeration of the necessary virtues (again in the form of a code for rulers 2.9), it can be confirmed: Moses was the best lawgiver of all (2.12; also recognized by non-Jews, 2.17). The proof of this is seen in the sacred books composed by him, and his laws are complete (2.12). A comparison with all other law codes shows that they have remained unchanged, even to the smallest detail (2.13ff.; cf. Josephus, *Ag. Ap.* 1.42). Not for nothing does Philo introduce into the LXX legend the idea of the *inspiration* of the translation.

A principal argument for the superiority of the Mosaic law is provided by the structure of the Bible (2.45ff.), that is, the anchoring of the story of the giving of the law in the creation story that precedes. The lawgiver is also the

---

[222] For the same reason Philo must also justify such things as the carrying off of booty.

[223] In *Decal.* the people (during the desert wanderings) are obedient; in *Vit. Mos.* they are rebellious. The Sinai theophany is missing in *Vit. Mos.* But the following difference should not be overrated: in *Decal.* Philo makes a distinction between the Word of God himself/itself and what he/it communicates through Moses, while in *Vit. Mos.* 2.188 he distinguishes the words of *God,* which he speaks through Moses as translator, and the words of *Moses,* which Moses speaks by inspiration. The distinction is not one of systematic theology, but of the psychology of religion.

[224] In the Greek democracies the lawgivers were an institution *sui generis.* The situation was, of course, different in the Hellenistic monarchies. 1.162 pictures this latter scene by representing the king as a living code of laws.

Creator. Thus, whoever lives by the law finds himself in harmony with the world and nature (2.48, 52; the counterpart 2.53).

One is almost tempted to conclude that Philo has the theme of heteronomy in his sights, as is indicated by what follows:[225] this order that binds together creation and law leads to freedom (2.50f.) and to the universality of the law (2.48, 51f.).

Josephus[226]

Josephus stands at the end of the history of the literary genre "apology," so far as this history is known to us.[227] He gathers up the apologetic approaches of his predecessors, combines them into a whole that he reinterprets and presents to the situation that had been completely changed by the Jewish War.[228]

As is the case with Philo, so also with Josephus: his works have been preserved and handed on by Christians.[229] For Jews he is an apostate.[230]

The whole of his work is an apology for the Jewish people.[231] We must here limit ourselves to the one writing (except for the *thematically* apologetic passages in the other works), in which the literary genre "apology" is continued (on the title, see below).

The *general* problems of Josephus studies can here be mentioned only in passing: for example, his biography, the evaluation of Josephus as a person, particular literary-historical issues such as the dating of the *Antiquities,* their conclusion and relations to the *Life,*[232] his Greek education,[233] his religion (or

---

[225] And the latent debate with Plato (2.49; cf. *Laws* 709ff.). When Philo thinks of law giving, his horizon is clearly not the *polis* but the world.

[226] Bibliography: L. H. Feldman, *Scholarship on Philo and Josephus (1937–1962),* Yeshiva University Studies in Judaica (New York, 1963); H. Schreckenberg, *Bibliographie zur Flavius Josephus* (Leiden: E. J. Brill, 1968).

[227] In addition to him, we should mention one completely different sprout from the root stock of Hellenistic-Jewish literature, which forces its way to our attention in a special area, "the intellectual resistance against Rome" (H. Fuchs, *Der geistige Widerstand*), namely, the Jewish parts of the *Sibylline Oracles* (which extended in part beyond the time of Josephus).

[228] See above. The legal standing of diaspora Jews was *not* changed. Palestine was, of course, a special case; Josephus, for his apologetic purposes, specifically calls attention to this (*J.W.* 7.100f.). This is presupposed also in his description of the position of the Jews in Alexandria (*Ant.* 19 *passim;* just so also in the two concluding chapters of *J.W.*) as it is also in the way in which he carries on his debate with Apion and his commander.

[229] A special case (?): H. Oellacher, *Griechische literarische Papyri II* (Baden bei Wien, 1939): *PGraec. Vindobon.* 29.810: an accurate copy that belonged to a book dealer, a codex, from the late third century with *J.W.* 2.576–79, 582–84.

[230] *Life* 423f. (cf. *J.W.* 7.447f.), 429.

[231] And for himself.

[232] And further, whether Josephus was used by Tacitus. The argument concerns especially the famous oracle, *J.W.* 3.352; 6.288ff., 312; cf. Tacitus, *Hist.* 5.13; Suetonius, *Vesp.* 4. Michel and Bauernfeind (*De bello Judaico* 2.2:190f.: Tacitus is dependent on Josephus).

[233] On authors mentioned by Josephus: See the list by G. Hölscher ("Josephus," *PW* 9:1964f.)

religiosity).[234] Of questions of this sort, only two are of particular interest for us: (1) the relation between the *Jewish War* and the later developments that appear in the *Antiquities*;[235] (2) the problem of the documents that are included in *Ant.* 14 and 16.[236]

In Josephus the theological issue posed by the whole apologetic enterprise is posed with particular urgency: How will the fundamental Jewish confession "*One* God, *one* people, *one* temple" (*Ant.* 4.200f.; *Ag. Ap.* 2.193) be concretely expressed in particular political decisions? The way in which God and people are bound together is in any case a hindrance for apologetic, especially so when one thinks of the Jewish hope for the future.[237] Nevertheless, there were points of contact already available that he could utilize to get over this hurdle. A first one was to be found in the contemporary polemic against tyranny: the kingdom of God (God's monarchy) cannot be appealed to as a cover for tyranny

and the indexes in Niese and LCL, *Josephus,* vol. 9. A few items stand out: Alexander Polyhistor is mentioned only *once,* and that incidentally (in connection with Cleodemus Malchus) (*Ant.* 1.240). Occasionally a whole patchwork of authors' names is pieced together, *Ag. Ap.* 1.218; 2.84. In the first passage the Jews Demetrius, Philo (the Elder), and Eupolemus are taken to be Gentiles. Josephus's wholesale judgments about the Greek historians (*Ag. Ap.* 1.13ff.; cf. also in the introduction to *J.W.*) are instructive for his educational horizon. He has no knowledge of Greek philosophy to speak of, as can be seen in precisely those passages where Plato or Platonic material appears: *Ag. Ap.* 1.7 (Plato, *Tim.*); 2.167f., 193 (see Thackeray ad loc.), 214, 256f., or when he refers to the Stoics (*Life* 12, where they are compared with the Pharisees; *Ag. Ap.* 2.168, with Moses) or the Epicureans (*Ant.* 10.277; 19.32).

[234] Schlatter, *Theologie;* G. Stählin, "Das Schicksal im Neuen Testament und bei Josephus," in *Josephus-Studien,* 319–43. A special problem: G. Delling, "Josephus und die heidnischen Religionen," *Klio* 43–45 (1965): 263ff.

[235] Hengel, *Zealots,* 8–9; Laqueur (*Der jüdische Historiker*), despite the questionableness of his theses, is still valuable especially if Thackeray is constantly consulted alongside.

[236] See below; H. R. Moehring, "The Acta pro Iudaeis in the Antiquities of Flavius Josephus," in *Christianity, Judaism, and Other Greco-Roman Cults,* Festschrift Morton Smith (Leiden: E. J. Brill, 1975) 3:124ff.

[237] F. J. Foakes Jackson, *Josephus and the Jews* (London: SPCK, 1930) 73ff.: "The Hope of Israel in Josephus"; Schlatter, *Theologie,* 252ff. ("The Coming One"); R. Marcus on *Ant.* 10.209ff.: Josephus passes over the details concerning the fourth kingdom in Daniel, certainly because he, like the rabbis, identified it with Rome and wanted to avoid problems. M. de Jonge, "Josephus und die Zunkunftserwartungen seines Volkes," in *Josephus-Studien,* 205ff. (on *Ant.* 10.210): the events of Dan. 2:44 for Josephus belong to the future; cf. *Ant.* 4.125. F. F. Bruce, "Josephus and Daniel," *ASTI* 4 (1965): 148ff.; M. Hengel, "Zeloten und Sikarier," in *Josephus-Studien,* 175–96: Josephus says that God has given the rulership of the world to the Romans *now.* "He does not say anything about the future; *sapiente sat*" ("he was wise enough" to refrain from doing so) (p. 180). In actuality, the whole work of Josephus is permeated with concealed references to the future. For the Jews, this meant God's promises to his people. For Jews *and* Romans this meant the hope of a restoration, when piety and political loyalty would be practiced by the Jews.

W. C. van Unnik (*Flavius Josephus als historischer Schriftsteller* [Heidelberg: Lambert Schneider, 1978] 66) observes concerning the relationship of Palestinian Judaism and Hellenistic Judaism in Josephus: "There is no trace in Josephus's writings that he was conscious of any difference between the Judaism in his homeland and in the Hellenistic world outside Palestine, but presupposed that the possibility was always there to live by the law."

(the Jewish insurgents).[238] A second: God ranges himself *against* his own people when they sin.[239] A third: the agitators that foment rebellion are a godless Jewish group (or groups), not the people itself.

The groups of rebels.[240] These are referred to as "bandits,"[241] sicarii,[242] Zealots,[243] along with their lawlessness[244] and desecration of the temple.[245] Cf. the speeches of the high priest Ananus and Jesus (*J.W.* 4.163ff., 238ff.), of Josephus (*J.W.* 5.362ff., 401ff.; 6.95ff.) and in contrast the speech of Titus (*J.W.* 6.124ff., 327ff.),[246] the passages about Judas the Galilean and the "fourth sect,"[247] and the Sicarii (even if this name did not appear until later).[248]

The Jewish War[249]

First, some preliminary comments on the significance of prophecy[250] and signs[251] in Josephus's religious-political picture of the world. Continuity with the Old Testament and Judaism appears in several ways: in conscious borrowings, specific references, and expositions, especially of the prophecies of doom; in the distinction between true and false prophecy; in the style in which he describes "signs."

---

[238] Tyranny: A. Schalit, *König Herodes*, 461ff. (cf. *Ant.* 16.1–5).

[239] Cf. Rest of Esther 14:9; *J.W.* 5.395ff.; O. Böcher, "Die heilige Stadt im Völkerkrieg," in *Josephus-Studien*, 65ff.: the city was not desecrated by the nations, but by the war of brother against brother.

[240] Hengel, *Zealots*, 24–75.

[241] A political designation! Hengel, *Zealots*, 25–46: it is probably taken over from Nicholas of Damascus; note that the term first begins to be used after the death of Herod, and the distinction made between the "bandits" and the moderate "Jews" in *J.W.* 2.517ff., etc.

[242] Hengel, *Zealots*, 46–53: not an independent party, but particular activists among the "bandits"; *J.W.* 7.253, 417ff.

[243] Hengel, *Zealots*, 59–73: in *J.W.* almost confined to books 4 and 5 (battles in Jerusalem); never used for the rebels as a whole, but only for a limited group.

[244] Hengel, *Zealots*, 183–86; *J.W.* 4.184; 6.102; cf. 5.393, 442; 4.258, 348; 5.343.

[245] *J.W.* 5.100ff.; 6.121ff.

[246] The attitude of the Romans: 4.180; 6.93ff., 101ff., 123.

[247] *J.W.* 2.117ff.; *Ant.* 18.2ff., 23ff. *Ant.*: "the fourth sect" resembles the Pharisees; but cf. 18.9: changes in the laws; in *J.W.*, it is an independent movement, mainly to blame for the war.

[248] On "liberation," see *J.W.* 5.365, 395f.: servitude began under Pompey, and God subjected the Jews to slavery because they were unworthy of freedom. In *J.W.*, Josephus lets the desire for freedom appear as a secular matter (2.259: deceivers, who promise "signs of liberation"; see above).

[249] Annotations in Michel and Bauernfeind; H. Lindner, *Die Geschichtsauffassung des Flavius Josephus im Bellum Judaicum* (Leiden: E. J. Brill, 1972).

[250] προφήτης, *TDNT* 6:821ff.; P. Vielhauer in E. Hennecke and W. Schneemelcher, *New Testament Apocrypha*, Eng. transl ed. R. McL. Wilson, 2 vols. (Philadelphia: Westminster, 1963, 1965) 1:601–7; Hengel, *Zealots*, 229–45; Weber, *Josephus und Vespasian*, 66, 77: "Josephus the historian covers himself with a prophetic garb"; Hengel, *Zealots*, 205; van Unnik, *Flavius Josephus*, 41ff.

[251] σημεῖον, *TDNT* 7:221ff.; Michel and Bauernfeind, 2.2:186ff.

In the first place, Josephus himself claims to be a prophet (*J.W.* 3.351ff.):[252] he has the gift of interpreting dreams[253] and the gift of interpreting ambiguous oracles from God; he takes his pattern from biblical models.[254] *J.W.* 3.354 indicates the relation to his understanding of salvation history: *Tyche* has been given over to the Romans, and Josephus has been chosen as prophet. Thus the way is prepared for the prophecy to Vespasian (3.399ff.).[255]

Survey

An anticipation of the signs to be given to Vespasian stands already in 1.23. Prelude: John Hyrcanus, 1.68ff.; 1.78ff. (par. *Ant.* 13.311ff.):[256] Judas the Essene.[257] 2.112ff. (*Ant.* 17.345ff.): Simon the Essene interprets a dream of Archelaus.[258]

Doom (4.388): An old oracle against "enthusiasts": Jerusalem will be conquered and the holy place burned. The Zealots do not reject it—and thus make themselves the means by which it is fulfilled (cf. 6.311).

Most clear of all is the tradition of the prophets of doom (6.300ff.):[259] Jesus, son of Ananias, constantly repeated his cry of doom for seven years, beginning four years before the war: φωνὴ ἀπ᾽ ἀνατολῆς, φωνὴ ἀπὸ δύσεως, φωνὴ ἀπὸ τῶν τεσσάρων ἀνέμων, φωνὴ ἐπὶ Ἱεροσόλυμα καὶ τὸν ναόν, φωνὴ ἐπὶ νυμφίους καὶ νύμφας, φωνὴ ἐπὶ τὸν λαὸν πάντα ("A voice from the east, a voice from the west, a voice from the four winds; a voice against Jerusalem and the sanctuary, a voice against the bridegroom and the bride, a voice against all the people"). And at the end, αἰαὶ Ἱεροσολύμοις, αἰαὶ πάλιν τῇ πόλει καὶ τῷ λαῷ καὶ τῷ ναῷ . . . αἰαὶ δὲ κἀμοί ("Woe to Jerusalem," then "Woe once more to the city and to the people and to the temple").[260] Finally, "Woe to me also."[261] Note his fate: he

---

[252] Van Unnik, *Flavius Josephus,* 43ff. He points out that it is worthy of note that when addressing Jews Josephus does not speak as a prophet (*J.W.* 5.362ff.).

[253] Dreams are granted to him as well (*Life,* 208f.).

[254] Scriptural interpretation: extensively in his speech in 5.375ff.; cf. (generalities) 6.291, 295.

[255] 4.622: Josephus addressed Vespasian as the emperor while Nero was still alive. Lindner (*Geschichtsauffassung,* 64ff.) comments: ἔτι ζῶντος Νέρωνος ("even in Nero's lifetime") does not fit the Flavian view of history. This does not provide a date for the prophecy, or falsely dates it. Cf. Tacitus, *Hist.* 2.78 (to Vespasian on Mount Carmel). Variations in Suetonius, *Vesp.* 5 and 7 (here: in Alexandria); 5: ". . . Josephus . . . constantissime asseveravit fore ut ab eodem brevi solveretur, verum iam imperatore" ("Josephus . . . declared most confidently that he would soon be released by the same man, who would then, however, be emperor") (Dio 66:1) (μετ᾽ ἐνιαυτόν) ("at the end of the year"). Lindner: Over against the Roman claims, Josephus reclaims the priority of the oracle for himself.

[256] 2.159. A general discussion of the gift of prophecy among the Essenes; on the Pharisees, see *Ant.* 17.43ff.

[257] The prediction of the death of Antigonus is politically neutral.

[258] In dependence on Joseph's dream.

[259] In connection with the prodigy that has just been mentioned (6.299).

[260] Cf. ναῷ–λαῷ ("temple–people").

[261] Jer. 7:14.

was persecuted by his own fellow countrymen, brought before the governor Albinus (who took no action against him, assuming he was crazy). His reaction: he neither cursed his persecutors nor thanked those who tried to help him; his only response was to continue to repeat his cry of doom. The famous χρησμὸς ἀμφίβολος ("ambiguous oracle"), that about that time someone from the land of the Jews would receive dominion over the whole civilized world, is documented in 6.312ff.[262]

Signs of doom[263] (6.288ff.; together with references to deceivers, see below).[264] The audition heard by all the priests in the temple is especially familiar (6.299): μεταβαίνομεν ("we are departing") (cf. μεταβαίνωμεν, "let us depart") ἐντεῦθεν ("hence").[265]

Deceivers[266] (2.258ff.; *Ant.* 20.167). They claim to be inspired, want to lead the people into the wilderness, promise "signs of liberation" (2.259). 6.283ff.: After the temple was already burning, a pseudo-prophet proclaimed that God had commanded the people to gather at the temple and await the "signs of deliverance." Many "prophets" thus spoke, and were urged on by the "tyrants."[267]

Quite apart from the fact that the whole work can be seen as an apology *sui generis,* this tendency comes to expression in condensed form in several passages. Especially the introduction[268] belongs in this category, as is the case with parts of the speeches that have been inserted into the narrative.[269]

---

[262] Tacitus, *Hist.* 5.13 (in connection with the extraordinary events of the exodus) . . . (according to an old priestly writing): eo ipso tempore fore ut valesceret Oriens, profectique Iudaea rerum potirentur. Quae *ambages* Vespasianum ac Titum praedixerat; sed vulgus . . . sibi tantam fatorum magnitudinem interpretati" ("this was the very time when the East should grow strong and that men starting from Judea should possess the world. This mysterious prophecy had in reality pointed to Vespasian and Titus, but the common people interpreted these great destinies in their own favor").

Suetonius, *Vesp.* 4: ". . . esse in fatis ut eo tempore Iudaea profecti rerum potirentur" ("it was fated at that time for men coming from Judea to rule the world"), etc. Norden, "Josephus und Tacitus" (Tacitus had not read Josephus).

[263] 5.409ff. (speech of Josephus). A miraculous spring for the benefit of Titus, alongside a reference to a biblical precedent.

[264] Concerning the false and the correct ways to interpret the prodigies (the latter through the scribes), see 6.291, 295.

[265] Cf. 3.354 (see above); 5.412. Again Tacitus, *Hist.* 5.13 is parallel, "et audita maior humana vox, excedere deos" ("and a superhuman voice cried: 'The gods are departing'").

[266] Hengel, *Zealots,* 229–33.

[267] 2.261 (*Ant.* 20.169ff.): the Egyptian pseudo-prophet; cf. *Ant.* 20.97ff.: Theudas; see on Acts 5:34ff.; 21:38.

[268] H. Lindner, "Eine offene Frage zur Auslegung des Bellum-Proömiums," in *Josephus-Studien,* 254.

[269] In addition there are several comments that indicate the political views of Josephus in an exemplary fashion. A selection follows.

A Selection of Individual Passages

1:27. The rage of the "tyrants" against the ὁμόφυλοι ("fellow-countrymen") and the φειδώ ("clemency") of the Romans toward the ἀλλόφυλοι ("alien race"). Titus wants to preserve the city and the temple.[270]

1.38. A recollection of the Maccabees, who had joined in friendship with the Romans. Josephus thus places himself in a Jewish tradition within which the rebels appear as apostates.[271]

2.1ff. A preview: During the disturbances after the death of Herod, people lost their lives in the temple.[272] Basic to his whole approach is that in establishing the blame for the war, Josephus works on a double front: (a) against the Roman governors;[273] (b) against the Jewish rebels.

From the Roman side, the program of Caligula was a prelude of things to come (2.196).[274] The general description of the conditions in the country throws light on both sides: (a) the conduct of the Roman governors; (b) the activities of the "bandits."[275]

On the "liberation" slogan (4.163ff., Ananus): Under the Zealots slavery will prevail instead of freedom. On the other hand, the Romans are the guarantors of law and order (4.184). They only require that Caesar be given his due (5.405). Of the Roman governors, Josephus concentrates especially on Gessius Florus as responsible for the war (2.293, 340f.; *Ant.* 18.25; 20.252ff., 257.

Both groups of warmongers are contrasted with the peace-loving Jewish people as a whole (including the ruling classes: 2.302 vs. 316, 336), but which is, of course, also partly responsible for the war because of this toleration of the intrigues of the rebels (4.163ff.; speech of Ananus). But the gap between the man of the people and the warmongers (2.320ff.) is constantly emphasized, along with the godlessness of the rebellious group. They prohibit non-Jews from offering their sacrifices (2.408ff.), which is irreligious (2.413).[276] Further typical outrages are breaking of oaths (2.453ff., with a view to their punishment); the συγγενικὸς φόνος ("slaughter of his kin") (2.469ff.).

4.150. Hubris against God and the desecration of the temple (151ff., 162f., 201); again in contrast to the conduct of the Romans (4.182).

5.19: the desecration of Jerusalem—once again opposed by the Romans.

---

[270] 1.152: The previous conduct of Pompey allows the plans of Titus to appear in a "Roman" light. Tacitus ostensibly saw these plans from a different point of view, according to Sulpicius Severus, *Chron.* 2.30.6 (Tacitus, *Hist.* frag. 2).

[271] For supplementary information, see 2.22: The Jewish political wish is for autonomy under direct Roman oversight; cf. 4.319 (358): "democracy"; *Ant.* 17.227. On Jews and Romans, see further 5.257, 363; 6.101.

[272] Accented in 2.30, 89; on the temple desecration, see 5.100ff.; 6.121ff., 262.

[273] More strongly emphasized in *Ant.* than in *J.W.;* Hengel, *Zealots,* 14–15.

[274] With the (constantly repeated) reference to the readiness of the Jews to suffer for the law.

[275] 2.254; the Sicarii; 2.264: imposters and bandits.

[276] 5.17: the altar venerated by Greeks and barbarians; 4.324: κοσμικὴ θρησκεία ("sacred vestments").

The religious background becomes visible: the Romans purify the desecrated city by fire (4.323; 5.19ff.). The Zealots destroy the due process of law.[277] 4.318: the murder of Ananus is the beginning of the downfall of the nations.[278] In general, perversion prevails (4.556ff.; 7.262ff.): παρανομία ("transgressions of law"), ἀσέβεια ("impiety").[279]

Religious and political aspects are intertwined. A political observation is made in 3.71: The Roman Empire is a fruit of ἀρετή ("glorious deeds"), not a gift of τύχη ("fortune"); 3.106: they have never won a victory by mere τύχη ("fortune"). Differently in 2.390 (Agrippa): Here the religious aspect comes forward: God has turned away from the Jews (cf. 3.354). 3.293: God is on the side of the Romans, bringing the catastrophe on the inhabitants of Galilee.

But in his affirmative statements about the Romans, Josephus does not distance himself from his own people—on the contrary![280] For he is a prophet and acts with a divine commission (3.361, 400). He must oppose the view that the war against the Romans is a holy war. It is only ostensibly such; the truth is, it is an unholy war (5.378). The outcome of the war is a manifestation of the judgment of God.

On the other side, the Romans are not simply praised or whitewashed. And God is the avenger of the Jews, when they suffer injustice (5.377). Even with all his political carefulness, Josephus still looks forward to what the future holds for the Jews; that this will have something to do with the Roman Empire is, of course, not said, though it is clear to every Jew; 5.19ff. gives a call to repentance and alludes to a possible restoration.[281]

The religious background of these apparently disparate statements is in fact united. The whole matter is to be understood against the background that is self-evident to every Jew, the doctrine of retribution (1.378). Although Josephus uses it for the benefit of the Romans, he does not use it against the Jewish people, but against the agitators, who, to be sure, invoke the name of God, but act contrary to the law, attack their own people, defile the holy place and finally destroy it (2.444ff.). God's justice prevails in history (5.395ff.).[282]

The mosaic that we have begun to piece together out of individual stones becomes a picture when we turn to the thematic summaries composed by Josephus.

---

[277] Hengel, *Zealots*, 183–86; Michel and Bauernfeind 2.1:211f.

[278] The "beginning" is also found in 5.3.

[279] As an illustration: 4.361ff.: the curse of Niger and its just fulfillment.

[280] Book 6, beginning: praise of the Jews; 6.17; 6.107: Josephus as Jew.

[281] But with a political warning to the Jews concerning the future (against influences from Palestine; *J.W.*, book 7). Such a warning is also indirectly contained in the portrayal of the Roman army (from whatever source it may have been taken, *J.W.*, book 3).

[282] 5.395ff.: a resumé of salvation history dealing with God, Jews, and Romans.

The Introduction

The purpose of this introduction is to place the Jewish War, and thereby the significance of the Jewish people as such, in the correct light from Josephus's own point of view. For (differently than in the Greek historians) only when this people and its achievement are understood, can the achievement of the Romans be understood (1.7).[283]

The Speeches

We read them as programmatic compositions of Josephus himself.

2.345-409. *The speeches of Agrippa II.*[284] If one compares them with the speech of the (non-Jew) Nicholas of Damascus in *Ant.* 16.31ff. (and reads this too as an expression of the political program of *Josephus;* see below), one thus receives an instructive insight into the intellectual range within which the Jewish argumentation functions.

Content and structure.[285] (a) The argumentation is at first purely political:[286] liberation and servitude; the relationship of the powers of the states to each other. (b) §§380ff.: And God's help? The *Romans* can be assured of that, on the basis of their successes (cf. above, on 3.71, 106). In wartime, the fulfilling of religious commandments is especially difficult.[287] Then follows the outlook for the diaspora[288] and the concluding appeal (§401).

5.362-419. *Josephus before Jerusalem.* (a) §§362-74: Josephus urges the defenders of Jerusalem to surrender. His appeal has a twofold basis: the Romans

---

[283] Josephus makes his own position clear by a sharp, fundamental critique of the Greek historians (no names are mentioned; a general judgment is pronounced, 1.13-16): in matters of business and affairs of the court, the Greeks have a nimble tongue.

In the writing of history they deal only with matters of the distant past, remaining prudently dumb about contemporary events. In the scholarly literature, the question of whom Josephus had in mind has become a curious guessing game. Nicholas of Damascus has been proposed, who has a dominant position among Josephus's sources in the first part of *Jewish War* and does not get off lightly; he is accused of being biased in favor of Herod (*Ant.* 16.183ff.). But one can dispense with the whole guessing game, when one takes into consideration the critique that is directed against the Greek history writers (and Greek scholarship as such) at the beginning of *Ag. Ap.* 1. He simply means all those he cites; the Greek writers generally including the historians, who, as Greeks, are not concerned with the truth.

[284] Here we have a summary of the content of the passages cited thus far.

[285] Lindner (*Geschichtsauffassung,* 21) divides the text as follows: (a) 345-49; (b) 350-61a; (c) 361b-401. 358-61a and 365-87 are bracketed as "insertions." This division is prejudiced by a particular source theory. Nothing relevant is settled thereby.

[286] Like the explanation presented above concerning the Roman Empire as a result of Roman efficiency. Just so Josephus pursues his goals with secular arguments, with a view to future prospects (as in the description of the Roman army).

[287] A bit much, in view of the history of Israel! For his (contemporary, Jewish!) opponents it was a matter of *holy* war.

[288] The reports of pograms provide illustrations. Josephus has in view here the continuing existence of the diaspora, but gives a warning for the future.

have reverence for Jerusalem as a holy place (§363; cf. 6.101: they have shown concern for our laws until the present). And their successes are a sign—*Tyche* has gone over to them (see above), and God is now in Italy (5.378: you are not making war against the Romans, but against God). (b) §§376–419: a survey of the way God has dealt with his people, from the point of view of the history of salvation. As to form, Josephus follows the traditional outline of salvation history (see the commentaries on Acts 7). God acts in accordance with the deeds of his people (§§395ff.).[289]

6.288-315. *The collection of prodigies.*[290]

7.323-36, 341-88. *The speeches of Eleazar.*[291] The first of these deals with the Zealot motto: "Serve no one except God."[292] The second is a kind of cooperative report.[293] Then comes the summary (see Lindner, *Geschichtsauffassung*, 142ff.), the point of which is the complaint in 5.29f., written from the perspective that deliverance might be a possibility after all.

The Antiquities[294]

This work too is an apology, taken as a whole, but on a different scale from *Jewish War*. The introduction already contains the formal elements of the apology (up to 1.17, and then 1.18ff.). It is helpful that the *Ant.* overlaps *J.W.* in part and allows us to see a version of some of the same events compared at a later date (around the end of the first century). This enables us better to trace the development of the political-apologetic attitudes of Josephus.[295]

The introduction gives information regarding the intention, desired readership, and the material on which the presentation is based.[296] Typical topoi are as follows:

---

[289] And see above: God has now already left the sanctuary.

[290] See above, Lindner (*Geschichtsauffassung*, 126ff.): Gentile sources are used. Michel and Bauernfeind, 2.2:179ff.: seven events from the apocalyptic tradition; two signs of salvation, cf. Isa. 60:1-4; pp. 296ff.: the transformation of a sign of salvation (Zech. 6:1) into a sign of doom.

[291] Michel and Bauernfeind, 2.2:276ff.

[292] Lindner, *Geschichtsauffassung*, 39f.: Josephus here characterizes his opponents. In §§327-33 he (falsely) attributes his own position to Eleazar. But in Josephus's sense the position of Eleazar in itself is thoroughly consistent. That is clear from the way Josephus presents his own activities before he was taken prisoner, from his internal involvement in the battle for Masada, and from the second speech. W. Morel, "Eine Rede bei Josephus (Bell.Iud. VII 341 sqq.)," *RheinMus* n.F. 75 (1926): 106ff.

[293] Morel, "Rede": (a) §§344-48 is Platonic school tradition; (b) §§349f. connections with Posidonius; (c) §§352-56 connections with the *Indica* of Megasthenes; cf. *Ant.* 10.227; *Ag. Ap.* 1.144.

[294] For bibliographies, see above (Feldman, Schreckenberg); bib. also in Schürer-Vermes-Millar, *History* 1:48ff.

[295] Hengel, *Zealots*, 12-15: In comparison with *J.W.*, the tendency of the *Ant.* is religious-ethical; that the Romans also bear a part of the blame is also emphasized more strongly. We may leave aside the comparison of the pictures of Herod in the two works, because this concerns the relationship to the exta-Jewish world only minimally; Schalit (*Herodes*) debates with Laqueur.

[296] The Bible (1.5; 1.17: without addition or omission). 1.6ff., a backward look at *J.W.*, and the relation of the new work to the previous one.

1.6. The origin of the Jews and their lawgiver; the goal of education as εὐσέβεια ("piety") and ἀρετή ("excellence") (1.14: obedience to the law). Further: the war with Rome was not wanted by the Jewish people.

The Jews do not attempt to keep their way of life secret; this is already proved by the translation of their Scriptures into Greek (1.10f.).[297] 1.15 alludes to the concept of God (cf. then 1.20) and rejects unworthy mythologies. The temporal scope is indicated: five thousand years (1.13).[298] In 1.18ff. Moses is compared with other lawgivers (1.21).[299] He does not begin with human conventions and rights, but with God and the creation of the world. As in Philo, the connection of creation and law is fundamental.[300] 1.23ff.: God and law belong together. None of it is unreasonable; all is in harmony with nature; the whole matter is highly philosophical.

Familiar motifs common to antiquity are given an *indirect* apologetic application, since they are drawn from Jewish writings:[301] the original paradisiacal conditions (1.40ff.), with features of the golden age; then came the great degeneration,[302] especially of faith in God (1.72). *Direct* apologetic is incidentally interspersed.[303] 1.113f.: turning away from God or else fear of him[304] results in tyranny. (Later [4.145ff.], the problem of law and freedom is thoroughly discussed: Zimri and Phinehas, Numbers 25.)

The topos of the proof of the antiquity of the Jews is also present, at least in its component parts: Abraham as teacher of the Egyptians (1.166ff.: Artapanus), with dependence on the common oriental understanding of the course of history: learning had progressed from the Chaldeans via the Egyptians to the Greek.[305] The description of the practice of circumcision and of amixia stands in the service of apologetic (1.192),[306] as does that of the relations of the Jews

---

[297] Of course the *name* of God remains secret (2.276); the manner in which the exact wording of the Decalogue is treated is peculiar (3.90).
[298] Cf. *Ag. Ap.* 1.1. Moses lived two thousand years previously (1.82); the flood happened 2,262 years after the creation. By this means the great mythical prehistoric period of the Greeks, which can never be checked anyway, is set aside, and their "historical" dates (the Trojan War) are undone.
[299] Cf. Philo, *Op. Mund.*
[300] Thackeray (on 1.21) assumes that Josephus has Philo, *Op. Mund.*, before him.
[301] 1.93: the flood: Berosus; §94, 107f.: oriental and Greek authors. §118: the building of the tower, and the Sibyls (cf. *Sib. Or.* 3:97ff.; see below), with polytheistic remnants that shimmer in the background: the gods (!) send storms; cf. *Sib. Or.* (Alexander Polyhistor).
[302] "Beginnings and degeneration"! 1.60ff.: Degeneration and *inventions*.
[303] 1.73 (giants), a passing shot at Greek mythology (another against the Greeks in 121).
[304] Nimrod argues in favor of this; now the fear of God is considered to be slavery (1.115). A foil from contemporary history was provided by the Greek enlightenment (Epicurus, Lucretius). The anti-Semitic picture of Moses should also be compared: Moses teaches contempt for religion. In opposition to this Abraham is made into an example of monotheism.
[305] §180: (Hiero)solyma goes back to the time of Abraham (cf. non-Jewish authors, who consider it to have been founded by Moses).
[306] For circumcision, reference is made to the Arabians (Ishmael) in 1.214. The charge of hatred of foreigners is diverted to the inhabitants of Sodom; cf. Wisd. of Sol. 19:13f. The prohibition of foreign marriages (cf. *Ep. Ar.*) is not here programmatically developed. In addition, it stands in

with other peoples.[307] A traditional apologetic affirmation is the statement that the Jews are not Egyptians, but originally derive from Mesopotamia (expressly against the false statements of the anti-Semites [2.177]),[308] along with the portrayal of the work of Joseph in Egypt (2.39ff.) and the "correct" description of the exodus (2.201ff.; contra the false descriptions [3.40]). Cf. also Artapanus (discussed above) for comparison with the Moses story.[309]

3.91ff. *The Decalogue* (cf. Philo). As in Philo, the Decalogue is followed by the "special" laws, under the schema πολιτεία ("government") and νόμοι ("laws"), 3.213; cf. 4.193f. (cf. §§224ff., 274ff., and the exposition in 4.196ff.). 3.245: fatherland and city/temple. 3.313: God and people; §§317ff.: the contemporary prestige of the Mosaic law is appreciated even by enemies of the Jews (§322).

Here is another instance of what is found elsewhere (cf. *Ep. Ar.*), the internal contradiction posed by the circumstance of defending the law over against non-Jews. It is typical, because unavoidable, as soon as one shifts from that which is generally valid, monotheism, to that which is particular—(a) God and his people; (b) the regulations that require segregation (cf. 4.137). Cf. further 4.114ff.: a promise to the people and the land for ever; §135: a look into the future (cf. §210—Daniel; a disguise); on the promise of the land forever, see also 5.93; 4.128: the present misfortune is only temporary. The diaspora is interpreted in terms of salvation history (4.190).

The great, comprehensive speech of Moses (Deuteronomy) looms up out of its context in 4.180ff.: monotheism, the special position of Israel; a summary of the law (§§196ff.); §200: *one* holy city, *one* temple, *one* altar (Deuteronomy 12); §201: *one* God and *one* people (cf. *Ag. Ap.* 2.193); §207: no slandering of foreign gods,[310] no robbing of temples (cf. Rom. 3:22). And §214: aristocracy—for Josephus a program for the political future of the Jews that has real relevance; cf. 6.36ff., 84 (*Ant.* 11.111: up to the Hasmoneans, with oligarchy); cf. the comments in 6.61 on theocracy (which in *J.W.* is the program of the godless rebels).

The story of Solomon, the sage who had power over the demons, also becomes useful for propaganda purposes (8.42ff.).[311] Among other things, this story illustrates Israel's confession of faith in one God and one temple (8.106ff.: a divine manifestation for the construction of the temple). This is combined with the *universal* character of Jewish religion: the world is the "everlasting

---

tension with 2.91ff. (the marriage of Joseph) and 2.25 (the Ethiopian wife of Moses).

[307] 1.220ff., 238ff.; cf. Malchus in Alexander Polyhistor (Heracles), 240. As a contrast: 1.278: hatred of Jacob in Canaan; 3.179: hatred of the Jews, to which Josephus responds not with a "refutation" but with an explanation of the ritual symbolism; cf. Philo, *Vit. Mos.* 2.88, 117ff.

[308] 3.265: the laughableness of the "leprosy" version; *Ag. Ap.* 1.279ff.

[309] Literary dependence, or the same traditions?

[310] Philo, *Vit. Mos.* 2.205; *Spec. Leg.* 1.53; Josephus, *Ag. Ap.* 2.237.

[311] On §§50ff., see above and 8.144ff. (Hiram).

house" of God.[312] §113: the promise to David is "forever"; §116 is again typically apologetic: prayer is offered not only for the Hebrews, but for all worshipers of God; and §117: we are not ἀπάνθρωποι ("inhuman") but wish God's blessings to come on all human beings.[313] In §120 we again have the affirmation: piety and happiness of the people forever, so long as they remain faithful to God. §§127f.: But apostasy and the worship of other gods leads to war, loss of the lands, and the destruction of the temple.[314]

8.161. *Jewish freedom.* §§191f.: Again the forbidden intermarriage with foreign women and the prohibition of the worship of foreign gods; §229: apostasy is the beginning of all evil (cf. §282). Such references are repeatedly sprinkled throughout the historical narratives (9.243, 256; 10.37ff.).

8.343ff. In the Elijah story the accent naturally falls again on monotheism and the polemic against polytheism.[315]

8.418f. Concerning the power of fate, which is characteristic of his concept of fate as such: fate is what God imposes; note the relationship with prophecy.

It corresponds to the "general line" as well as the currently relevant goal Josephus has set for himself, that in book 10 there is found an extensive discussion of the (first) destruction of Jerusalem. The theological background (along with the prospect of the later liberation [10.113]) is taken from Jeremiah.

In relation to the constant demarcation of the Jews from the Samaritans, 10.183 also becomes relevant: in regard to the two deportations it is stated (the first: 9.278) that Judea remained free of foreign settlers. Thus the Jews remain until the present—Jews.

The interpretation of Daniel 2, which remains a mystery to non-Jewish readers (10.208ff.), is of programmatic significance: The third king comes "from the West," and is thus Alexander (as among the rabbis). Then follows the *iron* kingdom—that is, Rome (likewise in agreement with the rabbis).[316]

It is to be expected that the application of the Esther story is conveniently available for repeated use (11.184ff.). It demonstrates the political loyalty of the Jews, who are unjustly persecuted (11.221, 230).[317]

In 11.212 we have a small compendium of charges against the Jews (cf. also §217: the charge of political disobedience, and of hatred against the monarchy).[318]

---

[312] Spiritualizing; somewhat reminiscent of the speech of Paul on the Areopagus; cf. Acts 17:27f.

[313] Cf. 1 Kings 8:43, the apologetic twin motifs!

[314] To be read on "two levels," in view both of the ancient story and the contemporary time, by which the destiny of the Jews is explained (8.129). History is made to serve apologetic purposes also in 8.144ff.=*Ag. Ap.* 1.116ff. (§147=*Ag. Ap.* 1.113ff.).

[315] §343: the other gods are only ὀνόματα ὑπὸ φαύλης καὶ ἀνοήτου δόξης πεποιημένα ("mere names invented by unworthy and senseless opinion") 10.50: ὡς οὐχὶ θεῶν ὄντων ("not really gods"); cf. 1 Cor. 8:4-6; Gal. 4:8.

[316] P. Volz, *Die Eschatologie der jüdischen Gemeinde im neutestamentlichen Zeitalter* (Tübingen: Mohr, 1934) 280ff.: the heathen world power as the object of judgment; Billerbeck, *Kommentar* 4/2:1004ff.

[317] §210: the ruler cult; incidentally: the Jews described as slaves by their enemies; cf. Cicero.

[318] Hecataeus. The charge is, in a certain way, confirmed by Josephus himself.

The *Legend of Alexander* (11.313ff.)[319] is developed into a paradigm: it demonstrates the political loyalty of the Jews in a splendid fashion (11.318; cf. 12.8). Alexander prostrates himself before the name of God (11.331);[320] sacrifice in the temple.[321] He permits life among the Jews to continue according to the divine laws (11.338f.), including those Jews who want to join his army.[322]

In 12.7f. the loyalty of the Jews is again illustrated (the transport of Jews to Egypt); cf. §§54; 55:[323] they offer sacrifice for the rulers.[324]

12.49ff. The privileges granted by the Seleucids, which were later confirmed by Vespasian and Titus (§121; *J.W.* 7.110f.).[325] The letters of Antiochus III are significant (12.138ff.).[326] Josephus feels free to enlarge on the episode of Antiochus IV, for it was, of course, the Romans who intervened against him (§§244, 246).[327]

12.281 (cf. 315). Concerning freedom, the Jews are prepared to die for it. One must ask whether this must have appeared to Roman readers to be dangerous (also for the future). But later (in book 16) Nicholas of Damascus will present the Romans as those who bring freedom to the nations (see below). And soon (§414) the treaty of the Jews with the Romans will be mentioned.[328]

13.54 offers yet another variation of the theme "*one* temple."[329]

13.245. The separateness of the Jewish way of life (Antiochus Sidetes).[330]

Books 14 and 16

These two books form a focal point of our study, since the position of the Jews in the Roman Empire is discussed thematically and in a manner mandated by the times.

What Josephus has to say is supported by documentary evidence, the content of which is clearly outlined. Thus these two books are foundational for all

---

[319] The use of a source: 11.305: καθὼς ἐν ἄλλοις δεδήλωται ("as has been related elsewhere").

[320] On the (secret) name, see above (2.276).

[321] See above, *J.W.* 2.408ff.: the rebels prohibit non-Jews from offering sacrifice. Thus, mentioned again with a view to the present.

[322] Cf. 12.45 (Ptolemies); §133 (Seleucids). And contrast: the Samaritans revolted; Curtius 4.8; now confirmed by archaeology.

[323] 12.22: cf. *Ep. Ar:* God −Zeus−ζῆν ("Life"=the infinitive of the verb "live"); cf. Aristobulus.

[324] 12.406; cf. Philo and Josephus concerning the sacrifice for the Roman emperor and Josephus on the cessation of the same as the signal for the beginning of the revolt.

[325] Cf. the anticipation *Ant.* 12.125ff. (Agrippa over against the Ionians); see below 16.27ff.

[326] On the question of authenticity, see R. Marcus, LCL 7:743ff.

[327] 12.276f.: In emergencies, fight on the Sabbath; there is a certain tension between this and the speech of Agrippa II in *J.W.* 2.345ff.

[328] Cf. 13.227, 259: Hyrcanus's friendship with the Romans (not in *J.W.*); §§266f.: a letter from Rome (Schürer-Vermes-Millar, *History* 1:204ff., treated as genuine); cf. 14.248ff.

[329] The temple in Egypt is mentioned too, in a harmless way (§§62ff.), with an appeal to Isaiah.

[330] Cf. Diodorus (Posidonius?).

work on the legal position of the Jews.[331] *The* historical problem, of course, is that of the authenticity of the documents.[332] Critical research has generally accepted them as authentic. A judgment on the matter is difficult, because of the desolate state of the tradition.[333]

A significant work for the most recent discussion is H. R. Moehring, "The Acta pro Iudaeis in the Antiquities of Flavius Josephus" in *Christianity, Judaism, and Other Greco-Roman Cults,* Festschrift Morton Smith (Leiden: E. J. Brill, 1975) 3:124ff.

Moehring considers the documents to be forgeries,[334] which does not necessarily mean that they were created from whole cloth by Josephus himself. Falsified documents were a (literary) commonplace.[335] The burden of proof rests on those who affirm authenticity. How could Josephus have obtained genuine documents of such a nature? If, according to his own statement, he reports only a selection (this, of course, only a literary device), then why is it so unreadable? The condition of the purported quotations can be explained neither by the supposition that Josephus drew them from archives nor by supposing that he derives them from Nicholas of Damascus. The invitation to check the original documents is merely an artifice.

The modern interpretations are apologetically motivated. The condition of the text invites emendations, because scholars want to find the desired sense in the "original" text.[336] Josephus does not mention that the archives in Rome were destroyed by fire in 69 C.E. (Josephus, *J.W.* 4.649 refers only to the temple on the Capitoline.) Of course they were restored—but not all the minor documents were replaced.[337] And how could ψηφίσματα ("votes"/"resolutions") of the Greek cities have been deposited in the capitol archives?[338]

---

[331] See pp. 1–43 above; Smallwood, *Jews under Roman Rule.*

[332] Along with the trustworthiness of the way in which the speech of Nicholas of Damascus is reported in book 16, see below.

[333] This can be used as an argument *for* authenticity; the text is supposed to have been corrupted in the course of transmission by copyists. In that case Josephus does not have the text directly from the archives.

[334] With good reason. *Ant.* 14.186f.: The Jews were not believed with regard to the Persian and Macedonian decrees, because they were not generally available, but had been preserved only by the Jews and barbarian peoples (where? at the time when Josephus is writing *Ant.*). An example: J.-D. Gauger, *Beiträge zur jüdischen Apologetik: Untersuchungen zur Authentizität von Urkunden bei Flavius Josephus und im 1. Makkabäerbuch* (Cologne: P. Hanstein, 1977) 138ff.; in particular on Josephus, *Ant.* 12.

[335] A test case for Josephus: the edict of Claudius concerning the Jews in Alexandria (19.280ff., 310).

[336] 14.149ff: Ὑρκανὸς Ἀλεχάνδρου (see R. Marcus).

[337] Why does Josephus not mention the fire? He obviously did not reckon with the fact that his readers might be aware of it.

[338] Schürer, *History* 1:85f.; Schürer-Vermes-Millar, *History* 1:52f. Moehring ("Acta," 131): a *senatus consultum* ("resolution of the Senate") is no law (p. 132); on fictitious decrees of the Senate, see Cicero, *Phil.* 5.12. On the familiarity of historians with decisions made in the Senate, cf. Livy 39.14.3–9 with *CIL* I² 581.

Summary. We will disregard the problem of authenticity, but will consider valuable for the reconstruction of the Jewish situation under Rome only what can be reliably confirmed from other sources, and thus will read the documents cited by Josephus (to the extent that they are readable at all) as documents of Josephus's apologetic from the time after the war. The problem will recur in book 16.

Details from Book 14:

§50: Do not fight against Rome![339] §72: The piety of Pompey.[340] §77: Hyrcanus and Aristobulus are responsible for the catastrophe in Jerusalem (not so in *J.W.!*)—one of the basic motifs of the *Antiquities*. §91: once again, aristocracy (cf. *J.W.* 1.170). §105: Crassus plunders the temple.[341] §§110ff.: the treasures of the temple; the diaspora and the contributions made to the temple (interesting, in the time of the *fiscus Iudaicus* ["taxes on the Jews"]).

§§114ff.: the Jews in Cyrene (cf. 16.160), Egyptians. §118 is peculiar: the Egyptian origin of the Jews—in contradiction to Josephus himself, thus a remnant from a source (Strabo).

§§185ff.: the high point: the documents, with an emphasis on their public availability (§186). The goal is securing the position of the Jews in the present situation.[342]

From Book 16:

For our purposes, the most important text is the speech of Nicholas of Damascus (§§31ff.).[343]

The speech of Nicholas. The extraordinary feature of this speech is that the defense of the Jews is inserted into the framework of the Roman idea of the state. By this procedure, the enemies of the Jews are themselves brought under suspicion (despite the Jewish war) §34: ὡς ἄμφω ἀδικοῦσιν ("they wrong both

---

[339] *J.W.* 1.135: their irresistible might. Laqueur: in *Ant.* Josephus has a freer attitude with regard to the Roman policy. But see R. Marcus on 72.

[340] Not in *J.W.* (1.152); but see 1.153; thus in the one sentence *Ant.* is more friendly than *J.W.;* in the next (*Ant.* 14.73) the matter is reversed.

[341] Not in *J.W.* Sources in *Ant.:* 104: Strabo alongside Nicholas of Damascus, then continuing with Strabo.

[342] Josephus has been careful to say that Vespasian and Titus confirmed even the *Seleucid* privileges. Cf. also *Life* 424: Vespasian's protection of Josephus from Jonathan; *J.W.* 7.438ff. What sort of *military* provisions were there as Josephus writes? What about the privilege to hold assemblies and to gather collections (§§214f., 241ff.)? The provisions in the documents in part presuppose the existence of Jewish client states (§265: Hyrcanus); thus their substance is derived from that time.

[343] Preceding, §14: the sacrifice of Agrippa in Jerusalem; the active help by Herod for Agrippa. For the *Roman* view, see Suetonius, *Aug.* 93: Augustus praises his grandson Gaius because while on a trip he left Palestine aside and did not perform any devotions in Jerusalem; Schalit, *Herodes,* 748.

§§27f.: the Ionian cities and the Jews; the main points are again (cf. book 14) the Jewish peculiarities, the temple tax, the military service.

parties"); §36: the εὐδαιμονία ("happiness") of all humanity through the Romans; §38: Rome's political-moral mission to the whole of the civilized world; §37: the universal right of peoples to worship their own gods.[344] A key point is affirmed in §40: freedom—through Rome, whose dominion has taken the place of the earlier βασιλεία ("kings") for the Greek states.

The difficulty in the line of argument comes to light in §§42ff.: the rejection of the charge of "hatred of humanity"; a positive presentation of the piety of the Jews and once again the affirmation that the Jews practice no secret rituals; material concerning the Sabbath and the study of the law; the Jewish ethos; the customs are wholesome and old (§44). And finally, once again the decrees are deposited in the capitol (§48; see below).

Schalit (*Herodes*, 426ff.) supposes that the basic ideas of this speech of a non-Jew for Jews derive partly from Nicholas himself and partly from the *Memoirs of Herod*.[345] This is the source of the combination with the Roman idea of the state. A component part thereof is the acknowledgment of the autonomy of each nation and the conviction that freedom and national law are only available because they are guaranteed by Rome. That Rome and its dominion represent the real theme of the speech is, according to Schalit, not merely flattery, but due to the fact that the speech represents the concept of empire current among the educated classes in Italy in that period (with which both Herod and Nicholas had associated themselves).[346] The fundamental motifs of this concept are the concept of justice,[347] and the idea that Roman justice secures freedom for the conquered territories.[348]

In §§162ff. the second cluster of documents follows: §164: protection for the sacred books of the Jews; §167: for their sacred monies. The apologetic character is compactly expressed in §§174–78; see the description of the purpose of the citation: reconciliation with the nations; this is possible, if all parties concerned allow themselves to be guided by justice. The Jews do this in any case—in loyalty to their own laws (§177); thus, away with anti-Jewish hatred![349]

Once again, near the conclusion of this lengthy work, the old position appears: the theocratic liberation movement is not a constituent part of the Jewish religion as such, but is the program of a particular party. But Josephus bumps against the edges of his own position: he too must acknowledge that for the Jews it is a given *status confessionis*, when it is a matter of reverencing a

---

[344] Cf. §41. Josephus conceals the fact that Jewish monotheism is exclusive.

[345] That would make no difference in the matter itself, since Nicholas is the court historian of Herod.

[346] See Cicero, *Resp.* 5.1f. already; Virgil; Horace; Livy 37.25: later the speech of Aelius Aristides on Rome.

[347] Thereto "dialectically" Carneades, Cicero, *Resp.* 3.6.9. Fuchs, *Widerstand*, 3f., 28f.

[348] Aelius Aristides, *Oration* 96; Schalit, *Herodes*, 445 n. 1041. In Josephus's sense this applies to the Jews after the war.

[349] Illustrations from this period: Tacitus on 17.227, see above (*J.W.* 2.22). 18.23: theocracy. The theocratic program and poor administration by Roman governors stand alongside each other.

human being as δεσπότης ("lord").[350] More on this in 18.55ff. (Pilate).[351] "Exhibit A" is, of course, Caligula (§§257ff.; significantly enough, Apion is also mentioned), who is a "negative" argument for all who come later. Thus the fundamental nature of the conflict can in this case be openly discussed (§§266ff.; cf. the reaction of Petronius [§§280f.]). Finally there is a look back at the (five) world empires.

Appendix: The Vita. We hear basically the same old song.[352]

Against Apion ("Concerning the Age of the Jewish People")[353]

Preview
In this writing Josephus has preserved the traditional forms of apologetic in their purest state.[354] Some main points that stand out are as follows (for the details, see below):

I. *A Historical Apology* (1.1ff.):
1. The determination of chronology: the world, and the Jewish people along with it, are five thousand years old.[355]
2. Their own history.
3. The settlement of the land.
4. The rejection of defamations against the Jews: these are in part the result of lies (against which: polemic) and in part the result of ignorance (against which: instruction).
5. The dependence of Greek philosophy on the orientals.[356]
6. A comparison: Greek historical writing is private and arbitrary, while the oriental is official, institutionally validated.
7. The laws (once again with a reference to the willingness of the Jews to become martyrs for it).

II. *A Brief, Moralistic-historical Apology* (1.60ff.)

---

[350] 18.23 on the fourth "philosophy" founded by Judas the Galilean. Further: this was written in Domitian's time!

[351] In §§24f., Josephus gets through the matter by cheating, by using Gessius Florus as a foil (concerning Gessius Florus, see 20.257).

[352] §20: Again to be read with side glances at the present; just so, for example, §§141ff., 299ff., 423ff. The Pharisees are loyal leaders; §§32ff.: internal splits among the Jews; §§230ff.: the people.

[353] On the title, see Origen, Eusebius: Περὶ τῆς τῶν Ἰουδαίων ἀρχαιότητος ("On the Antiquity of the Jews"). "Contra Apionem" first by Jerome; Schürer, *History* 1:89; Schürer-Vermes-Millar, *History* 1:55. Time of composition: after *Ant.;* see 1.1.54.

[354] On the points of contact with Philo's apology, see Wendland, *Therapeuten,* 709ff.; E. Kamlah, "Frömmigkeit und Tugend. Die Gesetzesapologie des Josephus in cAp 2,145–295," in *Josephus-Studien,* 220 n. 3 (supposition of a common source).

[355] Cf. no. 5. At one and the same time this declaration establishes the antiquity of the Jewish people and disposes of a mythical prehistorical period.

[356] This opinion is widespread also among the Greeks; Diogenes Laertius 1.

III. *A Complete Apology* is also found in 2.151ff.:

1. Moses, the first lawgiver; theocracy (cf. no. 3)
2. *One* God (the first commandment)
3. Secondary, dependent nature of the Greek philosophers.[357]
4. The law: it is sufficient, everything is regulated by it; faithfulness to the original law; it is unchangeable; it is simple, and thus is known by all. Its content: one God, no images; the temple. It is humane (thus no "hatred of humanity" among the Jews!). And again Jewish loyalty to it to the death is noted.
5. The religious-ethical immorality of the Gentiles is the foil for it.[358]
6. The *success* of the law; the spread of Judaism.[359]
7. The acknowledgment of the Jewish attitude and conduct by non-Jews.[360]

Commentary on the Apologies in Against Apion

(1) As a matter of course, 1.1f., introduces the γένος ("race") of the Jews: (a) (cf. *Ant.* 4.201) God is *one* and the race of the Hebrews is *one;* this is contrasted with τὸ πάτριον and τὸ ξενικόν (*Ant.* 9.96f.: ξενικοὶ θεοί) ("foreign gods"). (b) From the very beginning the division of humanity into two parts was implied.[361] (c) The age of the nation, drawn from data in the Holy Scriptures, is five thousand years (see above: the creation). The Jews are thus the oldest nation[362] τὴν πρώτην ὑπόστασιν ἔσχεν ἰδίαν ("the purity of the original stock").[363] (d) The settling of the land, ἣν νῦν ἔχομεν ("which we occupy today") (after the war).

(2) 1.2ff. (cf. 1.219): Response to the charge that our race actually originated later; in fact, it is not mentioned in the Greek historians. But (1.3) the false statements concerning the Jews are to be accounted for partly on the basis of prejudice against them and partly on the basis of ignorance (cf. 1.57ff.).[364]

---

[357] See no. 1 above; again, chronology serves an apologetic purpose.

[358] For this topos, cf. the line of development from Wisd. of Sol. 13–15 to Rom. 1:18ff.

[359] Cf. Philo, also for the continuation.

[360] Cf. already *Ep. Ar.*

[361] Cf. the twofold division in Rom. 1:16, "Jews/Greeks," parallel to the Greek "Greeks/Barbarians," Rom. 1:14. Schlatter, *Theologie,* 46ff.: the people of God; 237ff.: the relation of Israel to the nations.

[362] There was no mythical time before Israel; see above.

[363] The statement is somewhat ambiguous; what is clear, however, is that Israel is the *first* people of its kind—extremely important for the relationship of Israel to other peoples, and for apologetic purposes. H. Koester, ὑπόστασις, *TDNT* 8:583: "What is meant is the distinctive reality from which it derives its being." The opposite would be a derivation of *essence* (ὑπόστασις) and *origin* (παλαιότης) from some other people. L. Blum: "L'originalité de son noyau primitif" ("the originality of its primitive core") (*Contre Apion* [Paris: Leroux, 1930]). Thackeray: "the purity of the original stock." Note the competition with the idea of the Chaldean origin in 1.71. Makeshift translations!

[364] The respective authors are refuted by their own words. 1.58f.: The barbarians are better acquainted with the delineation of ancient history than the Greeks. Josephus draws the proper

(3) 1.6ff.: It is actually the Greeks who have a relatively short history.[365] This is based on information concerning the founding of their cities,[366] their knowledge of τέχναι ("crafts"),[367] their promulgation of laws,[368] their writing of history.[369] They in fact learned the art of writing from the Phoenicians.[370] Their documents are relatively recent; they do not even extend as far back as the Trojan War.[371] Their oldest philosophers are dependent on the Egyptians and the Chaldeans. Their historians contradict each other; in fact, they possess no *official* documents at all. Their guiding principle is not the truth, but rather the δύναμις of λόγος ("power of argument"). Thus they write out of rivalry and πρὸς χάριν ("seeking popularity") (§25).[372]

(4) 1.28ff. (cf. 1.8): The deplorable historiographical customs of the Greeks are contrasted with the secure manner in which traditions are handed on among the Orientals.[373] With this, Josephus has created a broad framework in preparation for his apologetic proper.

(5) 1.30ff.: Concerning the institutionalized securing of traditions within the *Jewish* community: (a) 1.31ff.: The διαδοχή ("succession") and their control, a control that extends to the wars inclusive of the most recent.[374] (b) 37ff.:

---

inference for the use of sources (1.8, 14, 70); he will only use sources as evidence that the Greeks consider to be reliable for ancient history.

[365] See Clement of Alexandria, *Strom.* 1.78.2.

[366] With this may be compared the generally accepted chronology; the Greek lists of kings (Argos, Silyon); Tatian 39; Clement of Alexandria, *Strom.* 1.79f. Synchronism: 1.103: The exodus was 393 years before Danus (Josephus overlooks the oldest Greek king, Inachus).

[367] The inventions of the barbarians: Tatian 41; Clement of Alexandria, *Strom.* 1.74ff.; the invention of writing (1.9ff.).

[368] For an example, 2.225 (Lycurgus).

[369] 1.8: compared with the Egyptians, Chaldeans, Phoenicians (not to speak at all of *us;* see 1.30ff.), the temporal priority of which the Greeks also acknowledge (1.14, 28, 58f.). The comparison of the Greeks with the Egyptians is particularly widespread (Herodotus, Plato). Tatian 36–38: Chaldeans, Phoenicians, Egyptians; 39: Greek historical writing began after Inachus (who was contemporary with Moses).

[370] The Greeks were also aware of this; Tatian 39.

[371] See the discussion of chronology above; Timaeus of Tauromenium, *FGH* 560; Eratosthenes of Cyrene, *FGH* 241.

[372] For comparison: (a) the introduction to *J. W.* and *Ant.;* (b) Greek theories concerning the style of historical writing, e.g., the debate concerning the "rhetorical" (Ephorus, *FGH* 70; Theopompus, *FGH* 115) and the "tragic" (Duris, *FGH* 76; Phylarchus, *FGH* 81) and the "pragmatic" program of Polybius. P. Scheller, *De hellenistica historiae conscribendae arte* (Diss., Leipzig, 1911); B. Snell, *The Discovery of the Mind* (Cambridge, Mass.: Harvard University Press, 1953); E. Schwartz, *Griechische Geschichtsschreiber* (1956); G. Avenarius, *Lukians Schrift zur Geschichtsschreibung* (Meisenheim/Glan, 1956).

[373] In Egypt through the priests; in Babylon through the Chaldeans. 1.29 gives a glimpse into the future: καὶ φυλαχθήσεται ("and they will continue to be preserved"). And 1.70 adduces a psychological argument in addition: what the Egyptians and Tyrians write about us is reliable, because they are hostile to us. The Chaldeans are, of course, τοῦ γένους ἡμῶν ἀρχηγοί ("the original ancestors of our race") (1.71,2).

[374] A note that is very revealing concerning Josephus's expectations for the future (near the end of his life). On genealogies, cf. the beginning of *Life.* Concerning Jewish genealogies, all too

Among us, not just anyone is permitted to write history.[375] The *prophets* (Josephus himself is one) are taught by God. (c) No contradictions are to be found in the Scriptures.[376] (d) The limited number of Scriptures contributes to clarity. (e) The period of time (extent) (temporal extent) of Jewish history can be easily surveyed (cf. 1.1).

(6) The comprehensive basic principle: οὔτε προσθεῖναι οὔτε ἀφελεῖν ("neither add nor omit anything").[377] In conclusion, the *obligatory* nature of the Jewish tradition in contrast to the Greek is established, for which the individual traditions are only λόγοι ("words," "sayings"). This obligation includes the obligation of martyrdom.

Thus far we have an essentially traditional basis that is arranged according to the needs of the current debate: the proof of the antiquity of the Jews in 1.60–68, with appeals to the validating sources in §§69–218; refutation of slanders in 1.219–2.144 (concerning the remainder of this document, to the extent that it pertains to our theme, see below).

At the beginning of the section on the proof of the antiquity of the Jews, once again the traits of a stylized apology stand out (1.60–80): for, of course, the data from the Greek historians must be opposed. The arguments based on the Greek sources are invalidated (cf. already the comment in 1.2 on their ignorance concerning the Jews), which leads once again into a brief description of the Jewish people.

1.60: The silence of the Greek historians concerning the Jews is explained by the geographical situation of Judea, which is remote from the sea and the traffic lanes of the world commerce.[378] To our nature belongs παιδοτροφία ("nourishing of children," a topos since Hecataeus), our laws and our religion. That is why there is no ἐπιμιξία ("mixing") with the Greeks. Among us there are no predatory raids, no wars of conquest.[379]

Once again a foundation is laid. Then follow the witnesses for the truth of Josephus's statements: Egyptians: Manetho (1.73); Phoenicians: Dios and Menander of Ephesus (1.106ff.); and the Greeks themselves, listed in order (1.161ff.).[380]

Then comes the *refutation of charges* (1.219ff.), with cross-references to the beginning section of the work (§219). Things began with the Egyptians (§223).

---

trustingly, see J. Jeremias, *Jerusalem in the Time of Jesus* (Philadelphia: Fortress Press, 1969) 278ff., 284ff.

[375] Although Josephus does it himself; still, he represents himself as a priest. This must be read with Greek eyes!

[376] Preview: If for once educated Greeks would read the Bible! Porphyry.

[377] *Ant.* 1.17; Rev. 22:18f.; W. C. van Unnik, *VC* 3 (1949): 1ff.

[378] 1.66: The Romans experienced the same thing for a long time! §61: In contrast to the commercial peoples, the Egyptians and the Phoenicians (with a passing shot at their greed).

[379] The matter was read differently among the Greeks.

[380] See pp. 45–133 above; in addition, 1.216 also gives a list; "But I have not read them all" — including those he names in his lists!

Then the main point is the arrival of the Jews and their exodus (cf. the extra-Jewish literature, which is hardly familiar with anything beyond the story of Moses and the exodus). The causes of the hatred against the Jews are the following: (a) Our ancestors had previously ruled Egypt (see the stories of Joseph and Moses in the *Ant.*), namely, the "shepherds" (which are identified with the Hyksos of Manetho). (b) Our good fortune after our return to our own country. (c) The difference between the Egyptian religion and ours, along with their envy of the success of our religion.

The debate with individual opponents, especially with Apion, is summarized in the third apology, which is again true to form (2.151ff.).

The Third Apology (2.151ff.)

(1) Moses is the first and oldest lawgiver.[381] But he did not take advantage of his situation and become a tyrant (2.158), but established a theocracy (2.165; cf. 184ff.). For the following holds true:

(2) *One* God (2.167; cf. 188ff.). Thus monotheism has immediate political consequences (including those of such nature that the Hellenistic opponents of tyranny must also be sympathetic to them).

That this God never came into being at a particular time but is eternal, etc., is obvious to the Hellenistic philosophy of religion.[382] 2.168: The Greek *philosophers* are also dependent on Moses.[383]

(3) 2.174ff.: The law regulates everything and is itself clearly arranged (cf. 1.38),[384] to keep us from sinning either intentionally or unknowingly.[385]

All Jews know the law (2.175ff.), which contains simple prescriptions (§§188ff.). Thus loyalty to it is possible (see 2.220ff.). The political result is the (generally known) Jewish ὁμόνοια ("oneness of mind") theologically expressed: appropriate to the fundamental principle of "one God/one people."

(4) The Jews are reproached for not having contributed any inventions to the world culture.[386] True enough—they do not in fact stray from the path laid out

---

[381] The proof of the antiquity of the Jews is illustrated: in comparison to Moses, Lycurgus, Solon, etc. are recent figures. 1.21: The Athenian memory does not extend back past Draco. 2.155: Homer does not yet even know the word νόμος ("law"); *TDNT* 4:1022ff., 1050ff.

[382] Philo; Josephus, *Ag. Ap.* 2.190; *Sib. Or. passim*, e.g., 3:11ff.; *Sib. Or.* frag. 3:3ff.; frag. 1:7ff.

[383] See above. The repetitions are to be explained form critically. Cf. the discussions of Artapanus, Aristobulus, and Numenius of Apamea above.

[384] That too is nicely said, and once again the repetition is due to the form of the apology with its fixed items of content.

[385] Josephus presupposes that the Jewish Scriptures are available to everyone. And everyone may worship in Jerusalem. In 2.82, according to the traditional (Latin) text, the cult is secret . . . "purissimam pietatem, de qua nihil nobis est apud alios effabile" ("the purest type of religion, the secrets of which we may not reveal to aliens"). Blum conjectures "*in*effabile." Concerning the whole business, see *Ag. Ap.* 2.94, 107.

[386] The background here is the Greek tradition concerning inventors and the countertradition concerning the barbarian inventors and inventions, e.g., astronomy, writing. In Jewish literature,

for them once and for all in the law.[387]

The stated themes (God; God and his people) are then expounded: (a) God: He rules the universe, is μακάριος ("blessed") (Greek!), αὐτάρκης, ἀρχὴ καὶ τέλος . . . τῶν πάντων ("sufficing [for all] [He is the] beginning and end of all things").[388] He may not be pictured in any image;[389] he is the Creator and can have only one sanctuary (§193; *Ant.* 4.200). (b) The theme "people of God" is developed in connection with particular commandments, whereby Josephus does not restrict himself to the Decalogue, but gives a more comprehensive description of Jewish ethics.[390] 2.199ff.: On the marriage commandments: Sexual relations are permitted only within marriage, for the purpose of conceiving children. The Jews do not expose their children, but rear them all. A further point: ἐπιείκεια to ἀλλόφυλοι ("equitable treatment of aliens") (2.209)— again in contrast to the reproach of hatred of humanity. §211: The commandment to act humanely applies also during war.[391]

The discussion proceeds further without any strict order: §§215ff.: punishment of misdemeanors.[392] §§220ff.: loyalty to the law (which everyone recognizes; see above).[393] §232: Is there even *one* or two known among us, who have betrayed the law or feared death, even though we are not talking about the easy death in battle (Josephus) but the hard death under torture?[394]

In connection with the emphasis on philanthropy (=the good attitude Jews have toward other peoples, not "charity"), Josephus also points out (2.237): We keep our own laws, but do not criticize those of others. Likewise, ridicule and blasphemy[395] of gods worshiped by others are forbidden to us.[396] Of course,

---

the patriarchs (Abraham) are pictured as inventors or propagators of culture. Of course, Josephus argues in this passage in a completely different manner.

[387] The *Christians* will make the charge against the Jews that they have in fact strayed from the path, by arguing that the cultic law was given for only a limited period of time; after Jesus, the Jews should have given it up.

[388] Orphic fragments 169 201, the gist: Ζεὺς κεφαλή, Ζεὺς μέσσα, Διὸς δ᾽ ἐκ πάντα τέτυκται ("Zeus is the beginning, midst, and end of all things"); Nilsson, *Geschichte* 2:427f.; Reitzenstein and Schaeder, *Synkretismus,* 69ff.; M. Dibelius and H. Greeven, *An die Kolosser, Epheser, an Philemon,* HNT 12 (Tübingen: Mohr-Siebeck, 1953) Beilage 1: *Ker. Petr.* 2.

[389] For comparison: the enlightened critique of images in Josephus's context; commentaries on Acts 17:29. The common denominator among Gentiles, Jews, and Christians is the *ridicule* of images. Jews: see above; Christians: see the discussion of the apologists below; Gentiles: Horace, *Satires* 8.1ff.; Lucian, *Jup. Trag.* 7.

[390] See Philo, *Hypoth.* 7.6; Pseudo-Phocylides.

[391] *Life* 128: It is forbidden to Jews to plunder even their enemies.

[392] §216: Prior to Josephus, robbery was a capital offense only in Philo, *Hypoth.* 7.2; differently in *Ag. Ap.* 2.215ff.

[393] Contrast the way the Greeks deal with Plato and Lycurgus.

[394] See 1.42; 2.279ff., 283; 1.190ff. (Pseudo-Hecataeus); Schlatter, *Theologie,* 134. Cf. also *Ag. Ap.* 217–18. (On immortality); the terminology is here different from that of *J.W.* 2.162ff.

[395] (And robbery of temples) Philo, *Spec. Leg.* 1.53; *Vit. Mos.* 2.205; Paul, Rom. 2:22; Josephus, *Ant.* 4.207; Billerbeck, *Kommentar* 3:113.

[396] Exod. 22:28 is taken as a basis for this; cf. Exod. 23:13 (the prohibition of speaking the names

when we are attacked, we cannot simply remain silent.

With that, Josephus returns to vigorous polemic: the Jewish position is a unified, self-contained whole. In contrast, the Greeks scold their most famous poets and lawgivers for their statements about the gods.[397] From the heavenly gods they have assigned to one the role of ruler, who in λόγῳ ("word") is called "Father," but who in ἔργῳ ("deed") is shown to be a tyrant.

Our attitude and conduct should be compared with that of the educated pagans concerning their gods, their sexual immoralities, etc.[398] In addition, there are other nations besides the Jews who are intolerant of foreign gods among their own people, as the conduct of the Athenians makes clear in the case of Socrates. Finally, the success of the law is brought in as evidence once again (see 1.225): there is no city and no pagan ("barbarian") nation where the law is not known and observed: the Sabbath rest, the fasts, the lighting of lamps, the observance of the food laws.[399]

The Jews are a model of internal cohesion, as they are of generosity, τὸ φιλεργὸν ἐν ταῖς τέχναις,[400] τὸ καρτερικὸν ἐν ταῖς ὑπὲρ τῶν νόμων ἀνάγκαις ("our devoted labour in the crafts, our endurance under persecution on behalf of our laws") (2.283).

A special nuance: the law has prevailed and won acceptance, even though it does not promise enjoyment (2.284).

2.287ff.: The summary specifies (with references to the *Antiquities*): (1) the age of the Jewish people; (2) the Jews were never Egyptians; (3) they returned to their own country of their own volition; (4) God and history testify to the ἀρετή ("excellence") of our lawgiver.

§§291ff.: Our laws speak for themselves. We have brought them to the other nations.

The Jewish Stratum of the Sibylline Oracles[401]

Preliminary Remarks

(1) The collection of *Sibylline Oracles* that has come down to us includes Gentile material, Jewish material, and a Jewish editorial stratum, to which

---

of other gods); see the preceding note on Philo and Josephus. The bifurcation is clear: on the one hand, the Jews can ignore the cult of the state gods and draw back into themselves. On another page polemic against polytheism is given, in the "private" realm that outsiders were intended to read, that is, an indirect literary defense and appeal.

[397] *The* paradigm is, of course, Plato's polemic against Homer (see 2.255ff.).

[398] A prominent topos of the *Christian* apologists.

[399] For illustrative material, cf. pp. 45–133 above.

[400] The Jewish evaluation of work! Cf. 1–2 Thessalonians.

[401] Bib. in *Sibyllinische Weissagungen*, ed. A. M. Kurfess (Berlin, 1951) 364ff. Editions: J. Geffcken, ed., *Sibylline Oracles: Die Oracula Sibyllina*, GCS 8 (Leipzig: Hinrichs, 1902); A. Kurfess (books 1–8, 11), Greek-German (not a scholarly edition) (1951). Translations: Kurfess; F. Blass in

Christian elements were then added (interpolations and whole books: 6–8). But entire books have preserved their Jewish character; the most important are 3–5.

(2) "Stratum" is not a literary judgment; from the literary point of view, we are dealing with materials from different times. But common elements of apologetic and polemic that correspond to our theme stand in the foreground of different strata. It is thus especially the redactional level that needs to be delineated.

(3) From the literary point of view, we meet here a completely new type, in comparison with all the literature previously discussed. The *form* is poetic (hexameter). The *content* is characterized by P. Vielhauer (Hennecke-Schneemelcher, *NT Apoc.* 2:600): "The Sibyllines represent the Apocalyptic of Hellenistic Diaspora Judaism."

The materials are heterogeneous, as in apocalyptic in general. They also correspond to other apocalyptic in that they are encoded. But the *Sibylline Oracles* are unlike "standard" apocalyptic in that they are written for Gentile readers, as the form of sayings of the Sibyls already indicates—although the element of address to Israel is not lacking. Schürer (*History* 3:553) sets them under the rubric "Jewish propaganda wearing a Gentile mask."

(4) Since neither the whole collection nor the individual books are literary units, literary analysis is indispensable, although it can be carried out with only a limited degree of success.[402]

Book 3

The extreme example with regard to problems, attempted solutions, and unresolvable issues is the most discussed book, namely, book 3.

Examples

3:1–96 does not belong to book 3. On the other hand, 3:97 (which begins with the building of the tower) is not the beginning of a book. Blass and Schürer attempt to find this in frags. 1 and 3 (in Theophilus, *Autol.* 2.36; differently Kurfess). Two passages have been inserted in 288 and 489—indications of redaction. Nor are the three parts of the books themselves a unity.

Kautzsch, *Pseudepigraphen* 2:177ff. (books 3–5). A selection of secondary literature: Schürer, *History* 3:555ff.; W. Bousset, "Sibyllen und Sibyllinische Bücher," *RE³* 18.265ff.; A. Rzach, "Sibyllen," *PW* 2 A: 2073ff. (Bib.); Geffcken, *Komposition;* V. Nikiprowetzky, *La troisième Sibylle* (Paris: Mouton, 1970).

[402] Schürer, *History* 3:570: "The collection in its present state is pure chaos, which even the most acute critical study will never be able to sort out and organize."

From the Contents

97–195: A historical survey from the building of the tower to the seventh Hellenistic king of Egypt (cf. 316ff., 608ff.),[403] the Romans, and the recovery of the Jewish people, with a ten-generation schema (108).[404]

105–217 is a section of euhemeristic "historical" narrative or exposition of mythology.[405] Here is found the famous "tower oracle."[406] The following may be mentioned as additional motifs: 159ff.: the series of world empires.[407] 196–294: concerning the ancestry of the patriarchs, after a prelude concerning the exodus (248), up to the time of the release and building of the new temple.

Within the following collection of oracles (295–488),[408] the threat of the revenge of the Orient against Rome (350ff.) deserves special attention; the "intellectual resistance against Rome" (Fuchs, *Der geistige Widerstand*, 35ff., 63ff.; see below) announces its arrival.[409] With no effort at harmonization, alongside this stands the threat against the Greeks: their enslavement by the Romans is a punishment for their idolatry (without mentioning the *Roman religion*).

Continuation of Apologetic

Tradition and redaction can be clearly distinguished in the double fragment in Theophilus 2.36 (frags. 1 and 3 in Geffcken) (however one arranges them; see above). Schürer, *History* 3:578: "The real program of the Sibyllines is indicated by these verses."[410] That applies, of course, only to their nonpolitical sections. The content as well as the structure reflects the apologetic tradition.

Fragment 1 contains the foundational section in the form of an appeal to "people" to be converted (cf. 3.8): *one* God, the Monarch, the Creator (cf. 3:11). The monotheistic confession is placed around the call to repentance as its framework (cf. 32).

---

[403] Ptolemy VII Physkon (170–164 and 145–117 B.C.E.)—an indication of the period in which these passages were composed.

[404] Such a scheme is found fairly often—in variations. The tower was built in the tenth generation; the human race lasts ten generations (4:20); in the tenth generation the last judgment and the advent of the time of salvation will occur.

[405] On the adoption of euhemerism by Jewish apocalyptic, see above.

[406] *Ant.* 1.118f.; cf. Alexander Polyhistor, *FGH* 273 F 79 (and Berosus, *FGH* 680 F 4 a, b); Abydenus, *FGH* 685 F 4. Bib.: W. Spoerri, *Untersuchungen zur babylonischen Urgeschichte des Berosos und zu den Turmbausibyllina* (Habilitationschrift, Hamburg 1964). The question of whether there was an extrabiblical legend of the building of the tower need not here concern us.

[407] Cf. 4:49ff.; Bousset: 159–91 is from the redactor; it is, in fact, a redactional transition.

[408] Composed almost entirely of threats, with an insertion on the coming time of peace (367-80).

[409] The passage belongs, of course, to the Roman period. See above on Josephus, *J.W.* 6.312; Tacitus, *Hist.* 5.13; Suetonius, *Vesp.* 4.

[410] Geffcken's thesis that we have a Christian fabrication here has appropriately found no followers.

It is no contradiction for this monotheism, when on the one hand it is declared that God's unknowability is proclaimed,[411] and on the other hand punishment is threatened for those who do not worship him or, more precisely, for those who have ceased to worship him and have turned aside to demons.[412] This style continues in the appeal for conversion that follows (25ff.), a conversion that is possible because God is in fact clearly revealed to all—that is, in creation. Here we find again the characteristic combination of monotheism and natural theology.

The second fragment too continues in the same style.[413] It too begins with the affirmation of the *one* God who never had a beginning and next elaborates his character as Creator, with his creative work reaching its climax when he installs humanity in its position of dominion over the animals (with some dependence on Genesis 1).[414] Then follows the reproachful speech (*Scheltrede*) (more extensive than in frag. 1). In the struggle against idolatry, the emphasis falls, more strongly than in the other apologies, on censuring the worship of animals—an indication of where this document was written. The fragment breaks off with a prospect of salvation: οἱ δὲ θεὸν τιμῶντες ἀληθινὸν . . . ἀέναόν τε ζωὴν κληρονομοῦσιν . . . ("those who worship the true God shall inherit everlasting life")[415] in paradise. (For documentation of this attribute, see the commentaries on 1 Thess. 1:9.)

The connection is clear between the elements of Sibylline traditional units along with their corresponding redactional sections and the usual Hellenistic-Jewish polemic.

Some nuances: the clearer orientation to the Egyptian religion; more important is the address to the pagan world that is more sharply polemical.[416]

Political Polemic[417]

Politically polemical tones could already be heard in the time of Ptolemy VII.[418] From Book 3:175ff.:[419] Polemic against Rome. The threat against

---

[411] See the Hellenistic negative attributes: e.g., ἀόρατος ("unseen") (who himself sees everything, 3.12).

[412] 20! The theory of an originally pure worship of God is intimated.

[413] 3.11ff. is very similar.

[414] 3.24ff., the "four-lettered" Ἀδάμ ("Adam") (i.e., ἀνατολή, δύσις, ἄρκτος, μεσημβρία) ("sunrise, sunset, north, south") stands out above all the other creatures.

[415] Thus as in frag. 1 "God" is a literary bracket within which a view of nature and a polemical argument are carried on.

[416] Thus the connection between God and *law* recedes (behind the connection between God and nature). This is related to what one might call the purified (from superstition) understanding of the *Jewish* religion, namely, the struggle against magic and manticism (3:218ff., 227ff.); in contrast, see Pseudo-Eupolemus (Abraham as teacher of astrology).

[417] In particular: the "intellectual resistance to Rome" especially in books 4 and 5; Fuchs, *Der geistige Widerstand.*

[418] On tradition and redaction: When redactors take up old oracles, e.g., against the Macedonians (e.g., 3:381ff.), the oracles are naturally redirected against Rome and widely so understood; "Macedonians" became a code name (like "Babylon").

[419] From 3:46–62 (does not belong in book 3, see above): A time is foreseen when Rome will

"Libya" (323ff.) is obviously camouflage, since it is directed against the "daughter of the West" because of the destruction of the temple. The short oracle 350–55 gives us our first view of the hatred against Rome that was widespread in Judaism and forms the background for this oracle.[420]

Book 4[421]

(1) Here the description "under a Gentile mask" does not fit; this is cast aside at the very beginning: here it is not the prophetess of the deceitful Phoebus (thus the Delphian sibyl; see Kurfess, 23f.), but the prophetess of "the Great God."

In comparison to book 3 (Philo, etc.) the times have changed, and in this later period a definite character of Hellenistic Judaism has developed more strongly.[422] The book contains nothing specifically Christian.

(2) The time of composition (ca. 80 C.E.) is derived from the following data: (a) Jerusalem has been destroyed (115–27).[423] (b) The eruption of Vesuvius (79 C.E.) is the punishment for this act (130–36).

3. This book does not belong in the category of nonpolitical apologetic. The motifs that coincide with this sort of apologetic (monotheism, opposition to the pagan images and sacrifices) are the common Jewish motifs, not organized in the schema characteristic of apologetic writing. Rather, what we have here is an apocalyptically determined picture of history, which surveys both the

rule Egypt. But then wrath falls on Rome too. Three men will bring things to ruin at the time when the greatest kingdom of the immortal king will appear. (An allusion to the second triumvirate? Bousset: A Christian addition referring to the three emperors before Vespasian.)

We may only briefly mention the puzzling verses 3:63–92 (par. 2:167ff.). Beliar will come from the *Sebastenoi*. People have long guessed that Simon Magus is intended (the section does appear to interrupt the context that deals with the triumvirate and Cleopatra (?). But the form is apocalyptic; therefore it means simply: Beliar. And what could Simon have to do with the "widow" who rises to rule the world (77). Some see Cleopatra here (ill advised); Bousset (*The Anti-Christ Legend* [London: Hutchinson, 1896]) sees Zenobia (probably too late). Schürer likewise sees a mythical figure.

[420] On the threatening oracle against Italy (464-69), Schürer: an interpolation, referring to the later Roman time. But why? It fits, for example, in the time of the civil war after the death of Nero.

[421] References to the book: since Justin, *Apol.* 1.20; Clement of Alexandria, *Prot.* 4.50, 62, etc.; Pseudo-Justin, *Coh.* 16; further in Kurfess, 303ff.

[422] In contrast to the political stance taken by Josephus, though the book comes from the same period.

[423] Cf. 5:154. Bousset, *Anti-Christ Legend:* The author has himself experienced the destruction of the temple and the preceding period of disintegration in besieged Jerusalem (Josephus!). – This is of course in principle possible, but cannot be proved; such information is available elsewhere than from personal experience: Josephus, *J. W.* 7.335ff.; Tacitus.

V. Nikiprowetzky, "Réflexions sur Quelques Problèmes du Quatrième et du Cinquième Livre des Oracles Sibyllins," *HUCA* 43 (1972): 66ff.: the subject of the verbs is not the Zealots, but the Romans.

past and the future from a politically anti-Roman point of view, even if this is expressed only with caution.[424]

(4) As we now come to the *motifs* of the book, that is, the means by which the Jewish religion is defended from attacks and commended to the world, we can concentrate on four main points: (a) First, an internal Jewish point: the decision concerning sacrifice after the destruction of Jerusalem. To be sure, the position that is taken is not absolutely clear. 8ff. indicates that it was possible not merely to be resigned to the loss of the temple and the consequent cessation of sacrifice, but that it could even be seen as a positive point: the great God does not need any earthly temple as his residence.[425] On the other hand, it is considered a punishable offense of which Rome is guilty.[426] (b) The picture of history is determined by the schema of the four world empires (47ff.).[427] (c) This schema is interwoven with that of the ten generations (49–80);[428] the Macedonians are the tenth generation. (d) This book is the oldest witness for the development of the Nero legend: 119ff.: Nero flees beyond the Euphrates, but is coming back[429] (137ff.). Rome repays Asia all the tribute exacted in past generations.[430] Finally the world conflagration is hinted at.[431]

---

[424] 35ff. The threat of judgment for those Gentiles who mock and defame the Jews, talk about their evil deeds, but do them themselves.

[425] Josephus, *Ant.* 8.227ff.; Acts 7:48; 17:24.

[426] The polemic against temple, altars, and blood sacrifices in 24ff. is problematic. Bousset (*Anti-Christ Legend*) sees this as proof of how quickly Judaism was about to separate itself from the concept of sacrifice. —But the polemic is constructed in prospect of a time when those people will be blessed who turn away from pagan worship and behold the glory of the *one* God. This is the typical style of speeches that call for conversion.

[427] Cf. 3:159ff. Geffcken; Bousset: 49–114: older, probably Hellenistic predictions. It is certainly the case that Hellenistic oracles are interspersed, e.g., 97f. (cf. Strabo 53C, 536C). And the schema of the four empires was pagan from the very beginning (the beginnings are found already in Herodotus 1.95; Ktesias, *FGH* 688); Diodorus 2.1ff.; Dionysius of Halicarnassus 1.2; Tacitus, *Hist.* 5.8; W. Baumgartner, "Zu den Vier Reichen von Daniel 2," *TZ* 1 (1945): 17–22; H. Fuchs, *Basler Zeitschrift für Geschichte und Altertumskunde* 42 (1943): 49f. n. 37. But that is no proof that our passage is Gentile. The schema became a naturalized Jewish citizen through its use in Daniel; frags. 1, 3.

[428] 5:20; see above, 3:107; further 2:15ff. Servius, *Ad Ecl.* 4; Horace, *Epod.* 16.53ff.; cf. 9ff.). So, e.g., Kurfess, *ZRGG* 8 (1956): 253ff.

[429] Cf. 5:28ff., 138–53, 216ff., 363ff.; 8:70ff., 140ff.

[430] Cf. 3:350ff.; Fuchs, *Die geistige Widerstand*, 66ff. Suetonius, *Nero* 40: a few fortune tellers had promised Nero that if he should be removed from office he would receive dominion over the Orient, others had promised in particular that he would rule over Jerusalem, and even more that he would be restored to his throne. E. M. Sandford, "Nero and the East," *Harvard Studies in Classical Philology* 48 (1938): 75ff.: in first-century Rome there was a growing resistance to oriental, and especially Jewish, ideas and customs. This reflects that they already had some influence in Rome. To what extent was Nero, who did keep his distance from the Senate, influenced by these ideas (Suetonius, *Nero* 37)? Note his oriental undertakings. Tacitus, *Ann.* 15.35 speaks of secret fantasies concerning the provinces of the East. A. Anderson, *Alexander's Gate: Gog, Magog and the Enclosed Peoples* (New York: Mediaeval Academy of America, 1932); W. Schur, "Die Orientpolitik des Kaisers Nero," *Klio* Beih. 15 (1923).

[431] See 2:196f., 3:53f., 84f.; Justin, *Apol.* 1.20. On the conviction that with the end of Rome the world itself must come to an end, see Tertullian, *Apol.* 32.

Book 5

We find in 1–51 (after a reference to Alexander the Great, who was a man, not a son of God) an enumeration of Roman emperors from Caesar to Hadrian (and his successors, 51) encoded according to the principles of gematria.[432]

A problem that can hardly be resolved is presented by the praise of Hadrian (48: πανάριστος ἀνήρ) ("a most excellent man"), which one cannot imagine having been written by a Jew after the Bar Kochba revolt (Hadrian prohibited circumcision!). When, where, and how this remarkable piece came to be included in this material can no longer be determined.[433]

The judgment of Schürer applies especially to book 5, namely, that in this loose conglomeration of materials we can no longer determine the time and place of origin of the particular units.[434] The *whole* is dated by most scholars still in the first century, because of the lamentations over the destruction of the temple.[435]

The same observation made of book 4 applies also here, where we find "classical" apologetic, but, so to speak, "in passing."[436] But taken as a whole the book contains an apologetic of a completely different sort, incomparably more extreme than that of book 4, the wildest eruption of hate against Rome in this literature. The opposition between Israel and "Babylon" is as radical as that between God and the idols.[437] The conceptual foundation is that of apocalyptic. In view of the chaotic condition of the book we can do no better in outlining its contents than to retain Bousset's convenient introductory comments, which distinguished three sections (key word: Nero):

---

[432] E.g., 16ff.: the first one to reign will bear a name the first letter of which is twice ten, that is, "K" (=Kaiser, emperor).

[433] From a Christian? On Hadrian, see Justin, *Apol.* 1.68. V. Nikiprowetzky ("Réflexions," 29ff.) contends that the section does in fact belong with the rest of the book, which he supposes to have been written in Hadrian's time, but before the Bar Kochba revolt. —In this case, of course, one would have to excise 5.51 (the emperor's successor) as an interpolation.

Several scholars also identify the section 256–59 as Christian: an allusion to Joshua/Jesus (cf. Josh. 10:12) is understood in terms of Jesus (so Schürer; Bousset, who still points out the catchword "Hebrews" and its use by the editor who reworked books 1 and 2); B. Noack, "Der hervorragende Mann und der beste der Hebräer (*Sib. Or.* V, 256–259)," *ASTI* 3 (1964): 122ff.

[434] That applies, e.g., to the predictions with an Egyptian accent, for example, 492–510. There appears to be here an allusion to the temple at Leontopolis, which stood until 73 c.e. (Josephus, *J.W.* 7.433ff.). Geffcken; Schürer, *History* 3:582 n. 174: what we have here is an idealized picture: a priest of Sarapis builds a temple to the highest God; this temple is then supposed to have been destroyed by the Ethiopians (504–10). But that is no explanation.

[435] 150ff., 397ff., 408ff. Bousset (*Anti-Christ Legend*) (as on 4:115ff.): the author had himself experienced the destruction of the temple; the Nero sections are older. Geffcken: the language of the book is homogeneous.

[436] E.g., the usual polemic against images (75ff., 495f.); the animal cult (279ff.).

[437] 158ff., 386ff., 434ff. On "Babylon" becoming fashionable as a code name for Rome, see Hunzinger, "Babylon," 67ff.

(1) 137–78 (including 162ff., the destruction of Rome); (2) 214–85; (3) 361–446.[438]

Proceeding from these sections as a starting point, one can get an overview of: (a) The apocalyptic world view that forms the conceptual foundation for all that is said. On the end of the world, see, e.g., 344ff. (because of sacrifice to idols); alluded to also in 476ff. On the key passage 512ff. that has been monstrously intensified, see below. Finally: the time of salvation for Israel, 247ff., 414ff. (cf. 3.569ff., 767ff.). (b) The two most important motifs by which the view of the world and history are actualized: the threatening speech against Rome and the announcement of the return of Nero.[439]

All that remains is the "finale" (512–31): the end of the world portrayed in astro-mythological style.[440]

SUMMARY: THE JEWISH APOLOGETIC

Jewish apologetic extends only over a short phase of Jewish history and is thus not a characteristic feature of Judaism as such. After a prelude in late Old Testament prophecy, its typical forms and elements of content were developed in Hellenistic Judaism, and they disappeared with it. Rabbinic Judaism did not carry on any apologetic—until this day. That is worthy of note for "dialogues between religions." The truth of Jewish teaching and the Jewish way of life was not, within Judaism, a subject for argument. Even when a friendly, *human* relationship was sought, this was done precisely with the presupposition that *this* was what was sought. So far as *religion* was concerned, the Christians continued to be seen as heretics with whom no compromise was possible. Jesus could not be acknowledged as the Messiah. One could only attempt to bring him back within Judaism where he belonged—as "our brother Jesus." But there were two insurmountable obstacles: (1) the law, and (2) where the object of faith was not the human being Jesus, but the exalted Lord—that is, where the

---

[438] Here in 386ff. is the sharpest attack on Rome and the Romans, to whom the label given Nero, "mother-murderer," was applied wholesale. On the charge of sexual perversions, see 3:175ff.

[439] Bousset (*Anti-Christ Legend*) appropriately notes that the picture of Nero shimmers in various colors. Sometimes he appears more humane, sometimes more demonic (incidentally, he does not come out of the underworld). This, of course, is due to the use of a variety of older materials; see 137–42; Geffcken, *Komposition*, 26.

[440] Blass (Kautzsch, *Pseudepigraphen* 2:183): "a lunatic finale." Completely different is F. X. Kugler, *Sibyllinischer Sternkampf und Phaeton* (Münster, 1927) (whose view is adopted by Kurfess): the original source document (which originated in Ethiopia) described real, natural events in astronomical terms. But even if the astronomy here has been reworked, this in no way changes the fact that the authors of the *Sibyllines* have interpreted it apocalyptically; cf. Revelation 12. The classic example of the use of astronomy in the poetry of antiquity is Ovid, *Met.* 2 (Phaeton); Seneca, *Herc. Fur.*

Christians themselves did not take on a Jewish coloration, there a compromise was excluded in principle.

No line of development can be drawn from this Jewish apologetic into the present. But it still has something to teach us, as an example of the association of Judaism with its environment on the foundation of monotheism and the law. We should keep before our eyes not only the paradigm of Jewish–Christian relations but also the paradigm of Jewish–Islamic relations, for in this case it is not only the religious but also the political actuality that is immediately clear.

IV

CHRISTIANS AND JEWS FROM THE BEGINNINGS OF CHRISTIANITY TO THE TIME OF ORIGEN

In the section devoted to Judaism there was one predominant theme: Monotheism as a political problem. This is now modified: What happens when the Jewish monotheism is, to be sure, adopted, but is conceived in terms of Christology or trinitarian theology? What happens when a historical person is thought of in terms of the bearer of the absolute revelation?[1] As in the consideration of Judaism, so here too the first question is not Which experiences did the Christians (or Jews) have with the pagan world? The prior question is rather, Which presuppositions did they bring with them in order to have any specific experiences at all? Politically speaking, what *can* they allow themselves on the basis of their faith, and what *must* they do? Which forms of argument are implicit in faith or even directly prescribed? Which forms are optional, and which are excluded (even if they in fact were practiced)?

PRELIMINARY REMARKS ON PERSPECTIVE

The historian must ask the question of the continuity of the events perceivable in history.[2] In this respect the sources available for reconstructing the history

---

[1] And what happens when the Christians take possession of the Jewish canon, but place alongside it a supplementary Christian canon (H. von Campenhausen)? It turns out that the Christians are then fighting a two-front war, or rather a three-front war, since the understanding of revelation was a disputed point within Christianity itself.

[2] Systematic theologians can, when they make use of history, subject the phenomena to the value judgments and needs of their systems and thus adjust to the "gaps" found in history and historical study.

of the early church present an extremely difficult problem for the attempt to write a continuous history of the church from the time of the earliest group of primary sources, the New Testament, to about the middle of the second century (the Apologists, Marcion). The writings from the intervening period (the Apostolic Fathers, fragments of anonymous "apocrypha," and individual authors such as Papias) provide only a minimum of information concerning the events of the period, though they do shed light on the (partially questionable) theological tendencies of the time, and some indications of the early forms of the later Christian canon.

Around the middle of the second century a new level of theological reflection becomes perceptible, in contrast to which the writings of the intermediate period appear somewhat primitive, not only theologically but also literarily. This is indicated by a new style of argument in the debate with Israel, determined in part by the formation of the *Christian* Bible with its canon of the "Old" and "New" Testaments.[3]

This new development poses afresh the question of the relationship between what Judaism and Christianity have in common and what is specifically Christian. This cannot be grasped simply by a comparison from the point of view of the history of religions. Rather, the self-understanding[4] of the Christians must itself be considered an important historical factor.

The conscious reflection could well have been quite simple at first,[5] but the substance of the problematic nature of the relationship was already there. Does the possibility of a successful argument exist at all when Christianity acknowledges the foundational documents of Judaism as divine revelation but seeks to wrest them from the hands of the Jews and claim them for themselves while at the same time rejecting integral elements (namely, the ritual laws), even though they too are commanded by God? Is it not precisely what they have in common that makes the conflict irresolvable?[6]

---

[3] The formation was itself a symptom of the new reflection.

[4] That is, self-understanding in reference not only to the canon as such, but to the history of salvation that it declares.

[5] C. Andresen (*Die Kirchen der alter Christenheit* [Stuttgart: Kohlhammer, 1971]) holds that Celsus confirms that around 180 Christianity had not yet managed to extricate itself from the shadow of late Judaism (p. 115) and that the church's *original* self-awareness was oriented toward the congregations of the Jewish minority (p. 131). In the *early Catholic church*, the counterpoint for Christian self-understanding was formed by *paganism*.

Previously, the Lukan concept — missionary activity directed to the whole world — was hindered by the diaspora mode of thought. But now it can develop freely. The nascent Catholic church operated with a conceptuality that lagged behind this development (Andresen, *Die Kirchen*, 29). See also F.-H. Kettler, "Enderwartung und himmlischer Stufenbau im Kirchen begriff des nachapostolischen Zeitalters," *TLZ* 79 (1954) 385ff.

[6] The question emerged: Is not finally the only feasible way that of Marcion, that of a fundamental separation?

Samples of the Perspectives and
Resulting Historical Pictures from Recent Research[7]

(1) J. Geffcken (*Apologeten*), working in the heyday of historicism with an immense outlay of materials that are still indispensable today, established the continuity between Jewish and Christian apologetic in their motifs and arguments. Indeed, this continuity derives from the fact that monotheism and the Old Testament are the common denominators between Jews and Christians.[8]

But we must go beyond such an inventory and make inquiry concerning the authentic *Christian* criteria: Where and how do they lead to modifications, even to opposition? A central point of crystallization was the question of the time of the advent of the Messiah: Has he already come—the central affirmation of the Christian creed—or is his advent the hope for the future—just as essential to Jewish belief?[9] With the answer to this question, a comprehensive judgment has been rendered concerning salvation history and non-Christian Judaism.[10]

(2) J. Juster (*Juifs*). This enormously learned work is also historically conditioned, this time from the perspective of a Jew.

History has been combed through in the search for measures and laws against the Jews, but all that has been found is Hadrian's prohibition of the Jews from entering Jerusalem (in addition to his prohibition of circumcision, which, of course, did not affect only Jews).[11] This is obviously the only law that remained in force under his successors.[12]

(3)H. Lietzmann (*A History of the Early Church* [Cleveland and New York: World, 1961] vol. 2)[13] presents both the points the two faiths have in common and the points of controversy under the theme "Christianity Face to Face with the World" (pp. 148ff.).[14] When the ritual law is omitted, the lifestyle of a

---

[7] The presentation will, of course, repeatedly refer to A. Harnack as its central figure.

[8] It was the Christians who preserved the writings of Hellenistic Judaism.

[9] A point on which it will never be possible for Jews and Christians to agree.

[10] Such a judgment is also given for the Christians concerning the Old Testament ritual law, which Christianity can do without, but not Judaism. Jewish Christianity is only apparently an exception, insofar as Christians continued to observe the Jewish ceremonies. This is possible, so long as these were not considered an essential part of salvation. Jews did not need to become renegades on the basis of *sola fide*.

[11] Ariston of Pella, Eusebius, *Hist. Eccl.* 4.6.3; Tertullian, *Adv. Iud.* 13, etc.

[12] Obviously it was gradually relaxed; see above, part I (Smallwood). But it is still cited by Origen (see below).

[13] "Around this time (i.e., in the second century), Judaism gradually begins to disappear from the historian's field of view" (p. 33 in the German original). Bertram Wolff (p. 44) translates the sentence: "About this time, Judaism began gradually to lose significance."

[14] The reference to the idea of martyrdom and its relation to the death of Jesus is significant. A characteristic change in contrast to the Jewish concept of martyrdom appears, precisely through its translation into a *historical* understanding; H. von Campenhausen, *Die Idee des Martyriums in der alten Kirche* (Göttingen: Vandenhoeck & Ruprecht, 1936).

Christian "was not essentially different outwardly from that of any contemporary with sound moral feelings" (p. 152).[15]

But still, distinctions need to be made: On the one hand, Tertullian's dictum was applicable (*Apol.* 41): "We are not Brahmans. . . . We do not despise any of the good gifts of God." On the other hand, there were specifically Christian prohibitions, which to a considerable degree coincide with those of the Jews: forbidden occupations.[16]

Although Lietzmann's portrayal is rather imposing, it too has its limitations. With regard to Aristides (p. 177), for example, he states that the discussion concerning the worthlessness of polytheism (with material drawn from Jewish polemic and the pagan enlightenment) would already have been possible in the time of Cicero; it is purely academic and quite dull. As a matter of fact, it is. But how did it come to be that Christianity was so alarming to the state, even for the masses, in that particular time and place? It was because the Christians so understood their faith in God that it necessarily included missionary activity, which in turn brought a renewed activation of the traditional arguments against polytheism.

(4) The dominant view of A. Oepke (*Gottesvolk*) is the idea of the people of God (which, of course, suggests continuity between synagogue and *ecclesia*). It is of particular importance that he pursues the connection of this idea with particular literary forms, which *theoretically* are concerned with the synagogue. The Letter to the Hebrews is an especially good example of such literature. Oepke comments in this regard, "The author had no interest at all in Judaism as it actually existed in his time" (p. 58). He carries on his conversation with the Old Testament, "whereby matters must constantly be dealt with, which after 70 were already over and done with in practice" (p. 67) It is not clear that the author had any personal acquaintance with Judaism at all.[17] But the issue is, whether the concept of the people of God is the appropriate overarching concept to include both continuity and discontinuity. It is itself, of course, a "historical" concept (even though it is also influenced by a historical ideology) and undergoes changes in the course of history, for example, by the inclusion of reflections on world history, reflections on the idea of a "third race."[18] But

---

[15] Cf., e.g., Aristides (Decalogue); Justin, who represents the church's ethical instruction as commands of Jesus; Clement of Alexandria; *Diogn.*

[16] Military service, public office; obviously, everything that had to do with idolatrous rites; prostitution. Tertullian; Origen; Hippolytus, *The Apostolic Tradition.*

[17] In addition, *Barnabas* and 5 Ezra belong here (H. Duensing, in Hennecke-Schneemelcher, *NTApoc.* 2:689). Further, Simon (*Verus Israel,* 135ff.) points out the theoretical character of the literature; Hans von Campenhausen (*The Formation of the Christian Bible* [Philadelphia: Fortress Press, 1972] 68ff.): the debate in Hebrews and *Barnabas* is less directly polemic and more a matter of internal Christian self-contemplation.

[18] Cf. the comments of Oepke (*Gottesvolk,* 266ff.) and Harnack (*The Mission and Expansion of Christianity* [New York: Harper & Brothers, 1961] 1:240–65, and esp. 266–78).

can a *salvation-historical* category adequately deal with actual historical events at all?[19]

(5) M. Simon (*Verus Israel*, 78-79) detects a shift from Christianity's consciousness of *newness* to Judaism's interest in establishing its *antiquity*. —But is that the appropriate alternative?[20]

His point of view is important (p. 133): "The Conflict of Orthodoxies." Simon points to the fact that the conflict led to an analogous development in both groups that resulted in an "orthodoxy."

It is also correct that the *Christian* evaluation of the law had not developed into a consistent position. On the one hand, it was considered to have been nullified by the New Covenant; on the other hand, it was viewed as invalid in and of itself. But this apt observation only raises for the first time the issue of material criteria by which the law may be evaluated.[21] Further, how do the concepts "law" and "Old Testament" stand in relation to each other, and how do "law/Old Testament" and διαθήκη ("covenant") relate to each other?[22] Is it possible to compose a summary portrayal, if one wants to avoid the fatal

---

[19] The unhistorical nature of "salvation-historical" value judgments is seen in Goppelt (*Christentum und Judentum*): from the Christian community's waiting on unbelieving Israel, as understood by the apologists, two parallel religious communities developed. The questions of (1) the messiahship of Jesus, (2) the attitude to the law, and (3) the rejection of Israel were no longer understood as a unit but disintegrated into three separate (!) didactic sections. "The early Catholic church is no longer the true Israel as was the community under the apostolic word . . ." (p. 319). A distinction was made between Old Testament Judaism, under the law, encompassed by the promise, as the enduring source (*Woher*) of Christian existence, and the post-Christian legalistic Judaism that was the enduring contrast to Christian existence.

Just try saying that to a Jew—as though it were the statement of a historical fact visible to anyone. How can it be said even to a Christian? If one continues this line of thought further, then the role of the Old Testament is replaced by contemporary Judaism. This would lead finally to the affirmation of the direct relevance of the state of Israel for faith, i.e., for one's own relation to God.

[20] That is, is it an alternative that can be established subjectively, in the consciousness of Christians, or objectively, through analysis of the sources?

[21] This is already the case in view of the fact that the "orthodox" Christians must carry on a "three-front war" (von Campenhausen, *Formation*, 96, with regard to Justin).

[22] On the Law and the Old Testament, see von Campenhausen, *Formation*, 61: "After the law had been dealt with, and the immediate threat from Judaism was past, the Old Testament was read, taught, and used with all the greater interest and delight." In the earliest period, Christ was justified by the Scripture. The opposite need, to justify the Scripture by Christ, had not yet appeared (p. 64). When one works with the *whole* Old Testament, the problem of the law is perceived in a new way. That was first noticed by the Gnostics, who solved the problem by a relativizing exposition. There were hardly any antibiblical Gnostics prior to Marcion (p. 77). The opponents of heresy did not charge the Gnostics with the *rejection* of Scripture, but with a *faulty interpretation* of it.

On the orthodox side, *Ker. Petr.* and Aristides are still naïve. Justin goes further. He was the first among the orthodox to have a thought-through doctrine of Scripture. As an alternative to Marcionism there were only two possibilities: typological exegesis or observing the difference in the times (von Campenhausen, *Formation*, 165f.). On διαθήκη ("covenant"), see W. C. van Unnik, "'Η καινὴ διαθήκη: A Problem in the Early History of the Canon," in *Studia Patristica* 4/2, TU 79 (Berlin: Akademie-Verlag, 1961) 212ff.

alternative between mere historical inventory (which only appears to be "objective") and nonhistorical "evaluation"? The question of the appropriate conceptuality should at least be raised.

The Issue of the Appropriate Conceptuality; Delimitations

(1) The concept "salvation history" can in fact be used to describe elements of the Jewish and Christian self-awareness. But if this concept is used as a solution to the Jewish–Christian problem, the result is that the problem is simply covered over. For the believing Jew, "salvation history" is a possible—perhaps even a necessary—aspect of faith, with the inseparable connection between faith and the (empirical) people Israel, with its past, present, and its future salvation that will one day be visible. But it is constitutive of Christian faith that its object is not visible and calculable in this world, that God's lordship over the world and history is in the strict sense a matter of *faith*. "Salvation history," however one defines it or attempts carefully to qualify it, is the transformation of faith into an objective, verifiable conception of the world, and that means a view of the world for which faith is not necessary. Faith then no longer originates "from hearing," but through the observation of "world history" (whatever theologians may mean by that) and through the acceptance of a conception of the world that Christians have constructed for themselves, which is thereby trapped in the relativity of various world views. In view of the theology of the ancient church, the question must then be raised whether or to what extent the church's tendency toward an objectification in the sense of "salvation history" actually got in the way of its own intention.

(2) Within the (only apparently neutral) category of *religion* (and "history of religion")[23] neither a polemical nor an irenic approach[24] is meaningful; only a limited description is possible—at best.[25]

(3) In order to make any progress, one must begin with the insight that the principal difficulty for a mutual understanding between Judaism and Christianity consists precisely in the fact that they have the same fundamental ideas and concepts:

---

[23] On the concept "religion" in the sense here used, see F. C. Grant, "Religio licita," in *Studia Patristica* 4/2, TU 79 (Berlin: Akademie-Verlag, 1961) 84–89.

[24] "Jewish–Christian dialogue."

[25] Which can be acknowledged as adequate neither by Christian faith nor by historical understanding. In Jewish–Christian dialogues the conversation is not at all objective—and should not be. The Jewish side expects—with historical justification—that a given in the conversation must be that Judaism is acknowledged as the mother of Christianity, while at the same time expecting that the question must remain open of whether the daughter can be acknowledged. This can be done if, and only if, the church gives up its proclamation of Jesus as the Messiah. At the moment, the Christian side appears at least partially willing to allow this point to recede, at least temporarily. Is this a service to real understanding? No. What can be hoped for, if a retreat is made to such a minimum on the basis of which nothing more can happen?

There is *one* God, who alone may be worshiped, the Creator. He has chosen one people for himself and has decreed the statutes by which his elected people must live. But, although "*one* God" refers to the same God in both religious communities, for the Christians he can be God only to those who "have" him as the Father of Jesus Christ.

It may be objected that among the Apologists one finds for the most part a "pure" monotheism;[26] true enough, but it is always presupposed that this monotheism is understood within the framework of the salvation provided by Christ. The church, its creed, and its Scriptures, which are already on the way to becoming a canon, are always assumed. Thereby a historical point of reference for faith in the one God is established, and that calls for a conceptual reworking of the historical relationship to Judaism.[27]

By so binding together God and Christ, the barrier posed by the ceremonial law was lowered, that is, the barrier between faith and freedom of movement in God's world; thus the connection between faith and an empirical *political* reality, one nation and its cultus, was dissolved.[28] This dissolution was *eo ipso* bound together with a judgment concerning Israel and its history.[29] *How* these two—the dissolution and the binding together—are related to each other was not worked out theoretically for a long time.

The privileged position of Israel during the epoch of the Mosaic law could be unconditionally acknowledged.[30] On the other hand, the explanation was also offered that the law had been given because of the intractability of Israel; it served the purpose of education, discipline, or even punishment.[31] This perspective on history became a relevant matter of practical concern when the view that Israel was being chastised by God (which could be supported especially from the prophets) was extended into the present by means of a theological judgment concerning the fate of the Jews through the destruction of Jerusalem and subsequent events.[32]

Corresponding to this interpretation of the *law,* there developed an interpretation of the *prophecies,* which in the Christian understanding had now been fulfilled.[33] Both judgments (concerning the law and the prophecies) are

---

[26] The famous saying of Bousset, that the Christianity of *1 Clement* was a shrunken diaspora Judaism that had become universal (*Kyrios Christos* [Nashville: Abingdon, 1970] 367, 369) may not be generalized (even if one—incorrectly—considers it valid for *1 Clement*).

[27] Or for the dissolving of this connection, as by the Gnostics and by Marcion.

[28] For the Jews, the affirmation still held true even after the destruction of the temple: *one* God, *one* temple.

[29] Justin, *Dial.* 46.

[30] Tertullian, *Apol.* 18–21; *Adv. Marc.* 1.10; *Praescr.* 8; Origen, *Contra Cels.* 3.2f.; 4.8, 31; 5.31, 43, 50.

[31] Justin; Irenaeus, *Adv. Haer.* 4.14f.; Tertullian, *Adv. Iud.* 2–4; *Adv. Marc.* 2.18.

[32] The current concern was especially the fact that the Jews had been prohibited from entering their holy city since the time of Hadrian; Tertullian, *Apol.* 21; *Pud.* 8; Hippolytus, *In Dan.* 4.58.3; Origen, *Contra Cels.* 4.22; 5.42.

[33] The New Testament as a whole, and, classically, Justin's *Dialogue.*

consequences of the *one* question that dominated the whole discussion from the earliest days of the church, namely, whether or not the Messiah had already come.[34]

The "practical" simplification of the way in which the life both of the individual and of the church would fit into the whole of God's world through the elimination of the ritual taboos had its counterpart in a complication of the way faith was conceptualized, which henceforth was directed to God *and* his Son/Logos; but the church was not yet aware how far this complication would develop.[35]

Continuity and Discontinuity in Particular Themes[36]

On the foundation of pure monotheism, agreement is possible (a) in accepting a "natural theology"[37] and (b) in the elaboration of a "negative theology."[38] In both cases, one finds oneself (along with the tradition of a metaphysic conceived in Greek terms) within a realm where the concept of God is formulated in a basically unhistorical manner. The combination of such a conceptuality with a historical person must in the long run[39] lead to reflection on the relationship between a transhistorical salvation and a particular historical event.[40] In this reflection one can recognize how the Christians adopted and adapted the Jewish "proof of antiquity"—and this brings us again to a controversial point between Jews and Christians.

This was unproblematic for the Jews, who simply relied on the data in the sacred documents. But when the Christians adopted this proof for themselves, thus claiming the history of Israel as their own, it became ambivalent, just as was the case with the Old Testament itself. The problem was not that they first

---

[34] In addition to Justin: Irenaeus, *Adv. Haer.* 4.33; Tertullian, *Adv. Iud.* 6; *Apol.* 21; *Adv. Prax.* 31; Origen, *Contra Cels.* 3.1, 28.

[35] It would take centuries for this development to be complete. Nevertheless, the theme is already expressed by Tertullian in formulations that are very rich in their implications (even though he too is still unaware of how far these extend).

[36] Geffcken (*Apologeten*) affirms that the continuity consists in the continuing apologetic. We ask: How is that possible with regard to the subject matter itself?

[37] On the foundations of a philosophy of religion; cf. the appropriation of Philo by the Christians.

[38] One can make the rough distinction: the first serves the interest of the knowability of God, the second that of his transcendence. In both cases a "supernatural" self-confidence of the theologian is presupposed. On the negative theology in Greek literature, see especially A.-J. Festugière, *La Révélation d'Hermès Trismégiste I–IV* (Paris: Lecoffre, 1950–54), vol. 4; on the negative attributes of God, see the index to the same volume (pp. 303f.). Sextus, *Spr.* 28: θεός ("God") is not the *name* of God. Wolfson, *Philo* 2:110ff.; H. Chadwick, *The Sentences of Sextus* (Cambridge: Cambridge University Press, 1959) 164f.; Festugière, *Révélation*, 4:65ff.

[39] Quite apart from the question whether the appropriate conceptual means of expression will be found at all.

[40] In this period the fixed historical point was considered to be the incarnation (not the death of Christ).

had to appropriate Israel's documents as their own—for in the Christian consciousness these documents had belonged to them from the beginning. Precisely for these reasons there developed an irresolvable conflict with Judaism.

Within the category of salvation history[41] the church cannot claim to be the true people of God without denying this status to the Jewish people (who live after Christ and do not accept the Christian faith).[42] The situation is hopeless, because on both sides "sacred" history is handed down in the tradition, is believed to report events that actually happened, and is affirmed to be perceivable *directly* as occurrences of divinely sent salvation or disaster, a situation that is essential for Judaism but that is for Christianity essentially impossible.[43]

(c) In the understanding of the *nature of human existence,* the problem materialized—again on both sides—as the doctrine (by early Christian standards: false doctrine) of *the freedom of the will.*[44] It appeared to the early Christian Apologists as the indispensable theoretical basis for the missionary-ethical appeal, for the debate with Judaism and paganism. It served as the barrier, on the one hand, against accepting the rule of chance, and, on the other hand, against the concept of Fate in the Stoic style. Incidentally: In Stoicism this concept is the theoretical foundation for the justification of manticism (Chrysippus); Pohlenz, *Stoa* 1:106ff., 2:62.

Cf. Justin, *Apol.* 1.41, 43f. (Stoa); Tatian 7ff.; Athenagoras 24; Irenaeus 4.37; Tertullian, *Exhortation to Chastity* 2 (with Sir. 15:17); *Adv. Marc.* 2.5f.

The View of the Future

Corresponding to the retrospective view of the church, by which the church saw the history of Israel as its own, the view of the future was directed toward the parousia of the lord. The church thus saw its own standpoint as between the two advents.[45] But as time went on, the view was more and more directed to the this-worldly history that unfolded between the two advents. Attempts to form a coherent view of the meaning of this period were at first tentative and groping. Efforts were made to see the contemporary period as the *third generation*—the first generation being that of the apostles.[46]

---

[41] That is, the objectification of faith into a particular view of history.

[42] That is, without demanding that the Jews be converted to Christianity. The conflict could only be averted by abandoning the historicity of the revelation "in Christ," by ignoring the fact that Jesus was a Jew (and for the Christians, the Jewish Messiah)—or by reducing his role to that of an ordinary teacher of the law.

[43] The unavoidable dilemma of every Christian "theology of history."

[44] Judaism: G. Maier, *Mensch und freier Wille* (Tübingen: Mohr-Siebeck, 1981).

[45] This arrangement has already been developed by Luke.

[46] The idea is implicit already in the prologue of Luke and in the Pastorals; if, in the fictitious framework of the Pastorals, the letters are sent to disciples of the apostles, this means that there is already a generation between the time of the apostle (Paul) and the time of the author. The "third generation" is to be fundamentally distinguished from the self-determination as the "third race," an idea not developed in a historical framework. For an attempt to link the third generation to

In this early period, the most interesting such attempt to periodize the history of the church from a theological perspective is probably that of Hegesippus (cf. Eusebius, *Hist. Eccl.* 4.22 with Eusebius's report in 3.20).

A SKETCH OF THE POLITICAL SITUATION

We do not choose as our point of departure for this discussion an outline of the external events and the problematic of the legal bases of the relation of the state to the Christians. We rather begin with the stance toward the world as such that was prevalent among the Christians, and—within this framework—with their political attitude.[47] Is the latter a necessary consequence of the former, or only a more or less incidentally accompanying phenomenon?[48]

We refer by way of example to two explanations of political policy, especially with regard to the Roman Empire, both of which manifest theological reflection: (a) Tertullian, *Apol.* 30–32: It is by the Christians' prayers for the well-being of the emperor that the imminent end of the world is postponed.

(b) Origen, *Contra Cels.* 8.70: If the Roman Empire were to become Christian, it would then be politically inviolable.

Even for the political thought of those days the first argument was, of course, considered to be an illusion,[49] and it was nullified by the simultaneous assurance that the Christians recognize only *one* government. (*Apol.* 38). The politicians even of that superstitious age considered the second not only to be absurd, but to be a contribution to the disintegration of the political mentality of the age.

Here we may take only a glance at the wider context of such views: Simon (*Verus Israel,* 212ff.) believes he has found a main point in the comparison with

---

the "second," see Irenaeus in Eusebius, *Hist. Eccl.* 4.14.1; Clement of Alexandria in Eusebius, *Hist. Eccl.* 5.11. On the determination of the extent of the apostolic age, see Epiphanius 51.33, from a source (Hippolytus?).

[47] Cf. the question of M. Dibelius: ". . . why was it that these experiences did not make Christians into enemies of the state?" ("Rom und die Christen im ersten Jahrhundert," *Botschaft und Geschichte* 2 [Tübingen: Mohr-Siebeck, 1956] 185).

[48] Of course one must take into consideration the unreflective picture of the political situation and the unfamiliarity with the actual government by those strata of society that were not immediately and actively participants in the political life—most of the early Christians. Harnack, *Geschichte der altchristlichen Literatur bis Eusebius.* Vol. 2, *Die Chronologie* (Leipzig, 1904) 1:161ff.: The Christians have no political program, but very definite political hopes (Revelation). He refers to the interest Christians had in the Roman emperor (e.g., Melito of Sardis, Eusebius, *Hist. Eccl.* 4.26.7). Christians of the second century dated events according to the year of the emperor (hardly according to the year of the consul, etc.), including dates of events in the internal history of the Christian congregation.

[49] Just as is the additional claim that since the advent of Christianity, the incidence of catastrophes has decreased (*Apol.* 40; Is he referring to political catastrophes since the time of Marcus Aurelius?).

Judaism in the Christian turning away from the world–the condemnation of the flesh and the asceticism and sexual morality that resulted from this view. But even if this wholesale judgment were correct, what would be the *political* significance of this supposed attitude toward the world, that is, its significance for the relation of the Christian to the state (and the resulting stance of the state to the Christian)? And what would it mean for the relation of Christians to Jews?

That this wholesale judgment is in fact erroneous is indicated precisely in the understanding of those documents that were the common possession of Jews and Christians, the Old Testament. Their effects among the Christians were ambivalent: As the creation of God, the world remains accessible, usable. For Christians it has in fact become even more accessible. On the other hand, new Christian taboos emerged: The kind of exclusiveness demanded by mono-theism–an exclusiveness shared by Christians and Jews–was even more radi-calized by the Christian sacraments. The extreme case of separation from the world was martyrdom, which again had its prototype in Judaism.[50]

The External Framework: The Roman State and the Christians[51]

Our theme is not the attitude of the state (and of the pagan population) as such, but only the extent that this attitude affected the development of the Christian self-understanding and the Christian debate with Judaism, as well as, of course, the connection between the attitude of the state to the Jews and its attitude toward Christians.[52]

A few distinctions are to be kept in mind: (a) Regional distinctions between the Greek East and the Roman West.[53] They are closely related to the origin

---

[50] In Judaism martyrdom was based on loyalty to the Torah, in Christianity on the confession of faith in the person of Jesus. In both cases it was a matter of belonging to the people of God. W. H. C. Frend (*Martyrdom and Persecution in the Early Church* [Oxford: Blackwell, 1965] 67): "Yet . . . martyrdom in Judaism remained something of a *Hamlet* without the Prince." The law for which one died remained impersonal; ultimately the Jewish martyr died as a member of the elect people. In order to give the idea abiding force, it required the death of Christ. Martyrdom became both the goal of the Christian life and the means of victory of the Christian religion. Ignatius, *Sm.* 4.2; *Trall.* 9.1; Tertullian, *Scorp.; Martyrium der Lugdunum* 5.1.16; the Spirit: *Passion of Perpetua* 3.3.

[51] Bib.: in G. Krüger and G. Ruhback, *Ausgewählte Märtyrakten* (4th ed.; Tübingen: Mohr, 1965), IIIff.; 130ff.; H. Grégoire et al., *Les persécutions dans l'empire romain* (Brussels, 1951); J. Vogt and H. Last, "Christenverfolgung" in *RAC* 2.1159ff.; R. Freudenberger, *Das Verhalten der römischen Behörden gegen die Christen;* Frend, *Martyrdom and Persecution;* J. Molthagen, *Der römische Staat und die Christen im zweiten und dritten Jahrhundert* (Göttingen, 1970); A. Wlosok, *Rom und die Christen;* Speigl, *Der römische Staat;* J. Moreau, *Die Christen Verfolgung im römischen Reich* (2nd ed.; 1971); R. Klein, ed. *Das frühe Christentum und der römischen Staat* (Bib.) (Darmstadt: Wissen-schaftliche Buchgesellschaft, 1971).

[52] See Frend, *Martyrdom, passim.*

[53] Speigl, *Der römische Staat,* 250: The persecution began in the Jewish communities in the East. But: Rome? See Frend below.

and geographical expansion of Christianity.[54] (b) Temporal distinctions, from the sporadic actions of Nero to the intense persecution at the end of the second century.[55] (c) Social distinctions. What effects did the social position of the Christian congregations have? How were the different political,[56] social,[57] religious[58] positions handled? All these distinctions were, of course, embraced by the rule of Rome from East to West.

The Puzzle of the Legal Situation

To this day the classical basis of the discussion is the debate between Theodor Mommsen and Adolf Harnack. It is concerned, among other things, with the concept ἀθεότης ("impiety, atheism").[59] "It was not the Jews, but the Christians whom the pagans regarded as denying the existence of God, ἄθεοι" ("impious, atheists").[60] Harnack's response:[61] That is not entirely correct, for in some circumstances conversion to Judaism was considered defection, *sacrilegium*, a capital offense. The crime of *laesae religionis* ("offense against religion") the Greeks called ἀθεότης ("impiety, atheism")[62] (see Tertullian, *Apol.* 24, 27), but the crime *laesae maiestatis* ("offense against authority, treason") (Tertullian, *Apol.* 28) they called ἀσέβεια ("ungodliness, irreligiousness"). Ἀθεότης ("impiety, atheism") is not found in Latin usage ("so far as I know") before the time of Arnobius and Lactantius,[63] and even after that time not among the jurists.[64]

---

[54] Harnack, *Mission*. Around 150 the spread of Christianity in the West was still essentially limited to Rome and some few strongholds in the Roman hinterland; the language of the Roman church remained Greek for a long time. The early Christian perspective can be seen in Rom. 15:14; Acts, etc.

[55] Here is the temporal boundary of our study. We might adduce as an additional reason for this date the modification of the legal situation of the subject peoples by the Constitutio Antoniana (212 C.E.); cf. Frend, *Martyrdom*, 312.

[56] Roman citizens: Pliny; *Mart. Lugd.* 5.1.44 (Attalus).

[57] Slaves; see Gülzow, *Christentum und Sklaverei in den ersten drei Jahrhunderten* (Bonn: Habelt, 1969).

[58] Christian congregational officers: Pliny; *Mart. Pol.*

[59] T. Mommsen, "Der Religionsfrevel nach römischem Recht," *Hist. Zeitschrift* 64 (1890): 396; ibid., *Römisches Strafrecht*, 575.

[60] This distinction is illuminating in itself: reports of Jewish worship of God are widespread in the literature. The Jews possess (or at least once possessed) a famous shrine, and they hold fast to their traditional faith.

[61] Harnack, *Vorwurf des Atheismus*, 3 n. 1.

[62] Mommsen, op. cit.: The word ἄθεος ("atheist") is borrowed from the Greek literary authors. The Roman lawyers were aware that such inflammatory language was no more applicable to the Christians than to the Jews. Harnack (*Vorwurf des Atheismus*, 9 n. 4): The Roman criminal code had nothing to do with "the denial that there is a god" but with a denial of the gods. ἀθεότης is more likely a *popular* reproach; cf. *Mart. Pol.*; Lucian, *Alex.* In the course of the third century the charge of "atheism" seems to have receded in the East; cf. the course of the proceedings in Eusebius, *Hist. Eccl.* 7.11. But is this a representative example?

[63] Beginning of the fourth century; Arnobius, *Adv. nationes* 1.29.

[64] Cf. periphrastic expressions such as Tertullian, *Apol.* 10ff.: "deos non colitis" ("not worshiping

Neither do the two familiar passages in Dio Cassius give exact definitions; quite apart from the fact that they refer to *Rome,* they give the late terminology of Dio himself:

(1) Dio 52.36.2 (the speech of Maecenas on the principles of Roman politics): μήτ᾽ οὖν ἀθέῳ τινὶ μήτε γόητι συγχωρήσῃς εἶναι ("Do not, therefore, permit anybody to be an atheist or a sorcerer").[65]

(2) Dio 67.14, 1: the case of Flavius Clemens under Domitian (81–96 C.E.). The characteristic Roman rubric is *superstitio.*[66] If one attempts to discover the legal basis of the Roman course of action in detail, one finds that there is no way to get behind[67] the exchange of letters between Pliny and Trajan.[68] The alternative sharply formulated by Mommsen between *coercitio* (confinement, punishment) of the authorities through the police and judicial *cognitio* (investigation) on the basis of a law has somewhat dissipated in the literature written since that time.[69] Thus it is advisable to take one's bearings from demonstrable facts (rather than from theoretical abstractions). Except for the actions of a few city officials in the early period,[70] the case was handled by the governor (or in Rome by the city prefects; Justin): Pliny, Polycarp, Karpus, etc.; Scillitanians: Lugdunensis; *Passion of Perpetua.* It was merely established that the person was a Christian or that they persisted in remaining a Christian.[71] Then followed the sentence of death.[72] For a summary treatment of the question of why being a Christian as such was forbidden, see Wlosok in *Das frühe Christentum,* ed. R. Klein, 282.[73]

---

the gods"). The difference between East and West is partially conditioned by the Caesar cult; for the West, see A. Wlosok in *Das frühe Christentum,* ed. R. Klein, 287.

Frend finds a qualitative difference: in the East the *Greek* measures against atheism (Justin, *Apol.* 1.6, cf. 4, 13; *Dial.* 17; *Mart. Pol.*) are supposed to have been combined with the *Roman* measures against disturbing the *pax deorum* (by astrologers, magicians), that is, *sacrilegium.* This judgment is too formalistic and is not supported by the sources. Cf. already the trial of Paul (in the East!) according to the report of Luke, then the fate of Ignatius, Polycarp. Pliny shows that Roman principles were also valid in the East. From the martyrologies and statements from pagan Gentiles concerning Christians, neither Frend's thesis nor any other strictly legal definition can be derived. For the picture of an eastern author, cf. Lucian, *Peregr.* 11ff.

[65] Speigl, *Der römische Staat,* 25: In Dio's time hardly anyone could have applied the term "atheist" to the Jews, but this term certainly could have been used of the Christians; cf. Lucian, *Alex.* 38; *Mart. Pol.* 3:2; Justin, *Apol.* 1.6; Minucius Felix 10.

[66] As previously for the Jews; Tacitus; Christians: Suetonius, *Nero* 16: "superstitio nova ac malefica" ("a new and mischievous superstition"). For the *positive* Roman counterpart "religious," see Wlosok, *Rom und die Christen,* 58ff. (Bib.: 77).

[67] We may consider the possibilities of interpretation to have been exhausted.

[68] On the supposed *institutum Neronianum* (Neronian decree), see below.

[69] Moreau, *Die Christen Verfolgung,* 61ff. (67); Wlosok in *Das frühe Christentum,* ed. R. Klein, 278 n. 12; popular: J. Bleicken, "Senatsgericht und Kaisergericht," *AAG* phil.-hist. Kl. 3. F No. 53 (1962).

[70] Philippi (A Roman colony), Acts 16; Thessalonica, Acts 17.

[71] On the treatment of Roman citizens, see Pliny; *Mart. Lugd.* (Attalus).

[72] The governor can also declare that he is unconcerned, Peregrinus, *Proteus.*

[73] Minucius Felix 6–8.

Certain *precedents* were already present in the measures that had been taken against foreign cults, astrology, magic, and so on (some of which had been in effect for a long time), in the interest of public security.[74] With the expulsion of magicians and astrologers by Agrippa (33 B.C.E.; Dio Cassius 49.43.5), we come to the period of the religious restoration of Augustus, which lays an official foundation for the future proceedings.[75] Tiberius took action against Egyptian and Jewish cults (19 C.E.).[76] Claudius is supposed to have expelled (the) Jews from Rome.[77] According to Dio, however, it was only a matter of the prohibition of assembly and had occurred already in 41 C.E.[78]

Unless one sees a reference to Christians in the comment of Suetonius "Iudaeos impulsore *Chresto* assidue inter se tumultuantes" ("Since the Jews constantly made disturbances at the instigation of *Chrestus*" . . . Claudius drove them from Rome), the Christians first come into public view during the so-called Neronian persecution.[79] This was an isolated instance, limited to the city of Rome.[80] Only Tacitus indicates a relationship to Judaism.

Speigl (*Der römische Staat*, 83ff.) believes he is able to document a further development in the relation between Christians and Jews in the time of Hadrian (117–138): the imperial prohibition against circumcision was the presupposition for the Christians dissociating themselves from this (*Barn.* 9). The Jewish wars under Hadrian brought about the "departure of the church from its original orientation to Judaism." Until then, it was the case that Christians were typically expelled by Jews. But now misgivings arose on the Christian side

---

[74] Survey: Moreau, *Die Christen Verfolgung*, 19ff. The measures taken against the Bacchanalia by the Romans in 186 B.C.E. are especially familiar (Livy 39.8ff.; Wlosok, *Rom und die Christen*, 11 n. 19; then the report of Valerius Maximus (1.3) concerning the driving out of the Chaldeans and the Jews because of their propaganda for the Sabazius cult (139 B.C.E.).

[75] Wlosok, *Rom und die Christen*, 65ff. (Marcus Aurelius 67).

[76] Tacitus, *Ann.* 2.32, 85; Suetonius, *Tib.* 36; Josephus, *Ant.* 18.81ff.

[77] Acts 18; Suetonius, *Claudius* 25; according to Horosius *Hist. contra Pag.* 7.6.15, in 49 C.E.

[78] Tacitus, *Ann.* 12.52, still in 52 C.E.: "de mathematicis Italia pellendis factum senatus consultum atrox et irritum" ("The expulsion of the astrologers from Italy was ordered by a drastic and impotent decree of the senate").

[79] The presumed martyrdom of Peter and Paul, about which we have no real information, preceded this. Acts 28 is not to be used as a source to support the view that Jews played a role in this. Likewise, one should not speculate on the possible role Jews might have played as informers for Nero (on the distinction between Jews and Christians), including the possible mediating role that could have been played by his mistress Poppaea Sabina, who is supposed to have been inclined toward Judaism (cf. Josephus, *Ant.* 20.195; *Life* 16); but she also protected the evil Gessius Florus (Josephus, *Ant.* 20.252). Contra Moreau, *Die Christen Verfolgung*, 37.

[80] On the interpretation of Tacitus, *Ann.* 15.44, see Fuchs, *Widerstand*, and Wlosok, *Rom und die Christen*, 7ff.; Fuchs also in the Pöschl edition of Tacitus (Darmstadt, 1969) 588ff., 591ff.; E. Koestermann, "Ein folgenschwerer Irrtum des Tacitus (Ann XV 44: 2ff.)?" *Historia* 16 (1967): 456ff.: The source used by Tacitus dealt with a nationalistic group led by Chrestus (see Suetonius, *Claudius* 25), which protested against the incorporation of the district of Agrippa I into the province of Syria. Tacitus mistakenly regarded these people as Christians. Contra: Molthagen, *Der römische Staat*, 22, 52; Wlosok, *Rom und die Christen*, 9 n. 11.

concerning the value of public disputes with the Jews. "Judaism withdrew more and more into itself." But against this must be said: (a) Dissociation from circumcision was present in Gentile Christianity from the very beginning; and Jewish Christianity continued to practice it.[81] (b) That Judaism withdrew into itself is only partially correct. It is correct, however, that the rabbis avoided public conflicts with the Christians.[82] (c) On the distancing of Christians from the Jews, see already Acts and the Gospel of John. On the other hand, the judgment of Aristides (14), who belongs in the same general period, was distinctly mild (compare his judgment concerning the Jews with that concerning the barbarians and the Greeks!). (d) The role that the Bar Kochba revolt played, or did *not* play, in the discussion between Christians and Jews, can be seen from the framework within which Justin's *Dialogue* is set.

FIRST EXPERIENCES OF CHRISTIANS WITH JEWS

Preliminary Remarks

In view of popularizing claims concerning the origins of "anti-Semitism," the following must be clearly stated: In the period we are discussing, the Jews were the externally superior number, both through their existence as a nation (and the Roman acknowledgment of this) and through their numbers. Wholesale judgments can only lead to confusion. For example, the situation in Palestine, in the eastern diaspora, and in the western diaspora was at that time very different.[83] And in Palestine it was basically changed by the Jewish revolts. If we thus place the situation in brackets, our first question should be concerning Jewish participation in the persecution of Christians,[84] and after that the internal appropriation and reworking of these experiences of persecution by the Christians.

The incentive that induced the Jews to take action against the Christians is clear: the claim of the Christians to be the true Israel, along with their claim on the sacred Scriptures and the Jewish cultus.[85] What we do *not* find in the

---

[81] And they are not denounced for it by Justin (*Dial.* 47). The schema by which the Jewish Christians were declared to be heretics was first developed by Irenaeus. And *Barn.* 9 is not at all oriented to contemporary history.

[82] But in Syria a lively contact between Jews and Christians continued; G. Strecker in Bauer, *Orthodoxy*, 241ff., esp. 249f.

[83] Despite the understandable spread of resistance movements such as occurred in Egypt and Cyrene after the destruction of Jerusalem (Josephus, *J.W.* 7.409ff.) and despite the eruption of riots in the diaspora under Trajan (Schürer, *History*, 1:661ff.; Schürer-Vermes-Millar, *History* 1:529ff.).

[84] Beyond the alternative of Jewish Christian and Gentile Christian, which in the Greco-Roman diaspora of the second century no longer had any significance for our question.

[85] Real, as long as the temple existed, and after that, ideal. But the ritual law remained.

sources is that the Christians also claimed the political privileges of the Jews for themselves.[86]

Will it be the case—rather, *can* it be the case—that the Christians will keep the commandment to bless and pray for those who persecute them, people who share with them faith in the same God and in the same holy Scriptures?[87] What effect will the Christians' own tradition have—a tradition of the death of Jesus and the participation of the Jews in it.[88]

What light do the sources throw on external events? The oldest document, 1 Thessalonians (2:14f.), refers to anti-Christian activities in Judea that correspond to the conduct of the pagans in Thessalonica.[89] Of a similar nature are the somewhat later, gloomy expectations expressed by Paul in Rom. 15:30ff. In his long list of troubles in 2 Cor. 11:24ff., Paul places suffering at the hands of Jews alongside suffering at the hands of pagans.

The picture offered by Acts is ambivalent. If one considers its political-apologetic tendency and the time in which it was written,[90] one notices a certain unevenness: on the one hand, it is concerned to make clear to the Romans the difference between Jews and Christians,[91] and, on the other hand, it underscores[92] the political loyalty of the latter.[93] Luke can of course already refer to the origin of the name "Christian" (Acts 11:26), which presupposes that the distinction between Jews and Christians had become a matter of public consciousness.[94]

On the basis of Acts one could come to the conclusion that the Jewish congregations of the East were the first opponents of the Christians.[95] Nevertheless, it was in the West that the persecution of Nero had occurred (already before the composition of Acts!). What was the situation under Domitian (the time in which "Luke" writes)?

---

[86] Tertullian's later rhetoric is another matter entirely.

[87] With their severe judgments against rebellious Israel.

[88] The view of the passion story in Luke and John.

[89] While Acts 17 emphasizes the activity of the local *Jews*. For Palestine and the environs, cf. in addition to persecution sayings such as Mark 13:9 par. the references of John to disciplinary measures against Jewish Christians (expulsion from the synagogue, John 9:22; 12:42; 16:2), and the whole debate carried on by Matthew against an Israel now led by Pharisees. The insertion of the "prayer against heretics" into the Eighteen Benedictions is not to be forgotten.

[90] After the destruction of Jerusalem; Luke 21:20ff.

[91] The Gentile portion of which is not bound to the Jewish law.

[92] By a fundamental loyalty to the *salvation-historical* thesis that Christianity is the true Judaism, which from time to time ignited the conflict.

[93] By carefully maintaining his silence concerning the death of Paul, although he in fact died under Nero.

[94] Which in fact was already the case in Rome in the time of Nero.

[95] So Speigl, *Der römische Staat,* 250. His further thesis that Rome at first attempted to keep the peace between the two groups is erroneous in view of the sources and the Roman religious policy as a whole.

In view of the state of the sources, it is no wonder that opinions differ radically concerning Jewish participation in the persecution.[96] A judgment concerning the role of the Jews must rest on a few striking expressions (already mentioned above), especially Tertullian, *Ad nat.* 1.14: "Quod enim aliud genus seminarium est infamiae nostrae?" ("For what other set of men [than the Jews] is the seed-plot of all the calumny against us?").[97]

Few actual *facts* have been preserved. The participation of the Jews in the martyrdom of Polycarp (*Mart. Pol.* 13, 17) is especially familiar. They are mentioned also in *Mart. Pion.* 4.8, 11; cf. 13; cf. further Justin, *Apol.* 1.31 (Bar Kochba); *Dial.* 16f., 95, 108, 133.[98]

The Beginnings

The conflict between church and synagogue[99] is inherent in the founding of the church itself, for it is inherently a *missionary* church.[100] Since the church originally consisted only of Jews and carried on its missionary work only among Jews, it was essentially an internal conflict. It did not understand itself as a new religion but as the true Israel, which believed that the promise to Israel was now being fulfilled.

Of course we do not find in this early period the level of reflection we later meet in the Apologists, especially in reference to the revelation of the Logos

[96] Harnack (*Mission,* 487) estimates this to have been considerable; differently Simon (*Verus Israel,* 115ff.): The Gospels and Justin's *Dialogue* were written in analogous situations: after 70 and after 135 one could assume a Roman disposition against the Jews. It is true that one could; only there is nothing of this in the sources. Just think of the stage setting for Justin!

[97] *Adv. Iud.* 13: "Ab illis enim incepit infamia" ("for it is from them that the infamy [attached to that name] began"); cf. *Scorp.* 10; Irenaeus 4.28.3. The anonymous anti-Montanist in Eusebius, *Hist. Eccl.* 5.16.12 asks: Is there anyone among the Montanists who has been persecuted by the Jews or killed by the lawless?

[98] *Mart. Pol.* 17.2 is found in the context of a section of von Campenhausen's "Gospel Redaction"; for the literary-critical data, see von Campenhausen, *Bearbeitungen und Interpolationen des Polykarpmartyrium* (Heidelberg: C. Winter, 1957) 24–26.

The martyrdom of Pionius and his companions may serve as an illustration of how Christians could confront Jews in a persecution situation (from the time of Decius, thus beyond the period we are considering, but obviously containing a deposit of traditional debate material). It is *the* document of complaints against the Jews from its whole period, not creative but worthy of note as an accumulation: the Jews affirm that Christ was a human being. The counterarguments are (a) the spread of Christianity, (b) the martyrs, (c) the power of Christians over the demons. In the persecutions, the Jews play the role of *spectators,* moral comrades of those who attempt to force the Christians to sacrifice to idols, and thus perverse even when judged by their own Scriptures.

The extensive Christian apologetic tradition was continued by the catalogue of sins that was carried over from the Old Testament, the climax of which was formed by the indirect accusation: "We have neither killed the prophets nor handed over and crucified the Christ" (13). The topos of the devastation of the Jewish land is given an original twist (4): Pionius has visited it himself and can tell of its natural phenomena and present condition.

[99] Proselytes: Justin, *Dial.* 122.

[100] H. Kasting, *Die Anfänge der urchristlichen Mission* (Munich: Kaiser, 1969).

and to salvation history.[101] But early on the "conflict" became a mutual separation. Hellenistic Jewish Christians cast off the ceremonial law.[102] And even before Paul, Gentile Christians were not required to keep such laws.[103] The basis for this freedom from the law (even though it was not yet completely thought through) was a fundamentally theological basis: the saving act of the *one* God (Rom. 3:29f.) was understood in universal terms. The program of world mission[104] was directed to a world and "world history"[105] that was seen in a thoroughly eschatological light. If the saving act in Christ is constitutive and thus the whole demand of God is summed up in the love commandment, then the ceremonial law cannot any longer be thought of as a condition of salvation, even if it was a long time before this was thought through in the church, which still consisted entirely of Jews (except for the special case of the "Hellenists").[106] This community soon became aware that *circumcision* is not necessary for salvation, which had been the understanding in the Gentile mission from the very beginning.[107]

To be sure, the faith itself produced antitheses that could not at all be overcome on the historical-empirical level.[108] Contrary to its own intent, the abandonment of the law[109] made the church *in fact* into a new religious

---

[101] Compare Romans 9–11 and John 1 with Justin and Irenaeus.

[102] Perhaps with an appeal to Jesus; see the commentaries on Acts 6–7; H. Hübner, "Mark 7, 1-23 und das 'Jüdische-Hellenistische' Gesetzes-Verständnis," *NTS* 22 (1975–76): 342ff.

[103] Galatians 2; Acts 15. That happened (despite Acts 15:10) not from tactical considerations (in order to make it easier to become a Christian). It would have been possible to have adopted the Jewish model and to have created a wider circle of "God-fearers" around the inner circle of full Christians. But that was excluded by the nature of faith itself: there can be no degrees in the matter of having faith. Nor was it necessary to have recourse to any such tactic, for success is given by the Lord himself; the church lives by the power of the Spirit.

[104] This existed neither in Judaism nor in the ministry of Jesus (J. Jeremias, *Jesus' Promise to the Nations* [2nd ed.; Philadelphia: Fortress, 1959]).

[105] On "world history" among Greeks and Jews, see Lietzmann, *History* 2:48ff. For the Christians (for the first centuries, see Africanus) the words are to be placed in quotation marks, since they cannot be essentially connected with a secular theory of history (e.g., origin and degeneration, the series of world empires, or a theory of the relation of world history to the role of Roman Empire) nor to Jewish, apocalyptic "history" phantasies. It is characteristic that the *Apocalypse of John* looks back on a history neither of the world, nor of Israel, nor of the church itself.

[106] If we only knew something about the line of argument followed by the "Hellenists"! *Jesus* did not demand the rejection of ceremonial observances as a general principle, but demonstrated freedom in occasional concrete actions (on Mark 7, see Hübner, "Mark 7"). Freedom as a *general* principle would have been "legalistic."

[107] Fundamentally expressed in Gal. 5:6, with the inference for the significance of law as such (5:3).

[108] One such antithesis is concerned with the coexistence of Jews and Gentiles in the same congregation (Gal. 2:11ff.); it still has effects in the effort to explain the nature of the church and mission among Jews, because the church replaces the mission to Jews with "religious dialogues" and seeks to justify this replacement theologically.

[109] This did not first happen through the delay of the parousia, that is, through an accidental historical development, but through a theologically necessary state of affairs.

community, but a community that found it necessary to maintain its continuity with Israel, if it was to remain a church and not degenerate into an unhistorical mystery cult.[110]

From its side, Judaism could do nothing except combat the new sect. From its perspective, too, the conflict was not incidental or a matter of psychology, but a conflict that was theological and necessary.[111] The full dimensions of this conflict were already grasped by Paul, who consistently postponed its "resolution" until the eschaton (Rom. 11:25ff.).[112] It must first be said that this is an effort to deal with the problem with the help of an apocalyptic perspective on the future. But the thrust of what Paul here wants to say is not to be grasped in terms of the items in an apocalyptic picture of the world.[113] This can be understood to point to the fact that the judgment concerning Israel is not made on *moral* grounds. It is concerned exclusively with faith.[114] For Paul it is not a matter of interpreting the meaning of "history" (or "salvation history"), but a matter of concrete confrontation through the preaching of the gospel, and this alone. In any case, Paul can portray the events of the eschatological drama without any reference to Israel: 1 Thessalonians 4–5; 1 Corinthians 15; 2 Corinthians 5—we must in fact say that this is normally the case. This indicates that his so-called salvation history is only an incidental means of interpretation. Thus, despite Romans 11 but because of Romans 9, empirical Israel is not *separated* (*geschieden*) from the "true" Israel, though it is surely to be *distinguished* (*unterschieden*) from it. Precisely for this reason Jews and Christians can live together in the world as fellow human beings.[115]

The point of all this is located in the *christological* understanding of the law, of which Christ is the end.[116] The *historical* crisis could only be resolved if the Christians were to renounce this thesis.[117] It is resolved *theologically* by the

---

[110] The beginnings of a development in this direction can be seen already in the Corinth of Paul's time. To this Paul first reacts in 2 Corinthians—negatively—through a consideration of the old and the new covenants; then he gives his positive response in Romans.

[111] That applies throughout the whole spectrum of Jewish groups. No group within Judaism can renounce the law, just as no group within Judaism can confess that the Messiah, Jesus of Nazareth, has already come.

[112] On Romans 9–11, see Luz, *Geschichtsverständnis*.

[113] Nor can it be communicated in terms of a speculative picture of the history of salvation from Adam to the eschaton. Luz, *Geschichtsverständnis*, 204: Past history as a whole comes in view only in Rom. 5:12ff. in all of Paul's writings. And how does this happen! Luz, 270ff.: "Israel's" capacity to be defined sociologically is broken through in Rom. 9:6.

[114] The whole line of thought in Romans 9–11 is based on this.

[115] This cannot happen, if a "Christian" ideology is developed around the present state of Israel and contemporary Judaism. Some Christians seem eager once again to give new wars the status of religious crusades.

[116] P. von der Osten-Sacken, *Römer 8 als Beispiel paulinischer Soteriologie* (Göttingen: Vandenhoeck & Ruprecht, 1975).

[117] This means recommending that we do away with *sola fide*. Luz, *Geschichtsverständnis*, 272f.: For Paul it is not a matter of the *possession* of the law but rather of the event of giving the law itself. And precisely because an inner historical continuity cannot be demonstrated, the possibility

consequence that follows from this thesis, namely, that Israel is henceforth a matter of theological concern only from the point of view of the law, that is, through the fundamental distinction between empirical and the true Israel (Rom. 2:27-29; 9:6f.; cf. 2 Corinthians 3).

Even though Paul's understanding of the law is to some extent historically conditioned, he still raises the issue of the law *in itself* as a factor in salvation, in terms of the fundamental freedom from the law instituted in Christ. This freedom prevailed in the church from the very beginning, even though it was Paul who first made it a principal theme of theological reflection. For if the Messiah has already come, then salvation depends exclusively on one's relation to him, that is, on faith.[118] This understanding of Paul was submerged in the history of the ancient church, even in Paul's own school, until around the middle of the second century (Marcion).

The letter to the Ephesians has no interest in either Israel or the law as such, but only in the present unity in Christ of those who were formerly Jews and Gentiles but are now together in the church created by breaking down the dividing wall that separated them, that is, the law (2:11ff.).[119] Consistent with this, there is no salvation-historical polemic.

The letter to the Hebrews[120] belongs to the genre of theoretical[121] debates with the synagogue. The decisive category is that of the new covenant by which the old is nullified, that is, both set aside and revealed in its typological meaning. Here, too, empirical Israel and its destiny are no theme of the Christian faith. That which is constitutive is the confrontation between God's erstwhile speech to the fathers and his speaking to "us" in these last days "through his Son."[122]

---

is given that the salvation-historical privileges will be granted to unbelieving Israel (Rom. 3:1ff.; 9:1ff.).

[118] The relationship of Jewish and Christian faith is misconstrued when one supposes that the inherently explosive problems can be defused by a historical relativizing of Paul's doctrine of the law. Such attempts make the "dialogue" not only unfruitful but also, at least from the Christian side, disappointing as conversations on the human level.

[119] Only Gentile Christians, who are to come to a better self-understanding, are addressed. Their past history is contrasted with that of those who were once Jews, in order to emphasize its *sola gratia* aspect. A. Lindemann, *Die Aufhebung der Zeit* (Gütersloh: Mohn, 1975) 145f., 155: "It is not meant that 'near' and 'far' are now united with each other, as though the Gentiles were incorporated into a previously-existing People of God; rather, it concerns the fact that those who 'once' were far from God are now near to him," that is, a matter of the incorporation of both Jews and Gentiles in Christ.

[120] Oepke, *Gottesvolk,* 17ff., 57ff.

[121] Not actual debates! The contrast Jew/Gentile is lacking, as is that of Jewish Christian/Gentile Christian; nor is the letter really polemical.

[122] Grässer, *Der Glaube im Hebräerbrief* (Marburg: Elwert, 1965) 162: "In chapters 5–6, Christianity has become a historical epoch in time." Historical newness replaces eschatology. Cf. *Barn.* 2:6; 5:7; 7:5; Hermas, *Vis.* 3.8.9; 12.3; *Sim.* 8.6.2; Tertullian, *Adv. Iud.* 3.

In connection with Paul,[123] Acts is still aware that freedom from the law and the inauguration of the Gentile mission were not incidental occurrences but necessary events in the history of salvation.[124] Precisely *because* (and not "although") the church is the Israel of promise,[125] the conflict can only be resolved if the Jews are converted[126] and thereby achieve the fulfillment of the promise (and thus become true Jews). The unbelieving Judaism of Acts is (differently than for Paul) only a secular reality and comes within Luke's purview only to the extent that the Jews make trouble for the Christians. Where Luke speaks directly to Gentiles, in the Areopagus speech (Acts 17; cf. 14:15ff.), Israel plays no role, but rather God's role over the whole inhabited earth from the creation to the day of judgment (17:31). There is no trace of the idea that Gentile Christians are somehow brought into a relationship to Israel; they are rather separated from Israel.[127]

Matthew[128]

Examples:

(1) G. Strecker discovers an ambivalent attitude toward the law in Matthew: On the one hand, it is completely accepted (5:17); on the other hand, substantial parts of it are dismissed. "As a result two things are excluded. The supposition that in comparison with the Old Testament the Matthean Jesus teaches a 'new law' is eliminated by the positive valuation of the 'old' law. On the other hand the negations make it clear that it is also not the case that Jesus simply repeats the old" (*Der Weg der Gerechtigkeit* [Göttingen: Vandenhoeck & Ruprecht, 1962] 147).

On salvation history: "If the time of Jesus is characterized by the revelation of the way of righteousness, so the time of the prophets is primarily characterized by reference to the central point in the history of salvation." Jesus signifies the definitive and final mission to Israel. "In contrast, after Israel is removed from the place of privilege, the course of salvation history is continued in the period of the church" (p. 188). The church has taken over the place of Israel (p. 189 n. 1).

---

[123] Quite apart from the question of to what extent his doctrine of justification was still understood and determinative for the theological course of thought.

[124] Cf. the report of the Apostolic Council in Acts 15 and the fundamental declarations in 13:46; 18:6; 28:25ff.

[125] W. Eltester, "Lukas und Paulus," in *Eranion*, Festschrift H. Hommel (Tübingen: Mohr-Siebeck, 1961) 1ff.; J. Jervell, *Luke and the People of God* (Minneapolis: Augsburg, 1972).

[126] Luke no longer takes this seriously as an actual possibility for his own time.

[127] The Gentile Christians are rather brought into a relationship to "the midst of time," the time of Jesus, which the Jews have missed.

[128] Hans Conzelmann, "Literaturbericht zu den synoptischen Evangelien: Die Theologie des Matthäus," *TR* n.F. 37 (1972): 261ff.

(2) W. Trilling: Israel is identical with the people of God. Israel's hardening did not first occur through the preaching of Jesus, but did then first become inexcusable, precisely through the fact that Jesus was sent only to Israel (*Das wahre Israel* [Munich: Kösel, 1964] 105).

(3) R. Hummel, *Die Auseinandersetzung zwischen Kirche und Judentum im Matthäusevangelium* (Munich: Kaiser, 1966) 150: "Unbelieving Israel is separated from its past. Israel's history becomes the history of the church, and is as such revered." But there is also continuity in the history of salvation; it is guaranteed by the law.

(4) Continuity is disputed by S. Schulz (*Die Stunde der Botschaft* [Hamburg: Furche, 1967] 234) and R. Walker (*Die Heilsgeschichte im ersten Evangelium* [Göttingen: Vandenhoeck & Ruprecht, 1967]): Israel is excluded. The Israel of the central period of salvation history (John the Baptist, Jesus, the disciples) is the collective of the evil ones.

The Gospel of John

The church in the Fourth Gospel is separated from empirical Israel. The Old Testament is preserved because of its witness to Jesus and precisely so is the unbelief of the Jews documented (5:39f.).[129] The church views "the Jews" only as one undifferentiated group, not in a racial, political, or national sense,[130] but as the enemies of Jesus and his own, for they are representatives of the world that the believers must hate in order to hold their own ground and maintain their own identity. In John too, the viewpoint is exclusively that of faith. And this faith is strictly related to the appearance of the Light and the crisis that this produced (3:18f.).[131] Through this revelation, sin becomes what it is (9:41). It is in this sense that the Jews are "children of the devil."[132]

---

[129] On the way the Bible is here understood, see von Campenhausen, *Formation*, 50ff., 60–61: The "paradoxical-ironic sense" of the Johannine technique of scriptural proof is not directed against the Jews, but against contemporary Christians. But the polemic is not yet directed against the Scripture as such; John is still oriented as an early Christian theologian. —But this judgment is one-sided. The text contains a clearly anti-Jewish point.

[130] This aspect can also appear from time to time (11:50), but it is not the dominant note; cf. the conversation of Jesus with Pilate.

[131] Or to the ἐγώ εἰμι ("I am") of the revealer, which is the same thing.

[132] On John 8:37-47, see E. Grässer in *Antijudaismus in NT?* (Munich: Kaiser, 1967) 157ff. (= *Text und Situation* [1973] 70ff.). He correctly observes that the national aspect has disappeared. Whoever believes, Jew or Gentile, belongs to "Israel" (1:44, 50); the "Jews" (who remain in unbelief) do not belong to Israel. Grässer's alternative (along with that of Schnackenburg's) is questionable, however: the basic tendency is directed to the internal life of the church, against the secularization of Christianity and the dangers of the world. But in the church, which has the assignment of being a witness to the world, internal policy and foreign policy cannot be separated. And it is not a matter of what the evangelist meant but how, after one hundred or one thousand or two thousand years, he is read.

The temple and the cult are no longer valid (4:21). There is no way for John to think of a future salvation of "Israel," since his concept of faith does not involve a temporal salvation-historical *linear* extent of time, but exclusively the *point* in time when the witness of faith and the response to it occur. Israel and its history cannot become a theme of theology for John.

The same can be said—despite the apocalyptic form—of the book of Revelation.[133] Its theology is by no means a "weakly Christianized Judaism."[134] The Jews are the "synagogue of Satan" (2:9; 3:9); but precisely this shows that for the author "Jew" has a *positive* meaning: they call themselves Jews but in reality are not.[135] Believers come from all nations (5:9). It was the earthly Jerusalem that crucified Jesus (11:8). In this role it represents the *world.* The temple is gone (21:22).

It is characteristic of the Christian reinterpretation of Jewish apocalyptic that a constitutive element of the latter is omitted, namely, the survey of history in the form of a prophecy by some fictitious figure of the past. The only period of time that interests the author of the Apocalypse is that which stretches out toward the future, toward the new heavens and the new earth. It is thus characteristic that the destruction of the temple is not mentioned (despite 11:13). The point of view for the separation of church and synagogue is the existence of the present people of God that looks toward the future.[136]

Summary

The conflict is inherent in the existence of the church itself. It will last as long as church and synagogue exist side by side. And it will be "human," if the

---

[133] Precisely when one attends to the difference between Gospel and Apocalypse.

[134] So Bultmann, *Theology of the New Testament* 2:175. Contra, W. G. Kümmel, *Introduction to the New Testament* (Nashville: Abingdon, 1975) 573; T. Holtz, *Die Christologie der Apokalypse des Johannes,* TU 85 (Berlin: Akademie-Verlag, 1962) 95ff., 212ff.

[135] M. Rissi, *Time and History* (Richmond: John Knox Press, 1966) 92. H. Kraft, *Die Offenbarung des Johannes,* HNT 16a (Tübingen: Mohr-Siebeck, 1974), on 2:9: A Jewish-Christian group is intended; on 3:9: This is not directed against authentic, circumcised Jews, but against "people who vacillate between synagogue and church." —An artificial "explanation."

[136] E. Lohse, *Die Offenbarung des Johannes* (Göttingen: Vandenhoeck & Ruprecht, 1971) 117. Rissi (*Time,* 105) finds "salvation history": In the coexistence of Jewish Christians and Gentile Christians in the *one* church (5:9f.) is revealed "the meaning of Jewish existence in the present." —This is borrowed from Paul. M. Rissi, *The Future of the World* (Naperville, Ill.: Allenson, 1972) 65f. on chap. 11: the judgment of Israel is limited in a threefold manner: (a) Provided that a remnant of Israel is preserved. —"Preservation"? It is precisely by this means that judgment on the pseudo-Jews is stressed. (b) Provided that Jerusalem does not continue without the message of God even in the time of desecration. —But the witnesses are killed and Jerusalem is called Sodom and Egypt. (c) Provided that the time of judgment is limited to three and a half days. —But that is no limitation, but rather an intensification. After this, the witnesses that have been killed arise and are miraculously transported out of Jerusalem. Then the earthquake comes as a sign, and seven thousand are killed καὶ οἱ λοιποὶ ἔμφοβοι ἐγένοντο καὶ ἔδωκαν δόξαν τῷ θεῷ τοῦ οὐρανοῦ ("and the rest were terrified and gave glory to the God of heaven") (11:13).

church understands its commission strictly and does not pervert it into a moralizing correction of others. It is precisely the event of salvation itself, the proclamation of *sola gratia/sola fide,* the doctrine of Christ as the end of the law, which make a moralizing, pseudo-historical anti-Judaism impossible. To this belongs, of course, the Christian insight that a Jewish state is a *political* reality, not a holy land, that it belongs to this world and possesses no eschatological dignity. If, in the name of Christianity, one attributes such a dignity to it, this would mean placing God and the world on *one* plane. Then it would be impossible to think of the state of Israel as a mere political reality, and one would have to think of war in behalf of Israel as a holy crusade—as though the world needed this and it were a Christian duty to encourage fanaticism, as though we did not have enough of that already.[137]

The Apostolic Fathers

Preliminary Remarks

The following presentation is restricted to the *explicit* debate with Judaism. The use of the Old Testament is mostly independent of this (*Didache; 1 Clement*). Concerning terminology: "Israel" is used in *1 Clement* and *Barnabas;* 'Ιουδαῖος ("Jew") is found only in Ignatius, *Sm.* 1:2, alongside 'Ιουδαϊσμός, ιουδαϊκός, ιουδαΐζειν ("Judaism, Jewish, to judaize"), also used by Ignatius. For (brief) recent bibliographies, in addition to F. X. Funk-K. Bihlmeyer-W. Schneemelcher, *Die Apostolischen Väter* (Tübingen: Mohr-Siebeck, 1956), see P. Vielhauer, *Geschichte der urchristlichen Literatur* (Berlin and New York: de Gruyter, 1975) throughout.

The Didache[138]

The parenetical material is essentially Jewish. It is all the more noticeable that a debate with Judaism is almost completely missing. Judaism obviously played no active role in the milieu where the book was edited. The single instance is the warning against "hypocrites" in chap. 8.[139] But one should be careful in drawing "positive" conclusions from this negative data.[140]

---

[137] The church should leave the political program of Zionism to the Zionists—not to the anti-Semites.

[138] R. Knopf, *Die Didache,* HNT, Ergänzungsband 1 (Tübingen: Mohr-Siebeck, 1920); J.-P. Audet, *La Didachè,* Études Bibliques (Paris: Lecoffre, 1955); H. Koester, *Synoptische Überlieferung* (Berlin: Akademie-Verlag, 1957) 159ff.; Vielhauer, *Geschichte der urchristlichen Literatur* (Berlin and New York: de Gruyter, 1975) 719ff.

[139] It is disputed whether this refers to the Jews in general or to the Pharisees in particular. The vocabulary and context speak for the first possibility. Koester (*Synoptische Überlieferung,* 203) assumes that it is a misunderstood reminiscence of Matthew (where the characteristic "hypocrites" is appropriate, though not in the *Didache*).

[140] Goppelt, *Christentum und Judentum,* 188f.: The *Didache* is doubtless the oldest Christian

First Clement[141]

A primary characteristic is the extensive and unreflective use of the Old Testament. Statements about Israel are unproblematically transferred to the church (29:2–30:1). "The fathers" are simply claimed as the author's own.[142]

How is it possible that this was so self-evident to him? It is obviously related to the lack of a salvation-historical confrontation of the church and Israel. What we have instead is the introduction—characteristically, only in passing—in one instance of the persecution of the righteous of the Old Testament by a ὁμόφυλος ("fellow tribesman"; Moses, 4:10) and through ἀλλόφυλοι ("Gentiles"; David, 4:13).

Ignatius[143]

He defends against ἰουδαΐζειν ("judaizing").[144] No salvation-historical perspective is apparent. The prophets are simply claimed for Christianity.[145] The opponents are not charged with legalism (e.g., with demanding circumcision), but with a biblicistic keeping of the Sabbath.[146] One cannot say "Christ" and at the same time ἰουδαΐζειν. ὁ γὰρ Χριστιανισμὸς οὐκ εἰς Ἰουδαϊσμὸν ἐπίστευσεν, ἀλλ' Ἰουδαϊσμὸς εἰς Χριστιανισμόν ("practice Judaism. For Christianity did not base its faith on Judaism, but Judaism on Christianity") (*Magn.* 10:3). Judaism is simply replaced by Christianity. Nor is the concept of οἰκονομία portrayed in terms of salvation history. [Translator's note: οἰκονομία means basically

---

writing in which the dissolution of the eschatological relation to Judaism and the judaizing of the church emerges. —But quite apart from the problem of the unclear terminology and the unhistorical postulate concerning the relation to Judaism (to which Judaism?), one must ask: Why, for example, is the letter of James—to be dated early according to Goppelt—excepted from such a judgment? It is clear: because it is in the canon.

[141] Ibid., 238ff.; K. Beyschlag, *Clemens Romanus und der Frühkatholizismus* (Tübingen: Mohr-Siebeck, 1966) on chaps. 1–7; L. W. Barnard, *Studies in the Apostolic Fathers and Their Background* (Oxford: Blackwell, 1966) 5ff. (*1 Clement* and the Domitian persecution); Vielhauer, *Geschichte der urchristlichen Literatur*, 529ff.

[142] Against this cf. the reflections of Paul concerning Israel in the categories of πνεῦμα ("spirit") and σάρξ ("flesh") or γράμμα ("letter") (2 Corinthians 3; Rom. 2:27ff.; on "father" Abraham, Galatians 3; Romans 4).

[143] L. W. Barnard, "The Background of St. Ignatius of Antioch," *VC* 17 (1963): 193ff.; idem, *Apostolic Fathers*, 19ff.; Vielhauer, *Geschichte*, 540ff.

[144] *Magn.* 8:1: εἰ γὰρ μέχρι νῦν κατὰ Ἰουδαϊσμὸν ζῶμεν, ὁμολογοῦμεν χάριν μὴ εἰληφέναι ("For if we still live according to the Jewish law, we deny that we have received grace").

[145] *Magn.* 8:2: οἱ γὰρ θειότατοι προφῆται κατὰ Χριστὸν Ἰησοῦν ἔζησαν ("For the most divine prophets lived according to Jesus Christ"); cf. 9:2.

[146] Biblicism: *Phld.* 8:2; *Magn.* 9:1f.: μηκέτι σαββατίζοντες, ἀλλὰ κατὰ κυριακὴν ζῶντες ("no longer living for the Sabbath but for the Lord's Day"). E. Molland, "The Heretics Combatted by Ignatius of Antioch," *JEH* 5 (1954): 1ff.; and von Campenhausen, *Formation*, 71 n. 58: the opponents are not Jews but are labeled thus by Ignatius because of their biblicistic obstinacy.

"household management," but when used in relation to the economy of salvation, it is translated "appointment, arrangement, dispensation," as below.][147]

The Letter of Barnabas [148]

This document is a special case, and not only in its own time. It is not representative of early Christianity, though it does indicate what a wide spectrum of possibilities were present then. Just the same, it was accepted, preserved in the tradition, and enjoyed high regard.[149]

The date of composition of *Barnabas* can be only approximately determined (the first half of the second century).[150] The determination of the literary character is more important: *Barnabas* belongs to the category of theoretical debates with the synagogue.[151] There is no indication that the church is experiencing any actual danger from Judaism as the author writes.[152]

---

[147] Oepke, *Gottesvolk:* This concept takes in the idea of the people of God. —But where and how? Cf. the New Testament letter to the Ephesians; Ignatius, *Eph.* 18:2: Christ was born of Mary κατ᾿ οἰκονομίαν θεοῦ ἐκ σπέρματος μὲν Δαυίδ, πνεύματος δὲ ἁγίου ("according to the appointment of God, of the seed of David, and by the Holy Spirit"). Cf. *Eph.* 19; 20:1: God's . . . οἰκονομία εἰς τὸν καινὸν ἄνθρωπον 'Ιησοῦν Χριστόν ("dispensation with respect to the new man, Jesus Christ").

[148] Windisch; *Der Barnabasbrief,* HNTSup 3 (Tübingen: Mohr-Siebeck, 1920); P. Prigent and R. Kraft, *Épitre de Barnabé,* Sources chrétiennes 172. (Paris: Cerf, 1971); Harnack, *Chronologie* 1:410ff.; *Mission* 1:67ff. R. Knopf, *Nachapostolisches Zeitalter* (Tübingen: Mohr, 1905) 346ff.; Oepke, *Gottesvolk,* 24ff., 46ff.; P. Prigent, *Les Testimonia dans le Christianisme Primitif* (Paris: Lecoffre, 1961); K. Wengst, *Tradition und Theologie des Barnabasbriefes* (Berlin: de Gruyter, 1971); Vielhauer, *Geschichte,* 599ff.

[149] Clement of Alexandria and Origen regarded it as an authentic letter of Barnabas. It was probably already known to Justin, then to the Gnostic Marcus, then to Irenaeus and Tertullian; see Windisch on *Barn.* 5:6f.

[150] Bib.: Speigl, *Der römische Staat,* 89 n. 32. The reference to the fourth animal in 4:5-7 (Dan. 7:7f.) is of no value in determining the date, since it is traditional and since it cannot be determined which emperor is intended.

16:3ff. refers to the destruction and rebuilding of the temple. But this more likely refers to a Gentile temple, that is, the rebuilding planned by Hadrian (ca. 130/131), rather than to the Jewish temple (differently, Barnard). Then one would have a *terminus post quem.*

Speigl thinks that *Barn.* 9 was occasioned by Hadrian's decree that prohibited circumcision (*Der römische Staat,* 87). That would point to the same period. But the passage does not refer to a contemporary event, but to the principle, and in fact presupposes the practice of circumcision. It was not Hadrian but God who abolished circumcision.

[151] Like Hebrews, 5 Ezra; Oepke, *Gottesvolk,* 24ff.; Wengst, *Barnabasbriefes,* 101f.

[152] Oepke, *Gottesvolk,* 26. Vielhauer, *Geschichte,* 605 (contra J. Schmid, *RAC* 1:1215): *Barnabas* does not want to tear the Old Testament out of the hands of the Jews; the document is no dialogue with the Jews. The occasion is obviously an inner-church controversy over the meaning of the covenant. —Logic?

Wengst undertakes a detailed analysis. Such an analysis is in fact necessary, even if it must remain hypothetical, since the letter itself manifests internal tensions. One of Wengst's theses is (with the exception of the Two Ways teaching that *Barn.* 18–20 has in common with the *Didache*): The framework is formed by chaps. 1, 17, 21; 4:9a, 6:5; 5:3, 7:1, 6:10 are redactional (p. 5f.). Later additions are found in 6:7, 9, then in 8:7, 9:1a, 3d; 10:12 (pp. 14ff.).

The Old Testament is interpreted in a radically unhistorical way,[153] even if there is one reference to the preparation of a "new people" by the Lord (5:7),[154] and likewise of a "new" law (2:6).[155] A radical critique is directed against Israel.[156]

This sharpness is present precisely because the God of the Old Testament—differently than for Marcion—is the God of Christian faith. The thesis that *Barnabas* advocates is not only that the old covenant has been replaced by the new, but that Israel, because of its sinfulness, had never accepted the covenant at all (4:6ff.; 14:1ff.).[157] Whoever teaches that "the covenant belongs both to them and to us" simply increases his own sins (4:6). Within this framework Old Testament polemic against Israel is taken up (which will also be widely practiced by the apologists).[158] Israel is attacked by the Gentile nations because of her sins (12:2). The apologists will extend this line into the present: the temple passed into the hands of the Gentiles (Luke 21:24 already is moving in this direction), and since the time of Hadrian the Jews are forbidden to enter Jerusalem (Tertullian, *Adv. Iud.* 13:4, etc.).

The Jews do not understand the Old Testament (chaps. 2f.; 10:2 etc.), for the ritual prescriptions and the food laws (10:9) were not at all meant literally. Thus, the whole worship life of Israel is not only superfluous; it is downright error. The prophets had already taught long ago that God does not desire sacrifices and feasts (chap. 2), fasts (chap. 3), temple (chap. 16; cf. *Diogn.* 4:1) and obviously did not command circumcision: literal fleshly circumcision is the result of being mislead by an evil angel (9:4).

In reading *Barnabas* one sometimes feels almost in the Gnostic realm of the transformation of Old Testament values.[159]

On the analysis of chaps. 2-16 (pp. 17ff.): Chaps. 2 and 3 are a coherent unit in themselves. The word νόμος ("law") is found only here, and only here is there reference to both (!) laws. Redactional material is found in the beginning of 2:1 (cf. 1:2), then in 2:2f., 4a; 3:6. 4:6-8, which clashes with its context, is traditional (see above: 4:9a); the continuation is in 5:1f.; 4:3-5 is an independent unit of tradition. Additional traditional material is found in 5:5-7 (Do 5:11f.; 5:13f. also belong to it?), then 6:1-4, etc. The tradition consists of individual units, products of a school (W. Bousset, *Jüdisch-christlicher Schulbetrieb in Alexandria und Rom* [Hildesheim: Olms, 1975]); cf. the dialogical style: μάθετε ("learn") 5:5 etc. The knowledge of Jewish rites was already found in the tradition (7:3ff.; 8:1) (Wengst, *Barnabasbriefes*, 67f., 68ff.: There is no indication that the author desired to correct his tradition; thus, it can be used in evaluating the author's own theology).

[153] W. Maurer, *Kirche und Synagogue* (Stuttgart: Kohlhammer, 1953) 20: "This radical christianizing of the Old Testament means of course that its historicity is entirely surrendered."

[154] According to Wengst, in a traditional section.

[155] So also Wengst.

[156] Windisch (*Der Barnabasbrief*) on chap. 16 (who compares it to *Diogn.* 4).

[157] Although Moses had already accepted and lived by it.

[158] E.g., 6:7 (Isa. 3:9f.; cf. Justin, *Dial.* 17; Tertullian, *Adv. Marc.* 3.22); 11:2 (Jer. 2:12f.; cf. Justin, *Dial.* 14, 114); 12:4 (Isa. 65:2; cf. the combination of quotations in Justin, *Apol.* 1:35; *Dial.* 97).

[159] See Cainites, Ophites/Naasenes. Cf., however, Windisch: later this statement is basically

The Jews are uncircumcised in heart (9:5; Jer. 9:26). Christ appeared in order to reveal their sin in all its fullness (14:5; cf. 5:11). Various other kinds of arguments are incidentally thrown in from time to time, for example, the topos that God has no need of sacrifice,[160] and the reference that other peoples practice circumcision (9:5).[161]

In summary: The "first" people did not receive the inheritance, but it is for "this" people, namely, "us" (chap. 13).[162]

We have already suggested that the document contains internal tensions: although Israel never had a covenant with God, *Barnabas* still speaks from time to time of a "first" (13:1) and a "new" (5:7) people of God, and of a "new law" (2:6).[163] And especially: How are chaps. 2f., 14 (abolition of the cult)[164] related to chaps. 7f. (allegorical interpretation of cultic prescriptions)? Similarly: How is 9:4f. to be related to 9:7f?[165]

These tensions are not only an indication that Barnabas was no profound thinker, but also point to the fact that the problematic of the Old Testament and Israel cannot be resolved in unhistorical[166] categories. The schema of promise and fulfillment that is conceived unhistorically in *Barnabas* (5:6f.) necessarily leads to unresolvable contradictions.

Appendix

In the *Shepherd of Hermas*, neither Israel nor the Old Testament becomes a theme to be discussed. The book may *in fact* be described as a judaizing of

---

taken back; the whole Pentateuch is in fact of divine origin. Several ideas and motifs are run together: (a) the tale about the evil angels (Genesis 6 in the Jewish haggadah; Enoch, etc.), (b) the tradition about the participation of the angels in the giving of the law (Gal. 3:19; Heb. 2:2). —Yes, but there remains a reversal of values that extends beyond what we have in Gal. 3:19. Wengst, *Barnabasbriefes*, 101f., on 9:4f. etc.: "Judaism here serves merely as the dark background against which he projects his own interpretation of the Bible." —But note what kind of background it is!

[160] Acts 17:25; Philo, *Det. Pot. Ins.* 55f.; Apollonius of Tyana in Eusebius, *Praep. Ev.* 4.12; *1 Clem.* 52.1; Justin, *Apol.* 1.10 etc.

[161] Justin, *Dial.* 28; Celsus in Origen 5.41 (cf. Origen 5.47).

[162] On the proof in 13:2, see Tertullian, *Adv. Iud.* 1.

[163] Wengst, *Barnabasbriefes*, 73: The new law is no other than the old. —That correctly states the author's view, but the salvation-historical manner of expression contained in his tradition is nonetheless apparent.

[164] Whether traditional or not.

[165] Windisch (*Der Barnabasbrief*) affirms that in 7:3 sacrifices and fasts are divine commands, differently than in 2f., 16. —True enough, but then how is the contradiction to be explained? Wengst, *Barnabasbriefes*, 80: For Barnabas it is no contradiction. For example, chaps. 7f. do not neutralize the fundamental abolition of sacrifice. —In the author's understanding, certainly not. Wengst continues: the validity of the Scripture is absolute, timeless (pp. 73ff.). Therefore a timeless meaning must be found for every sentence in the Scripture. It is thus not the case that its validity is relativized in the light of the advent of Christ. In precisely the same manner, it is not the case that the law, in its literal sense, is acknowledged to be valid only for a limited time (i.e., Israel's).

[166] This includes the "salvation-historical" category.

Christianity, but it makes no contribution to our theme, which is also the case with *2 Clement* and the letter of Polycarp to the Philippians.

The "New Testament Apocrypha"

Taken as a whole, the New Testament Apocrypha provide only a small amount of information concerning our theme (on the special case of Jewish Christianity, see below). This is in part due to the state of the tradition. Not much can be learned from documents that have been preserved only in more or less paltry scraps, and one must be wary of the argument from silence. In much of what has been preserved, Judaism no longer comes within the field of view. A historical understanding of the church (and its history) has been left far behind.

Since the materials cannot be examined in chronological order, we may best examine them according to their various literary types.

5 Ezra occupies a special place, since it is thematically concerned with Israel.[167] To gain an initial impression of the context of the book,[168] we set forth a few sample passages: "the shameful deeds of my people" (1:5); "sacrificed to strange gods" (1:6); "you still murmur and complain until this very day" (1:16); festivals, new moons, circumcision were never commanded by God (1:31); persecution of the prophets ("my servants") (1:32); a people will come from the East (Weinel, *Handbuch zu den Neutestamentlichen Apokryphen*, ed. E. Hennecke [Tübingen: Mohr-Siebeck, 1914] 334: unexplainable) (1:38); "Let destruction come upon them" (2:6); "scattered among the nations, your names will perish from the earth" (2:7). It would be easy to conclude from the polemic that the debate with Judaism was still a live issue. But is that really the case?

The *form* is that of an apocalypse. Classified according to its *content*, the book belongs in the category of theoretical literature dealing with the synagogue (see Oepke).

It contains two parts: (1) 1:4–2:9: A threatening speech against Israel, which, unlike *Barnabas*, does not dispute that Israel *once* was the elect nation of God. It contains the familiar topoi of the speeches that call Israel to repentance: God's mighty acts of salvation, the fate of the prophets, the threat of punishment—and finally hints of the possibility of salvation (1:4); 1:5: "my people"—Israel! (2) 2:10-47: A promise to the church.[169]

---

[167] It stands in the Vulgate as chaps. 1 and 2 of 4 Ezra. The original was Greek. The time of composition is uncertain. It is even less possible to obtain a date from individual allusions (1:11; 2:8) in the threatening speech, since it is permeated with allusions to the Old Testament. So also the glorification of the martyrs in the conclusion gives only an approximate indication. The consensus leans toward a date in the second century, or around 200.

[168] Against the thesis that a Jewish leaflet has received a Christian reworking in the first part of the document, see the critical remarks of Weinel, *Handbuch*, 2nd ed., 390f.; Duensing (Hennecke-Schneemelcher, *NTApoc.* 2:689) is inclined to accept the thesis.

[169] 2:10: "My people"=the (Gentile) church. Oepke characterizes this as polemic and parenesis, organically worked together. —But the parenesis has the less important role (except for 2:10-13).

The major salvation-historical aspect is that God leaves Israel and goes "ad alias gentes" ("to other nations," 1:24).[170] The cult has been rejected by God (1:31 Codex Sangermanensis and Codex Ambianensis; Isa. 1:13 etc.) or was never commanded by God in the first place. (1:31 Codex Mazarinaeus).

The characteristic tendency of the whole can be seen in 2:4ff.: In 2:4 the mother addresses her son: "Ite, filii, et petite a domino misericordiam" ("Go, my children, and ask for mercy from the Lord") 2:5f.: "Ego autem te, pater, testem invoco super matrem filiorum, quia non voluerunt testamentum meum servare, ut des eis confusionem et matrem eorum in direptionem, ne generatio eorum fiat" ("I call upon you, father, as a witness in addition to the mother of the children, because they would not keep my covenant, that you may bring confusion upon them and bring their mother to ruin, so that they may have no offspring").[171] In its stead, "my people" receives "the kingdom of Jerusalem, which I had wanted to give to Israel" (2:10). In 2:33f. the supplementary idea is found, which was already present in the New Testament: the Gentile mission is the result of the unbelief of Israel.

Thus: It is precisely the idea of a "new people of God" that allows this "new people" to take up the Old Testament as a weapon against the "old." On the basis of the Scripture, which is accepted without reservation, the sins of the "old" people of God are placarded before them. It is not the factual condition of the "new" people of God that is placed over against this catalogue of sins, but rather their eschatological purity (2:14ff.). The history of Israel and the eschatological promise are placed on the same plane.

Here too we see the problem with the concept of the people of God: it is not able to reach the individual directly (through evangelistic address), but addresses the collective mass, and the individual only as a part thereof.[172]

6 Ezra struggles on a front other than that of 5 Ezra, as is clear, for example, from 15:43: the destruction of Babylon. The Christian (!) *Sibyllines*[173] stand on this same front (e.g., 1:360: Israel will become drunk; 362: the wrath of the Highest God will come on the Hebrews; 366: Israel with abominable lips; 387: when Israel reaps the bitter harvest; 393: when the temple of Solomon will be destroyed; 395: the Hebrews will be driven out).[174] The content is encouragement in persecution and threats against the persecutors.

---

[170] On the manuscripts, see Weinel, *Handbuch*, 331f., and the Stuttgart edition of the Vulgate 1:xxixf.

[171] Does the Latin *super* (translated "in addition to" here) represent Greek ὑπέρ ("above") or κατά (an intensive use of the preposition that could mean *against* in this context)?

[172] The letter to the Hebrews also clearly indicates this.

[173] Weinel, *Handbuch*, 399ff.; Hennecke-Schneemelcher, *NTApoc.* 2:703ff. (Kurfess).

[174] Cf. Tertullian, among others, on the expulsion of the Jews from Jerusalem under Hadrian.

The Apocryphal Gospels

An Unknown Gospel of the Synoptic Type (POxy. 840)[175]

The fragment contains a conversation of Jesus with a Pharisaic "high priest" in the temple plaza.[176]

An Unknown Gospel with Johannine Traits (PEgerton 2)[177]

John 5:39 and 45 are cited against the leaders of the people: these Scriptures testify to Jesus, saying that Moses, on whom the leaders have set their hope, will accuse them. Their hostility is documented by utilizing John 7:30; 8:59; and 10:31. The papyrus also contains a variation of the question of tribute money, with a reference to Isa. 29:13; cf. Mark 7:6f.

The Gospel of Peter[178]

We may here leave aside the question of whether docetic traits are to be found in the Christology of this writing.[179] What is important for us is the intensification of a tendency that is already present in the canonical Gospels (Luke, John), that is, to shift the burden of guilt for Jesus' death from Pilate to the Jews (1:46). It is Herod who has Jesus led away to his execution by the people.[180] Supernatural signs make clear "to the Jews and the elders and the

---

[175] A. de Santos Otero, *Los Evangelios Apocrifos*, 2nd ed. (Madrid: Biblioteca de Autores Christianos, 1956) 78ff.; J. Jeremias, *Unknown Sayings of Jesus*, 3rd ed. (London: SPCK, 1963) 50ff.; idem, in Hennecke-Schneemelcher, *NTApoc.* 1:92–94; Aland, *Synopsis Quattuor Evangeliorum* (Stuttgart: Württembergische Bibelanstalt, 1964) 219.

[176] Jeremias considers it to be old tradition on the same plane as the Synoptic tradition, an exact parallel to Matt. 23:27f. The author is supposed to be well informed concerning the temple and its ritual, and the report is supposed to be full of Semitisms. —Against this may be said: The narrative is composed of broken fragments without a clear profile. There is no example of this discussion in the Synoptics. The "Semitisms" prove nothing in this primitive style. The content of the conversation indicates a complete moralizing of the critique of the ritual washings.

[177] Santos, *Evangelios*, 95ff.; Hennecke-Schneemelcher, *NTApoc.* 1:94ff. (J. Jeremias).

[178] E. Klostermann, *Apokrypha* I (Kleine Texte für Vorlesungen und Übungen 3; Berlin: de Gruyter, 1903); Santos, *Evangelios*, 375ff.; M.-G. Mara, *Évangile de Pierre*, Sources chrétiennes 201 (Paris: Cerf, 1973); J. Denker, *Die theologiegeschichtliche Stellung des PetrEv* (Bern/Frankfurt: Lang, 1975); Hennecke-Schneemelcher, *NTApoc.* 1:179ff. (C. Maurer); Vielhauer, *Geschichte*, 641ff.
On the points of contact with the Syriac *Didascalia*, see L. Vaganay, *L'évangile de Pierre*, 2nd ed. (Paris: Gabalda, 1930) 167ff. Strecker in Bauer, *Orthodoxy*, 247ff. (the *Gospel of Peter* used in Syriac *Didascalia*).
The question can be raised whether points of contact with *Barnabas* exist (cf. *Gos. Pet.* 17 with *Barn.* 5:11). But the similarity is too general to prove literary dependence.

[179] This is cautiously affirmed by Vaganay, denied by Vielhauer (*Geschichte*, 646f.). Denker (*Die theologiegeschichtliche Stellung*) decided that the Christology is Jewish, with angelological motifs; this is supposed to be the principal motif, with the docetic motifs only the by-products. The increase of the mythical element does not prove docetism.

[180] *Ascension of Isaiah* 11:19: the Adversary aroused the Israelites against Jesus: they delivered him to the king (they did not recognize him).

priests what a great evil they have brought upon themselves, so that they began to lament and to say, 'Woe to us because of our sins; the judgment and the end of Jerusalem has come near'" (25).[181]

The Gospel of the Egyptians
Not enough has been preserved of this work[182] to permit an interpretation.

Epistula Apostolorum[183]
This writing belongs to the literary type of conversations with the resurrected Lord with his disciples. It commands the mission in Israel and among the Gentiles (30 [41]) and abolishes the distinction from the point of view of the missionary enterprise. The Jew Saul becomes a preacher for the Gentile Christians (31 [42]). In 9 (20), Jesus is crucified, according to the Ethiopic version, "in the days of Pontius Pilate and the prince Archelaus" [sic!], and, according to the Coptic version, "by Pontius Pilate and Archelaus." The salvation-historical aspect is missing, as is the political (except for the allusions above).

The Protevangelium of James[184]
We mention only two passages: (a) In 17:2 Mary says, "Joseph, I see two peoples with my eyes, one that is crying and lamenting and one that is happy and shouting for joy."[185] (b) A secondary appendix is provided by the legend of the martyrdom of Zechariah (22–24), which offers a variation of the topos of the murder of the prophets.[186]

---

[181] Cf. Luke 23:48 v.l. On the judgment of the Jews, see Melito of Sardis. Denker emphasizes the Jewish-Christian character of the book. The author goes into a Jewish polemic, in which the passion of Jesus was in any case the work of the Jews. The Jewish-Christian praxis prevails: fasts, lamenting the Jewish-Christian brethren (!). The Jewish-Christian praxis was undertaken in the hope of converting the Jews (Die theologiegeschichtliche Stellung, 91, to § 27). –This would be a rather remarkable solicitation of the Jews. But the polemical tendency against the Jews cannot be conjured away, even with the best will.

[182] See Schneemelcher's suggested reconstruction in Hennecke-Schneemelcher, NTApoc. 1:166ff.; compare this with Klostermann, Apokrypha 2:15f.

[183] C. Schmidt, Gespräche Jesu mit seinen Jüngern nach der Auferstehung, TU 43 (Leipzig: Hinrichs, 1919); H. Duensing, Epistula Apostolorum, KlT 152 (1925); idem, in Hennecke-Schneemelcher, NTApoc. 1:189ff.; Vielhauer, Geschichte, 680ff.

[184] Text: PBodmer V (1958); Santos, Evangelios, 126ff.; Hennecke-Schneemelcher, NTApoc. 1:370ff. (German: Oscar Cullmann); E. de Strycker, La forme la plus ancienne du Protévangile de Jacques (Brussels: Société des Bollandistes, 1961) (text with French translation and commentary); R. H. Smid, Protevangelium Jacobi (Assen: Van Gorcum, 1965); Vielhauer, Geschichte, 667ff.

[185] Cf. Gen. 25:23; Luke 2:34f. Gen. 25:23 is a central point of apologetic, (Geffcken).

[186] On this, see the story of the birth of Mary in Hennecke-Schneemelcher, NTApoc. 1.387f.; H. von Campenhausen, Hist. Jahrb. 17 (1958): 383ff.

The Infancy Gospel of Thomas[187]
Thomas the Israelite preaches to the "brothers from among the Gentiles." A noteworthy feature is the undifferentiated references to the Jews, scribes, and Pharisees, as well as to the Law and the Prophets.

Appendix

The Gospel of Thomas from Nag Hammadi[188]

The theology is completely unhistorical. We need merely note the casual attitude toward the Jewish rites:

Logion 27: "If you do not keep yourselves from the world, you will not find the kingdom; if you do not keep the Sabbath as Sabbath, you will not see the Father."[189]

Logion 53: "His disciples said to him, 'Is circumcision profitable or not?' He said to them, 'If it were profitable, their father would beget them circumcised from their mother. But the true circumcision in Spirit has found complete usefulness.'"

Logion 89: "Why do you wash the outside of the cup?"

The Apocryphal Acts[190]

Despite the considerable quantity of material that has been preserved, we cannot expect much from the "apocryphal Acts" that is relevant to our question.[191] They contain, so to speak, no relation to history, nor any historical understanding.[192] One must resist speaking of theological reflection in them. To be sure, there are definite points of view expressed, and in different directions. But there is a certain negative point of view that they have in common, precisely in the lack of historical thinking mentioned above.[193]

---

[187] Santos, *Evangelios,* 282ff.; Hennecke-Schneemelcher, *NTApoc.* 1:388ff. (O. Cullmann); Vielhauer, *Geschichte,* 672ff.

[188] *Evangelium nach Thomas,* ed. A. Guillaumont et al. (1958); E. Haenchen, *Die Botschaft des Thomasevangeliums* (Berlin: Töpelmann, 1961); Vielhauer, *Geschichte,* 618ff.

[189] See Haenchen, *Botschaft,* 50: This is no command to observe the Jewish Sabbath; Logia 6, 14, 104 in fact reject fasting. The Sabbath is here a symbol of the Gnostic separation from the world.

[190] Hennecke-Schneemelcher is indispensable for their reconstruction.

[191] See the index to Hennecke-Schneemelcher, *NTApoc.,* under "Jews" and "Israel."

[192] See the appropriate evaluation of Schneemelcher, in Hennecke-Schneemelcher, *NTApoc.* 2:173.

[193] Concern for history is replaced by the basic motif of insisting on sexual abstinence. This motif is common to the Gnostic (*John, Thomas*) and non-Gnostic Acts. This common denominator is an indication that we must be very cautious in sorting the apocryphal Acts into "Gnostic" and "orthodox" categories as though these were clear alternatives (Hennecke-Schneemelcher, *NTApoc.* 2:266 n. 2).

Samples

Acts of John 94: πρὶν δὲ συλληφθῆναι αὐτὸν (Jesus) ὑπὸ τῶν ἀνόμων καὶ ὑπὸ ἀνόμου ὄφεως νομοθετουμένων ᾿Ιουδαίων ("before he was arrested by the lawless Jews, whose lawgiver is the lawless serpent").

Acts of Peter (*Act. Verc.* 1): Paul confutes the teachers of the Jews, who had laid hands on Christ, and dispels the ritual law and the Jewish traditions.

Acts of Paul: Reports additional correspondence between Paul and Corinth (3 Corinthians):[194] God sent the prophets to the Jews in order to save Israel, but the evil ruler killed them. "So they are not children of righteousness, but children of wrath, who have rejected the providence of God, in that they who are "far from faith" affirm that heaven and earth and all that is in them are not the work of the Father . . . they have the accursed faith of the serpent" (*3 Cor.* 3:19).

Gnosticism [195]

For our purposes, three points stand out as important: (1) The adoption of Jewish motifs. This aspect has been placed in a completely new light by the Nag Hammadi texts. (2) In particular, the relation to the Old Testament.[196] (3) The relation to Paul. The whole spectrum of possible relationships to the Old Testament and Judaism is present, from the acceptance of the Old Testament[197] to the revolutionary reversal of its values, for example, the positive valuation of the serpent or of Cain.[198]

---

[194] Hennecke-Schneemelcher, *NTApoc.* 2:340ff.; Vielhauer, *Geschichte,* 704f.

[195] The literature on this topic is so immense that it resists being surveyed, but see the reviews of recent research by K. Rudolph, serialized in *TLZ;* K.-W. Tröger, ed., *Gnosis und Neues Testament* (Berlin: Evangelische Verlagsanstalt, 1973). For literature on Nag Hammadi, see D. M. Scholer, *Nag Hammadi Bibliography 1948-1969* (Leiden: E. J. Brill, 1971), continued in *Novum Testamentum* (I–IV to date). Concerning new projects: M. Krause in *Proceedings of the International Colloquium on Gnosticism,* ed. G. Widengren (Stockholm: Kungl. Vitterhets Historie och Antikvitets Akademiens Handlingar, 1977) 179f.; K. Rudolph, ed., *Gnosis und Gnostizismus,* Wege der Forschung 262 (Darmstadt: Wissenschaftliche Buchgesellschaft, 1975); K. Rudolph, *Gnosis* (San Francisco: Harper & Row, 1983) (bib.); J. M. Robinson, *The Nag Hammadi Library* (San Francisco: Harper & Row, 1988) (complete English translation).

[196] R. McL. Wilson, in *Proceedings,* 164ff.; for a preliminary survey, see W. Foerster, ed., *Die Gnosis* II (Zurich: Artemis, 1971), which has a Scripture index.

[197] Against the widespread opinion that Gnosticism in general was hostile to the Old Testament, see von Campenhausen, *Formation,* 75–77; cf. the Gnostic appeal to the Old Testament, and Gnostic exegetical works. On the use of the Old Testament in the *Apocryphon of John,* see von Campenhausen, *Formation,* 76 n. 78.

[198] H. Jonas, *Gnosis und spätantiker Geist* I (3rd ed.; Göttingen: Vandenhoeck & Ruprecht, 1964) 227ff. E. M. Yamauchi, *Pre-Christian Gnosticism* (Grand Rapids: Eerdmans, 1973) 144f. Saturninus in Irenaeus, *Adv. Haer.* 1.24.2: the god of the Jews was an angel, and the purpose of Christ's advent was to destroy him.

This transvaluation also is manifest conceptually in the ways that Judaism is evaluated. One can even find—in the completely unhistorical thinking characteristic of Gnosticism—scattered traces of a kind of negative "salvation history."[199]

Basilides[200]

The prince of the angels, the god of the Jews, wanted to bring the other nations into subjection to them. Thus they turned against him. The prophecies are "a mundi fabricatoribus . . . principibus,[201] proprie autem legem a principe ipsorum, eum qui eduxerit populum, de terra Aegypti" ("derived from those powers who were the makers of the world, but the law was specially given by their chief, who led the people out of the land of Egypt").[202]

Heracleon

This author divides people into Gentiles, Jews, and Pneumatics. This is a typical point of view on the human race.[203] He has a double interpretation of John 4:22 (frag. 22, Völker, *Quellen*, 74f.): (a) Salvation is from Judea, since "he" was born there, but it is not *in* the Jews. (b) Allegorically, the Jews are symbols of the Pleroma.

Justin, Book of Baruch[204]

This contains a kind of Gnostic "salvation history." The course of the saving event is determined by the counteractions of Elohim and Edem (=the Earth). καλεῖται δὲ Ἐδὲμ αὕτη ἡ κόρη καὶ Ἰσραήλ ("This maiden is called 'Eden' and

---

[199] The Saturninus passage in the preceding note is an example of such.

[200] Irenaeus, *Adv. Haer.* 1.24.4; Clement of Alexandria, *Strom.* 2.36.1; Pseudo-Tertullian; Epiphanius 24.2.5; A. Hilgenfeld, *Die Ketzergeschichte des Urchristenthums* (Leipzig, 1884; reprinted Hildesheim, 1963) 2:196ff., 224.

[201] Cf. Simon Magus, according to Irenaeus, *Adv. Haer.* 1.23.3.

[202] Irenaeus, *Adv. Haer.* 1.24.5

[203] Frag. 20 (on John 4:21; W. Völker, *Quellen zur Geschichte der christlichen Gnosis* [Tübingen: Mohr-Siebeck, 1932] 73): οἱ πρὸ νόμου καὶ οἱ ἐθνικοί ("those before the law and all the Gentiles") worship the mountain=the cosmos. Jerusalem is the creation or the creator, ᾧ προσεκύνουν οἱ Ἰουδαῖοι ("whom the Jews serve"). Or the mountain is the creation, which is worshiped by the Gentiles, and Jerusalem is the creator, who is worshiped by the Jews. But *you*, as Pneumatics, should worship neither the creation, like the Gentiles, nor the creator, like the Jews. There is a certain analogy (of a non-Gnostic sort) to this three-fold division in the *Kerygma Petrou*, to which Heracleon refers (frag. 21 on John 4:22; Völker, *Quellen*, 74).

[204] Hippolytus, *Ref.* 26f.; Völker, *Quellen*, 27ff.; Foerster, *Gnosis* 2:65ff.; E. Haenchen in *Gott und Mensch* (Tübingen: Mohr-Siebeck, 1965) 299ff.

'Israel'") (26.2).[205] Baruch, the third of the paternal angels, repeatedly intervenes in earthly events (he is sent to do so): in paradise, by Moses, by the prophets— but without success, for his counterpart is also active, Naas, the third angel of Edem. Finally, in the days of Herod, Baruch is sent again and comes to Nazareth, where he finds Jesus, the son of Joseph and Mary, whom he meets as a twelve-year-old boy. Naas cannot get him to yield to his temptations. This makes him so angry that he finally has him crucified.[206]

Irenaeus, Adv. Haer., Concerning the Ophites

Another variation is found in 1.30: angry because human beings do not worship him, Jaldabaoth sends the flood. But Sophia wants to save them in the ark, "because of the remnants of that light that originally came from here." From the survivors Jaldabaoth chooses Abraham and makes a covenant with him. He then delivers the descendants of Abraham from Egypt, gives them the *law*, and makes them into *Jews*. "From these he selected seven gods . . . each of them, in order that his glory and deity might be proclaimed, selected a *prophet.* . . ."[207] But for her part, Sophia proclaimed many things concerning the first human beings and the immortal Aeon, concerning the heavenly Christ.

Letter of Ptolemy to Flora

The letter represents a unique variation.[208] Nothing is said concerning the *Jews*. The theme is not the Old Testament as such, but the *law*.[209] The concept of law is divided into two triads: (1) The law of the Old Testament consists of (a) the law of God, (b) the additions of Moses, and (c) the regulations of the elders. (2) The law of God is itself divided into three parts (a) the Decalogue is the pure law; (b) alongside this are laws that are bound up with evil: "an eye for an eye" . . .; this law is canceled by the Savior, for it is not in accord with his nature; (c) and finally there is the ceremonial law, which is to be understood

---

[205] Hilgenfeld, *Ketzergeschichte*, 274f.: "The whole pre-Christian history of religion, of Judaism as well as of paganism, is thus the unsuccessful struggle of the spiritual against the psychical." Judaism is divided into the revelation of Elohim to the spirit and the psychical power of Edem (Israel).

[206] 26.31: ὁ δὲ καταλιπὼν τὸ σῶμα τῆς Ἐδὲμ πρὸς τὸ ξύλον ἀνέβη πρὸς τὸν ἀγαθόν ("But he left the body of Edem on the Cross and went up to 'the Good'"). We here leave aside the matter of the secondary intermixing of pagan mythological elements about Heracles and Priapus.

[207] There follows a speculative allocation of the prophets to these gods.

[208] Epiphanius 33.3–7; Völker, *Quellen*, 87ff.; Foerster, *Gnosis* 1:204ff.; ed. G. Quispel, Sources chrétiennes 24 (2nd ed.; Paris: Cerf, 1966); von Campenhausen, *Formation*, 98ff.

[209] Von Campenhausen, *Formation*, 85: The relation of Jesus and the law is no longer understood within a salvation-historical perspective, but Jesus' words are considered to be the timeless criterion by which the law is measured. Further, p. 87: Under Gnostic presuppositions, a real acknowledgment of the canon is not possible. So also in the case of Ptolemy, "the situation is such that the canon as a normative entity in the strict sense is already disintegrating."

symbolically. This distinction is then transferred to the concept of God: the doctrine that the Old Testament law originated from the devil is strictly rejected.[210] On the other hand, it could not have come from the perfect God and so must have originated from an intermediate being, the Creator. Ptolemy thus finds himself struggling on two fronts: the one opponent does not recognize the God of justice; the other does not perceive the Father of the All.

Paul among the Gnostics

Finally, we must mention the Gnostic association with Paul.[211]

For H. Langerbeck,[212] this theme has fundamental importance for the understanding of Gnosticism as such. For him, Basilides and Valentinus are nothing else than radical Pauline theologians (who have adopted Platonic motifs).[213]

In view of the way in which these writers quoted (cf. n. 211) and interpreted Paul, this thesis cannot be accepted.

Marcion[214]

In the history of the early church's stance toward the Old Testament and Judaism, Marcion occupies an absolutely unique position, because of the combination of his evaluation of the Jews and his completely independent exegesis of the Old Testament, and because he based this on the "Gospel," which he exalted to canonical status (and it alone).[215] He also offered a solution for the

---

[210] Von Campenhausen, Formation, 87 n. 138; 86 n. 133. "Mention of attributing the Law to the devil must be a reference to Marcion." —But cf. also the Ophites (Irenaeus, Adv. Haer. 1.30; see above). On this passage, see also G. Quispel, "La lettre de la Ptolémée à Flora," VC 2 (1948): 17ff.

[211] See the index in Völker, Quellen; Foerster, Gnosis 2; on the Valentinian exegesis of Paul, see Elaine H. Pagels, The Gnostic Paul (Philadelphia: Fortress Press, 1975); C. Barth, Die Interpretation des Neuen Testaments in der valentinianischen Gnosis, TU 37/3 (Leipzig: Hinrichs, 1911).

[212] H. Langerbeck, Aufsätze zur Gnosis (Göttingen: Vandenhoeck & Ruprecht, 1967).

[213] Which was welcomed by the humanist Langerbeck. Whether such a "synthesis" is possible on the basis of Paul is another question.

[214] Harnack, Marcion: Das Evangelium vom fremden Gott (Leipzig, 1924; reprinted, Berlin, 1960); von Campenhausen, Formation, 147ff.; Bib.: B. Aland, "Marcion: Versuch einer neuen Interpretation," ZTK 70 (1973) 424 n. 21.

[215] On the dispute concerning the significance of Marcion for the development of the idea of the Christian canon, see Harnack; in connection with him, von Campenhausen, Formation, 148: "The idea and the reality of a Christian Bible were the work of Marcion. . . . This was no by-product of his theological endeavors, but their normative and most important result." The consequence for the church was: "She had lost her 'Scriptures,'" her claim "to be the religion of the most ancient wisdom and the religion of historical fulfillment" (p. 178). "Marcion's Bible tabled once and for all the question of a new canon, i.e., the question of the 'authentic' witnesses of the original gospel that was to provide the standard of all later tradition and the norm for the preaching of church" (p. 164).

Against this view, see I. Frank, Der Sinn der Kanonbildung, Freiburger Theologische Studien 90 (1971) (review: R. Pesch, BZ n.F. 17 [1973] 110ff.): (a) The idea of the canon is older than Marcion;

problem of the relationship of Christians and Jews, while the orthodox Christians were necessarily hindered in doing so precisely by their view of salvation history.[216] To be sure, Marcion's criticism of the Jews was severe: they are the worst national group; they sinned against God and killed the prophets.[217]

But orthodox Christians also said bad things about the Jews. In Marcion's statements, however, the meaning of such declarations first becomes clear against the background of unorthodox theology: the fundamental separation of Christian faith from the Old Testament, its God, its law, and its people, in connection with which Harnack's dictum must be kept in mind, namely, that this God and his law are *not evil* but *just,* and that it is precisely this that makes for the built-in disaster—for whoever serves this God.

Marcion's demand that the Old Testament be interpreted literally actually kept him closer to it than his opponents, who were forced into spiritualizing reinterpretations. Of course, Marcion's exegesis was not historical in the modern sense, but dealt with abstractions and principles. Its limited perspective is revealed with particular clarity in his judgment concerning the *prophets:* they made *true* predictions—which referred to the Messiah. The Jews were not mistaken in their messianic expectations.[218] *Their* Messiah has in fact not yet come. But he *will* come—and that means precisely the *Jewish* Messiah who is other than Jesus and who will be destroyed. The Christ of the true God gave warnings concerning him (Luke 21:8).[219] Thus the Jews can be reproached with killing their own prophets (Luke 6:23; 11:47); Marcion left 1 Thess. 2:15 in his New Testament.[220]

(b) contra Käsemann, Kümmel, Braun, the intention of the canon is to provide the basis for the *unity* of the church, on the basis of the Gospel of John (!); Muratorian Canon; Tatian; Irenaeus. —To be on the safe side, Frank draws his evidence from a later period.

[216] Their position is relevant today. The matter-of-fact manner in which the Old Testament is today customarily accepted as a Christian book is neither of any benefit for the understanding of the Old Testament or the New Testament, nor does it do the relationship with Judaism any good. See, most recently, A. H. J. Gunneweg, *Understanding the Old Testament* (Philadelphia: Westminster, 1978).

[217] Tertullian, *Adv. Marc.* 4.26; 5.15, etc.; Harnack, *Marcion,* 289*f. Harnack, *Marcion,* 22: Does his resentment against Judaism derive from the fact that he (or his family) came out of Judaism (as proselytes)? His knowledge of Jewish exposition of the Old Testament is unique among the Gnostics and among the church fathers. Cf. the agreement between Tertullian's polemic against the Jews and that against Marcion. Tertullian, *Adv. Marc.* 3.16: the Jews are "partiarii erroris tui" ("partakers of your heresy") (i.e., Marcion's). Harnack, *Marcion,* 67, 86.

[218] Contrary to the orthodox interpretation.

[219] Tertullian, *Adv. Marc.* 4.39.

[220] Although the reproach of the sins against the prophets was already a Jewish topos (cf. Acts 7:52; O. Steck, *Israel und das gewaltsame Geschick der Propheten* [Neukirchen: Neukirchener Verlag, 1967]) Marcion stands all these judgments on their heads. We then have a complete reversal of the Old Testament's own value system in the Gnostic style: Cain, the inhabitants of Sodom, the Egyptians, and the pagans generally are redeemed, as the Lord descends to the lower world; the just, Abel, the patriarchs, and the prophets cannot be redeemed. Harnack, *Marcion,* 129ff., 294 F 1. B. Aland, "Marcion," 432.

Marcion paid a price for his "solution": his concept of God had to be developed metaphysically, not historically; the world is withdrawn from his rule and receives an unhistorical, negative judgment. In truth, God is no longer God. He is removed from the history of human beings.[221] Consistent with this, the Marcionite church expressed its unworldliness *directly,* as asceticism, and this means in an intensified legalism.[222]

Jewish Christianity[223]

Here we have not only the historical beginning point of the church but also a model case of the problematic with which we are concerned. In Jewish Christianity the central problem, that of the law, is represented in an exemplary fashion—and indeed as a continuing problem from the very beginning.

Strecker rightly rejects the tendency to ignore Jewish Christianity as a sectarian group that early became unimportant.[224] Quite apart from its numerical strength in the East, the status of Jewish Christianity in the heresy–orthodoxy dispute was still an open question, even in the time of Justin and Hegesippus. Justin distinguished between Jewish Christians who themselves kept the Mosaic law but did not want to impose it on Gentile Christians and those who did want to subject Gentile Christians to it. He considered the former category to be authentic Christians, but not the latter (*Dial.* 47). In addition, he perceived an "Ebionite" Christology (*Dial.* 48) in the group, which he

---

[221] This is represented christologically by the fact that the Christ was not predicted but appeared unannounced; Tertullian, *Adv. Marc.* 3.2f.; 4.11; etc.; he was not born.

[222] In view of the present, we may well ask whether a solution to the problem of the church and the Old Testament/Judaism is not possible without the particular presuppositions of Marcion. For the Old Testament at least, Harnack has drawn the appropriate logical conclusions.

To the question, what *positive* significance it has in the church, no other persuasive answer can be given than that of the Pauline doctrine of justification, that is, through the distinction of law and gospel in such wise that the gospel is *necessarily* related to the law. This law, represented through the Old Testament, is understood as God's constitution for his world, a world in which believers still live—and that not only by necessity—but the world assigned to them as the place where god rules and the place where human beings live together, that is, the world as the place of faith.

[223] Since this expression has become commonly accepted, it may be used here even though it can lead to misunderstandings and is hardly adequate as a historical category; see now G. Luedemann, *Opposition to Paul in Jewish Christianity* (Minneapolis: Fortress Press, 1989) 1–32; Harnack, *The History of Dogma* (New York: Russell & Russell, 1958) 1:99. Bib.: G. Strecker, "Ebioniten," in *RAC* 4:487ff.; idem, in Bauer, *Orthodoxy,* 283ff.; A. F. J. Klijn and G. J. Reinink, *Patristic Evidence for Jewish Christian Sects,* Supplements to *Novum Testamentum* 30 (Leiden: E. J. Brill, 1973) (comprehensive collection of the patristic data); M. Simon, ed., *Aspects du Judéo-Christianisme* (Strassburg, 1965); *Judéo-Christianisme: Recherches historiques et théologiques offerts en hommage au Cardinal Jean Daniélou* (=*RSR* 60 [1972]: 1–160).

[224] In Bauer, *Orthodoxy,* 242 n. 2.

rejected, even though it was still a moderate version.[225] The Jewish Christian groups are still divided by Justin into Nazarenes and Ebionites.[226]

The Historical Question: In view of the paucity of source material, it is difficult to arrive at a judgment concerning the differing groups of Jewish Christians. Names of two groups have come down through the tradition: Nazoreans (or Nazareans)[227] and Ebionites.[228] On the other hand, both terms are used promiscuously.[229] Thus, caution is advised in using the names of groups as the basis for conclusions.[230]

Nevertheless, even within the paltry fragments of the Jewish Christian gospels, certain differences may be perceived, including some that have to do with their stance toward the law.[231]

Although the *Gospel of the Nazaraeans* does indeed contain legendary accretions, it does not manifest any particularly typical heretical tendencies. On the other hand, the *Gospel of the Hebrews,* in addition to peculiar christological ideas (the omission of Matthew 1–2),[232] also contains hostility to the cult and references to vegetarianism.[233] *Jesus* is the son of the (feminine) Spirit. There are additional indications of syncretistic motifs.[234]

The *Pseudo-Clementines* belong to a later period than that with which we are concerned, but they are indispensable for reconstructing the contours of Jewish Christianity.[235] Their outstanding feature is their opposition to Paul,[236] represented under the figure of Simon Magus, along with their doctrine of the false pericopes.[237] The doctrine of the syzygies is the characteristic substitute for

---

[225] On the use of the term αἵρεσις ("heresy"), see *Apol.* 1.26 and *Dial.* 80. According to *Apol.* 1.26, heresy came into being when human beings, at the instigation of demonic powers, claimed to be gods; this was the case with Simon and Menander. Then Marcion is placed among them, for he denied the creator; see *Apol.* 1.58. Alongside Hegesippus, Justin played a key role in the formation of the concept of heresy.

[226] The Jewish (!) heresies (*Dial.* 80).

[227] Epiphanius 29f.; Jerome, *Viri ill* 3.

[228] Since Irenaeus, *Adv. Haer.* 1.26.2.

[229] Precisely from Jerome (*Ep.* 112.12); Epiphanius 30.2.8f.

[230] Strecker, *RAC* 4:488; he regards as "Ebionites" "in general all those Jewish Christians . . . who continue to observe the Jewish law."

[231] I am following Vielhauer, in Hennecke-Schneemelcher, *NTApoc.* 1:117ff. in distinguishing *three* Jewish Christian gospels (*Gospel of the Nazaraeans, Gospel of the Ebionites,* and *Gospel of the Hebrews*).

[232] See Justin, *Dial.* 48.

[233] On hostility to the cult, see the syncretistic *Book of Elchasai* (Hennecke-Schneemelcher, *NTApoc.* 2:745ff.).

[234] Frags. 1–3 (Vielhauer) in Hennecke-Schneemelcher, *NTApoc.* 1:163f.

[235] As does the basic source document that is to be assumed. And the source document that is to be presupposed for the *Kerygmata Petrou* is located at the border of our period; Strecker, *Pseudoclementinen;* idem, in Hennecke-Schneemelcher, *NTApoc.* 2:102ff.

[236] In addition, see Irenaeus, *Adv. Haer.* 1.26.2 (Ebionites); Epiphanius 28.4.1 (Cerinthians); Origen, *Contra Cels.* 5.65 etc. (Ebionites and Encratites).

[237] *Hom.* 2.38; 3.43, 47ff.

salvation history: from Adam on, the True Prophet was embodied in a series of figures, each of which was accompanied by a negative partner (*Hom.* 3.17ff.). He brings the Gnosis, which is identical with the law.[238]

The Transition to Apologetic: Preliminary Forms

Hegesippus

Hegesippus is worthy of special attention[239] with regard to the development of a concept of the church and tradition determined by the idea of salvation history, as well as for the formation of a picture of early church history including the origins of heretical doctrine. This picture still has effects in modern times. Eusebius awarded him a high rank, both for his explanation of the origin of heresies (*Hist. Eccl.* 3.32.7; 4.22.4) and for the establishment of pure doctrine through the control of the succession of bishops.[240]

Unfortunately, Eusebius's statements are not entirely clear. There are doublets that differ considerably from each other.[241] We can hope for a clarification only by consistently attempting to interpret Eusebius's excerpts from Hegesippus in isolation from Eusebius's review of them.[242] The difference probably has to do with the desolate condition of the textual tradition that Eusebius found in the *Martyrdom of James.*

The most important point for us is that the concept of "apostle" probably

---

[238] *Hom.* 3.17ff. etc. R. M. Grant pursues a line of connection between Jewish Christianity and earlier Gnostic movements in "Jewish Christianity at Antioch in the Second Century" in *Judéo-Christianisme*, 97ff.: behind Simon and Menander (Justin, *Apol.* 26; Irenaeus, *Adv. Haer.* 1.23) stands a moderately speculative form of Jewish Christianity. Perhaps Menander developed his system in contrast to Christianity *and* Judaism. Was the anti-Jewish attitude of Saturninus (Justin, *Dial.* 35; Irenaeus 1.24) influenced by the Bar Kochba revolt? That Tatian resided in Antioch is first reported in Epiphanius 46.1.8. Theophilus mentions neither Saturninus nor Tatian; he speaks only about the heresies in general (2.14); he writes against Hermogenes and Marcion (Eusebius, *Hist. Eccl.* 4.24). What he defends is essentially Judaism; see 1.6 (see G. Kraetschmar, *Studien zur frühchristlichen Trinitätstheologie* [Tübingen: Mohr-Siebeck, 1956] 27ff.).

On Jewish Christian tendencies in Antioch, see still Eusebius, *Hist. Eccl.* 6.12; Serapion and the *Gospel of Peter* and Serapion's writing to Domnus, ἐκπεπτωκότα τινὰ παρὰ τὸν τοῦ διωγμοῦ καιρὸν ἀπὸ τῆς εἰς Χριστὸν πίστεως ἐπὶ τὴν Ἰουδαϊκὴν ἐθελοθρησκείαν ("a man who at the time of the persecution had fallen away from faith in Christ to Jewish will-worship") (cf. Col. 2:23).

[239] H. Kemler, *Der Herrenbruder Jakobus bei Hegisipp und in der frühchristlichen Literatur* (Diss., Göttingen, 1966).

[240] In Corinth and Rome, 4.22.1–3, with the famous passage: γενόμενος δέ ἐν Ῥώμῃ διαδοχὴν ἐποιησάμην μέχρις Ἀνικήτου ("On arrival at Rome I pieced together the succession down to Anicetus"). For an explanation, see H. von Campenhausen, *Ecclesiastical Authority and Spiritual Power in the Church of the First Three Centuries* (Stanford: Stanford University Press, 1953) 163ff.

[241] Thus the two passages concerning the origin of heresy mentioned above, and then the two catalogues of Jewish heresies (4.22.5, 7).

[242] See Kemler, *Herrenbruder.*

belongs not to Hegesippus but to Eusebius.[243] This concept plays no role whatsoever in Hegesippus's understanding of tradition.[244] A central place is occupied by the anti-Jewish motif of the profanation of the temple and the tradition of a church in which James, as the source of a stream of tradition, is the principal figure.

We should note also that James is associated with the title "apostle" in the excerpt in Eusebius, *Hist. Eccl.* 2.23.4 and in the review in 3.11. But in the first passage the "apostles" are introduced from the context (cf. 2.23.3); this is indicated by the comparison with 3.11: the assembly of the apostles who were still living had no value as a source alongside the relatives of the Lord.

On the origins of heresy, cf. (a) *Hist. Eccl.* 4.22.4ff. (quotation from Hegesippus): After the death of James he was succeeded by Simon, son of Clopas, as a relative of the Lord. Until then the church was a pure virgin. But it began to be defiled by Thebutis, who belonged to one of the seven Jewish sects. However, his motive was personal: he had not been elected as bishop. Christian sects then originated from these Jewish ones (only Gnostic sects are listed, 4.22.5); Simon heads the list. Here too we have a doublet, since the series of Jewish Christian sects is followed by a second catalogue of Jewish sects (22.7).[245] (b) Compare the quotation itself with the paraphrase in 3.32.7: Eusebius picks up on the key word "virgin." But at the time of her defilement he characteristically departs from Hegesippus by stating that it was after the sacred chorus of the *apostles* (along with their disciples!) had perished. A picture of early Christian history with enormous aftereffects!

Ariston of Pella

Although little of his writings has been preserved, he is worthy of our attention.[246] He is the author of a dialogue between a Jewish Christian, Jason, and an Alexandrian Jew, Papiscus, in which the Jew is (of course) converted.

---

[243] On Eusebius, *Hist. Eccl.* 2.23.4ff., see below.

[244] Kemler (*Herrenbruder,* 52) formulates it sharply: "The fundamental denial of apostolic tradition for the benefit of episcopal succession allows . . . a clear antithesis to the Christianity of the 'Great Church' to become visible." On this point Hegesippus and Eusebius are fundamentally different. —The latter inserts his concept of apostolicity into his references to Hegesippus.

[245] Harnack explains the doublets on the basis of the use of a second source, namely, Justin. To this Hilgenfeld (*Ketzergeschichte,* 33ff.) objects: the view of the origin of Christian heresy is completely different in the two places. "In Hegesippus Simon is not yet the first to indulge in self-deification, but is still connected with the seven Israelite heresies, with Dositheus etc., has Cleobius alongside him, and must share the honors of being the founder with Thebutis, whom Justin will not yet have known about, and is finally also related to Paul. . . . In any case, Hegesippus distinguished more clearly than did Justin between the public emergence of heresies since the death of the apostles and the immediate disciples of Jesus and its hidden working behind the scenes during the apostolic age" (p. 35).

[246] R. M. Grant, *Second Century Christianity* (London: SPCK, 1957) 56f.; Harnack, *RE³* 2:47; idem, *Literaturgeschichte* 1:92ff.

The data: (1) Eusebius, *Hist. Eccl.* 4.6.3 only cites from Ariston of Pella that on orders from Hadrian (after the Bar Kochba revolt) the Jews were not permitted even to glimpse their homeland from afar.[247] He does not mention the *Dial.* (2) Origen quotes Celsus as making a sneering reference to the "Antilogue" of Jason and Papiscus in his polemic against allegorical interpretation of Scripture. Origen defends it: the book enables a Christian to prove to a Jew, on the basis of their own Scriptures, that the predictions of the Messiah apply to Jesus.[248] Neither Celsus nor Origen gives the name of the author of the *Dial.*, but this can be confirmed on the basis of a passage in Maximus the Confessor.[249] From Jerome, *Quaest in Gen.* 2, we get a sample of his biblical exegesis: God created the heavens and the earth in the Son.

The Kerygma Petrou

Among the preliminary forms of apologetic the *Kerygma Petrou* occupies a rather important place.[250] It belongs in the first half of the second century.[251] It is often supposed that it was used by Aristides;[252] whether it was also used by Theophilus remains uncertain (cf. frag. 2 and Theophilus 1.10; 2.2).

We can agree with the characterization of E. von Dobschütz (*Kerygma*, 66) that the writing represents "a transition from earliest Christian literature to that of the apologists." Embryonic forms of both the formal structures and the contents of apologetic are found, but their philosophical manner of thought (Justin; Athenagoras) and their reflective hermeneutic (Justin, *Dial.*) are still lacking. One can say this much, despite the fragmentary character of what has been preserved. For this reason it is also problematic to reconstruct the structure of the writing. We will follow the order of the fragments in Clement of Alexandria, whose supplementary comments give some indications of the structure of the original.

We may confidently assume that the original order was Greeks-Jews-Christians (cf. Aristides; *Diogn.*).

Fragment 1 gives an indication of the Christology, which at first glance appears to be near to that of the apologists: the Lord (or σωτήρ, "savior") is

---

247 Justin, *Dial.* 16; Tertullian, *Adv. Iud.* 13.

248 Origen, *Contra Cels.* 4.52.

249 Harnack, *Literaturgeschichte*, and Grant, *Second Century Christianity*. Harnack assumes that Tertullian used *Dial.*

250 E. von Dobschütz, *Das Kerygma Petri kritisch untersucht*, TU 11/1 (Leipzig: Hinrichs, 1893); E. Klostermann, *Apocrypha* I (KlT 3) (1933); Hennecke-Schneemelcher, *NTApoc.* 2:94ff. (Schneemelcher, Bib.).

251 Already documented by Heracleon (Heracleon, frag. 21; Völker, *Quellen*, 74; Origen on John 13:17), and especially Clement of Alexandria. Harnack (*Chronologie* 1:472): It is used by an interpreter who also has taken Clement of Alexandria (*Strom.* 2.15.68) into consideration.

252 Harnack, *History of Dogma* 2:179; cf. Schneemelcher, in *NTApoc.* 2:95.

described as νόμος ("law") and λόγος ("word"). How important this is to Clement can be seen from the fact that he repeats it.[253] The combination of both concepts[254] has a long philosophical tradition.[255] The question, however, is whether one may read into these passages the developed Christology of the Apologists. This must be rejected, although in the Apologists too Logos stands beside Nomos.[256] The juxtaposition of these two words also has an Old Testament, nonphilosophical tradition. The hints that Clement himself gives are especially interesting. In *Ecl. Proph.* he connects the quotation mentioned above with Isa. 2:3: ἐκ Σιὼν γὰρ ἐξελεύσεται νόμος καὶ λόγος κυρίου ἐξ Ἱερουσαλήμ ("For the law shall go forth from Zion, and the word of the Lord from Jerusalem").[257] Hermas, *Sim.* 8.3.2 is instructive: ὁ δὲ νόμος οὗτος υἱὸς θεοῦ ἐστι κηρυχθεὶς εἰς τὰ πέρατα τῆς γῆς ("this law is the Son of God, proclaimed to the ends of the earth").[258]

Fragment 2 is introduced by Clement as follows: γινώσκετε οὖν ὅτι εἷς θεός ἐστιν, ὃς ἀρχὴν πάντων ἐποίησεν, καὶ τέλους ἐξουσίαν ἔχων ("Know then that there is one God, who made the beginning of all things, and holds the power of the end"). Εἷς θεός ("one God") is the fundamental confession of faith that Jews and Christians hold in common.[259] The εἷς θεός ("one God") formula, in connection with the first commandment, is a rejection not only of polytheism[260] but also of substituting the creation for the Creator.[261]

The use of the formula by the Christians is an indication that they identified their God with the God of the Old Testament. This includes faith in the unity of creation and redemption and the understanding of God as God and consequently the world as the place of faith.[262] At the same time, by means of the understanding of this confession in the sense of faith in Christ, the Christian

---

[253] *Strom.* 2.15.68 and *Ecl. Proph.* 58. Is that an indication that the christological article stood at the beginning?

[254] Von Dobschütz, *Kerygma*, 28f.; Pohlenz, *Stoa* I, index, under "Gesetz" and "Logos." Philo, *Ebr.* 142.

[255] Cf. the title of C. Andresen's book on Celsus, *Logos und Nomos.*

[256] Justin, *Dial.* 11: αἰώνιός τε ἡμῖν νόμος καὶ τελευταῖος ὁ Χριστὸς ἐδόθη ("an eternal and final law—namely, Christ—has been given to us") by which the old law is nullified); 42: Christ as αἰώνιος νόμος καὶ καινὴ διαθήκη ("eternal law and new covenant").

[257] Isa. 2:3 and *Protr.* 1.2; *Protr.* 10.95 on Isa. 1:20: νόμος ἀληθείας λόγος κυρίου ("the law of truth, the word of the Lord"). For the non-philosophical use of λόγος with reference to the law of God, cf. also *Protr.* 10.108; *Paed.* 2.1.6; *Strom.* 7.3.16, ὁ πάντων ἡγεμὼν . . . βασιλεύς τε καὶ γεννήτωρ τῶν καλῶν, νόμος ὢν ὄντως καὶ θεσμὸς καὶ λόγος αἰώνιος ("Leader of mortals and of immortals, King and Parent of what is good, who is truly law, and right, and eternal Word"). The combination is also used in Athenagoras 31 in an unspecific, un-christological manner (κατά τινα θεῖον νόμον καὶ λόγον, "according to a certain divine law and word").

[258] Cf. frag. 3; *Diogn.* 11.

[259] E. Peterson, Εἷς θεός (Göttingen: Vandenhoeck & Ruprecht, 1926).

[260] Cf. Philo and Josephus.

[261] Philo, *Op. Mund.* 170ff.

[262] *1 Clem.* 46.6; Hermas, *Mand.* 1.1.

faith was marked off as distinct from Judaism,[263] and revelation was conceived of historically in a new way. Thus the debate with Judaism was not merely a formal one;[264] it was a matter of a new apprehension of the historicality of the world and of human existence.[265] Under the presupposition of the revelation in Christ, Hellenistic-Jewish ideas about God could be adopted. In a comment typical of him, Clement says: "thus it should be clearly said that the leading personalities among the Greeks also worship the same God as we,[266] but without full understanding, since they have not gotten acquainted with the tradition about the Son. He thus says: 'Do not worship (not 'the gods that the Greeks worship,' but) in the *way* the Greeks worship.' He thus gives a new direction to the worship of God, but does not proclaim a new (God). Now the meaning of 'the way the Greeks worship' Peter himself makes clear. . . ."

Then follows a classic piece of apologetic in the Jewish tradition.[267] A glance at this, on the one hand, and, on the other hand, at the later Christian Apologists does indeed show that there is a continuous line of development but that we find ourselves here still in the preliminary stages of the apologetic thought developed later.

Clement again blurs the train of thought or else perverts it through an addition: "And since he thinks that we ourselves and the Greeks have come to know the same God, although not in the same way, he adds the following supplementary comment: μηδὲ κατὰ ᾿Ιουδαίους σέβεσθε ("Neither worship as the Jews").[268] καὶ γὰρ ἐκεῖνοι μόνοι οἰόμενοι τὸν θεὸν γινώσκειν οὐκ ἐπίστανται, λατρεύοντες ἀγγέλοις ("for they, thinking that they only know God, do not know Him, adoring as they do angels").[269] Then Clement continues: "He then adds the keystone of his investigation": νέαν ἡμῖν διέθετο· τὰ γὰρ Ἑλλήνων καὶ ᾿Ιουδαίων παλαιά, ἡμεῖς δὲ οἱ καινῶς αὐτὸν τρίτῳ γένει σεβόμενοι Χριστιανοί

[263] The means by which this marking off occurs in the *Kerygma Petrou* has perhaps already been provided by the way in which it is arranged. Early on, the double form εἷς θεός–εἷς κύριος ("one God–one Lord") (1 Cor. 8:6) is found (here in confrontation with polytheism).

[264] That is, whether the Messiah has already come or is still expected.

[265] And this is still the issue between Judaism and Christianity to this very day—when Christian theology remains Christian and the reference of faith to the historical revelation is not replaced with a Christian world view or, as people prefer to say, a Christian view of history—which makes faith into a religious law.

[266] That is a flat contradiction of the meaning of *Kerygma Petrou*, which is perfectly clear in Aristides and *Diogn.*: the tripartite division of humanity into Greeks, Jews, and Christians fundamentally excludes a pre-Christian revelation (despite the commonality of the εἷς θεός–εἷς κύριος) to the Jews, for what they lack, of course, is the Christian revelation, even if *Ker. Petr.*, Aristides, and *Diogn.* make some practical concessions to the Jews.

[267] Theophilus 1.10; 2.2.

[268] Jews: Aristides 14; *Diogn.* 3.1. On what follows, see Origen on John 13:17.

[269] Aristides 14.4. Origen, *Contra Cels.* 5.2ff.: Celsus charges the Jews with worshiping angels and says that they were following Moses' instructions in this. Origen responds with the question of where he found this in the writings of Moses. E. von Dobschütz (*Kerygma*) notes that Justin (*Apol.* 1.6) and Athenagoras (10.4) no longer make this charge against the Jews—precisely because they advocate a *Christian* worship of angels.

("He made a new covenant with us; for what belonged to the Greeks and Jews is old. But we, who worship Him in a new way, in the third form, are Christians").[270]

Despite their appeal to the Scriptures, the Christians do without the idea of a salvation-historical continuity. From the perspective of the *new* covenant, Gentiles and Jews are lumped together as "old." In the concept of the new covenant, the emphasis is entirely on the "*new*," that is, on the discontinuity.[271]

What is lacking in the *Kerygma Petrou* can be seen by a glance at Justin, *Dial.* 11: here too we find the ideas of the new covenant (Jeremiah 31), Christ as the eternal law, the selfhood of God. But there is a completely different level of hermeneutical reflection.

In frag. 3 the worldwide missionary commission of the apostles is explained (the missionary command given after the resurrection). The content of the message, among other things: sins that one unwittingly commits will be forgiven, if one repents and acknowledges God.

The church, faced with the prospect of the future judgment, is seen from the point of view of the world mission, of hearing and faith. But a salvation-historical look back at Israel is also missing from the concept of mission. A theology in the sense of an economy of salvation is not yet present.

In frag. 4 Clement says about Peter: "And somewhat later he adds the following statement, by declaring that the prophecies have come to pass by divine providence."[272]

The Presbyter in Irenaeus, Adv. Haer. 4.27.1–32.1[273]

The section deals with the proper use of Scripture, including the use of Scripture in relation to Israel. It is traced back to a presbyter who received his teaching from acquaintances and disciples of the apostles.

For the Israelites of the Old Testament, the admonitions and corrections given by the Scriptures were sufficient. *We* do not need to continue to offer the same rebukes that have already been made in the Scriptures. We cannot be more than the Master. The transgressions of Israel were written down for *our* admonition. Israel and we have the same God, and his righteousness is the

---

[270] Schneemelcher: "as the third race." Harnack, *Mission* 1:274f.: they worship God anew *in a third way;* Christians are not yet there called "the third race" (ibid.). Oepke substantially agrees: note the dative τρίτῳ γένει ("third race"). On the expression, see Aristides 16.4; *Diogn.* 1; Harnack, *Mission* 1:266ff.; its use by opponents of the Christians: Harnack, *Mission* 1:275ff.; Oepke, *Gottesvolk*, 266ff. See further on *Diogn.*

[271] This is a discontinuity that, otherwise than in *Diogn.* 11, is not bridged by a Christology of preexistence.

[272] Von Campenhausen, *Formation,* 88.

[273] Hennecke-Schneemelcher, *NTApoc.* 2:759ff.; G. Bornkamm, "Πρέσβυς," *TDNT* 6:677ff.; M. Widmann, "Irenaeus und seine theologischen Väter," *ZTK* 54 (1957) 156–73.

same. Both Testaments derive from the same God, the Creator.[274] The Lord descended into the underworld in order to bring the message of his advent to the Old Testament saints.[275] In the New Testament, faith in the Son of God is added to the recipe as an extra ingredient.

The relation of Jews and Christians, as it is determined through Christ: "If therefore the Jews had not become the murderers of the Lord (which they also did to eternal life), and if they had not killed the apostles and persecuted the church and thus fallen into the bottomless pit of wrath, then we could not have been saved. For just as they received salvation through the blindness of the Egyptians, we have attained it through the blindness of the Jews. . . ."[276]

Aristides[277]

With Aristides we find ourselves even more in the transitional phase toward a fully developed apologetic.[278] The problem of reconstructing the text poses a difficulty for analyzing and evaluating his work. R. Seeberg ("Die Apologie des Aristeides untersucht und wieder hergestellt," in T. Zahn, *Forschungen zur Geschichte der ntl. Kanons* 5/2 [1893]: 159ff.) argues for the primacy of the Syrian text (Syr). The Greek (G) text is preferred by Geffcken (whose text is also found in G. Ruhback, *Altkirchliche Apologeten* 1 [Gütersloh: G. Mohn, 1966]). The Syrian text is also the basis for the translation of K. Julius, *Die Apologie des Philosophen Aristides,* Bibliothek der Kirchenväter 12 (Munich: Kösel, 1913), which also gives an index of parallels.

H. Lietzmann (*History of the Early Church* 2:177) evaluates him as "a man of mediocre culture"; at first there is nothing particularly Christian. "The positive recommendation of Christianity only comes in at the end. Here again there is no discussion, nothing repudiated or proved, but simply something recounted" (p. 178).

The questions of date of composition and identity of the addressees[279] require that we again note the expression that describes Christians as the "third race"[280] (chap. 2).[281] And 16:4: "And truly, this is a *new* people." Harnack, *Mission* 1:277: the "explicit formula" of Christians as a "third race" is found, besides *Kerygma*

---

[274] Thus an anti-Marcionite polemic.

[275] *Adv. Haer.* 4.28; cf. Marcion above.

[276] *Adv. Haer.* 4.30: Christians in the world; the *pax romana;* "for everything that we unjustly obtained while we were pagans we have refined and ennobled as believers by using it in the service of the Lord, and are so justified."

[277] See above on *Kerygma Petrou:* Harnack, *History of Dogma* 2:179: used by Aristides; see Schneemelcher in Hennecke-Schneemelcher, *NTApoc.* 2:96.

[278] Geffcken, *Apologeten,* xxxix; C. Andresen, *RGG³*; see under the first Apology.

[279] Hadrian (Andresen; O'Ceallaigh, see below); Antoninus Pius (Harnack; Geffcken).

[280] *Ker. Petr.; Diogn.*

[281] The Syriac text divides them into four groups: Barbarians, Greeks, Jews, and Christians.

Petrou (but see above, Harnack, *Mission* 1:274f.) and Clement of Alexandria only in Pseudo-Cyprian (*De pascha computus* 17).[282]

Does a *literary* relation exist between Aristides and *Diogn.?* Compare Aristides 2: ὅτι τρία γένη εἰσὶν ἀνθρώπων ἐν τῷδε τῷ κόσμῳ, ὧν εἰσὶν οἱ τῶν παρ' ὑμῖν λεγομένων θεῶν προσκυνηταὶ καὶ Ἰουδαῖοι καὶ Χριστιανοί ("that there are three classes of people in this world, these being the worshipers of the gods acknowledged among you, and Jews, and Christians").

Aristides 16:4 "And truly, this is a new people," with *Diogn.* 1: οὔτε τοὺς νομιζομένους ὑπὸ τῶν Ἑλλήνων θεοὺς λογίζονται οὔτε τὴν Ἰουδαίων δεισιδαιμονίαν φυλάσσουσι . . . καὶ τί δή ποτε καινὸν τοῦτο γένος ἢ ἐπιτήδευμα εἰσῆλθεν εἰς τὸν βίον νῦν καὶ οὐ πρότερον ("they [=Christians] neither recognize those that are considered gods by the Greeks, nor hold the superstition of the Jews . . . and why this new race or practice entered into the present time of life and not earlier").

Diogn.	Aristides
2.3	3.2 (topos)
2.2	3.3
2.4, 7	3.2; 13.2
3.1-5	1.4; 13.4; 14
6.7	16.6
8.2	3.3; 4f.
10.2	1.3

---

[282] Clement of Alexandria, *Strom.* 3.10.70: συνῆγε λαοὺς τοὺς δύο, τρίτος δὲ ἦν ἐκ τῶν δυοῖν κτιζόμενος εἰς καινὸν ἄνθρωπον ("he was gathering the two peoples, and a third was being created from the two into a new human race") (cf. Eph. 2:15; also *Diogn.* 2). Further, *Strom.* 5.14.98; 5.15.42. Pseudo-Cyprian: the fiery furnace was not able to harm Hananiah, Azariah, and Mishael, "in mysterio nostro, qui sumus tertium genus hominum" ("in our religion, we who are a third race of humanity").

Tertullian appears to be acquainted with the phrase as a generic term but rejects it (*Ad. nat.* 1.8.1): "Plane, tertium genus dicimur" ("We are indeed said to be the 'third race' of men"). This designation makes sense neither chronologically nor in terms of the history of religion: "Cynopennae aliqui vel Sciapodes vel aliqui de subterraneo Antipodes. Si qua istic apud vos saltem ratio est, edatis velim primum et secundum genus, ut ita de tertio constet" ("What, a dog-faced race? Or broadly shadow-footed? Or some subterranean Antipodes? If you attach any meaning to these names, pray tell us what are the first and the second race, that so we may know something of this 'third'"). *Scorp.* 10: In the circus, people shout questions about how long this "third race" is going to be allowed to exist. *Ad. nat.* 1.20: Obscene ideas are connected with the expression: "Habetis et vos tertium genus etsi non de tertio ritu, attamen de tertio sexu. Illud aptius de viro et femina viris et feminis iunctum" ("You too have your 'third race'; not indeed third in the way of religious rite, but a third race in sex, and, made up as it is of male and female in one, it is more fitted to men and women [for offices of lust]").

P. Corssen (*Neue Jahrbücher für das klass. Altertum* 18 [1915]: 158ff.), contrary to Harnack, wants to explain the use of this designation in terms of the meaning "eunuch-ism," "perversity." Oepke, *Gottesvolk,* 267: *aptius* ("it is more fitted") indicates that Tertullian introduces this term as a new designation, for the sake of argument, but agrees that the pagan designation did not derive from the Christians.

The comparison indicates that no *literary* dependence can be established.[283] On the use of Paul: There are no quotations present. Allusions (but vague) are noted by K. Julius. There can be no talk of Paul's having played a role in the formation of the theology of Aristides (to the extent that one is willing to speak of such a theology at all).

The theme that dominates the beginning is the doctrine of the *one* God, the Creator.[284] God has no *names*. Names belong to created things.[285] G: There are three categories of human beings: polytheists, Jews, and Christians; the polytheists in turn are divided into Chaldeans, Hellenes, and Egyptians.

This arrangement provides a scheme for dealing with what then follows.[286] Into this framework are inserted the apologetic arguments and topoi, in the text as reconstructed by Geffcken: the Chaldeans (or else barbarians) worship the elements, that is, the creation instead of the creator, and they make images for themselves (G: of the heavens, the earth, the sea, the stars), shut them up in their temples, and worship them as gods. Their philosophers have also fallen into this same error (cf. *Diogn.* 8.2), the worship of transitory elements, which by nature are no gods (Gal. 4:8); the motif of "elements" is broadly elaborated.

The further error is that human beings are made into gods.[287] The Greeks erred even worse, these people who called themselves wise and thus became fools. As expected, next comes the critique of mythology, moralizing with an admixture of ridicule, as it has been indefatigably repeated from the time of Jewish apologetic (cf. still 13.8). The individual gods are dealt with in remarkable fullness. Everyone knows in advance what will be said about the Egyptians. According to the Syrian text they are the most evil, while the Greek text lumps the Egyptians, Chaldeans, and Greeks with their worship of images all together, again with a jab at the poets and philosophers. Then the critique of sacrifices from the old tradition is taken up again, with a reference to God's

---

[283] Geffcken, *Apologeten*, xxxiiiff.: Source criticism in the strict sense is not possible in Aristides. We can be confident only that he used the New Testament, especially Paul. Nor can the use of *Ker. Petr.* be established. And *Diogn.* is later.

[284] With the beginnings of a development toward a natural theology and the accumulation of negative predicates of God, which is reminiscent of *Ker. Petr.*

[285] Philo, *Somn.* 1.230. This is an essential point in the debate between Origen and Celsus (1.24); cf. Justin, *Apol.* 2.5; Tatian 4; Minucius Felix 18; Pseudo-Justin, *Coh.* 21. Thus it is a matter of rejecting the *pagan* monotheism: that *one* god is worshiped under many names; cf. *Ep. Ar.* 15; Seneca, *De mundo* 7; idem, *Nat. quaest.* 2.4.

[286] The Syriac text has a secondary variation: there are four categories—Barbarians and Greeks, Jews and Christians. Then follows a brief characterization of each, namely, the establishment of their origin, then a detailed debate with the Chaldeans (G) or Barbarians, Greeks, Egyptians, and then in a remarkable doublet, again with the Greeks.

[287] The Syriac text is clearly anti-euhemeristic, opposing the idea that men of the prehistoric period were gods.

aseity.[288] Then comes a reference to the laws of the Greeks, which is also a topos (13.7 or 8).[289]

Chapter 14 introduces the discussion of the Jews, whose monotheism is certified. "And they emulate God himself through their love of humanity." "But their knowledge of God too has become less than exact" through their cultic rituals, because they thereby "are directing their worship to angels and not to God" (see *Ker. Petr.* above).[290]

Finally comes the discussion of the Christians, who derive from the Lord Jesus Christ, the Son of the Most High God, who descends from heaven in the power of the Holy Spirit, was born of the Virgin, and took on human flesh. He was nailed to the cross by the Jews and arose from the dead after three days.

They know the Creator, keep his commandments, live in hope of the resurrection and the life of the new age (*Diogn.* 5). They do not practice sexual immorality; their women live pure lives; their fellowship is praised. "Just take their Scriptures and read them!" Once again they are contrasted with the Greeks. The book concludes with the prospect of the future judgment.

Even a first glance makes it apparent that we have here no work of art, that it was not cast as *one* piece but has been patched together from a variety of elements. There are traces of an overall plan but also interruptions in the pattern of thought, doublets, *non sequiturs;* in fact, all these are of such a nature that any effort to reconstruct the sources appears hopeless. Nevertheless, the attempt has recently been made: G. C. O'Ceallaigh, "'Marcianus' Aristides, on the Worship of God," *HTR* 51 (1958): 227ff. His thesis: The work is a Christian reworking of a Jewish protreptic-apologetic writing, not an apology for the Christians, but directed to a Hellenistic-Jewish proselyte, with Christian interpolations. This is seen in the contrast between the two Christian sections and the rest of the work.

The starting point of the discussion must be the first of the two items of information alleged by the title of the Syrian text: to Hadrian (only to him) concerning true religion (cf. Eusebius, *Hist. Eccl.* 4.3.3 Armenian). Note that the address alternates between addressing the ruler(s) in the singular and in the plural.[291]

---

[288] *Diogn.* 3.3; Athenagoras 13; Aristides 13.5: The poets and philosophers "muster their arguments and affirm that the *nature* of all their gods is *one* and they have never recognized God, our Lord, who, while he is *one,* is in all and everything." Then comes a critique of the mythology of the battles of the gods.

[289] Cf. already Josephus.

[290] On the reconstruction of chap. 14, see Geffcken, *Apologeten,* 82f.: The original form is to be derived from the Syrian text. "The Greek text has an absolutely foolishly tendentious portrayal, which even charges the Jews with frequent relapses into paganism. And of course the familiar angry outburst against the Jews for the crucifixion of Christ is not lacking, which is alien to the other apologists" (p. 82 n. 1).

[291] But what does this prove? There has, to be sure, been a reworking, but still not of the sort that O'Ceallaigh postulates. The Christians can hardly be removed from the basic source document so easily. Precisely because a *three*fold division of humanity was there originally, it is more likely

The Arguments

(1) The *Egyptians,* not mentioned in the preface of the Syrian and Armenian texts, receive three times as much space as the Jews. (What does this prove?) (2) Half of the material about the Christians derives from the description of the Jews (cf. chap. 15); the other half is interpolated.[292] (3) The barbarians are descended from Kronos and Rhea. That is in contradiction to the source (cf. chaps. 9f.): the *Greeks* consider Kronos to be their highest god (Rhea is also included here; see further on 11.5). It is not possible that the original author distinguished Greeks and barbarians, only then to state that the Greeks named as their first gods deities from whom the barbarians were descended.[293] (4) The *Greeks:* the author confuses Helena, the daughter of Zeus and Leda, with Hellen, the son of Deucalion and Pyrrha.[294] (5) The *Jews* receive this name in Egypt. Nowhere else is it said that the designation "Hebrews" was given by Moses.[295] There is no room in this context for the idea that the Jews descended from Abraham.[296] The Christian confession of faith in chap. 15 does not fit here and is in itself incorrect: Jesus is descended from the Hebrew race.[297] Behind the credo stands a text that referred to the fulfilling of the economy of salvation.[298]

---

to have been seen as a division between Greeks, Jews, and Christians than between barbarians, Greeks, and Jews; cf. also the alternation between barbarians and Chaldeans. And a contrasting of Jews and Christians can hardly be excluded.

Still, on the grouping of nations and peoples, cf. Josephus, *Ag. Ap.* 1.7f., 14, 70f.; Tatian 39; Theophilus 2.31.

What is said above does not exclude the possibility that Aristides made use of a Jewish apology. A Christian could incorporate a Jewish, monotheistic writing as the "first" article of his creed. The only question is whether a neat separation of sources is possible at all, especially in a work such as that of Aristides.

[292] The evidence for an interpolation is weak. And in the part that could be "Jewish," parallels are found to *Diogn.* and Minucius Felix; see further below on 14.4–15.3a.

[293] Thus it is to be concluded that the threefold schema originally contained not the *barbarians* but the Greeks (–Jews–Christians). Besides, the establishment of the aforementioned contradictions does not support O'Ceallaigh's thesis. Anyway, when the occasion arises he should spend some time studying the Kronos mythology.

[294] 8.1: "on the basis of which it is said that he is from Zeus." What was said in the preceding note applies, *mutatis mutandis,* also here.

[295] Philo, *Mut. Nom.* 117; Josephus, *Ant.* 1.146.

[296] In which? Obviously the Syrian. But why not? On Abraham as ancestor, see Reinach, *Textes,* index; Artapanus; Nicholas of Damascus, Stern, *GLAJJ,* no. 83; Josephus, *Ant.* 1.159f.; Pompeius Trogus 36.2, Stern, *GLAJJ,* no. 137; Theophilus 3.9.

[297] What is the problem with that? Perhaps the juxtaposition of virgin birth and Jewish origin?

[298] (a) The catchword "economy" does not prove that. (b) What support would this give to the hypothesis? (c) One can in fact bracket 14.4–15.3 as an interpolation. Then 15.4 applies to the Jews. But then other interpolations must be postulated: 15.12 and chaps. 16–17. (d) Concerning 14.4: the charge of angel worship presupposes Clement of Alexandria, *Strom.* 6.5.41 and Origen, *Contra Cels.* 1.26; 5.6–8. —See above: the passage from Clement of Alexandria is in fact *Ker. Petr.*

Results

The basic element is the polemic of a monotheist against the three pagan groups—the Chaldeans, the Greeks, and the Egyptians. Structure: (1) Introduction. (2) Exposition. (3) Brief conclusion. The same structure prevails in the description of the *Jews,* if the Christian elements are bracketed out. —Comment: (a) "If"! *petitio principii;* (b) mechanical.

According to O'Ceallaigh, the relation of Aristides to the later apologists is to be defined negatively: it is, to be sure, referred to the promise of the fathers, but neither the Old Testament nor the New Testament is quoted.[299] The whole Old Testament history of salvation is reduced to a few statements about the Jews: they are monotheists, have a lawgiver, are descended from Abraham. No positive relationship to the Christians is determined by this. —The author's acquaintance with the sources is inadequate. He attempts to apply his hypothesis to inappropriate materials.

The Letter to Diognetus (Diogn.)[300]

We will discuss this document here, even if it should be dated later (ca. 200), because the apologetic technique is only embryonically developed.[301] Even the expression already mentioned above in the discussion of *Kerygma Petrou* about the "new race" (chap. 1; cf. Aristides 16.4) does not lead to any more precisely

---

[299] Still, there are many allusions to the New Testament.

[300] Editions: Funk-Bihlmeyer, *Die Apostolischen Väter,* 144ff. (Bib.); H. I. Marrou, in SC (Paris: Cerf, 1951). Translations: Geffcken in Hennecke, *Neutestamentliche Apokryphen,* 2nd ed. (Tübingen: Mohr-Siebeck, 1942) 619ff.; G. Rauschen, *"Der Brief an Diognet"* in *frühchristliche Apologeten und Märtyrerakten,* Bibliothek der Kirchenväter 12 (Kampen and Munich: Kösel, 1913) 157ff. Literature: H. G. Meecham, *The Epistle of Diognetus* (Manchester: Manchester University Press, 1949); L. W. Barnard, *ZNW* 56 (1965) 130ff.; idem, *Apostolic Fathers,* 165ff.: "The Enigma of the Epistle to Diognetus": *Diogn.* 1–10 has *Jews* in view, but 11–12, Christians and catachumens; but it is the same author. Chapters 1–10 were written no later than 130; the Christology is more primitive than in Justin (an argument?); W. Eltester, "Das Mysterium des Christentums: Anmerkungen zum Diognetbrief," *ZNW* 61 (1970): 278–93; R. Brändle, *Die Ethik der "Schrift an Diognet,"* ATANT 64 (Zurich: Theologischer Verlag, 1975). For parallels, Marrou may generally be consulted. A. Lindemann, "Paulinische Theologie im Brief an Diognet," in *Kerygma und Logos,* Festschrift C. Andresen (Göttingen: Vandenhoeck & Ruprecht, 1979) 337ff.

[301] Contrast E. Molland, "Die literatur- und dogmengeschichtliche Stellung des Diognetbriefs," *ZNW* 33 (1934): 289ff.: In comparison with Aristides, *Diogn.* is more advanced. Lindemann emphasizes the strong Pauline coloration of the letter. He places *Diogn.* in the middle of the second century. —But any effort at trying to establish the date is a wasted labor of love. Marrou points out what is *lacking* in *Diogn.:* (a) a formal refutation of current widespread slanders; a discussion that deals with the legal aspects of the matter; (b) that the Christians were responsible for the catastrophes suffered by the empire (cf. Tertullian, *Apol.* 40f.; Origen, *Contra Cels.* 3.15); (c) problems associated with the resurrection; (d) an explicit reference to the Scriptures (but see the exception in chap. 12); no proof of antiquity; cf. *Ker. Petr.;* Aristides 16.5; on the other hand, see Justin, *Apol.* 1.58f.; Tatian 29, 31; Athenagoras 9; Theophilus 1.14; 2.9, 38; 3.26, 29f.

apologetic effort.[302] The expression has meaning in a perspective that divides all humanity into Gentiles, Jews, and Christians (see above on Aristides 2), a perspective in which "salvation history" is not only ignored but excluded. This denial is a basic motif of the whole letter (including chaps. 11–12).

The fundamental problem of "newness" and the historical period of revelation is presented in chap. 1.[303] The introduction[304] formulates the problem: that the Christians place little value on this world, despise death, do not accept the gods of the Greeks, and do not observe the δεισιδαιμονία ("religion, superstition"; cf. chap. 3) of the Jews.

Chapter 2 begins the response by first making an appeal to become a new person (cf. Eph. 4:24; Col. 3:10).[305] Then follows (in accordance with the typical topoi of the apologetic tracts) in the appropriate style the polemic against images, beginning with a reference to the material of which the gods are manufactured (as in *Ker. Petr.*), materials usually specified for a particular "secular" use. (cf. also *Ker. Petr.*). Derision is poured out on these practices in the customary manner: one must be careful that the valuable material such as silver, is not stolen! (cf. Aristides 3.2; Justin, *Apol.* 1.9; Minucius Felix 24). Inexpensive idols can be left unguarded, but valuable ones must be locked up to be on the safe side.

After the material, the next item in the line of topoi is that of the artists who manufacture the idols.

You hate the Christians, because they do not regard all this to be gods—and you yourselves ridicule it. A living God would not endure the stink of your offerings! (doublet of 2.8; 3.5). (Cf. Lucian's ridicule!) That should be enough of this sort of thing!

The Jews are next in turn, in chap. 3. (cf. Aristides 14). They have, of course, avoided the kind of idolatry that has just been portrayed, but they have gone astray in that they attempt to worship God in the same way as the pagans,

---

[302] Harnack (*Mission* 1:274) translates "This new race or institution." Rauschen: "This new way of living and worshipping God." Geffcken: "This new people, this completely new entity." Oepke, *Gottesvolk,* 266: In *Diogn.* 1 "the idea of a new national community has already emerged, but the author resists it."

[303] On the contextual relations, see Marrou, 202ff. Since "newness" is a category of thought here, *Diogn. cannot* give a "proof of the antiquity." Brändle sees the raising of the themes of "newness" as a response to a pagan charge. Especially Celsus is to be compared at this point. —But in *Diogn.* the dominant role is played by the positive presentation of the determination of the time of revelation from the point of view of his Christology (see under chap. 9, when it is read together with chap. 11). Marrou appropriately points out that the "optimistic" explanation of the problem of the (late) time of the Christian revelation by means of the idea of the education and preparation of humanity (Irenaeus, Clement, Origen) is missing in *Diogn.*

[304] Cf. Luke 1:1-4; Melito in Eusebius, *Hist. Eccl.* 4.26.12–13.

[305] There is a correspondence between the idea of the (old-) new Logos (cf. 11.4) and the new humanity that is manifest in the new human community, the Christians. Here too the idea of "newness" replaces the presumed continuity expressed in "salvation history."

namely, through the offering of sacrifice.[306] The topos of the aseity of the deity is extensively dealt with.

Chapter 4 discusses the Jewish rites in detail (like *Ker. Petr.* and Aristides) and castigates them.[307] The Jews also are subjected to ridicule. There is no mention of continuity between them and the Christians.[308]

The course of thought that leads to chap. 5 presents certain difficulties. Eltester suggests that it be improved by reversing the order of two sections, that is, by following 4.6 (concluding remarks about the falsehood of the Jews) directly with 5.3 (Christians are not advocates of a merely human doctrine).[309]

Thus, chap. 5 deals with the Christians: although they reside in Greek and barbarian cities, they preserve their indigenous way of life (5.5).[310] They are distinguished by their morality (5.6-12).[311]

Then follows a series of paradoxical affirmations in excellent rhetorical style.[312] Chap. 6.1: Briefly stated, Christians are to the world what the soul is to the body (cf. Aristotle, *Eth. Nic.* 1096 b 29). This is elaborated;[313] it is the Christians who hold the world together.[314]

Chapter 7: They are not entrusted with the management of human matters. God, the Creator, planted the holy Logos within humanity.[315] 7.7: "Do you not see how they are thrown to wild animals to make them to deny the Lord, and now they are not vanquished? Do you not see that the more they are punished, the more do others increase? These things do not seem to come from a human power; they are a mighty act of God. They are the proof of his presence" (Library of Christian Classics trans.) (cf. Minucius Felix 31.7). "As a

---

[306] Aristides 1.6; 13.4; *Ker. Petr.;* Justin, *Apol.* 1.10; Minucius Felix 33. So also *Diogn.:* as though there were something that God needed; cf. Aristides 13.4; Athenagoras 13; Tertullian, *Apol.* 30; *Sib. Or.* 8.390f.

[307] Here too the viewpoint is introduced, "which was intended for human use"; see above Minucius Felix 32.2.

[308] Also the concession in 3.2 is only as a background for the dissociation of Jews and Christians and the association of Jews and Gentiles in one category.

[309] Cf. the return to the subject in 7.1. The rearrangement hardly settles anything.

[310] The "worldliness" of Christians is contrasted (a) with the Jews, (b) with the Christians own unworldliness.

[311] For example, sexual purity (5.7): Aristides 15.4, 6; Justin, *Apol.* 1.15; Athenagoras 33 etc.; reminiscences of the familiar charges against the Christians; Athenagoras 31f.

[312] 5.17: ὑπὸ Ἰουδαίων ὡς ἀλλόφυλοι πολεμοῦνται καὶ ὑπὸ Ἑλλήνων διώκονται. καὶ τὴν αἰτίαν τῆς ἔχθρας εἰπεῖν οἱ μισοῦντες οὐκ ἔχουσιν ("they are attacked by Jews as aliens, and are persecuted by Greeks; and they who hate them cannot tell the reason of their hatred").

[313] On chap. 6, see Marrou, 130ff.: cf. Plato, *Phaedr.* 62b; Axiochus 365f.; Athenagoras 6; Aristides 16.1, 6. In comparison with Aristides, *Diogn.* manifests a certain popular philosophical trait: Stoicism.

[314] Aristides 16.6; Tertullian. On chap. 7, see Marrou, 181ff. For a defense against the charge that the Christians were uneducated, see Celsus; Minucius Felix 19ff.; cf. the corresponding charge against the Jews. The main thing, of course, is not the defense itself but the positive development of the idea of revelation; 7.2.

[315] Thus, a concept of revelation in the style of a cosmic Christology.

matter of fact, before he came, what man had any knowledge of God at all?" (Again: newness).

Then comes yet another polemic against the philosophers and acknowledging the elements as gods. No human being has ever seen or acknowledged God; but he has revealed the knowledge of himself.

There are variations on the "schema of revelation" (deutero-Pauline):[316] 8:9: "And when he had planned a great and unutterable design, he communicated it to his son [παῖς="son, child, servant") alone."

Chapter 9: Until then he lets us follow our own impulses.[317] This should bring to light that we cannot enter the kingdom of God by our own strength. But God has compassionately given his own Son as a ransom.[318]

Chapter 10: This faith leads to a knowledge of the Father, who loves humanity.

A parenetic section is introduced in 10.4, which has as its goal the strengthening of those who imitate God, in view of coming death and judgment.

Most scholars argue for the view that chaps. 11–12 are a secondary addition, but Marrou[319] has a very different view. "I am not speaking of things that are strange to me, nor is my undertaking unreasonable, for I have been a disciple of apostles, and now I am becoming a teacher of the Gentiles" (i.e., Scripture, tradition, but no salvation history), but the instruction that comes through the Logos (11.3), whom God sent in order that he might be revealed to the world.

Chapter 12: "You have become a Paradise of delight" (12.1). This is the place where the Tree of Knowledge and the Tree of Life have been planted. "It was not the Tree of Knowledge, however, which destroys; it is disobedience" (12.2). Concerning the story of paradise: There is no life without knowledge, and no sure knowledge without true life.[320] In this spirit the story is spun out to its end.

---

[316] From the point of view of this scheme, history is divided into two parts (cf. chap. 9).

[317] Although reference is later made to Genesis 1–2, there is no mention of Adam or the Fall; in place of salvation history there is a generalizing look at humanity before the coming of the revelation. The point in time when righteousness was revealed was not determined by the "fullness of time," but by the fact that sin had reached its full development (9.2).

[318] The role of δικαιοσύνη ("righteousness") and δικαιοῦν ("justify, make right") in chap. 9 is worthy of note. The modification of the Pauline doctrine of justification is to be examined with regard to its connection with the schema of revelation and is to be compared with the development from Paul to the deutero-Pauline writings (Ephesians).

[319] One can certainly establish differences in theological emphases: on the one hand, the Son, the Christians, and the Jews; and, on the other, the Word, the church, the Old Testament, and the prophets. But we have already seen several cases where the ways the relation of Christians to the Old Testament and to Judaism is expressed by one and the same author do not need to coincide. The shift of perspective does not prove that different authors are writing.

On the use of the Bible, see von Campenhausen, *Formation*, 98: Until the time of Justin the usual church use of the Bible was not at all "salvation-historically" oriented in the narrow sense.

[320] For confirmation, the apostle is quoted (1 Cor. 8:1).

THE FULLY DEVELOPED APOLOGETIC SITUATION

Justin

The External Relations between Jews and Christians

The intensification of the persecution of Christians in the course of the second century was a contributing factor to the external relations between Jews and Christians. Jews also participated in the persecution (*Diogn.* 5.17). This fact is not to be doubted, even if the Jews are not mentioned frequently in the stories of the martyrs. Their hatred of Christians is a substantial theme in Justin.[321] The Jews were the more powerful group. It is clear from Justin that even after the Bar Kochba revolt their influence in the Roman Empire was still strong.

The Christians were commanded to return hatred with love (*Dial.* 96). They held fast to the view that the Jews were their brothers and sisters (ibid.), although from the perspective of the persecution, Jews and Gentiles were on the same side. If they persist in their unbelief and continue the persecution, divine judgment is announced for both (*Diogn.;* for Justin, see below).[322] Hyldahl, *Philosophie,* 270f.:

> The theological problematic with regard to the relationship between Jews and Christians, in connection with the understanding of the Scripture that was bound up with this relationship . . . had by Justin's time *become a part of Christianity itself* [the author's own emphasis]. Thus it cannot be surprising that Justin here takes the same standpoint as Luke, since he stands on the same plane as Luke with regard to political-legal apologetic. Just as, according to Luke, the Jews are now called through the proclamation of the Christian message to demonstrate that they are truly (Israel) by accepting it, but remain merely (Jews) if they do not respond to the call, so according to Justin, anyone who wants to claim to inherit God's promises must keep the new law and the new covenant.[323] Those Jews who formerly had done what was customarily, naturally, and in every age has been considered good, will be saved, but not those Jews who now live according to the law and do not believe that Jesus is the Christ. . . . And it is precisely the same (rationalism) that is manifest in the way the Scripture is interpreted in both Luke and Justin: Christianity is not to be identified with nonsense, empty myths, or mere words

---

[321] A. Harnack, *Judentum und Judenchristentum in Justins Dialog,* TU 39.1 (Leipzig: Hinrichs, 1913) 47ff.; idem, *History of Dogma* 2:187 n. 1: Since Justin, the writings against the Gentiles are the anteroom of Christian knowledge; this is further developed in the writings against the Jews.

[322] These are especially emphasized in N. Hyldahl, *Philosophie und Christentum,* Acta Theologica Danica 9 (Copenhagen, 1966). Nor is Justin interested in attaining for the Christians the same status that the Jews have but wants to keep separate the problems of Jews/Christians and state/church (p. 266).

[323] There is a terminological difference between Luke and Justin here that is not to be overlooked.

that cannot be proven, but with truth and reason . . . ;[324] thus it was not, as Harnack argued, the apologists who first made Christianity into a rational entity,[325] but the rationality of Christianity springs from the way it understands Scriptures.[326] As for Luke the Jews do not understand the Scriptures and this is made into a charge against them because of their hardheartedness, so also for Justin. . . . Just as, according to Luke, the true prophecies of the Old Testament mirror the sovereign decision and saving plan of God and thus are divinely inspired, Justin too is convinced—in direct opposition to the Stoic understanding of the nature of prediction and the doctrine of fate (*heimarmenē*)[327]—that God so operates that he causes events to be predicted before they occur, and that the agreements between prediction and event can be proven. . . . Just as the events of Jesus' life are for Luke the demonstrable proof that the prophets had truly prophesied (seen most clearly in Luke 24:44), so for Justin the "memoirs of the apostles" contain the evidence that the prophets have spoken the truth. . . .

We should, of course, attend to the essential *difference* between Luke and Justin provided by the theological developments of the great Gnostic thinkers of the second century that had occurred in the meantime.[328] The debate that necessarily was associated with this development led to a new level of thought for the theological engagement with the pagan world, for the problem of the Old Testament, of the relation of Christianity and Judaism, and above all for the nature of Christianity itself. The problems of the Old Testament, Judaism, and Christianity are now seen to be more closely related.[329] Thereby a new reflection on history came into being, of which Luke was not yet aware—for now the Christians possessed their own canon of Scriptures.[330]

This decisive new turn of thought is found in Justin.[331] The step forward

---

[324] *This* theme is not yet developed by Luke, for whom also, of course, the Logos concept is missing. The hermeneutic in Luke 24 is fundamentally different from that of Justin.

[325] In any case Luke does not do this.

[326] Only: now, and to which understanding of the Scripture?

[327] *Apol.* 1.43. In Luke, philosophical reflection is entirely missing, along with engagement with philosophical themes such as freedom of the will.

[328] Whether one lumps Marcion together with the Gnostics or not is an idle question for us here. For Justin the reference in *Dial.* 35 is sufficient. It is concerned exclusively with the identification of the God of the Old Testament patriarchs with the Father of the revelatory Logos.

[329] Von Campenhausen (*Formation*, 88) refers to the still primitive standpoint of *Ker. Petr.*: "We opened the books that we have from the prophets, and found their predictions to be correct. . . ."

[330] In the novel "three-front war" (von Campenhausen, *Formation*, 96) against heretics, pagans, and Jews. The *Letter to Diognetus*, with its doctrine of the preexistent Logos on the one side, but its disputing of a "preexisting" revelation on the other side, from which the simplistic threefold division Gentiles–Jews–Christians and the corresponding understanding of "newness" arose, had not yet grown into these problems, or else they had not yet become apparent to the author. On the new turn of thought in the letter of *Ptolemy to Flora* along with its demarcation of its position over against that of Marcion, see von Campenhausen, *Formation*, 82ff.

[331] Von Campenhausen, *Formation*, 82ff.; R. Seeberg, "Die Geschichtstheologie Justins des Märtyrers," *ZKG* 58 (1939): 1ff.; a response to this in Hyldahl, *Philosophie*, 52ff.; C. Andresen, "Justin und der mittlere Platonismus," *ZNW* 44 (1952/53): 157ff.; a response to this in Hyldahl, 60ff.; W. Schmid, "Frühe Apologetik und Platonismus," in *Hermeneia*, Festschrift O. Regenbogen

made by him is namely that he was "the first orthodox theologian who had anything like a 'doctrine of Holy Scripture.' His formulation of it was not merely a response to the Jews." From *Dial.*, one can "clearly perceive how much he has been affected precisely by his opponents within Christianity."[332]

Preview of the Problems Involved in Interpreting Justin

The problem that has certainly attracted the most attention is that of the relationship between philosophy (especially the doctrine of the λόγος σπερματικός or σπέρμα τοῦ λόγου) ("generative word," "seminal word") and Christianity (especially the theology of salvation history in connection with the Old Testament).[333]

Sample Evaluations

Harnack suggests that Justin's thought moves on two rather independent tracks.[334] Lietzmann (*History of the Early Church* 2.185f.) expresses himself more sharply:

(1952) 163ff. H. Chadwick, "Justin Martyr's Defence of Christianity," in *BJRL* 47 (1965): 275ff.; P. Keseling, "Justin's 'Dialog gegen Trypho' (c. 1-10) and Platons 'Protagoras,'" *Rheinisches Museum für Philologie* n.F. 75 (1926): 223ff.: the introduction to the *Dialogue* is structured according to Plato's *Protagoras;* a response to this in Hyldahl, 90f.: Justin's style of dialogue is not Platonic. E. F. Osborn, *Justin Martyr* (Tübingen: Mohr-Siebeck, 1973).

Justin's relation to the Old Testament: J. Daniélou, *Message évangélique et culture hellénistique au IIe et IIIe siécles* (Tournai: Desclée, 1961) 185ff. P. Prigent, *Justin et l'Ancien Testament* (Paris: Lecoffre, 1964): a thorough analysis of the dialogue under the presupposition mentioned above. The structure of Justin's syntagma are reconstructed: (1) Recapitulation; (2) the Messiah as a heavenly being; (3) the virgin birth; (4) the name of Jesus; (5) preexistence; (6) the passion; (7) Israel after the resurrection; (8) the rejection of Israel and the offer of salvation to the Gentiles; (9) conclusion: call to decision. —Question: How is this reconstruction to be related to Justin's own summary, namely, refutation of (Christian) heresies?

On the form of the *Dialogue*: A. B. Hulen, "The 'Dialogues with the Jews' as Sources for the Early Jewish Argument against Christianity," *JBL* 51 (1932) 58ff.; M. Hoffmann, *Der Dialog bei den christlichen Schriftstellern*, TU 96 (Berlin: Akademie-Verlag, 1966).

On the addressees of the writings *Adversus gentes* and *Adversus Iudaeos*: H. Tränkle, *Q.S.F. [Quintus Septimius Florens] Tertulliani Adversus Iudaeos* (Wiesbaden: F. Steiner, 1964), introduction, LXXff.: The genre *Adversus Iudaeos* is also directed to Christians, to people who already have a certain understanding; the primary reason for writing is not to teach the Jews or to dispute with them. Tränkle, LXXII: The genre *Adversus gentes* is directed to people to whom Christianity is still entirely unknown. —But this alternative is formulated too mechanically. The purpose of the writing is to be determined not from its "genre" but from its content. In the case of Justin: it is obvious that the *Dialogue* is also involved in an inner-church dispute with heretics. But this does not replace the call to repentance directed toward the Jews. If this is not recognized, the internal coherence of the statements about the Bible, prophecy and the law, Israel (the reception of the prophets' call to repentance), and the later Judaism (direct appeal) will be incomprehensible.

[332] Von Campenhausen, *Formation*, 88; cf. *Dial.* 30.

[333] Reviewed by Hyldahl, *Philosophie* (see n. 322).

[334] Harnack, *History of Dogma* 2:184; critical response by Hydahl, *Philosophie*, 38ff.

It is obvious that Justin's Christianity is divided into two halves; one is a philo-sophical religion that clothes Greek ideas and conceptions in a loose Biblical garment, and that in the end issues in man's self-redemption ethically conceived; the second aspect is that of the unreasoned faith of the church[335] in which words of Jesus, sacramental mysticism, and church-life combined to form an active unity. . . . Nor as yet had Justin grasped the necessity of uniting the two parts.[336]

An answer to the question posed by C. Andresen concerning the place of Justin in the history of philosophy will serve to clarify the foreground of the problem as a whole.[337] Even if one does not agree with his being included among the Middle Platonists,[338] the question of the proportionate roles played by philosophical and by "Christian" or Old Testament components[339] in the development of a philosophy (or theology) of history is still not answered.

Examples of the Wide Variety of Hypotheses

(1) *R. Seeberg* ("Die Geschichtstheologie Justins des Märtyrers," *ZTK* 58 [1939]): The Logos doctrine of the Apologists "expresses especially the imper-ialistic historical consciousness of the developing Church" (p. 1).[340] In *Apol.* 1.1–29 and 2.1–15 there is no reference to the Old Testament. "Where is the pre-history of Christianity to be located, in Judaism or in Greek history as such?" (p. 30). With the help of the schema "prophecy/fulfillment," Christian-ity claimed the Old Testament as its own; with the help of the Logos doctrine, Christianity took possession of Greek culture (pp. 30f.).[341]

(2) *C. Andresen* wants to define the relationship of philosophical knowledge and scriptural proof on the basis of *Dial.* 7: "It is not the philosophical character of the Scriptures as such that confers its probative authority on them, but the historical proof that is associated with them" ("Justin und der mittlere Platon-ismus," *ZNW* 44 [1952–53]: 195). "With this proof from Scripture there is bound up a very specific understanding of history, which in Justin has become a distinctive theology of history" (p. 195). Platonism is not the key to Justin's approach to history. "He offers no point of contact for a line of argument that functions historically; this argumentation was found by Justin in the kind of theology that was expressed in the 'proof from Scripture' that had already been formulated before him" (p. 195).[342] Even if his Logos doctrine is conditioned

---

[335] Cf. *Dial.* 134.5; 111.3; *Apol.* 1.18-20.

[336] Any interpretation will have to attend to the question of whether Justin did or did not subjec-tively see differentiation and whether or not the beginnings of a development toward a synthesis are recognizable.

[337] Cf. W. Schmid, "Frühe Apologetik."

[338] Opposed by Hyldahl, *Philosophie*, 60f.

[339] How these "components" are to be defined more precisely is an issue that may remain open for the moment.

[340] Response: (a) evidence? (b) what would this explain?

[341] *Sic!* Cf. *Apol.* 1.46; Hyldahl, *Philosophie*, 52ff.

[342] How is this thesis to be related to Andresen's postulation of a kind of historical thinking by

by philosophical ideas, Justin holds fast to the kind of thinking oriented toward
a history of revelation. He "does not evaluate the witness of the prophets as
a product of literary activity, but sees them in the framework of his theology
of history" (*Logos und Nomos*, 342, on *Apol.* 2.10). The schema of promise/
fulfillment is elaborated by means of his Logos theology of history, so that
"Greek history and culture too belong to the background of Christianity"
(p. 343). In comparison with the contemporary philosophy, that was something new: the Platonists left history to the historians. But *now* there is a saving
plan in history. The heroes of Greek intellectual history are demoted to forerunners of Christianity. This attack must have had the same effect on a philosopher as a burglar alarm, especially when the concepts of *Logos* and *Nomos*
were introduced (p. 344).[343]

(3) *H. von Campenhausen* (*Formation*, 98 n. 195): The salvation-historical
thinking of Justin "is simply the inevitable result of his standing by the Old
Testament."[344]

(4) Against Seeberg and Andresen: Hyldahl (*Philosophie*, 52ff., 60ff., respectively): *Dial.* 7.2 does not, as Andresen supposes, deal with the relationship of
philosophical knowledge and scriptural interpretation.[345] "That Justin's understanding of Plato is congruent with middle Platonism does not necessarily
mean that he was a middle Platonist" (p. 68). The theory of the λόγος σπερματικός ("generative/seminal Logos/word") is not to be derived from Middle
Platonism.[346] The key passage is *Dial.* 2.1f. taken with 7.1–9.3, with the idea

---

the Platonist Celsus? Andresen's response to this question (*Logos und Nomos*, 308ff.) asks: "Is
Celsus' theory of history to be conceived as an answer to the theology of history of Justin?"
(p. 309). If the true *Nomos* has been revealed through Christ, then necessarily the laws of the pagans
must be critically evaluated (p. 328). "The problem of the relativity of the various laws is not seen
in moralistic terms, but . . . in metaphysical ones" (p. 329) The revelation of the *Logos* in history
has consequences for the *Nomos* (p. 330). "It means the stabilizing of a world in which everything
had begun to shake." Thereby a religious foundation was provided for juridical obedience (*Apol.*
2.9ff.). From the viewpoint of revelation, the whole pre-Christian period was summarized as a time
of hostility (*Apol.* 1.14). Cf. *Diogn.*, which knows no pre-Christian revelation.

[343] One must supplement: these intellectual heroes were demoted to disciples of *Moses.* —Can
one really speak here of a "historical background?"

[344] It is also the case that the additional investigations of the seminal *Logos*/word concept made
by R. Holte, "Logos Spermatikos: Christianity and Ancient Philosophy according to St. Justin's
Apologies," *ST* 12 [1958]: 109–68) have simply led to the conclusion that only a few of Justin's
concepts are embraced in the seminal *Logos*/word theme and that for Justin all the substantial doctrines of philosophy, to the extent that they are true at all, are derived from the Old Testament.

[345] The δέ ("and" or "but") in τὰ δὲ ἀποβάντα ("and those events that have happened") does not
indicate a contrast to philosophical knowledge but indicates a contrast to τότε ("then"): *then* no
proof for the truth of philosophy and prophecy was provided; but *now* it can be delivered.

[346] Hyldahl contrasts this with the effect of Posidonius (*Philosophie*, 120ff.). Cf. the doctrine of
the primeval condition of things and the theory of their later deterioration; Seneca, *Ep.* 90. For
the evolutionary theory, see Plato, *Phileb.* 16b; cf. Andresen, *Logos*, 155f.; Diogenes Laertius 7.129:
One should not let the διαφωνία ("disagreement") pose a barrier to philosophy. It is not the concept
of the λόγος σπερματικός ("generative word/Logos") (a divine potency) that is central, but that of
the σπέρμα τοῦ λόγου ("generative power of the word") (a human potency).

of the rediscovery of the original philosophy; *this* is what Christianity is. Justin's understanding of history is constructed out of purely Greek presuppositions (p. 234). The given point of departure is Christianity, as it was available to Justin (p. 259). Greek philosophy, as Justin knew it, was the challenge that stood over against him as a Christian. His apologetic is the response by which he overcame this challenge. *God's namelessness is not taken by Justin from Middle Platonism but is rather from Philo* and derives from the idea of God's transcendence (p. 286). This again is a response to the Stoa (p. 287).[347] It is not the case that "Justin, and with him the other apologists, present us with a remarkable 'fusion' of Christian and Greek culture, but an extraordinarily courageous and difficult attempt to proclaim the Christian message to Graeco-Roman cultural world of the second century and to elaborate its meaning in this context. So simple it is, and at the same time, so complicated" (p. 295).

The Utilization of a Conceptuality Derived from Philosophy

Our approach compels us to direct attention to particular aspects of the Logos doctrine:

(1) One such is the idea of freedom of the will.[348] The problem presented itself to Justin in connection with the doctrine of the prediction of future events.[349] From the Stoic point of view one could suppose that the Christians, who accepted the idea of prediction, believed that everything happened according to the necessity of Fate. Justin had to resist this: without freedom there can be no responsibility.[350] If Heimarmene (fate) were the cause of evil, it would contradict itself. Justin appeals to Moses (Deut. 30:19) and Plato (*Resp.* 10.618e).[351]

Like every theologian who advocates the doctrine of *liberum arbitrium* ("free decision"), Justin must pay the price of understanding the doctrine of election and reprobation in a shallow, practically trivial manner.[352]

---

[347] Even if the "Philonic" thesis should turn out to be correct, it is too simple merely to derive this from the idea of transcendence. As is clear from the Jewish and Christian apologetic (especially so in Origen), the doctrine of the namelessness of God serves to distinguish the Christian understanding from the pagan would-be monotheism, that is, the doctrine that the one supreme being has many forms in which it has appeared and correspondingly can be worshiped under many different names.

[348] *Apol.* 1.43f.; 2.7; Osborn, *Justin*, 149ff.

[349] Namely, with the Stoics in view, who base their view of the possibility of predictions of the future on their theory of the rule of Heimarmene; Chrysippus in Eusebius, *Praep. Ev.* 4.3.2; Osborn, *Justin*, 139ff.; Pohlenz, *Stoa* 1:106ff.; documentation in 2:61f.

[350] This is also important for him for the time *before* the revelation.

[351] Who, of course, is himself dependent on Moses; *Apol.* 1.59.

[352] For example, because responsibility in the time before Christ is moralized. For the creature as a particular person who exists in history, an abstract "free" subject is substituted. The word that directly addresses one in the proclamation of Christ is shifted into the form of communications

In fairness to Justin, we must note that a reminiscence of Paul does appear to shimmer in the background of his thought in one instance–*Dial.* 23.4 (cf. von Campenhausen, *Formation*, 98f.). This is an inkling (but no more than this) that the problem of the *law* is to be grasped in unity with that of the *cosmos* only from the point of view of the Pauline *sola fide* ("by faith alone"), that is, from the understanding of Christ as the end of the law and thereby (though Justin was not aware of it, it is the fact), from the recognition of the *servum arbitrium* ("decision-making service").[353]

(2) A further aspect to be considered is the interrelationship of Logos, cosmos, and history.[354] The Logos proves to be "a historico-theological principle of revelation" (Andresen, *Logos,* 316).[355] As was the case with creation, so also the eschatological revelation is understood chronologically.[356]

To be sure, there is yet no full-scale chronology in Justin.[357] But its presence is nonetheless an essential indication of the development of a historical consciousness, even if it at first serves only an apologetic goal (over against the pagans). But that in the wake of *Jewish* apologetic one grasps this means of defense, presupposes the self-consciousness of the people of God (see with reference to *Dial.* 119). And independently of apologetic, the construction of a chronology carries further the reflection on the place of Christianity within *world* history (Africanus), because, of course, the Old Testament history, along with the chronology contained in it, was claimed for Christianity. This is a history that begins with the creation and had already been related to the histories of other peoples within Hellenistic Judaism.

A fundamental distinction is to be drawn between the *proof of antiquity,* as this had already been carried on within Judaism, and the *proof from prophecy.*[358]

---

of abstract truths about God, the world, and humanity that are not capable of being *preached* but that, with the help of other sources, must be demonstrated. Even if the resources used for this are formally biblical, these are basically interchangeable with philosophical, moralistic resources (and, of course, today "psychological"–or at least what the average theologian today customarily understands by this term). The saving act of God in the fullness of time is made into a "salvation-historical" or "world-historical" (trans.: *weltgeschichtlichen;* he has the Pannenberg school in mind) theory, which one can analyze and evaluate without being directly encountered.

[353] *Dial.* 43 is interesting as an example of a text that has echoes of Paul while remaining distant from him with regard to the real subject matter.

[354] Andresen, *Logos,* 308ff.; Osborn, *Justin,* 154ff.

[355] Osborn, *Justin,* 165ff.: An antihistorical element is inherent in it/him (the identity of the Logos!). That also applies to Celsus. The idea of the fulfillment of Scripture is itself antihistorical.

[356] There are still only terse pointers in this direction: creation (*Apol.* 1.59); rudimentary temporal indications of the prophecy of the appearing of Christ (*Apol.* 1.31, cf. 42); the future (*Dial.* 81). The predictions reach back to five thousand years before the advent of Christ (cf. *Apol.* 1.32): Moses was the first prophet. Does this figure then refer to Adam? Cf. Tertullian, *De testimonio animae* 11: "Adam statim prophetiavit magnum illud sacramentum in Christum et ecclesiam" ("For, inasmuch as Adam straightway predicted that 'great mystery of Christ and the church,'").

[357] Contrast Tatian and Theophilus.

[358] Even if the association comes naturally.

The latter is interior to the Bible itself, while the former is related to the extra-biblical world.[359]

(3) Finally, the relationship Christ/Nomos is to be considered.[360]

Materials

Thesis

All the particular statements of Justin that are related to our subject are to be seen as the consequences of his understanding of the Bible taken as a whole. In this regard Justin is still of fundamental importance even today. Obviously it is not a matter of "taking over" his exegetical method,[361] or of particular interpretations of salvation history. Nor, on the other hand, is it a matter of giving him a stern reprimand from the point of view of some modern theological system. Rather, and more modestly, it is a matter of making a few probes under the guiding question, What can helpfully be proclaimed as authoritative? This can only be that faith which excludes salvation on the basis of human works (or even of human participation). This excludes also the demand of the one addressed in the kerygma that he accomplish some sort of intellectual work (even if it is only the negative work of a *sacrificium intellectus* ["sacrifice of the intellect"][362]), and thus excludes, for example, the requirement that one adopt a certain world view supposedly propagated in the name of faith. The real question is whether or not *all* portrayals of a "salvation history"[363] that can be simply seen in world history do not necessarily lead to consequences that cover up or distort the biblical foundations, and whether Justin's approach does not demand that the critical principle inherent in the subject matter itself be turned against his own results.[364]

---

[359] A negative purpose was the refutation of the charge of newness, with which the charge of revolution was associated. Cf. Celsus. On the problem of "newness," see *Diogn.* above.

Harnack (*History of Dogma* 2:179ff.) was of the opinion that the assertion of antiquity (of Moses over against Plato [*Apol.* 159]) was made basically superfluous by the doctrine of the *sperma* of the Logos. — This was not true for Justin, in any case, since the assertion of antiquity was based precisely on the Logos doctrine. The Logos is the Son of God the Father. Only from that point of view can its work in the pagan world be understood.

[360] *Apol.* 1.39 (Isa. 2:3f.); *Ker. Petr.* with the comments of Clement of Alexandria; *Apol.* 1.40 (Psalm 1).

[361] Which would not be possible in any case, although the typological interpretation of the Old Testament is still propagated to this very day, with a passion that is characteristic of it (and is substituted for method).

[362] This too falls under the verdict against all forms of sacrificial offerings as a form of worship to God.

[363] Exclusive of the concentration of the proclamation on the one point of the saving event in Christ.

[364] For Justin, the reservations of von Campenhausen are in any case to be noted: (a) that in evaluating the "rationalism" of Justin's method of proof, one should not overlook the fact that Justin himself knows "that for a genuine, spiritual understanding of the Scripture, spiritual illumination is necessary" (p. 90 n. 159); cf. *Dial.* 7.44, 78, 92; (b) that, with regard to the cancellation

Examples of the Promotion of This Idea (including contemporary attempts)

(1) The manufacturing of a "salvation history" through the incorporation of the "history of Israel"—whatever that may be—into the object of Christian faith with the help of a typological interpretation of the Old Testament, that is, the incorporation of a descriptive history and, where the "reconstruction" does not succeed, at least of certain "interpretations" of "history." The price is the factual surrender of the Old Testament as "old," in that it is draped in the garments of the "new."[365] Symptomatic of this is the widespread antinomianism among Old Testament scholars, which is disguised by playing up the concept of "covenant."

(2) A similar situation prevails in the program of a "biblical" theology. Quite apart from the fact that the issue of what "the Bible" is itself is carefully hushed up, as is the issue of what the object of faith should be (a "theology"?), the price is a blurring of the distinction between law and gospel, which results in the Old Testament's losing its specific significance.

(3) It is currently the fashion to offer "interpretations" of "world history," that is, in reality interpretations of what the average "systematic theologian" (who has had an inadequate education as a historian) imagines world history to be. And the suggestion of including pre-creation and post-eschatological in the category of "time" is purely speculative.[366]

Back to Justin

Which consequences of his sketch of salvation history are visible in his own work?

(1) A certain way of distinguishing between Israel and the Jews.[367] Here too the question must be whether this distinction is understood as a concretization of the doctrine of *sola fide*, that is, the end of the law as a way of salvation, or whether it is also required that one accept a supplementary view of history, a view that is internally coherent and independent.[368]

(2) The proof from prophecy.[369]

(3) What is the situation with the "proof from antiquity"?[370]

---

of the cultic regulations of the Old Testament, Justin expresses himself very briefly; see *Dial.* 114; von Campenhausen, *Formation*, 93 n. 172.

[365] The test is again: What is imposed on the hearer as a binding *requirement* of faith?

[366] Whoever makes such a proposal would have at least to believe that he or she is capable of making a trip to heaven. The one New Testament author who did have such an experience to report emphatically rejected such speculations; that is, he refused to make the person of the preacher into a second item of proclamation and object of faith.

[367] Cf. already Paul in Rom. 2:28f.; 9:6ff.; Luke.

[368] On this point, the comparison of Luke and Justin can in fact advance the discussion.

[369] See above: In Luke, the level of reflection attained by Justin has not been reached.

[370] Here too the criterion is appropriate, whether the *praeparatio evangelica* ("preparation for the Gospel") is to be made visible in certain—real or claimed—facts of history—which is something Paul does not do in Gal. 4:4.

(4) Concerning the application of the prophetic call to repentance and threat of punishment (a) on pre-Christian Israel, and (b) on post-Christian Judaism that continues in its unbelief: Will this preaching of repentance be carried on as the concretizing of the truth that there is salvation in no one else? Will the key signature of the whole composition be the insight that judgment begins at the house of God? Will it be recognized that the institutional church has salvation only in the hearing of faith and thus cannot carry on its business as though it were an institution authorized to dispense salvation, that is, that it cannot anticipate the judgment of God, in whose hands salvation finally rests.[371]

(5) In Justin's approach to the Bible, how is the double distinction applied (a) between the prophets and the giving of the law, and (b) between the ritual law and the ethical law?[372] This distinction raises the issue of the unity of God's demand, which cannot be answered by any theory of salvation history. One indication of this is the tears in the fabric of Justin's own argument; he must affirm side by side the unity of God's demand and the temporal restriction of the ritual law. What does he offer us as perspectives on the questions and efforts to solve them?

In *Apol.* 1.10 he bases the rejection of material sacrifices on the deity's aseity.[373] This is not a salvation-historical idea, but a rational theology. Concerning its importance, one would note that it had long been a topos, and thus possibly is included here only incidentally. One must inquire concerning the broader context of the idea: that God himself remains unchanging, that the God of the ancestors, the Creator and lawgiver, and the God of Christian faith, the Father of the revealer but who also is the source of redemption for the pagans (*Dial.* 35), is one and the same God, and thus the God to whom no material sacrifices must be brought.[374]

According to Justin, the only key to understanding the Old Testament—and this means not only the legal and cultic prescriptions but also the prophets[375]—is faith in Christ. On this matter it must be said that the Jews, who presumably possess the Scriptures as their own inheritance, do not in fact understand them.[376] This is why they hate the Christians and persecute them when they can, because the Christians claim that the Christ has already come. Thus they

---

[371] An insight that Paul develops in Romans 11.

[372] Cf. (a) Jesus: this distinction is not expressed theoretically, but practiced. (b) So also for Paul, the law is eliminated, while the moral law (Paul says simply "law"), summarized in the love commandment, remains (Romans 7; 13:9). (c) For Luke, cf. Acts 7 and 15 and his portrayal of the process of transition within earliest Christianity toward the Gentile Christian church.

[373] Cf. 1.13; Acts 17:25; Aristides 1.4; 13.4; *Diogn.* 3.3; Tatian 4.5.

[374] Further, should one burn up that which God created for our nourishment? On 1.13, see *Diogn.* 4.2; Minucius Felix 32.2.

[375] *Apol.* 1.37 (Isaiah against the temple, feasts, and sacrifice); *Dial.* 46; *Barn.* 2; *Ker. Petr.* 3; Aristides 14; *Diogn.* 4.5.

[376] *Apol.* 1.31; cf. 36: the words of the prophets were not spoken by *them*, but by the Logos. Because the Jews did not understand that, they did not recognize the Christ when he came. That is the salient point.

execrate them in the synagogues.[377] Justin incorporates this idea within a christological salvation-historical framework (*Dial.* 95f.).[378]

The transfer of imperial power to the Romans is also both politically relevant and, at the same time, based on this salvation-historical perspective (*Apol.* 1.32). It is directly related to the view of the universality of the offer of salvation to all nations.[379]

The doctrine that the Messiah has already come carries with it the corresponding doctrine of the *two advents*, the first in lowliness and the future in glory.[380] A biblical approach to the issue naturally carries with it the necessity that the indictments against the Jews and those against the pagans must turn out differently (*Dial.* 27ff.).[381]

Justin did not restrict himself to the topics of monotheism and the Jewish rituals, as his predecessors had done. It was his Logos doctrine that enabled him to do this. Rather, he included the prophets' indictments of the disobedience of Israel, because it was this disobedience that blocked the way toward understanding the Scripture and recognizing the Christ (cf. the context *Apol.* 1.36f.). He needed these indictments in order to make clear his own delineation of the nature of revelation. Thus it was not for him psychologically arbitrary, but a theologically necessary charge that the Jews crucified the Messiah.[382] By this means the framework was provided for the introduction of the prophetic threats against this sinful people who did not recognize the Lord (*Apol.* 1.37f.; *Dial.* 123). So also the declarations of punishment for the Jews stand in the service of the call to conversion (*Dial.* 118). The question remains whether all this does not remain prejudiced toward a kind of "legalism," if it is grounded in a view of salvation history.[383]

---

[377] An allusion to the prayer against the heretics in the Eighteen Benedictions. *Dial.* 16, 95, 133.

[378] Alongside this, he can once refer to the conduct of Bar Kochba against the Christians (*Apol.* 1.31) —a wink at the imperial power that reminds one of Luke: the Jews are those who fomented political unrest, while the Christians are bound by their religion to be loyal to the state (*Apol.* 1.12).

[379] We mention only incidentally that the Jews too charged the Christians with atheism (*Dial.* 17); compare this with the charge of the *pagans* (*Apol.* 1.6, 13; *Dial.* 108). We also note only in passing that the familiar commonplaces of the Gentile anti-Jewish literature are missing. For it is from the Bible that Justin knows the Jews (cf. his meager knowledge of extrabiblical Jewish history [*Apol.* 1.31] dealing with Herod).

[380] *Dial.* 14, 40, 45, 49, 52, 68, esp. 110f.

[381] For the (nonbiblical) preliminary forms of this distinction, see *Ker. Petr.;* Aristides; *Diogn.* In Justin's style (*Apol.* 1.49) this appears in such wise that the missionary point of view holds on to the call to faith: the pagans did not expect Christ, but they were given the opportunity to accept him. The Jews expected him, but did not recognize him when he came. That this happened in accordance with the prophecy of Scripture (Isa. 65:1-3) does not remove their guilt, but rather confirms it (*Dial.* 95; see also *Dial.* 27 and 29, which is the conclusion of a certain train of thought).

[382] Preliminary forms: Aristides 15.2; Justin, *Apol.* 1.35; *Dial.* 16, 85, 118, 133.

[383] Or the corresponding question, whether a salvation-historical approach, even if one attempts to think through the idea of a preexistent revelation in strictly christological terms, does not finally result in the charge of "murderers of God" against the Jews. This theological perversity, which even in our own time is not entirely dead, lies in the fact that historical data are confused with the

So that Justin is not judged or condemned in a one-sided, unhistorical manner, one must also look at the other side of the coin: *Dial.* 96: "You are still our brothers. I call on you to recognize the truth!" *Dial.* 133: The Christians pray, at the command of God, for all who persecute them.

But the fundamental issue is: *Can* the model of salvation history be ascribed to the christological approach of faith?[384]

It is important for us to point out two elements of this model: (a) the division of salvation history into periods; (b) the contrast of the Jews as a "non-people" with the Christians as the people of God.[385] One will certainly find in Justin a partially unharmonized juxtaposition of motifs and will have to be careful that he is not forced into a systematic straightjacket.[386] Nevertheless, we need to ask whether there are not lines of thought that run throughout Justin, lines that lie parallel to each other or cross each other. Some aspects relevant for our concern are the following:

Apol. 1.46 raises the temporal problem (cf. *Diogn.*): If revelation occurred in a certain period of history, how can people who lived before this period be made responsible? The answer is provided through the doctrine of the Logos. Thereby Justin is able to demonstrate the mutual coherence of creation and revelation. The world was never without God, therefore never without revelation.

The tension remains between the unity of God's rule of the world (God's identity: *Dial.* 11) and the—temporary—promulgation of the ritual law. The reason for this was the hardening of Israel (*Dial.* 22), the purpose was the prevention of idolatry (*Dial.* 92; objection: through animal sacrifice, of all things!). The temporal points are the commandment of circumcision to Abraham and the Sabbath commandment to Moses (*Dial.* 43). Beyond them lies the supertemporal validity of the ethical law; it is, of course, grounded in the nature of God himself.[387]

An important element in the periodizing of salvation history is that it—precisely because of its construction on the basis of the Old Testament—is laid

---

confession of faith—and precisely in the situation where it is thought that the Jews must be protected against this charge. Rather, the whole approach is to be rejected from the first line. The confession of faith declares rather that according to God's will Christ was crucified for *our* sins.

[384] A question that, *mutatis mutandis,* is to be directed also to Romans 9–11, if there were any kind of salvation-historical program outlined there, but that is to be disputed.

[385] In Justin's modification of the previous idea of the three categories of peoples (*Dial.* 119). The influence of this schema is indicated by the remark, superfluous in itself, that the Christians are not a barbarian people, and in the further comment that Jews have circumcision as the (only) distinguishing mark over against pagans and Christians.

[386] This lack of harmony is a result of, among other things, the fact that the nuclei of these motifs were already present before Justin and that he was the first who attempted to make a conceptual unit of them, which probably is not going to happen on the first try.

[387] *Dial.* 23. The opposition between the two laws was partially bridged through typological exegesis, for example, by interpreting circumcision as circumcision of the heart. But still the salvation-historical aspect is not thereby eliminated.

out as an extension of the Old Testament story (*Dial.* 43, 92). Two perspectives are revealed when the internal periodizing is examined. One can look at the problem of continuity and discontinuity in salvation history[388] retrospectively: the new law has made the law of Moses obsolete (*Dial.* 11); alongside this view stands the view that Christ is the eternal law. Or one can see the problem from the other perspective, beginning with the period Abraham-Moses and going forward from there. At this point Justin, in dependence on Paul, introduces a new perspective, that Abraham was justified by faith.[389]

In the retrospective view, Moses is seen as the first of the prophets; but the perspective is at the same time directed forward, beyond the Old Testament period: the Jews had their own rulers until the appearance of Christ. Then followed, as their punishment for rejecting Christ, the transfer of imperial power to the Romans. Here the interpretation of the historical fate of the Jews is incorporated: (a) the internal consequences—there are no longer any prophets in Israel (*Dial.* 82, 87f.; cf. Tertullian, *Adv. Iud.* 13); (b) the external consequences—judicial punishment has occurred, as predicted, in the devastation of the Jewish homeland (*Dial.* 110, 119; Minucius Felix 33), and no Jew is permitted to live in Jerusalem (*Dial.* 16; Tertullian, *Adv. Iud.* 3; *Apol.* 21).

The double aspect of the law leads to two series of statements: (a) The announcement of judicial punishment of the Jews, who trust in the ritual law and refuse to believe in Christ. To the extent that they were disobedient and remained unbelieving, their character as the people of God was denied. With this, the argument flows into an assertion that they (despite the dispersion that happened to them [*Dial.* 21]) were not distributed through the whole world (cf. the opposing statements of Philo, Josephus, *Sib. Or.*), in contrast to the Christians, the true people of God (*Dial.* 117, 119). This is the people promised to Abraham, but who could not be hoped for on the basis of the law (since the law cannot enlighten [*Dial.* 122]) but has its existence διὰ τῆς κλήσεως τῆς καινῆς καὶ αἰωνίου διαθήκης, τουτέστι τοῦ Χριστοῦ ("through the calling of the new and eternal covenant, that is through Christ").[390]

(b) It is interesting to note that alongside the collective aspect oriented toward salvation history, according to which the Jews are collectively threatened with judgment, there is also an individual perspective present that is determined by the concept of faith; here the view is focused on the salvation of the individual in the last judgment (*Dial.* 64). Concerning the individual, Justin does not want to anticipate or preempt God's judgment. The universal possibility of salvation is preserved by the declaration that saving knowledge is not

---

[388] Continuity is established by God's nature and by the harmonizing of the proclamations that have issued from his throne, while the discontinuity is indicated by the distinction between old and new.

[389] *Dial.* 23. In this passage Justin finds himself on the threshold of the promised land of the theology of justification *sola fide* (*Dial.* 119; *Apol.* 1.92, 23).

[390] On the new law and covenant, see *Dial.* 34, 43. It was getting the law out of the way that made the universality of salvation possible (*Dial.* 102).

reserved for an intellectual elite but is open to all (*Apol.* 1.60; 2.10; cf. Tatian 32; Athenagoras 12; Tertullian, *Apol.* 46; Origen, *Contra Cels.* 7.45f.). Those who have lived according to the Logos were Christians (Tertullian, *Apol.* 46; Socrates etc.); for there is no Logos apart from the Son of God. One is saved by right living. What that is has been revealed by God in all times and places and can be summarized in the double commandment of love to God and neighbor (*Dial.* 93).

From this point of view it can be seen how it is that for Justin salvation through faith and salvation through righteous living coincide. Thus the "Pauline" passages can be understood alongside the others: *Dial.* 43 (cf. 33), 92 along with 67: Jesus was himself circumcised in order to become righteous by the law.

Tatian[391]

Tatian stands only on the margin of our concern.[392] There is no pattern of salvation history in his work;[393] even in its approach, his thinking is unhistorical.[394] A characteristic indication of this is the fact that the Jews are mentioned only incidentally; they play no role in salvation history.[395] Thus neither are they a problem. On the other hand, the Old Testament, Moses, and the Prophets are unproblematically accepted as a Christian book.[396]

Because of the unhistorical orientation of Tatian's thought, we can eliminate or at least reduce a whole series of problems in advance: (1) the concept of God

---

[391] Edition: E. Schwartz, *Tatiani Oratio ad Graecus*, TU 4.1 (Leipzig: Hinrichs, 1888). Translations: A. Harnack, *Tatians Rede an die Griechen* (Giessen, 1884); R. C. Kukula in *Bibliothek der Kirchenväter* 12 (1913) 175ff.; Bib: A. Harnack, *Die Überlieferung der griechischen Apologeten;* E. Preuschen, *RE³* 19:386ff.; Lietzmann, *History of the Early Church* 2:186; R. M. Grant, "The Heresy of Tatian," *JTS* n.s. 5 (1954): 62ff.; idem, "Tatian and the Bible," in *St. Patr.* 1, TU 63 (Berlin: Akademie-Verlag, 1957) 297–306; M. Elze, *Tatian und seine Theologie* (Göttingen: Vandenhoeck & Ruprecht, 1960); H. Langerbeck, *Aufsätze zur Gnosis* (Göttingen: Vandenhoeck & Ruprecht, 1967) 167ff.; von Campenhausen, *Formation* (see index); Hyldahl, *Philosophie,* 236ff. (especially on Tatian's relation to Justin).

[392] This is not, of course, due to the fact that he is labeled "heretic" by us.

[393] Despite his relation to Justin and his chronology, which is more developed than Justin's, by which the "proof of antiquity" is supposed to be established.

[394] With Elze, against Hyldahl (see below).

[395] And the law appears in another frame of reference (see below). They are mentioned in the following passages: 36: Nebuchadnezzar led a campaign against the Jews and the Phoenicians; 37: King Solomon is incidentally mentioned for chronological purposes; 38: a synchronization of the exodus and Amosis-Inachus is produced (see below).

[396] The *Diatessaron* appears to represent a special case. Elze, *Tatian,* 124: This writing was (a) docetic, (b) ascetic, (c) *anti-Jewish.* According to Theodoret, Tatian omitted the genealogies and the descent of Jesus from David according to the flesh. Elze relates this to the demarcation of the Christian congregations in the East over against Judaism (*Tatian,* 125). See especially the Persian version (G. Messina, *Diatessaron persiano* [Rome, 1951], LXXIX).

as such (4),[397] especially since Tatian does not make any comments concerning Jewish monotheism in relation to it;[398] (2) the Logos concept (5);[399] (3) the polemic against fatalism (8ff.);[400] (4) the question of sources.

Sources

According to Langerbeck (*Aufsätze zur Gnosis*, 169), a reference to a handbook may already be found in Tatian's statement that his teaching is the result of his own study. According to Geffcken (*Apologeten*, 106), it is hardly the case that Tatian used Josephus, despite the passage about the age of Homer (36; cf. Josephus, *Ag. Ap.* 1.12). Rather, he used the same source, probably Alexander Polyhistor or a compendium that contained extracts from him.[401]

Harnack (*Überlieferung der griechischen Apologeten*, 218) on his aftereffects: Tatian's *Oratio* was not used by Athenagoras, Theophilus, Irenaeus (despite Irenaeus, *Adv. Haer.* 3.33.8, cf. *Or. Graec.* 8) nor Minucius Felix. Did both Tatian and Minucius Felix use a polemical pamphlet against gods, demons, and magical beings? Cf. the points of contact (they derive without exception from the apologetic repertoire):

Tatian	Minucius Felix
34.1	5.12 Phalaris
8.9	19.12 Minerva
10.4 Antinoos	24.1 Romulus became a god by perjuring himself.
21.5	21.11 What is born dies.
8.10 etc.	22.2
16f.	26f. the work of demons

The idea that the philosophers were dependent on the prophets also belonged to the repertoire (Tatian 20; Minucius Felix 34). A polemic against the theater: Tatian 22f.; Minucius Felix 37.11; Tertullian.

Harnack (*Überlieferung*, 220f.) not only assumes a common source for Tatian and Tertullian, *Apol.*, but also considers it probable that Tertullian read the *Oratio;* compare *Or. Graec.* 2 with *Apol.* 46.[402]

---

[397] Along with the approach that allows a natural knowledge of God and the typical rejection of sacrifices for the Nameless One who has no needs.

[398] The Jews are no special entity for him. Although he brings the Bible and paganism into a directly confrontative relationship with each other, he does not do this at all with the Jews as a people.

[399] For our purposes it is sufficient to point out the comment of Lietzmann (*History of the Early Church* 2:187) that Tatian and Athenagoras obviously did not want to acknowledge the spermata of the Logos in the extra-Christian world. —For the different understanding of Hydahl, see below.

[400] Since, differently than in Justin, it is not built into a salvation-historical framework.

[401] Compare the introduction in Tatian with that of Josephus, *Ag. Ap.* Cf. further *Or. Graec.* 37, Hypsicrates, with Josephus, *Ant.* 14.239; Mochus with 1.107, Menander with 8.144, 324; 9.383.

[402] Geffcken, *Apologeten*, 283 n. 1: Tertullian, *Apol.* 46.85 is from Tatian.

Harnack (*Überlieferung*, 224): Julius Africanus used Tatian (cf. Origen, *Contra Cels.* 1.16). It is not clear that Tatian was used in the *Cohortatio;* the common elements can be explained through the mediation of Africanus (p. 225).

Eusebius, in the preface to Tatian's *Chronicle,* names alongside Tatian also Clement of Alexandria, Africanus, Josephus, and Justin as his authorities for the age of Moses. But Eusebius probably knew Tatian only from Africanus. Harnack (*Überlieferung*, 225 n. 286): Eusebius, *Chron. Abr.* 915 is from Tatian.[403]

Concerning Tatian's Own Position[404]

Clement of Alexandria, *Strom.* 3.12.82.2: Tatian makes a sharp separation between the old and the new human nature. The old human nature, Adam, is identified with the law, the new with the Gospel; this new human nature breaks off its relationship with the law as though it were from another god.[405] Clement of Alexandria, *Ecl. Proph.* 38.1: Tatian understands the words "Let there be light" as the prayer of a subordinate deity to its superior. Irenaeus, *Adv. Haer.* 1.28 (Eusebius, *Hist. Eccl.* 4.29) subsumes him under the Encratites, who were descended from Saturninus and Marcion. It was only after the martyrdom of Justin that he separated from the church. Irenaeus, *Adv. Haer.* 3.23:8: Tatian constantly quoted, "In Adam we all die" (1 Cor. 15:22); but he overlooked the affirmation that "where sin increased, grace abounded all the more" (Rom. 5:20).[406]

In view of the content of the book, the question emerges, How is the unhistorical orientation of Tatian's thought related to the elaboration of a

---

[403] But H. Gelzer, *Sextus Julius Africanus* 1.22: Divergences and corruptions show that when the *Chronicle* was written Tatian was not directly used as a source.

In the *Praep. Ev.,* Tatian's words are exactly reproduced just as they stand in the Tatian manuscripts, with only *one* exception.

[404] That Tatian was an Assyrian or a Syrian—that is, a Semite, may not be exploited "psychologically"; with Elze, *Justin,* contra Preuschen, *RE.*

[405] Relationship with Valentinus: *Strom.* 3.13.92. Preuschen, 392: Unlike Marcion, Tatian certainly had no doctrine of two gods; cf. *Or. Graec.* 4. He does not juxtapose God to another god, as Marcion did, but to the devil, who originated marriage, law, and the physical senses. Langerbeck (*Aufsätze zur Gnosis,* 177): "Did Tatian really speak of the law as having come from another god, or did he only want to 'nullify,' to set it aside, as though it were not given by the one God? The first is the more likely, but with the stipulations that are found in the *Letter of Ptolemy to Flora.* There can be no question of an unrestricted Marcionite thesis advocated by Tatian."

[406] Von Campenhausen, *Formation,* 175 n. 139: Irenaeus appears to have made Tatian into a heretic rather one-sidedly. Elze, *Justin,* 108: it is noticeable "basically how little information Irenaeus actually has to report about the heresy of Tatian. . . . He has no philosophical education. . . ." Nevertheless, his charge is typical of him: "To teach the damnation of Adam means to practice theology without the concept of salvation history as understood by Irenaeus" (*Justin,* 109). Langerbeck (*Aufsätze zur Gnosis,* 178): The reports reveal a united picture: Tatian was a "Valentinian"—and that means in Langerbeck's understanding, a disciple of Paul.

Christology that extends far beyond what we have in Justin? And how is his unhistorical approach to the Old Testament related to the "proof of antiquity"? The determination of the literary type hardly contributes any information beyond the primary data that Tatian, barbarian philosopher from Assyria who had also studied Greek philosophy, in the name of barbarian wisdom turned to the confessors of Greek culture.[407]

Perhaps the question may be pressed: Who then are these Greeks and barbarians, if Tatian presents to the adherents of Hellenism the δόγματα ("doctrine") of the barbarians,[408] and Moses (in contrast to Homer) as τὸν δὲ πάσης βαρβάρου σοφίας ἀρχηγόν ("the founder of all barbarian wisdom") (31)? How is it established that the philosophy of the barbarians is also comprehensible to the uneducated? (30, 32f.).

Sample Efforts to Get Historical Information from This Data

Harnack (*History of Dogma* 2:192f. n. 6): "In Tatian's view barbarians and Greeks are the decisive contrasts in history." If one asks where the Jews and especially the Christians fit into this picture, one learns (*History*, 2:192 n. 4): "Tatian also cannot at bottom distinguish between revelation through the prophets and through Christ. See the description of his conversion in c. 29 where only the Old Testament writings are named, and c. 13 fin., 20 fin., 12 (p. 54) etc." (40: Greek sophists read Moses' writings and corrupted them).

Kukula (*Apologie*, 195 n. 1): "For the apologists, Ἕλληνες ("Greeks") refers to those who worship idols, Βάρβαροι ("barbarians") to the Christians, in neither case having any connotation of national or ethnic origin."[409]

This is opposed by Elze, *Justin*, 24: The contrast between philosophy and Christianity is for Tatian reduced to that between Greeks and barbarians—which is, of course, not a positive item of information. Elze, *Justin*, 25: "Barbarian" appears where one would expect the attribute "Christian," an expression that Tatian avoids. "Barbarians" are *Gentiles*. It is not the "Hellenes" who are the confessors of Greek culture, but rather the scholars (25.2f.). This would then mean that Tatian's self-understanding knows nothing of the

---

[407] Cf. the embarrassment of the different formulations: (a) Elze, *Justin*, 41ff.: not an apology, but an instructional lecture; "not an apology in the usual sense" (p. 41). —What is it then? (b) Langerbeck (*Aufsätze zur Gnosis*, 168f.): "Not an apology, at least not primarily, but a program of a teacher τῆς κατὰ βαρβάρους φιλοσοφίας ["of philosophy, as understood among the barbarians"]—seasoned, to be sure, with a heavy dash of polemic."

Nevertheless, there is plenty there of good apologetic material, e.g., the assurance of the political loyalty of the Christians (4) with the usual qualification: honor human beings as human, but worship God alone (cf. Justin *Apol.* 1.1). The critique on the multiplicity of pagan law codes is also standard apologetic (28).

[408] Cf. 35; 12: the βαρβαρικὴ νομοθεσία ("barbaric code of laws"); 29: the βαρβαρικαὶ γραφαί ("barbaric writings").

[409] Cf. Norden, *Die antike Kunstprosa* (5th ed.; Darmstadt: Wissenschaftliche Buchgesellschaft, 1958) 514 n. 1.

Christians as an independent community over against the Greeks and barbarians (Elze, *Justin*, 25). In this matter he is not at all oriented by the faith; for him, the contrast between Greeks and barbarians is rather merely a matter of the difference between the educated and the uneducated.[410] Elze sees this data within the framework of Tatian's lack of historical thinking, which is related to his concept of time.

Or. Graec. 26: τί μοι μερίζετε τὸν χρόνον, λέγοντες τὸ μέν τι εἶναι παρῳχηκὸς αὐτοῦ, τὸ δὲ ἐνεστός, τὸ δὲ μέλλον; πῶς γὰρ δύναται παρελθεῖν ὁ μέλλων, εἰ ἔστιν ὁ ἐνεστώς; ὥσπερ δὲ οἱ ἐμπλέοντες τῆς νεὼς φερομένης οἴονται διὰ τὴν ἀμαθίαν ὅτι τὰ ὄρη τρέχουσιν, οὕτω καὶ ὑμεῖς οὐ γινώσκετε παρατρέχοντας μὲν ὑμᾶς, ἑστῶτα δὲ τὸν αἰῶνα, μέχρις ἂν αὐτὸν ὁ ποιήσας εἶναι θελήσῃ ("Why do you divide time, saying that one part is past, and another present, and another future? For how can the future be passing when the present exists? As those who are sailing imagine in their ignorance, as the ship is borne along, that the hills are in motion, so you do not know that it is you who are passing along, but that time remains present as long as the Creator wills it to exist").

This understanding of time is seen by Elze within the context of Middle Platonism: time belongs within the category of those deceitful forms of empirical experience (cf. Andresen, *Logos*, 280). Elze, *Justin*, 105: "Like the Platonists, he (Tatian) can find no place in this system for either time or history."[411] Because Tatian's philosophy has a timeless orientation, it is *a theology without a soteriology*, a Christianity without a Christ. And whenever Tatian does let something like a Christology appear in his writings, he must necessarily give it a docetic character. 81: The Logos has an exclusively cosmological function; Tatian does not see it as having any relation to history or salvation history. 38: There is no internal connection between Tatian's unhistorical conception of things and the apologetic topos of the "proof of antiquity" and the Greeks having stolen from Moses, which he simply took over from the tradition. In Tatian, even the proof from prophecy loses its importance.[412]

Grant incorporates Tatian's understanding of time into another frame of reference, namely, that of the Stoics: the past and the future do not exist, only the present is real.[413]

Hyldahl too opposes Elze, but, of course, in a completely different regard than Grant.[414] He believes that he can establish the presence in Tatian of a concept of time and history similar to that of Justin and thus disputes the view that

---

[410] Contrast Justin's addresses to the barbarians, *Apol.* 1.5, 7, 46, 60; *Dial.* 119.

[411] Cf. the unhistorical sense of οἰκονομία ("household management/plan of salvation").

[412] But that is no evidence. Then why is the "proof of antiquity" not only taken over but explained? And the qualitative distinction between the "proof of antiquity" and the "proof from prophecy" is not recognized.

[413] H. von Arnim, *Stoicorum veterum fragmenta* 2:517f.; H. Diels, *Doxographi Graeci* (Berlin, 1879) 461f.; Pohlenz, *Stoa* 2:27.

[414] Hyldahl, *Philosophie*, 247ff.: A summary description of Tatian with a tendency to make him look like Justin.

Tatian's systematic thinking and the "proof from antiquity" are such divergent ideas: Tatian distinguishes the people of the primeval period (7) from the prophets who came after them (13). For him, Christianity is the oldest form of the wisdom of the barbarians.[415] In contrast to the Stoic doctrine of cycles (3), the world has a beginning and an end (4f.); it is a matter of the restoration of the ἀρχαῖον ("ancient times"), which has been perverted through the free will of humanity and the enticement of demons (on the combination freedom/ demons, see Or. Graec. 7f.). It is clear that nothing bad was created by God (11). The human condition of lostness is a matter of human freedom from beginning to end.[416] Hyldahl, Philosophie, 249: Tatian's theology is "a combination of the trichotomical doctrine in Dial. 5–6[417] and the theory of the Logos-Spermatikos." From this combination there also grows at the same time a theology of history that is akin to that of Justin, to the extent that a proof is given "that Christianity is as old as the world." Tatian believes, just as Justin and Melito had believed, that in Christianity the original philosophy has been rediscovered (Posidonius; Seneca, Ep. 90).[418] And the borrowing theory is firmly connected to the ἔναυσμα ("spark")-doctrine (13; cf. 15.1): at the beginning, the πνεῦμα ("spirit") lived in unity with the soul. But when the soul would not follow the leadership of the spirit, the spirit moved out. ἡ δὲ ὥσπερ ἔναυσμα τῆς δυνάμεως αὐτοῦ κεκτημένη ("Yet, retaining as it were a spark of its power"). As a result of the separation, it was not capable of recognizing the perfect. ζητοῦσα τὸν θεὸν κατὰ πλάνην πολλοὺς θεοὺς ἀνετύπωσε τοῖς ἀντισοφιστεύουσι δαίμοσι κατα-κολουθοῦσα. πνεῦμα δὲ τοῦ θεοῦ παρὰ πᾶσιν μὲν οὐκ ἔστι ("while seeking for God, it fashioned to itself in its wandering many gods, following the sophistries of the demons. But the Spirit of God is not with all"). But it did return to some whose manner of life was righteous and to these souls revealed prophecies of hidden things.[419] Hyldahl further argues that the content of the prophetic writing is quoted more precisely in Tatian 29 than in Justin, Dial. 7.[420]

If we attempt a summary, the result seems to be: in Tatian we find alongside each other (a) a theoretical denial of the reality of time; (b) the elaboration of a chronology—but without Jesus and Christianity; and (c) a divergence of the themes Israel and the Old Testament (the prophets and sacred writings: 12, 20,

---

[415] The contrary opinion in J. H. Waszink in Mélanges Christine Mohrmann (1963) 41ff.: Christianity is the newest form of the wisdom of the barbarians; Or. Graec. 35 does not mean "our barbarian teaching," but barbarian philosophy in the form in which it is advocated by us Christians. Hyldahl (Philosophie, 244) objects: Tatian never makes any distinction between the philosophy of Moses and Christianity.

[416] The Fall and the condition of humanity resulting from it are not thought of in historical categories, but in the unhistorical category of freedom of the will.

[417] An unhistorical section of Justin has intentionally been quoted out of context.

[418] What does that have to do with salvation history in Justin's sense? The original condition of things was something completely different; compare 20.3 with 15.1!

[419] Cf. in the same passage συζυγία ("union") of the divine Spirit with the soul.

[420] A dubious argument. How is the content then regarded? Or. Graec. 29 gives an unhistorical paraphrase of the content of the barbarian writings.

36).[421] The incarnation is not mentioned once (see 20.2); thus, no use is made of the (only) possibility of a historical understanding of salvation history. It is no problem for Christianity to reclaim *Moses*. The idea of the preexistence of the Logos is only used allusively in the "proof of antiquity" (7).

The Chronology (31ff.)

It is used by Clement of Alexandria (*Strom.* 1.21), copied by Eusebius (*Praep. Ev.* 10.11 [on Africanus, see 10.10]). The point of departure (and his own interest) for the proof of antiquity is the temporal relation between Moses and Homer, the oldest founder of the wisdom of the barbarians, as well as their oldest poet and historian (31). The date of Homer's activity is established with the help of Greek historians and grammarians (at the same time pointing out the contradictions within them). The material is taken from a handbook organized according to the Olympiads (and the Argive lists of kings). Cf. Pseudo-Justin, *Coh.* 9.[422] Then follows (36) the chronology of the Chaldeans (Berosus *FGH* 680; Stern, *GLAJJ*, p. 55f., no. 9), Phoenicians and Egyptians[423] with the synchronism Moses-Amosis-Inachus (from the Argive list of kings).[424]

We need not here pursue the details any further. The salient point is the proof that Inachus, the contemporary of Moses, lived four hundred years before the Trojan War (the beginning of the historical era for the Greeks) (39).[425]

Taken as a whole, the proof of antiquity is still somewhat primitive: the description of the great age of the barbarian cultural achievements at the beginning remains isolated from the argument as a whole and is composed of commonplaces: Babylonian astronomy; the Egyptians, whose ancient culture had long been accepted as canonical by the Greeks (Herodotus and his successors, Plato). The whole description is aimed at the refusal of the Greeks (1.7). With obvious inhibitions, the Greek lawgivers and sages are named, in order to

---

[421] There is no debate, either with the former or with his contemporary Judaism, and no hint of a historical function of the law. Hydahl, *Philosophie*, 269 n. 28: In Justin, Tatian, and Melito (Eusebius, *Hist. Eccl.* 4.26.7), the connection between Israel and the prophets is torn apart. That is to be disputed for Justin, but here it is constitutive.

[422] Where Josephus (cf. Theophilus 3.26ff.; Tertullian, *Apol.* 19) and Diodorus are also named. The *Coh.* also enlists the *Greek* historians in support of Moses. Schürer, *History* 3:542f.: they merely copy Africanus (contra v. Gutschmid, who, incorrectly assuming that the *Coh.* is older than Africanus, postulates a common source for both); cf. also Gelzer, *Sextus Julius Africanus* 1:24.

[423] See Josephus, *Ag. Ap.* 1.8, 14, 123ff.; *Ant.* 10.219ff.; Tertullian, *Apol.* 19.

[424] Cf. Justus of Tiberius, *FGH* 734 T 2 (with Clement of Alexandria, *Strom.* 1.21, 101; Africanus; Josephus). The reliability is confirmed by Juba of Mauretania, *FGH* 275 F 4; cf. Clement of Alexandria, *Strom.* 1.21; Jacoby *FGH* III, 328: "It is noticeable that Tatian-Clement cite Berossus from Juba, since Christian authors otherwise use Alexander Polyhistor (*FGH* 273 F 79)."

[425] The only item of interest for us in the list of sources in *Or. Graec.* 37f. is the fact that (as was already the case in Josephus) oriental historians are used: Laitus (*FGH* 784), Ptolemy of Mendes (*FGH* 711), Menander of Ephesus (Tatian incorrectly: Pergamon; *FGH* 783). In comparison with Josephus, the positive evaluation of Apion (*FGH* 616) is especially interesting.

conclude by rejecting them once again and finally. Except for the excursus on the barbarian cultural achievements at the beginning, the "proof of antiquity" is restricted to Moses. This limitation is possible for Tatian since there is no difference for him between Moses and Christianity.[426]

There can be no talk here of a chronicle of world history, of a comprehensive idea of the history of the world. For example, the Greek lawgivers are not brought into relation to Moses.[427] For Tatian, the Mosaic law had no inner-historical origin.

Thus, the excursion into chronology actually demonstrates the unhistorical nature of Tatian's thought. On the other hand, when the Old Testament is regarded as a document of revelation, Tatian is not at all conscious of any "other hand." The Old Testament is neither placed in a historical framework nor read as a document of salvation history. It is not the case that such an idea is rejected; it simply never appears on the horizon. Thus, Tatian has peace with the Jews, the peacefulness found in a cemetery, purchased at the price of relinquishing the saving revelation.

Athenagoras[428]

Despite the high level of excellence that Athenagoras has as apologist (one can read his work as an above-average, imaginative, and penetrating compendium), for our purposes he stands on the negative side of the ledger: he carries on his debate exclusively with the persecuting state and with Gentile culture. And this is no accident. The rule also applies to him: the reason he is not concerned with Israel and the Jews is part and parcel of the lack of any concern with salvation history and the historical problematic of the law, even though he bases the truth claim of Christianity on prophetic inspiration, which he anchors theologically and christologically (7, 9, 10, 18; 10: The Spirit is an emanation of God).

The following belongs in the apologetic repertoire: the popular charges against the Christians are listed (3). The legality of the proceedings against them is challenged; proof of the wrongdoing of Christians is called for—which cannot be found because of the irreproachable manner in which Christians live their lives,[429] despite their condemnation merely because of "the name" (1.3).

---

[426] So also in comparison with Theophilus, and then especially in the construction of the world chronology using Africanus.

[427] Again, a scanty doxographical compendium is copied out; cf. Cicero, *Nat. Deor.* 1.10ff.; Philodemus (Diels, 121ff.); Eusebius, *Praep. Ev.* 1.7f.; Athenagoras 4; Hermias; Minucius Felix 19, 21; Hippolytus, *Ref.* 1. The arrangement of such compendia: according to διαδοχαί ("succession") Aetius, *Placita* 1.3.7, Diels, 280; Hippolytus 1.5) or δόξαι ("popular repute"); (Hippolytus 1.17, on which see Diels, 144ff.; Diogenes Laertius, his introduction).

[428] *Athenagoras: Legatio and De Resurrectione*, ed. and trans. W. R. Schoedel (Oxford: Clarendon, 1972); G. Ruhbach, *Altkirchliche Apologeten;* L. W. Barnard, "God, the Logos, the Spirit, and the Trinity in the Theology of Athenagoras," *ST* 24 (1970): 70–92.

[429] The emphasis on sexual morality (33) is typical, to which the polemic against the theater is related (35).

No other people in the Roman Empire are hindered from loving τὰ πάτρια ("the ancestral customs of their own people") (1).[430] The political loyalty of Christians, their prayers for the rulers, is established (37; cf. *Acta Apollonii*, etc.). Monotheism is set forth with the familiar consequence: no sacrifices need be made for the One who needs nothing (13)! For Athenagoras too, animal sacrificial rituals are machinations of the demons.

The usual topoi are not missing from the polemic: the images, the material from which they are made, their construction by artists and craftsmen,[431] the animal worship of the Egyptians, the worship of the elements (Hera=air), the worship of the constellations. The reflections on the nature of the images are sharper than usual. Nor are these traditional arguments lacking: that which has an origin also has an end (cf. Artistides 1.4; Minucius Felix 34.2), then the moralizing and mocking critique of the myths, along with euhemeristic arguments (28). In the exposition of monotheism, the relation of God with his Son, the Logos, is fundamental.[432] Even though the imageless monotheism is expanded by including the emanations from God, the Logos, and the Pneuma (10.3), this is not done historically but in terms of a metaphysical cosmology. The crucifixion of the human being Jesus is just as absent as is the incarnation of the Logos itself. The ridiculing of the pagan philosophers by the "philosopher" Hermeias[433] contains nothing relevant to our study.

Melito of Sardis[434]

Just why his comprehensive work (Eusebius, *Hist. Eccl.* 4.26)[435] was lost is a matter of debate. Did he become suspect as a "eunuch" (Polycrates in Eusebius,

---

[430] Geffcken, *Apologeten*, 161ff.: That is precisely the issue, the customs of the fathers! *Cohortatio* 1; Minucius Felix 6.1. The dangerous charge is, of course, that the Christians did not worship the gods of the ancestors, the traditional gods (Athenagoras 13).

[431] This is carried through to the almost indispensable reference to the footbath of Amosis (26): *Diogn.* 2.2; Minucius Felix 24.7; *Acta Apollonii* 17.

[432] 4.2: The *one* God, who has created all through his word. 10: The only God, the eternal one, who can be perceived only through *nous* and *logos*. We also know a *Son* of God, but he is to be fundamentally distinguished from the mythological sons of the gods.

[433] Diels, 651ff.

[434] Editions: M. Testuz, *Pap Bodmer XIII* (Cologne: Bibliotheca Bodmeriana, 1960); O. Perler, Sources chrétiennes 123 (Paris: Cerf, 1966). Translations: J. Blank, *Meliton von Sardes. Vom Passa* (Freiburg: Lambertus Verlag, 1963) (reviewed by B. Lohse, *TLZ* 89 [1964] 363). Bib.: E. Peterson ("Ps-Cyprian, Adversus Iudaeos und Melito von Sardes," in *Frühkirche, Judentum und Gnosis* [Rome: Herder, 1959] 137ff.) points out the lack of philosophical terminology in the Christology; E. Werner, "Melito of Sardes: The First Poet of Deicide," *HUCA* 37 (1966): 191ff.; A. T. Kraabel, *HTR* 61 (1968) 642f.: the foil for Melito's polemic is the powerful Jewish community in Sardis; J. Daniélou, "Figure et évènement chez Méliton de Sardes," in *Neotestamentica et Patristica*, Festschrift O. Cullmann (Tournai: Desclée, 1962) 282ff.; Hyldahl, *Philosophie*, 269 n. 28: In Melito, as in Justin and Tatian, the connection between the prophets and Israel is torn apart.

[435] Up until the gradual rediscovery of the *Passover Homily* in the nineteenth and twentieth centuries.

Hist. Eccl. 5.5.24.5) because of his asceticism, or as a "prophet"[436] because of his stance toward Montanism?[437]

From what has been preserved, we can clearly perceive how he understood the connection between the canon and Judaism. The content of the canon is theologically activated in an original manner. We will limit our discussion to the line of thought of the *Passover Homily.*[438]

The way he begins is already typical: The Exodus passage is read forth and the words of the mystery are explained: πῶς τὸ πρόβατον θύεται καὶ πῶς ὁ λαὸς σῴζεται ("how the sheep is slain, and how the people is saved").[439]

Basic to the whole line of thought is the schema old–new (2-4), in specific applications: καινὸν καὶ παλαιόν, ἀΐδιον καὶ πρόσκαιρον . . . τὸ τοῦ πάσχα μυστήριον· παλαιὸν μὲν κατὰ τὸν νόμον, καινὸν δὲ κατὰ τὸν λόγον, πρόσκαιρον διὰ τὸν ⟨τύπον⟩ ("how new yet old, how temporal yet eternal . . . is the mystery of the Passover: old according to the law, but new according to the word; temporal through the [type]"; Perler: by a figurative expression; see further lines 23, 33) ἀΐδιον διὰ τὴν χάριν . . . ("eternal through grace").

The exposition of the theme reveals a high degree of hermeneutical reflection, on the one hand,[440] and, on the other, of specific reflection on salvation history, with the distinction between word and event (35, developed in the following).[441] The words and deeds of the Old Testament are distinguished from each other as anticipatory proclamations of the gospel, on the one hand, and prefigurations of it, on the other. The texts are explained by the gospel; the events are effected in the church. The problems of the meaning of Scripture

---

436 Tertullian, in Jerome, *Viri ill* 24.

437 On the aftereffects (Clement of Alexandria, see Eusebius, *Hist. Eccl.* 4.26.4), esp. in Origen; see J. Daniélou, *Origène* (Paris, 1948) 144ff. (trans. *Origen* [New York: Sheed & Ward, 1955]) (still has an influence on Irenaeus, Tertullian).

438 The debates about whether or not we have here a real "homily" can be ignored.

439 See Perler on this passage, although his interpretation is unlikely: the Scripture was read aloud in Hebrew and then translated into Greek, at which point its interpretation begins.

440 Daniélou is basic. Blank is too simplistic: He sees that *Barnabas* and Justin do not raise the hermeneutical question or do so only in passing (60). But it is not a very productive statement to say that it would not be Platonic to have model and truth appear in a temporal order (63). This statement is true enough in itself but is to be modified in accordance with the development that had occurred in Platonists such as Justin and Celsus.

441 35: [οὐδέν ἐστιν, ἀγα]πητοί, τ[ὸ] λεγόμε[νον καὶ γινόμενον] [δίχα παραβολῆς καὶ προκεντή-ματος. Πάντα ὅσα ἐὰν γίνεται καὶ λέγεται, παραβολῆς τυγχάνει]
[τὸ μὲν λεγόμενον παραβολῆς]
[τὸ δὲ γινόμενον προτυπώσεως]
("beloved, all the accounts and events are vain, except as a parable and a pattern. For whatever happened and whatever was recounted harmonizes with the symbol, the accounts with the parable").
Justin, *Dial.* 114: Sometimes the Holy Spirit causes things to happen that were types of coming events; sometimes the Spirit speaks words. . . . Daniélou: παραβολή ("parable") is not identical with τύπος ("figure"/"example") and does not describe the meaning of the *events,* but the exposition of the texts.

and the meaning of history are thus carefully distinguished.[442] Thus the twin phenomena exist side by side: direct prediction, the meaning of which is brought to light by proper exegesis, and the typological interpretation of salvation history.[443] No work of art is produced without a mode. But once it is created, the model (*typos*) is useless (37).

The specific reflections on time are important:

38: ἑκάστῳ γὰρ ἴδιος καιρός, τοῦ τύπου ἴδιος χρόνος, τῆς ὕλης ἴδιος χρόνος ("So, to each its own time, to the type its time, to the materials their time").[444]

40: ἐγένετο οὖν ὁ λαὸς τύπος προκεντήματος καὶ ὁ νόμος γραφὴ παραβολῆς τὸ δὲ εὐαγγέλιον διήγημα νόμου καὶ πλήρωμα ἡ δὲ ἐκκλησία ἀπο[δο]χεῖον τῆς ἀληθείας ("For the people were the pattern of the type" [Perler: "the outline of a plan"] "and the law the writing of a parable" [Perler: "the letter of a parable"] "but the gospel is the fullness of the law" [Blank: "the exposition of the law and its fullness"] "and the church the receptacle of reality").

Then the evaluation is given:

41: [ὁ λαὸς] ἦν τίμιος πρὸ τοῦ τὴν ἐκκλησίαν [ἀνα]σταθῆναι καὶ ὁ νόμος θαυμασ[τὸς] πρὸ τοῦ τὸ εὐαγγέλιον φωτισθῆναι ("that is, the people was prized before the church was raised, and the law was admirable before the gospel shed abroad").

In this way Melito is able to provide a basis for the cancellation of the old cultic ritual as well as the status of the Jewish people. Then follows a survey of salvation history from Adam on. The horizon is exclusively that of the Bible. Of course, the biblical history is accepted as the history of humanity in general. This history is not only permeated by terrible corruption; there is also a "typological" line of salvation events that is woven into it throughout: the sufferings of the Lord are reflected in advance in the patriarchs, the prophets, in all the suffering figures of the Old Testament from Abel on,[445] all focusing on the appearance of Christ (66ff.). Christ freed us from bondage to the cosmos, just as Israel was freed from the land of Egypt.

The idea of preexistence becomes a category of interpretation (69). Then a new course of thought begins (72ff.) according to which the fate of Christ became the standard by which the Jews are judged. His suffering was prophesied, but the prophecies are an accusation (cf. Justin, *Apol.* 1.48; *Dial.* 69). The

---

[442] The distinction is blurred by Origen, where he is not dependent on Melito; there he is only interested in the Scripture as an immense παραβολή; he reduces the τύπος to ἀλληγορία ("allegory").

[443] See further 35: [ἵνα ὡς ἂν τὸ γινόμενον διὰ τῆς προτυπώσεως δ]είκνυται, οὕτως καὶ τὸ λεγόμενον [διὰ τῆ]ς παραβολῆς φωτισθῇ ("so, as the events are unveiled by the example, so also, the accounts are made clear by the parable").

[444] Cf. Eccl. 3:1ff. Daniélou, "Figure et évènement," 287f.: of fundamental importance in the history of theological thinking; Melito was the first to show that the *typos* establishes the law of salvation history. τύπος ("figure"/"example") is a matter of prophecy, in between prefiguration and the reality itself.

[445] On 63 (Jer. 11:19), see Justin, *Dial.* 72; the quotation in Tertullian, *Adv. Iud.* 10.12; *Adv. Marc.* 3.19.3; 4.40.3. It is lacking in the Apostolic Fathers, Irenaeus, Clement of Alexandria.

"must" of the sufferings of Christ does not remove the guilt of those at whose hands he suffered. 75: it was necessary that he suffer, but not through you!

In this passage a crack opens up in the conception of salvation history, by which it is finally set aside, along with the idea of prophecy. On the one hand, the conduct of Israel is a matter of the past, but on the other, it affects the present (87ff.). The death of Christ is proclaimed (94): "Who is the murderer?" Israel gets to hear an outrageous portrayal of its deed: you caused the Lord to perish, and now you have utterly perished, and slump down as a corpse" (99; cf. Tertullian, *Adv. Iud.* 13). But this is the dark background for the praise of the exalted one (100ff.), for the meaning of his exaltation is the universal proclamation of salvation: death is destroyed, Hades has been trampled underfoot: "Thus it is that by this means all races of humanity . . . receive forgiveness of sins. For I am your forgiveness. . . ."[446]

The polemic against Israel attains its full pathos from the idea of preexistence: the Jesus who was killed is, in fact, the creator of the world and of Israel, the Lord of all salvation history. This objectification of Christology and salvation history effects an intensification. Now Israel is unavoidably isolated from humanity in general, until both are reunited in the universal call to repentance and the universal pronouncement of salvation.

From the *Apology* we need note further only the one item, the unique outlook on the political scene, namely, relating the gospel to the *pax romana* (Eusebius, *Hist. Eccl.* 4.26.7): Our philosophy, once having gained strength among the barbarians, blossomed and flourished under the rulership of your (sc. of Antoninus Pius) ancestor Augustus among your peoples, and caused your reign to flourish.[447]

---

[446] Blank (*Meliton*, 81ff.) offers an example of how one can attempt to hush up an attack on the Jews, even when it is conditioned by salvation history: a withdrawal to the position of an objective historian (what would that be?) was not possible. —But that still means that one sticks to the view of the historical verification of the "murder of God," but only quibbles about the way it is evaluated —appropriate for the times. Based on the history of revelation (!), a distinction should be made "between the Old Testament as revelation and post-Christian Judaism, the synagogue" (p. 83). But how? It is still the same old song! The theological view of salvation history is not to be criticized (p. 84). The hour will come "when Israel will recognize for herself this [which?] truth as the fruit [!] of an intensive dialogue with the revelation bestowed upon her [read: the Roman church]" (p. 86). —A verbatim quotation.

[447] For the issue itself, cf. Hippolytus, *In Dan.* 4.9; Origen, *Contra Cels.* 2.30; Eusebius, *Dem. Ev.* 3.7.30–35. Harnack, *Mission* 1:298: the most presumptuous expression of Christian self-confidence. Opposed by E. Peterson, *Der Monotheismus als politisches Problem*, 70: No, but mistrust of the empire, "which lays claim to a kind of ecumenicity that befits only the Church." Cf. the continuation in Melito, which contradicts Peterson's "ecclesiastically" desirable interpretation. Then too it is precisely the mentioning of the "bad" emperors Nero and Domitian, who had persecuted the Christians, which serves the purpose of the Christian ingratiation of the state. The contrasting point, a negative judgment against the empire, is found in Minucius Felix; see below.

The Letter of Theophilus of Antioch to Autolycus[448]

Harnack, *History of Dogma* 2:194 n. 2: "Theophilus merely looks on the Gospel as a continuation of the prophetic revelations and injunctions. Of Christ, however, he did not speak at all, but only of the Logos (Pneuma), which has operated from the beginning. To Theophilus the first chapters of Genesis already contain the sum of all Christian knowledge (II 10-32)" (cf. *Against Philosophy* 3.2f.).

Lietzmann, *History of the Christian Church* 2:187: He brings no new features to his portrayal of apologetic, but "wrote a more pleasing Greek, brought somewhat more of superficial learning to the front than did his predecessors. . . ."[449]

A sample of his level of education is given in 2.4: he places Stoic atheists, Epicurus, and Chrysippus all in the same category.[450] Whatever his educational level, he is still significant for his role in transferring the concept of inspiration to the New Testament (3.12).[451] It is important that the idea of inspiration is not bound up into epochs of the history of salvation. Theophilus does not have a concept of apostle or apostolic in some sense distinct from the inspired personages of the Old Testament. The vast resources of the Old Testament are simply seen as Christian documents of revelation, inspired by the same Spirit as the Gospels (3.12). The perspective of *unity* prevails: the *one* God, the unity of the triad God–Logos–Wisdom. There is thus *one* God and *one* law (1.7; cf. 2.10, 22; 3.23). There is no such thing as a *problem* of the law. It is not reduced to the moral law. The topic of the ritual law is missing, just as there is no topic "Israel."[452]

The Old Testament stories can be interpreted allegorically. In addition, the narratives of the Old Testament can be used for the proof of antiquity. The

---

[448] Editions: G. Bardy, Sources chrétiennes 20 (Paris: Cerf, 1948; French translation by J. Sender); R. M. Grant (with English translation), *Theophilus of Antioch: Ad Autolycum.* Oxford Early Christian Texts (Oxford: Oxford University Press, 1970); German translation: A. di Pauli, *Bibliothek der Kirchenväter* 14 (1913) 9ff.

[449] The thesis of F. von Loof, that Theophilus was a source for Irenaeus, cannot be discussed here (*Theophilus von Antiochien Adversus Marcionem,* TU 46.2 [Leipzig: Hinrichs, 1930]). Contacts with others (Geffcken, *Apologeten,* 250f.) hardly concern us; cf. e.g., 3.15 with Athenagoras 35; 2.15 with Philo, *Decal.* 104. On the praise of the creation (1.6); cf. Athenagoras 16.

[450] On the collection of quotations (2.8, 36f.), see Geffcken, *Apologeten,* 250; N. Zeegers van der Vorst, "Les citations poétiques chez Theophile d'Antioche," in *St. Patr.* 10, TU 107 (Berlin: Akademie-Verlag, 1970) 168-74.

[451] Von Campenhausen, *Formation,* 332f., who also deals with further developments (via Tertullian) up until Origen. 205 n. 290: Irenaeus does not yet speak of a specific "inspiration" of New Testament authors except for one time when he is in a tight spot exegetically (*Adv. Haer.* 3.16.2) (*Formation,* 205 n. 290). On the significance of Montanism in this connection, see *Formation,* 221ff.

[452] Moses is a διάκονος ("servant") of the law for the whole world, especially for the Hebrews, who are also called Jews. With this, the problem is set aside.

Old Testament history is the history of humanity in general.[453] Cf. the rupture in human history that occurred in connection with the spread of humanity over the whole earth after the flood (2.22) and the new beginning that was made through Moses (3.18). But this thread is pursued further only in terms of the *chronology*.[454] The chronology is of interest partly because it is used to refute the charge of newness (3.29; cf. Celsus and Diognetus).

Of course the concept of free will is also true and important for Theophilus (2.27), and with an apologetic slant: everything was created good, but evil entered only through human sin (2.17). Nor did Theophilus escape the consequence of this view, that through this doctrine a historical understanding of the law becomes impossible.[455] Despite the investiture in seemingly historical garments (2.32f.), his understanding of the issue is conceived unhistorically (2.34), which corresponds to the unhistoricality of his idea of inspiration. The connection of "history" with his concept of God is only a naïve philosophical connection: it is a matter of *creatio ex nihilo* (2.10, 4, 13), his concern being to refute the doctrine of the eternity of the world.

By means of the biblical chronology and the idea of creation, Theophilus can oppose both the philosophical claim of the eternity of the world (2.4) and the legendary accounts of the fabulous epochs at the beginning of human history.[456] With his presuppositions, he is able to extend the biblical chronology up to his own time (Marcus Aurelius). History is reduced to chronology (see above on Tatian). The period of time decisive for Christians, the time of the advent of Christ, consistently fails to appear: it would bring the "proof of antiquity" to naught. Thus, Theophilus also confirms the rule: Where there is no salvation history, there is no problem with the Jews.

Irenaeus

Our question is: Does not the evidence provided by Irenaeus refute the thesis that the Christian confession of faith conceived in terms of salvation history and the attitude toward Judaism are directly related? He was, in fact, the first to construct a theology that was systematically conceived in terms of salvation history and thus became foundational for all such later developments.[457] And

---

[453] The proof of antiquity embraces also the Greek lawgivers (3.23). This is nothing new; cf. already Josephus, *Ag. Ap.* 2.154.

[454] For a survey of this chronology, see di Pauli, 107ff.; Grant, *Theophilus*, xxiiiff.

[455] A detail from the history of humanity that has occasioned much racking of scholar's brains, the "Sibyl of the Tower Building" (2.31), was mentioned in other passages (*Sib. Or.* 3.97ff.; Alexander Polyhistor; Abydenus; W. Spoerri, *KlP*).

[456] And find fault with the shortcomings of secular historical writing (2.30, 33; 3.16, 26). He attempts to set Moses into a chronological framework with the help of Manetho, whom he knows only from Josephus, just as is the case with his knowledge of Berosus (3.29). (He does not know Berosus's numbers at all.)

[457] Harnack, *History of Dogma* 2:240: "According to this conception the central point of history was no longer the Logos as such, but Christ as the *incarnate God* . . ."; cf. 263f.

in his case this did not result in any thematic conflict with Judaism.[458] As a preview: the problem becomes more critical when the data in Tertullian and Hippolytus are taken into account, for in them the systematic role of salvation history is limited in comparison with Irenaeus,[459] but the topic of Judaism comes more strongly to the fore.

In order to make sense of the evidence, it is necessary to keep in mind the style of polemic—new since the time of Irenaeus—against the heretics and the new way in which the New Testament canon (von Campenhausen, *Formation*, 182ff.) was used. The New Testament now becomes the norm by means of which the debate is carried on. That implies holding fast to the Old Testament as well and carries with it not only the judgments of the Old Testament against Israel (the prophets) but the judgments of the New Testament against the Jews. There is thus a cumulative effect.

That the Old Testament could not be dispensed with was not only a matter of tradition but at the same time an actualization of the struggle against heresy. The first item on the agenda in this struggle was the identity of the highest God, who created the world and the Father of Jesus Christ.[460]

Irenaeus, *Adv. Haer.* 4.2.3: The writings of Moses are words of Christ, addressed to Jews (John 5:46f.). The unity of the two Testaments is developed thematically in 4.9: The master of the household (Matt. 13:52) gives the appropriate law to the slaves and to the free (those who are justified by faith). The Logos is the author of both Testaments, for he spoke with Abraham and Moses, and in the New Testament reestablished freedom and multiplied grace.[461]

However, the statements about Testaments, law, and covenant cannot all simply be made the various numerators of a common denominator. Tensions emerge: between the affirmation of the identity of the old and the new revelation, and the claim that the new covenant is superior (along with a constant emphasis on the fact that it was the same God at work in both covenants) (4.9, 11); between the foundational proof from prophecy and the pedagogy of God that works through salvation history; between the historical function of the ceremonial law as a reaction to the disobedience of Israel and its typological meaning (4.11.4).

---

[458] Ibid. 2:304. Harnack speaks of a "decay of anti-Judaism" (in the early Catholic fathers). For Irenaeus, the Jewish people is the representative of humanity (2:307). —Granted, but how?

[459] Cf. the characteristic judgment of Harnack (*History of Dogma* 2:257): "Here also the philosophical and cosmological interest prevails; the history of salvation appears only to be the continuation of the history of the world as such."

[460] Harnack, *History of Dogma* 2:249: The anti-Gnostic fathers consistently argue "on behalf of the Gnostic Demiurge and against the Gnostic supreme God. It never occurs to them to proceed in the opposite way and prove that the supreme God may be the Creator."

[461] Marcion's argument is turned around (*Adv. Haer.* 4.12.4): "quomodo finis legis Christus, si non et initium eius esset?" ("And how is Christ the end of the law, if he is not also the final cause of it?").

One can explain the tensions as the result of the reworking of apologetic tradition.[462] But one must look behind the "explanations" that are provided by the history of the times or by Irenaeus's psychology and ask the prior question of whether it is not the case that behind apparently divergent statements a unified background may not after all become visible, namely, a comprehensive plan of salvation history that embraces these tensive statements[463] and necessarily results in such divergent statements through the objectivizing of that which is essentially incapable of being objectified.

Irenaeus sets out to bridge these gaps. The affirmation of the identity of the law in the two covenants presupposes that it is summed up in the love commandment (4.12): There are agreements in content; but *now* the commandment is directed to those who are free, for the freeing of the soul. Thus from "thou shalt not commit adultery" is derived "do not lust" (4.13.3). So too in the case of the sacrificial laws, the purification of the old by the new is established (4.18), and thus the sameness of God is maintained against the heretics. It is in fact precisely the ceremonial law that proves the salvation-historical continuity: Jesus and his apostles keep the old regulations and thus make clear that the God who gave these regulations is the self-same God who is at work in them (3.12).

Biblical history is the history of humanity in general. That is the framework within which Israel will be spoken of.[464] But even in this there is a necessary tension: even if the Jews are the representatives of humanity in general, insofar as their history is the history of humanity, they are still a special people, as those who had received the prophecies and the commandments, the prophets, Moses, the temple, as the concrete people in and through whom humanity is educated.[465] But it is clear: the problem cannot be solved without remainder; things do not come out even. And that will become even more clear when the

---

[462] Tensions become visible in 4.16, for example: circumcision was only a mark of identification; the ceremonies in themselves do not at all have any justifying power. And why did God not make any covenant with the patriarchs? Because the law is not given for the righteous. The righteous patriarchs had the power of the Decalogue written on their hearts and thus required no external letter of the law.

[463] In this regard it is, of course, not to be disputed that here and there auxiliary structures were erected ad hoc, e.g., the charge that the Jewish leaders had corrupted the text of the Mosaic law (4.12).

[464] See above, Harnack, *History of Dogma* 2:307; N. Brox, "Juden und Heiden bei Irenäus," *MTZ* 16 (1965): 89ff.: The ideas concerning the Jews are not completely integrated. Many a saying about them actually functions as an argument against the Gnostics.

[465] A tension for us, but not for Irenaeus, since, of course, for him a secular understanding of humanity—that is, a humanity that is other than that of the biblical creation story—was inconceivable. Harnack, *History of Dogma* 2:307 n. 1: "To Irenaeus the heathen are simply idolaters, who have even forgotten the law written in their heart; wherefore the Jews stand much higher, for they only lacked the *agnitio filii* ("knowledge of the Son"; 3.5) etc." But a contradiction remains: "The pre-Christian righteous know the Son and do not know him, they require the appearance of the Son and do not require it." The knowledge of the Son is sometimes a *new* truth, sometimes is identified with the knowledge of the creator.

question is raised, What about the *future* of the Jews? On this, Irenaeus says nothing directly. In any case, after the appearance of the covenant of freedom, he has denied the Jews any significance.

So also in his chiliastic train of thought, the Jews as a people play no further role: The Antichrist comes from this people, and their holy city will be the headquarters for the earthly reign of Christ. "But the nation itself, which, according to this theory, had represented all mankind from Moses to Christ, just as if all men had been Jews, now entirely disappears."[466]

Particular Evaluations of the Jews

4.7.4: They mean the Father as he is in himself without being able to recognize the Word. They read incorrectly; cf. 3.6.2; 5.33; 4.26.1f.; 6.1 should be compared with Matt. 11:27! 13:11-15 etc. 4.11.4: they do not recognize the development of salvation history. They have a dishonest turn of mind: 4.2.6; 11.4; 12.1, 33.1. Each time the attitude of the Christians is presented in contrast.

4.23f.: The conversion of the Jews is given as one argument for the correct (Christian) exposition of the Old Testament.

4.27.4: The disobedience of the Jews and their punishment or forgiveness by God demonstrates the continuity of both Testaments. This is said against the heretics who use the transgressions of Israel as an argument for their distinguishing the Creator from the Father of Jesus Christ, while the fact is that the transgressions of the Jews have come to us in the tradition for the sake of our own improvement.

4.28.3: Just as the Jews were saved through the blindness of the Egyptians, so we receive salvation through the blindness of the Jews. The whole presentation is dominated by the struggle against Gnosticism. The Jews only appear where the schema of salvation history touches upon them.

The comparison with Justin is instructive. His teaching concerning postbiblical Judaism (see above): (a) the transfer of the rulership to the Romans (*Apol.* 1.32, cf. 52; Tertullian, *Apol.* 26) (b) the appearance of Christ in Jerusalem (*Dial.* 85); (c) the absence of the Spirit in Judaism (*Dial.* 87). In Irenaeus the matter appears thus: He too includes the destiny of Jerusalem in a salvation-historical framework, but the salvation history is not of a national character but a universal one, a schema of two epochs of slavery and freedom, with two kinds of laws. But it is the fruits of freedom that are sown over the whole earth. With that, the rule of Jerusalem comes to an end, "after it had brought forth its fruit in its time," that is, Christ and the apostles. *Jesus* fulfilled the law; *Jerusalem* fulfilled its time. With the advent of the new covenant, the law comes to an end. Further, an aspect of the role of Jerusalem is transferred to the end

---

[466] Harnack, *History of Dogma* 2:310. *Adv. Haer.* 4.4; cf. 5.10, the interpretation of Rom. 11:17; the salvation-historical hope of Paul is eliminated. Contrast Hippolytus.

of the world. The announcement of judgment is pronounced on the people, an appeal to their free will (4.4).

Irenaeus, too, divides the history of salvation into periods: (1) the time of the righteous, without circumcision, without covenant; (2) the time of the patriarchs, without the Mosaic law. This law was later given for the purpose of education and discipline, after God had been forgotten.

This is done without polemic against the Jews; they are in fact quasi-absorbed within human history in general.[467] But the polemic emerges when the consequences are drawn for the present: 4.18 puts forth the criteria for the true sacrifice, at the same time explaining the difference between the meaning of sacrifice in the synagogue and in the church: in the *church* it is a matter of *inner* purity. The Jews offer no pure sacrifices. "For their hands are covered with blood, because they do not accept the message that God is sacrificed." In addition, the survey of Israel given *without* polemic in 4.30 should not be overlooked, from the preaching of the presbyter (4.27–32).

Summary Review

The silence concerning the Jews is not a sparing of them based on feelings. There is no doubt that faith in Christ is the condition of salvation. Irenaeus chooses the path of refusing to enter into direct debate with the Jews by dealing with the Old Testament as an exclusively Christian book and by treating the story of the Old Testament as the story of humanity in general.

Is our thesis concerning the relationship of salvation-historical theology and the stance toward Judaism refuted by Irenaeus? Only if one understands it as a psychological thesis instead of a theological one. The thesis is *not* refuted, because in Irenaeus the Jews are incorporated into humanity and the judgment pronounced on it—in reality, humanity in general has been absorbed by Israel.[468] The thesis is in fact confirmed precisely by Irenaeus, when one looks at the other side of the coin, the Jewish side. Judaism can neither allow itself to be incorporated into humanity as a whole by setting aside the law as the separating wall, nor can it tolerate this use of the Old Testament or its being eliminated from eschatology.

One could even advocate the thesis that a Judaism that affirms itself to be a separate people (and there can be no other Judaism) is dealt with more severely by Irenaeus than by his predecessors.

Tertullian

His statements about the Jews stand in close relationship to his struggle against Marcion. Despite the sharpness of his invective, there is less substance in his

---

[467] Paganism also only comes into view incidentally, as that idolatry from which the Jews were led forth.

[468] *Epideixis* 97: "Through the invocation of the name of Jesus who was crucified under Pontius Pilate, a separation emerged within humanity."

declarations than one might expect. This is a by-product of the fact that salvation history plays a diminished role (see above), and of the blurring of the two profiles.[469]

Regarding the Way the Materials are Structured

We have already mentioned Harnack's judgment that the philosophical-cosmological interest dominates and that salvation history appears only as the continuation of the history of the cosmos (*History of Dogma* 2:257). Von Campenhausen, *Formation*, 269ff.: Now the New Testament is considered more authoritative than the Old Testament (cf. *Adv. Iud.* 3; *Adv. Marc.* 4.1.3). The understanding of the unity and structure of the Scripture is the same as in Irenaeus, that is, conceived in salvation-historical terms, but more flat and shallow. W. H. C. Frend ("A Note on Tertullian and the Jews" in *St. Patr.* 10/1, TU 107 [Berlin: Akademie-Verlag, 1970] 291ff.)[470] relates the statements of Tertullian on the situation in Carthage to its Jewish congregation; quite a few Jews spoke Hebrew; there were contacts between the Jewish and the Christian congregations. Christians observed the Sabbath (*De ieiun.* 14.3) and other Jewish regulations (*Apol.* 21.2). There were Jewish-Christian elements in the congregation (*Adv. Marc.* 4.8.1): "Nos Iudaei Nazarenos appellant" ("The Jews also designate us Nazarenes"). Several regulations point to Jewish practices (*De idol.* 20; *Ex.* 23.13).[471]

The Available Documents

Two groups of writings are important for our purposes: (1) *Adversus Iudaeos* (ed. H. Tränkle [Wiesbaden: F. Steiner, 1964]); this writing is bound up with *Adversus Marcionem* (book 3); (2) *Ad nationes*, his preliminary work for the *Apologeticum*.[472]

---

[469] If these were more sharply distinguished, the dispute concerning the relationship of Tertullian to Minucius Felix would not continue to be carried on so hopelessly.

[470] W. H. C. Frend, "A Note on Jews and Christians," *JTS* n.s. 21 (1970): 92ff.; idem, "Jews and Christians in Third Century Carthage" in *Paganisme, Judaïsme, Christianisme*, Festschrift for M. Simon (Paris: Boccard, 1978) 185–94. Frend sets himself in opposition to T. D. Barnes ("Tertullian's Scorpiace" *JTS* n.s. 20 [1969]: 105ff.; idem, *Tertullian* [Oxford: Clarendon Press, 1971]). Barnes denies that there was any Jewish influence on the formation of the Christian church in Africa and that there were any connections between Jews and Christians. Tertullian indicates a lack of contact between the two groups. When he talks about Jews, it is the Jews of the apostolic period that he has in view, not those of his own time. Frend: too one-sided; there were in fact debates; cf. *Adv. Iud.* 1.

[471] On the problem of theophoric place-names, see *b. Sanh.* 63b. On the problem of invitations to dinner parties (*De idol.* 16) see *b. 'Abod. Zar.* 1.3. In *De spect.* Tertullian obviously draws arguments from Jewish doctrine. *Scorp.* 10 refers to contemporary Jewish activities.

[472] C. Becker, *Tertullians Apologeticum* (Munich: Kösel, 1954) (Becker 2); idem, *Tertullian Apologeticum*, Latin-German (2nd ed.; Munich: Kösel, 1961) (Becker 1).

The problems of *Adv. Iud.* have to do with authenticity, sources, unity, intended readers, the relation to *Adv. Marc.* (reviewed by Tränkle). Harnack, *Chronologie* 2:288ff.: *Adv. Iud.* 1–8 is certainly genuine. Nowhere else does Tertullian assert so energetically that there have been no more prophets since the time of Christ (chap. 8, repeated twice more in 9–14, but not in *Adv. Marc.!*). The virtuosity of the polemicist had not yet developed.

A. *Kroymann* (Corpus Scriptorum Ecclesiasticorum Latinorum 10; Vienna, 1914): The book has been worked over by a second hand. *Tränkle:* The first half has remained a mere sketch, similar to the *Ad nat.* In contrast, chaps. 9–10 are clearly structured and composed with great power of expression.[473]

The intended reader: Tränkle advocates the thesis that the literary genre *Adversus Iudaeos* is also directed to Christians and for Gentiles who were open to Christianity (p. lxxi). This genre serves to give a more thorough introduction to understanding the Bible to those who already possess some understanding. The primary goal was not to combat Judaism or to instruct Jews.[474] The apology *Adversus gentes* is directed to people for whom Christianity was still completely foreign[475] (p. lxxii).

Supplementary notes: Concerning Tertullian's sources in general: A. Harnack, "Tertullians Bibliothek christlicher Schriften," *Sitzungsberichte der Deutschen Akademie der Wissenschaften zu Berlin* (1914/10, 303ff.): Greek language and culture were influential in Carthage (*Pass. Perp.* 13). *The Bible:* At least the most important parts already existed in Latin. A call to private reading of the Bible is found in *Ad ux.* 2.6. On the use of the Greek Bible: *Adv. Marc.* 2.9 etc. *Enoch:* *De Idol.* 4.15; *De Cult.* 1.3; 2.10. *4 Ezra: Praescr.* 3. Tertullian knows *Ep. Ar.*

---

[473] Tränkle, xliv: In 11.10, the punishment of the Jews *appears* to be forgotten at the end. The section that begins here is the concluding part. There is no longer any need to speak about the lot of the Jews. It is, in fact, dealt with only as a consequence of the death of Christ. 13.24–14.13 is an effort to supersede the incompletely developed section 10.17–12.2 (p. li). There has been a change in plans concerning the way Christology is handled between *Adv. Iud.* and *Adv. Marc.* To the original primacy of the Jews belongs also "ut de dei vocibus, quibus edocebantur, de promerendo deo et non offendendo praemonerentur" ("that for their instruction God spoke to them in special revelations, pointing out to them beforehand how they should merit his favor and avoid his displeasure") (pp. lxvif.). This is not found in *Adv. Iud.,* nor would it be fitting there.

[474] Is this the reason precisely this title was chosen? Is the method of proof *lucus a non lucendo,* that is, establishing false and fantastic points of contact—from an apologetic necessity?

[475] Such judgments are to be made not on the basis of "genre" (particularly so since one can hardly speak of such in this case) but on the basis of content.

On the question of the sources for *Adv. Iud.,* see further Tränkle, lxviii: Migne, *PG* 10:787ff. contains the fragment of a ὁμιλία πρὸς ᾿Ιουδαίους ἀποδεικτική ("demonstrative sermon against the Jews"). There is no point of contact with Tertullian, *Adv. Iud.* Tränkle, lxxxf.: Tertullian's dependence on Justin, *Dial.* is not to be proved with absolute certainty. *There* we first have the thesis of the abrogation of the old law; then come the individual regulations. But Tertullian deals with these first; then the thesis of the abrogation of the old law follows as the climax. —But this is more likely data for a *literary* connection. Further, *Justin, Dial.* 78 concerning Damascus in Arabia, the land from which the Magi come. Tränkle, lxxxvi n. 1: that is found only in Justin (*Dial.* 77f., 102, 106) and Tertullian, *Adv. Iud.* 9.12. —This too indicates a literary connection.

or its content (*Apol.* 18); *Josephus: Apol.* 19; "whether he had actually read him remains unclear" (Harnack, p. 312). Knowledge of Jewish legends: *Scorp.* 8; *Sib. Or.* 3.100ff.: *Ad nat.* 2.10, but most likely through an indirect tradition; otherwise there is no evidence of his awareness of the Jewish Sibylline literature. There is no trace of *1* and *2 Clem.*, Ignatius, Polycarp, *Phil.*, Papias, *Didache?*

Harnack, "Tertullians Bibliothek," 313: He does not know *Barnabas*, despite *Adv. Marc.* 3.7; *Adv. Iud.* 14 (*Barn.* 7); *Adv. Marc.* 3.18; *Adv. Iud.* 10 (*Barn.* 12). A different view in H. Windisch, *Barnabasbrief,* 301: the joint influence of *Barn.* and Justin is not an adequate explanation. Cf. Tränkle, lxxvi: The topos of the two rams (*Adv. Iud.* 14.9f = *Adv. Marc.* 3.7) can only derive from *Barn.* 7; Justin, *Dial.* 40.4 is too colorless.

Further data from Harnack: Tertullian knows *Hermas* and the *Acts of Paul* (*Bapt.* 17). On *Hermas:* In *Orat.* 16 he changes his judgment in *Pud.* 10, 20. "Barnabas" = the Letter to the Hebrews. Harnack, 315: *Acts of Pilate, Apol.* 21: from Justin; *Act. Perp: De an.* 55. *Justin* is mentioned only *once,* not as an apologist but as an anti-Gnostic writer. The apologetic literature as a whole is mentioned once: *Test. an.* 1. Justin's *Dialogue* appears especially frequently in *Adv. Iud.; Adv. Marc.* 3; See W. Otto on Justin, *Dial., passim.* Tatian: see Harnack, *Die Überlieferung der griechischen Apologeten des zweiten Jahrhunderts in der Alten Kirche und im Mittelalter,* TU 1.1 (Leipzig: Hinrichs, 1883) 200ff.; 297: Theophilus? There is much to suggest this, but it cannot be proved. *SAB* 318 n. 2: There were no connections between Tertullian and Alexandria.

On the Individual Writings

Adversus Iudaeos
A typological framework is erected in chap. 1: two peoples, two races, originated from Rebekah (Gen. 25:23). The Christians are the younger, which must be served by the elder. From the very beginning, the law was given to the whole world and all nations.[476] Righteousness already existed before Moses. As in Justin, time is divided into periods: Abraham did not yet keep the Sabbath. Circumcision was given to Israel as a mark of identification, so that they would be prohibited from entering the holy city because of their misdeeds (according to Isa. 1:7; cf. Justin, *Dial.* 26). The old law has been abolished, and the universal expansion of Christianity is an argument for the advent of Christ.[477]

Chapter 8 furnishes proof that Daniel 9 has been fulfilled (the appearance of

---

[476] For the following, cf. Justin throughout. Tertullian, *Ad nat.* and Justin: Becker 2, 81ff.

[477] On the awareness of the numerical strength of Christians, see Justin, *Apol.* 1.53; *Dial.* 110. The proof text is Isa. 54:1; on the history of the interpretation of this text, see Andresen, *Die Kirchen der alten Christenheit* (Stuttgart: Kohlhammer, 1971) 129f.

Christ and the destruction of Jerusalem). Since the advent of Christ there are no longer any prophets whose job it was to proclaim his advent.

The *conduct* of the Jews is described in the famous statement: "Ab illis enim incepit infamia" (13) ("for it is from them that the infamy [attached to that name] began").[478] And again the prohibition of the Jews' residence in the holy land is stated.

It is obvious to the reader: this brochure is not overburdened with either clarity or profundity. The extensive writing against Marcion[479] cannot make up for this lack, because there the Jews do not appear as an independent topic, but only as a by-product of the struggle against Marcion, the struggle to preserve the Old Testament and its God.[480]

Ad nationes and *Apologeticum*[481]

The one place where Jews are mentioned (see Becker 2, *Tertullians Apologeticum*, 244ff.) is in connection with the safeguarding of the authority of Scripture and the proof of antiquity. In this regard the connection between Jews and Christians is presented. The decisive reason is the struggle against paganism.[482] Cf. *Ad nat.* 1.11.4 with *Apol.* 16.3f.;[483] then *Ad nat.* 1.7.15 with *Apol.* 7.3. In

---

[478] See *Ad nat.* 1.14: "Quod enim aliud genus seminarium est infamiae nostrae?" ("For what other set of men is the seed-plot of all the calumny against us?").

[479] For the development of the beginnings found in *Adv. Iud.*, see, e.g., *Adv. Marc.* 2.17ff.; 3.3, 16, 23.

[480] *Adv. Marc.* 5.14.7 on Rom. 10:3f. (only here!): "Hic erit argumentatio haeretici quasi deum superiorem ignoraverint Iudaei, qui adversus eum iustitiam suam, id est legis suae, constituerint, non recipientes Christum, finem legis. Cur ergo zelum eorum erga deum proprium testimonium perhibet, si non et inscitiam erga eundem deum eis exprobrat, quod zelo quidem dei agerentur, sed non per scientiam, ignorantes scilicet eum, dum dispositiones eius in Christo ignorant consummationem legi staturo atque ita suam iustitiam tuentur adversus illum"

("Hereupon we shall be confronted with an argument of the heretic, that the Jews were ignorant of the superior God, since, in opposition to him, they set up their own righteousness—that is, the righteousness of their law—not receiving Christ, the end (or finisher) of the law. But how then is it that he bears testimony to their zeal for their own God, if it is not in respect of the same God that he upbraids them for their ignorance? They were affected indeed with zeal for God, but it was not an intelligent zeal: they were, in fact, ignorant of Him, because they were ignorant of His dispensations by Christ, who was to bring about the consummation of the law; and in this way did they maintain their own righteousness in opposition to Him.")

[481] Becker 1 and 2; 2, 31ff.: An analysis of *Ad nat.* as a preliminary work; 96: The second part of the *Ad nat.* is not a continuation of the first, but doublet of it; the first part is not taken into consideration in the *Apol.* 71f.: contacts with previous apologetic (2, 96).

[482] That is already indicated by the consistent point of departure, the monotheistic faith that Christians have in common with the Jews, and the struggle against polytheism as *the* common enemy; a firmly established component part of this is the fight against demonology (Becker 2, 246f.).

[483] Pompey found, as even the liar Tacitus must concede, no image of God in the Jerusalem temple.

the *Apol.* there is also the demarcation of Christians from the Jews.[484] The mentioning of the Jews in the service of a polemic against paganism is especially clear in *Apol.* 26.3.

If we now attempt to take stock of the evidence provided by the *Apol.*, the first item of business must be to consider Becker's thesis of two versions of the document[485] (independently of the relation of the *Apol.* to *Ad nat.!*). We will put aside for the moment the issue of the consequences for the relation of the *Apol.* to Minucius Felix and give a survey of the passages in Tertullian. For purposes of comparison we may use *Ad nat.* 1.13 and *Apol.* 16.[486]

Ad nat. 1.13.4: "Quod quidem facitis exorbitantes et ipsi a vestris ad alienas religiones: Iudaei enim festi sabbata et cena pura et Iudaici ritus lucernarum et ieiunia cum azymis et orationes litorales, quae utique aliena sunt a diis vestris. (5) Quare ut ab excessu revertar, qui solem et diem eius nobis exprobratis, agnoscite vicinitatem: non longe a Saturno et sabbatis vestris sumus."

("By resorting to these customs, you deliberately deviate from your own religious rites to those of strangers. For the Jewish feasts are the Sabbath and 'the Purification,' and Jewish also are the ceremonies of the lamps, and the fasts of unleavened bread, and the 'littoral prayers,' all of which institutions and practices are of course foreign to your gods. Wherefore, that I may return from this digression, you who reproach us with the sun and Sunday should consider your proximity to us. We are not far off from your Saturn and your days of rest.")

Apol. 16.11: "Aeque si diem solis laetitiae indulgemus, alia longe ratione quam religione solis, secundo loco ab eis sumus, qui diem Saturni otio et victui decernunt exorbitantes et ipsi a Iudaico more, quem ignorant." ("In the same way, if we devote Sun-day to rejoicing, from a far different reason than Sun-worship, we have some resemblance to those of you who devote the day of Saturn to ease and luxury, though they too go far away from Jewish ways, of which indeed they are ignorant.") Compare further *Ad nat.* 1.14 (the anecdote of Onocoetes) with *Apol.* 16.[487]

Ad nat. 1.14.2: "Et credidit vulgus Iudaeo" ("And the crowd believed this infamous Jew") (the Jew decked out like an ass) ("Jew" is missing in the *Apol.*).

[484] Becker 2, 287: in the *Apol.* Christology made necessary an explanation of the connections between Jews and Christians. Whereas *Ad nat.* 2.2.5 "speaks of the thievery of the philosophers from the sacred Scriptures, there is no reference at all to the Jews." Contrast *Apol.* 47.3. But the account still does not balance: *Ad nat.* 14.1 ascribes the caricature of Onocoetes to a Jewish apostate; *Apol.* 16.12 does not comment on his nationality (cf. Becker 2, 288 and n. 24).

[485] Survey of the two versions: Becker 2, 235ff.; on the *Fragmentum Fuldense*, sec. 149ff. A small example: In *Ad. nat.* 1.11:2 and *Apol.* 16.2 the fourth book of Tacitus's *Histories* is incorrectly quoted; in the final version of *Apol.* 16.2 this has been corrected; Becker 2, 200.

[486] Simon, *Verus Israel*, 286: *Ad nat.* 1.13 appears to be inspired by Josephus, *Ag. Ap.* 2.280ff. (and Philo, *Vit. Mos.* 2.20ff.); Josephus: The Jewish law is also widely accepted among the Gentiles; as examples he names the Sabbath, festivals, the lighting of lamps, and the food laws.

[487] Preceded by Tacitus's tale of the worship of the ass's head, who must admit that it stands in contradiction to his own statement about the imagelessness of Jewish worship.

Apol. 7.3: Motive for the hostility: "ex aemulatione Iudaei, ex concussione milites, ex natura ipsi etiam domestici nostri" ("the Jews, as was to be looked for, from a spirit of rivalry; the soldiers, out of a desire to extort money; our very domestics, by their nature").[488]

Apol. 18.5ff.: The origin of the Septuagint (with a reference to Aristeas): The prophets came from the Jews and were sent to them "scilicet ad domesticam dei gentem ex patrum gratia. Hebraei retro, qui nunc Iudaei" ("for from themselves, as a people dear to God for their father's sake. Now in ancient times the people we call Jews bear the name of Hebrews"). 18.6: Primam istis instrumentis auctoritatem summa antiquitas vindicat" ("Their high antiquity [i.e., the biblical writings], first of all, claims authority for these writings") (elaborated on in the *Fragmentum Fuldense*).

The central passage in Tertullian's work related to our topic is *Apol.* 20f.: *Christianity and Judaism regarded from the point of view of old and new* – in view of the fact that Christians appeal to the old Jewish writings, but that Christianity itself appeared only in recent times, under Tiberius (7.3; 21.1) and Pontius Pilate. Is Christianity seeking refuge in the shadow of "insignissimae religionis, certe licitae" ("an illustrious religion, one that has at any rate undoubted allowance of the law")? Well, the Christians have a right to appeal to the Jewish Scriptures. This right is based on the agreement in the concept of God, and that this God had prophesied the coming of his Son. This both poses the problem and proposes a solution: the relation of the former times to the historical advent of Christianity must be grounded theologically (God the Creator) and christologically (the preexistence of the Logos, through whom God created the world) (21.10ff.). Then the possibility is given of bringing into a coherent order all the aspects of antiquity and superhistoricality, supertemporality, and the distinction of periods within time, with the historicality of revelation, the continuity between Jews and Christians, and the relationship between their agreements and their differences. These agreements and differences are enumerated in 21.1ff.: they concern food laws, holy days, circumcision, and the names ("Jews"/"Christians").

That first becomes comprehensible when the background is illuminated and examined: the Jews concurred with the common opinion about Jesus and crucified him as an ordinary human being. Thus Christians can be considered to be worshipers of an ordinary human being. But we are not ashamed of Christ "neque de deo aliter praesumimus. Necesse est igitur pauca de Christo ut deo" ("nor do we differ from the Jews concerning God. We must make, therefore, a remark or two as to Christ's divinity") (21.3).

From this point of view the times are distinguished historically, that is, christologically, 21.4: "Totum ("through all time" or "completely") Iudaeis erat apud deum gratia, ubi et insignis iustitia et fides originalium auctorum" ("In former times the Jews enjoyed much of God's favor, when the fathers of the

---

[488] On the Jews: commentary in chap. 21.

race were noted for their righteousness and faith"). That is why their rule increased mightily. But they fell away (from God), which is proved by their present fate.[489] They are scattered, banished from their own land. Their fate was predicted, and the prophecies also extend into the future: in the last days God will choose true servants out of every nation, in order to pour out even greater grace on them.

21.5: The Jews, in fact, know about the coming of Christ through the prophets. But—and this is the decisive point—"adventum eius exspectant, nec alia magis inter nos et illos compulsatio est" ("The Jews, too, were well aware that Christ was coming . . . ; nor is there any other contention between them and us") (21.15). Tertullian too takes the burden of guilt from Pilate and places it on the Jews.[490] But Tertullian's major opponents are the Greeks.[491] *Apol.* 26 repeats the historical argument of 21:4.[492]

De spectaculis[493]

At the parousia, he would like to see "eos . . . qui in dominum desaevierunt. Hic est ille, dicam, fabri et quaestuariae filius (cf. Origen, *Contra Cels.* 1.28, 32, 69, etc.) sabbati destructor, Samarites et daemonium habens. Hic est quem a Iuda redemisti" ("those whose fury vented itself against the Lord. 'This,' I shall say, 'this is that carpenter's or hireling's son, that Sabbath breaker, that Samaritan and devil-possessed! This is He whom you purchased from Judas!'").

Scorpiace

Context: The Gnostics claim that martyrdom is not required by God. Here too Judaism is overshadowed by the conflict with heretics and pagans, even when Tertullian is discussing monotheism and the law (chap. 2), with its announcement of blessing and curse. Though this commandment is, of course, addressed to Israel, the point is that it is precisely against idolatry (chap. 3): the golden calf, Israel's misdeeds and punishment. This is told precisely to establish the identity of the God of Israel and the God of the Christians, as a warning example. Chap. 4: That will which has prevailed upon people to become

---

[489] Justin, *Apol.* 1.32; *Dial.* 16; Tertullian, *Adv. Iud.; Apol.* 26.3.

[490] Who was inwardly already a Christian (21.24); this passage refers back to the *Acts of Pilate* for its support; cf. the allusion in *Apol.* 5; Justin, *Apol.* 1.35, 48; see F. Scheidweiler, in Hennecke-Schneemelcher, *NTApoc.* 1:444.

[491] Their gods are subject to the power of the Christians; through their admissions, they must involuntarily confirm the Christian faith.

[492] By means of the familiar political-juridical line of argument (which does not concern us here), that the Christians pray for the preservation of the world and the postponement of the end (39.2). To be sure, there is an ambivalence in the political attitude of Christians: in the way their numbers are used as an argument. They form the mass of loyal citizens and would be in a position to revolt (37). The state is foreign to them; "unam omnium rempublicam agnoscimus, mundum" ("We acknowledge one all-embracing commonwealth—the world") (38).

[493] W. Horbury, "Tertullian on the Jews in the Light of *De spectaculis* XXX. 5-6," *JTS* n.s. 23 (1972): 455-59: In this section Tertullian is primarily citing Jewish polemic.

martyrs by its constant prohibition of idolatry and punishment of idolaters is the will of no other God than the God of Israel.[494]

Minucius Felix, Octavius[495]

Preliminary Remarks

In view of the issue that concerns us, we may put aside the problem of whether Tertullian's *Apologeticum* or *Octavius* is the prior document, a problem already interminably discussed.

The subject is here seen from a philosophical point of view, not that of the history of salvation. If Harnack has established that for Tertullian salvation history recedes, then we must say that for Minucius Felix it simply disappears, regardless of how the question of priority is seen. So also the "proof of antiquity" is reduced to a minimum. There is certainly no doubt that the philosophers are dependent on the predictions of the prophets (34). But it is not the *age* of the prophets that is here the point, but the correspondence between Christian and philosophical doctrine (which had been distorted by the philosophers!). And when the venerability of antiquity is contrasted with the newness of Christianity, this is done in a completely general way—and by the opponent, Caecilius (6.3).

The argument that the historical success of Rome is a religious argument (6.1ff.; 12.5) is rejected with a sharpness that places it in the category "the intellectual resistance to Rome" (25). This is a key passage for comparison with Tertullian (*Apol.* 25; on *Apol.* 26.3/*Oct.* 33.2f., see below).

Consistent with this, the subject "Jews" is brought up in only two passages (chaps. 10 and 33)—and note *how* this is done![496]

(1) On chap. 10: The passage is problematic for Minucius himself. The context is Caecilius's political line of argument for Rome (chaps. 6 and 12) against monotheism: just look at who it is that advocates it! "Iudaeorum sola et misera gentilitas unum et ipsi deum, sed palam, sed templis aris victimis caerimoniisque coluerunt" ("The lonely and miserable nationality of the Jews worshiped

---

[494] Thus the denial of the necessity of martyrdom and the denial of the identity of the Christian God with the God of the Old Testament belong immediately together. Chap. 10: The heretics postpone the situation of the confession that Christ requires until heaven. You heretics, you transfer to the heavenly world the hatred against Christians, and the synagogue of the Jews that fount of persecution, and the pagans who cry out in the circus "So where is the third race now?" On the "fount of persecution": in the context, Tertullian is speaking of the *historical* beginning of persecutions, against the apostles. On the "third race," see above.

[495] Editions: B. Dombart (with German translation) 2nd ed., 1881; J. P. Waltzing, *Octavius* (2nd ed.; Leipzig, 1926); J. Beaujeu, *Minucius Felix: Octavius* (Paris, 1964); B. Kytzler, *Octavius* (with German translation) (Munich, 1965), with brief bibliography.

[496] Is it at all conditioned by, or required by, the subject matter being discussed in the context? Here the issue of his relation to Tertullian certainly becomes relevant: Is the topic taken up merely on the basis of his prototype?

one God, and one peculiar to itself; but they worshiped him openly, with temples, with altars, with victims, and with ceremonies").

(2) Chap. 33: The section stands noticeably isolated in its context; it takes up Caecilius's reference to the political fate of the Jews in an antithetical fashion and contains a dark hint to the history of the Jews (including the extension of that history into the present). This is preceded (32) by an exposition of the rule of God, with an admixture of Stoic features.[497] Then, with a strange jump in the train of thought, 33:1: "Nec nobis de nostra frequentia blandiamur: multi nobis videmur, sed deo admodum pauci sumus. Nos gentes nationesque distinguimus: deo una domus est mundus hic totus" ("Neither let us flatter ourselves concerning our multitude. We seem many to ourselves, but to God we are very few. We distinguish peoples and nations; to God this whole world is one family").[498]

In chap. 34, Minucius Felix then comes to a discussion of the correspondence between Christian and philosophical doctrine mentioned above. In between, the brief excursus on the Jews stands in chap. 33 as an erratic boulder: Without any preparation Minucius picks up the familiar objection of Caecilius from chap. 10 that the Jews do not practice their monotheism (as the Romans did their polytheism): Just check their history! While as they religiously worshiped God, they grew from a few to a numberless multitude, from slaves to kings "Scripta eorum relege, vel si Romanis magis gaudes, ut transeamus veteres, Flavi Iosephi vel Antoni Iuliani de Iudaeis require" ("Carefully read over their Scriptures, or if you are better pleased with the Roman writings, inquire concerning the Jews in the books [to say nothing of ancient documents] of Flavius Josephus or Antoninus Julianus").[499] Then you will observe that they, through their *nequitia* ("wickedness"), have brought their fate on themselves: first they abandoned God; then they were abandoned by God.[500]

Appendix: Tertullian and Minucius Felix

Examples[501]

(1) R. Heinze (*Tertullians Apologeticum*, Verhandlungen der sächeschen Gesellschaft der Wissenschaften, Philologische-historische Klasse 62 [Leipzig,

---

[497] A reminiscence of Cleanthes and the Areopagus speech in Acts 17: "Unde enim deus longe est, cum omnia caelestia terrenaque et quae extra istam orbis provinciam sunt deo cognita plena sint? Ubique non tantum nobis proximus, sed infusus est" ("For from where is God afar off, when all things heavenly and earthly, and that are beyond this province of the universe, are known to God, are full of God? Everywhere He is not only very near to us, but He is infused into us").

[498] This is a remarkable, nonpolitical version of Tertullian, *Apol.* 37 (the number of Christians as a revolutionary potential), alongside the unanticipated cosmopolitan statement of *Apol.* 38.3; see above. The common element is the Stoic basis.

[499] Flavi Iosephi (Flavius Josephus) does not fit the context; the text may be corrupt (Beaujeu; Schürer, *History* 1:58; Schürer-Vermes-Millar, *History* 1:33).

[500] Cf. *Apol.* 26.3; Justin, *Apol.* 1.32; cf. *Dial.* 52 (*translatio*).

[501] Reviewed by Becker 2, 103ff.

1910] 281ff.): Tertullian is primary. Samples: on his exposition of the topos of ass worship (p. 369).[502] 372: Cf. *Apol.* 17 (creation of the world) "verbo quo iussit, ratione qua disposuit, virtute qua potuit" ("He who by His commanding word, His arranging wisdom, His mighty power") with *Oct.* 5: "verbo iubet, ratione dispensat, virtute consummat" ("He orders everything . . . by a word; arranges it by His wisdom; perfects it by His power"). Heinze: In Minucius Felix, this verb has no specific theological function, but is only a leftover. Cf. *Apol.* 17.2 with *Oct.* 18.8: Minucius Felix has written in his exaggerated style: artificially constructed sentences, clever antitheses (pp. 374ff.). The very thing that Tertullian emphasizes is lacking in Minucius Felix, namely, the positive complement to the negative qualifications (*Apol.* 17.3). *Apol.* 17.4–6 (*testimonium animae*, "testimony of the soul"): *Oct.* 18.11 has an ascending line. It is not the *testimonium animae* that stands at the beginning, but that of the nation. *Apol.* 25 castigates the irreligion of the Roman wars (p. 428). Minucius Felix combines this with the Carneadian-Ciceronian understanding of the Roman *iustitia* (justice).

(2) B. Axelson (*Das Prioritätsproblem Tertullian-Minucius Felix*): *Apol.* 39.8: We are your brothers by the law of nature, of the *one* mother, even if we cannot call you truly human, because you are bad brothers. With much more right we are called brother by those who have acknowledged God as the one Father.

Oct. 31.8: *We* call each other brother, "ut unius dei parentis homines" ("as being people born of one parent"). *You,* however, rage against each other in mutual hatred, are brothers only so that you may murder each other.[503]

(3) H. Diller ("In Sachen Tertullian-Minucius Felix"): If one does not assume dependence of one on the other, but the use of a common source, then this would have to be of an apologetic nature, since their agreements in the refutation of charges against them is especially strong; and this common source must have been in Latin, because agreements extend even to points of vocabulary. There are also agreements in regard to Roman circumstances and authors. Compare:

Apol.	*Oct.*
10.7	23.9
10.5, 11	24.1
11.1	21.1
21.23	24.1

---

[502] H. Diller, "In Sachen Tertullian-Minucius Felix," *Philologus* 90 (1935): 98ff., 216ff.: Minucius Felix combines the basically contradictory points of view of Tertullian and Justin; cf. B. Axelson, *Das Prioritätsproblem Tertullian-Minucius Felix* (Lund: Gleerup, 1941) 82f.

[503] Heinze (*Tertullians Apologeticum,* 451 n. 1) explains this as a secondary transference from another source. —But is it really a matter of primary and secondary, or rather a matter of a different style?

In Tertullian, the presentation of the evidence is subordinated to the overall train of thought: (a) untrue charges against the Christians (7–9); (b) true items of information, but that cannot be accepted as charges: the Christians do not worship the gods (10.1). Then a proof is given that these do not exist (10.2): they were originally human beings, who even before their death were not divine; cf. the transition, 11.1.

In contrast, *Oct.* restricts the proof to the apotheosis of the rulers. The procedure for presenting the proof is a unity in Tertullian; in Minucius Felix it falls apart into separate arguments. On *Apol.* 8.7ff. and *Oct.* 30.1ff.: Tertullian draws up an extremely precise counterclaim (9). His examples are also found in *Greek* apologists.

In Minucius these two are compiled and even expanded from Cicero, *Resp.* 4.15 and Livy 22.57.6. But the proof is no longer smoothly presented. A secondary thought from *Apol.* 9.4 (Saturn) becomes the main idea (*Oct.* 30.3). In the case of Jupiter (Latiaris), the point is broken off. Tertullian: He is honored by the murder of human beings. Minucius Felix: by the execution of a *criminal;* the opposition could, of course, use the same argument.[504]

Apol. 16 – *Oct.* 29: Concerning the adoration of the cross: Both turn the charge back on the pagans. But Minucius adds another idea from the Greek apologists that is not very appropriate here: that the figure of the cross is found in nature.[505] On the one hand, the quotations from Virgil in *Oct.* are garbled;[506] on the other hand, Minucius Felix expands the material from Virgil (19; 21.5, 7). It is unlikely that Tertullian would have omitted these.

Apol. 14 – *Oct.* 24: Virgil, *Aen.* 8 does not fit in this context (the unworthy ideas of the gods entertained by the poets; the line of argument derives from *Apol.* 11.6).

There are seams at the points where the material from Cicero has been worked in: The note in *Oct.* 7.3 concerning the "mater Idaea, quae adventu suo et probavit matronae castitatem et urbem metu hostili liberavit" ("the Idaean mother, who at their arrival both approved the chastity of the matron, and delivered the city from the fear of the enemy") does not fit. This is not refuted by the faith in oracles (26), but by the false pretenses of the demons (27.3); the subject is also presented this way in *Apol.* 22.12. Minucius has used this passage. It then had an effect on the way *Oct.* 7.3 was formulated.

Oct. 23.7: The chain of thought is at first not comprehensible: first come unworthy figures of the gods, then completely different examples: deifications. The transition is explained by Cicero, *Nat. Deor.* 3.41.

---

[504] The quip about the flowers stands between two other such humorous remarks in *Apol.* 42.6; in *Oct.* 38 it functions as a foreign element.

[505] Justin, *Apol.* 1.55. The meaning, of course, is precisely the adoration of the cross.

[506] *Oct.* 25.9, where Samia is meaningless (differently in *Apol.* 25.8).

(4) C. Becker would like to establish a new basis for Tertullian himself through his thesis of the reworking of the *Apol.*

> If *Ad nat.* is based in all essentials on the writings of the philosophers, and if the independent penetr .tion and formulation of the material that Tertullian here—in ever greater degree—undertakes, is continued in the *Apol.* in a manner that is not accidental but with an internal coherence with the *Ad nat.*, then Octavius, which is structured so differently, cannot have been the middle term between the apologetic of the Greeks to the apologetic of Tertullian, but Minucius Felix can only have written his *Dialogue* in dependence on Tertullian. (2, 309)[507]

(5) G. Quispel ("A Jewish Source of Minucius Felix," *VC* 3 [1949]: 113ff.): (a) *Oct.* 28.8 with *Pseudo-Clementine Homily* 10.16 (*Rec.* 5.20): *Hom.* 10.16 is inserted; (b) *Oct.* 29.4 with *Hom.* 6.23: The Egyptians worship a human being as a god; that is derived from a Jewish apology, which was misunderstood by Tertullian (*Ad nat.* 2.8) (Minucius Felix is primary in relation to Tertullian!). *Ad nat.* 2.8.8: "Aegyptiorum superstitiones . . . qui etiam bestias privatas colunt . . ." ("the superstitious practices of the Egyptians . . . ; for they worship even their native animals") (cf. *Oct.* 28.8f.; *Apol.* 24.7). *Ad nat.* 2.8.9f.: "Parum est, si etiam hominem consacraverunt, illum dico quem non iam Aegyptus aut Graecia, verum totus orbis colit et Afri iurant, de cuius statu quod conici potest, apud nostras litteras, ut verisimile videtur, positum est. Nam Serapis iste quidem olim Ioseph dictus fuit" ("It is therefore a small matter that they have also deified a man—him, I mean, whom not Egypt only, or Greece, but the whole world worships, and the Africans swear by; about whose state also all that helps our conjectures and imparts to our knowledge the semblance of truth is stated in our own (sacred) literature. For that Serapis of yours was originally one of our own saints called Joseph").[508]

---

[507] *Apol.* 14.3 intensifies the polemic against Jupiter and Juno, in comparison with *Ad nat.* This intensification recurs in Minucius Felix; but it is not the case that two additional supplementary examples contained in the *Apol.* are taken over (by Tertullian) from Minucius Felix, but rather are added in the course of arranging the material on the model of *Ad nat.* In Minucius Felix there is no organizing principle that corresponds to the structure of *Apol.* 14. Becker 2, 320f.: *Ad nat.* 1.12—*Apol.* 16.6ff. —*Oct.* 29.6ff.: Tertullian agrees in order and train of thought with Justin. Becker 2, 325f. on *Ad nat.* 2.17, 18 —*Apol.*, but again arranges the nations according to *Ad nat.*, but must omit the Amazons, whose king is only meaningful as the counterpart to the Vestal Virgins. He replaces the Amazons with the Greeks, resulting in the meaningless pair Greeks/Vestal Virgins.

The idea of the *anima naturaliter christiana* ("natural Christian life") was discovered by Tertullian, who in *De an.* 9 claims it for himself as a *novum testamentum* ("new [last will and] testament"). Becker 2, 331: Already the comparison of *Apol.* 17.5f. with the incidental Gentile names of *Oct.* 18.11 is sufficient to answer the question of priority.

[508] Cf. Firmicus Maternus, *Err.* 13. —A Jewish source cannot be established; cf. Isa. 31:3 LXX; Herodotus 2.144; Diodorus 1.13; Philo, *Leg.* 162ff.; Geffcken, *Apologeten*, 73ff.

Hippolytus[509]

The debate with the Jews stands within the framework of a far-reaching polemical discussion of history (*Ref.* 9.18ff.)[510]

On His Portrayal of History

Originally the Jews were a unity: one law, one teacher, one wilderness, one mountain, and one lawgiver, God (cf. Josephus, *Ant.* 4.201: one God, one people; *Ag. Ap.* 2.193: one God, one temple). After the crossing of the Jordan, they split into three familiar groups over the interpretation of the law (Josephus, *J.W.* 2.119ff.), from which the Essenes are chosen. An example of the relationship of Josephus and Hippolytus: According to Josephus, *J.W.* 2.155, the Essenes and the Greeks have the same understanding of the fate of departed souls.

Hippolytus 9.27: This agreement stems from the fact that the Greeks took over this view, along with others, from the Essenes and modified it in their own way. In this connection he appears not to have the Essenes particularly in mind, but the Jews as such: ἀπὸ τῆς 'Ιουδαϊκῆς νομοθεσίας ("from no other source than from Jewish legislation"). The Jewish religion is the oldest.[511]

9.30 summarizes: "All Jews are active in the service of God in a fourfold way": theologically, physically, ethically, and liturgically (cf. Clement of Alexandria, *Strom.* 1.176.1). They confess *one* God, Creator and Lord of the universe. They strive for a reasonable way of life, as it is prescribed in the law. They received the law from antiquity. They also have a highly developed form of worship.

---

[509] Oepke (*Gottesvolk*, 255) calls him the virtuoso among those who use the concept of the people of God. Andresen (*Logos*, 387ff.) finds traces of the use of Celsus in Hippolytus: his historical polemic (*Ref.* 10, prepared for in 9.31) is reminiscent of Celsus. Irenaeus was content to show that the heretics derived from philosophy. But Hippolytus carried on a historical polemic.

[510] On the relationship to Josephus: H. Schreckenberg, *Die Flavius-Josephus-Tradition*, 72f.: If the section in Hippolytus derives from Josephus, Hippolytus must have used other sources or a mediating source that already had departed from Josephus. *Ref.* 10.31 manifests obvious influence from Josephus, *Ant.* 1.122f. S. Zeitlin, "The Account of the Essenes in Josephus and the Philosophumena," *JQR* 49 (1958/59): 292ff.: a debate with Morton Smith, "The Description of the Essenes in Josephus and the Philosophumena," *HUCA* 29 (1958): 273ff. (a common source for Josephus and Hippolytus; in Josephus, the report concerning the Essenes is a digression within a digression within a digression). Zeitlin: there is no digression in Josephus, and the style and vocabulary are those of Josephus. A *Christian* excerpter stands between Josephus and Hippolytus, namely, Hegesippus; he used the word θεοσέβεια ("reverence for God"), which is not found in *J.W.* C. Burchard in A. Adam and C. Burchard, *Antike Berichte über die Essener* (2nd ed.; Berlin: de Gruyter, 1972) 41ff.: the divergences of Hippolytus from Josephus contain the characteristic idiomatic expressions of Hippolytus. The Essenes are christianized along the lines of the New Testament and the circumstances of the contemporary church. Formulations are adopted and presupposed that come from Josephus. Hippolytus has no other sources, though he does have supplementary traditions.

[511] Especially Pythagoras and the Stoics, who were taught by the Egyptians, are dependent on the Jewish religion.

There are differences among them. But they all agree on one point—namely, the expectation of a Messiah, a mighty warrior who will restore Jerusalem, and they reject the view that he has already come. For our purposes, we are justified in placing the *Chronicle* in brackets.[512]

The attitude toward the Jews is different than in Irenaeus. This is seen in the *eschatology*, in the way the Antichrist is presented, and it is, in a remarkable but not completely clear manner, somehow bound up with the attitude toward the Roman Empire.[513] In Irenaeus's eschatology, the Jews play no role (see above). The only statement made about the Antichrist is that he will come from the tribe of Dan (on the basis of Jer. 8:16).[514]

In Hippolytus, the sharpening of the political judgment corresponds to the increased interest in the Antichrist[515] and the subsiding interest in the thousand-year kingdom.

The description of this millennial kingdom in Irenaeus is not merely the result of a biblicistic compulsion: this kingdom is a firm component of his salvation history (*Adv. Haer.* 5.32). But scholars are divided on the question of whether the idea can even be found in Hippolytus.[516] In place of the bare reference to the Antichrist in Irenaeus, Hippolytus presents a massive elaboration of the biblical passages supposed to deal with the Antichrist, based primarily on Deut. 33:22 and Jer. 8:16 (*Antichr.* 14ff.).

Daniel is also of course fundamental, along with the Apocalypse. Not only is the *exposition* of Daniel to be taken into consideration, but the book itself, which is recognized as a political text and brought to bear as such. That which is kept carefully out of sight by Irenaeus, namely, the relation of the Antichrist

---

[512] Even if one considers it authentic, against P. Nautin, *Hippolyte et Josipe* (Paris: Cerf, 1947). It belongs to the genre of biblical chronicles; Gelzer, *Sextus Julius Africanus* 2:1ff.; R. Helm, in *Die Chronik*, ed. A. Bauer and R. Helm, GCS 46 (2nd ed.; Berlin: Akademie-Verlag, 1955): Hippolytus's primary concern was to fight chiliasm (better: the eschatological near-expectation), "while the Alexandrians who used him wrote a chronicle of world history" (Helm, *Chronik*, xxv). Hippolytus places the historical data in a line of argument to the effect that the end is not yet near. It will not come until after the collapse of the Roman Empire through the Antichrist and the establishment of his kingdom in Jerusalem.

[513] On the latter, see Fuchs, *Widerstand*, 75.

[514] And Irenaeus shows that this tribe does not belong to those who will be saved (*Adv. Haer.* 5.30.2; cf. Hippolytus, *Antichr.* 14f.). W. Bousset, *The Anti-Christ Legend* (London: Hutchinson, 1896) 113: This is quite an old idea, which is probably already present in Revelation 7, based on such traditions as Judges 11ff.; cf. *Test. Dan.* 5:6f.; cf. J. Becker, "Die Testamente der zwölf Patriarchen," in *Jüdische Schriften* 3/1: 350 n. 3: the passage does not belong to the original composition, and the subject matter does not fit the Antichrist tradition.

[515] Justin merely comments on the expected appearance of Elijah before the second coming (*Dial.* 49). On Elijah and Enoch, see Irenaeus, *Adv. Haer.* 5.5.1; Hippolytus, *Antichr.* 43; Tertullian, *De an.* 50:5.

[516] So G. Bardy and M. Lefèvre, *Commentaire sur Daniel*, SC 14 (Paris: Cerf, 1947) 33 n. 3: There is no trace of this in the Daniel commentary. Harnack, *History of Dogma* 2:296 n. 1: Hippolytus could not give up the idea itself because of its connection with the last thousand years of world history; but "it is not much more than a relic" (p. 473).

to the Roman Empire, is brought forward by Hippolytus: The fourth beast of Daniel's vision is the Roman Empire,[517] as is the harlot of Rev 17:3. However, the imperium is not itself the Antichrist. The relation of the Antichrist to the empire is strangely ambivalent. He will renew the fragmented and collapsed empire, will bring the world into subjection to himself, will make himself into a god (*Antichr.* 47.49ff., 56f.), and will regather the scattered Jewish nation (*Antichr.* 54; cf. 25). This artificial and unimaginable combination at least calls for an explanation.[518]

On the one hand, Hippolytus knows the doctrine that the Roman Empire is the last anti-Christian power. He knows that the first half of Revelation 13 refers to the Roman Empire. On the other hand, he also knows that the Antichrist, as the exact counterpart of Christ, must be a *Jew* (*Antichr.* 6, 14), and that he will make his appearance in the temple in Jerusalem.[519] He thus comes to the "solution" that although the first part of Revelation 13 does indeed refer to the Roman Empire, the Antichrist does not emerge until the second half of the chapter.[520]

It is obvious how artificial this construction is: on the one hand, the Antichrist restores the Roman Empire and its idolatry, and his rule is universal. While that is being described, it is forgotten that the Antichrist is a Jew, and the Jews themselves are forgotten (*Antichr.* 50, 52; the conquests, 56). On the other hand, as already mentioned, he will rebuild the Jewish temple and regather the Jewish people. How violently these two conceptions collide can be seen in *Antichr.* 56.[521] The old expectation of the "desolating sacrilege" in the temple, which had been destroyed, had to be modified in the direction that required that the temple be rebuilt (*Antichr.* 6; *In Dan.* 4.49.5).

It is, incidentally, unclear how the Antichrist and the devil are related to each other (Bousset, *Anti-Christ*, 88ff.). *Antichr.* 6: Καὶ αὐτὸς ἐν σχήματι ἀνθρώπου ἐλεύσεται ("he too will come in the form of a man"). *Antichr.* 14: γενηθήτω Δὰν

---

[517] Why is the fourth beast not identified? Each of the earlier ones represented a nation. But not so the power that is ruling at present: 4.8.7: it gathers together *all* the nations. This is the demonic counterpart of the rule of Christ. The rule of the Romans has flourished since the birth of the Lord (cf. Melito above) under Augustus; 4.9.3: the first census divided humanity into "Romans" and "Christians."

[518] Bousset, *Anti-Christ*, 77ff.: "The decline of the Roman Empire before the End." The decline: *Antichr.* 5; see already Irenaeus, *Adv. Haer.* 5.26 (according to Daniel 2 and Revelation 17): The Roman Empire will be fragmented into ten kingdoms. Then the Antichrist will come. Hippolytus relies on this in *Antichr.* 25, 54. Cf. Fuchs, *Widerstand*, 75ff.

[519] Irenaeus, *Adv. Haer.* 5.30; *Antichr.* 62f.; Bousset asks whether the idea of a Jewish Antichrist was already Christian.

[520] *Antichr.* 49. This, of course, leads to a confusing exegesis of Revelation 13; Bousset, *Anti-Christ*, 121f.

[521] οὗτος οὖν ἐπισυνάξας πρὸς ἑαυτὸν τὸν πάντοτε ἀπειθῆ θεῷ λαὸν γεγενημένον ("He then, having gathered to himself the unbelieving everywhere throughout the world"). In *Antichr.* 15 an apocryphon is quoted that is understood in a universalistic sense (Bousset, *Anti-Christ*, 127); the same saying is then restricted to the regathering of Israel in *Antichr.* 54.

ὄφις . . . ὄφις οὖν . . . ὁ ἀπ' ἀρχῆς πλάνος ὁ ἐν τῇ γενέσει εἰρήμενος ("Let Dan be a serpent . . . the serpent therefore . . . , that deceiver who is mentioned in Genesis"). Bousset, *Anti-Christ*, 89: "Of course it is not a matter of an actual identification of the two. But still, in Hippolytus the Antichrist is in any case the incarnation of Satan."

A careful discrimination is made in the times: the portrayal of the Antichrist throws a glaring light on the *present*, illuminating the church in its time of persecution, but it is a parenetic light, not an apocalyptic one. The scene is not drawn in such a way that the persecuting state is the Antichrist and the present is the last days of history—precisely this is *not* done. A warning is given against eschatological impatience (*In Dan.* 4.5.4; 15f.; 18f.). If the Lord still tarries, this means that he has graciously granted an extension (4.17.8f.): the church has crises, to be sure, but οὔπω τὸ τέλος! ("the End is not yet"). 4.5.6: to inquire about the dates of the final events ἀπίστων ἐστὶν ἀνθρώπων οὐ πιστευόντων ("is what unbelievers do, not what believers do"). The empire that rules at present is *not* the Antichrist, and it *alone* still has the authority to rule.[522] What is important is to have the right attitude to persecution and the readiness to become a martyr.[523]

It is thus in this context that the *Jews* are now discussed: they are the people of the Antichrist and the persecutors of Christians. Again, the secondary character of the combination is clear (but no less effective just because it is secondary; the contemporary and later readers were not interested in making motif analyses!):[524] the Antichrist gathers the Jews (54), gathers the unbelieving people from throughout the world (56), and thus begins the persecution of the saints. The conduct of the Jews in the past, the present, and the future is a unit (58). They have cast away their own redemption, were never in agreement with the truth, have transgressed the law, killed the prophets, crucified the redeemer, persecuted the apostles, are persecutors and traitors of the truth itself, are haters of God. In the present too, they make common cause with the pagans against the Christians.

The Daniel commentary in particular concentrates on this perversity:[525] 1.14f. is an exposition of the story of Susanna (Susanna=the persecuted church): οἱ δὲ δύο πρεσβύτεροι εἰς τύπον δείκνυνται τῶν δύο λαῶν τῶν ἐπιβουλευόντων τῇ ἐκκλησίᾳ, εἰς μὲν ὁ ἐκ περιτομῆς καὶ εἰς ὁ ἐξ ἐθνῶν ("the two

---

[522] *In Dan.* 4.17, 23. The chronology: from Christ to the parousia, five hundred years.

[523] Persecution by the Antichrist: Irenaeus, *Adv. Haer.* 5.29.1 (Matt. 24:21); 5.25.3 (Luke 18:1ff.); Hippolytus, *Antichr.* 56f., 61 (here the persecution and the flight of the believers are understood universally, in accordance with Revelation 12).

[524] Politically speaking, in comparison with the Christians, the Jews are still the more powerful force.

[525] Editions: M. Lefévre, SC 14 (text from N. Bonwetsch); attempt at dating: G. Bardy in Lefévre, 202ff.: Septimius Severus.

elders are to be taken as a type of the two peoples, that of the circumcision and that of the Gentiles, which are always enemies of the church") (1.14.6).[526]

1.15: They work together against the Christians: αὐτοὶ ἑαυτοῖς μὴ συμφω-νοῦντες . . . ὅτι ἐν μὲν τοῖς βρώμασι τοῖς ἐπιγείοις οἱ 'Ιουδαῖοι μετὰ τῶν ἐθνῶν οὐ συμφωνοῦσιν, ἐν δὲ ταῖς θεωρίαις καὶ παντὶ πράγματι κοσμικῷ τούτοις συνερχόμενοι κοινωνοῦσιν ("they parted the one from the other . . . in the matter of earthly meats the Jews and the Gentiles are not at one; but in their views, and in all worldly matters, they are of one mind, and can meet each other").[527]

Demonstratio adversus Iudaeos (Migne, PG 10:787-94)

1: Lend me your ears, you Jews. You have often bragged about the fact that you condemned Jesus to death.

3: ὅτε ἐκάλυψαν ἐντροπῇ τὸ πρόσωπόν μου οἱ 'Ιουδαῖοι, ὅτε ἀπηλλοτριωμένος ἐγενήθην τοῖς κατὰ σάρκα ἀδελφοῖς μου ("when 'they covered my face with shame,' that is to say, the Jews; when 'I became a stranger unto my brethren after the flesh'").

7: Why was the temple destroyed? Was it because of the golden calf? No—they were forgiven for that, as they were for their repeated idolatries—but it was because they put to death the Son of the Benevolent One.

Clement of Alexandria

Clement too, despite his general importance, is for our purposes to be mentioned only in a relatively negative sense—a major example that supports our thesis concerning salvation history. Even if it be granted that he can be labeled a "scriptural theologian" (Harnack, *History of Dogma* 2:33f.; von Campenhausen, *Formation*, 299ff.), in a more precise sense it is still clear that he is not interested in salvation history. He is, so to speak, absolutely devoid of historical thinking, and that despite—or because of—his preoccupation with chronology. No doubt he is completely caught up in the idea of the rule of the Logos in humanity from the very beginning;[528] but this rule is not thought of in terms of a "history" of salvation, but of an "economy" of salvation. For the terminology, see von Campenhausen, *Formation*, 266f.: Clement speaks—on the model of Irenaeus—of the two acts of covenant making. In addition, διαθήκη ("covenant") is already used for the old and new Scriptures.[529]

[526] 1.29.2 (on Susanna 52): Daniel addresses the one as a Jew, who knows the law, 29.3 (on Susanna 56), and the other as a Gentile.

[527] 1.19: ὦ παρανόμων ἀρχόντων . . . ταῦτα ὑμῖν παρέδωκε Μωϋῆς ("O wicked rulers . . . did Moses deliver these things to you?"). 4.50: The two witnesses, the great θλῖψις ("tribulation") that causes both Jews and pagans to rejoice.

[528] Harnack, *History of Dogma* 2:326: "Christianity is the doctrine of the creation, education, and redemption of the human race through the Logos."

[529] *Strom.* 2.29.2. On the missing temporal dimension (with reference to Rom. 1:17): "from faith

The decisive factor is the higher unity that embraces both acts of covenant making. The unhistoricality of the whole conception is classically formulated in *Strom.* 1.176.1: ἡ μὲν οὖν κατὰ Μωϋσέα φιλοσοφία τετραχῇ τέμνεται,[530] εἴς τε τὸ ἱστορικὸν καὶ τὸ κυρίως λεγόμενον νομοθετικόν, ἅπερ ἂν εἴη τῆς ἠθικῆς πραγματείας ἴδια, τὸ τρίτον δὲ εἰς τὸ ἱερουργικόν, ὅ ἐστιν ἤδη τῆς φυσικῆς θεωρίας. (2) καὶ τέταρτον ἐπὶ πᾶσι τὸ θεολογικὸν εἶδος, ἡ ἐποπτεία, ἥν φησιν ὁ Πλάτων τῶν μεγάλων ὄντως εἶναι μυστηρίων, Ἀριστοτέλης δὲ τὸ εἶδος τοῦτο μετὰ τὰ φυσικὰ καλεῖ ("The Mosaic philosophy is accordingly divided into four parts—into the historic, and that which is specially called the legislative, which two properly belong to an ethical treatise; and the third, that which relates to sacrifice, which belongs to physical science; and the fourth, above all, the department of theology, 'vision,' which Plato predicates of the truly great mysteries. And this species Aristotle calls metaphysics").

It is only the "proof of antiquity" that has any historical importance for him: the Greeks are newcomers.[531] And even the "proof of antiquity" is relativized by the proof of the rule of the Logos.[532]

Attitude to the Jews

The Bible is so obviously a Christian book that there is nothing here to be discussed. It is simply referred to as self-evidently the property of Christians (*Strom.* 1.109.4 [Judg. 3:8]; 109.5; 111.1). Even when Rom. 2:17 is referred to, this is only in order to portray the law in a positive light (*Strom.* 1.174). When in Rom. 3:10ff. the Jewish people are certified as a people that does not understand the law (*Strom.* 1.175.1), that is still to be understood within the framework of Clement's whole hermeneutic. The truth of Scripture is a mystery, even for Christians (*Strom.* 6.124.5; von Campenhausen, *Formation*, 303ff.). Clement hopes that his literary works will be just as useful for the Jews as they are for the Gentiles (*Strom.* 2.1.2). On the subject of Jews and

---

which is according to the covenant (διαθήκη) and the commandments, since these, which are two in name and time, given in accordance with the (divine) economy and in a manner appropriate to the time and stage of development (καθ' ἡλικίαν καὶ προκοπήν), the one old and the other new, but are one in power. They were given on the basis of the one divine plan of salvation (οἰκονομικῶς δεδομέναι), and are dispensed through the Son by one God."

Von Campenhausen, *Formation*, 318–19: The promise/fulfillment distinction "which takes cognizance of the gulf between the two eras," has basically lost its significance in the present. Ultimately there is only one single covenant, and one Testament, which has been given in different times, which now belongs to the elect in the one church under the one Lord (p. 319).

[530] A biblical judgment, not a historical one.

[531] Compare the chronology in *Strom.* 1.21; cf. 1.25.165f. On the thievery of the Greeks, see Tatian, who is also used by Clement (*Strom.* 1.21.102f.; 2.1; 5.14).

[532] Philosophy served to educate the Greeks, as the law did the Jews (*Strom.* 6.17, 159.9). The difference is already familiar to the Jews, but it is still only a relative difference: the law is available to every Jew, while philosophy is reserved for the few, and besides that, here is a multiplicity of philosophies (and only one law). For the Jews, this was a qualitative difference.

Christians, it should not be overlooked that the *Kerygma Petrou* was adopted and used by Clement.

Origen[533]

Origen has a special place in our study not only because of his exceptional importance in general but because he locates the issue of Judaism within a framework of meaning that cannot be compared to any of his predecessors. We have approached previous authors with the simple schematic question of whether or not they approached the issue with a frame of reference oriented to salvation history.[534] But Origen deals with the subject in such a way that it can be grasped neither from the point of view of his speculative system nor from his outline of salvation history, but only from the perspective of his biblicism, which, of course, includes his understanding of the economy of salvation.[535] He is different from the other Apologists in that for him the themes "Bible" (Old Testament) and "Jews" are inseparably bound together.[536]

---

[533] Bibliography: see under Celsus; A. von Harnack, *Der kirchengeschichtliche Ertrag der exegetischen Arbeiten des Origenes*, TU 42, 2 vols. (Leipzig: Hinrichs, 1918, 1919); H. Bietenhard, *Caesarea, Origenes und die Juden* (Berlin: Kohlhammer, 1974); N. R. M. de Lange, *Origen and the Jews: Studies in Jewish-Christian Relations in Third Century Palestine* (Cambridge: Cambridge University Press, 1976). The content of this book lies only on the margin of our concern: (1) within it, to the extent that the history of the relations between Jews and Christians plays a role; (2) outside it, to the extent that Origin is dealt with as a source for Judaism, especially of Palestinian Judaism, and (3) on the margin of it, to the extent that Origen's knowledge of Judaism is investigated.

[534] Clement of Alexandria too hardly gets beyond this. He merely finds it necessary to make a certain adjustment in the schema, since his basic understanding of an economy of salvation is in contrast to historical thinking (cf. the biblical model for the unhistorical approach to an "economy of salvation": Ephesians).

In Origen this distinction can be seen in quite a different degree. See Harnack, *History of Dogma* 2:343: (a) Origen denied the significance of the historical, incarnate Logos to the Gnostics. (b) "The objects of religious knowledge have no history, or rather, and this is a genuinely Gnostic and neo-Platonic idea, they have only a super-mundane one."

[535] Harnack, *Die kirchengeschichtliche Ertrag* 2:4 n. 3: "There has never been a theologian in the history of the church who wanted to be—and was—so exclusively an exegete of the Bible as was Origen." Cf. von Campenhausen, *Formation*, 307ff.; idem, *Die griechischen Kirchenväter* (1955) 40ff. (Eng. trans.: *The Fathers of the Greek Church* [New York: Pantheon, 1959]).

[536] Harnack, *History of Dogma* 2:348 n. 4: "Since Origen does not, as a rule, dispute the literal meaning of the Scriptures, he has also a much more favorable opinion of the Jewish people and of the observance of the law than the earlier Christian authors (but see Irenaeus and Tertullian). At bottom he places the observance of the law quite on the same level as the faith of the simple Christians. The Apostles also kept the law for a time, and it was only by degrees that they came to understand its spiritual meaning. They were also right to continue its observance during their mission among the Jews. On the other hand, he considers the New Testament a higher stage than the Old both in its literal and its spiritual sense. See *Cels.* II 1–4, 7, 75; IV 31 sq.; V 10, 30, 31, 42 sq., 66; VII 26."

According to von Campenhausen, this judgment is to be modified; see *Formation*, 318: When they affirmed the agreement of the Old Testament and the New, "Irenaeus and Tertullian in

Because of the biblical point of departure for his thought and/or the constant reference to biblical passages,[537] his statements about the Jews cannot be reduced to one common denominator but contain the same kind of variety as the Bible itself.[538] The fact also must be taken into consideration that Origen, standing in the tradition of Christian apologetic against pagans and Jews, also presents something of a compendium of this tradition.[539]

There is no question but that the God of the Christians and the God of the Jews is the same God,[540] which carries with it the uninterrupted continuity between the Old Testament and the New Testament.[541] The error of the Jews was not that they worshiped a false god, but that they did not attend to the prophecies (1.36f.). And to this extent they enjoyed a privileged position, which the Gentiles even today may not disdain (see below on Romans 11). But they did not understand the law.[542] Their literal interpretation missed the real meaning (5.60). It is the Christians who, basing their understanding on Moses and the prophets, attain to true knowledge (2.4); they have not fallen away from the law, but grant that it is proper honor by understanding it in its spiritual sense.

In Origen one can distinguish four groups of evaluative statements concerning the Jews, which are related to one another on the basis of their common biblical foundation.

(1) Since they did not recognize Moses and did not attend to the prophecies of Christ but rather killed the prophets, the natural result was that they did not recognize Jesus, but killed him (it was the Jews that did it, not Pilate [2.34]).

We thus once again stand before the question of the two advents as the

---

particular had made use of the idea of progress in the course of salvation history, thus explaining rather than removing the discrepancies; and the possibility of an allegorical reinterpretation of the obsolete law or of dealing with offensive stories by typology was brought in only as a supplementary measure." In Origen the situation is reversed. "Allegorical interpretation dominates, and history has become virtually insignificant." Cf. note 294: "In the problem of the old and new covenants, of law and Gospel, it can, of course, never be entirely omitted. In these contexts Origen speaks of preparation and fulfillment, shadow and reality, letter and spirit. Everything reaches its climax in Christ, and Christ also speaks through the Old Testament—spiritually understood."

[537] An especially instructive instance is the exposition of Romans 9–11 with the key statement of v. 25; see Bietenhard, *Caesarea,* 61ff., with documentation.

[538] Thus, alongside the threats of the prophets against disobedient Israel, there is the struggle of Paul against their unbelief (Romans 9–11) and the eschatological prospect at the conclusion of chap. 11.

[539] In the nature of the case this is found in an especially compact form in his writing against Celsus (the passages that follow are cited from this document).

[540] 5.6 (against Celsus's claim that the Jews worship angels; see 1.26: Where do you find that in Moses' writings? 7.35f.).

[541] This is related to the concern of Origen the scholar to study Judaism at its source (see Bietenhard, *Caesarea,* 24ff.). On the Jewish traditions in Origen, see G. Bardy, "Les traditions juives dans l'oeuvre d'Origène," *RB* 34 (1925): 221ff.; Bietenhard, *Caesarea,* 19ff.

[542] Namely, its true, spiritual sense (2.6; 5.20; 8.18ff.). On letter and spirit, see 7.20.

decisive issue. The Jews are still waiting for the first advent of the Christ. Their destiny corresponds to their past deeds: since the advent of Jesus they have been abandoned, and prophets or miracles no longer appear among them. Not only will they receive a more severe punishment than others in the *future* judgment; they are already being punished. They are forbidden to enter their own capital city.[543] 4.22: They will never be able to return to their previous circumstances. The Christians have now taken their place as those who have the laws of God, laws that are appropriate for a universal kingdom.

But the other side of the coin also calls for attention: (a) The Old Testament not only includes threats against Israel but also statements that Israel will time and again be converted (7.18). (b) Alongside the negative judgment of Rom. 11:3, the promise of 11:4f. is not ignored: a remnant remains.[544] (c) The Jews have received the special honor that Moses, the prophets, and Jesus appeared among them.[545] (d) They have preserved their original *language*, because they have not withdrawn from the East. They have become the Lord's own portion (5.31).

In such statements we find ourselves still in the realm of the relative. But the ultimate verdict was given in response to their treatment of Jesus.

(2) Their present *conduct* corresponds to their *fate:* they curse Jesus and attempt to get Christians to deny their faith (8.69). It is not the pagans, the idolaters, that they hate, but the Christians, the very ones who have been converted to the God of the Jews (!).[546]

(3) Since the issue between Jews and Christians is exclusively a matter of the faith (as is universally the case in the debates Christians had with others), Origen does not hesitate impartially to defend the Jews against the unjustified charges and slanders of Celsus.[547] He refutes the attacks on their intelligence and their writing of history,[548] and makes a case for the excellence of their ethics and general disposition (4.31).

(4) He gives a biblical perspective on the issue of the Jews in connection with Romans 11.[549] Jesus did not want the Jews to disbelieve. But he foresaw that they would not believe and used their disbelief to prepare the Gentiles for faith.

---

[543] See Justin; Tertullian. The classic passage Isa. 1:7 cannot be omitted, of course (see 2.76). Here too the threats of the Old Testament against the Jews are brought up again.

[544] This is a salvation-historical remnant, which the standpoint of Origen allows to appear in a softer light but is not qualitatively different either from earlier or later Israel.

[545] This is confirmed by Paul, but it is not an *eschatological* priority – not even in the concluding verses of Romans 11 (contra most commentaries).

[546] This is the reason for the warning against visiting Jewish synagogues and participating in Jewish festivals.

[547] See above, for example, against the charge of angel worship.

[548] With which Celsus, in a series of anti-Semitic topoi, connects the charge of the Jews' lack of culture (1.14, 16, 18).

[549] Despite the allusion to future punishment, see above; on Romans 11 in Origen, see Bietenhard, *Caesarea*, 61ff.

The Gentile Christians are indebted to the Jews for the opportunity to come to faith.[550] The rejection of the Jews means the reconciliation of the world. So the Gentiles should not boast. It is through the failure of the Jews that they have salvation.

* * *

We Stand Again at the Beginning Point

The only issue between Jews and Christians is the issue of faith.[551] This issue cannot be avoided psychologically—by being polite to each other—nor can it be avoided by having one side or the other reduce their articles of faith (in the present situation this is a temptation only on the Christian side).

Rather, from the Christian side the insight must be brought to bear that the Christian faith is not an ideological standpoint and that correspondingly the church is not a "people" (*Volk*) in the sense that it is one ideological group among others, but that the only statement necessary for determining the essential nature of the church is: "est autem ecclesia congregatio sanctorum in qua evangelium pure docetur et recte administrantur sacramenta" ("a holy congregation in which the pure Gospel is taught and the sacraments are rightly administered") (Calvin).

Within this definition, the Jews cannot be seen as some special *eschatological* category. Within this definition, all human beings, Christian and non-Christian, are directly confronted by God—and that not in terms of the accidental circumstances of history, nor in psychological or other categories, but in terms of the theology of the Word. They are confronted by this Word not as Jews or Gentiles, Greeks or barbarians, but simply as human beings, i.e., as sinners who must renounce all boasting before God, including boasting that they are Christians, since the renunciation of all such boasting is inherent in faith. All are justified before God in exactly the same way, by faith alone, which Paul in Rom. 3:30 bases on the confession that God is *one*.

---

[550] Bietenhard, *Caesarea,* 73 n. 28 (passages that deal with Rom. 11:25).

[551] In Origen, as in the other church fathers, the issues of the "murder of God" and of the two advents are issues of the faith. Because of his biblicism, Origen is usually (not always) milder in his vocabulary than the others, but concerning the substance of the faith itself he is (despite or even because of Rom. 11:25) not one whit milder. For him the issue of faith is ultimately not relativized.

BIBLIOGRAPHY

PRIMARY SOURCES

Greek-Roman

Acta Alexandrinorum. Edited by H. Musurillo. Oxford: Clarendon Press, 1961.

Cassius Dio. *Roman History.* Edited, with English translation by E. Cary. 9 vols. Cambridge, Mass.: Harvard University Press; London: William Heinemann, 1914ff.

Celsus. *Origenes contra Celsum.* Edited by P. Koetschau. 1899.
    German: P. Koetschau. 1926–27; R. Bader, *Der ΑΛΗΘΗΣ ΛΟΓΟΣ des Kelsos.* Stuttgart and Berlin: Kohlhammer, 1940.
    English: H. Chadwick. Reprint. Cambridge: Cambridge University Press, 1965.

Chairemon. Edited by H. R. Schwyzer. 1932.

Corpus Hermeticum. Edited by A. D. Nock and A. J. Festugière. 4 vols. Paris: Belles Lettres, 1954–60.

Diels, H. *Doxographi Graeci.* 1879.

——, and W. Kranz. *Die Fragmente der Vorsokratiker.* 3 vols. 11th ed. 1964.

Dio Chrysostom. Edited, with English translation by J. W. Cohoon and H. L. Crosby. 5 vols. Cambridge, Mass.: Harvard University Press; London: William Heinemann, 1932ff.

Diodorus Siculus. Edited, with English translation by C. H. Oldfather et al. 12 vols. Cambridge, Mass.: Harvard University Press; London: William Heinemann, 1933ff.

Herodotus. Edited, with German translation by G. Felix. 2 vols. 1963.

Jacoby, F. *Die Fragmente der griechischen Historiker.* Teil I–III mit Kommentarbänden. Leiden: E. J. Brill, 1923ff. Supplements by H. J. Mette in Lustrum 21, 1978.

Juvenal. Edited, with English translation by G. G. Ramsay. Cambridge, Mass.: Harvard University Press; London: William Heinemann, 1918.

Livy. Edited, with English translation by B. O. Foster et al. 12 vols. Cambridge, Mass.: Harvard University Press; London: William Heinemann, 1919ff.

Martial. *Epigrams.* Edited by W. A. Ker. 2 vols. Cambridge, Mass.: Harvard University Press; London: William Heinemann, 1919f.

Müller, C., and T. Müller. *Fragmenta Historicorum Graecorum.* 1841–72.

Nauck, A. *Tragicorum Graecorum fragmenta.* 3rd ed. 1964.

Oellacher, H. *Griechische literarische Papyri II.* 1939.

Papyri Graecae Magicae. Edited by K. Preisendanz. 2 vols. 1928.

The Greek-Magical Papyri in Translation. Edited by H. D. Betz. Chicago: University of Chicago Press, 1986.

Plutarch. *Moralia V (De Iside et Osiride).* Edited, with English translation by F. C. Babbitt. Cambridge, Mass.: Harvard University Press; London: William Heinemann, 1936.

Polybius. Edited by W. R. Paton. 6 vols. Cambridge, Mass.: Harvard University Press; London: William Heinemann, 1922–27.

Posidonios. L. Edelstein and I. G. Kidd. *Posidonius I. The Fragments.* Cambridge: Cambridge University Press, 1972.

Pseudo-Longinus. *De sublimitate.* Edited, with commentary by D. A. Russell. Oxford: Clarendon Press, 1964.

Reinach, T. *Textes d'auteurs Grecs et Romains relatifs au Judaïsme.* Paris: Presses universitaires de France, 1895.

Stern, M. *Greek and Latin Authors on Jews and Judaism.* 3 vols. Jerusalem: Jerusalem Academy Press, 1974–84.

Tacitus. *Historiae.* Edited by E. Koestermann. Heidelberg, 1969.

Latin-German: F. Borst and H. Hross. 1959.

German: W. Sontheimer. 1959; F. Eckstein. 1960.

Varro. R. Agahd, M. *Terentii Varronis Antiquitates Rerum Divinarum. Theologischer Jahresbericht, Phil. Suppl.* 24. 1989.

A. G. Condemi. M. *Terentii Varronis Antiquitates Rerum Divinarum Librorum I-II Fragmenta.* 1964.

Wehrli, F. *Die Schule des Aristoteles III.* 1969.

Jewish

Adam, A. *Antike Berichte über die Essener.* KIT 182. 2nd revised and enlarged edition by C. Burchard. Berlin: de Gruyter, 1972.

Apokalypse Abrahams. Edited by G. N. Bonwetsch. 1897. Reprint, 1972.

Aristeas, Letter of. Edited by P. Wendland. 1900. Edited, with English translation by M. Hadas. New York: Harper & Brothers, 1951.

Edited, with French translation by A. Pelletier. SC 89. Paris: Cerf, 1962.

The Babylonian Talmud. Translated by L. Goldschmidt. 12 vols. London: Soncino, 1929–36.

Charles, R. H. *The Apocrypha and Pseudepigrapha of the Old Testament.* 2 vols. Oxford: Clarendon Press, 1913.

Corpus Inscriptionum Judaicarum. Edited by J. B. Frey. 2 vols. Rome: Institute of Christian Archaeology, 1936, 1952.

Corpus Nummorum Palaestinensium. Edited by L. Kadman. 3 vols. 1956–60.

Corpus Papyrorum Judaicarum. Edited by V. A. Tcherikover and A. Fuks. 3 vols. Cambridge: Harvard University Press, 1957–64.

Denis, A.-M. *Fragmenta Pseudepigraphorum . . .* Leiden: E. J. Brill, 1970.

———. *Introduction aux Pseudepigraphes Grecs d'Ancien Testament.* Leiden: E. J. Brill, 1970.

1 Esra: Esdrae liber I. Edited by R. Hanhart. Septuaginta, Acad. Sc. Gott. 8/1. Göttingen: Vandenhoeck & Ruprecht, 1974.

Esther. Edited by R. Hanhart, Septuaginta. Acad. Litt. Gott. 8/3. Göttingen: Vandenhoeck & Ruprecht, 1966.

Josephus. *Flavii Iosephi Opera.* Edited by B. Niese. 6 vols. 2nd ed. Berlin: August Raabe. Reprint, 1955.

——. Edited, with English translation by H. St. J. Thackeray, R. Marcus, and L. H. Feldman. 10 vols. Cambridge, Mass.: Harvard University Press; London: William Heinemann, 1926ff.

——. *Contre Apion.* Edited, with French translation by T. Reinach and L. Blum. Paris: E. Leroux, 1930.

——. *De bello Judaico.* Edited, with German translation by O. Michel and O. Bauernfeind. 4 vols. Munich: Kösel, 1959–69.

Jüdische Schriften aus hellenistisch-römischer Zeit. Edited by W. G. Kümmel et al. Gütersloh: Mohn, 1973ff.

Kautzsch, E. *Die Apokryphen und Pseudepigraphen des Alten Testaments.* 2 vols. Tübingen: Mohr-Siebeck, 1900.

Kindler, A. *Coins and Documents for Israel's Ancient History, Antiquity and Survival.* 1957–58.

3 Maccabees. *The Third and Fourth Books of Maccabees.* Edited, with English translation by M. Hadas. New York: Harper & Brothers, 1953.

Maccabaeorum liber III. Edited by R. Hanhart. Septuaginta Soc. Litt. Gott. 9/3. Göttingen: Vandenhoeck & Ruprecht, 1960.

Paraleipomena Jeremiou. Edited, with English translation by R. A. Kraft and A. E. Purintun. Missoula, Mont.: Scholars Press, 1972.

Philo of Alexandria. *Opera quae supersunt.* Edited by L. Cohn and P. Wendland. 7 vols. 1896–1930.

——. Edited, with English translation by F. H. Colson, G. H. Whitaker, and R. Marcus. 10 vols. Suppl. 1–2. LCL. Cambridge, Mass.: Harvard University Press; London: William Heinemann, 1929–62.

——. Edited, with French translation by R. Arnaldez, J. Pouilloux, and C. Mondésert. 32 vols. Paris: Cerf, 1961–72.

——. *Philonis Alexandrini Legatio ad Gaium.* Edited, with introduction, English translation, and commentary by E. M. Smallwood. 2nd ed. 1970.

Reifenberg, A. *Ancient Jewish Coins.* 4th ed. Jerusalem: Rubin Mass, 1965.

Riessler, P. *Altjüdisches Schrifttum ausserhalb der Bibel.* Heidelberg: Augsburg, 1928.

Robert, L. *Nouvelles Inscriptions de Sardes, Ier Fascicule.* 1964.

Rosenstiehl, J.-M. *L'Apocalypse d'Elie.* Paris: Guethner, 1972.

Schermann, T. *Prophetarum Vitae . . .* TU 31.3. Leipzig: Hinrichs, 1907.

Sibylline Oracles: Die Oracula Sibyllina. Edited by J. Geffcken. GCS 8. Leipzig: Hinrichs, 1902.

——. *Sibyllinische Weissagungen.* Edited, with German translation by A. Kurfess. 1951.

Testament of Abraham. Edited, with English translation by M. E. Stone. Missoula, Mont.: Scholars Press, 1972.

Wisdom of Solomon: The Book of Wisdom. Edited, with English translation by J. Reider. New York: Harper & Brothers, 1957.

Christian

Athenagoras. *Legatio and De Resurrectione.* Edited, with English translation by W. R. Schoedel. Oxford: Oxford University Press, 1972.

Bihlmeyer, K. *Die Apostolischen Väter.* With a supplement by W. Schneemelcher. 2nd ed. 1956.

Clement of Alexandria. *Protrepticus und Paedagogus.* Edited by O. Stählin. GCS 12. Leipzig: Hinrichs, 1936.

———. *Stromata I–VI.* Edited by O. Stählin and L. Früchtel. GCS 52. 3rd ed. Berlin: Akademie-Verlag, 1960.

———. *Stromata VII–VIII.* Edited by O. Stählin. GCS 17. Leipzig: Hinrichs, 1909.

Diognetus, Letter to. Diognetbrief. Edited by K. Bihlmeyer and W. Schneemelcher. Edited, with French translation by H. I. Marrou. SC 33. Paris: Cerf, 1951.

Epiphanius. *Panarion Haer.* Edited by K. Holl. 3 vols. GCS 25, 31, 37. Leipzig: Hinrichs, 1915–33.

Epistula Apostolorum. Edited by H. Duensing. KlT 152. 1925.

Eusebius. *Kirchengeschichte.* Edited by E. Schwartz. Kleine Ausgabe. 5th ed. 1952.

———. *Praeparatio evangelica.* Edited by K. Mras. GCS 43. 1/2. Berlin: Akademie-Verlag, 1954, 1956.

———. *Demonstratio evangelica.* Edited by I. A. Heikel. GCS 23. Leipzig: Hinrichs, 1913.

———. *Die Chronik.* Translated from the Armenian by J. Karst. GCS 20. Leipzig: Hinrichs, 1911.

Goodspeed, E. J. *Die ältesten Apologeten.* Göttingen: Vandenhoeck & Ruprecht, 1914.

Hennecke, E., and W. Schneemelcher, eds. *New Testament Apocrypha.* English translation edited by R. M. Wilson. 2 vols. Philadelphia: Westminster, 1963, 1965.

Hippolytus. *Refutatio omnium haeresium.* Edited by P. Wendland. GCS 26. Leipzig: Hinrichs, 1926.

———. *Kommentar zum Buche Daniel.* Edited, with German translation by N. Bonwetsch. GCS 1/1. Leipzig: Hinrichs, 1897.

———. *Commentaire sur Daniel.* Edited, with French translation by M. Lefèvre. Introduction by G. Bardy. SC 14. Paris: Cerf, 1947.

———. *De Antichristo.* Edited by H. Achelis. GCS 1/2. Leipzig: Hinrichs, 1897.

———. *Die Chronik.* Edited by A. Bauer und R. Helm. GCS 46. 2nd ed. Berlin: Akademie-Verlag, 1955.

Irenaeus. *Adversus haereses.* Edited by W. W. Harvey. 2 vols. Cambridge: Cambridge University Press, 1857.

Kerygma Petri. Edited by E. Klostermann. *Apocrypha I.* KlT 3. 2nd ed. 1908.

Krüger, G., and G. Ruhbach. *Ausgewählte Märtyrerakten.* 4th ed. Tübingen: Mohr, 1965.

Melito of Sardes. *Sur la Pâque.* Edited, with French translation by B. Dombart. 2nd ed. 1881.

Edited by J. P. Waltzing. 1st ed. 1926.

Edited by J. Beaujeu. 1964.

Edited, with German translation by B. Kytzler. 1965.

Musurillo, H. *The Acts of the Christian Martyrs.* Oxford: Clarendon Press, 1972.

Origen. *Contra Celsum.* Edited by P. Koetschau. 2 vols. Leipzig: Hinrichs, 1899.

German: P. Koetschau. BKV 52.53. 1927.

English: H. Chadwick. Cambridge: Cambridge University Press, 1965.

Edited, with French translation by M. Borret. SC 132, 136, 147, 150, 227. Paris: Cerf, 1967, 1968, 1969, 1976.

Peter, Gospel of. Edited by E. Klostermann. *Apocrypha I.* KlT 3. 2d ed. 1908.
    Edited, with French translation by M.-G. Mara. SC 201. Paris: Cerf, 1973.
    Denker, J. *Die theologiegeschichtliche Stellung des PetrEv.* Bern and Frankfurt: Lang,
    1975.
Pseudo-Clement. *Homilies.* Edited by B. Rehm and I. Irmscher. GCS 42. Berlin:
    Akademie-Verlag, 1953.
———. *Recognitions in Rufin's Translation.* Edited by B. Rehm and F. Paschke. GCS 51.
    Berlin: Akademie-Verlag, 1965.
Ptolemy to Flora, Letter of. Edited, with French translation by G. Quispel. SC 24. 2nd
    ed. Paris: Cerf, 1966.
Robinson, J. M. *The Nag Hammadi Library.* San Francisco: Harper & Row, 1988.
de Santos Otero, A. *Los Evangelios Apocrifos.* Madrid: Biblioteca de Autores Chris-
    tianos, 1956.
Tatian. *Oratio ad Graecos.* Edited by E. Schwartz. TU 4.1. Leipzig: Hinrichs, 1888.
Tertullian. *Opera, Corpus Christianorum.* 2 vols. 1954.
———. *Adversus Iudaeos.* Edited by H. Tränkle. Wiesbaden: F. Steiner, 1964.
———. *Adversus Marcionem.* Edited, with English translation by E. Evans. Oxford:
    Clarendon Press, 1972.
———. *Apologeticum.* Edited, with German translation by C. Becker. 1st ed. Munich:
    Kösel, 1961.
Theophilos of Antioch. *Ad Autolycum.* Edited, with English translation by R. M.
    Grant. Oxford: Clarendon Press, 1970.
Völker, W. *Quellen zur Geschichte der christlichen Gnosis.* 1932.
von Otto, C. T. *Corpus Apologetarum Christianorum saeculi secundi.* 9 vols. Jena: Frider,
    1847–61.

DICTIONARIES AND REFERENCE WORKS

Beyerlin, W. *Religionsgeschichtliches Textbuch zum Alten Testament.* ATD Erg.reihe 1.
    Göttingen: Vandenhoeck & Ruprecht, 1975.
The Cambridge Ancient History. 12 vols. Plates I–V. Cambridge: Cambridge University
    Press, 1923ff.
Encyclopaedia Judaica. 10 vols. 1928–34.
Gressmann, H. *Altorientalische Texte zum Alten Testament.* Berlin: de Gruyter, 1926.
*Der kleine Pauly: Lexikon der Antike von Pauly's Realencyclopädie der classischen Alter-
    tumswissenschaft..* Edited by K. Ziegler and W. Sontheimer. Stuttgart: A.
    Druckenmüller, 1964–75.
Paulys Realencyclopädie der classischen Altertumswissenschaft. Neue Bearbeitung. Edited
    by G. Wissowa, W. Kroll et al. Stuttgart: Metzler, 1893ff.
Reallexikon für Antike und Christentum. Edited by T. Klauser. Stuttgart: Hiersemann,
    1950ff.
Die Religion in Geschichte und Gegenwart. Edited by K. Galling et al. 3rd ed. Tübingen:
    Mohr-Siebeck, 1957–62.
Theological Dictionary of the New Testament. Edited by G. Kittel and G. Friedrich.
    Grand Rapids: Eerdmans, 1964–76.

SECONDARY LITERATURE

* =Additions to Bibliography of the German edition.

Abel, E. L. "Were the Jews Banished from Rome in 19 AD?" *REJ* 127 (1969): 383ff.

Aberbach, M. "The Conflicting Accounts of Josephus and Tacitus Concerning Cumanus' and Felix' Terms of Office." *JQR* 40 (1949–50): 1ff.

——. "The Historical Allusions of Chapters IV, IX and XIII of the Psalms of Solomon." *JQR* 41 (1950–51): 379ff.

Adriani, M. "Note sull' antisemitismo antico." *Studi e materiali di storia delle religioni* 36 (1965): 63ff.

Alfonsi, L. "Motivi tradizionali del giovane Aristotele in Clemente Alessandrino e in Atenagora." *VC* 7 (1953): 139ff.

——. "Traces du jeune Aristote dans la 'Cohoratio ad gentiles' faussement attribuée à Justin." *VC* 1 (1948): 65ff.

Alon, G. "The Attitude of the Pharisees to the Roman Government and the House of Herod." *Scripta Hierosolymitana* 7 (1961): 53ff.

——. "Jews, Judaism and the Classical World." In *Studies in Jewish History in the Times of the Second Temple and Talmud*, 18–47. Jerusalem: Magnes, 1977.

Aly, W. *Strabon von Amaseia, Strabonis Geographica.* Vol. 4. Bonn, 1957.

Anderson, A. *Alexander's Gate: Gog, Magog and the Enclosed Peoples.* 1932.

Andresen, C. *Logos und Nomos: Die Polemik des Kelsos wider das Christentum.* Berlin: de Gruyter, 1955.

Andriessen, P. "The Authorship of the Epistula ad Diognetum." *VC* 1 (1947): 129ff.

Applebaum, Shimon. "Cyrenesia Judaica." *JJS* 13 (1962): 31ff.

——. "The Jewish Community of Hellenistic and Roman Teucheria in Cyrenaica." *Scripta Hierosolymitana* 7 (1961): 27ff.

——. "Josephus and the Economic Causes of the Jewish War." In *Josephus, the Bible, and History*, edited by Louis H. Feldman and Gohei Hata, 237–64. Detroit: Wayne State University Press, 1989.*

Archamabault, G. *Justin, Dialogue avec Tryphon.* 2 vols. Paris, 1909.

Arenhoevel, D. *Die Theokratie nach dem 1. u. 2. Makk.* Mainz: Matthias Grünewald, 1967.

Armstrong, A. H., ed. *The Cambridge History of Later Greek and Early Medieval Philosophy.* Cambridge: Cambridge University Press, 1967.

Attridge, Harold W. "The Philosophical Critique of Religion under the Early Empire." In *ANRW* II.16.1, edited by W. Haase, 45–78. Berlin and New York: de Gruyter, 1978.*

Avenarius, G. *Lukians Schrift zur Geschichtsschreibung.* Meisenheim/Glan, 1956.

Avi-Yonah, M. *Geschichte der Juden im Zeitalter des Talmud.* Berlin: de Gruyter, 1962.

——. *The Holy Land from the Persian to the Arab Conquests (536 B.C. to A.D. 640).* Grand Rapids: Baker, 1966.

Aziza, Claude. "L'Utilisation polémique du récit de l'Exode chez les écrivains alexandrins (IVème siècle av. J.-C.–Ier siècle ap. J.-C.)" In *ANRW* II.20.1, edited by W. Haase, 41–65. Berlin and New York: de Gruyter, 1987.*

Baer, Y. "Israel, the Christian Church, and the Roman Empire from the Time of Septimius Severus to the Edict of Toleration of AD 313." *Scripta Hierosolymitana* 7 (1961): 79ff.

Balch, David L. "Two Apologetic Encomia: Dionysius on Rome and Josephus on the Jews." *JSJ* 13 (1982): 102–22.*

Baldwin, Barry. "Fronto on the Christians." *Illinois Classical Studies* 15 (1990): 177–81.*

Ball, A. B. "Josephus the Satirist." *JQR* 67 (1976): 16ff.

Baltz, H. R. "Anonymität und Pseudepigraphie im Urchristentum." *ZTK* 66 (1970): 403ff.

Bammel, Ernst. *Judaica.* Vol. 1. Tübingen: Mohr-Siebeck, 1986.*

———. "Die Neuordnung des Pompeius und das römisch-jüdische Bündnis." *ZDPV* 75 (1959): 76ff.

Bardy, G. "Le souvenir de Josèphe chez les Pères." *RHE* 43 (1948): 1789ff.

Barnard, L. W. "Athenagoras: De Resurrectione." *ST* 30 (1976): 1ff.

———. "God, the Logos, the Spirit, and the Trinity in the Theology of Athenagoras." *ST* 24 (1970): 70–92.

———. "Judaism in Egypt AD 70–135." *CQR* 160 (1959): 320ff.

———. *Justin Martyr: His Life and Thought.* Cambridge: Cambridge University Press, 1967.

——— *Studies in the Apostolic Fathers and their Background.* Oxford: Blackwell, 1966.

Barnes, J., et al. *Science and Speculation: Studies in Hellenistic Theory and Practice.* Cambridge: Cambridge University Press, 1983.*

Barnes, T. D. "Porphyry Against the Christians: Date and the Attribution of Fragments." *JTS* n.s. 24 (1973): 424ff.

———. *Tertullian.* Oxford: Clarendon Press, 1971.

———. "Trajan and the Jews." *JJS* 40 (1989): 145–62.*

Barnett, P.W. "'Under Tiberius all was Quiet,'" *NTS* 21 (1974–75): 564ff.

Baron, S. W. *A Social and Religious History of the Jews.* vols. 1–2. 2nd ed. New York: Columbia University Press, 1952.

Barraclough, R. "Philo's Politics: Roman Rule and Hellenistic Judaism." In *ANRW* II.21.1. edited by W. Haase, 417–553. Berlin and New York: de Gruyter, 1984.*

Bartlett, J. R. *The First and Second Books of the Maccabees.* 1973.

———. *Jews in the Hellenistic World.* Cambridge: Cambridge University Press, 1989.*

Barzano, Alberto. "Cheremone di Alessandria." In *ANRW* II.32.3, edited by W. Haase, 1981–2001. Berlin and New York: de Gruyter, 1985.*

Bauckham, R. "The Martyrdom of Enoch and Elijah: Jewish or Christian?" *JBL* 95 (1976): 447ff.

Bauer, W. *Orthodoxy and Heresy in Earliest Christianity.* Philadelphia: Fortress Press, 1971.

Baumann, U. *Rom und die Juden: Die römisch-jüdischen Beziehungen von Pompeius bis zum Tode des Herodes.* Frankfurt: Peter Lang, 1983.*

Baumbach, G. "Zeloten und Sikarier." *TLZ* 90 (1965): 727ff.

Beaujeu, J. *La Religion romaine à l'Apogée de l'Empire.* Paris: Belles Lettres, 1955.

———. *L'incendie de Rome en 64 et les Chrétiens.* Coll. Latomus 49. Paris, 1960.

Beavis, M. A. L. "Anti-Egyptian Polemic in the Letter of Aristeas 130-165 (The High Priest's Discourse)." *JSJ* 18 (1987): 145–51.*

Becker, C. *Tertullians Apologeticum.* Munich: Kösel, 1954.

Belkin, S. *The Alexandrien Halaka in the Apologetic Literature of the First Century C.E.* Philadelphia: Jewish Publication Society, 1936.

———. "The Alexandrien Source of Contra Apionem II." *JQR* 27 (1936): 1ff.

Bell, I. H. *Cults and Creeds in Graeco-Roman Egypt.* Leipzig: Hinrichs, 1953.

———. *Juden und Griechen im römischen Alexandreia.* 2nd ed. 1927.

Bellen, H. "Συναγωγή τῶν 'Ιουδαιων καὶ Θεοσεβῶν. Die Aussage einer bosporanischen Freilassungsinschrift (CIRB 71) zum Problem der 'Gottfürchtigen.'" *Jahrbuch für Antike und Christentum* 8/9 (1965–66): 171ff.

Bellinzoni, A. I. *The Sayings of Jesus in the Writings of Justin Martyr.* NovTSup 17. Leiden: E. J. Brill, 1967.

Beloch, J. *Die Bevölkerung der griechisch-römischen Welt.* 1886.

Ben-Chorin, S. *Jüdischer Glaube.* 1975.

Bengtson, H. *Herrschergestalten des Hellenismus.* 1975.

Benko, S. "The Edict of Claudius of A.D. 49 and the Instigator Chrestus." *TZ* 25 (1969): 406ff.

———. *Pagan Rome and the Early Christians.* Bloomington: Indiana University Press, 1984.*

Bergmeier, R. "Loyalität als Gegenstand paulinischer Paraklese: Eine religionsgeschichtliche Untersuchung zu Röm 13, 1ff. und Jos. B. J. 2,140." *Theokratia* 1 (1967–1969): 51ff.

Bernand, A. *Alexandrie la Grande I–II.* 1966.

Berwig, D. *Mark Aurel. und die Christen.* 1971.

Betz, H. D. *Lukian von Samosata und das Neue Testament.* TU 76. Berlin: Akademie-Verlag, 1961.

Betz, O., K. Haacker, and M. Hengel, eds. *Josephus-Studien,* Festschrift O. Michel. Göttingen: Vandenhoeck & Ruprecht, 1974.

Bickermann, E. J. "Anonymous Gods." *Journal of the Wartburg Institute* 1 (1937–38): 187ff.

———. *Chronologie.* Ithaca, N.Y.: Cornell University Press, 1968.

———. "The Colophon of the Greek Book of Esther." *JBL* 63 (1944): 339ff.

———. "Die Datierung des Pseudo-Aristeas." *ZNW* 29 (1930): 280ff.

———. *Four Strange Books of the Bible.* New York: Schocken Books, 1967.

———. "The Jewish Historian Demetrius." In *Christianity, Judaism and Other Greco-Roman Cults,* Festschrift M. Smith, 3:72ff. 3 vols. Leiden: E. J. Brill, 1975.

———. *The God of the Maccabees.* Translated by H. R. Moehring. Leiden: E. J. Brill, 1979.

———. "Une question d'authenticité: Les privilèges juifs." *Annuaire de l'institut de philologie et d'histoire orientales et slaves* 13 (1953): 11ff.

———. "Ritualmord und Eselskult." *MGWJ* 71 (1927): 255ff. Reprinted in *Studies in Jewish and Christian History,* 225–55. Leiden: E. J. Brill, 1980.*

Bidez, J., and F. Cumont, *Les Mages Hellénisés.* 2 vols. Paris: Belles Lettres, 1938.

Black, M. "The Tradition of Hasidaean-Essene Asceticism: Its Origins and Influence." In *Aspects du Judéo-Christianisme,* 19ff. 1965.

Blanchetière, Francois. "Au coeur de la cité: le chrétien philosophie selon l'à Diognète 5-6." *RSR* 63 (1989): 183–94.*

Bleek, F. "Über die Entstehung und Zusammensetzung der uns in acht Büchern erhaltenen Sammlung sibyllinischer Orakel." *TZ* 1 (1819): 120ff.; 2 (1820) 172ff.

Blowers, Paul M. "Origen, the Rabbis, and the Bible: Toward a Picture of Judaism and Christianity in Third-Century Caesarea." In *Origen of Alexandria: His World and His Legacy,* edited by Charles Kannengiesser and William L. Petersen, 96–116. Notre Dame, Ind.: Notre Dame University Press, 1988.*

Blumenkranz, B. *Die Judenpredigt Augustins.* Basel: Helbing & Lichtenhahn, 1946.

Boccaccini, Gabriele. *Middle Judaism: Jewish Thought, 300 B.C.E.–200 C.E.* Minneapolis: Fortress Press, 1991.*

Bokser, Baruch M. "Recent Developments in the Study of Judaism: 70-200 C.E." *The Second Century* 3 (1983): 1–68.*

Borgen, Peder. "Aristobulus and Philo." In *Philo, John and Paul: New Perspectives on Judaism and Early Christianity,* 7–16. BJS 131. Atlanta: Scholars Press, 1987.*

———. "Debates on Circumcision." In *Philo, John and Paul: New Perspectives on Judaism and Early Christianity,* 61–71. BJS 131. Atlanta: Scholars Press, 1987.*

———. "Philo of Alexandria: A Critical and Synthetical Survey of Research since World War II." In *ANRW* II.21.1, edited by W. Haase, 98–154. Berlin and New York: de Gruyter, 1984.*

———. "Philo's Writings." In *Philo, John and Paul: New Perspectives on Judaism and Early Christianity,* 17–60. BJS 131. Atlanta: Scholars Press, 1987.*

———. "The Sabbath Controversy in John 5:1-18 and Analogous Controversy Reflected in Philo's Writings." In *Studia Philonica Annual III,* 209–21. BJS 230. Atlanta: Scholars Press, 1991.*

Bousset, W. *The Anti-Christ Legend.* London: Hutchinson, 1896.

———, and H. Gressmann. *Die Religion des Judentums im späthellenistischen Zeitalter.* 3rd ed. Tübingen: Mohr-Siebeck, 1926. Reprint, 1966.

Bowersock, G. W. "A Roman Perspective on the Bar Kochba War." In *Approaches to Ancient Judaism,* edited by W. S. Green, 2:131–41. Chico, Calif.: Scholars Press, 1980.*

Brändle, R. *Die Ethik der "Schrift an Diognet."* ATANT 64. Zurich: Theologischer Verlag, 1975.

Braun, R. *"Deus Christianorum." Recherches sur le vocabulaire doctrinal de Tertullien.* Paris: Presses universitaires de France, 1962.

Bréhier, E. *Les Idées philosophiques et religieuses de Philon d'Alexandrie.* 3rd ed. Paris: Vrin, 1950.

Briessmann, A. *Tacitus und das flavische Geschichtsbild.* Hermes Einzelschriften 10. Wiesbaden, 1955.

Brooks, Roger. "Straw Dogs and Scholarly Ecumenism: The Appropriate Jewish Background for the Study of Origen." In *Origen of Alexandria: His World and His Legacy,* edited by Charles Kannengiesser and William L. Petersen, 63–95. Notre Dame, Ind.: Notre Dame University Press, 1988.*

Broshi, Magen. "The Credibility of Josephus." *JJS* 33 (1982): 379–84.*

———. "The Role of the Temple in the Herodian Economy." *JJS* 38 (1987): 31–37.*

Brox, N. "Antignostische Polemik bei Christen und Heiden." *MTZ* 18 (1967): 265ff.

———. "Juden und Heiden bei Irenäus." *MTZ* 16 (1965): 89ff.

———. "Zum literarischen Verhältnis zwischen Justin und Irenäus." *ZNW* 58 (1967): 121ff.

———. "Zum Problemstand in der Erforschung der altchristlichen Pseudepigraphie." *Kairos* n.F. 15 (1973): 10ff.

Bruce, F. F. "Tacitus on Jewish History." *JJS* 29 (1984): 33–44.*

Bruce, I. A. F. "Nerva and the Fiscus Judaicus." *PEQ* 96 (1964): 34ff.

Brüchlmeier, M. "Beiträge zur rechtlichen Stellung der Juden im römischen Reich." Diss., Münster, 1939.

Burke, Gary T. "Celsus and Justin: Carl Andresen Revisited." *ZNW* 76 (1985): 107–16.*

Burr, V. *Tiberius Iulius Alexander.* Bonn: Rudolph Habelt, 1955.

Burrows, Mark S. "Christianity in the Roman Forum: Tertullian and the Apologetic Use of History." *VC* 42 (1988): 209–35.*

Canevet, Mariette. "Remarques sur l'Utilisation du Genre Littéraire Historique par Philon d'Alexandrie dans la *Vita Moysis,* ou Moïse Général en Chef-Prophète." *RSR* 60 (1986): 189–206.*

Cardauns, Burkhart. "Juden und Spartaner." *Hermes* 95 (1967): 317ff.

——. "Varro und die römische Religion zur Theologie, Wirkungsgeschichte und Leistung der 'Antiquitates Rerum Divinarum.'" In *ANRW* II.16.1, edited by W. Haase, 80–103. Berlin and New York: de Gruyter, 1978.*

Case, S. J. "Josephus's Anticipation of a Domitianic Persecution." *JBL* 44 (1925): 10ff.

Casey, S. R. P. *The Excerpta ex Theodoto of Clement of Alexandria.* London: Christophers, 1934.

Causse, A. "L'humanisme juif et le conflit du judaïsme et de l'hellénisme." In *Mélanges F. Cumont,* 525ff. 1936.

Cazeaux, J. "Philon d'Alexandrie, exégète." In *ANRW* II.21.1, edited by W. Haase, 156–226. Berlin and New York: de Gruyter, 1984.*

Cerfaux, L., and J. Tondriau. *Le culte des souverains dans la Civilisation Gréco-romaine.* 1957.

Chadwick, H. *Early Christian Thought and the Classical Tradition.* Oxford: Oxford University Press, 1966.

——. "Justin Martyr's Defence of Christianity." *BJRL* 47 (1964–65): 275ff.

——. *The Sentences of Sextus.* Cambridge: Cambridge University Press, 1959.

Charlesworth, James H. "A History of Pseudepigraphical Research." In *ANRW* II.19.1, edited by W. Haase, 54–88. Berlin and New York: de Gruyter, 1979.*

——. "Jewish Interest in Astrology During the Hellenistic and Roman Period." In *ANRW* II.20.2, edited by W. Haase, 926–50. Berlin and New York: de Gruyter, 1987.*

——. "The Triumphant Majority as Seen by a Dwindled Minority: The Outsider According to the Insider of the Jewish Apocalypses, 70-130." In *"To See Ourselves as Others See Us": Christians, Jews, "Others" in Late Antiquity,* edited by Jacob Neusner and Ernest S. Frerichs, 286–316. Chico, Calif.: Scholars Press, 1985.*

Christ, K. "Zur Herrscherauffassung und Politik Domitians." *Schweizerische Zeitschrift für Geschichte* 12 (1962): 187ff.

Christiansen, I. *Die Technik der allegorischen Auslegungswissenschaft bei Philon von Alexandrien.* Tübingen: Mohr, 1969.

Clark, K. W. "Worship in the Jerusalem Temple after A.D. 70." *NTS* 6 (1959–60): 269ff.

Clarke, G. W. "Four Passages of Minucius Felix." In *Kyriakon,* vol. 2, edited by P. Granfield and J. A. Jungmann, 2:499–507. Münster: Aschendorff, 1970.*

Cohen, A. A. *The Myth of the Judeo-Christian Tradition.* New York: Harper & Row, 1970.

Cohen, N. G. "Josephus and Scripture." *JQR* 54 (1963–64): 311–32.

Cohen, Shaye J. D. *From the Maccabees to the Mishnah.* Philadelphia: Westminster, 1987.*

——. *Josephus in Galilee and Rome: His Vita and Development as a Historian.* Leiden: E. J. Brill, 1979.*

——. "Respect for Judaism by Gentiles According to Josephus." *HTR* 80 (1987): 409–30.*

——. "The Significance of Yavneh: Pharisees, Rabbis, and the End of Jewish Sectarianism." *HUCA* 55 (1984): 27–54.*

Cohon, S. S. "Theology of Judaism according to Josephus." *JQR* 26 (1935–36): 152ff.

———. "The Unity of God: A Study in Hellenistic and Rabbinic Theology." *HUCA* 26 (1955): 425ff.

Colin, J. *L'empire des Antonins et les martyrs gaulois de 177.* Bonn: R. Habelt, 1964.

Collins, J. J. *Studies in the Sibylline Oracles.* Missoula, Mont.: Scholars Press, 1972.

———. "A Symbol of Otherness: Circumcision and Salvation in the First Century." In *"To See Ourselves as Others See Us": Christians, Jews, "Others" in Late Antiquity,* edited by Jacob Neusner and Ernest S. Frerichs, 163–86. Chico, Calif.: Scholars Press, 1985.*

Collomp, P. "La place de Josèphe dans la technique de l'historiographie hellénistique." *Weg der Forschung* 84 (1974): 278–93.

Comfeld, E., ed. *Daniel or Paul: Jews in Conflict with Greco-Roman Civilisation.* 1962.

Correns, D. *Mischna Schebiit.* Berlin: de Gruyter, 1960.

Corssen, P. *Die Altercatio Simonis Iudaei et Theophili Christiani auf ihre Quellen geprüft.* 1890.

Dalbert, P. *Die Theologie der hellenistisch-jüdischen Missionsliteratur unter Ausschluß von Philo und Josephus.* Hamburg: Reich, 1954.

Daniel, J. L. "Anti-Semitism in the Hellenistic-Roman Period." *JBL* 98 (1979): 45–65.*

Daniélou, J. "Figure et évènement chez Méliton de Sardes." In *Neotestamentica et Patristica,* Festschrift O. Cullmann. 282ff. Tournai: Desclée, 1962.

———. *Histoire des doctrines chrétiennes avant Nicée.* 2 vols. Paris: Desclée, 1958, 1961.

———. "Judéo-Christianisme et Gnose." In *Aspects du Judéo-Christianisme.* 1965.

———. *Message évangélique et culture hellénistique au IIe et IIIe siècles.* Tournai: Desclée, 1961.

———. *Origène.* Paris, 1948.

Daoust, J. "La Guerre juive selon Tacite." *Bible et Terre Saint* 118 (1970): 4ff.

———. "Pline l'ancien et la Judée." *Bible et Terre Sainte* 125 (1970): 20f.

Davies, W. D., and L. Finkelstein. *The Cambridge History of Judaism.* Vol. 2. Cambridge: Cambridge University Press, 1989.*

de Boer, Martinus C. "Images of Paul in the Post-Apostolic Period." *CBQ* 42 (1980): 359–80.*

de Faye, E. *Clément d'Alexandrie.* Paris, 1906. Reprint, Frankfurt/Main: Minerva, 1967.

Deissmann, A. *Light from the Ancient East.* London: Hodder & Stoughton, 1911.

de Labriolle, P. *La réaction païenne.* Paris: L'Artisan du Livre, 1934.

de Lange, N. R. M. *Origen and the Jews: Studies in Jewish-Christian Relations in Third Century Palestine.* Cambridge: Cambridge University Press, 1976.

Delcor, M. "Le Livre de Judith et l'epoque Grecque." *Klio* 49 (1967): 151ff.

———. "Le temple d'Onias en Egypte." *RB* 75 (1968): 188–205.

Delling, G. "Die Begegnung zwischen Hellenismus und Judentum." In *ANRW* II.20.1, edited by W. Haase, 3–39. Berlin and New York: de Gruyter, 1987.*

———. "Josephus und die heidnischen Religionen." *Klio* 43–45 (1965): 263ff.

———. *Studien zum Neuen Testament und zum hellenistischen Judentum.* Edited by F. Hahn, T. Holtz, and N. Walter. Göttingen: Vandenhoeck & Ruprecht, 1970.*

———, in cooperation with M. Maser. *Bibliographie zur jüdisch-hellenistischen und intertestamentarischen Literatur 1900–1970.* 2nd ed. 1975.

Denis, A.-M. "Les pseudépigraphes grecs d'Ancien Testament." *NovT* 6 (1963): 310ff.

Denker, J. *Die theologiegeschichtliche Stellung des PetrEv*. Bern and Frankfurt: Peter Lang, 1975.

De Savignac, J. "Le messianisme de Philon d'Alexandrie." *NovT* 4 (1960): 319ff.

Dihle, A. "Zur hellenistischen Ethnographie." In *Grecs et barbares. Entretiens Hardt* 8 (1962): 207ff.

Di Lella, A. A. "Conservative and Progressive Theology: Sirach and Wisdom." *CBQ* 28 (1966): 139ff.

Dilke, Oswald A. W. "The Interpretation of Horace's 'Epistles.'" In *ANRW* II.31.3, edited by W. Haase, 1837–65. Berlin and New York: de Gruyter, 1984.*

Dinkler, E. "Eirene: Der urchristliche Friedensgedanke." *SAH* (1973): 1.

———. "Schalom-Eirene-Pax." *RivAC* 50 (1974): 121ff.

Dodds, E. R. *Pagan and Christian in an Age of Anxiety*. Reprint. Cambridge: Cambridge University Press, 1968.

Doran, Robert. "The Jewish Hellenistic Historians Before Josephus." In *ANRW* II.20.1, edited by W. Haase, 246–97. Berlin and New York: de Gruyter, 1987.*

Dornseiff, F. *Echtheitsfragen antik-griechischer Literatur*. Berlin, 1939.

———. *Echtheitsfragen II*, 128ff. Würzburger Jb. 1. 1946.

Dörrie, H. "Zur Methodik antiker Exegese." *ZNW* 65 (1974): 121ff.

Dozemann, Thomas B. "*Sperma Abraam* in John 8 and Related Literature." *CBQ* 42 (1980): 342–58.*

Drexler, H. "Untersuchungen zu Josephus und zur Geschichte des jüdischen Aufstandes 66–70." *Klio* 19 (1925): 277ff.

Dubnow, S. *Weltgeschichte des jüdischen Volkes III*. Berlin: Jüdischer Verlag, 1926.

Dunn, James D. G. *The Parting of the Ways*. London: SCM Press; Philadelphia: Trinity Press International, 1992.*

Efron, Joshua. *Studies in the Hasmonean Period*. Leiden: E. J. Brill, 1987.*

Efroymson, David P. "The Patristic Connection." In *Antisemitism and the Foundations of Christianity*, edited by Alan Davies, 98–117. New York, Ramsey, Toronto: Paulist Press, 1979.*

Ehrhardt, A. *Die Kirche der Märtyrer*. Munich: Kösel, 1932.

Eising, H. "Der Weisheitslehrer und die Götterbilder." *Bib* 40 (1959): 393ff.

Eissfeldt, O. *The Old Testament: An Introduction*. New York: Harper & Row, 1965.

Eleney, N. J. "Orthodoxy in Judaism of the First Christian Century." *JSJ* 4 (1973): 19ff.

Elsas, C. *Neuplatonische und gnostische Weltablehnung in der Schule Plotins*. 1975.

Elter, A. *De Gnomologiorum Graecorum historia atque origine commentatio I–IX*. Bonn: Universitätsprogramme, 1893–95.

Eltester, W. "Das Mysterium des Christentums: Anmerkungen zum Diognetbrief." *ZNW* 61 (1970): 278–93.

Elze, M. *Tatian und seine Theologie*. Göttingen: Vandenhoeck & Ruprecht, 1960.

Eppstein, V. "When and How the Sadducees were Excommunicated." *JBL* 85 (1966): 213ff.

Fauth, Wolfgang. "Römische Religion im Spiegel der 'Fasti' des Ovid." In *ANRW* II.16.1, edited by W. Haase, 104–86. Berlin and New York: de Gruyter, 1978.*

Feldman, L. H. "Abraham the Greek Philosopher in Josephus." *TAPA* 59 (1968): 145ff.

———. "Anti-Semitism in the Ancient World." In *History and Hate: The Dimensions of Anti-Semitism*, edited by D. Berger. Philadelphia, 1986.*

———. "Asinius Pollio and his Jewish Interests." *TAPA* 84 (1953): 73ff.

———. "Flavius Josephus Revisited: The Man, His Writings, and His Significance." In *ANRW* II.21.2, edited by W. Haase, 763–862. Berlin and New York: de Gruyter, 1984.*

———. "The Identity of Pollio, the Pharisee, in Josephus." *JQR* 49 (1958–59): 53ff.

———. "Jewish 'Sympathizers' in Classical Literature and Inscriptions." *TAPA* 81 (1950): 200ff.

———. *Josephus: A Supplementary Bibliography.* New York and London: Garland, 1986.*

———. *Josephus and Modern Scholarship (1937–1980).* Berlin and New York: de Gruyter, 1984.*

———. "Josephus' *Jewish Antiquities* and Pseudo-Philo's *Biblical Antiquities.*" In *Josephus, the Bible, and History,* edited by Louis H. Feldman and Gohei Hata, 59–80. Detroit: Wayne State University Press, 1989.*

———. "Origen's Contra Celsum and Josephus' Contra Apionem: The Issue of Jewish Origins." *VC* 44 (1990): 105–35.*

———. "Philo-Semitism among the Ancient Intellectuals." *Tradition* 1 (1958–59): 27ff.

———. "Pro-Jewish Intimations in Anti-Jewish Remarks Cited in Josephus' Against Apion." *JQR* 78 (1988): 187–251.*

———. "A Selective Critical Bibliography of Josephus." In *Josephus, the Bible, and History,* edited by Louis H. Feldman and Gohei Hata, 330–449. Detroit: Wayne State University Press, 1989.*

———. "The Sources of Josephus' Antiquities, Book 19." *Latomus* 21 (1962): 320ff.

———, D. Flusser, D. Ladouceur et al. "The Meaning of Josephus." *Midstream* 32 (1986): 26–33.*

———, and Gohei Hata, eds. *Josephus, the Bible, and History.* Detroit: Wayne State University Press, 1989.*

Festugière, A.-J. *La Révélation d'Hermès Trismégiste.* 4 vols. Paris: Lecoffre, 1950–54.

Fink, W. "Der Einfluß der jüdischen Religion auf die griechisch-römische Religion." Diss., Bonn, 1932.

Finkel, Asher. "Yavneh's Liturgy and Early Christianity." *JES* 18 (1981): 231–50.*

Forni, Giovanni. "Pompeo Torgo come fonte di storia." In *ANRW* II.30.2, edited by W. Haase, 1298–1362. Berlin and New York: de Gruyter, 1982.*

Fraser, P. M. "Hadrian and Cyrene." *JRS* 40 (1950): 77ff.

———. *Ptolemaic Alexandria.* 3 vols. Oxford: Clarendon Press, 1972.

Frede, Michael. "Chaeremon der Stoiker." In *ANRW* II.36.3, edited by W. Haase, 2067–2103. Berlin and New York: de Gruyter, 1989.*

Freimann, M. "Die Wortführer des Judentums in den ältesten Kontroversen zwischen Juden und Christen." *MGWJ* 55 (1911): 555ff.; 56 (1912): 49ff., 164ff.

Frend, W. H. C. *Martyrdom and Persecution in the Early Church.* Oxford: Blackwell, 1965.

———. "A Note on Jews and Christians in Third-century North Africa." *JTS* n.s. 21 (1970): 92ff.

———. "A Note on Tertullian and the Jews." *St. Patr.* 10/1, 291–96. TU 107. Berlin: Akademie-Verlag, 1970.

———. "Open Questions concerning the Christians and the Roman Empire in the Age of Severi." *JTS* n.s. 25 (1974): 333ff.

———. "The Persecutions: Some Links between Judaism and Early Church." *JEH* 9 (1958): 141ff.

Freudenberger, R. "Christenreskript: Ein umstrittenes Reskript des Antoninus Pius." *ZKG* 78 (1967): 1ff.

———. *Das Verhalten der römischen Behörden gegen die Christen im 2. Jh. dargestellt am Brief des Plinius an Trajan und an den Reskripten Trajans und Hadrians.* Munich: Beck, 1967.

Freudenthal, J. *Hellenistische Studien.* 2 vols. Breslau: H. Skutsch, 1874, 1875.

Freyne, Sean. "Vilifying the Other and Defining the Self: Matthew's and John's Anti-Jewish Polemic in Focus." In *"To See Ourselves as Others See Us": Christians, Jews, "Others" in Late Antiquity,* edited by Jacob Neusner and Ernest S. Frerichs, 117–43. Chico, Calif.: Scholars Press, 1985.*

Friedländer, M. *Geschichte der jüdischen Apologetik.* Amsterdam: Philo Press, 1903.

Früchtel, U. *Die kosmologischen Vorstellungen bei Philo von Alexandrien.* Leiden: E. J. Brill, 1968.

Fruin, R. "Abraham en Damaskus." *Nieuwe Theol. Tijdschr.* 15 (1926): 3ff.

Fuchs, H. *Der geistige Widerstand gegen Rom in der antiken Welt.* 1938. 2nd ed. Berlin: de Gruyter, 1964.

Fuks, A. "The Jewish Revolt in Egypt (A.D. 115–117) in the Light of the Papyri." *Aegyptus* 33 (1953): 131ff.

Fuks, Gideon. "The Jewish Revolt in A.D. 115–117." *JRS* 52 (1962): 98ff.

———. "Josephus and the Hasmoneans." *JJS* 41 (1990): 166–76.*

Gager, J. G. "The Dialogue of Paganism with Judaism: Bar Cochba to Julian." *HUCA* 44 (1983): 88–118.*

———. *Kingdom and Community: The Social World of Early Christianity.* Englewood Cliffs, N.J.: Prentice Hall, 1975.

———. *Moses in Greco-Roman Paganism.* Nashville: Abingdon, 1972.

———. *The Origins of Anti-Semitism: Attitudes Toward Judaism in Pagan and Christian Antiquity.* New York: Oxford University Press, 1983.*

———. "Pseudo-Hecataeus Again." *ZNW* 60 (1969): 130ff.

Gardner, A. E. "The Relationship of the Additions to the Book of Esther to the Maccabean Crisis." *JSJ* 15 (1984): 1–8.*

Gaston, Lloyd. "Judaism of the Uncircumcised in Ignatius and Related Writers." In *Anti-Judaism in Early Christianity,* vol 2, *Separation and Polemic,* edited by Stephen G. Wilson, 33–44. Waterloo, Ont.: Wilfrid Laurier University Press, 1986.*

Gauger, Jörg-Dieter. *Beiträge zur jüdischen Apologetik: Untersuchungen zur Authentizität von Urkunden bei Flavius Josephus und im 1. Makkabäerbuch.* Cologne: P. Hanstein, 1977.

———. "Zitate in der Jüdischen Apologetik und die Authentizität der Hekataios-Passagen bei Flavius Josephus und im Ps. Aristeas-Brief." *JSJ* 13 (1982): 6–46.*

Geffcken, J. *Der Ausgang des griechisch-römischen Heidentums.* 1920.

———. "Der Bilderstreit des heidnischen Altertums." *ARW* 19 (1919): 286ff.

———. *Komposition und Entstehungszeit der Oracula Sibyllina.* TU 23.1. Leipzig: Hinrichs, 1902.

———. *Zwei griechische Apologeten.* Leipzig and Berlin: Teubner, 1907.

Geiger, Joseph. "The Earliest Reference to Jews in Latin Literature." *JSJ* 15 (1984): 145–47.*

Gelzer, H. *Sextus Julius Africanus, und die byzantinische chronographie.* 2 vols. Leipzig: Hinrichs, 1880–98.

Gelzer, M. "Die Vita des Josephos." *Hermes* 80 (1952): 67ff.

Georgi, Dieter. *Theocracy in Paul's Praxis and Theology.* Minneapolis: Fortress Press, 1990.*

Gero, Stephen. "Apocryphal Gospels." In *ANRW* II.25.5, edited by W. Haase, 3969–96. Berlin and New York: de Gruyter, 1988.*

Giangrande D. "Emendations to Josephus Flavius' Contra Apionem." *Classical Quarterly* n.s. 12 (1962): 108ff.

Gichon, Mordechai. "New Insight into the Bar Kokhba War and a Reappraisal of Dio Cassius 69.12-13." *JQR* 77 (1986): 15–43.*

Giet, S. *L'apocalypse et l'histoire.* 1957.

———. "Un courant judéo-chrétien à Rome au milieu du IIe siècle?" In *Aspects du Judéo-Christianisme,* 95ff. 1965.

Gilat, Yitzhak D. "The Nature of the Sabbath in Extra-Talmudic Sources." Paper Presented at the Eighth World Congress of Jewish Studies. Jerusalem, 1981.*

Ginsburg, M. S. *Rome et la Judée: Contribution à l'histoire de leur relations politiques.* 1928.

Golan, David. "Hadrian's Decision to Supplant 'Jerusalem' by 'Aelia Capitolina.'" *Historia* 35 (1986): 226–39.*

Goldenberg, D. "The Halacha in Josephus and in Tannaitic Literature." *JQR* 67 (1976): 16ff.

Goldenberg, Robert. "The Jewish Sabbath in the Roman World Up to the Time of Constantine the Great." In *ANRW* II.19.1, edited by W. Haase, 414–47. Berlin and New York: de Gruyter, 1979.*

———. "The Place of Other Religions in Ancient Jewish Thought, with Particular Reference to Early Rabbinic Judaism." In *Pushing the Faith,* edited by Martin Marty and Frederick E. Greenspahn, 27–40. New York: Crossroad, 1988.*

Goldstein, J. A. "Jewish Acceptance and Rejection of Hellenism." In *Aspects of Judaism in the Greco-Roman Period,* edited by E. P. Sanders, 64–87. Philadelphia: Fortress Press, 1981.*

Goodenough, E. R. *By Light, Light.* New Haven: Yale University Press, 1935.

———. *Jewish Symbols in the Greco-Roman Period.* 11 vols. New York: Pantheon Books, 1953ff.

———. *The Jurisprudence of the Jewish Courts in Egypt.* New Haven: Yale University Press, 1929.

———. *The Politics of Philo Judaeus.* New Haven: Yale University Press, 1938.

Goodman, Martin. "A Bad Joke in Josephus." *JJS* 36 (1985): 195–99.*

———. "The First Jewish Revolt: Social Conflict and the Problem of Debt." *JJS* 33 (1982): 417–27.*

———. "The Origins of the Great Revolt: A Conflict of Status Criteria." In *Greece and Rome in Eretz-Israel.* Haifa and Tel-Aviv, 1985.*

———. *The Ruling Class of Judaea: The Origins of the Jewish Revolt Against Rome, A. D. 66–70.* Cambridge: Cambridge University Press, 1987.*

———. *State and Society in Roman Galilee, AD 132-212.* Totowa, N.J., 1983.*

Goppelt, L. *Christentum und Judentum im ersten und zweiten Jahrhundert.* Gütersloh: Bertelsmann, 1954.

Gorday, Peter. "Moses and Jesus in *Contra Celsum* 7.1-25: Ethics, History, and Jewish-Christian Eirenics in Origen's Theology." In *Origen of Alexandria: His World and His Legacy,* edited by Charles Kannengiesser and William L. Petersen, 313–36. Notre Dame, Ind.: Notre Dame University Press, 1988.*

Grabar, A. "Le thème religieux des fresques de la synagogue de Doura (245–256 après J.-C.)." *RHR* 123 (1941): 143ff.; 124 (1941): 5ff.

Grabbe, Lester L. *Judaism from Cyrus to Hadrian.* 2 vols. Minneapolis: Fortress Press, 1991.*

Grant, F. C. "Religio licita." *St. Patr.* 4/2, 84–89. TU 79. Berlin: Akademie-Verlag, 1961.

Grant, R. M. "Aristotle and the Conversion of Justin." *JTS* n.s. 7 (1956): 246ff.

———. "Charges of 'Immorality' Against Various Religious Groups in Antiquity." In *Studies in Gnosticism and Hellenistic Religions,* edited by R. van den Broek and M. J. Vermaseren, 161–70. Leiden: E. J. Brill, 1981.*

———. *Christian Beginnings: Apocalypse to History.* London: Variorum Reprints, 1983.*

———. "The Chronology of the Greek Apologists." *VC* 9 (1955): 25ff.

——— "Five Apologists and Marcus Aurelius." *VC* 42 (1988): 1–17.*

———. *Greek Apologists of the Second Century.* Philadelphia: Westminster, 1988.*

———. "The Heresy of Tatian." *JTS* n.s. 5 (1954): 62ff.

———. "Notes on the Text of Theophilus, Ad Autolycum III." *VC* 12 (1958): 136ff.

———. *Second Century Christianity.* London: SPCK, 1957.

———. "Studies in the Apologists." *HTR* 51 (1958): 123ff.

———. "Tatian and the Bible." *St. Patr.* 1, 297–306. TU 63. Berlin: Akademie-Verlag, 1957.

———. "The Uses of History in the Church before Nicea." *St. Patr.* 11, 166–78. TU 108. Berlin: Akademie-Verlag, 1972.

Grégoire, H., et al. *Les persécutions dans l'empire romain.* Brussels, 1950.

Guignebert, C. *The Jewish World in the Time of Jesus.* New York: E. P. Dutton, 1939.

Gülzow, H. *Christentum und Sklaverei in den ersten drei Jahrhunderten.* Bonn: R. Habelt, 1969.

Gunther, J. J. "The Epistle of Barnabas and the Final Rebuilding of the Temple." *JSJ* 7 (1976): 143ff.

Guterman, S. L. *Religious Toleration and Persecution in Ancient Rome.* London: Aiglon Press, 1951.

Gutmann, Joseph. *Ancient Synagogues.* Chico, Calif.: Scholars Press, 1981.*

Guttman, A. "The End of the Jewish Sacrifical Cult." *HUCA* 38 (1967): 137ff.

Guttmann, H. *Die Darstellung der jüdischen Religion bei Flavius Josephus.* Breslau: Marcus, 1928.

Hadas, M. "Aristeas and III Maccabees." *HTR* 42 (1949): 175ff.

———. *Hellenistic Culture: Fusion and Diffusion.* New York: Columbia University Press, 1959.

———. "Plato in Hellenistic Fusion." *Journal of the History of Ideas* 19 (1958): 3ff.

———. "Third Maccabees and Greek Romance." *RR* 13 (1948–49): 155ff.

Hadas-Level, Mireille. *Flavius Josèphe: Le Juif de Rome.* Paris: Fayard, 1989.*

Hamerton-Kelly, R. G., and R. Scroggs, eds. *Jews, Greeks, and Christians,* Festschrift W. D. Davies. Leiden: E. J. Brill, 1976.

Hann, Robert R. "Judaism and Jewish Christianity in Antioch: Charisma and Conflict in the First Century." *Journal of Religious History* 14 (1987): 341–60.*

Hanson, R. P. C. *Studies in Christian Antiquity.* Edinburgh: T. & T. Clark, 1985.*

Hardwick, Michael. *Josephus as an Historical Source in Patristic Literature Through Eusebius.* Atlanta: Scholars Press, 1989.*

Hare, D. R. A. "The Rejection of the Jews in the Synoptic Gospels and Acts." In *Antisemitism and the Foundations of Christianity*, edited by Alan Davies, 27–47. New York, Ramsey, Toronto: Paulist Press, 1979.*

———. *The Theme of Jewish Persecution of Christians in the Gospel according to St Matthew*. Cambridge: Cambridge University Press, 1967.

Harnack, A. *Die altercatio Simonis Judaei et Theophili Christiani*. TU 1.3. Leipzig: Hinrichs, 1883.

———. *Das Edict des Antoninus Pius*. TU 13.4. Leipzig: Hinrichs, 1895, 1ff.

———. *Geschichte der altchristlichen Literatur bis Eusebius*. 4 vols. Leipzig, 1893–1904.

———. *Judentum und Judenchristentum in Justins Dialog*. TU 39.1. Leipzig: Hinrichs, 1913.

———. *The Mission and Expansion of Christianity*. Vol. 1. New York: Harper & Brothers, 1961.

———. *Die Überlieferung der griechischen Apologeten des zweiten Jahrhunderts in der Alten Kirche und im Mittelalter*. TU 1.1. Leipzig: Hinrichs, 1883.

———. *Der Vorwurf des Atheismus in den ersten drei Jahrhunderten*. TU 18.4. Leipzig: Hinrichs, 1905.

Harris, Bruce F. "The Defence of Christianity in Athanagoras' *Embassy*." *Journal of Religious History* 15 (1989): 413–24.*

Hayward, Robert. "The Jewish Temple at Leontopolis." *JJS* 33 (1982): 429–43.*

Heine, Ronald, trans. *Origen's Commentary on the Gospel According to John, Books 1–10*. Washington: Catholic University Press, 1989.*

Heinemann, I. *Philons griechische und jüdische Bildung*. 1932. Reprint. Hildesheim: G. Olms, 1962.

Helck, W. *Unterschungen zu Manetho und den ägyptischen Königslisten*. Berlin, 1956.

Hengel, M. "Anonymität, Pseudepigraphie und 'Literarische Fälschung' in der jüdisch-hellenistischen Literatur." In *Pseudepigrapha I*, 231ff. Geneva: Fondation Hardt, 1972.

———. *Jews, Greeks, and Barbarians*. Philadelphia: Fortress Press, 1980.

———. *The 'Hellenization' of Judaea in the First Century After Christ*. London: SCM Press; Philadelphia: Trinity Press International, 1991.*

———. *Judaism and Hellenism*. Philadelphia: Fortress Press, 1974.

———. *Property and Riches in the Early Church*. Philadelphia: Fortress Press, 1974.

———. "Die Synagogeninschrift von Stobi." *ZNW* 57 (1966): 145ff.

———. *The Zealots*. Edinburgh: T. & T. Clark, 1989.

———. "Zeloten und Sikarier." In *Josephus-Studien*, Festschrift O. Michel, 175ff. 1974.

Henrichs, A. "Pagan Ritual and the Alleged Crimes of the Early Christians." In *Kyriakon*, vol. 1, edited by P. Granfield and J. A. Jungmann, 1:18–35. Münster: Aschendorff, 1970.*

Herrmann, L. *Chrestos: Témoignages païens et juifs sur le christianisme du premier siècle*. 1970.

Herrmann, P. *Der römische Kaisereid*. 1968.

Heubner, H., and W. Fauth. *P. Cornelius Tacitus, Die Historien*. Heidelberg: Carl Winter Universitätsverlag, 1982.*

Hilgenfeld, A. *Die jüdische Apokalyptik in ihrer geschichtlichen Entwickelung*. Amsterdam: Rudupi, 1857. Reprint, 1966.

———. *Die Ketzergeschichte des Urchristenthums*. Leipzig, 1884. Reprint. Hildesheim, 1963.

Hilgert, E. "Bibliographia Philoniana 1935–1981." In *ANRW* II.21.1, edited by W. Haase, 47–97. Berlin and New York: de Gruyter, 1984.*

Hochner, H. W. *Herod Antipas.* Cambridge: Cambridge University Press, 1972.

Hoffmann, M. *Der Dialog bei den christlichen Schriftstellern der ersten vier Jahrhunderte.* TU 96. Berlin: Akademie-Verlag, 1966.

Holladay, Carl R. *Fragments from Hellenistic Jewish Authors, I, Historians.* Chico, Calif.: Scholars Press, 1983.*

———. *Fragments from Hellenistic Jewish Authors, II, Poets.* Atlanta: Scholars Press, 1989.*

Holm-Nielsen, Svend. "Religiöse Poesie des Spätjudentums." In *ANRW* II.19.1, edited by W. Haase, 152–86. Berlin and New York: de Gruyter, 1979.

Holte, R. "Logos Spermatikos: Christianity and Ancient Philosophy according to St. Justin's Apologies." *ST* 12 (1958): 109–68.

Hopfner, T. *Die Judenfrage bei Griechen und Römern.* Prague, 1943.

Horbury, William. "The Benediction of the Minim and Early Jewish-Christian Controversy." *JTS* 33 (1982): 19–61.*

Hospers-Jansen, A. M. A. *Tacitus over de Joden.* Groningen, 1949.

Howard, George. "The Gospel of the Ebionites." In *ANRW* II.25.5, edited by W. Haase, 4034–53. Berlin and New York: de Gruyter, 1988.*

Hruby, K. *Juden und Judentum bei den Kirchenvätern.* Zurich, 1971.

———. *Die Stellung der jüdischen Gesetzeslehrer zur werdenden Kirche.* 1971.

Hulen, A. B. "The 'Dialogues with the Jews' as Sources for the Early Jewish Argument against Christianity." *JBL* 51 (1932): 58ff.

Hummel, R. *Die Auseinandsetzung zwischen Kirche und Judentum im Matthäusevangelium.* Munich: Kaiser, 1966.

Hunzinger, C.-H. "Babylon als Deckname für Rom und die Datierung des 1. Petrusbriefes." In *Gottes Wort und Gottes Land,* Festschrift H.-W. Hertzberg, 67ff. Göttingen: Vandenhoeck & Ruprecht, 1965.

Huzar, Eleanor. "Claudius—the Erudite Emperor." In *ANRW* II.32.1, edited by W. Haase, 611–50. Berlin and New York: de Gruyter, 1984.*

Instinsky, H. U. *Die alte Kirche und das Heil des Staates.* 1963.

Isaac, Benjamin. "Judaea after AD 70." *JJS* 35 (1984): 44–50.*

———, and Aharon Oppenheimer. "The Revolt of Bar Kokhba: Ideology and Modern Scholarship." *JJS* 36 (1985): 33–60.*

Isser, S. J. *The Dositheans: A Samaritan Sect in Late Antiquity.* Leiden: E. J. Brill, 1976.

Jackson, F. J. F. *Josephus and the Jews.* London: SPCK, 1930.

Jaeger, W. *Diokles von Karystos.* Berlin, 1938.

———. *Early Christianity and the Greek Paideia.* Boston: Belknap Press, 1963.

———. "Greeks and Jews." *JR* 18 (1938): 127ff.

Jaubert, A. *La notion d'alliance dans le judaïsme aux abords de l'ère chrétienne.* Paris: Sevil, 1963.

Jellicoe, S. "Aristeas, Philo and the Septuagint Vorlage." *JTS* n.s. 12 (1961): 261ff.

———. "St. Luke and the Letter of Aristeas." *JBL* 80 (1961): 149ff.

———. "The Occasion and Purpose of the Letter of Aristeas." *NTS* 12 (1965–66): 144ff.

Jervell, J. *Imago Dei.* Göttingen: Vandenhoeck & Ruprecht, 1960.

Johns, A. F. "The Military Strategy of Sabbath Attacks on the Jews." *VT* 13 (1967): 482ff.

Johnson, S. E. "Asia Minor and Early Christianity." In *Christianity, Judaism and other Greco-Roman Cults,* Festschrift M. Smith, 2:77ff. Leiden: E. J. Brill, 1975.

Johnson, William A. "Anti-Semitism in John's Gospel. In *From Ancient Israel to Modern Judaism*, vol. 1, edited by Jacob Neusner, Ernest Frerichs, Nahum M. Sarna, 149–70. Atlanta: Scholars Press, 1989.*

Jonas, H. *Gnosis und spätantiker Geist I.* 3rd ed. Göttingen: Vandenhoeck & Ruprecht, 1964.

Jones, A. H. M. *The Later Roman Empire.* I. Norman, Okla.: University of Oklahoma Press, 1964.

———. "Die soziale Hintergrund des Kampfes zwischen Heidentum und Christentum." In *Das frühe Christentum im römischen Staat*, edited by R. Klein, 337ff. 1971.

Judge, E. A. "The Beginning of Religious History." *Journal of Religious History* 15 (1989): 394–412.*

Juster, J. *Les Juifs dans l'empire Romain, leur condition juridique, économique et sociale.* 2 vols. New York: Burt Franklin, 1914, 1965.

Kahrstedt, U. "Die Märtyrerakten von Lugdunum 177." *RheinMus* 68 (1913): 395ff.

Kanael, B. "Notes on the Dates Used During The Bar Kokhba Revolt." *IEJ* 21 (1971): 39ff.

Kant, Laurence H. "Jewish Inscriptions in Greek and Latin." In *ANRW* II.20.2, edited by W. Haase, 672–713. Berlin and New York: de Gruyter, 1987.*

Kasher, Arye H. *The Jews in Hellenistic and Roman Egypt.* Tel Aviv: Tel Aviv University, 1978. (Hebrew)*

———. *The Jews in Hellenistic and Roman Egypt: The Struggle for Equal Rights.* Tübingen: Mohr-Siebeck, 1985.*

———. "The propaganda purposes of Manetho's libellous story about the base origin of the Jews." In *Studies in the History of the Jewish People and the Land of Israel*, edited by B. Oded et al. 1974.*

Katz, Steven T. "Issues in the Separation of Judaism and Christianity after 70 C.E.: A Reconsideration." *JBL* 103 (1984): 43–76.*

Kee, Howard C. "The Transformation of the Synagogue after 70 C.E." *NTS* 36 (1990): 1–24.*

Keresztes, P. "The Jews, the Christians, and Emperor Domitian." *VC* 27 (1973): 1ff.

———. "Marcus Aurelius a Persecutor?" *HTR* 61 (1968): 321ff.

Keseling, P. "Justins 'Dialog gegen Trypho' (c. 1-10) und Platons 'Protagoras.'" *RheinMus* n.F. 75 (1926): 223ff.

Kinzig, Wolfram. "Der 'Sitz im Leben' der Apologie in der Alten Kirche." *ZKG* 100 (1989): 291–317.*

Kisch, G. *Judaistische Bibliographie.* 1972.

Klassen, William. "Anti-Judaism in Early Christianity: The State of the Question." In *Anti-Judaism in Early Christianity*, vol. 1, edited by Peter Richardson, Waterloo, Ont.: Wilfrid Laurier University Press, 1986.*

Klavinghaus, J. *Die theologische Stellung der Apostolischen Väter zur alttestamentlichen Offenbarung.* 1948.

Klein, G. *Der älteste christliche Katechismus und die jüdische Propagandaliteratur.* Berlin: Reimer, 1909.

Klein, R., ed. *Das frühe Christentum im römischen Staat.* Darmstadt: Wissenschaftliche Buchgesellschaft, 1971.

Klijn, A. F. J. "Das Hebräer- und das Nazoräerevangelium." In *ANRW* II.25.5, edited by W. Haase, 3997–4033. Berlin and New York: de Gruyter, 1988.*

———. "The Influence of Jewish Theology on the Odes of Solomon and the Acts of Thomas." In *Aspects du Judéo-Christianisme,* 167ff. 1965.

Knox, W. L. *Some Hellenistic Elements in Primitive Christianity.* London, H. Milford, 1944.

Köves-Zulauf, Thomas. "Plinius d. Ä. und die römische Religion." In *ANRW* II.16.1, edited by W. Haase, 188–288. Berlin and New York: de Gruyter, 1978.*

Koschorke, K. *Hippolyts Ketzerbekämpfung und Polemik gegen die Gnostiker.* Leiden: E. J. Brill, 1975.

Kraabel, A. T. *The Diaspora Synagogue* (forthcoming).

———. *Judaism in Western Asia Minor under the Roman Empire, with a Preliminary Study of the Jewish Community at Sardis, Lydia.* Leiden: E. J. Brill, 1968.

———. "Paganism and Judaism: The Sardis Evidence." In *Paganisme, Judaïsme, Christianisme,* Mélanges M. Simon, 13ff. Paris: Boccard, 1978.

———. "The Roman Diaspora: Six Questionable Assumptions." *JJS* 33 (1982): 445–64.*

———. "Synagoga Caeca: Systematic Distortion in Gentile Interpretations of Evidence for Judaism in the Early Christian Period." In *"To See Ourselves as Others See Us": Christians, Jews, "Others" in Late Antiquity,* edited by Jacob Neusner and Ernest S. Frerichs, 219–46. Chico, Calif.: Scholars Press, 1985.*

Kraft, Robert A. "In Search of 'Jewish Christianity' and its 'Theology': Problems of Definition and Methodology." In *Judéo-Christianisme,* 81ff. 1972.

———. "Christian Transmission of Greek Jewish Scriptures: A Methodical Probe." In *Paganisme, Judaïsme, Christianisme: Mélanges offerts à Marcel Simon,* 207–26. Paris: Boccard, 1978.*

———, and George W. E. Nickelsburg, eds. *Early Judaism and Its Modern Interpreters.* Atlanta: Scholars Press, 1986.*

Kraemer, Ross S. "On the Meaning of the Term 'Jew' in Greco-Roman Inscriptions." *HTR* 82 (1989): 35–53.*

Kraus Reggiani, Clara. "I rapporti tra l'impero romane e il mondo ebraico al tempo di Caligola secondo la 'Legatio ad Gaium' di Filone Alessandrino." In *ANRW* II.21.1, edited by W. Haase, 554–86. Berlin and New York: de Gruyter, 1984.*

Krause, W. *Die Stellung der frühchristlichen Autoren zur heidnischen Literatur.* 1958.

Kreissig, H. "A Marxist View of Josephus' Account of the Jewish War." In *Josephus, the Bible, and History,* edited by Louis H. Feldman and Gohei Hata, 265–77. Detroit: Wayne State University Press, 1989.*

———. *Die sozialen Zusammenhänge des judäischen Krieges.* 1970.

———. "Zur Rolle der religiösen Gruppen in den Volksbewegungen der Hasmonäerzeit." *Klio* 43–45 (1965): 174ff.

Kretschmar, G. "Die Bedeutung der Literaturgeschichte für die Frage nach der Kontinuität des Judenchristentums in nachapostolischer Zeit." In *Aspects du Judéo-Christianisme,* 113ff. 1965.

Krüger, P. *Philo und Josephus als Apologeten.* Leipzig, 1906.

Kuhn, K. G. "Weltjudentum in der Antike." In *Forschungen zur Judenfrage,* 1:79ff. 1st ed. 1943.

Kukula, R. C. *Tatians sogenannte Apologie.* Leipzig, 1900.

Lagrange, J.-M. *Le judaïsme avant Jésus Christ.* Paris: J. Gabalda, 1931.

———. *Le messianisme des Juifs.* Paris: Gabalda, 1909.

Langerbeck, H. *Aufsätze zur Gnosis.* Göttingen: Vandenhoeck & Ruprecht, 1967.

Laqueur, R. *Der jüdische Historiker Flavius Josephus.* Giessen, 1920.

Larcher, C. *Études sur le Livre de la Sagesse.* Paris: Gabalda, 1969.

Latte, K. *Römische Religionsgeschichte.* Munich, 1960.

Lebram, J. C. H. "Apokalyptik und Hellenismus im Buche Daniel. Bemerkungen und Gedanken zu Martin Hengels Buch über 'Judentum und Hellenismus.'" *VT* 20 (1970): 503ff.

Lémonon, J.-P. *Pilate et le Gouvernement de la Judée.* Études Bibliques. Paris: Gabalda, 1981.*

Leon, H. J. *The Jews of Ancient Rome.* Philadelphia: Jewish Publication Society of America, 1960.

Lesky, A. *History of Greek Literature.* New York: Crowell, 1966.

Levine, L. I. *Caesarea under Roman Rule.* Leiden: E. J. Brill, 1975.

Lévy, I. *La légende de Pythagore de Grèce en Palestine.* Pythagore, 1927.

———. "Ptolémée Lathyre et les Juits." *HUCA* 23 (1950–51): 127ff.

———. "Tacite et l'origine du peuple juif." *Latomus* 5 (1946): 331ff.

Lewy, H. "Aristotle and the Jewish Sage according to Clearchus of Soli." *HTR* 31 (1938): 205ff.

———. "Hekataios von Abdera περὶ 'Ιουδαίων." *ZNW* 31 (1932): 117ff.

Leytens, J. "Les Esséniens dans l'oeuvre de Flavius Joséphe et des Philosophumena d'Hippolyte de Rome." Diss., Louvain, 1962.

Lieberman, S. *Greek in Jewish Palestine.* New York: Jewish Theological Seminary of America, 1942.

———. *Hellenism in Jewish Palestine.* New York: Jewish Theological Seminary of America, 1950.

Liebig, Janis E. "'John and the Jews': Theological Antisemitism in the Fourth Gospel." *JES* 20 (1983): 209–34.*

Liebmann-Frankfort, T. "Rome et le conflit judéo-syrien." *L'Antiquité Classique* 38 (1969): 101ff.

Lietzmann, H. *A History of the Early Church.* Cleveland and New York: World, 1961.

Lifshitz, B. "Beiträge zur griechisch-jüdischen Epigraphik." *ZDPV* 82 (1966): 57ff.

———. "Inscriptions de Césarée." *RB* 74 (1967): 50ff.

———. "Notes d'épigraphie Grecque." *RB* 76 (1969): 92ff.

———. "Une synagogue Samaritaine à Thessalonique." *RB* 75 (1968): 368ff.

Lightstone, Jack. "Christian Anti-Judaism in its Judaic Mirror: The Judaic Context of Early Christianity Revised." In *Anti-Judaism in Early Christianity,* vol. 2, *Separation and Polemic,* edited by Stephen G. Wilson, 103–32. Waterloo, Ont.: Wilfrid Laurier University Press, 1986.*

———. *The Commerce of the Sacred: Mediation of the Divine Among Jews in the Graeco-Roman Diaspora.* Chico, Calif.: Scholars Press, 1984.*

Limbeck, M. *Die Ordnung des Heils: Untersuchungen zum Gesetzesverständnis des Frühjudentums.* 1971.

Lindars, Barnabas, ed. *Law and Religion.* Cambridge: James Clark, 1988.*

Lindemann, A. "Paulinische Theologie im Brief an Diognet." In *Kerygma und Logos,* Festschrift C. Andresen, 337ff. Göttingen: Vandenhoeck & Ruprecht, 1979.

Lindern, Amnon, ed. *The Jews in Roman Imperial Legislation.* Detroit: Wayne State University Press; Jerusalem: Israel Academy of Sciences and Humanities, 1987.*

Lindner, H. *Die Geschichtsauffassung des Flavius Josephus im Bellum Judaicum.* Leiden: E. J. Brill, 1972.

Linton, O. *Synopsis historiae universalis.* 1957.

Liver, J. *The House of David.* 1969. (Hebrew)

Loewe, Malcolm. "Real and Imagined Anti-Jewish Elements in the Synoptic Gospels and Acts." *JES* 24 (1987): 267–84.*

Loewe, R. "Jewish Counterpart to the Acts of the Alexandrians." *JJS* 12 (1961): 105ff.

———."'Salvation is Not of the Jews.'" *JTS* 32 (1981): 341–68.*

Lohse, E. *Märtyrer und Gottesknecht.* 2nd ed. Göttingen: Vandenhoeck & Ruprecht, 1963.

Luz, U. *Das Geschichtsverständnis des Paulus.* BEvT 49. Munich: Kaiser, 1968.

MacDonald, Margaret Y. "Early Christian Women Married to Unbelievers." *Studies in Religion/Sciences Religieuses* 19 (1990): 221–34.*

Mack, B. L. "Exegetical Traditions in Alexandrian Judaism." *Studia Philonica* 3 (1974–75): 71ff.

———. "Philo Judaeus and Exegetical Traditions in Alexandria." In *ANRW* II.21.1, edited by W. Haase, 227–71. Berlin and New York: de Gruyter, 1984.*

McKnight, Scot. *A Light Among the Gentiles: Jewish Missionary Activity in the Second Temple Period.* Minneapolis: Fortress Press, 1991.*

MacLennon, Robert. *Early Christian Texts on Jews and Judaism.* BJS 194. Atlanta: Scholars Press, 1990.*

———. "Four Christian Writers on Jews and Judaism in the Second Century." In *From Ancient Israel to Modern Judaism,* vol. 1, edited by J. Neusner, E. Frerichs, and N. Sarna, 187ff. Atlanta: Scholars Press, 1989.*

MacMullen, Ramsay. *Christianizing the Roman Empire.* New Haven and London: Yale University Press, 1984.*

———. *Paganism in the Roman Empire.* New Haven and London: Yale, 1981.*

Madden, F. W. *History of the Jewish Coinage.* 1864.

Maier, J., and K. Schubert. *Die Qumran-Essener.* 1973.

Mantel, H. *Studies in the History of the Sanhedrin.* Cambridge, Mass.: Harvard University Press, 1965.

Marache, René. "Juvénal – peintre de la société de son temps." In *ANRW* II.33.1, edited by W. Haase, 592–639. Berlin and New York: de Gruyter, 1989.*

Marcovich, Miroslav, ed. *Hippolytus Refutatio Omnium Haeresium.* Berlin and New York: de Gruyter, 1986.*

———. "Pseudo-Justin ΠΡΟΣ ΗΔΔΗΝΑΣ." *JTS* n.s. 24 (1973): 500ff.

Marcus, R. "The Sebomenoi in Josephus." *Jewish Social Studies* 14 (1952): 247ff.

Mason, Steve. *Flavius Josephus on the Pharisees.* Leiden: E. J. Brill, 1991.*

———. "Josephus on the Pharisees Reconsidered: A Critique of Smith/Neusner." *Studies in Religion/Sciences Religieuses* 17 (1988): 455–70.*

Maurer, K. *Kirche und Synagoge.* Stuttgart: Kohlhammer, 1953.

May, G. *Schöpfung aus dem Nichts: Die Entstehung der Lehre von der Creatio ex Nihilo.* Berlin: de Gruyter, 1978.

Mayer, G. "Aspekte des Abrahambildes in der hellenistisch-christlichen Literatur." *EvT* 32 (1972): 118ff.

Meagher, John C. "As the Twig Was Bent: Antisemitism in Greco-Roman and Earliest Christian Times." In *Antisemitism and the Foundations of Christianity,* edited by Alan Davies, 1–26. New York: Paulist Press, 1979.*

Meeks, Wayne A. "Breaking Away: Three New Testament Pictures of Christianity's Separation from the Jewish Communities." In *To See Ourselves as Others See Us*": *Christians, Jews, "Others" in Late Antiquity*, edited by Jacob Neusner and Ernest S. Frerichs, 93–115. Chico, Calif.: Scholars Press, 1985.*

Meisner, N. *Untersuchungen zum Aristeasbrief.* Berlin: Kirchliche Hochschule, 1973.

Mendelson, Alan. *Philo's Jewish Identity.* BJS 161. Atlanta: Scholars Press, 1988.*

Meshorer, Y. "New Denominations in Ancient Jewish Coins." *Israel Numismatic Journal* 2 (1964): 4ff.

Metten, D. H. *The Ancient Synagogue at Sardis.* 1965.

Meyer, E. *Die Entstehung des Judenthums.* 1896.

———. *Ursprung und Anfänge des Christentums II.* 4th and 5th eds. Stuttgart: J. G. Cotta, 1925.

Michel, O. "Die Rettung Israels und die Rolle roms nach den Reden im 'Bellum Iudaicum.' Analysen und Perspektiven." In *ANRW* II.21.2, edited by W. Haase, 945–76. Berlin and New York: de Gruyter, 1984.*

Millar, F. *A Study of Cassius Dio.* Oxford: Clarendon Press, 1964.

Moehring, H. R. "Joseph Ben Matthia and Flavius Josephus: The Jewish Prophet and Roman Historian." In *ANRW* II.21.2, edited by W. Haase, 864–944. Berlin and New York: de Gruyter, 1984.*

———. "The Persecution of the Jews and the Adherents of the Isis Cult at Rome." *NovT* 3 (1959): 293ff.

Molland, E. "Die literatur- und dogmengeschichtliche Stellung des Diognetbriefes." *ZNW* 33 (1934): 289ff.

Molthagen, J. *Der römische Staat und die Christen im zweiten und dritten Jahrhundert.* Göttingen, 1970.

Momigliano, Arnaldo. "The Disadvantages of Monotheism for a Universal State." In *On Pagans, Jews, and Christians*, edited by Arnaldo Momigliano, 142–58. Middletown, Conn.: Wesleyan University Press, 1987.*

———. "Religion in Athens, Rome, and Jerusalem in the First Century B.C." In *Approaches to Ancient Judaism*, edited by William S. Green, 1–18. Atlanta: Scholars Press, 1985.*

———. "Some Preliminary Remarks on the 'Religious Opposition' to the Roman Empire." In *On Pagans, Jews, and Christians*, edited by Arnaldo Momigliano, 120–41. Middletown, Conn.: Wesleyan University Press, 1987.*

———. "In torno al Contro Apione, Rivista di Filologia e d'Istruzione." *Classica* n.s. 9 (1931): 485ff.

———, ed. *On Pagans, Jews, and Christians.* Middletown, Conn.: Wesleyan University Press, 1987.*

Mommsen, T. *Römisches Strafrecht.* 1899.

Montefiore, H. W. "Josephus and the New Testament." *NovT* 4 (1960): 139ff., 307ff.

Montet, P. "Le roi Amenophis et les impurs." Festschrift Radet, 263ff. 1940.

Moore, C. A. "On the Origins of the LXX Additions to the Book of Esther." *JBL* 92 (1973): 382ff.

Moore, G. F. "Fate and Free Will in the Jewish Philosophies according to Josephus." *HTR* 22 (1929): 371ff.

———. *Judaism in the First Centuries of the Christian Era: The Age of the Tannaim.* 3 vols. Cambridge, Mass.: Harvard University Press, 1927–30.

Mor, Menachem. "The Bar-Kokhba Revolt and Non-Jewish Participants." *JJS* 36 (1985): 200-209.*

Morel, W. "Eine Rede bei Josephus (Bell.Iud. VII 341 sqq.)." *RheinMus* n.F. 75 (1926): 106ff.

Morgenstern, J. "The King-God among the Western Semites and the Meaning of Epiphanes." *VT* 10 (1960): 138ff.

Morr, J. "Die Landeskunde von Palästina bei Strabon und Josephus." *Philologus* 81 (1926): 250ff.

Mühlenberg, E. "The Divinity of Jesus in Early Christian Faith." In *St. Patr.* 17, edited by Elizabeth A. Livingstone, 136-46. Oxford: Pergamon Press, 1982.*

Munier, C. "A Propos des Apologies de Justin." *RSR* 61 (1987): 177-86.*

——. "La Méthode Apologetique de Justin le martyr." *RSR* 62 (1988): 90-100.*

——. "La Méthode Apologetique de Justin le martyr (suite)." *RSR* 62 (1988): 227-39.*

Murray, Robert. "'Disaffected Judaism' and Early Christianity: Some Predisposing Factors." In *"To See Ourselves as Others See Us": Christians, Jews, "Others" in Late Antiquity,* edited by Jacob Neusner and Ernest S. Frerichs, 263-81. Chico, Calif.: Scholars Press, 1985.*

Mussner, Franz. *Tractate on the Jews.* Translated by Leonard Swidler. Philadelphia: Fortress Press; London: SPCK, 1984.*

Nautin, P. *Hippolyte et Josipe.* Paris: Cerf, 1947.

——. "Notes critiques sur Théophile d'Antioche Ad Autolycum Lib. II." *VC* 11 (1957): 212ff.

Neher-Bernheim, R. "The libel of Jewish ass-worship." *Zion* 28 (1963): 106ff.*

Nesselhauf, H. "Tacitus und Domitian." *Hermes* 80 (1952): 222ff.

Neufeld, K. H. "'Frühkatholizismus'–Idee und Begriff." *ZKT* 94 (1972): 1ff.

Neusner, Jacob. "The Conversion of Adiabene to Judaism." *JBL* 83 (1964): 60ff.

——. *Judaism and Christianity in the Age of Constantine: History, Messiah, Israel, and the Initial Confrontation.* Chicago and London: University of Chicago Press, 1987.*

——. *A Life of Rabban Yohanan Ben Zakkai.* Leiden: E. J. Brill, 1962.

——. *The Origins of Judaism.* 13 vols. New York and London: Garland Publishing Inc., 1990.*

Nickelsburg, George W. E. *Resurrection, Immortality and Eternal Life in Intertestamental Judaism.* Cambridge, Mass.: Harvard University Press, 1972.

——. "Revealed Wisdom as a Criterion for Inclusion and Exclusion: From Jewish Sectarianism to Early Christianity." In *"To See Ourselves as Others See Us": Christians, Jews, "Others" in Late Antiquity,* edited by Jacob Neusner and Ernest S. Frerichs, 73-91. Chico, Calif.: Scholars Press, 1985.*

Niebuhr, Karl-Wilhelm. *Gesetz und Paränese: Katechismusartige Weisungsreihen in der frühjüdischen Literatur.* WUNT 2.28. Tübingen: Mohr, 1987.*

Niese, B. "Zur Chronologie des Josephus." *Hermes* 28 (1893): 194ff.

——. "Der jüdische Historiker Josephus." *Historische Zeitschr.* 40 (1896): 193ff.

Nikiprowetzky, Valentin. "Josephus and the Revolutionary Parties." In *Josephus, the Bible, and History,* edited by Louis H. Feldman and Gohei Hata, 216-36. Detroit: Wayne State University Press, 1989.*

——. *La Troisième Sibylle.* Paris: Mouton, 1970.

Nilsson, M. P. *Geschichte der Griechischen Religion II.* 2nd ed. Munich: Beck, 1961.

Nissen, A. *Gott und der Nächste im antiken Judentum.* Tübingen: Mohr, 1974.

Noack, B. "Are the Essenes Referred to in the Sibylline Oracles?" *ST* 17 (1963): 90ff.

Norden, E. *Agnostos Theos.* Leipzig and Berlin: Teubner, 1913.

――. "Josephus und Tacitus über Jesus Christus und eine messianische Prophetie." *Neue Jahrbücher für das klass. Altertum* 16 (1913): 637ff.

Oepke, A. *Das neue Gottesvolk.* 1950.

Olmstead, A. T. "Intertestamental Studies." *JAOS* 56 (1936): 242ff.

Oppenheimer, Aaron. *The 'Am Ha-Aretz: A Study in Social History of the Jewish People in the Hellenistic-Roman Period.* Leiden: E. J. Brill, 1977.

――. "Jewish Lydda in the Roman Era." *HUCA* 69 (1988): 115–36.*

Osborn, E. F. *Justin Martyr.* Tübingen: Mohr-Siebeck, 1973.

Palmer, D. W. "Atheism, Apologetic, and Negative Theology in the Greek Apologists of the Second Century." *VC* 37 (1983): 234–59.

Pantle-Schieber, Klaus. "Anmerkungen zur Auseinandersetzung von ἐκκλησία und Judentum im Matthäusevangelium." *ZNW* 80 (1989): 145–62.*

Pellegrino, M. *Studi sull' antica apologetica.* 1947.

Pelletier, A. *Flavius Josephus adapteur de la lettre d'Aristée.* Paris: Klincksieck, 1962.

Perler, O. "Das vierte Makkabäerbuch, Ignatius von Antiochien und die ältesten Märtyrerberichte." *RivAC* 25 (1949): 47ff.

Petersen, H. "Real and Alleged Literary Projects of Josephus." *American Journal of Philology* 79 (1958): 259ff.

Peterson, E. *Die Kirche aus Juden und Heiden.* 1933.

――. *Der Monotheismus als politisches Problem.* 1935.

Pfaettisch. J. M. *Justinus' des Philosophen und Märtyrers Apologie.* 2 vols. 1912, 1913.

Pfeifer. G. *Ursprung und Wesen der Hypostasenvorstellungen im Judentum.* 1967.

Pfeiffer, R. H. *History of New Testament Times.* New York: Harper & Brothers, 1949.

Pohlenz, M. *Herodot.* Leipzig: Teubner, 1937.

Poirier, Paul-Hubert. "Éléments de Polémique Anti-Juive dans l' AD Diognetum." *VC* 40 (1986): 218–59.*

Pöschl, V., ed. *Tacitus.* Darmstadt, 1969.

Preuss, H. D. *Verspottung fremder Religionen im Alten Testament.* Stuttgart: Kohlhammer, 1971.

Prigent, P. *L'épître de Barnabé I-XVI et ses sources.* Paris: Cerf, 1961.

――. *Justin et l'Ancien Testament.* Paris: Lecoffre, 1964.

Puech, A. *Les apologistes Grecs.* Paris: Hachette, 1912.

Pummer, R., and M. Roussel, "A Note on Theodotus and Homer." *JSJ* 13 (1982): 177–82.*

Qalders, G. J. D. *Political Thought in Hellenistic Times.* 1975.

Quispel, G. "L'Evangile selon Thomas et les origines de l'ascèse chrétienne." In *Aspects du Judéo-Christianisme,* 35ff. 1965.

――. "A Jewish Source of Minucius Felix." *VC* 3 (1949): 113ff.

――. "La lettre de la Ptolémée à Flora." *VC* 2 (1948): 17ff.

Radice, R., and D. T. Runia, eds. *Philo of Alexandria: An Annotated Bibliography.* Leiden: E. J. Brill, 1988.*

Radin, M. *The Jews Among the Greeks and Romans.* Philadelphia: Jewish Publication Society of America, 1915.

Rahnenführer, D. "Das Testament des Hiob in seinem Verhältnis zum Neuen Testament." Diss., Halle, 1967.

Rajak, Tessa. "Contrasting Worlds in First-Century Palestine." *JRS* 72 (1982): 170–75.*

———. "The Hasmoneans and the Uses of Hellenism." In *A Tribute to Geza Vermes*, edited by Philip R. Davies and Richard T. White, 161–80. Sheffield: Sheffield Academic Press, 1990.*

———. "Jews and Christians as Groups in a Pagan World." In *"To See Ourselves as Others See Us": Christians, Jews, "Others" in Late Antiquity*, edited by Jacob Neusner and Ernest S. Frerichs, 247–62. Chico, Calif.: Scholars Press, 1985.*

———. *Josephus: The Historian and His Society.* London: Duckworth. 1983.*

———. "Josephus and the 'Archaeology' of the Jews." *JJS* 33 (1982): 465–77.*

———. "Was There a Roman Charter for the Jews?" *JRS* 74 (1984): 107–23.*

Rappaport, U., ed. *Josephus Flavius: Historian of Eretz-Israel in the Hellenistic-Roman Period.* Jerusalem, 1982.*

Reese, J. M. "Plan and Structure of the Book of Wisdom." *CBQ* 27 (1965): 391ff.

Reider, J. *The Book of Wisdom.* New York: Harper, 1957.

Reinhardt, K. *Poseidonios über Ursprung und Entartung.* Heidelberg: C. Winter, 1928.

Reinhartz, Adele. "The Meaning of *Nomos* in Philo's *Exposition of the Law.*" *Studies in Religion/Sciences Religieuses* 15 (1986): 337–45.*

———. "The New Testament and Anti-Judaism: A Literary-Critical Approach." *JES* 25 (1988): 524–37.*

Reitzenstein, R. *Historia Monachorum und Historia Lausiaca.* 1916.

———. *Poimandres.* Leipzig and Berlin: Teubner, 1904.

Remus, Harold. "Justin Martyr's Argument with Judaism." In *Anti-Judaism in Early Christianity*, vol. 2, *Separation and Polemic*, edited by Stephen G. Wilson, 59–80. Waterloo, Ont.: Wilfrid Laurier University Press, 1986.*

Rengstorf, K. H., and S. von Kortzfleisch. *Kirche und Synagoge I.* Stuttgart: Ernstklett, 1968.

Richardson, Peter. *Israel in the Apostolic Church.* SNTSMS 10. Cambridge: Cambridge University Press, 1969.*

———. "Law and Piety in Herod's Architecture." *Studies in Religion/Sciences Religieuses* 15 (1986): 347–60.*

———, and S. Westerholm. *Law in Religious Communities in the Roman Period.* Waterloo, Ont.: Wilfrid Laurier University Press, 1991.*

Ricken, F. "Gab es eine hellenistische Vorlage für Weish 13–15?" *Bib* 49 (1968): 54ff.

Robert, L. *Nouvelles inscriptions de Sardes I.* Paris, 1964.

Rordorf, W. "Un chapitre d'éthique judéo-chrétienne: les deux voies." In *Judéo-Christianisme*, 109ff. 1972.

Rosen, G. *Juden und Phönizier.* 1929.

Rost, L. *Einleitung in die alttestamentlichen Apokryphen und Pseudepigraphen einschließlich der großen Qumran-Handschriften.* Heidelberg: Quelle & Meyer, 1971.

Rudolph, K., ed. *Gnosis und Gnostizismus.* 1975.

———. *Gnosis.* New York: Harper & Row, 1983.*

Russell, D. S. *Between the Testaments.* Philadelphia: Muhlenberg Press, 1960.

Safrai, S., and M. Stern, with D. Flusser and W. C. van Unnik, eds. *The Jewish People in the First Century.* 2 vols. Philadelphia: Fortress Press, 1974, 1976.

Saldarini, Anthony. *Pharisees, Scribes and Sadducees in Palestinian Society.* Wilmington, Del.: Michael Glazier, 1989.*

Sanders, E. P. "Purity, Food and Offerings in the Greek-Speaking Diaspora." In *Jewish Law from Jesus to the Mishnah*, 255–308. London: SCM Press; Philadelphia: Trinity Press International, 1991.*

Sandford, E. M. "Nero and the East." *Harvard Studies in Classical Philology* 48 (1938): 75ff.

Sandmel, Samuel. "The confrontation of Greek and Jewish Ethics: Philo, De decalogo." In *Judaism and Ethics*, edited by D. J. Silver, 163-78. New York: Ktav, 1970.

——. *Judaism and Christian Beginnings*. New York: Oxford University Press, 1978.*

——. "Philo Judaeus: An Introduction to the Man, his Writings, and his Significance." In *ANRW* II.21.1, edited by W. Haase, 3-46. Berlin and New York: de Gruyter, 1984.*

——. *Philo of Alexandria: An Introduction*. New York and Oxford: Oxford University Press, 1979.*

——. *Philo's Place in Judaism*. New York: Ktav, 1971.

Sandvoss, E. "Asebie und Atheismus im klassischen Zeitalter." *Saeculum* 19 (1968): 312ff.

Saperstein, Marc. *Moments of Crisis in Jewish-Christian Relations*. London: SCM Press; Philadelphia: Trinity Press International, 1989.*

Saulnier, Christiane. "La Persécution des Chrétiens et la Théologie du Pouvoir à Rome." *RSR* 58 (1984): 251-79.*

Scarpat, G. "Cultura ebreo-ellenistica e Seneca." *Rivista Biblica* 13 (1965): 3ff.

Schaeder, H. H. *Studien zum antiken Synkretismus*. Leipzig and Berlin: Teubner, 1926.

Schäfer, Peter. *Der Bar Kokhba-Aufstand: Studien zum zweiten jüdischen Krieg gegen Rom*. Tübingen: Mohr, 1981.*

——. "The Causes of the Bar Kokhba Revolt." In *Studies in Aggadah, Targum and Jewish Liturgy in Memory of Joseph Heinemann*, edited by J. J. Petuchowski, 74-94. Jerusalem: Magnes, 1981.*

——. *Geschichte der Jüden in der Antike: Die Jüden Palästinas von Alexander des Grosses bis zur arabischen Eroberung*. 1983.*

——. "Hadrian's Policy in Judea and the Bar Kokhba Revolt." In *A Tribute to Geza Vermes*, edited by Philip R. Davies and Richard T. White, 281-303. Sheffield: Sheffield Academic Press, 1990.*

——. *Rivalität zwischen Engeln und Menschen*. Berlin: de Gruyter, 1975.

Schalit, A. "Die frühchristliche Überlieferung über die Herkunft der Familie des Herodes." *ASTI* 1 (1962): 109ff.

——. "Josephus und Justus: Studien zur Vita des Josephus." *Klio* 26 (1933): 67ff.

——. *König Herodes*. Berlin: de Gruyter, 1969.

——. "The Letter of Antiochus III to Zeuxis regarding the Establishment of Jewish Military Colonies in Phrygia and Lydia." *JQR* 50 (1960): 289ff.

——. "Roman Policy in the Orient from Nero to Trajan." *Tarbiz* 7 (1936): 159ff. (Hebrew)

——. *Die Vita des Josephus*. 1925.

Schaller, B. "Hekataios von Abdera über die Juden: Zur Frage der Echtheit und Datierung." *ZNW* 54 (1963): 15ff.

Scheele, J. *Zur Rolle der Unfreien in den römischen Christenverfolgungen*. 1970.

Scheidweiler, F. "Zur Kirchengeschichte des Eusebios von Kaisareia." *ZNW* 49 (1958): 123ff.

Schelkle, K. H. *Paulus, Lehrer der Väter: Die altkirchliche Auslegung von Römer 1-11*. Patmos, 1956.

Scheller, P. "De hellenistica historiae conscribendae arte." Diss., Leipzig, 1911.

Schiffman, Lawrence. *From Text to Tradition*. Hoboken, N.J.: Ktav, 1991.*

Schlatter, A. *Geschichte Israels von Alexander d. Gr. bis Hadrian*. 3rd ed. Stuttgart: Calwer, 1925.

——. *Die Theologie des Judentums nach dem Bericht des Josefus.* Gütersloh: Bertelsmann, 1932.

Schmid, W. "Frühe Apologetik und Platonismus." In *Hermeneia,* Festschrift O. Regenbogen, 163ff. 1952.

——. "Die Textüberlieferung der Apologie des Justin." *ZNW* 40 (1941): 87ff.

Schnabel, Eckhard J. *Law and Wisdom from Ben Sira to Paul.* WUNT 2.16. Tübingen: Mohr-Siebeck, 1985.*

Schnabel, P. *Berossos und die babylonisch-hellenistiche Literatur.* Berlin: Teubner, 1923.

Schneemelcher, W. "Kirche und Staat im Neuen Testament." In *Kirche und Staat,* Festschrift. H. Kunst, 1ff. 1967.

Schoedel, William K. *Ignatius of Antioch.* Philadelphia: Fortress Press, 1985.*

Schoeps, H. J. "Das Judenchristentum in den Parteikämpfen der alten Kirche." In *Aspects du Judéo-Christianisme,* 53ff. 1965.

Scholer, D. M. "Tertullian on Jewish Persecution of Christians." *St. Patr.* 17, edited by Elizabeth A. Livingstone, 821–28. Oxford: Pergamon Press, 1982.*

Schönfeld, H. G. "Zum Begriff 'Therapeutai' bei Philo von Alexandrien." *Revue de Qumran* 3 (1961): 219ff.

Schrage, W. *Die Christen und der Staat nach dem Neuen Testament.* Gütersloh: Mohn, 1971.

Schreckenberg, Heinz. *Bibliographie zur Flavius Josephus.* Leiden: E. J. Brill, 1968.

——. *Die christlichen Adversus-Judaeos-Texte und ihr literarisches und historisches Umfeld (1.-11. Jh.).* Frankfurt/Main and Bern: Peter Lang, 1982.*

——. *Die Flavius-Josephus-Tradition in Antike und Mittelalter.* Leiden: E. J. Brill, 1972.

——. "Louis H. Feldman: *Josephus and Modern Scholarship (1937–80)*." *Gnomon* 57 (1985): 408–15.*

——. *Rezeptionsgeschichte und textkritische Untersuchungen zu Flavius Josephus.* Leiden: E. J. Brill, 1977.

Schuhl, P.-M. "Sur un fragment de Cléarque." *RHR* 147 (1955): 124ff.

Schüller, S. "Some Problems Connected with the Supposed Common Ancestry of Jews and Spartans and their Relations during the Last Three Centuries B. C." *JSS* 1 (1956): 257ff.

Schüpphaus, J. *Die Psalmen Salomos.* Leiden: E. J. Brill, 1977.

Schur, W. "Die Orientpolitik des Kaisers Nero." *Klio* Beih. 15, 1923.

Schürer, E. *A History of the Jewish People in the Time of Jesus.* 3 vols. 3rd and 4th eds. New York: Scribner, 1901–1909.

——. *The History of the Jewish People in the Age of Jesus Christ.* A New English Version Revised and Edited by G. Vermes and F. Millar. Edinburgh: T. & T. Clark, vol. 1, 1973; vol. 2, 1979.

Schüssler Fiorenza, E., ed. *Aspects of Religious Propaganda in Judaism and Early Christianity.* Notre Dame, Ind.: University of Notre Dame Press, 1976.

Schwabe, M. *Index of Articles Relative to Jewish History and Literature.* 1971.

Schwartz, D. R. "On Some Papyri and Josephus' Sources and Chronology for the Persian Period." *JSJ* 21 (1990): 175–99.*

Schwartz, E. *Griechische Geschichtsschreiber.* 1956.

Schwartz, J. "Aspects politiques du judaïsme au début du IIIe siècle P. C." *L'Antiquité Classique* 39 (1970): 147ff.

——. "Note sur la famille de Philon d'Alexandrie." In *Mélanges I. Lévy, Annuaire de l'Institut de philologie et d'histoires orientales et slaves* 13, 591ff. (1953).

——. "Philon et l'apologétique chrétienne du second siècle." In *Hommages à A. Dupont-Sommer,* 497ff. 1971.

———. "Du Testament de Lévi au Discours véritable de Celse." *RHPR* 40 (1960): 126ff.

Schwartz, K. H. "Das angebliche Christengesetz des Septimius Severus." *Historia* 12 (1963): 185ff.

Schwartz, Seth. "The Composition and Publication of Josephus's *Bellum Iudaicum* Book 7." *HTR* 79 (1986): 373–86.*

———. *Josephus and Judaean Politics.* Columbia Studies in the Classical Tradition 18. Leiden: E. J. Brill, 1990.*

———. "The 'Judaism' of Samaria and Galilee in Josephus's Version of the Letter of Demetrius I to Jonathan (Antiquities 13.48-57)." *HTR* 82 (1989): 377–91.*

Scullard, H. H. *From the Gracchi to Nero.* 5th ed. London: Methuen, 1982.*

Seeberg, R. "Die Apologie des Aristeides untersucht und wieder hergestellt." In T. Zahn, *Forschungen zur Geschichte des ntl. Kanons* 5.2, 159ff. 1893.

Seel, Otto. "Pompeius Trogus und das Problem der Universalgeschichte." In *ANRW* II.30.2, edited by W. Haase, 1363–1423. Berlin and New York: de Gruyter, 1982.*

———. *Die Praefatio des Pompeius Trogus.* 1955.

Segalla, G. "Il problema della volontà libera in Filone Alessandrino." *Studia Patavina* 12 (1965): 3ff.

Sellers, O. R. *The Citadel of Beth-zur.* 1933.

Sevenster, J. N. *Do you know Greek? How much Greek could the First Jewish Christians have known?* Leiden: E. J. Brill, 1968.

———. *The Roots of Pagan Anti-Semitism in the Ancient World.* Leiden: E. J. Brill, 1975.

Sherwin-White, A. N. "Philo and Avillius Flaccus: a Conundrum." *Latomus* 31 (1972): 820ff.

———. *Racial Prejudice in Imperial Rome.* Cambridge: Cambridge University Press, 1967.

Shohet, A. "Die Anschauungen des Josephus über die Zukunft Israels und seines Landes." In *Jerusalem,* ed. M. Isch-Scholom et al., 43ff. 1953. (Hebrew).

Shukster, Martin B., and Peter Richardson. "Temple and Bet Ha-midrash in the Epistle of Barnabas." In *Anti-Judaism in Early Christianity,* vol. 2, *Separation and Polemic,* edited by Stephen G. Wilson, 17–32. Waterloo, Ont.: Wilfrid Laurier University Press, 1986.*

Shutt, R. J. H. *Studies in Josephus.* London: SPCK, 1961.

Sider, R. D. "On Symmetrical Composition in Tertullian." *JTS* n.s. 24 (1973): 405ff.

Siebeneck, R. T. "The Midrash of Wisdom 10-19." *CBQ* 22 (1960): 176ff.

Siegert, F. "Gottesfürchtige und Sympathisanten." *JJS* 24 (1973): 109ff.

Sijpesteijn, P. J. "The Legationes ad Gaium." *JJS* 15 (1964): 87ff.

Siker, Jeffrey S. "Abraham in Graeco-Roman Paganism." *JSJ* 17 (1987): 188–208.*

———. *Disinheriting the Jews: Abraham in Early Jewish Controversy.* Louisville: West-minster/John Knox Press, 1991.*

Sild, O. *Das altchristliche Martyrium in Berücksichtigung der rechtlichen Grundlage der Christenverfolgungen.* 1920.

Silver, D. J., ed. *Judaism and Ethics.* New York: Ktav, 1970.

Simon, M. *Le judaïsme et le christianisme antique d'Antiochus Épiphane à Constantin.* 1968.

———. "La migration à Pella: Légende ou réalité?" In *Judéo-Christianisme,* 37ff. 1972.

———. "Problèmes du Judéo-Christianisme." In *Aspects du Judéo-Christianisme,* 1ff. 1965.

———. *Recherches d'histoire judéo-chrétienne.* Paris and The Hague: Mouton, 1962.

——. "Réflexions sur le Judéo-Christianisme." In *Christianity, Judaism and other Greco-Roman Cults,* Festschrift M. Smith, 2:53ff. 1975.

——. "Sur les débuts du proselytisme juif." In *Hommages à A. Dupont-Sommer,* 509ff. 1971.

——. *Verus Israel: A Study of the Relations Between Christians and Jews in the Roman Empire (135–425).* Oxford: Oxford University Press, 1986.*

——, and A. Benoit. "Alexandre le Grand, juif et chrétien." *RHPR* 21 (1941): 177ff. (=*Recherches d'histoire judéo-chrétienne. Études juives* 6 [1962]: 127ff.).

Sint, J. A. *Pseudonymität im Altertum.* Innsbruck: Wagner, 1960.

Skarsaune, O. "The Conversion of Justin Martyr." *ST* 30 (1976): 53ff.

Smallwood, E. M. "The Alleged Jewish Tendencies of Poppaea Sabina." *JTS* n.s. 10 (1959): 329ff.

——. "The Chronology of Gaius' Attempt to Desecrate the Temple." *Latomus* 16 (1957): 3ff.

——. "Domitian's Attitude toward the Jews and Judaism." *Classical Philology* 51 (1956): 1ff.

——. *The Jews under Roman Rule.* Leiden: E. J. Brill, 1976.

——. "The Legislation of Hadrian and Antoninus Pius against Circumcision." *Latomus* 18 (1959): 334ff.

——. "Palestine c. A.D. 115–118." *Historia* 11 (1962): 500ff.

——. "Some Notes on the Jews under Tiberius." *Latomus* 15 (1956): 314ff.

Smith, M. "The Description of the Essenes in Josephus and the Philosophumena." *HUCA* 29 (1958): 273ff.

——. "Goodenough's 'Jewish Symbols' in Retrospect." *JBL* 86 (1967): 53ff.

Smit Sibinga, J. *The Old Testament Text of Justin Martyr, I. The Pentateuch.* 1963.

Snell, B. *The Discovery of the Mind.* Cambridge, Mass.: Harvard University Press, 1953.

——. *Scenes from Greek Drama.* Los Angeles and Berkeley: University of California Press, 1964.

Speigl, J. *Der römische Staat und die Christen: Staat und Kirche von Domitian bis Commodus.* 1970.

Speyer, Wolfgang. *Frühes Christentum im antiken Strahlungsfeld.* Tübingen: Mohr-Siebeck, 1989.*

——. *Die literarische Fälschung im heidnischen und christlichen Altertum.* Handbücher der klass. Altertumswissenschaft. Munich: Beck, 1971.

——. "Religiöse Pseudepigraphie und literarische Fälschung im Altertum." *Jahrbuch für Antike und Christentum* 8/9 (1965–66): 88ff.

Spoerri, W. *Späthellenistische Berichte über Welt, Kultur und Götter.* 1959.

Stählin, G. "Josephus und der Aristeasbrief." *TSK* 102 (1930): 324ff.

Stegemann, V. "Christentum und Stoizismus im Kampf um die geistigen Lebenswerte im 2. Jahrhundert nach Christus." *Welt als Geschichte* 7 (1941): 295ff.

Stein, E. *Die allegorische Exegese des Philo aus Alexandria.* Giessen: Töpelmann, 1929.

——. *Alttestamentliche Bibelkritik in der späthellenistischen Literatur.* 1935.

——. "De Celso Plantonico Philonis Alexandrini imitatore." *Eos* 34 (1932–33): 205ff.

——. *Philo und der Midrasch.* Giessen: Töpelmann, 1931.

Stemberger, Günter. "Die Beurteilung Roms in der rabbinischen Literatur." In *ANRW* II.19.2, edited by W. Haase, 338–96. Berlin and New York: de Gruyter, 1979.*

Stern, Menahem. *History of Eretz-Israel: The Roman Byzantine Period: The Roman Rule from the Conquest until the Bar Kochba Rebellion (63 B.C.E.–135 C.E.).* Jerusalem: Keter, 1984.*

———. "The Jewish Diaspora." In *The Jewish People in the First Century,* edited by S. Safrai and M. Stern, 1:117ff. CRINT. Philadelphia: Fortress Press, 1974.

———. "The Jews in Greek and Latin Literature." In *The Jewish People in the First Century,* edited by S. Safrai and M. Stern, 2:1101ff. CRINT. Philadelphia: Fortress Press, 1976.

Stevenson, J., ed. *A New Eusebius.* Revised by W. H. C. Frend. London: SPCK, 1987.*

Stockton, David. "The Founding of the Empire." In *The Oxford History of the Classical World,* edited by J. Boardman, J. Griffin, O. Murray, 531–59. Oxford and New York: Oxford University Press, 1986.*

Stone, Michael, ed. *Jewish Writings of the Second Temple Period: Apocrypha, Pseudepigrapha, Qumran, Sectarian Writings, Philo, Josephus.* Philadelphia: Fortress Press, 1984.*

Strange, J. F. "Archaeology and the Religion of Judaism in Palestine." In *ANRW* II.19.1, edited by W. Haase, 646–85. Berlin and New York: de Gruyter, 1979.*

Strecker, G. *Das Judenchristentum in den Pseudoklementinen.* TU 70. Göttingen: Vandenhoeck & Ruprecht, 1958.

Surkau, H. -W. *Martyrien in jüdischer und frühchristlicher Zeit.* Göttingen: Vandenhoeck & Ruprecht, 1932.

Taeger, F. *Charisma: Studien zur Geschichte des antiken Herrscherkultes.* 2 vols. 1957, 1960.

Tannehill, Robert C. "Israel in Luke-Acts: A Tragic Story." *JBL* 104 (1985): 69–85.*

Tappe, G. "De Philonis libro, qui inscribitur Ἀλέξανδρος," Diss., Göttingen, 1912.

Taylor, J. E. "The Phenomenon of Early Jewish Christianity: Reality or Scholarly Invention." *VC* 44 (1990): 313–34.*

Taylor, K. E. "Attitudes of the Fathers toward Practices of Jewish Christians." TU 79, 504ff. 1961.

Tcherikover, V. "The Decline and Fall of the Jewish Diaspora in Egypt in the Roman Period." *JJS* 14 (1963): 1ff.

———. *Hellenistic Civilization and the Jews.* 3rd ed. Philadelphia: Jewish Publication Society of America, 1966.

———. "The Ideology of the Letter of Aristeas." *HTR* 51 (1958): 59ff.

———. "The Third Book of Maccabees as a Historical Source of Augustus' Time." *Scripta Hierosolymitana* 7 (1961): 1ff.

———. "Was Jerusalem a Polis?" *IEJ* 14 (1964): 61ff.

Theiler, W. "Philo von Alexandria und der Beginn des kaiserzeitlichen Platonismus." In *Parusia,* Festschrift J. Hirschberger, 199ff. 1965.

Thoma, Clemens. "Die Auswirkungen des jüdischen Krieges gegen Rom (66–70/73 n.C.) auf das rabbinische Judentum." *BZ* n.F. 12 (1968): 30ff., 186ff.

———. "The High Priesthood in the Judgment of Josephus." In *Josephus, the Bible, and History,* edited by Louis H. Feldman and Gohei Hata, 196–215. Detroit: Wayne State University Press, 1989.*

Thompson. L. A. "Domitian and the Jewish Tax." *Historia* 31 (1982): 329–42.*

Thornton, T. C. G. "The Crucifixion of Haman and the Scandal of the Cross." *JTS* 37 (1986): 419–26.*

Thyen, H. *Der Stil der jüdisch-hellenistischen Homilie.* Göttingen: Vandenhoeck & Ruprecht, 1955.

Tiede, David. L. *The Charismatic Figure as Miracle-Worker.* Missoula, Mont.: Scholars Press, 1971.

——. "Religious Propaganda and the Gospel Literature of the Early Christian Mission." In *ANRW* II.25.2, edited by W. Haase, 1705-29. Berlin and New York: de Gruyter, 1984.*

Timpe, D. "Römische Geschichte bei Flavius Josephus." *Historia* 9 (1960): 474ff.

Toaff, A. Sulla. "'Archeologia Giudaica' de Tacito." *La Rassegna Mensile di Israel* Ser. 3, 29 (1963): 394ff.

Tov, Emanuel. "Die griechischen Bibelübersetzungen." In *ANRW* II.20.1, edited by W. Haase, 121-89. Berlin and New York: de Gruyter, 1987.*

Townsend, John. "The Gospel of John and the Jews: The Story of a Religious Divorce." In *Antisemitism and the Foundations of Christianity,* edited by Alan Davies, 72-97. New York, Ramsey, Toronto: Paulist Press, 1979.*

——. "The New Testament, the Early Church, and Anti-Semitism." In *From Ancient Israel to Modern Judaism,* vol. 1, edited by J. Neusner, E. Frerichs, and N. Sarna, 1:171-86. Atlanta: Scholars Press, 1989.*

Trebilco, Paul R. *Jewish Communities in Asia Minor.* SNTSMS 69. Cambridge: Cambridge University Press, 1991.*

Treu, K. "Die Bedeutung des Griechischen für die Juden im Römischen Reich." *Kairos* n.F. 15 (1973): 123ff.

Trevett, Christine. "Prophecy and Anti-Episcopal Activity: A Third Error Combatted by Ignatius?" *JEH* 34 (1983): 1-18.*

Trisoglio, F. "L'Intervento divino nelle vicende umane dalla storiografia classica greca a Flavio Giuseppe e ad Eusebio di Cesarea." In *ANRW* II.21.2, edited by W. Haase, 977-1104. Berlin and New York: de Gruyter, 1984.*

Trocmé, Etienne. "The Jews as Seen by Paul and Luke." In *"To See Ourselves as Others See Us": Christians, Jews, "Others" in Late Antiquity,* edited by Jacob Neusner and Ernest S. Frerichs, 145-61. Chico, Calif.: Scholars Press, 1985.*

Troeger, K. W., ed. *Gnosis und Neues Testament.* Berlin: Evangelische Verlagsanstalt, 1973.

Trüdinger, K. *Studien zur Geschichte der griechisch-römischen Ethnographie.* 1918.

Tugwell, Simon. *The Apostolic Fathers.* Harrisburg, Penn.: Morehouse, 1989.*

Turcan, Marie. *Les Spectacles.* Tertulline. SC 332. Paris: Cerf, 1986.*

Turcan, R. *Sénèque et les religions orientales.* 1967.

Turner, E. G. "Tiberius Julius Alexander." *JRS* 44 (1954): 54ff.

Urbach, E. E. *The Sages: Their Concepts and Beliefs.* 2 vols. Cambridge, Mass.: Harvard University Press, 1979.

——. "Self-Isolation or Self-Affirmation in Judaism in the First Three Centuries." In *Aspects of Judaism in the Graeco-Roman Period,* edited by E. P. Sanders, 269-98. Philadelphia: Fortress Press, 1981.

van der Horst, P. W. *Chaeremon: Egyptian Priest and Stoic Philosopher.* Leiden: E. J. Brill, 1984.*

——. "Chaeremon: Egyptisch priester en antisemitisch Stoïcijn uit de tijd van het Nieuwe Testament." *Nederlands Theologisch Tijdschrift* 35 (1981): 265-72.*

——. *Essays on the Jewish World of Early Christianity.* Göttingen: Vandenhoeck & Ruprecht, 1990.*

——. "The Jews of Ancient Crete." *JJS* 39 (1988): 183-200.*

――. "The Way of Life of the Egyptian Priests According to Chaeremon." In *Studies in Egyptian Religion Dedicated to Prof. Jan Zandee,* edited by M. Heerma van Voss et al., 61–71. Leiden: E. J. Brill, 1982.*

van Unnik, W. C. " Ἡ καινη διαθήκη – a Problem in the Early History of the Canon." In *St. Patr.* 4.2, 212ff. TU 79. Berlin: Akademie-Verlag, 1961.

――. *Flavius Josephus als historischer Schriftsteller.* Heidelberg: Lambert Schneider, 1978.

Veil, H. *Justinus' des Philosophen und Märtyrers Rechtfertigung des Urchristentums.* 1894.

Vermès, G. "Essenes and Therapeutai." *Revue de Qumran* 3 (1961): 495ff.

――. "The Etymology of 'Essenes.'" *Revue de Qumran* 2 (1959–60): 427ff.

――. *Jesus the Jew.* 2nd ed. Philadelphia: Fortresss Press, 1973.

――. *Scripture and Tradition in Judaism.* Leiden: E. J. Brill, 1961.

Villalba i Varneda, P. *The Historical Method of Flavius Josephus.* ALGJ 19. Leiden: E. J. Brill, 1986.*

Virgilio, B., ed. *Studi Ellenistici, II.* Pisa: Giardini Editori e Stampatori, 1987.*

Vischer, L. "Le prétendu 'culte de l'âne' dans l'église primitive." *RHR* 139 (1951): 14ff.

Vogt, Ernst. *Tragiker Ezechiel.* Jüdische Schriften 4.3. Gütersloh: Mohn, 1983.*

Vogt, J. "Zur Religiosität der Christenverfolger im römischen Reich." SAH 1962.

Völker, W. "Das Abrahambild bei Philo, Origenes und Ambrosius." *TSK* 103 (1931): 199ff.

von Albrecht, M. "Minucius Felix as a Christian Humanist." *Illinois Classical Studies* 12 (1987): 157–68.*

von Borries, B. *Quid veteres philosophi de idolatria senserint.* Göttingen: Dieterich, 1918.

von Campenhausen, H. *The Formation of the Christian Bible.* Philadelphia: Fortress Press, 1972.

――. *Die Idee des Martyriums in der alten Kirche.* Göttingen: Vandenhoeck & Ruprecht, 1936.

von Dobschütz, E. *Das Kerygma Petri kritisch untersucht.* TU 11.1. Leipzig: Hinrichs, 1893.

von Gutschmid, A. *Kleine Schriften.* Vol. 2. Leipzig, 1890. Vol. 4, 1893.

von Wahlde, Urban C. "Literary Structure and Theological Argument in Three Discourses with the Jews in the Fourth Gospel." *JBL* 103 (1984): 575–84.*

Vrugt-Lentz, J. Ter. "Horaz 'Sermones': Satire auf der Grenze zweier Welten." In *ANRW* II.30.2, edited by W. Haase, 1827–35. Berlin and New York: de Gruyter, 1981.*

Wacholder, Ben Zion. "Biblical Chronology in the Hellenistic World Chronicles." *HTR* 61 (1968): 451ff.

――. *Essays on Jewish Chronology and Chronography.* 1976.

――. *Eupolemus: A Study of Judaeo-Greek Literature.* Cleveland, Oh.: Hebrew Union College–Jewish Institute of Religion, 1974.

――. "Josephus and Nicolaus of Damascus." In *Josephus, the Bible, and History,* edited by Louis H. Feldman and Gohei Hata, 147–72. Detroit: Wayne State University Press, 1989.*

――. *Nicolaus of Damascus.* University of California Publ. in History 75. Berkeley and Los Angeles: University of California Press, 1962.

――. "Pseudo-Eupolemus' Two Greek Fragments on the Life of Abraham." *HUCA* 34 (1963): 83ff.

Walser, G. *Rom, das Reich und die fremden Völker in der Geschichtsschreibung der römischen Kaiserzeit.* 1951.

Walsh, J. J. "On Christian Atheism." *VC* 45 (1991): 255–77.*

Walter, Nikolaus. *Fragmente jüdisch-hellenistischer Epik: Philon, Theodotes.* Jüdische Schriften 4.3. Gütersloh: Mohn, 1983.*

———. "Frühe Begegnungen zwischen jüdischem Glauben und hellenistischer Bildung in Alexandrien." *Neue Beiträge zur Geschichte der Alten Welt* 1 (1964): 367ff.

———. "Jüdisch-hellenistische Literatur vor Philon von Alexandrien." In *ANRW* II.20.1, edited by W. Haase, 68–120. Berlin and New York: de Gruyter, 1987.*

———. "Zu Pseudo-Eupolemos." *Klio* 43–45 (1965): 282ff.

———. "Der Thoraausleger Aristobulos." TU 86. Berlin: Akademie-Verlag, 1964.

———. "Zur Überlieferung einiger Reste früher jüdisch-hellenistischen Historiker." *St. Patr.* 7:314–20. TU 92. Berlin: Akademie-Verlag, 1966.

———. *Untersuchungen zu den Fragmenten der jüdisch-hellenistischen Historiker.* Habilitationsschrift, Halle, 1968.

Walzer, R. R. *Galen on Jews and Christians.* Oxford: Oxford University Press, 1949.

Wardy, Bilhan. "Jewish Religion in Pagan Literature during the Late Republic and Early Empire." In *ANRW* II.19.2, edited by W. Haase, 592–644. Berlin and New York: de Gruyter, 1987.*

Wasser, N. "Die Stellung der Juden gegenüber den Römern nach der rabbinischen Literatur." Diss., Zurich, 1933.

Waszink, J. H. "Der Einfluß des Platonismus im frühen Christentum." *VC* 19 (1965): 129ff.

———, and J. C. M. van Winden, eds. *Tertullianus De Idololatria.* Leiden: E. J. Brill, 1987.*

Weber, W. *Josephus und Vespasian.* Stuttgart: Kohlhammer, 1921.

Weiss, H. -F. "Zur Frage der historischen Voraussetzungen der Begegnung von Antike und Christentum." *Klio* 43–45 (1965): 307ff.

Wendland, P. *Die hellenistisch-römische Kultur in ihren Beziehungen zu Judentum und Christentum: Die urchristlichen Literaturformen.* 2nd and 3rd eds. Tübingen: Mohr, 1912.

———. *Die Therapeuten und die philonische Schrift vom beschaulichen Leben.* 1896.

Wengst, K. *Tradition und Theologie des Barnabasbriefes.* Berlin: de Gruyter, 1971.

Werner, E. "Melito of Sardes: The First Poet of Deicide." *HUCA* 37 (1966): 191ff.

Westerberg, F. *Die biblische Chronologie und Flavius Josephus.* 1910.

Westermann, W. L. *Upon Slavery in Ptolemaic Egypt.* 1929.

Whittaker, Molly. *Jews and Christians: Graeco-Roman Views.* Cambridge: Cambridge University Press, 1984.*

———, trans. and ed. *Tatian Oratio ad Graecos and Fragments.* Oxford: Clarendon Press, 1982.

Widengren, G. *Sakrales Königtum im Alten Testament und im Judentum.* Stuttgart: Kohlhammer, 1955.

———. "Royal Ideology and the Testaments of the Twelve Patriarchs." In Festschrift S. H. Hooke, 202ff. 1963.

Wiefel, W. "Die jüdische Gemeinschaft im antiken Rom und die Anfänge des römischen Christentums." *Judaica* 26 (1970): 65ff.

Wilcken, U. "Urkunden-Referat. (II. PER Inv. 24552 gr.)." *Archiv für Papyrusforschung* 12 (1937): 221ff.

Wilde, R. *The Treatment of the Jews in the Greek Christian Writers of the First Three Centuries.* Cleveland, Oh.: J. T. Zubal, 1949; Reprint, 1984.

Wilhelm, A. "Zu dem Judenerlasse des Ptolemaios Philadelphos." *Archiv für Papyrusforschung* 14 (1941): 30ff.

Wilken, Robert L. *The Christians as the Romans Saw Them.* New Haven and London: Yale University Press, 1984.*

———. *Judaism and the Early Christian Mind.* New Haven: Yale University Press, 1971.

———. "Judaism in Roman and Christian Society." *JR* 47 (1967): 313ff.

Williams, A. L. *Justin Martyr: The Dialogue with Trypho.* London: SPCK, 1930.

———. *Adversus Judaeos.* Cambridge: Cambridge University Press, 1935.*

Williams, Margaret H. "Θεοσεβὴς γὰρ ἦν – The Jewish Tendencies of Poppaea Sabina." *JTS* 39 (1988): 92–96.*

———. *Adversus Iudaeos.* 1935.

Williamson, Clark M. *Has God Rejected His People?* Nashville: Abingdon, 1982.*

Williamson, G. A. *The World of Josephus.* 1964.

Williamson, R. *Philo and the Epistle to the Hebrews.* Leiden: E. J. Brill, 1970.

Willrich, H. *Das Haus des Herodes zwischen Jerusalem und Rom.* Heidelberg: C. Winter, 1929.

———. *Judaica.* Göttingen: Vandenhoeck & Ruprecht, 1900.

———. *Juden und Griechen vor der Makkabäischen Erhebung.* Göttingen: Vandenhoeck & Ruprecht, 1895.

Wilson, R. McL. "Jewish Literary Propaganda." In *Paganisme Judaïsme, Christianisme: Mélanges offerts à Marcel Simon,* 61–74. Paris: Boccard, 1978.*

Wilson, Stephen G. "Marcion and the Jews." In *Anti-Judaism in Early Christianity,* vol. 2, *Separation and Polemic,* edited by Stephen G. Wilson, 45–58. Waterloo, Ont.: Wilfrid Laurier University Press, 1986.*

———. "Passover, Easter, and Anti-Judaism: Melito of Sardis and Others." In *"To See Ourselves as Others See Us": Christians, Jews, "Others" in Late Antiquity,* edited by Jacob Neusner and Ernest S. Frerichs, 337–56. Chico, Calif.: Scholars Press, 1985.*

Windisch, H. "Die Orakel des Hystaspes." Koninklijke Akademie von Wetenschappen, AFD. Letterkunde 28, no. 3. Amsterdam: Koninklijke Akademie von Wetenschappen, 1929.

———. "Der Untergang Jerusalems (Anno 70) im Urteil der Christen und Juden." *TT* 48 (1914): 519ff.

Winston, David. "Judaism and Hellenism: Hidden Tensions in Philo's Thought." In *Studia Philonica Annual II,* 1–19. Atlanta: Scholars Press, 1990.*

———. *The Wisdom of Solomon.* Anchor Bible 43. Garden City, N.Y.: Doubleday & Co., 1979.*

Wirgin, W. "Juda Maccabee's Embassy to Rome and the Jewish-Roman Treaty." *PEQ* 101 (1969): 15ff.

Wlosok, A. *Rom und die Christen.* 1970.

———, ed. *Römischer Kaiserkult.* 1978.

Wolfson, H. A. "Philo on Free Will and the Historical Influence of his View." *HTR* 35 (1942): 131ff.

———. "Philo on Jewish Citizenship in Alexandria." *JBL* 63 (1944): 165ff.

———. *The Philosophy of the Church Fathers I.* Cambridge, Mass.: Harvard University Press, 1956.

Wright, A. G. "The Structure of the Book of Wisdom." *Bib* 48 (1967): 165ff.

———. "The Structure of Wisdom 11–19." *CBQ* 27 (1965): 28ff.

Yadin, Y. *Bar Kochba*. New York: Random House, 1971.

Yoyotte, J. "L'Égypte ancienne et les origines de l'anti-judaïsme." *RHR* 163 (1963): 133ff.

Ze'ev, Maria Pucci Ben. "Greek Attacks Against Alexandrian Jews During Emperor Trajan's Reign." *JSJ* 20 (1989): 31–48.*

———. "New Perspectives on the Jewish-Greek Hostilities in Alexandria during the Reign of Emperor Caligula." *JSJ* 21 (1990): 226–35.*

Zeitlin, S. "The Account of the Essenes in Josephus and the Philosophumena." *JQR* 49 (1958–59): 292ff.

———. "Herod: A Malevolent Maniac." *JQR* 54 (1963–64): 1ff.

———. "The Pharisees." *JQR* 52 (1961–62): 97ff.

———. "Proselytes and Proselytism during the Second Commonwealth and the Early Tannaitic Period." In *H. A. Wolfson Jubilee Vol. II*, 871ff. 1965.

———. *The Rise and Fall of the Judaean State*, vol. 1, *332–37 B.C.E.* 2nd ed., 1968. Vol. 2, *37 B.C.E.–66 C.E.* Philadelphia: Jewish Publication Society of America, 1967.

———. "Slavery during the Second Commonwealth and the Tannaitic Period." *JQR* 53 (1962–63): 185ff.

———. "A Survey of Jewish Historiography: From the Biblical Books to the Sefer Ha Kabbalah with Special Emphasis on Josephus." *JQR* 59 (1968–69): 171ff.; 60 (1969–70): 37ff.

———. "The Temple and Worship." *JQR* 51 (1960–61): 209ff.

———. "Zealots and Sicarii." *JBL* 81 (1962): 395ff.

Ziegler, J. *Der Kampf zwischen Judentum und Christentum in den ersten drei christlichen Jahrhunderten*. 1907.

Zielinski, T. "L'empereur Claude et l'idée de la domination mondiale des Juifs." *Revue de l'Université de Bruxelles* 32 (1927): 128–48.

Zuntz, G. "Aristeas Studies." *JJS* 4 (1959): 21ff., 109ff.

SCRIPTURE INDEX

APOCRYPHA AND PSEUDEPIGRAPHA

OLD TESTAMENT

NEW TESTAMENT

ANCIENT SOURCES

GREEK AUTHORS

ROMAN AUTHORS

HELLENISTIC-JEWISH LITERATURE

EARLY CHRISTIAN LITERATURE

MODERN AUTHORS